Salvaging a Teenage Wasteland

Salvaging a Teenage Wasteland

Origins of the Recovery High School Movement

Andrew J. Finch

OXFORD
UNIVERSITY PRESS

OXFORD
UNIVERSITY PRESS

Oxford University Press is a department of the University of Oxford. It furthers
the University's objective of excellence in research, scholarship, and education
by publishing worldwide. Oxford is a registered trade mark of Oxford University
Press in the UK and certain other countries.

Published in the United States of America by Oxford University Press
198 Madison Avenue, New York, NY 10016, United States of America.

Library of Congress Cataloging-in-Publication Data
Names: Finch, Andrew J. (Andrew Jaffry), 1970– author.
Title: Salvaging a teenage wasteland : origins of the recovery high school
movement / Andrew J. Finch.
Description: New York, NY : Oxford University Press, [2024] |
Includes bibliographical references and index.
Identifiers: LCCN 2024020109 | ISBN 9780190645502 (paperback) |
ISBN 9780190669980 (epub) | ISBN 9780190645519 (updf) | ISBN 9780190645526 (digital online)
Subjects: LCSH: Teenagers—Counseling of—United States. |
Teenagers—Alcohol use—United States. | Teenagers—Drug use—
UnitedStates. | Alcoholics—Rehabilitation—United States. | Drug
addicts—Rehabilitation—United States. | Alternative schools—
UnitedStates. | Recovering addicts—Education (Secondary)—United States. |
Addicts—Rehabilitation—United States.
Classification: LCC HV1431 .F55 2023 | DDC 373.14/60973—dc23/eng/20240625
LC record available at https://lccn.loc.gov/2024020109

DOI: 10.1093/oso/9780190645502.001.0001

Printed by Integrated Books International, United States of America

To Deb, Michael, and David

In Memoriam

Dr. Paul Moberg (1949–2022),
Trailblazer for recovery school research

Contents

16. SOCK AND BUSKIN

EPILOGUE: THE FATE OF THE SCHOOLS

Acknowledgments

This project has been the most rewarding academic project I have attempted, but researching and writing the book was a challenge. Nine years passed from preparing a prospectus to publication, and along the way the world endured such life-altering events as an opioid epidemic, the Black Lives Matter movement, and, of course, the COVID-19 pandemic. The work was disrupted multiple times by life, but through commitment and perseverance, there is now a published history of recovery high schools. Completing the book was only possible, though, with the support and encouragement of several people.

Thank you to Sarah Harrington and Oxford University Press for believing in this topic and contracting with me on the research. I appreciate your patience as the project was much more complex than I anticipated it would be, requiring years more time to complete. And I am grateful to Phoebe Aldridge-Turner and everyone on the OUP editorial staff for the support you provided in bringing the final product into fruition.

Research of this magnitude requires assistance, and I benefited from the talents of three student researchers from Vanderbilt University—one doctoral student (Emily Hennessy), one master's student (Billie Anderson), and one undergraduate student (Emma Rosenberg). All three have since graduated and are now making contributions in research, counseling, teaching, and parenting. Many of the ideas and quotes cited in the manuscript are products of their work, and the book benefited immeasurably from their efforts.

Paul Proia is a historian, author, and friend, who combed through countless genealogical documents and newspaper articles. He helped over the full nine years of the project, answering calls for assistance at all hours and receiving only gratitude in return. Paul's attention to detail is unparalleled, and the stories told here are richer thanks to him.

Thank you to the librarians and archivists, too numerous to name individually, from Vanderbilt University, the Library of Congress, Rice University, the Bureau of Prisons, the Minneapolis Public Library, the Minnesota Secretary of State records office, the Gale Family Library at the Minnesota History Center, the Silver Spring Historical Society, and the St. Louis Park Historical Society. There is one archivist who must be named—Rob Jensen at the Montgomery County Archives. He went above and beyond to find documents about the Phoenix School, and his discovery of a report compiling dozens of parent and student testimonials (from which he then redacted all identifiable information) was invaluable.

Some people both shared memories of their personal experience and also became research assistants by helping me find archival data. Shirley Mikell, Michael

Durchslag, Mike Bucci, Brian Berthiaume, Sally Eller, Patty Winters, John Cates, Barbara Schmidt, and Carol Robson in particular answered numerous calls and emails, contacted other participants, and shared historical documents that deepened the history. These data often were not available anywhere but your own personal files and lived experience, and I cannot thank you enough.

Dr. Ken Winters and Dr. Paul Moberg inspired my recovery high school research, and both made this book possible by suggesting potential publishers, helping me compile data, and encouraging me through my career. We lost Paul in the spring of 2022, and I wish he could have seen the final work. I am forever indebted to them both.

My family has been a rock. Your patience, support, and encouragement saw me through days in which I thought this would never be finished. My children, David and Michael, were ages 10 and 13, respectively, when I started, and they are both now in college. You have literally grown up with the writing and probably do not remember a time when Dad was not "working on the book." My wife Deb had to fly solo for hundreds of hours taking care of family responsibilities while I did that work, and she has been a source of reassurance not only for the nine years of research and writing, but for twenty-five-plus years of marriage. I love you, and I hope you enjoy the book.

Finally, to all the participants who gave hours of their time to share their memories, their photos, and even their homes with me and my research assistants, I cannot say enough how much we appreciated it. Beyond the time given for this research, the innovators who started recovery high schools deserve special praise. For you, I owe much of my career, and there are thousands of people who can thank you for a better quality of life, if not for life itself. I can only hope this book does your stories justice. You may not have intended to start a movement, but that is exactly what you did.

Introduction: Opening the Door

"School to open doors to teen addicts."[1]

The Tennessean headline grabbed my attention as I made my everyday morning commute. Reaching a traffic light, I read on.

"In what might be the first private initiative of its kind," began the article, "The Oasis Center [a local nonprofit agency] plans to open a new school in Nashville this fall targeted for teens recovering from alcohol and drug addictions."

Only a year removed from earning my master's degree in school counseling, I was headed to my job as a school-based therapist in July 1997. I had recently completed the additional coursework for a community counseling specialization, and I also identified as an adult child of an alcoholic. A school providing therapeutic services for youth in recovery thus appealed to me on multiple levels. Professionally, a high school focused on substance use recovery aligned with both my school and clinical training. Personally, I had felt the impact of addiction having had a parent who struggled with substance use and co-occurring disorders. I had experienced firsthand the dynamics of what is often called a "family disease," and I had developed a passion to help prevent the spread of that malady to future generations. And vocationally, the opportunity to help start such an innovative program with the potential to save lives held tremendous appeal. I picked up the phone that day to call and express my interest in a counseling position at the school, and a month later I was hired.

My first day as a counselor for the Oasis Center's new Oasis Academy was August 1, 1997, about one month before the school was scheduled to officially open. The principal and the only teacher there at the time was Judy Ide, and she and I set about interviewing families, creating the curriculum, and devising procedures for the new program from scratch. A local foundation provided us with almost $100,000 of seed funding, but while we were waiting for the doors to open and the first tuition checks to arrive, I found myself helping tutor adults in a GED program also run by the Oasis Center.

Starting something original was exciting, but we had no blueprint or road map to guide us. The Oasis Center in Nashville had opened in 1970, and since then, it had served more than 100,000 youths and their families. Its centerpiece was a program called the "Runaway Shelter" for teens who had chosen to leave their homes for various reasons, often just to get a break from their families, but their services had expanded to over twenty programs including family and individual counseling, suicide prevention, and crisis intervention. Both the GED program and the shelter

Salvaging a Teenage Wasteland. Andrew J. Finch, Oxford University Press. © Oxford University Press 2024.
DOI: 10.1093/oso/9780190645502.001.0001

had provided educational services, and, initially, we thought those teaching methods would work at Oasis Academy.

A full-fledged high school, however, was new to the organization. And this type of school, a sober school, was particularly unusual.[2] I was only aware of one other school like it in the nation, and in fact, only fifteen sober schools had ever existed before that time. The Oasis Center had spent two years doing a market study and needs assessment, which informed them that Nashville could sustain four sober schools, each with a maximum enrollment of forty students—the standard enrollment for the best-known recovery school at the time, "Sobriety High," in Edina, Minnesota. Access to information was far more limited than today, and communication was still primarily by phone or in-person.

According to the article that originally had piqued my interest, Oasis Academy was modeled after "Unity High" in Phoenix that had opened in 1992.[3] In reality, Sobriety High in Minnesota had been more influential. Our principal, Judy Ide had shown me a video from *Dateline* that featured Sobriety High, with interviews of staff and students, and showing the school and a graduation ceremony in 1995. Viewing that story had inspired the Oasis Center—and I later found out many others across the country—to create a similar program. That video and a few phone calls to those two schools, Unity High and Sobriety High, was basically all the preparation I had.

General structures such as small classes—individualized instruction, and requirements of abstinence from alcohol and drug use—were fairly easy to adopt from the other schools. However, as the month of August progressed, we ran into early challenges. Only seven students qualified for enrollment and were able to pay the $595 monthly tuition. We also discovered that it was common for a student to slip and return to use, and we did not have strategies in place to discourage this. Treatment facilities instructed us to expel any student who used alcohol or drugs at all while enrolled, but, with such a small enrollment, we would have had no school had we followed their advice. As a result, we developed a graduated "relapse" policy, with random drug screening for accountability—this was something Sobriety High refused to do because of their students' ability to tamper with and skew the results of urine tests.

While Sobriety High had full-time teachers for each of the four major subject areas—math, English, science, and social studies—our initial budget did not allow for any paid staff beyond Judy Ide and me, which quickly proved to be insufficient. We started adding volunteer teachers, most of whom came from the recovery community and were looking for service opportunities. As a private school, we had some flexibility with who could teach, but having a staff filled with volunteers led to inconsistent faculty from one day to the next. As the school counselor, I took on the responsibility of revising student schedules daily to account for which teachers were available and which had decided not to volunteer at the last minute.

Families wanted assurance that credits would transfer and be accepted by colleges, which would ultimately mean hiring certified teachers and providing approved curriculum. The Oasis Center decided not to continue the program when the initial grant expired after year two, so Judy Ide and I decided to create a board of directors and form our own nonprofit agency, Creative Recovery Communities, to raise the money needed for an expanded program. Oasis Academy would no longer work as the name, since we had left the Oasis Center, so in 1999, we renamed the school "Community High School." Despite our best efforts, the school, was never able to secure public education funding, and the annual tuition of about $12,000 constrained enrollment. Not enough families were willing or able to pay tuition for such a specialty program with no empirical evidence of its value. Far from reaching a forty-student enrollment, let alone four sites, the school typically enrolled twenty to twenty-five students at a time, which proved financially unsustainable. Community High School remained open until 2008, relocating twice, but ultimately succumbing to the financial pressures of raising a quarter of a million dollars annually.

In the years since, I have compared the process of our first two years to building a house, tearing it down, and rebuilding it multiple times to create a stable structure. We were learning how to support the students' recovery as we went. Our first commencement, in May 1998, featured two graduates, one of whom matriculated to one of the earliest collegiate recovery communities at Texas Tech University. The other, we later discovered, had started using again, and was actively using by the time we held our ceremony. That revelation was hard to process at the time. I wondered then if we actually had helped anyone as we were figuring things out.

Then I recalled the comments from our students. From the first days, the students at the school were filled with gratitude that our school existed to provide them a recovery community. One early student was quoted in the *Tennessean* saying, "I wouldn't be alive today if it wasn't for the people here."[4]

It was a common sentiment, and one that kept me going. I still remember one of the first seven students sitting in a daily check-in group saying, "I wish everybody who needed a school like this could go to one."

Comments like these became a sustaining influence, as did the goal of helping others avoid the pitfalls we faced. As I completed my doctoral studies and wrote my dissertation on the topic of recovery high schools, it became apparent how little information existed on schools like Community, Sobriety, and Unity High Schools. When those programs started, there had been no published research. At most, schools had conducted their own internal evaluations, which were not widely accessible to the general public. While sober school staff at other schools occasionally reached out, no standards existed, nor was there a directory of schools to help people locate schools around the country. Instead, those of us doing the work had to find and support each other, and then go back to our silos.

As my career progressed, I helped research recovery schools, develop standards and accreditation criteria, and, in 2002, start a national organization of high schools and colleges, the Association of Recovery Schools (see Figure I.1). Recovery high schools opening today have a strong network to lean on and many more resources. One thing still missing, however, is an accurate account of the history of recovery schools.

Figure I.1. The Association of Recovery Schools' inaugural conference was held at the Renaissance Hotel in Washington, DC, July 15–17, 2002. The attendees are pictured here, including several who were prominent in the establishment of recovery high schools: Kellie Winter of P.E.A.S.E. Academy (row 2, third from left), Judy Ide of Oasis Academy (row 3, fourth from left), Judi Hanson of Sobriety High (row 2, sixth from left), and Dave Hadden from the StepUP Program at Augsburg College (standing in the back). The author is pictured in the fourth row (standing, first from left), and the keynote speaker was singer-songwriter Paul Williams (row 2, first from left). (Source: Andy Finch.)

For a long time, there was disagreement about whether Sobriety High or another program called "P.E.A.S.E. Academy" (for "Peers Enjoying a Sober Education"), opened their doors in Minnesota first. Regardless, the generally accepted notion of the time was that sober schools started in Minnesota in the late 1980s. Preeminent recovery school historian William White and I even made that claim in a manuscript.[5] In fact, we now know neither of those schools was the first, and furthermore, the first recovery high schools originated outside Minnesota over a decade earlier.

Part of the confusion was not having a formal definition of what constituted a "recovery high school," a term that was not used regularly until the advent of the Association of Recovery Schools. We now denote recovery high schools as alternative school settings that provide an academic, credit-bearing, curriculum while simultaneously offering recovery supports throughout the school day. When the first recovery high schools opened in the 1970s and 1980s, few beyond the people associated with those schools knew of their existence—and all believed that their school was the first of its kind.

Another issue contributing to the lack of awareness about recovery high schools was not having a national network until 2002. For the most part, recovery high schools operated regionally and only found out about other schools by chance. There was, and currently is, no requirement to promote one's school on a national level, and without common terminology, there was no guarantee a program would promote itself as a recognizable "sober" or "recovery" high school. Indeed, some schools actively *avoided* publicizing their alcohol and drug focus to protect the anonymity of their students. If nothing was ever published, and a school was not promoting itself as a sober or recovery high school, a school could exist in relative obscurity beyond the staff and families of the programs themselves. The only published accounts are scattered among organizational reports, board minutes, newspaper stories, and professional publications, and the unpublished narratives reside in the memories of the school founders. There have been, thus, many gaps and inaccuracies in the published record to date.

This book gathers such accounts into an accessible volume both to chronicle the rise of recovery high schools as a legitimate component of the adolescent substance use disorder continuum of care and to provide a resource upon which future researchers can draw. The book attempts to close knowledge gaps and provide an accurate historical account of the origins of the recovery high school movement. From their beginnings in the alternative schools of the 1970s that overlapped with the first adolescent substance use treatment programs, the book explores the development of the earliest recovery-based education programs in South Carolina, Texas, Maryland, and Minnesota, which served as roots for later growth.

Recovery high schools have become a key setting supporting the adolescent recovery process, and our understanding of them has evolved along with our understanding of addiction and recovery. It is hoped that knowledge of how recovery high schools started and developed will inform our understanding of this program modality and lead to further application in existing recovery school environments and publications. Discovering recovery high schools that have closed and left little historical residue is akin to both an archaeological dig and a detective investigation. Our awareness and knowledge of this history continue to evolve, and no work can be considered final—but we must start somewhere.

Prologue

Setting the Stage for Recovery and Education

Asking "Where did it start?" is like asking where a river starts.
You have to go upstream, where you probably will find no single source,
but several little streams flowing together.[1]

As the sun rose above Max Yasgur's Farm in Bethel, New York, on Sunday morning, August 17, 1969, guitarist Pete Townshend looked out at a crowd of almost half a million people at the Woodstock Music and Art Fair. Roger Daltrey was singing the finale to The Who's new album *Tommy*, a rock opera about a boy who enters a dissociative, catatonic state after witnessing the murder of his father, and Townshend was struck by the "absolute desolation of teenagers at Woodstock, where everybody was smacked out on acid and twenty people, or whatever, had brain damage."[2] He later wrote a powerful anthem, "Baba O'Riley," inspired in part by that day, in which he referred to the crowd as a "teenage wasteland," because they were all "wasted."[3]

The Sunday sunrise at Woodstock is an apt place to begin the story of recovery high schools, because recovery high schools are descended in many ways from 1960s America. Almost exactly a decade after that Woodstock sunrise, Montgomery County (Maryland) Public Schools opened the Phoenix school in Silver Spring, making it the first recovery high school operated by a public school district. The school district had approved the school after a series of drug raids in local schools had led to the arrest of over three hundred high school students in a three-month period. Most of the arrested students had been in elementary school during Woodstock and had been raised in its aftermath. In fact, the same spiritual master—Meher Baba—who inspired Pete Townshend to write the song "Baba O'Riley" for The Who in 1971 also influenced teacher and social worker, Brian Berthiaume, to start the Phoenix recovery high school in 1979.

The origin of recovery high schools represents a confluence of innovative ideas spurred by two human service movements: the advent of treatment for adolescent substance use disorders and the growth of alternative schools of choice. The schools also characterize the juxtaposition of drug and education policies between White, middle-income families and their counterparts of color and lower-income families. While the schools themselves were not formerly or intentionally segregated, the early schools were predominantly White. They arose in an era when White families were fleeing from desegregated urban schools, and drugs were being framed as a problem being pushed upon White youths by dealers who were stereotypically people of color.

Recovery high schools provided a continuing care option that would keep youths from falling into the abyss of lifelong, hard-drug usage—images that were often racialized in public perception as having young, White victims with Black and Latino perpetrators.[4]

There is no clear "beginning" for recovery high schools, as the schools still do not have one definitive model, and none of the first efforts to provide recovery support in a school setting look exactly like the recovery high schools of today. This ambiguity has caused many different schools to believe they were the first and to claim originality, including, at various times, each of the schools profiled in this book. In actuality, the idea for specialty schools to support student recovery emerged over several years through the interaction of personalities, politics, and ideologies in a time period and geographical locations fertile for such programs.

Historical Context

While the seeds for adolescent treatment and the alternative school movement were planted throughout the twentieth century, they took root in the 1970s, a decade known for challenging convention and the expanding use of drugs by teenagers in the years after Woodstock and in the shadow of Vietnam and Watergate and the new War on Drugs. William White, the preeminent addiction and recovery historian, wrote this of the period:

> The 1960s and 1970s witnessed America's first widespread youthful polydrug epidemic. Marihuana, and to a lesser extent LSD, became sacraments within a drug-experimenting youth subculture that by the 1970s usually involved alcohol, cannabis and an assortment of newly popular hallucinogens (PCP), stimulants, barbiturates, and "look-alike" drugs. This period was marked by an increased perception of marihuana as a relatively benign drug, a growing acceptance of marihuana use, and proposals for decriminalization of marihuana coming from the highest levels of government.[5]

In 1979, just ten years after Woodstock, adolescent drug-use in the United States reached the highest level before or since, with 54.2% of high school seniors reporting they had used an illicit drug in the last year. In 1978, 10.7% of seniors had reported using marijuana daily, and by 1981, the largest percentage of seniors ever (65.6%) reported having used an illicit drug in their lifetimes.[6] The rates were even higher for alcohol, with 93% of high school seniors reporting having a drink in their lifetimes in 1979, and 71.8% having had alcohol in the prior month.[7] By comparison, in 2019, the last pre-pandemic year, only 47.4% of seniors reported ever trying an illicit drug in their lifetime, and only 58.5% reporting ever having alcohol in their lives.[8]

Parental backlash was loud and reverberated all the way to White House, as the First Lady, Nancy Reagan, told kids to "Just say No" to drugs, and schools of choice

were promoted as the antidote to public schools that had placed our nation "at risk."
The environment was rich for specialty programs to help adolescents recover from
substance use disorders, especially in suburban areas with higher concentrations of
middle-to-upper income White families, and recovery high schools were one of the
models to emerge from what Pete Townshend had called a "wasteland." [*]

Rise of the Teen Drug Culture

Psychologist G. Stanley Hall is widely credited with defining "adolescence" as a
distinct period of human development in his two-volume work, *Adolescence: Its
Psychology and Its Relations to Physiology, Anthropology, Sociology, Sex, Crime,
Religion, and Education*, which was published in 1904.[9] Hall felt adolescence was a
period of "storm and stress," characterized by emotional and behavioral upheaval.[10]
While Hall defined adolescence as the years 14 to 24, as the twentieth century progressed, adolescence became synonymous with the teenage years, and J. J. Arnett
claims that Hall's description of this stage of life "accords remarkably well with current findings in our scientific psychology."[11] As the years went by, teenagers were
increasingly seen as distinct from adults, requiring workforce protections and compulsory schooling.

All drugs, including alcohol under most circumstances, are, of course, "illicit" for
adolescents. Views of adolescent drug use are particularly complex and have been
driven by fear and an evolving yet uncertain science. The science was particularly
sparse during the first part of the twentieth century, when the first commissioner of
the Federal Bureau of Narcotics, Harry Anslinger, perpetuated anxiety and conflated
the use of marijuana with narcotics. Anslinger wrote, "Marijuana is the unknown
quantity among narcotics. No one knows, when he smokes it, whether he will become
a philosopher, a joyous reveler, a mad insensate, or a murderer."[12] Today, though, the
Drug Enforcement Administration (DEA) has clearly defined narcotics not to include marijuana, equating narcotics instead only with opioids:

> The term "narcotic" comes from the Greek word for "stupor" and originally re-
> ferred to a variety of substances that dulled the senses and relieved pain. Though
> some people still refer to all drugs as "narcotics," today "narcotic" refers to opium,
> opium derivatives, and their semi-synthetic substitutes.[13]

By the 1950s, though, concern about teenagers dissolving into "reefer madness"
had created hysteria and sewed confusion.[14] The lines of response were also being
drawn along racial lines, as M. D. Lassiter writes:

> Since the 1950s, state institutions and American political culture have repeatedly
> constructed the war on drugs through the framework of suburban crisis and posi-
> tioned white middle-class youth as innocent victims who must be shielded from

both the illegal drug markets and the criminal drug laws. Scholars primarily have analyzed the U.S. drug war as a racial system of social control of urban minority populations, an extension of the punitive war on crime and the foundation for the "new Jim Crow" in the contemporary era of mass incarceration. Numerous studies have documented the systematic disparities generated by racially and geographically targeted enforcement policies, which have insulated most white youth from the carceral state. By 2000, according to Sentencing Project data, African Americans and Latinos represented three-fourths of all drug offenders in state prisons, even though whites constituted a large majority of illegal drug users and dealers in the United States.[15]

The Narcotics Act of 1956 allowed dealers of narcotics to juveniles to be put to death, and while that law was limited specifically to suppliers of heroin, the tone was set for harsh penalties around any drug trafficking, with, as Lassiter pointed out, "Mexican, African American, and Italian American traffickers on one side of the law; helpless white prostitutes and desperate suburban addicts on the other."[16]

Prejudice was built into the very terminology used to refer to substances. For example, the US government began using the term "marijuana," and its colloquial spelling "marihuana" instead of "cannabis." Martin A. Lee's thorough social history of cannabis, *Smoke Signals,* suggested the intent was "to turn people off to smoking pot by [exploiting] prejudice against despised minority groups, especially Mexican immigrants."[17] A similar linguistic distinction would be drawn between "crack" and "cocaine" decades later, situating the former with predominantly urban Black populations and the latter with wealthier White subgroups in the 1980s.[18] And regardless of the phrasing, White teenagers were often presented as victims who required rehabilitation and specialized programs to escape a life of drug addiction.[19]

Interestingly, the same apprehension and harsh standards were not applied as much to youth alcohol sales and consumption. Prior to the start of Prohibition in 1919, there was no federal drinking age. Some states had a drinking age, but most did not enforce it. After the passage of the Eighteenth Amendment, purchase and consumption of alcohol were illegal for all ages from 1920 to 1933. Then, when the Twenty-First Amendment repealed Prohibition in December 1933, the federal legal drinking age was set at twenty-one, which corresponded with the voting age at the time. Until the 1970s, there was variance across the states with regards to legal age to purchase and to consume alcohol, as well as different ages for types of alcohol (i.e., beer and wine sometimes had lower ages than other alcoholic beverages).[20]

The Vietnam Draft lottery set the age that men could be drafted into the armed services at 18, and this started a movement to lower the voting and drinking ages. In July 1971, the Twenty-Sixth Amendment lowered the voting age from 21 to 18, and from 1970 to 1975, twenty-nine states lowered their minimum drinking age to 18, 19, or 20.[21] High school aged youth still were not legally allowed to drink, but like illicit drug use, alcohol use among teenagers increased through the 1970s. Between 1975 and 1979, the annual prevalence-of-use rate rose from 85% to 88%, the monthly rate from 68% to 72%, and the daily rate from 5.7% to 6.9%. Just like cannabis use, 1979 was the peak year for annual use of alcohol for adolescents.[22] And, just like other drugs, after 1979, alcohol use among high school students started to decline.

Regardless of the laws restricting alcohol and other drug use, adolescent recreational drug use became much more common in the 1960s, especially among middle-income, White teenagers, and this growth continued through the 1970s. An article published by the *American Journal of Public Health* at the start of the new decade highlighted multiple substances of concern (italics added for emphasis):

> Drug dependence . . . may be associated with the minor *tranquilizers* or anti-anxiety drugs—meprobamate, chlordiazepoxide; *sedatives and hypnotics*—barbiturates, glutethimide, chloral hydrate; *stimulants*–amphetamines, methylphenidate, phenmetrazine, cocaine; ethyl *alcohol and nicotine*; the natural and synthetic analgesics–*opiates*, pentazocine; *hallucinogens*–LSD, STP, and, of course, *cannabis*.[23]

The author of that prescient article, Dr. K. D. Charalampuous, was an associate professor of psychiatry at the University of Texas Medical School at Dallas. He had presented the paper at the 98th Annual Meeting of the American Public Health Association in October 1970 in Houston, and he punctuated it with this point, "Drug abuse is not just a fad and a fashion and will not go away, but it will create many victims."[24]

Charalampuous's presentation came at a time when the US government was wrestling with the best way to attack the issue of drugs and the rising use of substances by teenagers. The science available to understand the differential impact of drugs on human beings was relatively new, and precise neurological information on how drugs affected the developing brain was almost nonexistent. For this reason, federal and state drug policies were driven heavily by ideology and behavioral indicators, which were often still simply interpreted by ideology.

For many teenagers, drug use was representative of the period's political dissent. Parents trying to raise their children in the 1960s and 1970s in the midst of the Vietnam War and a civil rights movement were left to figure out how to address alcohol and drug use with conflicting messages coming from experts, a lack of scientific rigor behind educational materials, and growing acceptance of drug use in the media and popular culture. J. Hudak writes, "The youth movement transformed American thinking for decades to come and made older generations nervous. Worried about their boys overseas, Americans also worried about the fabric of their society at home. The tensions were linked. Youths associated with the counterculture were painted as less valuable than youths drafted into war. That conflict intensified feelings on both sides, driving protests to grow louder and the government's response to be stronger."[25]

Federal Drug Policies

Societal drug laws and treatment programs evolved gradually throughout the twentieth century. Starting in 1906, numerous federal acts were passed creating penalties for selling and using drugs, but most did not distinguish youth from adults.[26] Federal drug policies were passed by each of the first nine presidential administrations of the twentieth century, from Theodore Roosevelt through Dwight D. Eisenhower.[27] And with the notable exception of the Twenty-First Amendment that ended Prohibition, virtually all the acts had strengthened the federal role over and criminal definition of drug distribution, possession, and use. Most of these policies had been enacted under the direction of Commissioner Anslinger. As Massing writes in his chronicle of the drug war, however, "The national mood began to change" about drug use, coinciding with the election of John F. Kennedy as president in 1960.[28]

By the 1960s, addiction and alcoholism was coming to be seen by the medical community as a disease or psychological condition more than a criminal or immoral act.[29] The American Medical Association famously proclaimed alcoholism to be a disease in 1956, and in 1962, the Supreme Court ruled in *Robinson v. California* that a California law that criminalized being addicted to narcotics was unconstitutional. In the concurring opinion, Justice Potter Stewart wrote that drug addiction was a disease, and that it was unconstitutional under the Eighth Amendment's prohibition of cruel and unusual punishment to impose punishment for having a disease.

The federal offices overseeing drug policy also had started to change, and with the change, the divergent needs of young people came more into focus. President Eisenhower had created the Department of Health, Education, and Welfare (HEW) in 1953 as a new cabinet-level department. Health and education policy thus would be managed by the same federal department through the 1960s and 1970s, until President Carter created a separate Department of Education in 1979. The National Institute of Mental Health (NIMH) had been created in 1949, and it ultimately became a division of HEW. Policies concerning drug use and abuse increasingly diverged from the enforcement of drug trafficking, which had mostly been patrolled by the Federal Bureau of Narcotics. Commissioner Anslinger retired as head of the Federal Bureau of Narcotics in 1962, and in 1966, a distinct Bureau of Drug Abuse Control was formed under the FDA. Just two years later, the Bureaus of Narcotics and Drug Abuse Control merged to form the Bureau of Narcotics and Dangerous Drugs (BNDD). Federal offices were essentially realigning to acknowledge the two heads of the global drug problem—one to control trafficking and *supply*, and the other to reduce the *demand* for illicit substances through treatment and rehabilitation.

Just a few months after Charalampuous's presentation in Houston, Congressmen Morgan F. Murphy (D-Illinois) and Robert H. Steele (R-Connecticut) submitted a report to the House Committee on Foreign Affairs in May 1971. Murphy and Steele had met with officials responsible for narcotics control in nine countries, including South Vietnam, during April 1971, to gather information about illegal trafficking of heroin. In the opening paragraph of the report, Murphy and Steele expressed concern with the rise in use of opium-based drugs, and "the rapid increase in heroin addiction with the United States military forces in South Vietnam"[30] and wrote, "To combat this growing menace around the world and at home the United States must use every resource available."[31]

The Murphy and Steele report stoked the fears of narcotics and rising crime, which had been affirmed by research from Dr. Robert DuPont in August 1969, which reported 44% of inmates entering the Washington, DC, jail system had tested positive for heroin.[32] Within weeks of the Murphy and Steele report, President Richard Nixon declared a "war on drugs" on June 17, 1971 (see Figure P.1). In a press conference, Nixon stated, "America's public enemy number one in the United States is drug abuse. In order to fight and defeat this enemy, it is necessary to wage a new, all-out offensive."[33] The president appointed Dr. Jerome H. Jaffe as "Special Consultant to the President for Narcotics and Dangerous Drugs" and announced that Jaffe would "have the responsibility to take all of the Government agencies, nine, that deal with the problems of rehabilitation, in which his primary responsibilities will be research and education, and see that they work not at cross-purposes, but work together in dealing with the problem."[34] The office would be called the Special Action Office for Drug Abuse Prevention (SAODAP).

Figure P.1. President Richard Nixon declared a "War on Drugs" on June 17, 1971. In a press conference, Nixon stated, "America's public enemy number one in the United States is drug abuse." The war resulted in a huge increase in federal drug spending and spurred a reorganization of the federal alcohol and drug service offices. This photo was taken at a drug control meeting in November 1973. (Source: Associated Press.)

In essence, the government's approach to drug abuse prevention could be divided into reduction of demand (which encompassed prevention and treatment programs) and reduction of supply (which involved law enforcement and the military). Initially, Dr. Jaffe made treatment a main focus of the efforts, especially methadone treatment for heroin addicts. Massing described Jaffe's goal as a creating comprehensive public health approach for drug addiction, with the following principles:

- Chronic drug users are at the heart of the nation's drug problem;
- Users are a heterogenous group, requiring a diverse array of services;
- Government has a responsibility to make sure services are available and effective; and
- Law enforcement has a role to play in curtailing drug abuse, but only as an adjunct to rehabilitation, and those two functions should remain separate.[35]

Dr. Jaffe oversaw a massive increase in federal drug spending. When Nixon took office in 1969, the federal budget for drug programs was $81 million, with just over half going to treatment. By 1973, federal spending ballooned to $420 million, with *demand*-reduction (i.e., treatment and prevention) funding getting about two-thirds of the budget. As Massing wrote, this approach was the "reverse of what might have been expected from the hawkish Nixon."[36] That same year, the first publicly funded high school for teenagers with alcohol and other drug problems opened in Charleston, South Carolina.

President's Nixon's War on Drugs also spurred a time of reorganization around the federal alcohol and drug service offices, especially on the demand-reduction side. The Comprehensive Alcohol Abuse and Alcoholism Prevention, Treatment, and Rehabilitation Act of 1970 had created the National Institute on Alcohol Abuse and Alcoholism (NIAAA) as a separate institute within the NIMH. Two years later, the federal Drug Abuse and Treatment Act of 1972 established the National Institute on Drug Abuse (NIDA). This meant there were two distinct institutes overseeing alcohol and drug services and research.

The recently appointed Assistant Secretary for Health, Education, and Welfare, Charles Edwards, created a Mental Health Task Force in 1973 to consider the best structure for handling the disparate requirements of research, services, and training in the areas of alcoholism, drug abuse, and mental health. Elmer Gardner, a psychiatrist and researcher, chaired the task force, which recommended that the drug abuse and alcohol abuse fields should be combined, in part due to the growing number of people who had problems with both.[37] The task force also acknowledged differences between the fields of substance use and mental health.[38] In response to the task force's report, Assistant Secretary Edwards administratively established the Alcohol, Drug Abuse, and Mental Health Administration (ADAMHA)—composed of the NIAAA, the NIDA, and NIMH—as the successor organization to the Health Services and Mental Health Administration (HSMHA), which had only been in existence itself since 1968.[39] ADAMHA would exist for almost twenty years until a Congressional reorganization replaced it with the Substance Abuse and Mental Health Services Administration (SAMHSA) in 1992.[40]

In time, however, the *supply*-reduction side would begin receiving most of the funding and became more synonymous with the drug war itself. The Office of Drug Abuse Law Enforcement (ODALE), directed by a former Customs Department Commissioner, Myles Ambrose, was established in January 1972 to assist local officials in enforcing drug laws.[41] New York Governor Nelson Rockefeller then proposed mandatory life imprisonment for drug dealers in January 1973. Rockefeller wanted his law to become a national model, and he got the attention of the Nixon administration. Dr. Jaffe submitted his resignation in June 1973, and, in July, ODALE was consolidated into a new single federal agency, the DEA, merging with the Bureau of Narcotics and Dangerous Drugs, the Office of National Narcotics Intelligence, and elements of the US Customs Service that worked in drug trafficking intelligence and investigations.[42] A few months after that, another reorganization placed the DEA inside the Department of Justice. By 1976, supply-side federal enforcement spending would finally catch up with the demand-reduction treatment and prevention budget, a trend that would continue for the next forty years.[43]

Much has been written about Nixon's actual intentions, ranging from criminalizing Black people[44] to an attack on his political enemies (i.e., anti-war liberals and hippies),[45] and a full discussion of the rationale and sociological impact of the drug war is beyond the scope of this work. What is most salient for the development of recovery high schools is that Nixon's drug war generated the funding, bureaucracy, and public consciousness that made it possible for recovery schools to open in three states during the war's first decade.

Decriminalization and Legalization Movements

In the wake of the 1960s, advocates on the West Coast had begun cannabis legalization campaigns. Keith Stroup founded the National Organization for the Reform of Marijuana Laws (NORML) in 1970, and the group lobbied for decriminalization of cannabis. Soon after the drug war was declared in 1971, full-legalization bills failed in California and Oregon in 1972. In 1973, however, the Oregon state legislature voted to remove criminal penalties for marijuana possession, making it the first state to decriminalize pot.[46] This started a wave of similar efforts in statehouses across the country, and between 1973 and 1978, eleven more states would follow suit: Colorado (1975), Ohio (1975), Alaska (1975), California (1976), Maine (1976), Minnesota (1976), South Dakota (1977), Mississippi (1977), New York (1977), North Carolina (1977), and Nebraska (1978) (Dufton, 2013, 1).[47] The typical legislation would allow personal possession of up to one ounce of cannabis, and if a person was caught smoking cannabis, a civil fine would be assessed, similar to a parking ticket.

The voice of decriminalization advocates was heard in Washington, DC. After Nixon resigned, the Domestic Council Drug Abuse Task Force issued a report to

President Gerald Ford in September 1975, titled "White Paper on Drug Abuse."[48] The report noted that any claims to winning the drug war had been premature, and that "we probably will always have a drug problem of some proportion."[49] The report instead recommended the following:

> The Domestic Council Task Force on Drug Abuse strongly endorses the concept of a Federal program which balances the effort to control and, ultimately, reduce the supply of drugs with an effort to control and, ultimately, reduce the demand for drugs. We believe that this concept should continue to be the cornerstone of the Federal strategy.[50]

Notably, the White Paper suggested not all drug use was "equally destructive," and that federal enforcement efforts be focused on drugs that posed the greatest risk. "Public policy should be most concerned with those drugs which have the highest social cost."[51] Heroin, amphetamines, and barbiturates, were suggested to be of the greatest priority. While cannabis was said to be the "most widely used illicit drug, with an estimated 20 percent of Americans above the age of 11 having used it at least once," the paper also recognized "a great deal of controversy exists about marihuana (sic) policy" and noted "the relatively low social cost associated" with its recreational use.[52] Not enough was known at the time about the "new 'in' drug" cocaine, but the task force suggested paying attention to it in future years, and, summarized their position as follows:[53]

> The task force endorses this moderate view and expects the lower priority that has been established for marihuana will also be reflected in our demand reduction efforts by the elimination of many non-compulsive marihuana users now in our treatment system.[54]

When Jimmy Carter took office in 1977, his administration continued to view marijuana as a low priority drug, and Carter's administration announced that it favored decriminalization of cannabis (see Figure P.2).[55] In a speech to Congress in August 1977, President Carter said, "I support legislation . . . to eliminate all federal criminal penalties for the possession of up to one ounce of marijuana. This decriminalization is not legalization. It means only that the federal policy for possession would be reduced, and a person could receive a fine rather than a criminal penalty."[56] It seemed as though the United States was on the path to national decriminalization.

Parents pushed back. In the 1970s, heroin use was seen as a problem in major urban areas, but it was not yet seen as the significant threat to the wealthy suburban, predominantly White, youths, as Dufton writes:

> The "parent movement," as these activists became known, consisted of groups of generally white, suburban, middle-class mothers and fathers who were horrified that their nation was legalizing pot and fearful that their children would become

"Penalties against possession of a drug should not be more damaging to an individual than the use of the drug itself.

PLAYBOY

... Nowhere is this more clear than in the laws against possession of marijuana in private for personal use. ... The National Commission on Marijuana and Drug Abuse concluded 5 years ago that marijuana use should be decriminalized, and I believe it is time to implement those basic recommendations.

"Therefore, I support legislation amending Federal law to eliminate all Federal criminal penalties for the possession of up to 1 ounce of marijuana."
—President Jimmy Carter
Message to Congress, 8/2/77

Today repressive pot laws are still disrupting the lives and careers of responsible, productive people — and wasting millions of tax dollars on fruitless police and court action. NORML has helped win the fight for humane laws in ten states. We need your help to finish the job once and for all.

Figure P.2. President Jimmy Carter announced in a speech to Congress in August 1977 that he supported legislation "to eliminate all federal criminal penalties for the possession of up to one ounce of marijuana." The National Organization for the Reform of Marijuana Laws placed this advertisement in *Playboy* to raise money for its advocacy efforts. (Source: New England Reserve website.)

a generation of zombies, utterly incapacitated by the drug's surging use. Less concerned about the rising rate of narcotics abuse by adults than they were about the growing potential for adolescent experimentation with marijuana, parent activists launched a war on drugs of their own, using education and "parent peer groups" to mobilize against the "drug culture" they saw surrounding pot use.[57]

Smoking pot was a much more prominent concern for suburban parents, who led an effort to present cannabis as a primary public health concern. According to Peter Bourne, the Drug Czar under President Jimmy Carter, though, fears about marijuana were largely manufactured. In an interview for the PBS series on the Drug Wars in 2015, Bourne said the following:

Marijuana really was not seen as a serious public health problem—then, or today. It was viewed as very much a secondary issue. Subsequently, there was an effort to imply that marijuana was a public health problem, to justify the tough measures taken against those who experimented with it. But it was really a very phony effort. It was policymakers trying to hide behind the skirts of science, trying to say that marijuana poses a threat to the health of young people.[58]

Martha "Keith" Schuchard and her husband, Ron, were horrified to learn in August 1976 that their 13-year-old daughter had smoked pot. Ron was an assistant professor at Emory University, and Keith had a PhD in English literature in Georgia and taught at a local community college. They lived in the affluent Druid Hills neighborhood near Atlanta, in Jimmy Carter's home state.[59] They pulled together a meeting with about thirty parents of their daughter's friends—a group the teenagers called the Nosy Parent Association. Bourne, perhaps with a touch of cynicism, summarized their message as "Carter's too liberal on drugs. We don't want treatment. We want more aggressive law enforcement. These people aren't sick, they're criminals, and we want to lock them all up and put them in prison. Heroin isn't the issue, it's marijuana smoking by suburban white kids—our children—that we're worried about."[60]

According to Bourne, the parent advocacy effort was emboldened by "ebbing support for President Carter," and they got the attention of the NIDA in Maryland.[61] NIDA was then led by Dr. Robert DuPont, who had conducted heroin studies on DC jail inmates in 1969. Keith Schuchard contacted Dr. DuPont, who had expressed concern about the spread of marijuana among young people, but also favored decriminalization. DuPont visited Atlanta in 1977, where he met Schuchard and a group of students who noted how pervasive drug use was in their school. DuPont was so disturbed by what he saw in Atlanta, he commissioned Schuchard to write a drug prevention handbook, "Parents, Peers, and Pot," which reportedly became the agency's most requested publication ever.[62] Dufton wrote this in the Atlantic:

What began as a small organization of concerned parents in Keith Schuchard's living room morphed with unprecedented speed into an influential nationwide gestalt. Led by organizations like National Families in Action—organized by Schuchard's friend Sue Rusche in 1978—and the Parents' Resource Institute on Drug Education (PRIDE)—formed by Schuchard and Buddy Gleaton in 1977— activists like Keith oversaw the formation of thousands of individual parent groups across the nation. Over 4,000 of these groups had formed by 1983, and by Ronald Reagan's second term as president, they were influencing national drug policy.[63]

Schuchard and Gleaton's PRIDE organization launched a student survey in 1982, and since that time, thousands of school systems have used the Pride Questionnaires for millions of students in grades 4–12. Accord to PRIDE, the survey archives now form "the world's largest database on student use of illicit drugs, alcohol, tobacco products, and violence."[64]

Dufton notes that the Parent Movement was not suggesting lifelong abstinence. The groups actually "insisted that their children not use drugs while they were too young and vulnerable to handle the psychological, physical, and social hazards involved."[65] Whether it was the alarms sounded by the Parent Movement, a backlash against the Carter Administration, or the conservative influence of the Reagan Administration in the 1980s, the decriminalization movement stalled for years. After 1978, not a single state would eliminate criminal penalties for recreational marijuana use for over two decades, until Nevada finally did so in 2001.[66]

Unlike the response to marijuana and other illicit substances, though, the parental response to teenage alcohol use tended to be driven less by reefer madness hysteria and more by the measurable consequences of alcohol use. One of the major factors in moving drinking ages back up again was the high incidence of alcohol-related traffic accidents. In the mid-1970s, alcohol was a factor in over 60% of traffic fatalities, and two-thirds of traffic deaths among persons aged 16 to 20 involved alcohol.[67] In 1984, the National Minimum Drinking Age Act outlawed the purchase of alcohol by people under the age of 21, with the main federal penalty to states being restriction of highway funds. Public sale and use of alcohol and other drugs remains forbidden for all high school-aged youths. Many states, however, do still allow for private consumption of alcohol for teenagers under the supervision of parents in the home or in religious ceremonies.[68]

Evolution of Adolescent Drug Treatment

While teenage drug use may have peaked in the 1970s, there have been programs for young people with alcohol and drug problems since the nineteenth century.[69] In the 1800s, recovery support societies sponsored "cadet" branches for young problem drinkers, and they launched "youth rescue crusades."[70] Early addiction treatment programs often included young alcoholics, and according to White, youths between the ages of 15 and 20 represented about 10% of admissions to nineteenth century "inebriate homes and inebriate asylums," and children as young as 12 were being admitted to hospitals for detoxification.[71]

Early adolescent treatment programs were not limited to alcohol. Opiates have long been an issue for young people, and a focus of treatment interventions. In the years following World War I, the morphine maintenance clinics that operated in the United States between 1919 and 1924 enrolled teenagers.[72] According to Hubbard, almost 10% of the seventy-five hundred addicts registered at the Worth Street Clinic in New York City in 1920 were under the age of 19.[73] New York City established Riverside Hospital in the 1920s as a specialized facility for treating narcotic/opiate addiction, but so many of the people treated returned to regular use quickly upon release that the facility closed.[74]

Despite the existence of a program such as Riverside Hospital in New York, most adolescents with drug problems were sent to municipal correctional institutions. After Riverside closed, most people with addictions were forced into federal prison hospitals, and according to White and colleagues, adolescents were "viewed as miniature versions of adult addicts and were mainstreamed via the indiscriminate application of adult treatment methods."[75]

Adolescent narcotics addiction continued to grow in the 1940s and 1950s, especially among urban African American and Puerto Rican populations. Hospitals, churches, and law enforcement were most likely to handle young people with substance use disorders. In addition to addiction wards in community hospitals that sprang up across the country, two public health hospitals treated both drug offenders and people with drug problems voluntarily seeking help—one in Lexington, Kentucky, which opened in 1935, treated people from East of the Mississippi, and the other in Fort Worth, Texas, treated people from West of the Mississippi.[76] The two hospitals became known as "narcotics farms," and admissions of persons under age 21 at those two facilities increased from 22 in 1947 to 440 in 1950.[77] Churches saw young people with substance use disorders as a missionary opportunity, creating programs such as St. Mark's Clinic in Chicago, the Addicts Rehabilitation Center in Manhattan, the Astoria Consultation Service in Queens, and Exodus House in East Harlem during the 1950s.[78]

Adolescents and adults were usually treated in programs together as only one specialized adolescent treatment facility existed in the 1950s.[79] Riverside Hospital re-opened on July 1, 1952, as a 141-bed residential treatment facility exclusively for juveniles addicted to narcotics, thus becoming the first dedicated adolescent addiction treatment program. Riverside provided detoxification, psychiatric and medical evaluations, psychological testing, individualized programs of therapeutic, educational, vocational and recreational activities, and outpatient follow-up via community clinics after three-to-six months of inpatient treatment. There were three wards for boys and one for girls. The program lasted for nine years but closed in 1961 after a study showed that 39% of the 247 former patients had returned to heroin use following their discharge.[80]

From the 1950s through the 1960s, new options arose for adolescents beyond narcotics programs. Alcoholics Anonymous—which formed in 1935 in Akron, Ohio—soon developed "young peoples' meetings." The organization first published a pamphlet titled, "Young People and A.A." in 1953, the same year that Narcotics Anonymous (NA) launched in Los Angeles. NA groups provided another space for adolescents, along with the creation of modified therapeutic communities for adolescents, and the appearance of adolescent chemical dependency programs based on the "Minnesota Model,"[81] Faith-based programs also continued to evolve beyond churches, with the creation of religious-affiliated programs like Teen Challenge and the Samaritan Halfway House Society in the early 1960s.[82]

With rising adolescent drug use and a federal government intent on waging war on it, a handful of innovative programs started emerging to treat youths, often with loosely or noncredentialed staff. Some used rather harsh behavior modification approaches. One such program was the Seed, which opened in Fort Lauderdale, Florida, in 1970. Founded by a former night club comedian, Art Barker, the program became known for its harsh psychological reconditioning, which some described as brainwashing. Barker once stated the Seed's goal as "a kid being totally off drugs, his whole attitude toward life being changed, he loves himself, he loves others, loves God, loves country, is totally honest and aware."[83] With little oversight or standards in the field of early adolescent treatment programs, claims of abuse later arose. In one scathing expose, Stack Jones posted a blog claiming: "After spending only a short time at The Seed many gladly opted for incarceration over the brutal psychological, emotional, and physical torture they received at the hand of Barker, and his untrained and unskilled staff."[84]

Not all early adolescent programs were so harsh or experimental. One of the first attempts at modifying a more traditional, clinical drug treatment programs for adolescents was at St. Mary's Hospital in Minneapolis. St. Mary's piloted an "Adolescent Drug Detox" in 1974, and the full treatment center opened in 1975, with "rehabilitation/treatment" geared toward adolescents.[85] Through the 1960s and 1970s, though, adolescent treatment approaches were developmentally attuned to youths. The programs primarily used adult models and treated teenagers alongside adults. Adolescent-only units would not become widespread until the 1980s and 1990s.[86]

Alternative School Movement

As educational institutions, recovery high schools were not only a product of the 1970s drug culture battles. They also emerged from an alternative school movement. If teenage drug use in the 1960s and 1970s was a counter-cultural expression of behavior, alternative schools took a counter-cultural approach to education.

In the early twentieth century, US high schools increasingly became a place for vocational counseling and emotional and behavioral supports. From 1900, just before

Hall defined adolescence, to 1920, the mean legal age for leaving school rose from 14 years and 5 months in states that had compulsory education laws to a mean age of 16 years and 3 months. By 1920, thirty-one of the forty-eight required school attendance until age 16, and five required it until age 18.[87]

US schools of the late nineteenth and early twentieth centuries had highly regimented classrooms. Education was essentially rote learning, grades were clearly defined, and there were distinct expectations for students.[88] Based on the industrialization occurring in the country and the principles of scientific management being espoused by the likes of Frederick W. Taylor for the business sector, urban schools had started to resemble factories with socialization, structure, and preciseness driving the mechanism.[89] At the same time, more and more rural, one-room schoolhouses, were beginning to consolidate, and by the 1950s, the "little red schoolhouse" of lore had begun to vanish in the United States.[90] Industrialization and consolidation forced schools to focus less on the learner and more on what was being learned.

In the midst of this era emerged the first of three ideological movements advocating for looser boundaries in schools and the creation of child-centered or "alternative" schools: the progressive movement, free schooling, and charter schools. Recovery high schools have historical roots among all three of these schooling movements. Historian Lawrence A. Cremin (1961) gives a thorough accounting of the first period, which he calls the *progressive movement*.[91] According to Cremin, the progressive movement began around 1890, peaked in the 1920s and 1930s, and closed in the 1950s. Interestingly, the forefather of adolescent psychology, G. Stanley Hall, also influenced the progressive, child-centered movement in schools. In response to the Committee of Ten report in 1890 directing secondary schools to teach every subject in the same way, Hall wrote, "This principle does not apply to the great army of incapables, shading down to those who should be in schools for dullards or subnormal children."[92] As insensitive as Hall's comment might sound today, this was his way of advocating for an individualized curriculum, and one of Hall's students at Johns Hopkins University, John Dewey, became the leader of the progressive movement. Dewey opposed the formalistic nature of US public schools, and his Dewey School in Chicago—which he operated from 1896 to 1904 while teaching at the University of Chicago—promoted integrated, project-oriented, experiential learning based on the student's interests. While the Dewey School was not representative of other public schools in Chicago and was not heavily replicated in other cities, the writings of John Dewey and other prominent thinkers such as Boyd Bode, George Counts, Francis W. Parker, Caroline Pratt, and Helen Parkhurst, influenced many educational leaders of the time to consider loosening the reins on students.[93]

Cremin suggests the progressive movement began to collapse in the 1950s due to internal factionalism, erosion of political support, the rise of an "articulate opposition" associated with post–World War II conservatism, and ideological inflexibility.[94] One event in 1958, though, contributed more than any other to keep progressive schools from becoming the predominate model of schooling in the United States. That year, Russia launched the first human-made satellite, Sputnik, and many believed a lax educational system was to blame for allowing Russia to beat the United States into space. These fears helped bring closure to the progressive movement and caused widespread reform emphasizing science, math, and language and a compartmentalized curriculum rather than the integrated, experiential one espoused by Dewey.[95]

The 1950s also brought two Supreme Court decisions addressing segregation of schools. First, *Brown v. Board of Education of Topeka* was a landmark ruling that found state laws establishing racial segregation in public schools were unconstitutional.[96] The unanimous decision famously stated that "separate educational facilities are inherently unequal." The ruling, though, gave no guidance about how states should achieve desegregated schools, so in 1955, the Court issued a second decision, "Brown II" ambiguously ordered states to desegregate "with all deliberate speed."[97]

While formal, compartmentalized, and large schools became the norm in the United States, the Cold War and the Civil Rights Era desegregation policies opened school leaders to the idea of alternative models of instruction for some students. In some cases, policies provided White families the impetus and opportunity to flee from state-imposed desegregated schools; in others, people saw an opportunity to create schools that would empower marginalized groups. In both instances, the groundwork was laid for innovative, usually small, schools, and their inspiration came from across the Atlantic. In 1960, A. S. Neill published *Summerhill: A Radical Approach to Child Rearing* to document the boarding school he had founded in Suffolk, England, in 1921(see Figure P.3).[98] *Summerhill* became a best-seller and signaled the beginning of an ideological jump toward *"free schooling"* in the United States. Similar to the earlier progressive movement led by Dewey, this era had its ancestral roots in Jean-Jacques Rousseau's (1762/1979) classic French tale of Emile, an imaginary pupil whom the author plans to educate naturally so that Emile will learn by experience.[99] Rousseau wrote, "In leaving him thus master of his will, you will not be fomenting his caprices. By never doing anything except what suits him, he will soon do only what he ought to do."[100] At Summerhill, which operates still today, lessons are optional until the student "wants to learn"; there are no exams (except occasionally "for fun"); all school rules are voted on by the entire school; all discipline, direction, suggestion, moral training, and religious instruction are "renounced"; the director, Neill, is "the children's equal"; and "visitors cannot tell who is staff and who is pupil."[101] Now calling itself a democratic school, Neill's Summerhill launched an alternative school movement aimed at empowering students.

Neill's book coincided with the social consciousness—and increased teenage drug use—brewing in the United States in the 1960s, and it became the first of a series of radical treatises on public schools. According to D. Ravitch, the 1960s saw "the zeitgeist in American education swing wildly toward the liberationist, pseudo-revolutionary consciousness that was roiling the rest of the culture . . . Requirements became anathema."[102] By 1979, when the first school district-operated recovery high school opened its doors, over thirteen hundred alternative schools were in operation.[103]

Popular books of the time included John Holt's *How Children Fail,* Jonathan Kozol's *Death at an Early Age,* Herbert Kohl's *36 Children,* and Ivan Illich's *Deschooling Society,*

Figure P.3. A. S. Neill published *Summerhill: A Radical Approach to Child Rearing* in 1960. The book documented the boarding school he had founded in Suffolk, England, in 1921. *Summerhill* became a bestseller and signaled the beginning of an ideological jump towards "democratic" and "free schooling" in the United States. This is a photo of the Summerhill main building as it appeared in 1993. (Source: Axel Kühn at German Wikipedia.)

each of which criticized the ineffectiveness of public schools and promoted social consciousness and civic engagement.[104] Holt would later urge parents to "unschool" their children, becoming the foremost advocate of home-schools. The trumpeters of the cause, however, often disagreed wildly about which aspects of the new alternative schools should be emphasized. Duke finds seven configurations of goals among the alternative schools which emerged in the 1960s.[105] One of the configurations features "therapeutic goals," devoting considerable time to "introspection, values clarification, and exploratory 'rap' sessions."[106] While Duke can find no single cause for the rise of alternative schools, he does say they were all accessible by choice rather than assignment. Still, he also contends the schools enrolled "hardly a percentage point of the entire body of students presently enrolled in American elementary and secondary schools" by 1978.[107]

Graubard saw the concept of freedom as a theme common to the schools of this period, hence the classification of the period as the "free school" or the "open school" movement.[108] The schools designed by this philosophy were literally open and free. Duke provides a list of terms used to describe these schools, many of which speak directly to the abolishment or blurring of traditional boundaries: "free schools, storefront schools, continuation schools, three R's schools, magnet schools, mini-schools, street academies, schools-without-walls, and schools-within-schools."[109] Students would often gather in hallways or in businesses within the surrounding community for classes. Existing schools often knocked down walls, and new schools were built without them. Educational Facilities Laboratories, Inc., a nonprofit corporation established by the Ford Foundation in 1958 to research educational facilities, published blueprints for designing "open-space" schools titled *Profiles of Significant Schools: Schools Without Walls*.[110] The EFL manual describes schools without walls as "an educational process unbound by the barriers built into the conventional schoolhouse with its rows of standard classrooms. The major aim in these open-space schools is to provide an environment which encourages greater interaction between teacher and pupil, and between teacher and teacher. There are no partitions to fragment learning . . . no halls to funnel children . . . Each child finds his own place, creates his own path."[111] Other schools-without-walls, such as Chicago's Metro High, used the entire community for learning. Most classes would meet in spaces donated by institutions around Chicago, and up to 30 minutes travel time was allotted between classes.[112] The idea of peer and community support was integral to the alternative free school movement, and it was an ideology that inspired the leaders of each recovery high school described in this book.

Ultimately, distractions and the inability of teachers to exercise the traditional right to shut their doors to outside distractions doomed schools-without-walls. Indeed, the entire free school ideology faced stiff critique virtually from its beginning. In a review of Charles Silberman's promotion of open education and student freedom from 1970, organizational theorist Amitai Etzioni called the approach "impractical and misguided" and suggested Silberman was asking members to act selfishly to "maximize freedoms."[113] Cremin, whose classic work *The Transformation of the School* gave an historic account of the first progressive movement led by John Dewey, compared the free school movement to Dewey's era and essentially predicted its downfall.[114] Casting the "new progressive movement" as "ahistorical and atheoretical," Cremin wrote, "It is utter nonsense to think that by turning children loose in an unplanned and unstructured environment they can be freed in any significant way. Rather, they are abandoned to the blind forces of the hucksters."[115] Cremin's concerns proved to be prophetic when, just three years later, the publication of *A Nation at Risk* charged the nation's schools as the culprits in the failure of US students to achieve at the same levels of their international counterparts.[116] Any momentum that may have begun for alternative schools slowed once again as schools were jolted back to basics and away from freedom.

As researchers rushed in to diagnose the illness afflicting US schools in the 1980s, a variety of reform efforts and prescriptions were presented. An early 1980s study by James Coleman and his colleagues examined the national dataset, "High School and Beyond," and determined that Catholic schools did a better job of educating disadvantaged students than public schools.[117] This began a long-running discussion of the virtues of private schooling compared to the challenges of public education. H. M. Levin espoused the benefits of bringing market and public choice to public schools.[118] C. E. Finn said the nation's school system needed to provide more choice to families because, among other reasons, "the alternative is incompatible with American democracy."[119] While the *choice movement* was aimed at improving public schools, nonpublic schools served as both a frame and a competitive foil for the philosophical discussion. Chubb and Moe claimed, "Choice is being embraced by liberals and conservatives alike as a powerful means of transforming the structure and performance of public education—while keeping the public schools public."[120] Driven by these arguments, efforts to grant students the freedom to attend schools outside their zoned boundaries expanded during the late 1980s and early 1990s, including measures such as vouchers to fund private school placements, income tax credits for private school families, and the creation of magnet schools and charter schools.[121]

By design, charter schools are more autonomous than other public schools in that they are released from many of the state and local regulations governing traditional schools, and students attend voluntarily. Unlike the full-fledged "free schools" of the 1960s and 1970s, however, charter schools face stricter accountability to the public. As publicly funded schools, if they fail to perform at certain standards, their charters can be revoked. Additionally, the freedom from restrictions varies from state to state depending on the charter laws. Initially promoted as incubators of innovation, the free-market philosophy embraced by many charter advocates have made the schools targets of many democratic/free school advocates from the 1970s, such as Deborah Meier and William Ayers. Charter schools have even been accused of resegregating public schools and underserving their students (Ravitch, 2000).

The first recovery high school operated entirely by a public school district opened in Maryland at the end of the free school movement, just before the release of *A Nation at Risk* report, and the first major wave of schools occurred in Minnesota as part of the school choice movement, which was fueled by the same report. Unlike many of the public compensatory and punitive alternative schools existing today, many of which employ some form of behavior modification, recovery high schools have voluntary enrollment and would describe themselves as progressive, community-based, and child-centered—similar to the early Dewey-era schools. Most receive some type of public funding. Coincidentally, Minnesota, which passed the first charter school law in 1991, began operating "contracted alternative schools" of choice many years before charters were legalized. The first two recovery high schools in Minnesota were contract alternative schools, and both later became charter schools. Rapid expansion of recovery high schools occurred throughout the 2000s, in part by taking advantage of new charter school laws across the nation.

Merging of Substance Use Programs and Schooling

In reviewing the literature on substance use programming in schools, the first school-based programs arose in response to the exploding teenage drug use of the 1960s and

1970s and initially emphasized prevention. By the mid-1970s, the limits of those prevention programs were already apparent. Bard (1975) provided a critical analysis of early school-based drug use programs,= titled, tellingly, "The Failure of Our School Drug Abuse Programs," which focused on the preventative role of drug education programs within the general school population.[122] Bard states that the costs of drug abuse education programs had risen to about $100 million annually by 1975.[123] The typical progression would be for communities to see drug problems from afar, until the local community was impacted. Schools would then attempt to offer some type of programming to stem the tide. Often the impact of such programming would be to exacerbate the drug problem rather than to reduce it.

Several school-based intervention programs designed specifically for active drug users opened in the 1970s. Like the recovery schools that would evolve later, the high schools in the early years of adolescent alcohol and drug programs were also explicitly providing an education to young people in recovery from substance use disorders, before the terms "substance use disorder" or "recovery high school" existed. Schools in treatment centers and alcohol and drug services in alternative schools are common today, but in the early 1970s, they were just beginning. What made them different from how we now understand recovery high schools was that the education component was either adjunct to a treatment program (in the case of treatment schools), or not every student enrolled was in recovery from alcohol or drug issues (as was the case with alternative schools).

One type of program was *a school operating within an inpatient or out-patient treatment program*. These "treatment schools" provided academic classes for patients in alcohol and drug treatment facilities, usually leading to either a diploma, a high school equivalency certificate, or help to transition back into regular schools. Adolescent patients might remain in some of these treatment programs for one to two years, which made schooling a necessity. The two earliest examples were both in New York and they served diverse populations of students, mostly from lower-income communities: the Odyssey House and the Canarsie Youth Center. Odyssey and Canarsie could be considered the forerunners of the recovery high school movement—the main difference being their primary purpose was drug treatment, as indicated by their names. School was just one of the many wraparound services the early treatment schools provided, and education was framed as advancing treatment goals.

Dr. Judianne Densen-Gerber founded Odyssey House in New York in 1966, and it grew to include multiple sites in the city, eventually expanding both nationally and internationally. Odyssey House was a residential treatment program utilizing the therapeutic community approach, and it featured typical TC elements, such as encounter group, marathon sessions, and a "hierarchical normative system of social control." Odyssey also modified its program for specific populations, people with psychiatric disorders, those with gifted intelligence, and, starting in 1969, adolescents.[124]

The Odyssey House Adolescent Program was created for youths aged 12 to 19 "to respond to the sudden epidemic of addiction in the New York City population of adolescents, which at that time accounted for 332 deaths or twenty-five percent of the addiction deaths in the city."[125] The program featured "communal living" and "shared responsibility," and in 1970, it began operating a school on-site for its treatment residents, "Public School (P.S.) 203M." The school billed itself as "the first publicly funded adolescent treatment unit featuring a full-service residential high school."[126] P.S. 203M employed three teachers and a principal assigned exclusively to Odyssey, and the school was woven into the Adolescent Treatment Units as well as into its Parents' Program, with the teachers trained in TC methods. Students obtained a high school diploma or were "channelled back to regular high schools after making a satisfactory adjustment."[127] Founder Dr. Densen-Gerber described the school in this way:

> P.S. 203M conducts small classes within the aforementioned facilities with the objective of upgrading educational deficiencies of residents as well as minimizing the disculturation that often accompanies institutionalization. Those who have attended P.S. 203M at Odyssey House have ranged in age from ten to fifty, the older residents from other facilities attending at the Adolescent Units. In the stages of early treatment, attendance in the regular New York school system is prohibited because of widespread drug availability within the schools.[128]

One year after Odyssey House started its on-site school, another treatment school opened in a converted warehouse on Rockaway Avenue in Brooklyn. The Canarsie Youth Center transitioned in 1971 from a therapeutic community behavior-modification program modeled after Synanon into a humanistic "drug rehabilitation center."[129] The new director, April Vandetta, created a center for "psychologically addicted" persons rather than "physically addicted" ones requiring detoxification.[130] In order to receive funding from New York State Office of Drug Abuse Services, the program needed to assert that all its students were drug users, but in fact, Lawson writes, not all the students used drugs. They were "young human beings in a special education program designed to assist them with special problems," and they were referred by a "manifestation of adjustment problems, involving truancy, and minor drug offenses."[131]

The center assigned four counselors to the school who provided individual counseling, in-home visitations, and workshops in areas such as cooking, nutrition, drama, videotaping, writing, woodwork, ceramics, typewriting, silk-screening, yoga, movement therapy, music, chess, checkers, health care, and child care."[132] Similar to Odyssey House, the school had three teachers—two assigned by the New York City Board of Education and the other from the Canarsie staff. Clients were in academic classes for three hours per day in English, Math, and Social Studies, and they could take a six-hour test to earn a High School Equivalency Diploma.

The Alpha School, another treatment program with a school, also opened in Brooklyn in March 1971.[133] In introducing the program, New York Mayor John Lindsay called it "the nation's first public school that will seek to rehabilitate former addicts while they continue their high school education."[134] Designed for a capacity of sixty students, Alpha was funded by the Narcotics Addiction Control Commission and the New York's Addiction Services Agency and employed a therapeutic community (TC) milieu. Students would "sleep and eat" at the school, similar to the therapeutic boarding schools of today. Half the twelve-person staff were encounter group leaders in recovery who had been treated at local treatment centers such as Phoenix House and Synanon, and the other six staff members were teachers.[135]

The Alpha School had four classrooms and was located in what once had been a milk factory. Most of the students "were dropouts from (nearby) Thomas Jefferson High School. Almost all of them were heroin addicts; most had records of juvenile delinquency."[136] Students spent up to a year in the school, where they would take classes to stay on-track academically while receiving intensive counseling. They would then return to Thomas Jefferson, where they were expected to "counsel their peers about the dangers of drug abuse."[137] As evidence of the stigma associated with substance use, their school records would not indicate that they had attended the Alpha School.

The New York programs were trailblazers in recognizing that schooling was critical for teenagers receiving treatment for alcohol and drug problems. Whereas Odyssey House's P.S. 203M, the Canarsie Youth Center, and the Alpha School were schools located within treatment centers, another approach for drug intervention programs was to embed rehabilitation programs in schools serving the general population. A few traditional high schools employed substance use programs. San Francisco, for example, established "crash pads" in four high schools to provide treatment services on-site in the early 1970s. The programs were a partnership between the health department and the school district and were staffed by psychiatric professionals, doctors, nurses, student aides, and social workers. One teacher described the crash pads as "a rap center, where kids can get accurate drug information, with no moralizing and relatively little judging; where they can talk about personal problems with other students, social workers or teachers—and feel safe doing it."[138]

More common than embedding treatment programs in traditional high schools was providing substance use services in alternative schools. The alternative schools of choice emerging in both the private and public sectors during the 1970s were efforts either to educate children who were not succeeding in the traditional system or to provide a better education for youths who might succeed in traditional schools, but for whom the traditional school was not seen as sufficient. According to Hawkins and Wall, alternative schools in the 1970s predominantly attracted two groups of students, often divided along racial lines: "(1) white, middle class 'opt-outs' who were bored or disillusioned with traditional schools; and (2) inner city, low income, primarily minority youth who had given up on school and/or had been expelled."[139] In either case, alternative schools of choice were usually seen as better schools for families attracted to them. Compulsory alternative schools also existed to reform students with discipline problems and were often viewed as dumping grounds. Recovery high schools emerged less from the expulsion/compulsion model than from the alternative schools of choice approach—the idea being that kids who did not want to stop using drugs would only "dry out" for a few weeks or months in a forced program, while kids who were motivated to be clean and sober would fare better in a choice school.

Bard suggested that alternative schools were more effective at addressing drug problems than embedding drug abuse programs within traditional schools, not necessarily because they could offer focused drug abuse programming (which they could), but rather because they might engage disaffected students in such a way as to make drugs less compelling.[140] Interestingly, in the 1970s era of lower drinking ages, methadone management programs, and marijuana decriminalization, complete abstinence from drug use was not universally seen as the best goal for school-based drug programming. Rather, programs emphasized helping students make healthy decisions and learn self-regulation to reduce or stop drug abuse—precursors of the harm reduction approach. For some, peer supports and a humanistic milieu were viewed as the key factors for alternative schools to help teens stop abusing drugs, rather than focusing on abolishing drug use for life.[141] The main distinction between an alternative school with a drug program and a recovery high school was that the former was not limited to students in recovery from substance use disorders. Still, more and more schooling options were created throughout the 1970s, and as attention paid to drug use programs in schools increased, recovery high schools for students with substance use disorders became a logical extension.

The Association of Recovery Schools published a typology of school programs for students with substance use disorders, categorizing general program modalities other than recovery high schools in which students might receive both therapeutic interventions for their substance use problems and academic coursework to help them earn a high school diploma.[142] The categories include therapeutic boarding schools, alcohol and drug treatment center schools, nontraditional/alternative schools, and traditional secondary schools.

Each of the school types can and do provide recovery support services, such as individual and group counseling, peer accountability, drug-screening, level-systems, drug-free social functions, and the like. Indeed, in the early years of adolescent alcohol and drug programs, there were so few programs that none were making such granular distinctions as is possible today. There were no education standards or best practices for the schools embedded in the substance use programs, and there was no research to guide school development. The schools associated with those early programs would try to catch patients up or keep them on track until the treatment was completed and they transferred back into the original schools.

In the 1970s, of course, the Association of Recovery Schools did not yet exist (it was created in 2002), and the delineation between a "recovery high school" and other school alternatives with drug abuse programming was murkier. Even the term "recovery high school" likely was not used itself in association with specialty schools until 1992 when a school named "Recovery High School" opened in Albuquerque, New Mexico.[143] Although each recovery high school operates differently depending on available community resources and state standards, they do share the following characteristics:[144]

- The primary purpose of a recovery high school is to educate and support students in recovery from substance use or co-occurring disorders. Their main identity is a school. Recovery high schools are not treatment programs and are not designed to provide primary treatment for substance use or co-occurring disorders.
- Recovery high schools meet state requirements for awarding a secondary school diploma. Recovery high schools offer credits leading to a state-recognized high school diploma, and their students are not just getting tutored or completing work from another school while there. While many schools transition students back to traditional schools, numerous students graduate from recovery high schools, and a few have spent all their high school years in a recovery high school.
- All students are working an abstinence-focused program of recovery as agreed upon by the student and the school. Recovery high schools promote abstinence and a drug-free environment for all youth who choose to attend. Recovery high schools usually do not require prior treatment or a set number of days without using for admission, though some have and do. Recovery high schools enroll students following different pathways to recovery, but they do not supplant or replace treatment.
- Recovery high schools are available to any student in recovery who meets state or district eligibility requirements for attendance. While some recovery high school students will need both treatment and a recovery high school, the schools are not simply the academic component of a primary or extended-care treatment facility or therapeutic boarding school, where the primary purpose is treatment. Some students may not benefit from a recovery high school, based on where they are in the stages of change. Recovery high schools are uniquely situated to refer these youth to the services they need.

Methodology and Scope of the Project

This book will trace the origin stories for six of the first recovery high schools. The study was reviewed by the Vanderbilt University Institutional Review Board, and data collection included **interviews** with staff members, students, families, and community advocates / stakeholders, a thorough **literature search** of historical documents and media, and **site visits** to gain an understanding of the physical and environmental context for school operations. Through the examination of transcript, observational data, and document analysis, the research focused on the following questions:

1. What were the factors that led to the establishment of the earliest recovery high schools, including the background and inspiration of the founders?
2. What were similarities and differences across the featured recovery high schools?

3. What challenges did the featured recovery high schools face?
4. What influence did the recovery high schools have on their students?

Except for one school that prepared its students for a General Educational Development (GED) certificate, all six exhibited the four characteristics stated by ARS to some degree, and all identified as schools first. These six schools were selected either because they were the earliest schools of their kind, or because they were influential in the nascent recovery high school movement.

Book Outline

This prologue and chapter 10 establish the context for the creation of recovery high schools, and the epilogue will give a synopsis of what happened to those schools and their founders. An afterward will then summarize themes that emerged from the research, including lessons learned about recovery high school development, the potential for growth, and issues and barriers on the horizon. The main text will provide the stories of six foundational recovery high school programs:

The Freedom Road School in South Carolina (chapters 1–2), which opened in 1973, was the first school located off the site of a treatment center in which all students were working on their recovery. Like the Odyssey House, the Canarsie Youth Center, and the Alpha School in New York, Freedom Road used teachers employed by the local school district. What made Freedom Road unique and thus a focal point here was that the treatment and recovery services were embedded in the school rather than the other way around. The Freedom Road School also went a step beyond the New York schools by developing an arrangement with the local school district to enroll any student expelled for drug use. Furthermore, while the counselors were affiliated with the local public health center, which had a treatment program, some students were only enrolled at the school, and thus did not participate in the other treatment components. The primary identity of Freedom Road was as a school, making it the first program of its kind, and a direct ancestor of today's recovery high schools.

The Palmer Drug Abuse Program GED School in Houston (chapter 3) opened in 1976. While the students were preparing for a GED rather than a high school diploma, they attended classes in a school building and had a commencement ceremony. This school began independent of any other organization, initially operating out of its founder's apartment. It was the first school with no connection to a treatment center, but it did merge with the nation's first alternative peer group (APG)—an adolescent recovery support model that integrates recovering peers and prosocial activities.[145] The recovery high school–APG partnership approach would later thrive in Texas, and become the foundation for one of the most influential schools, Archway Academy in Houston, as well as a model for other schools around the nation.

The Phoenix School in Silver Spring, Maryland (chapters 4–9) opened in 1979, and it was the first recovery high school owned and operated completely by the local school district, and some thus consider it the first full-fledged recovery high school. Montgomery County Public Schools funded the school, provided its staff, and set its policies. The school in Silver Spring was so successful that the county opened a second campus in Gaithersburg called *Phoenix II* (chapter 9) in 1983, for which the district used local industrial arts classes to construct a facility. The two schools lasted over thirty years.

Sobriety High in Minnesota (chapters 11–13, and 16) opened in 1987, under the name New Dimensions. It began as a private school, but eventually forged a contract with Edina (Minnesota) Public Schools. Sobriety High received national publicity that sparked the creation of many other schools nationwide. It was so well-known relative to the schools that had come before it that many believed it was the first recovery high school.[146] Perhaps the most impactful school influenced by Sobriety High was the Holos School, which opened in Minneapolis in 1989. Interestingly, the people who started Holos did so, in part, because they had observed Sobriety High and felt they could create a better program. The first Holos students voted to change the name to *Peers Enjoying a Sober Education (P.E.A.S.E.) Academy* (chapters 14–16) in its first semester, and today, the school is the longest continually operating recovery high school.

A Note on Privacy

This project was submitted to the Vanderbilt University Institutional Review Board, which determined the study posed minimal risk to participants, in part because the events happened decades ago. All participants were provided information about the topic and nature of the study as well as the intention to publish the story in a book, and the author received verbal consent from all participants before conducting and recording interviews. In some cases, participants requested that birth names be used rather than married or changed names. Typically, the name a person was using when the events occurred is the name used in the book. In instances where a person or their family wished to remain anonymous, their names and other identifiable information are not included. Each of these situations are explained in notes throughout the book.

Many of the historical documents, such as newspaper and magazine articles, school yearbooks and records, correspondence, and evaluation reports, revealed the names of people and their personal information. Some of the details include specific stories about mental health distress, problematic alcohol and drug use, family discord, self-harm, and suicide attempts, and many of the people of interest to this work were minors at the time of their inclusion in the artifacts. Their stories may have been shared freely at the time, and most are available in published sources. Those stories, however, were usually only published once, with the descriptions provided by the reporters and researchers of the time. No additional context or verification was available, and while those events may have happened long ago in a person's past, that person may not wish to have them shared today. Thus, if it was determined by the author and publisher that a person's story might potentially be distressing to them or their family if revealed here, their names were excluded to respect their privacy. The only exceptions made were if a person was sharing their story in a public forum (such as a professional or governmental meeting or fundraiser), or if it was featured in multiple publications over time—evidence that the person was intentionally making their story available for the benefit of their audience or readers.

Several direct quotes from news accounts and other historical documents are included, and citations are noted for each. All other direct quotations were transcribed from interviews conducted by the author and research assistants. In the interest of space, those interviews are not included with other references, except in cases where a fact was shared by a participant and not cited elsewhere.

Scope

The people involved with creating these schools did not realize they were part of a movement, and they did not have a model to follow—which is what makes their own backgrounds intriguing. Understanding the roots of an innovator helps discern why the innovation happened, and this book will trace the creators' paths. The stories told here stretch from the beginning of Alcoholics Anonymous through the turbulent 1960s; the declaration of the War on Drugs through the advice for kids to "Just Say No"; and from the *Brown vs. Board of Education* decision to desegregate schools through the Summerhill free school movement and onto the *A Nation at Risk* report. Each of those events played a role in the development of recovery high schools and will provide the context for the school narratives.

As a few of the schools existed over decades, the complete story of those schools is beyond the scope of this work, though the epilogue will discuss the general fate of each. Future research can explore in depth the expansion of the movement, the closure of schools, and the establishment of the national Association of Recovery Schools. The focus here will be how recovery high schools started and established a key role in helping the United States avoid becoming a teenage wasteland.

Figures

PART I

OUT OF THE WILDERNESS

1
Carrying the Message

Dr. C. Sidney Jordan Jr. arrived in Charleston, South Carolina, in the summer of 1969 after traveling nearly three thousand miles from San Francisco. Jordan was fresh from a yearlong postdoctorate fellowship at the Langley-Porter Neuropsychiatric Institute, trading the fog off the Pacific Ocean for the thick humid air at the confluence of the Ashley and Cooper Rivers flowing into the Atlantic. He had grown up on a farm in Georgia, in a small town with only eighteen hundred people, and, as a Southerner, the trip was a homecoming of sorts.

"Everybody was the parent," said Jordan of his childhood. "We were a village raising children in a small town."

Jordan graduated from Emory University in Atlanta, and he got his master's and PhD at the University of Georgia, before making the trek west to the heart of psychedelia for his postdoctorate work. The southern drawl in Sid Jordan's voice and the cadence of life would feel more familiar to the residents of Charleston than to the revolutionaries in the Bay Area.

By the late 1960s, it appeared as though there was not much that Northern California and South Carolina had in common. In the years before Sid Jordan moved to San Francisco, the region had come to define the counterculture movement. The movement had been established in the late 1950s by the Beat Generation authors, such as Allen Ginsberg, Jack Kerouac, and William S. Burroughs. The works, most notably Ginsberg's *Howl*, Kerouac's *On the Road*, and Burroughs's *Naked Lunch*, had inspired what was known as the Silent Generation of people born during the Great Depression and World War II.[1] The Beat writers were part of a culture that rejected materialism, experimented with drugs, and promoted sexual liberation.[2] Many of the Beat writers had met in and around New York City in the 1940s, and by the early 1960s, several had relocated to the West Coast during the San Francisco Renaissance, where their writing would influence a new generation—the Baby Boomers.

The Baby Boomer Generation, which technically began in 1946, came of age during the 1960s, with the first of the children born after World War II graduating from high school around the time of President John F. Kennedy's assassination and Martin Luther King's "I Have a Dream" speech during the March on Washington—both occurring in 1963. A counterculture movement had exploded in the United States as a synthesis of many forces following JFK's death, including the burgeoning civil rights movement and the acceleration of Vietnam War.

In 1967, an estimated one hundred thousand people flocked to the Haight-Asbury district of San Francisco to experience the "Summer of Love," the epitome of the

Salvaging a Teenage Wasteland. Andrew J. Finch, Oxford University Press. © Oxford University Press 2024.
DOI: 10.1093/oso/9780190645502.003.0001

counterculture movement. David Hinckley described the "hippies" who converged on Haight-Asbury in a retrospective newspaper article:

> Hippies were themselves a cultural hybrid. Suspicious of the system, they were widely sympathetic to the peace-and-equality agenda of the Left, which was fast piling onto the anti-Vietnam War train. On the other hand, many preferred sex, drugs and rock 'n' roll to speeches, which also gave them spiritual kinship to the 1950s beatniks, whose 1967 remnants included the Fugs[3] singing "Kill for Peace" at the Players Theater by night and lead Fug Ed Sanders running the Peace Eye book-store on E. 10th St. by day. While the occasional icon like Allen Ginsberg straddled all counterculture factions, and while Pravda[4] wrote that hippies might be just the kind of subversives who could overthrow capitalism, much of the Summer of Love crowd was less primed for revolution than just sick of summer jobs, the suburbs or the old man's rules.[5]

Drug use and experimentation was a prominent part of the movement for many young people. It was in the Bay Area that former Harvard professor Dr. Timothy Leary urged people to "Turn on, tune in, drop out," most prominently at the "Human Be-In" at Golden Gate State Park. Leary would later write, " 'Turn on' meant go within to activate your neural and genetic equipment.[6] Become sensitive to the many and various levels of consciousness and the specific triggers engaging them. Drugs were one way to accomplish this end."

Haight-Ashbury was at the core of the hippie movement, and in the process has be-come its icon.[7] Anthony Ashbolt described the ethos as follows:

> Hundreds and then thousands of "flower children" had flocked to San Francisco in search of love, peace, community and self. They sought refuge from an American dream that was crumbling quickly in suburban wastelands and urban hothouses, as well as the jungles of Vietnam. The Haight-Ashbury district of San Francisco was the focus.

At that beginning, the revolution was hopeful and utopian,[8] as captured by anthems such as "San Francisco (Be Sure to Wear Flowers in Your Hair)" by Scott McKenzie; "Happy Together" by the Turtles; and "Are You Experienced?" by Jimi Hendrix. Not everyone, though, idealized the movement. Consider this poem distributed on a flyer in 1968. It was titled "An Open Poem to the Prophets and Their Apostles,"[9]

> *Ruling guru greybeard bards*
> *Having new fun in yr rolling rock renaissance.*
> *Have u passed thru the Haight*
> *Lately?*
> *Have u seen yr turned on kids?*
> *U promised them Visions & Love & Sharing.*

They got
Clap, hepatitis, fleas, begging & the gang-bang.
Sure you didn't want to see the scene go that way
But that's how the shit went down.
And I do not hear your "Howl."
I do not see u exorcising demons.

That flyer had been written around the time Sid Jordan moved to San Francisco in July 1968, which was just months after Martin Luther King Jr. and Robert Kennedy had been assassinated. Jordan's office was at the Langley-Porter Institute on the campus of the University of California-San Francisco Medical Center, only five minutes from Haight-Asbury.[10] Being so close to "the Haight," Jordan could not avoid exposure to the cultural revolutionaries, in the form of artists, poets, musicians, and hippies:

"I met the drug culture of the Haight-Ashbury scene the first day in making my way to Langley-Porter on the hill above the Haight and Golden Gate Park. One of my colleagues in the fellowship was assigned to the drug clinic in the Haight, so I remained informed and had some direct experience with the hippie culture in the Haight and Berkeley, where there was rebellion and tear gas in the streets of Telegraph Ave."

The hippies and counterculture revolutionaries wanted a transformation from many traditions, and in the field of mental health, Langley-Porter embodied the spirit of the age by rooting psychology in the community. It was California's first neuropsychiatric institute, and preeminent researchers such as psychologist Paul Ekman and anthropologist Gregory Bateson had worked there.[11]

"We had a fantastic set of supervisors," said Jordan. "We had psychoanalysts. I had a psychologist as my supervisor. We had social workers. We had an anthropologist who was an urban anthropologist, who had vast experience in Oakland. It was a fantastic group of people."

His postdoc was in community mental health, and one prominent characteristic was that the training required immersion in the community. It was through his community training that Jordan began working with schools.

"Eighty-percent of our time was spent doing consultations in the community, and I focused on schools," Jordan recounted. His research concentrated on the efficacy of preschools assisting a child's early development through third grade. One of his findings was that the positive impact of preschool regressed over time—an idea that would be supported by later research of the Head Start program, which launched in 1965.[12] Jordan attributed the structure of the school system for the decline (see Figure 1.1).

"Later research supports that idea," said Jordan, "that the public school system, which is a colonialized, industrialized school system, takes away all individuality and freedom of a student."

The schools Jordan studied were not in Haight-Ashbury. Jordan was immersed in a community about thirty minutes away in the southeastern part of the city

Figure 1.1. Dr. C. Sidney "Sid" Jordan Jr. was the director of mental health services for the new Franklin C. Fetter Family Health Care Center, a comprehensive program being created to service low-income residents in Charleston, South Carolina. He would spend five years in that role, ultimately leading the effort to launch one of the first high schools for youth in recovery from substance use disorders. This photo is of Dr. Jordan as he appeared during the writing of this book. (Source: Neohumanist College website.)

called Hunters Point. The two landmarks of the area were Candlestick Park and the Hunters Point Naval Shipyard. The shipyard housed the Naval Radiological Defense Laboratory (NRDL) after the war, and its activities contaminated the area so badly it was declared a Superfund site due to the presence of radioactive materials.[13]

The offices at UCSF and the communities of Hunters Point and nearby Bayview had been impacted by discriminatory housing policies. Many Black people had been driven out by red-lining and expensive housing, and they had chosen to move to the Bayview-Hunters Point area, which they found to be more racially accepting and financially affordable. In the 1950s and 1960s, the shipyard also had attracted African American workers from across the country as part of the Great Migration, so by the time Jordan arrived, the Bayview-Hunters Point residents were predominantly Black.[14] At the same time, most of the police officers were White, some recruited from the South. A local activist organization opined, "From this point onwards, racial discrimination–in terms of the environment, housing, employment, and policing—shaped the development of the Bayview Hunters Point and further contributed to its segregation from the rest of the city."[15]

In contrast to the counterculture revolution occurring in the Haight, which was predominantly White, the heavily Black Bayview-Hunters Point region was more recognizable to a Southerner like Dr. Sid Jordan.

"It felt like home to me having been brought up on a farm in Georgia and raised by Black people as much as my White family," said Jordan. "People that lived out there all came from Mississippi, Alabama, Georgia, Louisiana. And it was like going home."

"I loved it when, in the first meeting with psychologist Betty Kalis, one of the developers of Crisis Intervention Therapy, she asked me if I would like to work in Hunter's Point."

Langley-Porter trained Jordan in an indirect "community mental health" approach more likely than direct service to establish rapport and empower the local residents—an approach that proved effective for a White, male psychologist with a southern accent immersed in a low-income Black community.

"I was trained as a mental health consultant, which is an indirect service, not a direct service," said Jordan. "It taught me how to not be an expert, but to listen to people, and help them use their talent. Not come in as an expert but come in as someone to help foster the talent that is sitting in front of you with these agencies that you work with, with the schools, with the people from the community. It's about fostering their competence, and not being an expert with explaining everything and directing everything."

If the community desired Jordan's services, UCSF would establish a contract to offer consultation that could be client-centered, consultee-centered, or program-centered concerning the mental health issues they encountered.

"In all cases," said Jordan, "It was about recognizing the positive contributions being made and how to have a positive impact on the mental health issues related to the clients, consultees, or programs by doing collective problem solving."

An Opportunity in Charleston

Jordan had started consulting in Charleston, South Carolina, while still in San Francisco completing his fellowship. The night before he took the assignment in Hunters Point, the chair of the Department of Psychiatry at the Medical College of South Carolina, Dr. Layton McCurdy, had offered Jordan a position upon completion of his postdoc, and a stipend while doing his fellowship to help develop mental health services at a new community health center. Jordan accepted the job, so during his year at Hunters Point, Jordan made the three-thousand-mile trip to Charleston every three months to consult there as well. Working as a consultant while still completing his postdoc assignment meant Jordan would be learning and training simultaneously, and his experience at Hunters Point naturally influenced his approach in Charleston.

"We'd sit down once a week with (our supervisors at the Langley Porter Institute) and share our experience," Jordan said. "And they would come in, and they make very wise comments, using that indirect style, nonjudgmental style, and supportive style. It was like the kind of parenting you'd always wanted. Without that training, I wouldn't have known what to do in that community."

That training would serve Jordan well in the social cauldron that was Charleston in the summer of '69. Jordan settled into his new home in the midsummer, after relocating from San Francisco to Charleston at the completion of his postdoc, and he essentially had taken on three jobs at once. He had accepted an appointment to the faculty of the Department of Psychiatry at the Medical University (formerly the Medical College) of South Carolina as well as a position as a clinical psychologist at the Charleston Area Mental Health Center. His most prominent position, though, would be as the director of mental health services for a new Comprehensive Health Care Center being created to service low-income residents in the Eastern part of town. He would spend five years in that role, ultimately leading the effort to launch one of the first high schools for youth in recovery from substance use disorders.

While in San Francisco, Jordan had been near some of the most publicized protests of the sixties. Charleston, however, had managed for the most part to stay on the sidelines.

"Charleston of 1969 was an anachronism," wrote Brian Hicks, in his biography of Joe Riley, who served as its mayor for forty years.[16] "Once among the nation's largest and most sophisticated cities, it was now merely a small, quiet seaside town most noteworthy for a large collection of antebellum homes protected by the nation's first serious preservation movement."

"The greatest–perhaps only–signs of growth were the new buildings going up around the Medical College."[17]

That growth was partly what brought Sid Jordan to South Carolina, and it was also what would allow Charleston to become one of the first cities in the world to have an alcohol and drug treatment program specifically designed for adolescents– something that did not exist in Charleston or anywhere else in August 1969. It would be a few years, though, before that treatment began. To get there, Jordan would have to navigate social dynamics older than the nation itself, and steeped in generations of segregation, aristocracy, discrimination, and white supremacy.

When describing the Charleston ecology, Jordan said, "It was not all roses. It was a tough road to hoe, working with the implicit biases in the community toward the Black community, and their implicit biases toward the White community, and towards law enforcement. And I put myself in the middle of all these dynamics."

"But that's what I was trained to do at Langley-Porter (in California)," he said.

"While Birmingham and Montgomery were torn apart by violence," wrote Hicks, "Charleston sat idle through the fight for equal rights with little more than a few lunch counter sit-ins. There had always been an uneasy détente among Black and White Charlestonians, as if matters of race were meant to be avoided. Such unpleasantness had no place in a polite town of Southern manners. And so the town limped along."[18]

There were signs, however, that Charleston was entering a more progressive moment. Just weeks before Jordan landed in town, the Medical College itself was embroiled in a historic strike that had threatened that "détente."[19] In March, twelve Black workers took over the Medical College Hospital president William McCord's office to protest discriminatory work conditions. After returning to work, they were fired, and their union voted to strike. The union demanded their workers be rehired, a grievance procedure to be adopted, the union to be recognized, and the minimum hourly wage to be raised 30-cents to the federal standard of $1.60.[20] In response to the demands, President McCord declared, with not so subtle hints of white supremacy, he would not "turn a twenty-five million dollar complex over to a bunch of people who don't have a grammar school education," and by the end of the month Charleston County Hospital workers joined the strike.[21]

The strike would last over three months, during which civil rights leaders such as Dr. Ralph David Abernathy and Andrew Young traveled to the city, and Dr. Abernathy was arrested multiple times. In April, Governor Robert McNair ordered five hundred National Guardsmen with fixed bayonets onto the streets. Coretta Scott King delivered a speech at the Emmanuel A.M.E. Church, just over a year after her husband, Dr. Martin Luther King Jr. had been assassinated in Memphis, and then she led a march in the hospital area.[22] The day after the march, Governor McNair declared a state of emergency and imposed a curfew.[23] In June, Senator Strom Thurmond joined with President McCord in refusing a settlement.[24] Dr. Abernathy went on a hunger strike in his jail cell,[25] the AFL-CIO threatened to close the Port of Charleston, the federal Department of Health, Education, and Welfare threatened to halt federal funds, and the White House sent mediators as sporadic violence broke out. "Finally," wrote Hicks, "the pressure was too great to ignore any longer. Local civil rights activists, including Bill Saunders of Johns Island, were able to broker a deal with officials from the two hospitals."[26]

If Jordan's time in San Francisco trained him how to engage with such a contentious environment, the hospital strike provided a lesson on who held the power in both the White and Black communities, and the people willing and able to bridge the cultural divide.

"It's a small community with a very systematic political infrastructure," said Jordan. "That's what made things work well in this town, and as a social engineer, training in community mental health and indirect consultation services, I was always interested in that level of interaction."

Beyond the administrators of the Medical University, the gatekeepers included White legislators such as Strom Thurmond and Ernest "Fritz" Hollings, South Carolina's two US senators, who each had also served terms as governor, and Black leaders, such as Bill Saunders and Rev. Henry L. Grant—each of whom would be integral to bringing public alcohol and drug treatment services to Charleston.

Saunders had negotiated on behalf of the hospital strikers, and he had grown up in Charleston on Johns Island, attending the segregated Mt. Zion Elementary School. He attended two Black high schools—Burke High School and Laing High School, the first public high school accredited by Charleston County.[27] The reason for attending two schools was that he left high school at age fifteen to join the army and fight in Korea, lying about his age to do so.[28] Wounded in Korea, he was not awarded a Purple Heart until 2002.[29]

While Charleston may not have been as active in the civil rights movement in the 1960s as other cities, Bill Saunders was. As a Black Power advocate, he spoke out in print through the *Lowcountry Newsletter*,[30] and on-air as a host on WPAL, Charleston's first radio station targeting African Americans and promoting Black culture. Saunders created a self-defense group and established the Committee on Better Racial Assurance (COBRA), a mediation and communications organization. In 1970, he cofounded South Carolina's fourth political party, the United Citizens Party.[31] Here, Sid Jordan discusses Saunders influence on himself and on the community:

> When the Black Panthers came to town, COBRA ushered them out of town, took them to the edge of town, and said, 'We'll handle things here.' They had eight different factions of the black community, from mulatto to the A.M.E. church, the Episcopal Church, and they all had an understanding about what was going to happen in the black community. And they didn't want the Black Panthers handling the politics. They had a direct channel with the mayor's office and with the City Council, with people like Henry Grant.

Rev. Grant had only lived in Charleston since 1960, but he had become a dominant figure in race relations. He was dubbed a "bridge of communication between the races" who "commands attention on both sides of whatever racial gap exists."[32] Grant directed the St. John's Episcopal Mission and was "priest-in-charge" of St. Stephen's Church in East Charleston.[33] Jordan called Grant a "political force." His congregants called him simply "the Rock."[34]

"He was a bit of a Napoleon in his diplomacy, but he got things done," said Jordan. "And I could always rely on him if I had a problem in the community, or even a problem with the politics of the health care center. He said, 'Don't worry about it. I'll take care of it.' He was very supportive of every program that I had. And without him a lot of things couldn't happen. He took care of the backroom caucus."

It took the work of each of these civic leaders and many others to bring better health care services to Charleston's poor and Black communities, but none of them had a primary interest in substance use disorders. Not that they were opposed; it was just they had other expertise and priorities. Even psychologist Sid Jordan had engaged in community mental health more broadly and preschool education more empirically. In the late 1960s, alcohol and other drug addiction carried stigma, and the stigma was even more pronounced in Charleston's social ecology. Addiction was something to be hidden both for poor Black families not wanting to draw negative attention and for wealthy White ones trying to maintain a veneer of respectability.

"To start a drug treatment program in Charleston was a threat to a lot of blue blood Charlestonians South of Broad,[35] whose children were involved also in active addiction," said Jordan. "So, it was tricky business to deal with a whole set of people from a poor Black community and from White [folks] who were from South of Broad—very prominent families in Charleston."

Addiction treatment did, however, find its way onto the agenda and into the federal grants that would fund the community health care center, largely because of the activism of one person with deep Carolina roots. This advocate had been fighting for services for over twenty years by the time Dr. Jordan arrived—carrying the message day after day, year after year, for all people suffering from substance use disorders, regardless of race, gender, or social status. Like Dr. Jordan, he had grown up in a rural area far from the "blue blood Charlestonians," and he too had learned how to navigate South Carolina's political morass. Ultimately, the adolescent treatment program that emerged and spawned a high school was named D. Ceth Mason, in his honor.

A Trusted Servant

D. Ceth Mason's South Carolina roots ran deep. He was born David Ceth Mason Jr., on September 13, 1913, near Clarendon County, and raised in Summerton about eighty miles from where the first shots of the Civil War were fired. Like his father before him, he chose to go by his middle name, which was also the first name of his great-grandfather, Ceth Smith Land. Land served in the Confederate Army during the Civil War, rising to the rank of major in the 26th South Carolina infantry. Indeed, Major Ceth Land served most of the war, entering on July 1, 1862, and not mustering out until his regiment, serving under General Robert E. Lee, surrendered to Ulysses S. Grant and the Union Army at Appomattox Courthouse on April 9, 1865. His family would refer to him as Major long after his death, in recognition of his service to the confederacy.

The family continued to serve South Carolina in elected, appointed, and military roles through the next century and beyond. It is impossible to overlook the segregation and discrimination inherent in many public policies and social programs developed and sustained in South Carolina in the early-to-mid twentieth century. It is also interesting that David Ceth Mason, both Sr. and Jr., preferred to use their confederate military ancestor's name as their own in public. It is, however, equally important to note that both also took substantial steps to improve the lives of the poor and the marginalized people of the state during their lifetimes, a large percentage of whom were Black.

This service can be seen in one of Mason Sr.'s publicized actions that served the African American community. D. Ceth Mason Sr. was a land administrator for the Federal Land Bank before WWII, and as such, he was put in charge of resettlement for families displaced by the new Pinopolis Dam being constructed in Berkeley County in 1941. The flooding of the basin would force the resettlement of over nine hundred Black families, most of whom were direct descendants of enslaved persons that had been deeded those lands by "former masters in appreciation of the loyalty of their former slaves and for the practical purpose of keeping them on the plantations."[36] Mason Sr. had succeeded the original resettlement director and was credited with "the final culmination of the problem," enacting an intricate plan to move the families in groups along with their "churches, schools, lodges, and cemeteries . . . and to provide the best of sanitary conditions."[37]

D. Ceth Mason Jr. continued his family's civic engagement. Beginning on September 16, 1940, the United States required all men between the ages of 21 and 45 to register for the military draft,[38] and Mason did so in October.[39] In the early days of World War II, which the United States entered in December 1941, and in the months just before it, the United States started churning out cargo vessels, and they needed crews to staff them. Recruiters urged people to join the Merchant Marine, which staffed the supply and passenger ships. Some came out of retirement to answer this call, while others, unable to serve the military due to age or disability also joined.[40] While not technically enlisted in the armed forces, the Merchant Mariners faced great danger providing services in both the North Atlantic and Pacific theaters, according to the American Merchant Marine at War webpage:

> Merchant ships faced danger from submarines, mines, armed raiders and destroyers, aircraft, "kamikaze," and the elements. About 8,300 mariners were killed at sea, 12,000 wounded of whom at least 1,100 died from their wounds, and 663 men and women were taken prisoner. (Total killed estimated 9,300.) Some were blown to death, some incinerated, some drowned, some froze, and some starved. 66 died in prison camps or aboard Japanese ships while being transported to other camps. 31 ships vanished without a trace to a watery grave. 1 in 26 mariners serving aboard merchant ships in World WW II died in the line of duty, suffering a greater percentage of war-related deaths than all other U.S. services. Casualties were kept secret during the War to keep information about their success from the enemy and to attract and keep mariners at sea.[41]

D. Ceth Mason Jr. became one of those mariners in 1941, serving first as a clerk[42] on the US Army Liberty Ship (a transport ship) *Samuel F. B. Morse*, in Europe, and later as a chief electrician on the US Army Hospital Ship (USAHS) *Thistle*, operating in the South Pacific.[43] In all, his service bridged the length of the US involvement in World War II and covered both major theaters of the war. While he was not in combat or a direct medical role, Mason likely was exposed to traumatic suffering on a regular basis for a prolonged period.

A newspaper feature detailed this time of his life as one that also plunged him into alcoholism. "He often found himself miserably alone as a street drunk in unfamiliar settings. New York City. Scotland. Tunisia. California. Italy. The Philippines. Hawaii. Remote areas in South Carolina."[44]

"Ask any addict about that awful gut feeling," Mason told the interviewer. "It's the unnamed fear that always is with you. It gnaws, it makes life hell. I wasn't drinking to be happy; I was drinking to live."[45]

By his own account, he started drinking in his hometown of Summerton, South Carolina, when he was only 14 years old, drinking "corn whisky" in part to earn approval from his friends, as it often starts.[46] He continued drinking heavily for 20 years, moving beyond whisky to shaving lotion, vanilla extract, paint thinner, and drugs such as marijuana, cocaine, morphine, and heroin.[47] Mason described his behavior as "hell drinking,"[48] and he labeled himself a "public drunk."[49]

"I've played it man," he told an interviewer. "I've played the field." He described himself as "hopelessly lost with nowhere to go."[50]

His drinking and using encompassed the entire time of his first marriage to Annie Lou Byrd,[51] which ended in divorce in less than five years,[52] as well as his years as a Merchant Mariner. While it is not known for certain when and how his substance use developed into a disorder, it may have been both a cause and a symptom in the divorce from his first marriage, and likely a factor in a brief second marriage. He married 19-year-old Gloria Emily Smith—who herself had already been divorced and lost a child in infancy—in Charleston in October 1944,[53] but his second marriage did not last long either. Mason's drinking may have been an understandable coping mechanism for the monotonies of naval life as well the horrors of war, but it also played a role in ending two of his marriages.

Reaching bottom, a couple years after the war, Mason said he would even steal from friends to fund his addiction.[54] It was friends, however, that would ultimately help him stop using, and in 1947 he got sober.[55] Alcoholics Anonymous (AA) had only existed about twelve years when Mason got sober, as it was founded in Akron, Ohio, in 1935. But Mason worked the program of AA, and once he did, he embraced the Twelfth Step as much as any person before or since:

Having had a spiritual awakening as the result of these steps, we tried to carry this message to alcoholics, and to practice these principles in all our affairs.

When Mason got sober, Strom Thurmond was governor of South Carolina. Thurmond had been elected governor in 1947, and he had immediately proposed a four-year "good government" reorganization plan during his inaugural address. In January 1948, he added twenty-three new recommendations during his State of the State Address to the general assembly, including a new penitentiary, a secret/Australian style ballot, a state bureau of investigation, and an "industrial school for negro girls." Thurmond's slate of proposals also included alcoholism:

I recommend that there be established, under the direction of the State Hospital, a clinic for treatment of the disease of alcoholism and that an educational and information program be conducted to educate the public on alcoholism as a disease.

As the idea of alcoholism as a disease was not settled at the time, the fact that a governor would call for such a program in a State of the State address was itself notable. Two weeks later, the house committee on the state hospital held a "lengthy hearing" on a proposed $60,000 "program of care," including a statewide clinic and education initiative "to inform the public that alcoholism is a disease and is curable."[56] Governor Thurmond took to the airwaves in May to affirm his good government initiative in a radio address, during which he specifically named the clinic to treat alcoholism. As a signal of how intertwined segregation and alcoholism service might be in the state, Thurmond would become the Dixiecrat candidate for president that summer, leading a party formed in part to oppose the civil rights plank adopted at the 1948 Democratic National Convention. Author Pat Conroy, a Charlestonian himself, wrote an anecdote into his novel *South of Broad,* set in 1969 Charleston, to show what African Americans thought of Thurmond and his policies. The main character, a White teenager named Leo King, asks Anthony Jefferson, his African American football coach, what the worst name the coach's Black son could call the White Leo, and the coach replies, "He's got to call you Strom Thurmond. That's about as big an insult as a black man can yell at a white man."[57]

Thurmond remained governor after losing the Presidential election, but he continued to promote the alcoholism clinics during public speeches, including one of his first speeches after losing the presidential election, which was given to South Carolina school administrators in December.[58]

The attention the governor was paying to alcoholism was part of a larger effort underway both in the state and nationwide to treat the issue as a disease rather than a moral failing or poor choice. The 1948 State Hospital annual report echoed the governor's pleas, including the segregationist undertones:

> It is earnestly hoped that the General Assembly will immediately take the necessary steps to make provisions for the care of the alcoholic, the aged, and the mentally deficient Negro. Of necessity, having to deal with the problem has become an enormous one for the hospital.[59]

That year was in fact a consequential one for recovery both in the state of South Carolina and for D. Ceth Mason himself. Mason had only recently gotten sober, but he took up the charge for the alcoholism initiative. Though there is no official record of a meeting, it is possible he met Marty Mann that spring. Mann was known as the First Lady of AA, because she was purported to be the first woman to achieve long-term sobriety through Alcoholics Anonymous.[60] She visited Charleston in May 1948, just before Thurmond's radio address, representing the National Committee for Education on Alcoholism (NCEA)—a nonprofit organization, distinct from AA, which she had founded in 1944. It would later become the National Council on Alcohol and Drug Dependence (NCADD). Similar to how Sid Jordan later would involve the community in developing Charleston's health services, Marty Mann wrote that the object of the NCEA was "community action," which,

> in the form of local committees in cities or states or both, armed with sound scientific knowledge, can make a start at really solving this problem. With the aid of the

Yale Plan for Alcohol Studies, the National Committee will be provided always with information and literature that are unbiased and abreast of the newest developments in scientific research. The National Committee will disseminate this knowledge by all possible means, and help form local committees wherever possible.[61]

Years later, the *Charleston Evening Post* published a photo of Mason presenting Marty Mann with an "etching of a Charleston scene" in honor of a speech she gave there in 1961.[62] Following Mann's lead, community action would become D. Ceth Mason's life work, as would be carrying the message of AA The first ever South Carolina assembly of Alcoholics Anonymous was held in Charleston in July 1948, and while there is no record of Mason's attendance, he was likely among the four hundred or so who did.[63] Many things converged for D. Ceth Mason that year: publicly funded addiction clinics, community action on recovery, and Alcoholics Anonymous as an institution in South Carolina. Then, on December 4, he got married a third time, and this time it lasted. About a year after he stopped drinking, Mason married another divorcee, Carrie Hilton. Hilton had been one of the friends who helped Mason abstain from drug use, and they would remain married the rest of his life.

"If that gal hadn't stuck with me," Mason told an interviewer. "I couldn't have made it. You got to have somebody you can respect. You can't be a dog like I was and kick this habit."[64]

The efforts of 1948 bore fruit in 1949, and this meant D. Ceth Mason was present at the creation of alcohol and drug services in South Carolina–a process that was directly influenced by people responsible for the recovery movement in the United States. In mid-January, the formation of a group modeled on the Yale Plan for Alcoholism— which was created in part by Dr. E. M. Jellinek in 1944 and provided the foundation for Marty Mann's organization—was announced.[65] Also in January, after planning a clinic "for some time," the Medical College of the State of South Carolina hosted a two-day Institute on Alcoholism. One of the featured speakers was Yvelin Gardner, the assistant to the executive director, Marty Mann, at the National Committee for Education on Alcoholism.[66]

While other states, mostly in the North, such as Minnesota and New York, have received much more attention for their seminal efforts in the development of alcohol and drug treatment programs, South Carolina was active in the movement in the late 1940s and 1950s, and Mason would assume the leadership. Mason, along with about thirty other concerned citizens, established the first state-level treatment and education department on alcoholism, based on the Yale Plan and NCEA's disease model of addiction, in 1949. This department would later become the South Carolina Commission on Alcoholism. He was instrumental in starting the Charleston Council on Alcoholism in 1957, and then helped start similar councils in other cities across the state over the next decade. These councils were nonprofit organizations composed of doctors, police officers, business leaders, and service organizations. When Charleston hosted the 13th AA State Convention in 1960, Mason was its chairperson.[67] Mason was appointed to the state commission the same year, and in 1967, he was named chairman of the commission.[68] When the Charleston Council needed to be reactivated in the mid-1960s, Mason was asked to chair the effort.

Mason started to have success professionally as well. He had been an appliance salesman before joining the Merchant Marine, and he returned to that occupation after the war. He later moved into investment financing, and over time, Mason rose to become president of the Installment Finance Corporation of Charleston. As both a business leader and a champion of recovery causes, Mason commanded respect in South Carolina, and he started to use his influence to make sure as many people as possible had access to recovery—including Black people in the heavily segregated South.

One striking aspect of treatment and recovery services is the historically segregated nature of their delivery. While people of color receive substance use treatment at rates equal to or higher than White people, they are more likely than White folks to be mandated to that treatment by the criminal justice system.[69] Mason felt that alcoholism was an equal opportunity disease, and that community-based treatment services should be available to anyone. In his role as chairman of the South Carolina Commission on Alcoholism, he realized in 1971 "whether an alcoholic is treated depends largely on who he is . . . a prominent businessman has no problem getting admitted to a hospital for detoxification . . . but in many places, including Charleston, there is no treatment available for the average person."[70] Mason applied pressure where he could to try to change that.

It is not clear exactly when Mason developed a desire to help people across racial lines, but there are hints. He grew up attending the Clarendon County Schools, which were segregated and alleged to be unequal in the court case Briggs vs. Elliott. That suit would become the first of five to be bundled into the *Brown v. Board of Education of Topeka* case brought by Thurgood Marshall and the NAACP to the Supreme Court, which in 1954, famously ruled that school segregation was unconstitutional. There were White people in Clarendon County, however, that favored better treatment for Black people, and even supported integration. One of those White families was the Land family. John Calhoun Land III was born in 1941, grew up in Summerton, and would become a state senator. *Newsweek* featured Senator Land in an article commemorating the fortieth anniversary of the *Brown* decision:[71]

> John Land is a curious figure. "He's difficult to peg," says Gil Thelen, executive editor of The State newspaper. "Fiscal conservative, a defender of traditional power relationships in the state-and a deeply committed progressive on human-rights issues." Senator Land says the last was something of a family tradition.

Levi Pearson, who was Black, had been the original plaintiff against the Clarendon County schools, filing a suit for a school bus in 1947.[72] The suit resulted in a backlash against Pearson and other Black families in the community. According to *Newsweek*, "The white banker cut off the family's credit, and they couldn't buy fertilizer. The white neighbors wouldn't loan the harvesting machine as they had in the past, and the

Pearsons' crops were left to rot in the field."[73] But Land's family stood by the Pearsons. His dad ran a service station, and his uncle owned the local Sinclair Oil dealership. They "quietly defied the boycott against the Summerton blacks; as a teenager, John Land delivered kerosene to blacks like Levi Pearson, who'd been cut off by all the other white merchants in the area."[74]

D. Ceth Mason was John Calhoun Land III's cousin. They both were descended from the confederate major, Ceth Land, and they both grew up in Summerton. Senator Land even carried on the family legacy by naming his youngest son William Ceth Land. And they apparently also shared the family tradition of progressivism on human rights. Senator Land was born in 1941, the year D. Ceth Mason's father had helped resettle a Black community during the construction of the Pinopolis Dam. Mason Sr. had tried to help them rebuild their lives in a respectful way, and that also was the same year that Mason Jr. joined the Merchant Marine, which was more racially integrated than the military branches themselves.[75]

One sign that D. Ceth Mason had adopted his family's inclusive mindset was where he attended church. After he got sober, Mason chose to worship at one of the oldest churches in Charleston, the Circular Congregational Church, which was established in 1681.[76] The church was and still is a progressive community. The first words on the website's homepage are "Whoever you are, and wherever you are on life's journey, you are welcome here!"[77] That welcoming spirit would be a salve for someone in recovery who was trying to reestablish connections strained by addiction. The website also states, "We welcome and celebrate people of every race and ethnicity, gender identity, sexual orientation, and life experience as we work together to create a more just world for all."[78] While the concept of inclusivity has likely expanded since the 1950s, the mission of acceptance and justice were present then and would have certainly influenced its leadership. The church's mission is notable, as D. Ceth Mason, with just about seven years sober, was elected president of the congregation at the Circular Church's 273rd annual meeting in 1954—the same year as the Supreme Court's *Brown vs. Board of Education* school desegregation decision.

The Church's history notes Circular's congregation has worshiped on the same spot in Charleston, South Carolina, since 1681, its name coming from the fact that one of its earliest sanctuaries was indeed round.[79] A church history notes, "From its beginning, the congregation challenged the established order, and this tradition has continued throughout our history. Circular is a vibrant and theologically progressive church with a clear voice for social justice. We took a stand for the integration of churches in the 1960s."[80]

Though the church remained segregated during Mason's term, it voted to integrate in 1965.[81] When Mason was elected president, Circular was affiliated with the Congregational Association, which would soon become the United Church of Christ in 1957—the progressive affiliation it retains today. Two of the many community groups to which the church has provided space over the years are Alcoholics Anonymous and Narcotics Anonymous, which were obviously important to Mason.

Circular Church was not the only historic and progressive institution in Charleston with which Mason worked. The McClennan-Banks Hospital, a hospital and training institution for Black nurses, had opened as the Cannon Street Hospital in 1897. In the Jim Crow era, when White hospitals segregated Black patients or denied them service altogether, Cannon Street "provided desperately needed health care for Charleston's African American citizens with twenty-four beds, nurses' dormitories, a dining hall, an operating room, a reception room, and an office."[82] By the 1940s, the Cannon Street building had deteriorated, and the new Medical Director, Dr. Thomas McFall, started pursuing funds for renovation or replacement. Not only did Dr. McFall, who was African American, reach out to the Black community, but he also lobbied the Charleston County Council for funds.[83] One of the people who supported funding a new hospital was D. Ceth Mason,[84] who by that time was actively involved in establishing alcohol commissions statewide,[85] and surely saw a synergy of marginalization between Black people and alcoholics, both Black and White, in his home state. The County Council approved $88,000 for a new hospital in 1956, which would be relocated and named in honor of its founder, Dr. Alonzo C. McClennan, and its first head nurse, Anna DeCosta Banks: the McClennan-Banks Hospital.[86]

In the coming years, Mason and the Charleston County Substance Abuse Commission would work with Dr. McFall to provide addiction services at McClennan-Banks, but, at first, they needed to do so under cover of darkness. It was unorthodox at that time for a prominent White man and a prominent Black man in Charleston to work so closely together on a project, but that is what they did to aid people suffering from substance use disorders. In the 1960s, Charleston still did not have any place for alcoholics who were in severe withdrawal, which could be deadly. People with substance use disorders were still the object of ridicule, often called names like "skid row bums" or "public drunks." Few physicians were trained in how to treat substance use disorders, and the risk of death was real. Furthermore, hospital care was still quite segregated, so a Black doctor, like Dr. McFall, treating White patients was frowned upon. Mason as a public official and Dr. McFall as a hospital administrator were taking great risk personally and professionally in facilitating these services off the books, but they did so to save lives across racial lines.

At first, Mason turned to a friend of his who owned a Pawn Shop on Carver Avenue in North Charleston. The owner had been living above the shop, but had decided to move, and Mason rented the place from him.[87] When nobody else wanted the liability of detoxing people in withdrawal, Mason provided a place, and he asked Dr. McFall to provide the care. In time, Dr. McFall moved those services to his own rooms in McClennan-Banks, at the back end of the hospital. At night, they would bring in patients in severe distress from alcohol dependence on withdrawal, and Dr. McFall would treat those persons for three days, and then would release them through the back door.

This covert treatment continued through the 1960s. The Charleston County Substance Abuse Commission eventually merged with other commissions to become the Trident Council on Alcoholism and set a goal of establishing a formal detoxification center.[88] Dr. Thomas McFall would not live to see that happen. In June 1969, after a brief illness, Dr. McFall died at the age of 60. His brother, Dr. John McFall, succeeded him as the administrator of McClennan-Banks, and he made sure the detox unit became a reality. It took two more years, but in September 1971, McClennan-Banks opened a small, three-bed detoxification facility. It needed a donation of materials and labor by the Plumbers and Steamfitters Local Union 470 to make it happen, but detox finally came out of the shadows, in a hospital created to train Black nurses. And in the newspaper photo announcing the "special unit," standing next to Dr. John McFall, was D. Ceth Mason.[89]

Mason had used his status to cut through generations of racial disparities to reach those who might not have received substance use disorder services otherwise. A White man who chose to use the name of an ancestor who fought for the Confederacy and surrendered at Appomattox, and whose initial advocacy efforts benefited from the support of Dixiecrat Strom Thurmond, was also adamant about including Black citizens in the movement—and not only as clients in segregated programs, but as leaders of integrated ones. To that point, most of Mason's efforts were directed at adults and in setting up treatment programs. During the last phase of his career, though, specifically helping youths started to become a focus. When he crossed paths with a young paraprofessional educator, a treatment school also came into the picture. And once again, it was people of color who took a leading role.

Shirley Jackson was born in Charleston in 1946, about a year before Mason got sober. Jackson, who is Black, graduated high school in 1964 and moved about three hundred miles north to study education and library science at Bennett College, a private historically Black liberal arts college for women in Greensboro, North Carolina. Her father became ill, however, so Jackson withdrew after only two years to return home and care for him.[90] She married Herman Beckett in 1968 and became Shirley Beckett.[91] Though Beckett had left college early, she was still able to use her training in library science to get hired as a paraprofessional in the library at Mount Zion Elementary School, an African American school for kindergarten through eighth grade, on Johns Island, South Carolina—the same elementary school that civil rights activist Bill Saunders had attended years earlier.

The year Beckett graduated high school—1964—was the year President Lyndon Johnson declared his War on Poverty, and the Office of Economic Opportunity (OEO) was the agency created to administer most of Johnson's Great Society programs. Bailey and Duquette studied the OEO, and said it was established by the Equal Opportunity Act (EOA) to "empower the poor to transform their own communities."[92] They noted two key provisions in the EOA. First, each state received money based on a formula, but there were no restrictions on how the money could be spent within states. Second, the government could fund local organizations directly rather that the common way of channeling grants through the state or local governments. Bailey and Duquette wrote that this had the effect of encouraging "the development of customized programs to combat the root causes of local poverty and also allowed the federal government to work around widespread *de jure* racial segregation, which had restricted the political participation of African Americans, and *de facto* exclusion of the poor from the policymaking process."[93]

Rev. Henry Grant, the Charleston civil rights advocate known as "the Rock," seized the opportunity to apply for direct federal funding. He was appointed chairperson of the Charleston County Office of Economic Opportunity Commission, and under his leadership, the county requested a $1.1 million federal OEO grant to establish an outpatient medical facility for Charleston's low-income community. The facility would provide comprehensive medical services to residents of Charleston, and the grant would also provide education and training programs. The intent was to allow patients to receive all services in one location, rather than moving clinic to clinic. The Medical College of South Carolina had been running clinics, but those had become overcrowded. At the new center, Medical College doctors would staff the programs and manage the funding, and the college's dean, Franklin C. Fetter, would be the director.[94] This was the program that ultimately brought Dr. Sidney Jordan to Charleston.

Just as Rev. Grant had seized an opportunity to fund health services for Black and low-income residents, D. Ceth Mason saw an opening to assist people with substance use disorders. There had been efforts for over two decades to improve services for substance use disorders, including the State Hospital's 1948 annual report calling for the General Assembly "to make provisions for the care of the alcoholic." Mason had led much of the advocacy himself, and now he worked with Rev. Grant to make sure treatment for alcoholism and drug addiction would be included in the OEO program. While the initial media coverage did not mention an addiction clinic, by the time the center opened, mental health services were in the plan, which would later pave the road for substance use treatment.

The fact that the funding was federal meant that services must be integrated, and because it was a War on Poverty initiative, locating the program near where people of color and lower-income residents lived made sense. Rev. Grant and Bill Saunders led the planning and advocacy for the center, and they worked closely with Senator Ernest "Fritz" Hollings. Hollings became a champion of the project, mainly because of the medical services rather than mental health care, and he made sure the grant was funded.[95] The grant would be managed by the Medical College of South Carolina, but it stipulated that the college would only be a temporary home. A permanent facility would need to be built.

After Dr. Fetter's death, Dr. Leroy Anderson was named the new project director, and he announced plans to construct a multimillion-dollar facility on Nassau Street, not far from Shirley Beckett's home in East Charleston. The program had been designed to provide preventative medicine, mental health counseling, pediatric care, family planning, eye care, and dental care for low-income residents in the Charleston area. When conceived, the center set a goal of twenty-six thousand persons served, but it would always be hampered by funding challenges. Because it was administered by the Medical College of South Carolina, staff needed to meet the qualifications to be staff at the College—hence the recruitment of Dr. Sidney Jordan from California.

When Dr. McCurdy asked Jordan to start consulting in Charleston, community volunteer programs like those in San Francisco's Hunters Point became a centerpiece. With the funding limitations, volunteers would be needed to provide services at the intended scope.[96]

During Shirley Beckett's time as a librarian at Mount Zion Elementary School, some seventh grade students began to act strangely, and they said they had been smoking marijuana. Beckett had no knowledge of marijuana or any drugs except for alcohol, which she notes was not at that time considered a drug, so she asked their permission to have their "drug" analyzed at a drug clinic near her home in East Charleston (see Figure 1.2). It turned out to be oregano and thyme, and Beckett realized how much she, and her students, needed to learn about drugs. Through that job, she saw many families with children being impacted by actual alcohol and drugs, and she wanted to help.

With the new health center launching services near her home, she came into contact with Dr. Jordan and others associated with the medical college, and they informed her of the community volunteer opportunities. This led to her meeting D. Ceth Mason and Dr. McFall at McClennan-Banks Hospital, and Beckett quickly developed respect for Mason.

"His reality was, no matter what race you are, you're a human being, and you're suffering, and he didn't want to see you die," said Beckett.

Figure 1.2. Shirley Beckett was born and raised in Charleston. Beckett would become an alcohol and drug counselor in Charleston, and she helped establish the Freedom Road School. She would later become the director of Certification and Education for the National Association for Alcoholism and Drug Abuse Counselors. This picture was taken in the mid-1970s in front of a public housing development and one of the first treatment sites in Charleston. (Source: Shirley Beckett Mikell.)

"When I was a kid, so to speak, volunteering, people would throw up on us or pee on us. [Mason] would tell us, 'You know, if you want to see somebody die, go home just because you got a mess.' And [Mason] said, 'Go home and change. And they may die by the time you get your ass back here.'"

White supremacy and racial discrimination remained omnipresent in Charleston at the time and stood as a reminder to just how divergent D. Ceth Mason was to work so closely with the Black community to provide addiction services. It was under this climate of disparities that Shirley Beckett, an African American working in a segregated school, had started to volunteer.

In the middle of the 1969 hospital strike, the South Carolina legislature had moved to give the Medical College university status, effectively changing its name to the Medical University of South Carolina (MUSC), and that would be the governing body for the new facility. A decision was made to name the facility in honor of the late dean, Dr. Franklin C. Fetter, who had spent the last years of his life working on the creation of the center, and a dedication and ribbon cutting ceremony was held in March 1970.[97] MUSC President McCord, Center director Anderson, and Senator Hollings all participated in the event, less than a year after the labor protests. The media coverage of the dedication listed the aims of the Franklin C. Fetter Family Health Care Center, including "a reduction in the incidence of . . . mental health problems."

"Fritz Hollings was a big supporter of the Franklin C. Fetter Health center," said Jordan. "At the inauguration of Franklin C. Fetter Health Center, Fritz Hollings said, 'We need more medical services. We don't need all these psychologists.' He failed to observe that one-third of the program was mental health. It was a medical, dental, and mental health grant for Franklin C. Fetter. But in his inauguration speech he made the error of downplaying mental health."

Addiction services were not explicitly funded, but D. Ceth Mason, Dr. Jordan, and others were working to make substance use a focus of the health center. In fact, Mason had started banging his drum as loud as ever through his committee work.

"He was so very highly respected," Beckett said. "(Mason) never wanted to be a politician. He had been offered up to run for office, but he refused that because he couldn't speak his mind."[98]

Indeed, while Mason was appointed to many leadership positions in his life, he also embraced the second tradition of Alcoholics Anonymous: "Our leaders are but trusted servants; they do not govern."[99] His governance roles held to a singleness of purpose—to help those still suffering from substance use disorders. The AA publication, *Twelve Steps and Twelve Traditions*, provides what could have been D. Ceth Mason's creed:

When by devoted service to family, friends, business, or community we attract widespread affection and are sometimes singled out for posts of greater responsibility and trust, we try to be humbly grateful and exert ourselves the more in a spirit of love and service. True leadership, we find, depends upon able example and not upon vain displays of power or glory . . . True ambition is the deep desire to live usefully and walk humbly under the grace of God.[100]

Mason felt he could exert the most usefulness and influence from his appointments on the state and regional drug commissions. Mason was chairman of the South Carolina Council on Alcoholism in 1969, when he stated his vision for a Charleston alcohol information center in an interview with reporter Jean May.

"We would hope to be established under a charter which would assure our qualification for state and federal funds. However local capital would be needed." As the article described it, the information center would operate by "pulling together all related area agencies into a cohesive action unit and serving as an easily accessible haven of help for the alcoholic and his family." The "blanket approach" would include multiple facilities, including the new comprehensive health center.[101]

The alcoholism councils of Berkeley, Charleston, and Dorchester Counties had formed the "Trident Council on Alcoholism" a few years before, and the Council announced it was reorganizing as an " 'action-oriented' group" in February 1970.[102] A steering committee was formed, and D. Ceth Mason would serve as an ex officio member. Their priorities included a detoxification center and cooperative use of the Medical University and Veterans Administration Hospitals for the information and referral center. Such information centers were necessary so "the public's opinion can be reshaped so that the community will accept the reality of the disease."[103]

At the same time, with little funding for substance use treatment services, Dr. Jordan was continuing to build volunteer resources. In August 1970, he oversaw the creation of a volunteer "hot line for persons with drug problems or problems related to drugs."[104] As he described the program, a volunteer would answer the call, discuss the problem with the caller, and refer as needed. The hotline was sponsored by a citizen's group called "Furthur, Inc.," chaired by Charleston native David Furchgott, who told a local newspaper the phones would be staffed by two volunteers at a time: one adult and one youth. This was thus one of the first ventures into youth peer substance use counseling.[105]

"Young people are more likely to contact another young person," said Dr. Jordan. "When a young person has a 'bad trip' he doesn't call a physician, he doesn't call a hospital. He is more likely to contact another young person who is level-headed . . . The spontaneity and sensitivity of the young person is immeasurably important."[106]

Progress toward an actual substance use treatment program in Charleston, however, was slow. By March 1971, detox facilities were available, but they were sparse. The County Hospital had a few beds, and McClennan-Banks was a few months from opening their small, four bed unit. The Office of Economic Opportunity had just started an outpatient program, and that rehabilitation program had about thirty clients.[107] Both Mason and Jordan continued lobbying for better care.

"The ideal situation would be to have access to a hospital and to be covered by insurance as with any other illness," Mason said in a newspaper interview. "Drunks are very sick people and withdrawal is a very dangerous period."[108]

Dr. Jordan was attributed in the same article as claiming "100 per cent of all hospitals with detoxification units . . . have found the units are successful and do not interfere with normal hospital routine."[109]

There were still no services for youths other than the Furthur Hotline. Advocates, though, started using the rate of adolescent drug usage to help make the case for more treatment services. The fact that use was increasing among the young Charleston population was something that got people's attention. And considering most legislators were White, the growth of drug use among the White high schools was likely to provoke concern.

Dr. Martin Keeler, a professor at the Medical University of South Carolina, testified before a Special Legislative Committee on Drug Abuse in late 1970, to urge for comprehensive treatment facilities. Law enforcement officials and volunteers from the hotline also testified. Dr. Keeler noted that heroin use was increasing in Charleston, and "spoke of a pattern of 'fairly heavy use' of amphetamines developing in area high schools, and of a 'disproportionate amount' of young people being treated at the hospital for psychological problems."[110]

Inspector Joseph Hodge, a narcotics agent, testified that youths aged 13 to 20 were "the most common ages of marijuana smokers."[111] In segregated South Carolina, though, it was Hodge's emphasis on racial demographics that may have struck to the loudest chord. He estimated that two years earlier (about 1968), Black youths had represented 75% of marijuana arrests. By 1970, that trend had almost completely "reversed," with about 65% of those arrested for marijuana being White, and LSD was "strictly a white community problem."[112] Those racial data, combined with his estimate that "marijuana is the biggest problem in high schools in Charleston County, with LSD following and then amphetamines," helped sound an alarm not only for more treatment services, but for more youth programs.[113]

Jesse Purvis, an African American from Charleston who would later become one of the city's first substance use treatment counselors, summed it up directly, "It really didn't become a problem until the White kids started using the damn drugs. That's when it became a damn problem."[114]

Months after the legislative hearing, President Richard Nixon declared a "war on drugs" in June 1971. Opportunities for federal funding suddenly expanded, and another opportunity window opened for D. Ceth Mason, Dr. Jordan, and the faculty at the Medical University of South Carolina. Charleston County applied for a federal grant to start a county-wide substance use disorder treatment program, and MUSC, the governing body of the Fetter Family Health Center, submitted funding proposals as well.[115] Purvis credits Dr. Jordan for leading the funding effort.

"Dr. Sidney Jordan was the man who had the impetus about starting drug treatment in Charleston," said Purvis. "He wrote the programs and all that to get the federal funds. He was the guy that started this whole thing."[116]

The politics lined up in their favor, as Senator Strom Thurmond had switched to the Republican Party—also President Nixon's party—in 1964. While governor two decades earlier, Thurmond had made an alcoholism clinic one of his "good government" priorities, and the new drug war was now a Republican initiative. Even though demand reduction (i.e., treatment) was not nearly as well funded as supply reduction (i.e., the "drug war"), Senator Thurmond would be on his party's side by supporting

President Nixon's call to arms. Thurmond had supported Nixon's candidacy in 1968 and had a close relationship with the administration.[117] This eased the path for federal money to flow into South Carolina, and in May 1972, Senator Thurmond announced a one-year grant of over $2 million to the Charleston County Equal Opportunity Commission for "a full range of comprehensive family health services for 26,000 low-income residents of Charleston," to be administered by the Medical University of South Carolina.[118]

Mason was applying pressure locally as well. Dr. Anderson, the director of the Fetter Center, was still hesitant to include drug treatment services under the Fetter umbrella because he did not want that kind of responsibility and liability. Mason worked hard to convince Dr. Anderson to include addiction treatment, and the turning point was a training program. While they were waiting for the federal funding to get approved, the state and regional alcohol and drug commissions had planted seeds with what little funding they could muster. The Trident Council on Alcohol and Drug Abuse and the State Commission on Alcoholism each presented a $700 check to the Charleston County Office of Economic Opportunity (OEO) in January 1972. The checks were contributions for a new drug counselor training program, and Dr. Jordan also wrote and received a large training grant. These efforts meant that MUSC would be hiring and training several counselors who would ultimately need a physical space to practice—something Dr. Anderson found palatable.

"There was all this training going on," said Beckett. "And nobody really wanted to give us a home."

Dr. Anderson finally relented, and Fetter's alcohol and drug program would open later that summer. A photo from the check presentation for the training program was published in the *Charleston Evening Post,* and standing next to the Charleston County OEO director, with a smile on his face, was D. Ceth Mason.[119]

2

Freedom Road

"I think we've discovered something very important about the treatment of the adolescent."[1]

That is what Lon DeLeon told a newspaper reporter in May 1974. DeLeon was the director of the Drug and Alcohol Program at the Franklin C. Fetter Family Health Center, which had opened in August 1972. The program was one of the comprehensive initiatives funded by a grant from the Office of Economic Opportunity to the Medical University of South Carolina in spring of that year. D. Ceth Mason had fought for decades to get funding for substance use treatment in Charleston, and once the funding came, the program grew in ways he likely had never anticipated, including adolescent treatment and recovery services and the employment of a counseling staff, mostly with people of color.

The grant specified $262,000 for drug and alcohol programming, which would include methadone maintenance as well as treatment services for both adults and youths.[2] The Fetter Center had already opened the first methadone clinic in South Carolina with funding from the Office of Economic Opportunity in May 1971, and this new program would be one of the first in the United States to provide alcohol and drug counseling for adolescents. The original grant provided enough resources to counsel about 30 people, but demand was so high that funding was increased to $778,000 to allow for 250 adult and adolescent clients by March 1974.[3]

Creating an adolescent alcohol and drug program in Charleston would be a community effort, and Dr. Sid Jordan took the lead under Mason's guidance.

"Ceth Mason was a mentor for many of us," said Jordan. "He was very well known and respected and was important in the recovery of many alcoholics. I worked with him on many individuals who (got into) recovery through the Charleston County Substance Abuse Commission."[4]

Dr. Jordan had arrived in Charleston in 1969 as a faculty member in the Department of Psychiatry at MUSC, and he devoted his first five years to developing mental health, alcohol, and drug services. He also credited his colleagues for their contributions, such as a physician he said had survived the Holocaust and later developed the children's mental health services for MUSC. Beyond the college, narcotics agents and police officers were watching the methadone program closely to make sure it was "well put together."[5]

Salvaging a Teenage Wasteland. Andrew J. Finch, Oxford University Press. © Oxford University Press 2024.
DOI: 10.1093/oso/9780190645502.003.0002

"Chief (John) Conroy and the judges and the narcotic agents were all having surveillance of our program," recalled Jordan. "And we finally won the respect of all those people, including the Mayor, Joe Riley, who was very supportive. And the judges started working with us on decriminalizing drug addicts and allowing them to be a part of the program . . . They started to see that what we were doing was legitimate."

The original grant had provided funding for twenty-four staff, but the reality was that alcohol and drug treatment was a relatively new field, and it would take time to train that many people. Dr. Jordan had requested and received a $75,000 grant to train new counselors.[6] His time in San Francisco working in the Hunters Point community had shown him the importance of integrating the local community into the programming, so he made hiring people of color part of the design.

"I was interested in them developing their careers," said Jordan. "I had a grant to train these counselors to become good counselors, and many of them went on to develop their education further. That was an interest of mine . . . creating a career ladder for people that came from a poor community."

The University of Miami had received a grant for a pilot program to train ten candidates from each of eight states, including South Carolina, so the Charleston staff were sent there for three weeks of addiction training.[7] One of the trainers was Dr. Beny Primm, a prominent African American physician who had founded some of the earliest methadone clinics in New York City in the 1960s. Dr. Primm would later advocate for changing public policies for intravenous drug users during the AIDS epidemic, work for which he was named to Ronald Reagan's Presidential Commission on the Human Immunodeficiency Virus Epidemic in 1987.[8] Part of the training program thus involved traveling to Brooklyn to visit Dr. Primm's methadone program.

The first wave of trainees was selected in early 1972, before Fetter's alcohol and drug program opened, and the training included eight local residents from a variety of backgrounds. There were ten selected, but two were struggling with their own drug problems and were unable to follow through with the training program.[9] Shirley Beckett had been volunteering for Dr. Jordan for a few years by then, and she was one of the counselors selected for the training program. In addition to the fact that Beckett was a Black woman in segregated South Carolina, she was also an educator. Even though it was not his intention to choose an educator for training, Dr. Jordan had set the stage for bringing schools into the treatment sector.

Another one of the trainees selected along with Beckett was Jesse Purvis, who at the time was selling insurance in Charleston.

"I'd worked in the worst job I ever had, trying to sell insurance," said Purvis. "Yeah, I had to get rid of that. So, they had this opening at Fetter, and they had just started the drug program. I applied. Shirley applied. We started very small. And as we grew, we trained more people under the auspices of the psychologists and physicians and things of that nature."

Jesse Purvis, who was Black, grew up in Charleston and attended the Avery Normal Institute. Avery was started in 1865 by the New York based American Missionary Association (AMA), and it was the first accredited secondary school for African

Americans in Charleston.[10] Established as a private school, Avery transitioned to a public school in 1947 and was closed in 1954, coinciding with the US Supreme Court's desegregation decision, *Brown v. Board of Education*.[11]

"Most of us came from very educated families," said Purvis. "I had the best people. My daddy was a pharmacist, a good businessman. I had the best of everything as I was growing up, and then we had the public health service of Dr. (Charles) Banov.[12] He made sure all the children in Charleston County, at that time, received whatever vaccinations or vaccines that were available. Because, although we were deeply segregated against, (Dr. Banov) understood that all children needed to be protected."

Purvis recalled that most of the early recruits for counseling training were people of color—a Puerto Rican female, another African American male and female. Beckett noted, "Because [it was] federal funding for treatment services and medication services, they couldn't help but allow integration."

Most of the counselors, though, had little if any personal experience with drug use or drug users. For that reason, the University of Miami training included popular films and novels, such as Claude Brown's book, *Manchild in the Promised Land*, and the Al Pacino movie, *Panic in Needle Park*.

"They showed it as a part of our training," said Purvis. "We had to watch the movie because, none of us knew nothing about no drugs, what drug addicts looked like or what they did, see. And because the normal educational system didn't teach people how to deal with drug addicts, that's why they trained us . . . Because drug addicts at that time, people were afraid of them."

At the time, alcohol and drug treatment was still in its infancy, and the treatments for alcohol and drugs were seen as distinct modalities. Shirley Beckett recalls how little was known about successful interventions, and how much stigma existed. "They had shut down methadone services [in the United States] because of deaths, misuse of methadone, and mis-prescribing, misuse by the clients," said Beckett. "The federal government decided it was going to train individuals to work in opioid treatment services, and with alcohol and drug clients, respectively. That's really how we were hired. [Purvis] was hired as an alcohol counselor; I was hired as a drug counselor. That's really how foreign treatment was in those days."

The multiple training experiences were spread out over a year, and this was intentional.

"There was such a hysteria in the United States," Beckett explained, "About treatment itself and also the mixture of White and Black clients in treatment settings that were funded federally. So that was what they were trying to quelch by saying that they had qualified individuals who had gone through a year-long training program that was under the auspices of the University of Miami."

As the director of addiction servicers at MUSC, Dr. Jordan oversaw all the training at both the University of Miami and MUSC. He would continue to provide clinical supervision for the counselors, and the plan was to also have him direct the treatment services at the Fetter Health Center. As the grant had stipulated that MUSC could only be the temporary home for the program, however, this would have required Jordan eventually to surrender his appointment with the Medical University. Not wanting to lose his seniority or his position in the Department of Psychiatry at MUSC, he declined the leadership role with Fetter.[13]

Instead, a few months after those early hires, Lon DeLeon, who, like Jordan, was a White male, was recruited from Yale to become director of the Alcohol and Drug Program in fall 1972. DeLeon had been born and raised in Connecticut, and he had worked four years at Yale University's drug dependency program, which was housed in their department of psychiatry. After the new counselors had gone through their training in Miami, they met with DeLeon and began developing services under him.

DeLeon was himself using methadone to treat a heroin dependency. He thus needed to receive federal approval and provide knowledge of his treatments to Fetter and MUSC. DeLeon's contract stipulated he had eight months to be "totally detoxified," but before that period ended, an upset assistant director brought his methadone use to the press. Ronald Free, who was also a person in recovery, had been a project director for the drug counselor training grant.[14] According to a news account, Free, who was White and a native of Charleston, had expected to be promoted to director of the alcohol and drug program. When DeLeon was recruited for the position instead of him, Free became angry at being passed over and was eventually fired. Free was accused of using his home to counsel Fetter clients and of "shortcutting" procedures for admitting people to the program. Free then chose to make DeLeon's addiction public. DeLeon responded by calling Free a "misinformed, very sick person."[15]

As the dispute played out in the newspaper, DeLeon's colleagues and supervisors came to his defense, informing the public that the methadone was used for treatment rather than to get high. The program's medical director, Dr. Jerome Duckman, described DeLeon as a "very effective director of this program because he has been through the drug world himself."[16]

"I don't know what I would do if he weren't here," said Duckman. "[DeLeon] is hard working, dedicated, very honest . . . a dynamo."[17]

DeLeon emerged from the controversy with his job intact, and he built a staff that included five counselors for adults and three youth drug counselors, as well as a training director and an education coordinator.[18]

"He did a marvelous job," recalled Purvis.

As they were building a successful methadone program and securing funds to train alcohol and drug counselors, Dr. Jordan began consulting with local high schools about the drug use occurring among their students. Vice principals were treating drug use as a disciplinary issue to be punished, while counselors wanted to counsel the students.

"They were at odds with one another," said Jordan. "Vice principals were sending these children home and discharging them from school, and counselors were trying to counsel them. They had a psychology division, and they asked me to do a consultation. And that was a very tough consultation, you can imagine, because the principal was caught between the School Board and the parents. And they have to maintain order and discipline. And that didn't always go along with counseling. It went along with sometimes being strict and punitive and discharging students from school."

DeLeon had hired three youth drug counselors at Fetter, and the youth aspect of the program was immediately popular. By April 1973, there were 119 adolescents participating in drug counseling.[19]

"These teenagers—they had a big, hell of a drug problem in Charleston at that time," said Purvis.

Jordan said, "We saw that a lot of these students no longer could matriculate in high school, and we said they need a program. We need to create an alternative high school for them and help them with their addiction issues and include the parents in the program."

The Fetter clinical staff was well-suited to help students, as Shirley Beckett had worked for years in a school. Indeed, her first connection with alcohol and drug services had come when she tried to get help for her families on Johns Island.

"I'd worked in schools, because I worked on Johns Island," said Beckett. "And I'd also substitute taught in the schools in the city of Charleston. So, I had a background already in education and understood school settings and school room behaviors."

Another Fetter staff member, Marie Cole, also had a background in education. Cole was from Puerto Rico, and her mother was a vice principal. Cole also had done some substitute teaching in the schools of Puerto Rico.

"She bought another culture and awareness of educational components," said Beckett. "That really helped us to figure things out. We didn't really have to go into the schools themselves, because it had been so recent for us."

Beckett mentioned Fetter also had a staff member who had recently graduated from a two-year college. Fetter's staff thus would be able to bring skills and knowledge from their own classroom experiences into the development of classroom settings in a new alternative school. DeLeon had proposed to "use education as prevention in drug abuse cases," but the original grant for Fetter was only to provide counseling. This meant that regardless of their staff's educational experience, they would need a partner if they wanted to create a school. Beckett recalled contacting a school principal who she knew, and the principal introduced her to the Charleston County Schools superintendent, Dr. Alton C. Crews. Dr. Crews was a seasoned administrator who had led the Huntsville (Alabama) City Schools and Cobb County (Georgia) Schools before coming to Charleston. He had the foresight to recognize that having Fetter provide counseling services within an alternative school setting would solve the dilemma between discipline and therapy and shift much of the responsibility away from his campuses. Dr. Crews threw his full support behind the school concept and approved the funding of two teachers during 1973–1974 school year, as well as approving the enrollment of Charleston students in the new school.

The school had a vision, students, teachers, and counselors, and the Catholic Church stepped forward with a building. Once again, Charleston's history with segregation and efforts to integrate its institutions played a role. The Immaculate Conception School had been a parochial school built for African Americans established in 1916 and staffed by the Oblate Sisters of Providence, an early Black Roman Catholic holy order in the United States.[20] The school moved to a newly constructed red-brick facility with fourteen grammar and high school classrooms at 200 Coming Street in 1930. DuBois wrote that the school developed an excellent academic reputation, but it came to represent class division within the African American community:

> With the new school and the skills of the sisters, Immaculate Conception School at 200 Coming Street became one of Charleston's most prestigious learning institutions for African Americans. Next to the Avery, Immaculate Conception became the best location for anyone within the city's African American community wanting an advanced education curriculum. Yet unintentionally this heightened sense of prestige came with a disadvantage. Due to the high tuition, not everyone within Charleston's African American population was able to attend Immaculate Conception School. This contributed to the class divide within Charleston's Black population. Charleston's middle- to upper-class African American families were able to afford to send their children to the private Immaculate Conception. At the same time, those who could not were forced to use schools with less funding and no advanced courses.[21]

The structure built in 1930 still stands today, but by the 1960s, it had fallen into disrepair. As the rest of Charleston's schools were beginning to desegregate, Bishop Ernest L. Unterkoefler decided that instead of investing the large sum of money needed to upgrade the facilities, they would phase out the school. Immaculate's high school students thus relocated in 1968 and integrated with the all-White Bishop England High School. The grammar school operated a few more years, but it too closed during the 1972–1973 school year.[22] By fall 1973, when Fetter happened to be looking for a school building, the red brick building on Coming Street was vacant.

"It had everything," said Dr. Jordan. "It had a school yard. It had classrooms. It had a gymnasium. It had a cafeteria. It had everything that constituted a school plant, and it was totally unoccupied. And so, we put it to good use."[23]

Fetter's counselors would provide the substance use recovery program, but they asked the school district to provide teachers and curriculum. With the support of superintendent Crews, the Board of Education approved the school under its Home Bound instructional program, which allowed it to fund and supervise teachers.[24] At the time, students with alcohol and drug problems qualified for special education in South Carolina, so this allowed the district to place one exceptional education teacher for every ten students enrolled in the school. If a teacher was not certified in exceptional education, they would be required to take additional courses to teach at the school.[25]

With all these pieces in place, the school opened in October 1973.[26] By the end of the school year, twenty-six students were attending the school, which allowed for two teachers: Derril Edwards and James Gordan. Those first students also came up with the name of the school: the "Freedom Road."[27]

"It means the freedom to learn. To be yourself. To kick the habit," recalled Lewis Sloan, who later became Fetter's Youth Substance Abuse Program Director.[28] As one newspaper feature described the school, "Education and therapy is the freedom road for teen-agers with drug abuse."[29]

The school developed a structured admission procedure, including an evaluation period before full admission, as not every student was referred by the schools, courts, or counselors. Some were self-referred.[30] Fetter's staff would conduct a psychological evaluation both with the student and the student's family, a physical examination, tests, and a review of the referral information.[31]

Freedom Road was designed to allow young people to stay on-track academically while receiving substance use treatment. Arthur Hunt became the educational supervisor for Freedom Road, and in a newspaper feature on the school he noted, "the therapy is always there, and when new students come in, we lean more towards the therapy at first."[32]

"They were definitely in treatment in order to attend that school," said Jesse Purvis. "We didn't have any student with non-drug problems, no, everybody in that school had drug problems, believe me."

Today, the school likely would be categorized more as a treatment-center school than a recovery high school, but it appears to have been the first publicly funded high school for students with substance use disorders that was not located in a treatment facility. Treatment was the initial point of the program, with a return to traditional schools being the goal. Over time, however, the school allowed students who had completed treatment to remain until they finished their high school credits or attained a certificate of high school equivalency.[33] In essence, though most of the students were receiving primary treatment, several of them had completed treatment and were in recovery while attending the school. As reporter Donna Scott wrote in 1976, Freedom Road was "the only public school of its kind in this country."[34]

One of the reasons Fetter's staff saw a need for a school was the length of time students would be in treatment for their drug use. The minimum length of stay when the school opened was three months, and according to one news account, it could be as long as fifteen months.[35] The minimum time eventually expanded to four months.[36] Additionally, many of the students who were referred to Freedom Road had been expelled from their school, which usually meant finding an alternative school. If the expulsion involved drug use, a school with a substance use treatment curriculum would be the best option.

"The process takes place outside of the normal school environment where the student first became involved with drugs," said DeLeon.

"Superintendent (Crews) was extremely supportive," said Shirley Beckett. "He referred them to us for that school. They may have been referred by a prevention specialist or counselor within the school system because of issues, and then quote, unquote, 'expelled,' but then the option that they had to continue their education was to come to [Freedom Road]. So those children were required, even though the term expulsion had been applied, that if they ever intended to apply or reapply to get back into school, because of their being identified as substance abusers, they had to go through [Freedom Road] in order for them to even be able to reapply to go back to school."

"It was our really great surprise that the superintendent at that time was so open minded to work that agreement with us and with his principals. He didn't want the trouble anyway. We really kept the kids out of their hair."[37]

The alcoholism councils of Berkeley, Charleston, and Dorchester Counties had collaborated to form the Trident Council on Alcoholism in the late 1960s, appointing D. Ceth Mason as an ex officio member to retain his expertise and influence. Freedom Road followed suit by opening its doors to students from those same three counties. Students would come from many miles away, as the other counties had not developed the same therapeutic programs. The superintendents of Dorchester County (about fifty miles away) and Berkeley County (about twenty-five miles away) worked with Charleston County to transfer students to Charleston in order for them to continue their education.

"The school was, of course, under the Charleston County school district's regulations," said Beckett. "But they worked that out; they worked that out for those kids."

Students were transported those long distances by their parents because there was not a bus system for the school. In some cases, the expelled students had a family member in Charleston, and the students would move in with them.

"There were a lot of concessions made by parents to help the kids," said Beckett.

Fetter now also saw the need for adolescent residential services. Transportation to the center for counseling was a hardship for many families, and some of the youths needed more intensive services as well as a break from their neighborhood and home environments. While the original substance use programming had been outpatient, in 1974, Fetter opened a residential "therapeutic community for adolescents with drug problems."[38] The program would house up to fifteen teenage boys, and it used a positive behavior-modification program modeled after the Synanon adult therapeutic community (TC) founded in California in 1958. The Odyssey House Teen Leadership Center in New York City and Canarsie Youth Center in Brooklyn had also utilized the TC approach for youths when they opened a few years earlier. Funding would come from federal and municipal agencies, which made the housing accessible to low-income families. Jesse Purvis was made director of the residential program, and Shirley Beckett became a counseling supervisor. The program utilized group therapy and individual counseling and implemented a contract and goal system to incentivize the residents. A level system was created to grant privileges as rewards for progress, and residents typically stayed nine to twelve months at a time. Most attended the Freedom Road school.

"We would always reward good behavior," said Purvis. "We didn't punish or things like that, but we tried to reward good behavior. And we fed the children there fabulous meals, because we wanted them to have something to look forward to. They had good accessibility for medical problems by the staff and psychiatric examinations."[39]

One of the financial backers was the Charleston County Substance Abuse Commission, which at the time was chaired by D. Ceth Mason. Mason turned 61 in 1974, and he had remained active in advocacy for substance use services, though he bristled at that terminology. While "substance use disorder" is now the more accepted term for alcoholism and drug addiction, Mason believed the term substance abuse would damage advocacy efforts.

"The average citizen doesn't know what substance abuse is," said Mason.[40] He felt the naming was "caught up in sophistication," and he preferred keeping the specific words "drugs" and "alcohol" in the commission's name. While the reference to substances remained, his larger goal of expanding treatment access was getting closer to reality, and he believed reaching young people was critical.

"He dedicated his life to try to help people recover from alcoholism," said Purvis. "He was very helpful and ended up politically and culturally in the recovery business of alcoholics. It was his idea to try to treat the children; to try to get ahead of the problems in life."

To honor Mason's vision and dedication, the residential program was named in his honor, the D. Ceth Mason House.

"He was a fine old Southern gentleman," said Purvis. "He was a White man, but he was a fine old gentleman. We named the program after Ceth Mason to make him feel good. He was proud. We called it at first 'Mason House,' but he said, 'Oh, no, no. You got to call it D.' His name was D. Ceth Mason."

Mason was also suffering from various forms of cancer, including cancer of the jaw.

"Half of his face had been cut out because of the cancer," recalled Beckett. "He had cancer in the jawbone, and even that didn't stop him."

"That's really what I always admired about him. As disfigured as he was, it did not stop him from going into Washington and testifying before Congress and challenging the fundraisers and challenging the governor of the state of South Carolina. He was not alone. There were many with him, but he was he was a gang leader as I called him."

The residents of the D. Ceth Mason House along with the students from schools across three counties caused the Freedom Road enrollment to swell. According to news accounts, the school could have enrolled as many as one hundred students, but, as Beckett recalls, the most at one time was sixty-seven.[41] This allowed the school to add teachers. The school ended up with six teachers covering academic subjects like history, math, and English/literature, as well as vocational/technical training in plumbing and auto mechanics. The school also had two "floaters" who could fill in when other teachers could not be there.[42] A federal "manpower" program provided four additional aides.[43] Teachers were interested in Freedom Road because they wanted to have the opportunity to teach outside of a regular classroom and in a less formal atmosphere.

"They were excited," said Beckett, "because we told them we did not want them coming there in suits and ties. So, to have them be able to come in jeans and tennis shoes was a relaxing opportunity for them to be able to still teach and kind of introduce some non-traditional forms of teaching." This atmosphere would become a hallmark of recovery high schools.

"I called it experimental at that point," said Beckett. "Because they were not the same teaching accoutrements that they would be using in their regular high schools. We had some very ingenious people working at that school. Watching them as they were able to garner the respect and also to engage the students on a regular basis, because of the non-traditional methods of teaching that they used—they were really phenomenal."

The students also appreciated the alternative environment, in which they were on a first name basis with their teachers.

"The majority of the students we teach couldn't handle large group teaching at regular schools," said Lewis Sloan. "That's one reason they are with us."[44]

"There is a lot of interaction with the kids from the standpoint of being human," one of the teachers, Dorothy Fairey, explained in a newspaper interview. "If I am asked something I don't know, I tell them and say, 'Let's read the book.' I learn something new every day. Taking courses in special education was a requirement for me to teach here. But most of the kids are exceptional, not on the remedial level."[45]

The school was not completely unique. The schedule went Monday through Friday, from 9 a.m. to 2 p.m., and classes were fifty-minutes long.[46] The facility had served as a high school for decades, so students felt like they were in an actual school building. Inside that traditional casing, however, the curriculum and the milieu reflected its non-traditional staff and student population. Class sizes were about ten to fifteen students (see Figure 2.1.) Each student was provided with an individualized schedule and a weekly "work contract" that needed to be completed for the student to get a satisfactory grade.

Figure 2.1. Teachers were interested in Freedom Road because they wanted the opportunity to teach outside of a regular classroom and in a less formal atmosphere. Creative projects were common, as they could provide academic instruction, recreation, and therapeutic support. This picture shows a sample of wooden lamps crafted by Freedom Road students. (Source: Shirley Beckett Mikell.)

"It can seem unstructured," said Sloan, "But really it is more structured than regular school programs. These students even have an outlined status structure."[47]

The real historical contribution of Freedom Road lay beyond the academics. D. Ceth Mason himself was integrally engaged in the philosophy, goals, and objectives of the recovery program.

"We had the wherewithal to treat the drug problem, and they (i.e., the public schools) had the wherewithal to treat the education problem, so that's why we came together," said DeLeon.[48]

"The therapeutic interventions were great," said Beckett. "But if [the students] lost that connecter to further their education and then their careers, they'd have nothing. So, the intent was to make sure there was a strong connector between their need for education and the need for treatment as well."

Terry Fox was a longtime teacher at Freedom Road, and he explained, "There are two distinct staffs. One deals with therapy and counseling and the other with teaching.[49]

Counselors from Fetter's staff were at the school all day. Two were there in the morning for monitoring. If the teachers had any issues, they immediately had a referral source. There was always a counselor there to assist with any issues that came up. In the afternoons, there were four counselors on hand either to conduct groups or for individual needs and crises. There were therapy groups during the school day, peer group counseling after school from 2 to 3 p.m., and family groups every other week.[50] Fetter's counselors were present for each of the groups. According to Beckett, who oversaw the counseling component, the groups were more like traditional therapy groups than mutual aid or AA meetings.

"The immersing of AA into group therapy was something that we tried to avoid," Beckett said. "Because we referred them. They didn't have sponsors. They didn't really have AA connectors for adolescents anyway. We tried not to have the idea of a counselor being a sponsor. We really tried to veer away from that because that was a free service, one. And two, we wanted, we wanted them to seek that service outside of us. So, the therapeutic interventions that we did were traditional."[51]

The family component was more educational than family therapy. Families had to attend an orientation group, and family groups were held every other week.

"We wanted them to understand the types of interventions we've been working with the kids on, the rules and regulations they were following, and how they could impose those in their homes. So, it was kind of teaching more than a group activity. It was more of teaching them how to be parents."[52]

Beckett oversaw the counseling component, and she made sure counselors checked in with students at the beginning of every school day.

"The reason that I thought the treatment should be early in the morning was because we don't know what they're dealing with at home," said Beckett. "We really don't understand sometimes if it's their issue, trying not to use and their parents are using, and a lot of that needed to be talked through or worked out before they could concentrate on English, math, reading skills, whatever else."

"That was how we started developing: What do we do in the mornings? What is most essential for the afternoons? Are you teaching the courses every day or every other day? What's the focus? What's the need from the public-school perspective of what they had to do? So that's really how we looked at the curriculum from the public school. And then we put together therapeutic curriculum from there."

The school did urine screening to hold students accountable, but consistent with the therapeutic community approach, peers provided much of the discipline. A "peer group government" was created, and they would meet weekly to discuss student concerns.

"The kids make decisions," Sloan said in a newspaper feature about the school. "The program works better because of that."

Despite the diverse staff, the connection to a predominantly Black public health center, location in a Black community, free services, and a school facility that had served as an all-Black parochial school up to just a short time prior to the school opening there, Freedom Road's student body was almost entirely White. The same was true for the Mason House. A predominantly White student body was not the intention of Fetter's leadership, and certainly not for the Black leaders such as Purvis and Beckett. The student demographics can be understood through the Charleston ecology.

"We opened up the first methadone program in Charleston," recalled Purvis. "We were in a predominantly Black neighborhood, but I bet you out of the first fifty people that came in [to the methadone clinic], forty of them were White. And then the Mason House, let's see, when we first started, we didn't have any Black kids in there. No, we started with twelve, they were all White children."

Then, at Freedom Road, Purvis said, "When they first started, most of the children came from well-to-do families."

Beckett agreed with that description, saying the student body was 95% White, with 70% to 80% coming from middle-to-upper income families. Furthermore, the students were mostly male. The Mason House was exclusively male when it opened, though it later admitted girls to retain federal funding.[53] Beckett explained that even with the students not residing in the house, the students were mainly boys.

"There was resistance to referring girls," said Beckett. "Ironically enough, fewer girls were being identified, although we knew that there had to be. But there was still the resistance in the South of labeling or identifying any young lady or women even with substance use disorder or substance use issues."[54]

Beckett said that one reason for the mostly White student population was the referrals. In the mid-1970s, desegregation was still moving slowly in Charleston, and the mainly Black schools were not referring students at the same rate as the mainly White schools.

"I can't say [the Black schools] were ignoring the problem," said Beckett. "They weren't. But they did not choose to engage in the referrals. I never understood why. We visited them. We did presentations to a few of the classrooms. We worked with the counselors, but we couldn't ever get them to see that that was of benefit to their students. I don't know whether it was familial. I don't know. I don't know whether it was their attitudes. I've never have been able to figure that out."

"All the years that we had that school open, the school system itself never referred [Black students]. There were opportunities from other venues where some Black kids were referred, but it didn't happen through the schools themselves."

Dr. Sidney Jordan, who was White and who helped start the mental health and substance use services at Fetter, suggested Black families in the South generally distrusted the system, and they were hesitant to be labeled with a mental health diagnosis. This hesitancy was especially true for their children.

"We were taking referrals," said Jordan about Fetter's mental health clinic. "And still, even in the Black community where we were trying . . . that we had a storefront where people could walk in, and we didn't have a sign that says, 'Mental Health.' Because the [Black families] at that time were very much opposed to being considered that they had any mental problem. That was cultural, and we were trying to get by that by not identifying ourselves as psychiatrists, psychologists, mental health addiction specialists. We were people who wanted to help them develop themselves in their community. In other words, we deemphasized the mental health aspect of it in terms of how we advertised ourselves, and how we presented ourselves.

"But when we had the program for the school, the high school students, the referrals we got, they had to be voluntary. And I'm sure that [Black families] didn't want to be identified as having, they didn't want their children to be identified as having a drug problem. And [White families] were more open to wanting to have them identified. And so, it had a skewed population that was a problem that we had trouble overcoming."

Dr. Mario Fantini, an education researcher and university administrator, affirmed Jordan's assessment in a 1973 commentary published a special issue of the *Phi Delta Kappa* focused on alternative schools.

"Minority communities resisted alternatives because they were different from the normal forms of education," wrote Fantini. "The resentment was expressed by such remarks as, 'Why are you giving us something different? Aren't we normal like others? We want what the [White families] have—not something different.' In short, those accepting an alternative would be admitting that something was wrong with them—a verdict already rendered by white society."[55]

In the adult programs, adults were choosing to attend programs themselves, which resulted in a big mixture of White and Black folks in the adult drug treatment program.

"But when you had parents involved with children," said Dr. Jordan, "I'm sure that some of their biases were being manifest in not supporting referrals. It was predominantly White. That's a weakness that we didn't overcome."

Jordan also recalled that there were several schools in South Carolina that wished to remain Black, even after desegregation began, because their identity was protected. "They didn't want to be integrated into oblivion, so to speak. They would become less important citizens." To the extent that Freedom Road was perceived as a predominantly White school, therefore, some Black families may have had no interest in helping diversify it.

Conversely, many White families did not like the idea of their children mixing with Black children or being taught or counseled by Black staff members.

"Ironically enough, [Freedom Road] was a segregated school," said Beckett. "And that was another issue with the community as well. The treatment programs, because of the federal funding for treatment services and medication services, they couldn't help but allow integration. But when it came to those kids being together, oh my god, that was . . . we'd have sometimes people picketing outside. The church property had a brick wall that always was there, so they didn't come in, because we did lock the gates, but they'd be picketing sometimes on the streets."

As Beckett explained, if a parent wanted their child who had a severe addiction or alcohol dependence to be treated, and they did not have the money, they could not complain about where they got the free treatment. Freedom Road crossed that line, however, by partnering with the school district for educational services. There was a different threshold for public acceptance of integrated services when it came to schools.

"That kept the community from picketing [the treatment program] as much as they wanted to, making us think about what was going on in the treatment program," said Beckett. "But when it came to the school and there were children [involved], that was a very different issue. Although their children had serious problems, that was not the issue, because treatment was going on. Outpatient counseling was also being held in that school for those children with behavioral issues."

Dr. Jordan further noted that the discomfort with Black teachers and counselors may have cut both ways, suggesting internalized oppression. Using Fetter's community health services as an example, Jordan recalled that while the center had hired several Black physicians, most of their doctors were White.

"And here's my take on that," said Jordan. "The Black people didn't trust Black doctors. That had been so ingrained in them. This is part of the history of segregation. It is creating a sense of inferiority in Black people about their own race, and trusting their own race, that a 'real' doctor was a White doctor. That was part of the implicit bias in Black people . . . It was teaching them to respect their own people. Part of the lesson is we were doing diversity training."

This may provide part of the explanation about the resistance of Black schools and families to utilize services of a treatment program with so many Black counselors and staff. Shirley Beckett, though, suggested yet another possibility: the Black schools' unwillingness to admit their own shortcomings.

"Those teachers knew that those kids were being put out on the street with nothing to do," said Beckett. "The reality, as a Black Southern female, with a Black director of another treatment service, the residential service [i.e., Jesse Purvis], with two Black teachers, really, we had two Black teachers, what I said to them was, 'I don't think that you see that your kids are worthy of this.' "

"Back then in Charleston in particular, I think they themselves were afraid to admit *their* failure (to create similar programs). And so rather than say, 'There's an alternative that may do well for my students that *I* didn't do . . .' I believe that it was more ego than it was anything else. I really do."

Ultimately, regardless of the rationale, the result was that many African American youths did not get services that may have prevented larger problems later. Interestingly, as schools and other community-based programs desegregated in the following decades, Black students were more likely to get punished rather than treated for alcohol and drug problems due to implicit bias on the part of White administrators. In the case of Charleston's segregated system in the 1970s, though, resistance of *Black families and professionals* to refer to a treatment program staffed by Black counselors, teachers, and physicians may have contributed to the same outcome.

"They ended up in the justice system because they weren't referred for their health," said Beckett. "They were expelled from school. They had no recourse; they were in the street, you know, began to use other drugs, also became involved in crime, and ended up in prison. But the reality is that the school system, then a Black school system, could have done more to refer them and kept them out of that altogether."

"Many of those kids, we already had notification through our counselors who were assigned to some of those schools, ended up in prison. It was just very heartbreaking for me to know that the help was available, that the teachers did not cooperate to get their students referred. They just needed to make the referral; the school district would have done the rest. They only needed to make the referral."

The students who did come to Freedom Road typically stayed no more than three or four months.

"Most wanted to get back to their original environments," Beckett said.

But for some, Freedom Road became their final destination. Five students received high school diplomas from the school in 1975, making them the first graduates of the Freedom Road School.[56] The actual diplomas were awarded by their home schools, as the school was not yet accredited on its own, but their final credits had been earned at Freedom Road. Three of the five were planning to attend college the next fall. The commencement was a moment of celebration that the staff would long remember as an indicator of the program's success and its potential.

The financial structure of the school, however, had always been tenuous, and ultimately, finances led to the school closing. The school relied on funding braided through several sources, and those braids started to untangle soon after the school began. Beckett, Purvis, and the other therapeutic staff members were funded by Fetter; Charleston County Public Schools placed the teachers; and the space was provided by the Catholic Diocese. The Freedom Road School was a community effort in every sense, but it was not sustainable. Fetter's funding had initially come from the federal Office of Economic Opportunity, but the same year the school opened, the Nixon administration began dismantling this Johnson administration agency (President Ford formally shuttered the OEO in 1975), and many of the OEO's programs, including the Fetter Family Health Center, were transferred to other offices.[57]

Fetter's funding shifted to NIDA and NIAAA, and in 1976, Fetter laid off thirty-three employees after federal funds were cut by $500,000.[58]

"What happened tragically, is that the Republican administration cut mental health associated with neighborhood health care centers," said Dr. Jordan. "It was the Nixon era.... They thought it was a duplication of services because we still had the mental health center system. So, we really got rid in this country of the public mental health system. We totally took it out of the budget. And it's still missing. It's been criminalized mental health; children and adults have been criminalized. It meant the end of the Freedom Road School, because of the political shift in where we wanted to spend money."

All Fetter programs were transferred under the control of the Charleston County Substance Abuse Commission on July 1, 1977.[59] The commission paid for a few much-needed renovations to the Immaculate Conception building, and the school changed its name to the "Lowcountry School," which was descriptive of the regional nature of the school.[60] While the Commission, still receiving advising from Mason, remained supportive of the school, the school district leadership did not. Dr. Lawrence G. Derthick took over as superintendent in 1978, and he did not have the same commitment to the Freedom Road/Lowcountry School as his predecessor. Dr. Derthick had been the US Commissioner of Education under President Eisenhower from 1956 to 1961, the years immediately following the *Brown v. Board of Education* desegregation decision. On April 3, 1979, Dr. Derthick sent a letter to Eugene Hall, then executive director of the Charleston County Substance Abuse Commission, announcing the district's decision to end its affiliation with the school. According to a newspaper account, the department of instruction had recommended the move because the school "was too expensive to run and was in danger of losing its accreditation from the S.C. Department of Education."[61] The district was making plans for opening a more general alternative school "that would address all problem students, not just those with a history of drug and alcohol problems," and the drug program would be rolled into that larger school.[62] One of the reasons the school had become too expensive was that the state had reclassified students with substance use disorders as "regular" high school students. In the past, they had been classified as "severely mentally handicapped," which had qualified them for additional special education funding.[63] The removal of that funding reduced the budget available for placing teachers at the school.

The school board eventually reversed course and decided to extend their contract through the 1979–1980 school year—thanks in part to pleas from the Substance Abuse Commission. A major blow, however, came when the building's lease ended on June 30, 1980, and it was not renewed. The school district did not offer a new space, as it was proceeding with plans to fold the program into the larger alternative high school.[64]

"The reality was that the Catholic Diocese of Charleston had been allowing us to use the building for free, and the building was in disarray," recalled Beckett. "And there were some safety issues. We needed another space, but we could not find anything. We tried renting a house, and of course, the neighbors didn't want the children in their neighborhood."

According to Beckett, families dropping kids off added to neighborhood traffic. Students standing in the yard during breaks or playing games during recess upset some local residents. The house only allowed space for one or two classes at a time, which was not satisfactory to the school district, especially with a more comprehensive school in the works. The school continued looking for a suitable space within Charleston County but could not find one.

"So, we ended up having to close the school," said Beckett. "That was a heartbreaking situation for all of us."

The school closure may have been more heartbreaking to one person than anyone else: D. Ceth Mason. By 1980, Mason was starting to succumb to the cancer that would ultimately end his life at age 69 on New Year's Eve, 1982. Mason had retired from his investment finance career in 1975 to become a full-time projects administrator for the South Carolina Commission on Alcohol and Drug Abuse, and he spent the rest of his life fighting for the survival of programs like the Freedom Road School and the Mason House. Just three months before he died, Mason was awarded the prestigious Order of the Palmetto by South Carolina Governor Richard W. Riley. The honor was in recognition of his thirty-plus years of service to "bring alcoholism to the forefront in South Carolina as a disease to be treated openly."[65]

In accepting the award, Mason acknowledged South Carolinians as "special citizens for recognizing the importance of the problems of addictions and making the state a leader in treatment."[66] And nothing had been more representative of that leadership than the trailblazing Freedom Road School.

3

Spontaneous Generation

Hermann Park sits on 445 acres in the Museum District of Houston, across the road from Rice University. The park was established in 1914 in the spirit of another municipal greenspace, Central Park in New York.[1] As a large, public place, Hermann Park has hosted many community events in its century-plus existence. This meant Hermann Park was the site of protests against the Vietnam War. One event in particular captured the zeitgeist of the youth subculture soon after the 1960s. On April 12, 1970, Abbie Hoffman, the antiwar activist and Chicago 7 member, gave a speech at Hermann Park (see Figure 3.1). Less than one year before, Hoffman had interrupted the Who's performance of their rock opera, *Tommy*, at Woodstock—the same concert that would later inspire guitarist Pete Townshend's lyric about a "teenage wasteland" in the song "Baba O'Riley." Hoffman, apparently high on LSD, was forever captured on the Woodstock soundtrack as shouting, "I think this is a pile of shit, while John Sinclair rots in prison!" Sinclair was a Detroit poet who had been arrested in Michigan for marijuana possession and given a ten-year prison sentence just weeks before the Woodstock festival. Townshend was not happy with the interruption. He bonked Hoffman with his guitar and yelled, "Fuck off my fucking stage!"[2]

Rice University had refused to allow Hoffman onto campus, so he spoke instead in Hermann Park on that warm, spring day in 1970.[3] About five hundred people made a three-mile anti-war demonstration march to the park, and the crowd swelled to five thousand people as Hoffman spoke.

"The youth of this nation is going to replace the government," said Hoffman. "And we are going to keep it."[4]

Many of those youths had taken to drinking and using drugs in spacious Hermann Park, and that had started to concern a local minister. Palmer Memorial Episcopal Church is situated directly between Hermann Park to the east and Rice University to the west. As the legend goes, Father Charles Wyatt-Brown, the rector of Palmer Church, made a bold decision in the spring of 1971. Father Charlie, as he was known, had been Palmer's rector for five years, and he felt called to help teenagers like those in the nearby park, some of whom he had gotten to know when they came over from the park to use the restrooms in the church (see Figure 3.2).[5] He had been hosting Twelve Step meetings for adults at the parish house, and he decided to begin also hosting group meetings for the youths struggling with drug use themselves (Alcoholics Anonymous) or in their families (Alateen).[6]

One of the adults attending meetings at the church was 27-year-old Bob Meehan. Meehan had recently moved to Houston and found work on the grounds crew at

Salvaging a Teenage Wasteland. Andrew J. Finch, Oxford University Press. © Oxford University Press 2024.
DOI: 10.1093/oso/9780190645502.003.0003

Figure 3.1. Abbie Hoffman was a prominent social and political activist in the United States during the 1960s and 1970s. Hoffman was known for his advocacy of the countercultural movement, and he cofounded the Youth International Party ("Yippies"). He frequently used theatrical tactics to challenge authority and promote social change, which included interrupting The Who during their set at Woodstock. (Source: Associated Press.)

nearby Rice University "digging ditches and doing other manual labor."[7] He had recently been released from one of the original federal narcotics farms in Lexington, Kentucky,[8] where he had served time for theft related to his substance use disorder.[9]

Journalist Daniel Kolitz writes the following about Meehan:

> At 27, (Meehan) was mostly toothless—he wore dentures—and bald, save for a grimy curtain of hair running from the peak of his scalp down to his shoulders. A Fu Manchu mustache drooped past his chin. He'd mostly stopped using drugs but still wrestled with booze, and after another short stint in jail, this time for burglary and public drunkenness, he began attending Alcoholics Anonymous meetings at Palmer Memorial Episcopal Church.[10]

Meehan claimed to have been using drugs since he was a teenager, and his parents had notified him that they would no longer bail him out of trouble, so he was on his own. As Palmer Church was across the street from Rice, Meehan had begun eating lunch and attending meetings there. He claimed he had stopped using heroin by then, but he was "still drinking and taking other drugs."[11] According to another account, "Someone suggested that Bob attend a meeting at Palmer. Since Bob didn't have anything else going for him except a fresh heroin habit, he agreed to go."[12]

Though stories vary with regards to Meehan's drug use at the time, the narratives concur that after attending the Twelve Step meetings for a while, Meehan tried to stop

Figure 3.2. Father Charles Wyatt-Brown ("Father Charlie") was rector of Palmer Memorial Church in Houston from 1966 to 1980. In the spring of 1971, Father Charlie felt called to help local teenagers by hosting group meetings for youths struggling with drug use themselves or in their families. He befriended Bob Meehan, with whom he created the Palmer Drug Abuse Program (PDAP). This is a photo taken by the author of a portrait hanging in the Palmer Church. (Source: Andy Finch.)

using drugs. Meehan also got Father Charlie's attention by speaking up at meetings, and Father Charlie invited Meehan to have lunch with him regularly in the church cafeteria to talk about "himself, his past, and his dreams for the future." Through those discussions, Father Charlie came to care for Meehan, and Meehan valued their lunchtime meetings. Meehan credited the rector for turning him around.

"I believe," Meehan told an interviewer, "It would have to be the unconditional love shown to me by Father Charlie . . . He immediately made me feel different. Here was a man that I had respect for, who said he loved me . . . I believe that that did something to me about how I saw me. His love for me started me changing me."[13]

Finder of the Founder

Looking around at the teenagers attending the support groups at the church, as well as those from Hermann Park just using the facilities, Father Charlie asked himself, "What if teenagers who were on the brink of making all the mistakes Bob had made could hear where it would get them, from someone who had been there?"[14]

Father Charlie believed that Bob Meehan's struggles might help young people decide to avoid drug use themselves. It is impossible to know for sure how much of Meehan's story that compelled Father Charlie is factual or apocryphal, but there are basic details passed down through historical interviews with Meehan and Father Charlie and published in the PDAP organizational literature. Everyone who provided accounts of the founding of PDAP for this book shared essentially this same story, though only Meehan and Father Charlie were there for all the events, and Father Charlie passed away in 2000.

Meehan was born in Baltimore in June 1943. His father, Joseph Meehan, was a traffic patrol officer with the Baltimore Police Department from 1943 to 1959, when he retired and began selling "ecclesiastical apparel."[15] Interestingly, Joseph Meehan was still selling religious clothing when his son started meeting with Father Charlie at Palmer Episcopal.

Meehan graduated from St. Bernardine school in 1961. St. Bernadine Catholic Church is in West Baltimore's Edmondson Village neighborhood, and in the 1950s, it housed one of the largest Catholic parishes in the city.[16] Meehan attended school there just as the neighborhood was beginning to transform. According to a church history, in the 1960s the area faced "blockbusting" change, from "Catholic to non-Catholic residents of Edmondson Village, from predominantly white to predominantly African American neighbors."[17] The parish dwindled and declined in membership, and the church nearly closed.

The Catholic school system in Baltimore at the time tracked students into the Business Course or the College Preparatory sequence. Meehan was on the college prep track, and he had a music scholarship.[18] According to St. Bernardine's 1961 yearbook, he was a member of the band all four years and played volleyball his junior year. The charisma that later impressed Father Charlie apparently was evident in his youth too, as Meehan was on the Student Council for three years, including the Executive Committee as a senior.

The clean-cut, blond-haired, smiling teenager in the yearbook photo was already actively using drugs according to Meehan's later narrative, though it is unclear exactly when he started using. One interview stated, "From age 12 to 27, he was addicted to what he calls 'mind-changing chemicals.'"[19] In his own book, though, Meehan reported that he "used drugs for 10 years," getting sober at age 27. That would suggest he had just started using around the time the senior photo was taken. The distinction seems important, as the first account that had him starting at age 12 would allow him to relate better to the teens Father Charlie wanted to counsel.

"I was playing music," said Meehan. "I was a drummer, and I was playing music back then . . . And yes, I was getting high then. And I was drinking all the time. Well, the guys in the band were older than me. So, you know, they were drinking and using and they just kind of brought me along."

One of his early drug incidents ended up in the *Baltimore Sun* in May 1964. Meehan, was 20 when narcotics officers caught him and another 20-year-old with two hundred amphetamine pills. The article described Meehan and the other young man as "employed," "first offenders," and "only occasional users of the pills."[20] While it isn't known what if any influence his father, who had retired from the police force five years earlier, exerted in the case, Meehan and the other defendant were given probation. The newspaper mentioned that this was only his first offense, even though he claimed later to have been using drugs anywhere from three to eight years by that time.

Meehan wrote of his parents' lifelong support of him in his book, *Beyond the Yellow Brick Road: Our Children and Drugs.*[21]

"My parents had always helped me," wrote Meehan. "My father, a policeman, often had used his connections to bail me out of trouble. My mother had always been comforting and nurturing. If I had debts, my folks paid them. When I needed medical care, they never hesitated to help. No matter what I did, I could always depend on my father or mother to rescue me."[22]

One of the last times Meehan's father helped him was when he had been sentenced to prison for a drug offense. Though Meehan said he had been arrested several times before that, none of the crimes had been federal ones, which ultimately worked in his favor, thanks to Joseph Meehan.

"I had been up in Holmesburg State Penitentiary in Philadelphia," said Meehan. "I got out. I was out for two weeks, and I got busted again. So, I called Dad. Dad got me transferred into the federal system. So now I'm a *first* offender in the federal system, and I got to go to Lexington [the narcotics farm] with some great possibilities that came down. It's such a God trip, it's unbelievable."[23]

Meehan's book mentioned that he tried to quit using drugs "31 times" unsuccessfully, listing his parents, teachers, friends, neighbors, and a "Christian group" as all trying but failing to help him. He said he even was given methadone at Johns Hopkins Hospital in his hometown of Baltimore, which, if true, would have made him one of the earliest methadone recipients in Baltimore.[24] According to Meehan, upon his release from the narcotics farm, he signed papers saying if he could avoid a drug conviction for five years, he would receive a full pardon, and his first stop was the Hopkins Drug Abuse Clinic.[25]

"I came out of Lexington penitentiary, and Johns Hopkins was like my parole," said Meehan in an interview for this book. "I had to go to Johns Hopkins, and they put me on methadone."[26]

Methadone clinics had begun in New York in 1965, spread to Chicago in 1968, and eventually to Washington, DC, in 1969, due in large part to the influence of Jerome Jaffe and Robert DuPont.[27] Both Jaffe and DuPont would later serve as US Drug Czars. Johns Hopkins Hospital had started treatment programs in East Baltimore in the late 1960s. Then, in 1971, Hopkins worked with Baltimore public officials to expand substance abuse treatment in the city, requesting $3.3 million "to support methadone maintenance and other treatment programs rather than education or counseling."[28] Dr. Leon Wormser directed the Hopkins Drug Abuse Center.[29]

"As they saw it, you know, 'at least it'll keep them from stealing our color TVs,'" said Meehan of his methadone treatment. "I was on 90 milligrams a day, which is a pretty heavy dose. Dr. Wormser decided to make me his poster-boy and asked me to speak at schools.... But at the time, I was not sober. I was still on methadone. I was still drinking wine, you know, but claiming I was straight. To me, it was really straight. I wasn't shootin' dope."[30]

Meehan had a great aunt who lived in Houston, and she told him there was "a lot of work there, and I should come down there."[31] Because his father had gotten him switched to a federal prison, his parole was also federal, which allowed him to move outside the state. So, after finishing the Hopkins program, Meehan moved to Houston. He was screened regularly for drugs, but said he kept drinking and soon got arrested for "burglary and public drunkenness." This time his parents denied his request for help. According to Meehan, "Now they were cutting the cord. They stood united against me."[32]

Meehan quoted the letter from his mother, Elizabeth Meehan, in his book, "Dear Bobby: Your Father and I thought that leaving town would help you. Apparently, it hasn't. Maybe more time behind bars will."[33]

On the first page of his book, Meehan describes the behaviors he had put his parents through leading up to their "cutting the cord." He lists the drugs he used, including marijuana, heroin, cough syrup, cocaine, speed, and alcohol.

By Meehan's own account, he would spend "three years in penitentiaries and jails."[34]

"I used to rob people, hurt people, and scare people." And Meehan claimed that after joining the Palmer meetings, "I no longer do those things, because I have found a way to live that is better than the way I lived before."[35]

These stories held messages of challenge and redemption that Father Charlie thought could help straighten the path for the youth at his church, so he hired Meehan as a sexton/janitor for about a hundred dollars per week, with specific instructions to talk with the youths coming to the church and to share his story with them (see Figure 3.3).[36]

"I said, 'Bob, we have children here that are having problems with drugs,'" said Father Charlie. "So, keep your eye on them, and if the hall doesn't get vacuumed right on-time, that's alright. You turn your attention to the child who has a need."[37]

As Father Charlie recalled in an interview posted online in 2013, Meehan started "surrounding himself" with about four boys aged 17 or 18, and they would

Figure 3.3. Bob Meehan founded the Palmer Drug Abuse Program in 1971 after befriending Father Charles Wyatt-Brown. Meehan's work with PDAP had a significant impact on addiction treatment methods for adolescents, and it inspired similar programs, now called "Alternative Peer Groups," nationwide over the next fifty years. (Source: PDAP/John Cates.)

meet almost every day. According to Meehan, "after a few months, 25 to 30 kids were coming every day to the church to listen to me talk, play cards, make music and sing songs, or just to smoke cigarettes and horse around."[38]

The eventual job Father Charlie envisioned would be that of a "youth counselor," and Father Charlie reached out to the local community to fund such a position.

"Father Charlie got the funding together," said John Will, who would later also work for Palmer. "The oil industry has been more than generous to us. Of course, [Palmer] is in an oil land."

"How Father Charlie pulled off letting me do this was a mind blower," said Meehan. "And he's a beauty. He stayed my sponsor for thirty years. He called himself the finder of the founder."[39]

The rector was able to raise enough funding to hire Meehan as a youth counselor for four months, and in July 1971, Meehan held the first meeting of what they would later start calling the "Palmer Drug Abuse Program" or "PDAP."[40] It was not yet known as an "Alternative Peer Group" or "APG," but PDAP was the first such program. According to PDAP's historical account, six teenagers between the ages of 13 and 16 attended that first meeting:

> The original group of teenagers discovered that if they loved, accepted, and supported one another, they could stop using drugs and alcohol and stay that way. They also learned that through loving and helping each other, they began to feel

good about themselves. They also discovered the strength and unity and power that comes from the love of the group.[41]

Meehan was careful to distinguish PDAP's recovery support model from "treatment."[42]

"The word 'treatment' seems incompatible with the concept of self-help," Meehan wrote. "The program I describe is a free, non-profit, self-help group . . . An 'opportunity for recovery' is a much better way to describe what my programs offer because recovery implies that one gradually overcomes the drug disease by strengthening himself."

He also asserted the originality of PDAP.

"The Palmer Drug Abuse Program (PDAP) that I founded in 1971 was never actually 'conceived.' Heads never got together and hatched the idea for a teenage drug program. At first glance, PDAP's birth more closely fits the definition of spontaneous generation."[43]

"But it only *seemed* to spring out of nothing," he clarified. "In fact, there was something going on all the time that I was unaware of. I knew there was a method of kicking chemical dependency that worked—the Twelve Steps of Alcoholics Anonymous."

Indeed, PDAP even rewrote a version of the Twelve Steps to better fit the teenage population they were serving.

"What I did—unwittingly at first, but quite consciously later on," wrote Meehan, "was package the Twelve Steps so that young people could benefit from them."

Meehan noted that in the early 1970s, Twelve Step groups were not as accessible to young people as they are today. Most were attended and run by "middle-aged alcoholics," and thus were not welcoming to a younger generation. He realized the need to include parents; PDAP thus had two main components: youth groups and parent groups. They also involved social activities beyond the meetings, including "outings, parties, concerts, round robins (all-night gatherings), and dances . . . to make the program attractive."[44]

Meehan and Father Charlie clearly struck a chord with Houston-area families. Under their leadership, PDAP was so successful that in just over six months, they opened a second counseling center in Houston in February 1972.[45]

PDAP eventually grew beyond youth programming. In November 1972, a "counselor" was hired for an "Older Group satellite for those 17 to 25 years old."[46] This meant PDAP now had programs for youths 13 to 16 and for young adults 17 to 25. In the early 1970s, the term "counselor" did not yet imply licensure or certification; PDAP typically hired young people who could relate to the teenagers—mostly people who had once attended the program, and Meehan would train them himself.

Anne Wingfield and her twin sister were two of the Houston teenagers who started attending PDAP meetings in 1974 at the age of 15, and Anne eventually became a PDAP counselor.[47] The Wingfields' older brother had been a member of PDAP, and when he realized his sisters were smoking pot and drinking, he encouraged them to attend a meeting.

"My brother was worried," said Wingfield.

Her brother said, "Girls, you have to go to PDAP."

"Why?" they asked.

" 'Because you shouldn't be smoking pot. That's really bad for you."

"So, we went, and let me tell you something," said Wingfield. "It was so much fun, and there were so many good-looking boys. And it was like, okay, we'll give this a try. We won't drink, we won't smoke."[48]

Wingfield's mother had left home when she was only thirteen, and her father was raising her and her six siblings. Six of the seven Wingfield children would ultimately join PDAP, and the seventh, who had physical and behavioral disabilities, would also regularly attend events. For them and many of their fellow teenagers, PDAP filled a void, even if many, such as Wingfield, did not consider themselves "addicts" or "alcoholics." The labels did not matter as much as the community they could join.

"It became a lifestyle choice for us, you know, and it was really helpful," said Wingfield. "We didn't have a lot of structure at home. Dad was doing his best, but he was trying to raise six kids, including Danny."

"We found PDAP, and it was like, 'Wow!' People who can relate and talk and be emotional."

"It was fucking awesome," said Wingfield, in an interview. "It really was."[49]

Campouts might draw a thousand sober people, and as Wingfield recalled, "Whatever you wanted to do, somebody else enjoyed it, and you went and did it sober."[50]

PDAP was not a school, but like most of the early recovery high schools, it was predominantly, if not exclusively, White. Pictures from its early days show mostly White youths, and BIPOC teens would not have seen many people who looked like them in the crowded PDAP meetings.[51] The dearth of inclusivity did not, however, stem the growth of PDAP. On the contrary, its cunning message, charismatic leadership, and free services led to rapid expansion.

"In no time," wrote Meehan, "the program grew too big for the Palmer Church, so we opened another one at a different church, then another, and another, until we were all over Houston and its suburbs."[52] PDAP literature says this growth occurred "within four years," at which time, "the rector of the Church of Incarnation in Dallas established the first satellite outside of Houston."[53] According to Meehan, the growth would continue "like a wildfire" across Texas in Fort Worth, San Antonio, Austin, and Beaumont,[54] and in 1976, one PDAP member even started his own school.

"Houston's First Ex-Drug Fiend Education School for Ex-Drug Fiends Taught by an Ex-Drug Fiend"

The first independent recovery school (i.e., not connected to a public school district or health center) was not, in actuality, a high school, but it considered itself a school.

They made a yearbook, and the graduates donned robes and received diplomas at a commencement ceremony.[55] The program actually tutored students preparing for the GED, and it was created by a PDAP member.

The GED stands for General Education Development exams and is a battery of tests developed during World War II. The GED is used as a standard measure to ascertain high school–level academic knowledge, as many young people called into military service had not completed high school. The idea was to give service members credentials that would help them find employment after the war. New York became the first state to offer the GED to civilians as a high school equivalency test in 1947, and over the next twenty-five years, other states followed suit. By 1974, all fifty states were using the GED to award high school certificates equivalent to a diploma, and the state of Texas issued 7,636 GED credentials in 1976.[56]

While critics have charged that the GED option encourages people to drop out of high school,[57] many of the young people found themselves either unable or unwilling to go back to high school after getting clean and sober, and the GED was another option. Students could be expelled for using or possessing drugs at school, and throughout the 1970s, drug use among adolescents was steadily increasing every year. Students could legally drop out of Texas high schools at age 17, and many teens wanting to be sober, facing the choice of confronting drug use every day, chose to do just that.[58]

Drug-free school options were limited in Houston in 1976. While the Odyssey House and Canarsie in New York had started providing "full-service" high schools in their adolescent treatment units as early as 1970, such programs were essentially adjunct to the treatment its young patients were receiving.[59] Once the treatment was completed, students would no longer need to be in a rehabilitation program, nor, by default, the school. There were also no such programs in Texas. For high school students wanting to work on their day-to-day recovery while attending a school within a drug-free and supportive environment, the educational landscape was bleak.

"Houston had a couple of alternative high schools," said John Will, an early PDAP member who later became a director. "Namely, if you could not function in a regular school, you could go to the alternative high school downtown, and it had rooms like the Moody Blues room and the Rolling Stones room. The rooms didn't have numbers, they had names, and stuff like this. It was really hip and cool, and some of the kids would go to that. We had a lot of kids who had gone through school, and they couldn't go back. They had gotten kicked out. The schools didn't want them back. They were getting to the point of being too old, where the schools could say, 'You can't come back.'"[60]

While the GED was another pathway to a high school credential, it was not a guarantee. Though critics have suggested the GED is too easy, not everybody who took the test was prepared to pass it. In 1976, 37% of the Texans who took the test failed—a total of 4,455 people.[61]

Into this academic void stepped an older PDAP member who also happened to be a licensed teacher. John Carrington Cates was born on May 30, 1951, in Galveston,

Texas, which means he was just shy of his 25th birthday on March 5, 1976, the day he claimed as his sobriety date. The PDAP program had added an "Older Group" for people aged 17 to 25 in 1972, and Cates had found his way to that group as his life was falling apart for all to see through the Houston media.

Cates described himself as coming from a religious family. "My great-grandfather was a traveling minister. My grandmother was the kindest church-starting Baptist lady. I never heard her say an unkind word about anybody. My father was an absolute hero—a deacon in the church. My mother and he were active." Winfred Hiram Cates, his father, was a veteran of both World War II and Korea.[62]

"I had no toxic parenting in my background," said Cates.[63]

Cates has stated in multiple interviews that he did not start using drugs until he was 17, though the details have varied.

"I was a good boy," said Cates. "I went to church; I went to Bible School, but I really didn't know Christ."[64]

He claimed he first used cannabis "with a girl,"[65] after which, "I had been stoned every night from the time I was 17 years of age until the night I got arrested (at age 24)."[66]

Cates graduated from high school in 1969 and then attended the University of Houston, where he majored in elementary education and minored in psychology.[67]

"I was one of those weird guys who stayed in school," said Cates. "I was the poster child of 'Here's a guy who can do his dope and his dope not do him.'"[68]

While in college, Cates married his "high school sweetheart," Joan Miller, two days after Christmas 1970. He said that at the time, "We were both high-functioning users."[69]

Cates became an elementary teacher's aide in January 1971, and he worked at two different elementary schools in the Houston Independent School District: Dunbar Elementary and Park Place Elementary. After earning his teaching license, Cates began teaching at Pugh Elementary in January 1973, and he later transferred to Nat Q. Henderson Elementary. He was teaching sixth grade at Henderson as his drug problem worsened.[70]

"I was posing as a teacher in the daytime and an absolute criminal at night," said Cates. "I carried a gun; started dealing dope on the side. I've held the gun on people, made folks lie down in parking lots, told them I would shoot them."[71]

He also admitted to selling drugs to fellow teachers.[72]

"School officials obviously had no idea of what I was doing."[73]

Cates had begun working on his master's degree in educational administration when the police finally caught up with him. On October 14, 1975, Cates and his roommate, Michael Drane, sold twelve ounces of heroin to an undercover agent, and they both were arrested by state and federal agents on charges of possession and delivery of heroin, a second-degree felony. The transaction had occurred on a Tuesday night at 7:30—a school night. Cates said that he and his lawyer were hoping for only a thirty-year sentence, and he later noted that prosecutors were requesting ninety years.[74]

Cates life began to unravel with his arrest.

"I was down to 136 pounds at 6-1," said Cates, "and I was put in the old Harris County Jail—terrified, kicking heroin. I was, you know, going through withdrawals."[75]

He also lost his teaching job, was briefly out of work, and his "first marriage blew up." Joan left him and by September 1976, their divorce was final.[76]

While waiting about nine months for his day in court, Cates said, "My attorney suggested I get back to church and get a job."[77]

At first, Cates was able to find work at a concrete yard, but his coworkers were using drugs there too. This made it difficult for him to stop his own use, as he had not received any formal treatment. Cates's attorney thus had another strategic idea: to get involved with the Palmer Drug Abuse Program—"because it could influence the court," said Cates.

At the time, PDAP was four years old, and it had garnered quite a following in Houston. It was also beginning its expansion beyond Houston into other Texas communities. Cates went to see a PDAP counselor, whom he recalled had two years sober and no certification beyond his training at PDAP.

"I walked in and got arrogant on him," said Cates, who at 24 was at the upper end of the 13 to 25 age range. "I analyzed the process and thought I had conned them."

The counselor said he could help Cates, but he "would need to hang around PDAP," which was a standard requirement (see Figure 3.4). Cates had stopped using heroin

Figure 3.4. John Cates was a Houston schoolteacher and an early participant in the Palmer Drug Abuse Program (PDAP). Cates combined his training as an educator with his experience as a person in recovery to start a GED program in his apartment in 1976. Initially a private venture, Cates eventually turned the program over to PDAP. Cates spent most of the rest of his career running alternative peer groups and creating schools associated with them. (Source: PDAP/John Cates.)

but was still "smoking dope and drinking." The turning point came during, of all occasions, a spring break trip.

"PDAP was getting ready to go on a campout," said Cates. He went along for three days in early March, and he stayed sober. According to Cates, March 5, 1976, has remained his sobriety date ever since.

Cates quickly assimilated into the PDAP culture and built friendships that remain to this day. Anne Wingfield had been in PDAP since 1974, and she remembers when Cates started attending.

"When John came to PDAP, we met him, and he was just the sweetest young man," said Wingfield.

About four months after that Spring Break trip, Cates had his trial on July 13, 1976, in the Harris County District Court, with Judge George L. Walker presiding. Cates went in expecting to be given a long prison sentence. Cates's involvement in PDAP may have impacted the judge's decision, as he had four months of sobriety by that point and was turning his life around.

"We heard that he had to go to court, and it was serious, and he might go to prison, and he needed support," said Wingfield.

So, Wingfield and enough PDAP members to fill two rows of seats in the courtroom attended the hearing.

"My twin sister and I and a whole bunch of girls, we went to that courtroom," said Wingfield. "And we sat there. And they said to the judge, 'This is his support group now. Look at him.' And it was fantastic."

Instead of a jail sentence that day, Judge Walker placed Cates on probation for "not less than two nor more than ten years … upon advice from the district attorney's office."[78]

"I walked out not knowing what had happened," said Cates. "Nobody knew."

In addition to being given probation, Cates would benefit from a "youth offenders" law which said if a person had committed their first felony before age 25, the conviction would be erased after serving probation. Since Cates had been 24 when he was arrested, it would be as if the event had never happened.[79]

"My relationship with God had grown to the point that I slept like a baby the night before court," Cates later reflected. "I was looking for what was the adventure [God] had for me."[80]

And an opportunity indeed presented itself. By getting probation instead of jail time, Cates was given the chance to remain in Houston, among the PDAP community. And he hit upon a way to converge his training as an educator with his experience as a person in recovery. With so many young people in PDAP seeing the GED as their most viable pathway to a high school certificate, and the Texas pass rate sitting at only 63%, Cates could fill a need.

"When I didn't get to prison and I had a few months sober, I wanted to help," said Cates. "People were getting kicked out of school, and there was a very large group of recovering young people [in PDAP]. It got much larger than that, but it was pretty good sized then. There were a couple hundred of them. Of that couple of hundred, there were dozens who had not finished high school or were still of high school age, but really no place for them to go."[81]

Cates had been trained in the University of Houston School of Education, and he recalled "in those days, it was kind of a big deal to be in the field of education, to go to U of H. They had just built this thing called the Kiva, and all the new designs for classroom furniture was coming out like the trapezoidal tables, so you can do differentiation.[82] I was right in the midst of that."

According to Cates, University of Houston students were taught how to "break curriculum into learning modules and do the diagnostics and pre- and post-tests and all that kind of thing." This training was particularly well suited for preparing students to take the GED, which was broken into different subject areas.

"Some of them really had been kicked out early, junior high, and they were way, way behind educationally," said Cates.

Cates threw himself into the new venture. He quit his job at the concrete yard and set up his apartment, which he was sharing with a roommate named Bill P., as a classroom to prepare students for the GED (see Figure 3.5).[83] Cates set a tuition of thirty dollars per month for the school and created flyers on a mimeograph machine to promote it. The flyer, a copy of which Cates had framed and still hangs in his office decades later, is one of the most descriptive artifacts we have of what became the first

Figure 3.5. This apartment complex was the original site of the GED school started by John Cates in 1976. Cates bought TV trays to use as desks, so the program would feel as much like a school as possible. The apartment had a large living room with a connected dining room, and students would be spread through the rooms. Students were charged thirty dollars per month to attend, and there might be up to a couple dozen students in the apartment at a time. After a few months, Cates moved the school out of his apartment to office space on the second floor of a pharmacy near Rice University. (Source: John Cates.)

independent educational program for students in recovery.[84] The words were hand-written, and across the top, in large, bold, underlined, capital letters, taking two lines was the proclamation, IF YOU ARE WILLING?!? . . .

Under the heading, the flyer said, "Announcing: Houston's First Ex-Drug Fiend Education School for Ex-Drug Fiends taught by an Ex-Drug Fiend." By emphasizing the label "drug fiend," the announcement was co-opting a derogatory word, "fiend," and thus disarming it, similar to how the LGBTQIA community later would embrace the word "queer." Such reframing of negative concepts was something common to the PDAP vernacular. Indeed, the next line on the flyer did the same thing with the word, "junkie": "Featuring: Houston's First and Most Infamous Junkie, Teacher: John Cates Now Residing in Houston for a limited time of not less than two nor more than ten years as a guest of the State of Texas and The Palmer Drug Abuse Program." The last line obviously referred to Cates's probation terms, which he would wear as a badge of legitimacy and relatability.

The flyer next provided a six-point outline of the school's curriculum, designed to appeal to its target audience of students who had left high school either voluntarily or through expulsion:

1. *No Boring Lectures.*
2. *Cover only what you need to know.*
3. *No Lifetime financial involvement.*
4. *No wondering if you will pass.*
5. *No grades, report cards, keeping in your seat.*
6. *Taught in one hour a day sessions of 3 people each.*

The last point in particular distinguishes the GED school as an educational program rather than a full-fledged high school. While the intent was to create a schooling experience, the curriculum was tutorial in nature and would not lead to a high school diploma per se. The actual goal was emphasized by a sentence written sideways along the left edge of the flyer: "Get Your G.E.D. the Quickest, Easiest Way Possible!"[85]

The flyer concluded with two sentences about how to enroll: "For More Information, Call 526-5058 or talk to John in person before or after any of a number of PDAP meetings. Call Soon, Due to uniqueness of Course and singularity of teacher, there will be a limited enrollment."

These last points indicated that (a) the program would be targeted at PDAP members; (b) there was not another program like it; and (c) Cates would be the only teacher. Even though it was his own private business and did not yet belong to PDAP, Cates asked for approval to start distributing the flyers at PDAP meetings.

"I got permission," said Cates. "(PDAP) said, 'Sure, go ahead, whatever.' They were worried about whether I could even pull it together. I only had four months sober. They were sitting around taking bets on whether this guy was going to make it."[86]

The flyer had predicted the school would be popular, and it was. According to Cates, the school opened with forty students, which would make it among the larger recovery high schools today.

Wayne Cloud was one of the first students to sign up, and he was actually a PDAP counselor who had grown up near the University of Texas in Austin and dropped out of high school early in his academic career. A self-described child of an alcoholic, he had started using substances in his teens and always struggled with school. Due to his family situation, Cloud had changed schools many times before he eventually stopped attending altogether.[87]

As PDAP began expanding beyond Houston, one of its early satellite cities was Austin. Cloud had started trying to get sober through AA when he turned 18, but there was not much of a youth presence in AA at the time, and he had limited success. Once he started attending the fledgling PDAP groups around 1973, things changed. He met Bob Meehan, who recruited Cloud to become a counselor. Cloud recalls moving to Houston and attending about six weeks of training during fall 1973, during which time he turned 21. In the early days, PDAP had not required its counselors to have diplomas.

"We had some counselors on the staff that had minus fifteen minutes sobriety," said John Will. "It was like, 'If you sober up, you look good, you talk good, we'll hire you.' We had these kids that we wanted to hire as staff, but they'd been kicked out of school. They were attractive to staff members because of their experience, their stories, and they had gotten high. They knew the game. They knew all the stuff, and they knew about recovery, but they'd gotten kicked out school, so they didn't have a high school diploma or a GED, but we thought, 'We need to hire these people.' "[88]

The job was an ideal fit for the newly sober Cloud.

"I was working with Palmer, and I loved my job and couldn't wait to get up and go to work each day," said Cloud. "And I thought, 'What a great thing. Something I want to do, and I get paid for it. I didn't get paid much, you know, like $400 a month or so. It wasn't much, but, I mean, it was perfect. I couldn't have asked for anything better.'"

As PDAP grew as an organization, they added a requirement that counselors have a GED or high school diploma, and that was the incentive Cloud needed to go back to school, and the timing worked well. Cates had just launched the school in his apartment.

"That's what actually inspired me to get it done," said Cloud. "Like, 'Oh, okay, I need to do this.' Before that, I just never had any interest in learning, 'cause I was just busy getting high.'"

Cates bought TV trays to use as desks, so the program would feel as much like a school as possible. Most of the students would be age 18 and over, but not all. Some were still of high school age but had been kicked out or dropped out of their school.

"I bought some GED books, the standard curriculum manuals, broke them down, expanded on the pre-test and pro-test elements," remembered Cates. "I filed it and set it up to where we could shift and go through different things."

"We started to use the word tutor, but we thought, 'That's not really accurate here. There's mentoring going on.' It's not just about how to tie down the curriculum, it's about how to interact with it, how to assimilate it."[89]

Though the program was run by Cates and not PDAP, it was an outgrowth of the PDAP social structure. As PDAP had grown, its membership criteria were similar to AA and other Twelve Step groups, i.e., a desire to stop drinking and using drugs. Many young people had started showing up at PDAP as much for the peer connections as the sobriety.

"We've made [social activities] an integral part of [PDAP]," wrote Meehan. "For some kids, they are the program." "Enthusiasm about sobriety" was a major element of PDAP.[90]

One of those young people for whom the social activities were the program was Vicki Bernholz. Bernholz had grown up in Houston, and she described herself as a "surfer girl."[91]

"We had a beach house in Surfside," said Bernholz. "So really all my weekends, all my summers, all the holidays, we just drove an hour and fifteen minutes away from house to house."

Bernholz stayed close to home for college, where she attended the University of Houston and majored in psychology. She graduated in four and a half years, and received her diploma in December 1975. Bernholz described herself as a social drinker, but certainly not an "addict" or "alcoholic."

"I've never had any kind of drug or drinking issues," said Bernholz. "I just don't. I never have, never will."

After finishing college in her hometown, Bernholz was looking for some new friends whose lives did not revolve around alcohol and drug use.

"Back in that time of the world, it was hard to find people who weren't getting high," she said. "I just didn't do all that stuff when everybody was doing it."

It just so happened that a neighbor in her apartment complex was in PDAP, and through this friend, Bernholz discovered a new social group.

"These people were sober; they were fun," said Bernholz. "And so for me, I got involved with PDAP because it was a way for me to have a social outlook . . . a social world without people getting drunk and getting high all the time, in the throes of everybody doing it.

"I got involved with PDAP as one of the few people who came in just sober for social."

This made Bernholz, in her words, an "anomaly." Bernholz even adopted a sobriety date: December 28, 1975.

"Of course, when you're there, you don't drink or anything," said Bernholz. "I had to maintain all that, and that's fine. I didn't care."

"And people always go, 'Well, you can't be here if you don't have a problem.' I said, 'I do have a problem. I don't have any friends.'"

One of the new friends she met in PDAP was John Cates, who would get sober himself in PDAP during those same winter months. Cates, like Bernholz, was a University of Houston alum, though he had taken a very different path to PDAP. Once their paths converged, they became close. When Cates started running a school in his apartment, Bernholz would frequently hang out there, and they dated for a time.[92]

"I absolutely remember the TV trays, and I can remember the apartment," said Bernholz. "I was there, [but] I wasn't really helping with the school."

Similar to PDAP, the new school had its own social attraction. Many students were drawn to Cates's apartment as much for the peer interaction as the educational programming.

"Going over to John and Bill's apartment was like a big deal. All the girls wanted to go do that," said Bernholz. "These are young guys, Bill in particular. And both handsome guys. Now there's two new guys in PDAP that are sober, and lots of girls going, 'Oh wow, that's great.'"

"The problem is we would go over there, and we'd start on the school," said Wayne Cloud. "But we'd spend a lot of time just talking about getting recovery, you know, which made it even more nice. I enjoyed going over there, 'cause I got to meet John and talk to him, 'cause you know, he's quite a guy."

Once they were there, though, Cates did try to create an experience that was more or less like a classroom. Unlike the three-students-at-a-time that was promoted, there might be up to a couple dozen students in the apartment for GED lessons. Cates recalled, "I would have maybe fifteen, twenty, twenty-five people in the room." As advertised, when the school began, he was the sole teacher. The apartment had a large living room with a connected dining room, and students would be spread through the rooms. Cates would move person to person to assist with the modules.

"John would talk, and they would go through things," said Bernholz. "It was more of what I would consider a teaching format, a classroom format. We're going to be very generous with the word there, right? And then, you know, people would get into it, and figure out it was hard, and they had to study."

And so it went for the first few months of the John Cates GED School, through the summer of 1976. Cates would provide instruction to groups of students, based on the GED prep guides. Students would stay enrolled until they were ready to take the test. The daily schedule varied depending on the student's schedules, but Cates said, "I would run it all day, up until about 7:00 p.m., then I'd shut it down. Every day I would pull out the TV trays."

By this time, the PDAP program itself was five years old, and the number of youths involved required an expansion of its counselor base and the addition of satellite sites. PDAP counselors typically were people who had participated in PDAP and had shown leadership qualities. Bob Meehan had created a training program for counselors that took about four months to complete. Even though Cates had less than a year of sobriety, he was a person who had shown the qualities Meehan was looking for, and in May 1976, Cates had turned 25, which meant he was about to age out of the program himself. With a bachelor's degree in education, a minor in psychology, and a few courses in administration, Cates served as an ideal candidate to direct one of the early satellite programs outside Houston. Meehan would have wanted someone he could trust for that role, and in a few short months, Cates had apparently earned that trust.

As summer moved into fall, PDAP thus asked Cates to go through the four-month counselor-training program, which he would ultimately complete in two-and-a-half months.

"They apparently needed me really badly," said Cates.

In October, Cates was sent to Fort Bend County, just southwest of Houston, and home to the city of Sugar Land, to start a young PDAP group. In 1976, Sugar Land had not quite exploded in population.

"It was a different Sugar Land [than today]," said Cates. "It was all cow pastures. There were plenty of kids getting high. Not as many as now, but plenty."

Cates's counselor training and subsequent move to Fort Bend, meant the GED school needed new leadership. The school had remained his own, private program from July through September 1976. In October, Cates decided to find someone else to run it, though he would stay involved.

When considering possible candidates to take over the school, Vicki Bernholz was a logical choice (see Figure 3.6). After graduating with her bachelor's degree in psychology, she found herself with few options in that field.

Bernholz asked herself, "What are you gonna do with an undergraduate degree in psychology?"

She had thus taken a job as a secretary-receptionist for a "two-man CPA firm in Houston."

"It's insightful into my personality," said Bernholz. "You know, they wanted me to get them coffee. Like, 'the coffee machine is two feet from you, dude. Why do you need me to walk in here and pour it for you?'"

"I did fine, but inside I didn't do well. It was demeaning to me."

While Bernholz could make ends meet with part-time work and support from her parents, she was also drawn to what she was observing in Cates's new school, and Cates thought she would be a good fit.

"I needed help," said Cates. "I had a lot of people, and [Vicki] was on top of it, knew what was going on, had some education. The delivery of the curriculum was very simple. It was the backup, the personal involvement that required some kind of [assistance]."[93]

Considering the backgrounds of the students in the GED School, Bernholz's psychology training was also an asset.

"[We] were working with those modules and those people hands-on," said Cates. "They weren't just being handed [the materials] and told, 'Go over and do that.' We were right there on top of them. If they had trouble, we talked to them about it."[94]

"It just was a natural," said Bernholz. "Like, 'I'm available here.' And my parents were like, 'You're doing what?' Because there was no pay in it."

Other than new leadership, the school also needed a new space. With Bernholz running the day-to-day, Cates's shared apartment would no longer work.

Figure 3.6. Vicki Bernholz grew up in Houston and majored in psychology at the University of Houston. Bernholz became friends with people in Palmer Drug Abuse Program (PDAP), including John Cates. She would frequently hang out at his apartment and became familiar with the GED school. After Cates moved to Sugar Land to start a PDAP program there, Bernholz took over the school in October 1976. This is a picture of her at the first commencement ceremony. (Source: PDAP/John Cates.)

"It just wasn't tangible for me to meet with people at the apartment," said Bernholz. "And John's roommate was having enough of it at that point too . . . I mean enough is enough."

So, Cates and Bernholz found some office space on the second floor of a pharmacy near Rice University, and thus also not far from the Palmer Church.

"It was an odd space that they were really trying to get rid of," said Cates. "It kind of stuck out in the middle, at the top of the stairs, and it was windows all the way around."[95] The windows, though, faced a hallway. Bernholz described it as a "big empty room with a couple of tables" at the top of a flight of stairs.

"I imagine it was not easy to rent," said Cates. "I don't remember how much we paid. It was cheap."

Still, the tuition of thirty dollars per month was meager revenue to support a full-time salary, rent, and materials.

"It wasn't enough," said Bernholz, who turned 23 about the same time she took over the school. "I didn't need a lot then, which is good, but it wasn't enough to have a living out of."

Though they continued to support their daughter, her parents were also leery of the unorthodox nature of PDAP. They would have preferred she stay at the CPA firm.

"In the beginning, they were supportive," said Bernholz, "but not wildly enthusiastic."

"And they weren't gonna flip the bill either."[96]

Cates was now working for PDAP, and Bernholz herself had remained actively involved with PDAP for almost a year, regularly attending meetings.

"I would go to meetings," she said. "Even without a drug problem, there are many, many wonderful things to be learned by listening to the Twelve Steps and applying the Twelve Steps and listening to what people learn in life."

"I was always able to find benefit in it, even if I didn't apply some of the literal stuff to it."

And even though membership in PDAP was not a requirement, PDAP had remained the exclusive referral source for students. Word-of-mouth had proven sustaining enough that Cates had only had to print one set of promotional flyers.

"I always got my students through PDAP," said Cates. "They all came from PDAP."

Cates said he had considered having it part of PDAP from the beginning, but said they were not so sure.

"I wanted a whole school, a real school," said Meehan. "But we had so much else going on, with the recovery factor, which was our first goal—to get them to a place [without which] nothing else was going to matter. There was so much there that we just gave it whatever time we could. So, I'd say that sounds like an excuse. Not an excuse. We really were that busy."[97]

"I had always thought of it," said Cates. "I understand their reluctance to feel certain that I was going to make it. Plus, nobody had ever done anything like that. They were like, 'What?'[98] There weren't any education agencies to solve that issue. There wasn't anything out there that they had ever seen."

Cates and Bernholz had shown PDAP that a GED school was viable, and the school's popularity had made it an asset.

"It was a good selling tool for PDAP," said Bernholz, "But it wasn't part of PDAP."

They thus approached Bob Meehan and the other leaders at PDAP about assuming control of the school and its new lease for the space above the pharmacy.

"Can you bring it into PDAP?" asked Bernholz. "Then I can just be on staff, and then I can have a paycheck, a regular paycheck and keep it going. Because it was a good tool for PDAP, and we talked about [how] 'this makes sense for PDAP as much as it makes sense for me.' "It was sort of like, 'Either you guys gotta help me out here, or I can't keep going.' I couldn't afford to keep doing it."

Meehan and the other PDAP leaders realized a GED school would be more manageable than running a full high school.

"Let's talk about what's needed for [the GED]," recalled Meehan of the decision. "All you got to do is go take the damn test. What do we have to do?"

"We just all said, 'This works for everybody,'" said Cates. "So, they just put me on staff, and then it was just part of PDAP."

And with Cates's time now more limited running the satellite program, PDAP put Bernholz in charge, giving her the title, "Educational Coordinator." In addition, since all PDAP services were free to their youth, the thirty dollar monthly tuition was eliminated. The free PDAP GED School was born.

GED School Grows

Bernholz felt the GED School was essential for the sobriety of its students.

"A big motivation for me in the school was to help people stay sober," said Bernholz. "I've always been a big believer in education and to help people stay sober, because not having an education always affected their choices . . . And then seeing the connection between people changing their lives and education making a difference in what they could do with the rest of their life, those connected super easily for me."

With the thirty dollar a month fee removed and the addition of a monthly lease and Bernholz's salary, the school needed funding. One benefit of coming under the PDAP umbrella was PDAP's status as a 501c3 nonprofit organization, meaning all donations to the program would be tax deductible. Moving forward, fundraising would be one of Cates's primary roles in keeping the school alive, and an early benefactor he approached was Frank Abraham, a senior partner in the Houston law firm, Kronzer, Abraham, and Watkins. Abraham had founded the firm with John Hill and James Kronzer in 1951, and the firm would have been commemorating its silver anniversary the year the GED school opened. During his career, Abraham rose to prominence as director of the State Bar of Texas, and he mentored many fledgling attorneys. He valued education, establishing student exchange programs at multiple universities and serving as the president of the nonprofit Student Aid Foundation.[99]

Parents were integral to PDAP's programming, and Frank Abraham also happened to be the father of a PDAP member. His firm's website now proclaims the following message:

Our founding attorneys created an environment of giving back to the community in service and leadership—an environment that our attorneys continue to foster today.

The PDAP GED school was part of that community commitment. A few years earlier, the firm had purchased and renovated an historic dry goods building in downtown Houston, where Bernholz remembered visiting to get paperwork signed for the costs of students to attend the program.[100]

"I would go to his office with these students," said Bernholz. "We would fill out this literally one-page application about [why] 'they wanted to go [to the school], [how] they qualified, [if] they were in PDAP, how long they'd been sober,' and then he would pay for their quote unquote GED education."

Abraham would provide the funds in a lump sum that Bernholz would budget for salary, rent, and expenses.

"He actively paid for individuals to go through the school and get done what they needed to be done."

"That worked for a while, but it still was just not enough," said Bernholz.

One of the most expensive costs was rent, and as PDAP was starting to expand, it followed its initial approach of seeking space in church buildings—a model many recovery high school follow to this day. Church spaces were especially appropriate for a school, as churches often have rooms for Sunday school and other meetings that are not used much if at all during the week. Furthermore, helping teenagers stay away from drugs and alcohol fit nicely into a church's mission, so churches were willing to provide their space at no cost to PDAP. In the case of the GED school, St. Luke's Presbyterian Church on Timberside Drive offered use of a large multipurpose room for a classroom and office space for its coordinator.[101] Thus, with the expiration of the school's lease, Bernholz packed up and moved the school about three miles south. St. Luke's was generous, giving the school a room with a wall of windows and plenty of space.

"A huge room," said Bernholz. "And me. Sitting there with a table. It was hilarious. And all my little GED books stacked up."

Yearbook photos show long folding tables, at least two, set up with another folded and leaning against the wall. There is a small chalkboard on one wall, adjacent to a wall with windows and drawn curtains. Along one wall is a mail-slot for student papers, and a photo shows a student sitting at a desk typing on an electric typewriter above the caption, "Future Secretary."[102] Many of the photos show students both in the school and on social gatherings away from the school drinking bottles of soda and smoking cigarettes. The atmosphere appeared to be collegial and informal. Bernholz usually would work with three to eight students at a time, for about one to three hours. Sometimes, it might only be Bernholz and one other student. The schedule was flexible to meet the needs of the students.

Wayne Cloud had continued in the GED program since its first days in Cates's apartment. As the program moved to the room over the pharmacy, Cloud's job demands as a PDAP counselor increased as PDAP's reach was growing. His time as a student became more sporadic, but he never gave up. When the school moved to St. Luke's, he became more dedicated to completing the process. He remembers many sessions in which Bernholz worked with him one-on-one, and it was during that time that she discovered Cloud had dyslexia.

"Vicky recognized that and said, 'Well, this is what you have going on. Let's go and get you tested for dyslexia.' And that changed a lot of my learning, you know, understanding. I had to be slower at what I do, take my time, just focus, those kinds of things. But that environment was critical for me . . . It was just a very supportive, nurturing kind of environment," said Cloud.[103]

Cloud's story represents one of the benefits of a recovery high school's small enrollment. In Cloud's case, his dyslexia had caused him to struggle in school, and his drug use, frequent moves, and family dysfunction had diverted attention from an actual, unidentified learning disability. For many students, it takes getting into a small school and off alcohol and drugs for other mental health and emotional issues to be properly understood.

Cloud recalled of his prior educational experience, "It was just, 'There's something wrong with you.' You know, that was what you always felt. And people would wonder, 'Why aren't you doing this? How come you're not catching on?'"

"So that was part of my motivation to not care, after a period. But what the [PDAP GED] school offered was an environment and understanding of that."

Cloud finally sat for the GED at the University of Houston in late 1977, and he passed the exam on his first try.

Fundraising and Program Evolution

John Cates continued raising money for the school through donations and grants, and over time, PDAP added a variety of other programs. A PDAP promotional pamphlet from 1979 read as follows:

> Several appendage services have been established to assist members and provide opportunities to enhance sobriety. These services include Adult Probation Counseling Services; Employee Assistance Programs offered to businesses, corporations and public agencies; Foster Parent Program; GED school to obtain high school equivalency for high school dropouts; Juvenile Probation counseling services; school district programs to alleviate discipline and truancy problems related to drug abuse; and vocational program to obtain jobs and vocational training.

One program of note was the Foster Parent Program. Many of the teenagers in PDAP had strained relationships with their families, and others lived far from Houston and needed housing to access PDAP programs. About the same time that they took over the GED school, PDAP opened houses to board youths who wanted to move out of their homes for up to six months. There were two separate houses, one for boys and one for girls, and each had a foster parent who lived with about six youths, most of whom were still enrolled in high school. They were called simply, "The Girls House" and "The Boys House." The Girls House was a four-bedroom ranch house, with a master bedroom suite with a bathroom and three bedrooms with another bathroom on the other side of the house. There were two girls per room.

With the addition of the houses came an evolution in the GED School. Because the houses were far from where many of the youths attended high school, Bernholz started providing instruction for the boarders so they would not fall too far behind in their studies. She would get homework and assignments from the students' schools, and they would work on it at the St. Luke's site alongside the GED students.

One of Bernholz's friends in PDAP was Anne Wingfield, who had been a member since 1974, when she was 15. Both had been competitive surfers off the Gulf Coast in Texas, and both had joined PDAP primarily for the community. PDAP allowed youths to train as counselors when they turned 17, and Wingfield had become the junior counselor at one of PDAP's satellites. She graduated high school in 1976, and after she had been a counselor for about a year, PDAP asked her to be the live-in foster parent at the Girls House, in Southwest Houston.

"These were girls who were either getting kicked out of the house or had been kicked out of their house," said Wingfield. "They didn't have a place to go, but they wanted to get sober."

"It was rough! Texas licensed me as a foster mother at 18 years old," said Wingfield. "But it was a really good experience. I did that for a year, which consisted of just trying to keep those girls sober, taking them to meetings, taking them to the school so they can get on with their schoolwork."

"They needed to do schoolwork, and it was someplace to take them to get structure and help."

The houseparents would drop off the residents of both the boys' and girls' houses at St. Luke's. Bernholz would go over their assignments with them, help as needed, and get new assignments from their teachers when necessary. Until the foster houses closed in the late 1970s, this is how the school would continue operating, providing GED instruction for students who had dropped out of high school, and tutoring other students who were temporarily boarding away from their own high schools. The program was easily replicable, and as PDAP expanded into Dallas and Denver, it started GED schools at those sites as well.

As Wingfield recalled, the PDAP school was providing an essential service for its students.

"Back then, you could do a lot with a very limited education, even just high school," said Wingfield. "But if you didn't have high school, you were really screwed. It was the equivalent of a bachelor's today."

Years later, John Will recalled how proud PDAP was of the GED school.

"We were doing something that no one else had done," he said. "We knew there wasn't anything like it. We got people who were stuck. They were out of high school. They needed to get their GED.... A lot of these folks were in their early recovery, they weren't functioning all that well yet, and we could say, 'Not only will we help you get sober, but we had a school environment where they could get sober,' and the people who were running it knew how to deal with them."

By the late 1970s, PDAP was offering multiple educational programs, including the GED school, tutoring, vocational training, and Meehan's counselor preparation program. PDAP began calling its portfolio of academic services the "PDAP Continuing Education System," and in 1978, the GED School published a thirty-nine-page yearbook, with the title *Dreams Realized*. On its cover was the picture of the PDAP's symbolic "monkey fist" leather knot, which members would receive to celebrate their sobriety.[104] The second page featured a large picture of a sunrise with the inscription, "We proudly dedicate this first annual to the man who started it all, JOHN CATES." Included with pictures of Bernholz and the graduates were photos of attorney and benefactor Frank Abraham; Denver director James Welborn; Meehan; and Cates, who was by then, director of Houston PDAP.

The GED school held its first formal graduation in the St. Luke's auditorium in the spring of 1978. All students who had gone through the program and passed the GED exam since Cates had started the school in his apartment in the summer of 1976 were considered graduates of the school, and according to the yearbook, the total was twenty-five—all of whom were named or pictured in the book.

PDAP created a traditional commencement experience. There was a stage, a podium, caps and gowns, and diplomas. Even though the number of graduates was modest, there was a large crowd in attendance. In addition to the graduates and their families, the audience included current students (forty-three names are listed in the yearbook), donors, PDAP staff, and many youths from local PDAP groups, which numbered around three thousand members by that time.[105]

John Will recalled, "We were sitting around going, 'We are a bunch of dope fiends, and we got our own high school graduation.' That literally was a line that was used at times."

In her remarks to the attendees, Bernholz said, "There are twenty-five miracles graduating tonight."

One of those miracles was Wayne Cloud, who was asked to be the graduation speaker. As Cloud remembered many years later, he was the "valedictorian person" (see Figure 3.7). While the exact speech has faded from his memory, he had just been married a year, and his wife Carol was in the audience and remembered the highlights decades later.

"He said that he'd never really read much because he had trouble reading. And that the one book that he read was the Big Book of AA, and it got him sober. And that now he's finished up his education by getting his GED. The two best things that happened to him was getting sober and being able to finish [his GED], and they were connected, because if he hadn't gotten sober, he wouldn't have gotten in the GED class and gotten his [diploma]."[106]

After the ceremony, Cloud remembers a good old fashioned, substance-free, PDAP celebration and fundraiser.

"We just had events all the time," said Carol. "We had dances. We had garage sales. We would always make a fun event, and everybody would come, and you'd make a little bit of money."[107]

Figure 3.7. Wayne Cloud attended the GED program beginning with its first days in John Cates's apartment. Cloud, who had dyslexia, remained a student as the school changed locations twice, and he passed the GED in 1977. When the school held its first commencement ceremony, Cloud was chosen to be the graduation speaker. He later referred to himself as the "valedictorian person." Vicki Bernholz called Cloud and the other two dozen graduates, "miracles." (Source: PDAP/John Cates.)

As PDAP partied into the evening, little did the attendees realize that the commencement celebration would mark a pinnacle of sorts in the PDAP story, and certainly it was the high point for the GED school. In less than two years, the school would be gone.

Not long after the first graduation, Vicki Bernholz transitioned into an administrative role, and Anne Wingfield took over as the Houston education coordinator. GED schools had opened in Dallas and Denver, and at least one more graduation ceremony was held in late spring 1979.

As Cates recalled, by the summer of 1979, PDAP's growth had been explosive.

"What happened was it opened up in Dallas," said Cates. "It was getting bigger. It opened in Denver. It was getting too big for Bob [Meehan] to be able to run Houston, because Houston was the biggest of the cities." Cates thus became director over all the Houston PDAP programs.

The demand for new centers was so strong that Meehan spent more and more time away from Houston and on the road speaking and opening programs. Meehan asked Cates to take over the Houston programs around 1977.

"I think we had nine centers [in Houston] at that time," said Cates. "Nine centers and the school. I took it over [from Meehan], which freed him up to go ahead and open up all the other cities and do all of that ... Within about eighteen months, it grew to twenty-three centers here in Houston."

Meehan even started a rock band. According to Meehan's high school yearbook, he had been in the Calvert Hall College High School band in Towson, Maryland, all four years, 1957–1961.[108] Meehan remained interested in playing music, and as a hobby, he started a rock band called "Freeway" with other PDAP members.[109] Meehan invited Cates to sing with the band. Another singer was Cathie (Alexander) Beard, who had recently married Frank Beard—the drummer for the rock band ZZ Top since 1969.[110] Frank Beard, who grew up in Texas and graduated from Irving High School in the 1960s,[111] had developed a drug addiction and gotten into recovery through the Twelve Steps.[112] He became so close with Cates that he would serve as Cates's best man when John got remarried a few years later. Beard produced Freeway's one and only album, "Off the Streets," which was released in 1979. The song titles show a clear recovery influence, including "Program Pusher," "Let Go of Your Past," "Power of Choice," "You Can Get High," "Promises," and "Sober Up." The album lists Meehan on piano and Cates on vocals.

Freeway did concerts, which resonated with people in recovery. Years later, someone posted the song, "Hard Left," on YouTube, with an autographed picture of Meehan at the piano.[113] Among the comments posted in reaction was one person who attended a Freeway show at Houston's Astro Arena and another who wrote, "I LOVED this highly inspirational album. Cathy's Victory was one of my favorite songs and has helped me greatly thru life. Oh, I miss this! All the songs were so great. I would give anything to have another copy." The post was dated 2012, over thirty years after the album's release.[114]

Soon after joining the band, Cates was transferred to Dallas to help run their PDAP satellite program in 1979. PDAP had started contracting counselors to school districts, and by 1979, Cates estimated there were 205 full-time counselors and 3700 young people involved. PDAP had offices in three hospitals and was operating two halfway houses for adults and the foster care houses for adolescents.

"In Houston we were doubling every year," said Cates. "We thought we were on the verge of hitting that 51st percentile of young people saying it's cool to stay sober, verbally saying it—which would change the dynamics. That's what we dreamed of."

And then Joe Hamilton called about his daughter, Carrie. Bernholz was in the office when Hamilton called.

"I was there when Joe Hamilton called, and I didn't know who Joe Hamilton was," said Bernholz. "'Cuz there's a million of them, right? Like he's some guy named 'Joe Hamilton,' and then I give the call to Bob [Meehan], and Bob comes out going, 'Oh my God! Do you have any idea who that was?'"

Joe Hamilton was Carol Burnett's husband, and Carrie was their 15-year-old daughter. Burnett was virtually a household name in the United States in 1979, most famous for her comedy show on television. In June 1979, Carrie had entered Deer Park General Hospital in Houston, which housed PDAP's intensive individual and group therapy. She would move into a foster home and become a PDAP member, and on October 1, 1979, *People Magazine* ran a story with this headline on the cover: "Carol Burnett's Nightmare: For the first time, she reveals her daughter's battle to conquer drugs." The cover featured a photo of a smiling Burnette and her daughter.

Suddenly, a national spotlight shone on PDAP, and everybody in America started learning about its novel treatment approach. Media wanted to interview Bob Meehan, and he started doing the talk show circuit. For example, TV listings for the *Mike Douglas Show* on Tuesday, November 20, noted the cohost that night was television star Ed Asner, and the guest list included Bob Meehan, Carol Burnett, Joe Hamilton, and Carrie Hamilton.[115]

"Bob and [Meehan's wife] Joy just started to believe their own press," said Bernholz. "And if they said jump, they expected you to say, 'How high?' And they started to be, um, to be interfering in people's lives and dictating decisions. And 'You can date this person. You shouldn't date that person. You need to break up with this person. You should go tell your parents this.'"

"I literally got completely out, because it started to feel too cultish."

Bernholz is not the only person to make such a comparison; many of the people interviewed for this book made similar statements.

"People who watched it in action would say, 'It looks like a frigging cult,'" said John Will. "When this school works right, it will look like a cult, because when people think of cults they think of those, 'Hi there, how are you doing? Come on in. Join us. We're doing this. We're doing that.' They call it in cults 'love bombing,' this giving of unconditional acceptance and high regard. That, for a kid who is miserable, who is struggling, is the most attractive thing in the world."

Being linked to a cult was particularly toxic in 1979. Much of America was focused the concept of cults at that time, because on November 18, 1978—exactly one year to the day before Bob Meehan appeared on the *Mike Douglas Show*—more than nine hundred members of the religious group called the Peoples Temple, now commonly construed as a cult, died after drinking poison at the urging of their leader, the Reverend Jim Jones, in a Guyana settlement known as "Jonestown."[116] Parents everywhere feared their teenagers might be lured into cults, and they were hypervigilant of any insinuation that a group was functioning as one. And as people started looking closely at PDAP, such accusations arose.

Dan Rather traveled to Houston in December 1979 to investigate PDAP for the CBS news program, *60 Minutes.* Another crew from ABC started asking questions for its own show, *20/20,* which had only recently been given a regular Thursday-night slot by the network. At first, it may have seemed like another opportunity to promote the positive aspects of the PDAP, so Meehan and others spoke openly. In a critical expose of Meehan and his approach titled, "The Love Bomb," Daniel Kolitz wrote the following:

> An early memo written by a [CBS] producer described PDAP as a force for good and Meehan as "ebullient, funny, caring." But during the reporting process, that view changed considerably. In a later memo, the same producer wrote, "All the people I've talked with who have left the Palmer Drug Abuse Program agree on two things: that Bob Meehan is a superb con man, and that he's 'dangerously unstable.[117]

When it became clear that both the *60 Minutes* and *20/20* portrayals would not be positive, the PDAP board asked Meehan to resign his position as executive director retroactive to January 1, 1980, and many other staff members resigned as well—some in support of Meehan, and others to distance themselves from what PDAP had become as it had grown in prominence. The *60 Minutes* and *20/20* episodes aired in late January 1980—Rather's piece played right after Super Bowl XIV, which was watched by over 76 million viewers, the second-most watched Super Bowl to that point[118]— and many negative news articles followed. Beyond accusations of cultish behaviors, the news reports homed in on questionable business practices and a few unhappy staff.[119]

Dan Rather has made many of his PDAP investigative documents public, and he has posted numerous files, including interview transcripts, on the Internet.[120] One fascinating document was a list of staff and counselor resignations. Rather lists twenty staff members and counselors who resigned from June through December 1979, and that was *before* the news pieces aired in January.

John Cates was one of the people who stepped down in early 1980, and with him went many of the fundraising connections, as well as leadership of certain ancillary programs like the GED School.

"When John left," said Anne Wingfield, who had taken over the Houston GED school after Bernholz, "all the funding that he had set up for these different places went away. We went back to, 'Okay, yes, this is wonderful that they have all these extraneous things. You have all that, the school, and the juvenile probation, and the houses. But we need to refocus back to the original commitment, and that is helping kids get off drugs. Let's do it the way we did it in the beginning.' "

PDAP's alternative peer group continues to operate to this day in Houston, and there have been many other APGs created in its image, though now with credentialed staff and more professional business practices. All the GED schools, though, had ceased operation by early 1980. They have, in fact, become a footnote to the larger Palmer Drug Abuse Program story. As Bob Meehan was becoming a national celebrity of sorts in 1979, however, another recovery school was launching in his homestate of Maryland. Unlike the GED School, that program would be a full-fledged high school, and it had no connection to PDAP in any way. While the people who started the Maryland school did not know Bob Meehan or John Cates or Vicki Bernholz, they likely had some awareness of what was happening halfway across the country in Texas from the news reports. They had no idea, though, about the graduation celebration that had occurred in the St. Luke's auditorium in the spring of 1978—a ceremony similar to ones they would hold for the next thirty years. And unknown to the graduation revelers that day at St. Luke's was that halfway across the country, the Montgomery County police were making plans during the summer of 1978 to raid the local high schools looking for drugs. It would be a firestorm from which Phoenix, the first recovery high school run by a school district, would rise.

PART II

PHOENIXES ARISE

4

A Lighthouse District

Eight teenagers are beginning a journey into a dark cave. The picture shows four girls and four boys standing in a pasture with miners' caps on their heads, preparing to go spelunking, donned in jeans and flannel plaid shirts with voluminous hair—it's the 1980s. The teens huddle close together, with their arms around each other. Seven of the youths are standing, while the eighth lies on the ground. One of the boys standing is holding his hat in his hands, but the others have helmets situated firmly on their heads. And the lights from their helmets, not lit yet, will help guide the way. They're not smiling; you really can't tell what they're thinking. But it makes the photo all the more real.

They are teenagers on a caving trip. But they are not just teenagers; they are students. And this isn't just a caving trip; it's a school trip, sponsored by their school, Phoenix II—one of the first of its kind—a recovery high school. The students were able to go caving, during normal school hours; and the entire school—staff and students included—were able to participate. And since they were students in a recovery high school, all eight of the students in the photograph, as well any of the other twenty or so students on the journey, were actively working programs of recovery from substance use disorders. Had any of these students been in a more traditional school at that hour, many of them would have been high on drugs, both because of a desire to use drugs and their availability. Instead, this group is likely sober and ready to embrace the adventure.

The story of Phoenix is a story of a journey into a dark unknown educational landscape, at the beginning of an education movement. Phoenix was one of the first attempts to approach adolescent substance use disorders differently from adults. The first Phoenix campus represented the first attempt by a school district to create an entire high school exclusively for students with substance use disorders. Before that, high schools had attempted to provide prevention and intervention programs, and treatment programs such as Oxford House and Canarsie in New York had created schools within their walls for students in treatment. The Freedom Road School had enrolled students from the Charleston Public Schools and other districts who had drug problems or who had been expelled for drug usage, but it was operated by a public health center. The PDAP GED school for students in recovery had begun in Houston three years earlier, but it was a private school and essentially prepped students to take the GED exam. Until Phoenix opened its doors in 1979, a school run by a public school district for recovering students was unchartered territory. The first Phoenix was so successful that a second campus, Phoenix II, launched in 1983. By

Salvaging a Teenage Wasteland. Andrew J. Finch, Oxford University Press. © Oxford University Press 2024.
DOI: 10.1093/oso/9780190645502.003.0004

the time the Phoenix Schools faded into larger alternative schools in the early 2000s, a national movement had begun. Over thirty schools were operating by then, and a national Association of Recovery Schools had been formed.

The first Phoenix recovery high school was a response to a growing youth drug problem in Montgomery County, Maryland, that sprang into public consciousness in the spring of 1978 at the suburban Bethesda-Chevy Chase High School. The setting was a progressive county bordering the nation's capital, and home to many Washington DC, employees and their children.

A drug overdose and an undercover drug sale on school grounds by a school newspaper reporter caught the attention of the local police department, leading to four months of drug raids that fall. By end of the fall semester, the Montgomery County School Board had approved of a "Pilot Program" that would become the Phoenix School.

The main cast in the story of Phoenix's development included four transplants from the Northeast, each of whom embraced transformative and progressive concepts for their sectors—education, justice, and health. And the protagonist was a man inspired by the same spiritual master that had influenced rock star Pete Townshend, and from whose mind the notion for a recovery high school was forged.

Brian Berthiaume

Tracing the pathway to something original requires understanding both the context of the creation as well as the influences upon the creator. Brian Berthiaume was the central figure in the creation of the Phoenix recovery high school, and in reviewing his background, one can see many influences. These include family dysfunction, school struggles, teaching in an experimental school, drug use, and a spiritual master. Brian became an adult and began his career during the 1960s and 1970s, during a time of educational innovation, and he worked in Montgomery County, Maryland, which was known for progressive social service policies. A catalyst for the school came through local events involving the police chief, the school superintendent, and publicized drug use in the district high schools. These events converged with Brian's experiences, and what emerged was the Phoenix school.

Raised Feeling Rejected

Brian Berthiaume recalls his childhood as being a series of rejections and failures from his family to his education to a military career, beginning in infancy when his young mother abandoned him at a neighbor's house. Brian was raised in a working-class family that he describes as "dysfunctional." Brian's father, Harvey Brian Berthiaume, was born in 1908 in Quebec, Canada, and he was the third of eight children of Joseph and Leona Berthiaume.[1] Joseph and Leona moved the Berthiaume family to the

United States in 1911, when Harvey was three.[2] Joseph supported the family with blue-collar jobs such as driving a coal wagon[3] and working in a lumber mill.[4] The family lived in Massachusetts for a time before settling in Keene, New Hampshire. Harvey maintained perfect attendance, until dropping out only after two years of high school.[5]

Brian's mother, Bethel Evelyn Barlow, was born in September 1919 to Frank and Iva Barlow. She was the second of two children for the couple that was married in 1918, when Frank was 28 and Iva was 18.[6] A native of Keene, New Hampshire, Frank was a traveling salesman. He and Iva eventually settled in Greenfield, Massachusetts, where Bethel was raised. According to Census records, by the time Bethel was three-months old, Iva and the children had moved in with Iva's parents, Rockey and Genie Nicklaw. Iva divorced Frank, took a job as a salesperson at a dry goods store to make ends meet, and eventually got remarried to Potter Ford while Bethel was still a child.[7] In 1936, in the midst of the Great Depression, Bethel dropped out of high school at age 16 and went to work.[8]

Bethel Barlow was 21 years old when she married Harvey Berthiaume in Greenfield in June 1941.[9] Harvey was from her birth-father's hometown of Keene, and he was twelve years her senior. By that time, Harvey had risen to assistant foreman at a leather tannery, and Bethel was working as a waitress.[10] Japan bombed Pearl Harbor in December, thrusting the United States into World War II, just under six months after Bethel and Harvey's wedding. Nine months into the War, Harvey joined the Army as a private on August 19, 1942.[11] According to military records, he enlisted "for the duration of the war plus six months subject to the discretion of the President."[12]

Bethel gave birth to Harvey Brian Berthiaume Jr. on October 9, 1943.[13] While Harvey was off in the service, Bethel was alone with baby Brian in Greenfield, and she decided to leave. She asked someone to take care of Brian, and she fled. Harvey came home on leave one day to find his wife gone and his son living with neighbors. As he was still enlisted and thus not able to raise the boy by himself, Berthiaume's father moved the child in with his parents, Joseph and Leona, in North Swanzey, New Hampshire, a small community just outside Keene.[14] Harvey then sued for a divorce from Bethel, citing "such treatment as to seriously injure health and endanger reason." The divorce was granted in April 1945, when Brian was not yet two years old.[15]

Brian's French-Canadian grandparents raised him until his father re-married. He remembered his grandmother Leona as being a deeply spiritual person, and that he initially misunderstood her faith as a rejection of him.

"My grandmother took me to church all the time with her," Brian recalled. "I was raised by my grandmother, and she was super religious. I saw her praying all the time. Every time I'd come home from school, she'd be praying."

One day, Brian asked her, "Why are you always praying?"

"I'm preparing for death," she said.

"So, I thought," Brian said, " 'you're preparing to die. Well, what about me? I mean, you're the only person raising me, and you're preparing to die.' It felt like another rejection. So, when she died I went to the funeral and remember not crying or anything, because I thought she got what she wanted. It took me years to finally figure out that what she was doing—there's nothing wrong with that. She was a spiritual person. She was really into her faith."

Faith would later play a major role in Brian's own adult development and vocational discernment.

After the war, Brian's father, Harvey, moved back home to Keene, where he met Irene Marie Lamoureux. Like Harvey, Irene had also been married once before, though she was much younger.[16] In June 1946, less than one year after the end of the war, Harvey and Irene got married. Irene was 22 years old when she married Harvey Berthiaume, who was 38.[17]

Brian believes his father married Irene primarily to provide him a mother, and they did not tell Brian she was his stepmother. When Brian was 12, he was rummaging through the attic and found a letter from Bethel. That letter was how he finally discovered that she was his real mother. Bethel would go on to marry at least two more times before she died at age 84 in 2003.[18] She updated her name to Bethel Maillie in 1947, to Bethel Durand in 1954, then Bethel Berthia—only to die and have her record restored to Bethel Durand.[19]

The Berthiaume household was rocky during Brian's childhood. He describes Irene, who became a licensed beautician in Keene,[20] as being a verbally abusive stepmother, and sometimes she would hit as well. Brian recalled that his stepmother "didn't like me. She had anger problems." His parents rarely disciplined him, though, letting Brian get away with whatever he wanted.

"[My father] never disciplined me," recalled Brian. "Except one time, I broke his bottle on a Sunday. He tried disciplining me by beating me up, but we don't call that discipline, right?"

Alcohol played a prominent role in Brian's family. He described his father, Harvey, as being an alcoholic, and when the large Berthiaume family gathered, liquor was flowing.

"When I think of my youthful years," Brian said, "the Berthiaumes would all get together on weekends and get drunk. All of them."

During Brian's youth, Harvey worked in a factory, where he had authority over the tool crib.[21] This meant that the other workers in the factory had to get permission from Harvey to use tools. While he had some authority, the work was hard and the hours long. By Brian's account, his father "worked all the time." Harvey must have realized the value of an education, though, because it was the one piece of advice Brian remembered getting from his father.

"My father only said one thing his whole life to me—he said, 'Get an education.' And somewhere I read a book that talked about how we end up living the unlived life of a parent. So, I think about my dad saying that one thing."

Brian did indeed dream of higher education, though he admits at the time it was "because all the cute girls and cool kids were going to college." Brian did ultimately graduate from high school in 1961, something neither of his birth parents had done, but the Keene High School principal dissuaded him of his college notions, saying

Brian was not "college material" due to a poor academic record. His lack of discipline had had a negative impact on his schooling, which led to a school ranking near the bottom of his graduating class.

Brian applied to Keene State anyway, but as his principal predicted, Brian was not admitted. Harvey thus got Brian a job at his factory, which came with some cache, due to Harvey's position as keeper of the tools.

"I was like a celebrity," said Brian. " 'Oh, you're Harvey Berthiaume's kid.' Everyone loved my dad. At home he was quiet, disconnected from my stepmother. But I was treated like a superstar [because of Harvey]."

Still, the work was not glorious. The job Harvey got his son was washing and waxing the floors from midnight to 8:00 a.m.

"I couldn't do it," said Brian. "I mean, I wasn't good at it. That wasn't going to work for me."

Brian was compelled to look at other options. His principal had suggested that kids with his academic record were better off joining the military, so Brian followed in his father, Harvey's footsteps and enlisted in the Air Force. He was stationed at a base near the University of Oxford in England. During his four-year commitment to the Air Force, he never lost his desire to attend college, and Brian used the opportunity of being stationed so close to Oxford University to enroll in a night course in US History.

After completing his military service, Brian used the G.I. Bill to enroll at the University of Maryland at College Park, because his best friend wanted to go there. He started off as an English major, then switched to psychology, and even tried drama. Initially, he found he did not have the study skills to do well in school, but he began dating someone who was a straight-A student, with great study skills. Brian followed her example and his grades improved; by the time he graduated, he said, "I was pretty much an A-student." At this point, Brian Berthiaume's life started turning around.

"I had felt like a failure in the family and in school and in the Air Force," said Brian. He later would tell his students, "I still turned it around, and so can you. Just as the apple falls from the tree when its ripe, they don't have to stay in that failure mode. I think my life is an example of that. Find people to care about. Because, when I was at Maryland, and I was away from the dysfunctional family and started to get some meaningful relationships going, it all started to change."

After shifting from studying English to psychology in college, Brian took a public speaking class, where he excelled.

"What you studied were the great speakers, Emerson, King, and Lincoln," said Brian. "I was in a competition nationwide. I played Abraham Lincoln, the Gettysburg Address. I didn't win, but I was in the competition. For me, who had always felt like I wasn't even college material, to be selected to do that was the beginning of me feeling like I did have some talent."

Interestingly, Brian says he chose to pursue public speaking even though it was something that initially caused him anxiety. "I'm counter-phobic. I go towards things I'm afraid of. I was afraid of public speaking, I would get anxious, but it interested me. I've always been like that. Give me a challenge, and I try to do the impossible."

Brian graduated from the University of Maryland-College Park with a degree in communications, but when he started looking for a job, he quickly realized that his public speaking degree alone did not lead to many employment opportunities.

Eventually, a friend suggested Brian was becoming a "bum," which hurt his feelings but was enough to convince him to start looking for a job. In this process, though, Brian quickly realized that his public speaking degree alone did not lead to many employment opportunities. One of Brian's roommates had heard that Montgomery County had opened an experimental school and named it in honor of John F. Kennedy who had been assassinated just a few years before in November 1963. Kennedy High School, located on Randolph Road in Silver Spring, Maryland, was about five minutes from where the Phoenix school would one day be housed. Kennedy initially enrolled students in seventh through tenth grades, but by the fall of 1966, it had changed to a ninth through twelfth grade format.[22] The school graduated its first full twelfth grade class in the spring of 1967. Berthiaume's roommate felt Brian would be perfect as a substitute teacher there, because it was known to be a school for "liberal, hippy kids."

To foster self-motivation, Kennedy High School did indeed feature open classes with no grades, and it did not require attendance. According to one recollection, Kennedy was known as "Hippie High," and the school featured "open classrooms without walls, there were no bells between classes, students graded their own tests, and academics took a back seat to self-actualization and free expression—it was OK to attend school barefoot and getting stoned between classes was common."[23] Another account noted many Kennedy students "hung out in the halls, rode tricycles and listened to rock music blaring over the intercom. Rumors abounded of drugs done in the parking lot."[24] To Brian Berthiaume, who admired the classic open-schooling book, *Summerhill,* this workplace sounded ideal, so he made the decision to start substitute teaching at Kennedy.

"All the teachers there had long hair," said Brian. "Some of them would be teaching classes on LSD, which was really interesting to listen to. They were like radical, out there, but it was exciting. As I think about it now, it was wrong, but at the time I wasn't thinking it was wrong. I was just thinking, 'Oh, this is different. It's kind of, what's going on here?'"

Brian described his first days as a substitute teacher at Kennedy. The first impression left a deep mark on him.

"The first day I went there as a sub, and I'm sitting in on some classes just to get the feeling," said Brian. "One of the teachers said, on the first day of class, 'I wanted to let you all know everyone in here has an A. Right now, you have an A. If you come to class, or if you don't come to class you still have an A.' All of a sudden, he's removed the motivation to go to class to get an A.

"But the teacher was so charismatic, you wouldn't miss his class, because it was like going to a rock star's class; he was like a rock star. He was a classical musician. He played the piano like a concert pianist. Some people are just so charismatic, you can't *not* listen to him, and he was like that. So, I think every kid showed up. I used to go there for the fun of it just to see him teach. I was just struck by that everybody got an

A, but he didn't want you coming to class for the A. He wanted you to come to class to learn. It was an interesting notion. And it actually worked. But only under certain circumstances will that work, if you know what I mean."

Brian himself became so popular at Kennedy that many teachers would call him to sub for them.

"Sometimes I ended up at other schools, but [Kennedy] was my primary school," said Brian. "When you're a sub, you get around, and people get to know you. The kids always liked me, because quite frankly I never made them do the substitute teacher lessons. I've always been a bit of a maverick; that's good and bad."

"When I would go into a classroom, I would take all the classroom chairs and put them in a circle. So instead of us sitting in lines, with me at the head, we'd be in the circle, and I'd say, 'Today we're going to talk about something that's happened to you in your life that's interesting.' And we'd have a go-around, or we would go out and do Yoga if it was nice weather, you know. And it was an experimental high school, so no one really cared if I did traditional class with chairs in lines anyway because it wasn't a traditional high school."

In time, the permeable boundaries around attendance, drug use, and sexual promiscuity created a parental backlash, and some parents refused to send their children to Kennedy. Others demanded the school be shut down, and eventually, the school erected walls and installed more traditional school policies. Berthiaume, though, took away many positives from the experimental approach of Kennedy.

"I think at its essence the ideology of the hippie movement was pure and innocent and beautiful," said Berthiaume, "but it got corrupted by the flaws of human beings for indulgences."

While his connection to open schooling would persist, Berthiaume was soon introduced to the philosophy of a spiritual master that would transform his views on drug use in schools.

Meher Baba

Meher Baba was an Indian spiritual master born in 1894. Baba believed he was "the Avatar of the Age" (see Figure 4.1).[25] According to Merriam-Webster, "Avatar" derives from a Sanskrit word meaning "descent," and it referred to the descent of a deity to the earth—typically, the incarnation in earthly form of Vishnu or another Hindu deity.[26] In 1925, Baba committed himself to silence for the rest of his life. Baba would communicate through disciples using hand gestures and an alphabet board, and he became well known, traveling for appearances, and doing charity work. Baba also published poems of enlightenment using the penname, "Huma." Interestingly, Huma is the Persian word for Phoenix, which would inspire Brian Berthiaume in naming the first recovery high school.

While Meher Baba's home was in India, he sent two of his early disciples, Elizabeth Chapin Patterson and Princess Norina Matchabelli, to establish a center for his work

Figure 4.1. Meher Baba (1894–1969) was a spiritual master in India. Baba inspired Pete Townshend to write the song "Baba O'Riley" for The Who in 1971 and influenced teacher and social worker Brian Berthiaume to start the Phoenix recovery high school in 1979. This poster was distributed throughout the United States and India in the 1960s. (Source: Meher Baba's Life & Travels website.)

in the United States in 1941. Though he did not specify where to locate the center, according to Patterson, Baba had five requirements for the place: "an equitable climate; virgin soil; ample water; soil that could be made self-sustaining to a large number of people; and the property should be given from the heart." After three years, Patterson decided land belonging to her father, Simeon Chapin, in Myrtle Beach, South Carolina, met each of Baba's requirements. Meher Baba agreed, and in 1944, work began to establish the Meher Spiritual Center.[27]

Baba traveled to the Spiritual Center three times during the 1950s, and by the 1960s, the growing drug culture in Western society began to concern him. In Meher Baba's 1966 publication, *God in a Pill*, he wrote:

"The fast-increasing number of drug addicts forms an appalling chain of self-sought bondage! Even as these drugs hold out an invitation to a fleeting sense of ecstasy, freedom or escape, they enslave the individual in greater binding. LSD, a highly potent 'mind-changing' drug differing from the opium derivatives and being used in the research of mental science, is said to 'expand consciousness and alter one's personality for the better.' In America it has become tragically popular among the young, used indiscriminately by any and many. They must be persuaded to desist from taking drugs, for they are harmful—physically, mentally, and spiritually."[28]

Meher Baba's ideas caught the attention of academics and celebrities such as Timothy Leary at Harvard and movie star Gary Cooper. His anti-drug message attracted followers, including Brian Berthiaume. One of the most prominent "Baba lovers" was guitarist Pete Townshend. Baba's teachings influenced many of Townshend's works, including the rock opera *Tommy*, and his song "Baba O'Reilly." Townshend had been introduced to the ideas of Meher Baba in 1967 by artist and journalist Mike McInnerney, and the next year, he asked McInnerney to do the cover art for *Tommy*.[29] McInnerney wrote about it:

"I have this memory snapshot, back in '68, sitting in Pete T's kitchen, showing him the finished artwork for the Tommy cover and trying to find a way of bringing God into the cover copy. The Indian word for God is 'Avatar' and, for us, his name was Meher Baba and the cover credit list was where we put him. Somehow, giving God a job description on the album, juxtaposing the ordinary with the extraordinary, seemed appropriate to the project. It was a contrast that wove its way throughout the Opera."[30]

Indeed, on the back cover of the *Tommy* album, released in May 1969, the credits include "Opera by Pete Townshend; Cover Design—Pete McInnerney; Avatar—Meher Baba" (see Figure 4.2). *Tommy* was a hit album, and The Who performed most of its songs at the legendary Woodstock Music & Art Fair in August 1969. *Tommy's* popularity introduced Meher Baba to thousands of people, including Brian Berthiaume, who was a fan of the album.

Berthiaume, initially, did not make the connection between *Tommy*, Meher Baba, and the anti-drug message. Then one day, Brian used LSD while under the supervision of a psychologist, and he had a "profound drug experience" that led him to feel like he was "being one with the universe." Brian asked the psychologist why *he* was not using LSD, and the psychologist responded that he followed Meher Baba, and "he's against drug use."

His second trip on LSD was not the same. "It was just vibrating walls," said Brian. "It was empty, and I didn't have that profound feeling. But I wanted to get to that profound deep place, and I found out the way you do that is not with drugs." So, Brian Berthiaume began to stop using drugs.

Brian met his future wife, Cathleen Crocker, in Maryland, in January 1969, the same week Meher Baba died in India. As Brian recalls, he "conned Cathleen to go out to coffee," and they talked for eight hours. He believed right then that he would marry her someday, and he told her so. On June 11, 1970, Brian Berthiaume and Cathleen Crocker did indeed marry, and they made plans to spend their honeymoon surfing

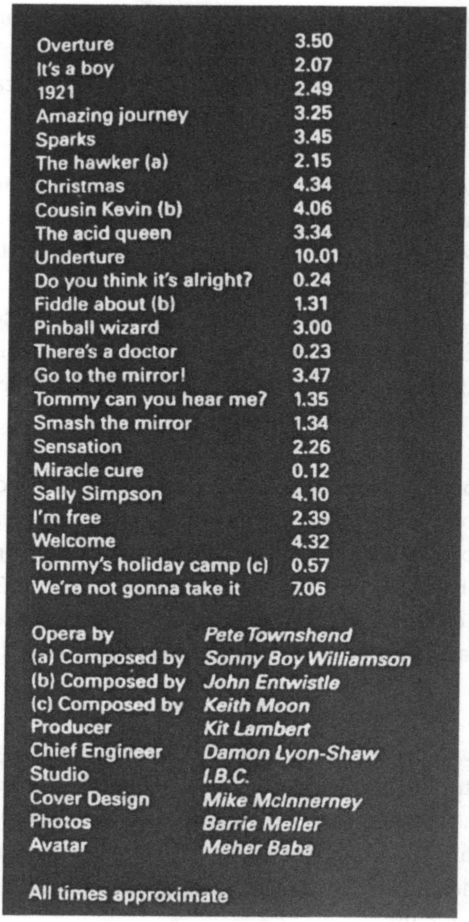

Overture	3.50
It's a boy	2.07
1921	2.49
Amazing journey	3.25
Sparks	3.45
The hawker (a)	2.15
Christmas	4.34
Cousin Kevin (b)	4.06
The acid queen	3.34
Underture	10.01
Do you think it's alright?	0.24
Fiddle about (b)	1.31
Pinball wizard	3.00
There's a doctor	0.23
Go to the mirror!	3.47
Tommy can you hear me?	1.35
Smash the mirror	1.34
Sensation	2.26
Miracle cure	0.12
Sally Simpson	4.10
I'm free	2.39
Welcome	4.32
Tommy's holiday camp (c)	0.57
We're not gonna take it	7.06

Opera by	*Pete Townshend*
(a) Composed by	*Sonny Boy Williamson*
(b) Composed by	*John Entwistle*
(c) Composed by	*Keith Moon*
Producer	*Kit Lambert*
Chief Engineer	*Damon Lyon-Shaw*
Studio	*I.B.C.*
Cover Design	*Mike McInnerney*
Photos	*Barrie Meller*
Avatar	*Meher Baba*

All times approximate

Figure 4.2. The back cover of *Tommy* (shown here) included the credits, "Opera by Pete Townshend; Cover Design—Pete McInnerney; Avatar—Meher Baba." *Tommy's* popularity introduced Meher Baba to thousands of people, including Brian Berthiaume.

at Cocoa Beach, Florida. Myrtle Beach, South Carolina, happens to be on the way to Cocoa Beach, and a friend told him the story of Elizabeth Patterson and the Meher Spiritual Center. Intrigued after his experience with LSD and the supervising psychologist, Brian and Cathleen decided to stop at the Center on their way to their honeymoon. As Brian explains, "I was not really into it; just kind of interested."

Brian visited the room where Meher Baba had met with people individually during his visits to Myrtle Beach, the last of which had been in 1958. In that room, Brian, who had not yet completely stopped using drugs, said, "I had this spiritual experience, and I threw away all my marijuana. I had it in my bag, and I just poured it down the toilet." At that point he completely stopped all drugs.

Working with "Crazy Kids"

A few months after his honeymoon visit to the Meher Baba Center, Brian's career took a step further down the path toward starting the Phoenix recovery high school during the 1970–1971 school year. Subbing at the Kennedy school showed Brian how much he enjoyed working in a nontraditional school environment, but his spiritual growth was steering him away from the drug-using high school culture. While Brian did have a college degree, he was not a certified teacher. Thus, he was limited in the teaching positions he could accept.

One position for which he was qualified was teaching in the Home Study Program in Prince George's County, Maryland. This would be a full-time, unlicensed, hourly job with no benefits, but it provided experience that would prove invaluable later in designing his own school curriculum. In the Home Study Program, Brian provided an educational program for individual students who were not attending their public school due to emotional problems.

The school system assigned each student a teacher to work on academics individually, in their homes, and Brian was one of the teachers. Just as he did at Kennedy, Brian felt a connection with students who did not fit a traditional mold. Recalling his own years of "acting out" in school, Brian said, "I could like the kids nobody else liked, because in high school I was not liked."

After a year in the Home School Program in Prince George's County, a position opened back in Montgomery County. The Department of Education's Department of Home Instruction was providing academic instruction for students living in a residential drug treatment center, similar to the programs at Oxford House and Canarsie Youth Center in New York. Brian's experience as a home-school teacher prepared him well for teaching outside a school setting, and in 1971, Montgomery County made Brian the Academic Director of the Young Adult Rehabilitation Center. While there, Brian developed an education program to be provided on-site for young people with drug-related problems.

One year later, Brian left the Rehabilitation Center to accept a full-time job as a middle school teacher at the Developmental School of Washington in 1972. Similar to the treatment center program, the Developmental School was not in a traditional school site. This school, though, was an independent school on the children's unit in a mental hospital called the Psychiatric Institute in Washington, DC. Brian still did not have a teaching license, but he did not need one in a private school.

"I started working with crazy kids, and I really liked that," said Brian. "I really liked crazy kids, because they just did whatever they wanted. It's kind of strange, but they were very interesting to work with. They were not on the straight and narrow. They weren't doing things the way they were conditioned to be."

Brian continued using a nontraditional approach to teaching at the Psychiatric Institute (see Figure 4.3). "I was a teacher, but I was always more interested in asking them questions. 'We're going to study history, but you know what? We're going to

Figure 4.3. Brian Berthiaume was the central figure in the creation of the first full-fledged recovery high school. Berthiaume described himself as a "maverick," and as a teacher. Berthiaume used nontraditional methods to make material more interesting. In this photo, Berthiaume brings a character to life. (Source: Brian and Cathleen Berthiaume.)

do it a little different. We're going to find out *your* history instead of the history of the country. Let's find out your history, like where you were born.' So, my history class was the history of each individual person. Actually, it was a lot more interesting to me than the other traditional history. It was good, but I was always getting in trouble."

One example of Berthiaume's trouble was the lesson he taught about the composition of hot dogs, after which many students stopped eating hot dogs.

"I was into Yoga, and during lunch time, I'd be standing on my head for half an hour. All of a sudden, all the kids would come into my classroom, where I was at during my lunch hour, and then they would all be on their heads. The psychiatrist walked by, and he said, 'What the hell are the kids doing in there with Berthiaume? They're standing on their heads!' I'd be doing some Yoga with them, and then it turned out that the kids would end up telling me everything, and they weren't telling the therapist. So, I was always in trouble."

The Other Way

In the 1970s, Montgomery County was innovative in its social services and education system. If there was a need, the county tried to create a program to handle it, and this was especially true with youth issues. In 1973, the Montgomery County Health Department started a program called the Other Way School for dysfunctional families. Brian was still teaching at the Psychiatric Institute middle school when he applied for a position at the Other Way. Brian interviewed with Dr. Robert P. Jardin, Chief of the Department of Alternatives and Counseling Services for Adolescents and their Families in Montgomery County Health Department. Dr. Jardin, who was a leader in the Montgomery County Health Department for fifteen years, from 1971–1986, wanted to know what type of curriculum Brian would use if hired. Berthiaume recalled, "Half of it was stuff like Yoga and doing meditation, but he hired me anyway, and I got to do sort of a creative, innovative [school]."

One day in the early 1970s, Cathleen and Brian bought a Baba painting from a man who lived at the Meher Center in Myrtle Beach. The artist was nearly blind and exclusively did paintings of Baba. On New Year's Eve, instead of going out, Cathleen wanted to do something more meaningful. She decided to sit in front of the Baba painting and meditate. Brian liked what she was doing, joined her, and dedicated his life to doing Baba's work.

"I wanted him to use me to do his work."

Brian and Cathleen traveled to India three times, in 1973, 1974, and 1977. During those trips, they heard more about Meher Baba's teachings regarding drug use, and Brian met with Eruch Jessawala, an interpreter of Baba's alphabet board and his unique sign language. Jessawala told Brian the best thing a person could do was get off drugs oneself or to help other people get off drugs. This message resonated strongly with Brian. Through the comments of Eruch Jessawala and his own New Year's Eve dedication to Meher Baba's work, Brian Berthiaume had discerned his vocation.

"If you're going to be spiritual, you really can't be doing drugs," Brian said. "It's the antithesis to a spiritual life."

Soon after his first trip to India in 1973, Brian started the Other Way school with a personal priority of stopping the students' drug use, though that was not the stated priority of the program. Dr. Jardin, the administrator who hired Brian, had been trained just a year earlier at Georgetown University under the tutelage of psychiatrist Murray Bowen, the legendary pioneer of family systems therapy.[31] His vision for the Other Way program thus centered on family work. Jardin and Berthiaume had different visions of how to help kids, and according to Brian, this would continue to cause some friction between the two.[32]

"The mental health program in the health department was more committed to family therapy for kids with a variety of problems—school attendance, anger, depression, school phobia," said Brian. "But I had my private little agenda with the drugs because of the Meher Baba thing."

Berthiaume's official title was Educational Alternatives Counselor, but he did a little of everything. He was the school administrator, ran therapy groups, taught classes, and handled in-takes and withdrawals. Brian had been hired before the Other Way School even had a building, and he claimed his first class was in his car with one student. In time, he was provided a room in a local library, and eventually, the program got a building. Much of the experience he gained working at the Other Way would be useful years later at Phoenix.

The Other Way's enrollment grew steadily from one student to two to five, ten, fifteen, and about twenty. Berthiaume was the lone teacher in the school for its first two years, but when the enrollment reached the high teens, Montgomery County Public Schools assigned two teachers to the school. In supplying the County Health Department with two teachers employed by the public-school system, the Other Way school transitioned from a health department program to an "interagency program," functioning cooperatively with the education department—similar to how the Freedom Road school had functioned in Charleston.

At the time, there were about a dozen interagency programs in Montgomery County. The school operated that way for several years. Brian was a health department employee, and the other teachers were public school employees. This type of progressive cross-sector collaboration facilitated the creation of the Phoenix school. In many states and counties today, funding remains in silos, such as health, education, and justice. Students may receive services from various sectors, but the funding streams today rarely intersect. In the 1970s, however, health and education for youth were not seen so distinctly. Since President Eisenhower created a new cabinet-level Department of Health, Education, and Welfare in 1953, federal education and health policy had been governed by the same department. Prior to that time, federal education programs were operated by the Office of Education, which was a non-cabinet bureau. The Department of Education Organization Act was only signed into law by President Jimmy Carter on October 17, 1979, and it did not begin operating until May 4, 1980. The law divided this once unitary agency into two offices: the Department of Education and the Department of Health and Human Services.

Students who attended school at the Other Way did not just have drug problems; according to Brian, they also had problems with anxiety, anger, and school attendance. All the students had mental health diagnoses, and there was no predetermined length of stay in the program. Students would usually stay about a year, and the main eligibility factor was whether the families would be consistent with family therapy.

"In the health department," said Berthiaume, the philosophy was any problem that a kid had—depression, drug usage, anger—that wasn't the problem; that was simply the tip of the iceberg. It was a symptom. The problem was family dysfunction. If you don't do family therapy, you're not getting to the core of the problem."

If the family stopped going to family therapy, the Health Department could remove the children from the school. Brian could only recall one time a student actually had to withdraw because the family had quit therapy, but "just the fact the parents knew that that would happen—and they were really desperate to have the kids in the school—they didn't drop out."

The National Association of Counties (NACo) honored the Other Way program in 1975 with its Achievement Award, which recognized innovative county government programs. The Other Way school was becoming a prominent resource for Montgomery County, and by 1976, Brian Berthiaume was garnering the attention of county leaders.

Education and Justice in Montgomery County

Montgomery County shares the same birth-year as the United States, both being created in 1776. As the nation celebrates its milestones, so does Montgomery County. The suburban county covers about 495 square miles, and the geographical location bordering on the nation's capital has influenced the demographics of the region, making it a wealthy and well-educated county. It has been said there are "more Congressmen per square foot in Montgomery County than anywhere in the United States."[33] Many legislators, staffers, and federal officials essentially would wage policy battles on Capitol Hill on weekdays and raise their families in Montgomery County on nights and weekends. In fact, many federal employees do not even have to leave the county, as over time, several federal offices have been located in Montgomery County, including many that have been integrally involved in federal drug programs, such as the Department of Health and Human Services (HHS), the Food and Drug Administration (FDA), the National Institutes of Health (NIH), and the Substance Abuse and Mental Health Services Administration (SAMHSA). As much as a person might try to compartmentalize work and home, a symbiotic relationship likely would have existed between home and families and work and policy. Though it is impossible to know exactly how much one influenced the other, what was happening culturally with rising teenage drug use in the 1970s was impacting families in Montgomery County, and the operationalization of federal drug programs was being carried out by many heads of those families. Interestingly, the offices in Montgomery County, where the Phoenix recovery high school opened in the nascent years of the drug war, have had more of a treatment and prevention role, whereas the enforcement agencies, such as the Bureau of Alcohol, Tobacco, Firearms and Explosives (ATF), the Drug Enforcement Administration (DEA), and the Office of National Drug Control Policy (ONDCP) have remained anchored in Washington, DC, or its Virginia suburbs.

Montgomery County in the mid-1970s could be characterized as affluent, diverse, and socially progressive, and in its bicentennial year of 1975–1976, both the school system and the police department hired new leaders. Montgomery County

Public Schools hired Dr. Charles M. "Charlie" Bernardo in fall 1975 as its new superintendent, and one year later, in November 1976, the police department hired Robert J. di Grazia, giving him the newly created title of "Chief." Both men came to Montgomery County from New England—Bernardo from Providence, Rhode Island, and di Grazia from Boston, Massachusetts–and both men broke contracts with their prior employers to accept their positions in Maryland. Both men were relatively young—di Grazia was 48 when the county made him its Chief, and Bernardo was 37 when hired by Montgomery County Public Schools (MCPS), making him the county's youngest superintendent.[34] Both men also had histories of staying in jobs for brief periods and ruffling feathers before they left. Their Montgomery County experiences would be no different. Both would make political waves during their tenures, and both would be ousted in the same month—December 1979—culminating with the launch the Phoenix recovery high school at the same time as they were exiting their jobs.

At the start of the 1975–76 school year, Montgomery County opened three new schools, bringing its total to 205. The district's enrollment was 122,000, which made it the 17th largest district in the nation. According to census records, though, the decade of the 1970s was a period of population stagnation and even decline for some areas of the county.[35] Montgomery County faced many of the same issues as other large US districts, including racially imbalanced schools, declining enrollments, and budget problems.

Montgomery County had experienced a 65% population increase in the 1960s, from 340,000 in 1960 to 522,000 in 1970.[36] The population growth had ballooned MCPS enrollment from 80,557 in 1960 to 125,334 in 1970.[37] After 1970, though, population growth leveled off, growing only about 10% to 579,000 in the 1980 census.[38] School enrollments began a steady decline, due in part to the end of the Baby Boom and a declining birth rate that was occurring nationwide, called the "Baby Bust."[39] In 1975, enrollment had dropped to 122,000, and by 1980, there were less than 100,000 students enrolled in Montgomery County Public Schools.

Montgomery County had developed a high percentage of white-collar workers, and typically has had one of the largest proportions of college graduates of any major metropolitan area in the nation. Montgomery County residents historically have been politically active and supported socially liberal policies.[40] Progressive as the county was, however, it was not immune to discriminatory policies, such as segregated housing ordinances. Such ordinances passed in the 1960s had led to racially imbalanced schools, whereas only 7.5% of the county population was non-White in 1970, schools ranged few non-White students to over 70% non-White enrollment in Rosemary Hills Elementary School in 1973.[41] Like many urban districts, the dynamics of racial integration impacted the demographics of the neighborhoods, the schools, and school leadership.

In the 1970s, the MCPS Board of Education had seven seats and held elections every other year. Board terms were four years, and either three or four seats were up for grabs each election cycle. This rotation meant that a majority of the Board votes would be dislodged every other election. With a socially liberal and educated electorate, the Board of Education tended to elect left-leaning, degreed members. The year 1974 was one of those elections, with four liberal members elected: Herbert Benington (a Rhodes Scholar), Verna Fletcher (a former elementary school teacher), Roscoe Nix (an Alabama native with a bachelor's degree and the only African American on the Board), and Elizabeth Spencer (a Kansas native with a Master of Education degree). Those new members, along with veterans Marilyn Allen, Thomas Israel, and Harriet Bernstein, were presented with demands from the Citizens Advisory Committee on Minority Relations, which had formed a year earlier and in 1974 had issued a "sweeping and in-depth final report that identified some of the sources of racial difficulties in the county's schools."[42] In response, the Board of Education appointed a number of task forces to improve the quality of the education and relations across races in the district and held a retreat to discuss desegregation issues.

Superintendent Charles M. Bernardo

In March 1975, the Board of Education was given disappointing news when the superintendent, Dr. Homer Elseroad, announced he had accepted a job with the Education Commission of the States in Colorado, and his resignation would be effective June 30. After eleven years on the job, he wanted a slower pace, and he thought regular change in leadership was a good thing for school districts. Vice Chair Harriet Bernstein was quoted as saying the news was a "total surprise" and "upsetting to the Board."[43] She also noted it had come at a "critical time," and the man they chose as his replacement, Dr. Charles M. Bernardo, was a Northeasterner whose ideology aligned with most of theirs. He was only 37 years old.

Dr. Bernardo was one of the rising leaders in school administration. Born in Yonkers, New York, in September 1937, Bernardo attended public elementary schools before enrolling in the highly selective, independent Trinity School in New York City for secondary school. After graduating from Trinity in 1955, he joined the Marine Reserve for six years, serving six months of active duty. Bernardo also enrolled at New York University, where he received a bachelor's degree in science and health education. He then earned a master's degree in secondary school administration from Columbia.[44]

Bernardo was a leader from the time he became an educator, serving as department chair and teacher of physical education and health at Nathaniel Hawthorne Junior High in Yonkers, and then as baseball coach and a teacher of science and physical education at Oceanside High School on Long Island. Like many schoolteachers, Bernardo worked during the summers to earn extra income, though his job may have been more thrilling than others. He put his military training to use as a member of the Westchester County, New York, Police Department, patrolling the beat and controlling the crowds of the historic Playland Park in the city of Rye, which had opened in 1928.[45]

Bernardo was also an academic, becoming a Research Associate at the Columbia University Institute of Administrative Research. He earned his doctorate at Columbia in 1966, defending his dissertation on school finance titled *Performance of School Districts on Fiscal and Other Factors in Relation to Agencies of Budget Approval.* One year later, the small Oxford, Massachusetts, school district hired the 29-year-old to be its superintendent. Charlie and his wife, Carolynn, packed up and moved with their two young children from New York to Massachusetts.[46]

His would be a short stay. Since receiving his bachelor's degree in 1959, Bernardo had only stayed at schools for about two years before moving to a different school. This trend would continue as he became a district administrator. His term as Oxford superintendent began a series of leadership appointments that Bernardo would leave about two years into his term, each time for a larger district. In May 1969, Bernardo was named superintendent of the relatively new Owen J. Roberts School District in Chester County, Pennsylvania, which had been founded just two years earlier. Bernardo signed a four-year contract and started his job in July, at age 31. He saw himself as "a manager of change in the philosophy and practice of teaching."[47]

While having the backing of the school board, his attempts to "revolutionize" approaches to education and increase involvement of local citizens in district planning ultimately drew opposition from more conservative residents, and he would not finish his contract. In September 1970, unbeknownst to the Owen Roberts school board, Bernardo applied for the Providence, Rhode Island, superintendent's job. He was one of fifty applicants, and in December, he was offered the position. In January 1971, Bernardo made a surprise announcement that he was resigning two years early to become the superintendent in Providence, a district with a relatively large but declining enrollment of thirty-four thousand students. Bernardo was then 33 years old, and according to newspaper accounts, the hiring made him "the youngest chief executive school administrator in a major urban system in the country."[48]

Bernardo signed a three-year contract, and unlike his prior administrative jobs, he would stay in Providence for four years.[49] His time there would prepare him for many of the issues he would face in Montgomery County—budget cuts, school facilities in need of repair, school desegregation, and teacher labor issues. The teacher's union contract with the district was set to expire in August 1971, soon after Bernardo assumed his post. The district had also begun a voluntary racial integration program in 1965. The racial balancing plan, which included busing to achieve desegregated schools, had started in elementary schools in 1969 and middle schools in 1970, and would now be implemented in high schools under his watch. The programs initially had led to sporadic racial violence, but Bernardo was proud to note that problems were almost nonexistent by the time high schools started an integration plan in 1974.

During his years in Providence, Bernardo took bold, and sometimes unpopular, moves such as closing schools at the start of the 1972 school year after the teachers' union rejected contract offers,[50] cutting school staff,[51] reorganizing the central office,[52] and recommending the closing of several older school buildings.[53]

His method was exemplified by his approach to his own central office staff, where he eliminated all seventy-three central office positions (except his own), reclassified positions, and then required former employees to reapply for jobs.[54] In describing his efforts in Providence, Bernardo was quoted at the time as saying, "We're working on the quality of what a child will experience at the end of the bus ride."[55]

Though he had signed another three-year contract in 1974, by 1975, Bernardo was looking for his next step. He was a finalist for superintendent positions in Milwaukee and St. Louis but was not chosen for either. Montgomery County, however, was impressed enough by his credentials to offer him the position. The MCPS Board of Education received seventy-seven applications for the opening, and they saw Bernardo as a person who had experience in the issues they saw as most pressing to the district—racial balancing, declining enrollment, budget cuts, and contract negotiations. In selecting the 37-year-old Bernardo, they also chose the youngest person ever to occupy to role of MCPS superintendent, and the vote was unanimous. On August 21, 1975, the Board voted 7–0 to approve of Bernardo's hiring.[56]

Adolescent Drug Use in Montgomery County

Adolescent drug use was one issue not mentioned in the press accounts of Dr. Bernardo's hiring. Like many places in the United States in the 1970s, however, youth drug use was on the rise in Montgomery County when Bernardo was hired in summer 1975. Perhaps this is because the spectrum of teenage drug use was just starting to come into focus. 1975 was the first year that the University of Michigan's Institute for Social Research conducted its annual National High School Senior Survey, best known as Monitoring the Future (MTF), a study of substance use and related factors among US adolescents. MTF has conducted the federally funded study every year since, and in that first year, the research found that 90% of high school seniors had drunk alcohol in their lifetime, 55% had used an illicit drug, and 47% had smoked marijuana. In this era of lowered drinking ages and states starting to decriminalize marijuana, these percentages would go up every year for the rest of the decade—with the minor exception of alcohol, which ticked down only from 93.1% to 93.0% in 1979.[57]

Just up the road on Capitol Hill, the federal response to drug problems had begun shifting away from treatment and toward enforcement. Gerald Ford had taken over the presidency in 1974, and it was around the same time as Bernardo's hiring in summer 1975 that the Domestic Council on Drug Abuse Task Force issued its "White Paper on Drug Abuse" to the President.[58] Even though the report had suggested "a high priority analysis of treatment capacity," the analysis never occurred, and the Ford Administration instead doubled down on supply reduction and enforcement. By 1976, federal spending on drug enforcement would for the first time catch up with that on treatment and prevention.[59]

Following the tone being established by the federal government, the Montgomery County police did make a brief effort at enforcement in the local high schools. In spring 1975, the year Brian Berthiaume's Other Way therapeutic school had earned a national honor for the county, the Montgomery County police conducted a three-month-long undercover investigation of adult drug dealers.[60] Then, on May 29, 1975, the police raided four Montgomery County high schools, and arrested twenty-two people, including nineteen students, on charges of distributing drugs on school grounds. The 1975 raids, however, were an isolated event and did little to quash the festering drug use in the Montgomery County Public Schools.

The next two school years, Bernardo's first years in MCPS, were quiet with regards to police interventions at the local high schools, with the occasional school administrator contacting police about suspicious activity or active drug use on campus. This quiescent period of police activity in the schools, however, would soon end. A new police chief arrived in the county in 1976—a figure who was arguably even more of trailblazer than Bernardo. Their professional paths would quickly become intertwined, and their jobs in Montgomery County would end abruptly within days of each other in December 1978.

Police Chief Robert di Grazia

The Montgomery County police force had grown to 784 officers by 1976, and that year the title of the head of the MCPD was changed from "Superintendent" to "Chief."[61] The county also conducted a national search that year for a new police chief, and their attention was drawn toward Boston and its outspoken leader, Robert di Grazia.

Di Grazia was well-known as a reformer who had "hobnobbed with the social elite,"[62] and he had been considered one of the most popular people in Boston.[63] Di Grazia also had built a reputation as one of the most liberal commissioners in the nation, battling corruption, cronyism, and police brutality.

Born in 1928 in San Francisco, di Grazia left a career as a Macy's retailer to join the Marin County, California, police department beginning his career in law enforcement at age 31.[64] After about a year in Marin County, di Grazia became chief of the twenty-seven-man force in the new Novato, California, Police Department, at age 35. At 41, he left his home state to become Superintendent of the St. Louis County, Missouri, police department. It was in St. Louis that di Grazia's controversial style started to breed dissent by pushing against convention. He developed a system for assigning officers' duties according to their expertise rather than rank and introduced women into the patrol through a foundation's "women in policing" project.[65] He even considered a plan to place constraints on when officers could fire a gun, causing an outcry from the local residents and officers themselves who felt it would leave the community vulnerable.[66]

On November 1, 1972, at age 44, di Grazia accepted an unsolicited offer to become police commissioner in Boston. He stocked his staff with a small cadre of young, liberal academics called the "Whiz Kids," many of whom accompanied him from St. Louis.[67] Rather than promoting rank-and-file officers based on seniority or patronage, di Grazia leaned heavily on his Whiz Kids, who, like him, were interested in testing out innovations in policing.[68]

Di Grazia cut an imposing figure, standing 6-4 with thick hair in an era where John Travolta's hair in *Saturday Night Fever* (first seen by the public in winter 1977) would reach iconic status (see Figure 4.4). Di Grazia served as police commissioner during a tumultuous time in Boston. The early 1970s were years in which the Bulger brothers were rising to great power on the streets and in the statehouse. Whitey Bulger was an infamous mobster who ruled South Boston, and brother Billy was starting his tenure of twenty-five years in the state Senate, having just finished serving five terms in the Massachusetts House of Representatives. While di Grazia was battling corruption that had been going on for years before he arrived in Boston, on June 21, 1974, federal Judge Arthur Garrity issued an order that would thrust the city and its police force into a firestorm.

Twenty years after the Supreme Court's *Brown v. Board of Education* ruling had determined the nation's segregated schools were unconstitutional in 1954, Judge Garrity

Figure 4.4. Robert di Grazia served as police chief in Montgomery County, Maryland, from 1976 to 1978. Di Grazia built a reputation as one of the most liberal commissioners in the nation, battling corruption, cronyism, and police brutality. He also approved the drug raids in Montgomery County high schools that were an impetus in the creation of the Phoenix School. (Source: Wikimedia/City of Boston.)

found that Boston had created two separate school systems, one Black and one White. His solution was to require students from predominantly Black sections of town and from predominantly White areas to attend schools in the other students' neighborhoods.[69] Desegregating Boston's schools would be accomplished by busing. Unlike Dr. Bernardo's experience of relatively smooth racial integration that only resulted in scattered incidents in Providence, busing in Boston exploded in violence.

The busing decree was issued at the beginning of summer 1974 to take effect that fall, which gave the police department just under three months to prepare—though the case had taken eighteen months for Judge Garrity to decide, so the possibility had loomed on the horizon for the police for a while before the ruling. The first phase of busing was to be implemented in two of the poorer sections of town, Roxbury (which was 90% Black) and South Boston (which was almost entirely White). Families in these areas would have less financial ability to transfer to private schools, which only fueled the anger. Di Grazia was at the helm as the city erupted into violence immediately upon implementing the directive on the first day of school, September 12, 1974.

As the buses arrived at South Boston High that day, White parents shouted angrily as di Grazia's officers shepherded Black and White students though separate doors. People hurled eggs, bricks, and bottles at the Black students. Only about one hundred of the thirteen hundred Black students assigned to South Boston High School had chosen to make the journey that first day. For white students, it was even more sparse—only thirteen of the South Boston White students assigned to Roxbury chose to attend school on the first day.[70] The city never fully embraced the busing plan, and over time, thousands of White students would leave Boston Public Schools for private schools.[71] The heaviest of the riots occurred from 1974–1976, under di Grazia's watch. His police officers had to don military gear and utilize reinforcements from the National Guard and State Police to handle the mobs. To his credit, perhaps with an assist from Whitey Bulger who did not want negative attention from the police in South Boston, nobody died during the violence that erupted during the first two years of the desegregation.

While the nation witnessed the violence erupting in Boston, di Grazia's penchant for proclamations captured the attention of the media, and the school busing era battles enhanced that image. He spoke regularly on police reform, becoming active in the Police Foundation, which had been founded in 1970 as "an independent, non-partisan, and non-membership organization dedicated to improving policing through innovation and science."[72] The Foundation convened a conference of law enforcement officials and scholars in Washington in April 1976, and di Grazia was invited to speak. In his speech, di Grazia accused the nation's police chiefs of caring more about protecting their jobs and their pensions than having compassion for the poor.

"Few of our colleagues," he said, "are questioning traditional practices and promoting innovations, demanding increased productivity and upgrading personnel, encouraging serious research and advocating the hiring of women and members of minority groups."[73]

He continued, "There is one other thing few police chiefs are doing—leveling with the public about crime. Most of us are not telling the public that there is relatively little the police can do about crime. We are not letting the public in on our era's dirty little secret; that those who commit . . . violent street crimes are, for the most part, the products of poverty, unemployment, broken homes, rotten education, drug addiction and alcoholism, and other social and economic ills."[74]

Instead, he said police chiefs "let politicians get away with law-and-order rhetoric that reinforces the mistaken notion that the police . . . can alone control crime." The politicians, di Grazia contended, "end up perpetuating a system by which the rich get richer, the poor get poorer and crime continues." Most damning of all was that most police chiefs behave like "pet rocks unable to move, grow, change, or innovate . . . They bend to the political winds and offer little leadership"[75]

His words that day would follow him the rest of his career. In particular, the pet rock quote cemented his legacy as a reformer in opposition to entrenched, "good ol' boy" leadership that was only satisfied with the status quo. Most assuredly, Robert di Grazia would never gather moss as a pet rock, and when he took action, he intended to transform so that people took notice. His style alienated him from the traditional rank-and-file officer. Chester J. Broderick, chairman of the Boston police union, was one of di Grazia's loudest critics. Broderick told the *Washington Post*, "He was a dirty rotten, vicious man who supported people's civil rights only as long as [the people] didn't work for him."[76]

In the public eye, di Grazia was improving conditions at the Boston police department and helping keep a lid on the simmering school system. As his popularity grew, though, his celebrity status may have threatened Boston Mayor Kevin White, who had won a narrow re-election victory in 1975. It was suggested di Grazia may have had an interest in running for mayor himself. Still, the pace of reform was not quick enough for di Grazia, and with signals of resistance from Mayor White, di Grazia allowed his name to be included in the search for a new Montgomery County police chief. Montgomery County formerly offered di Grazia the position in November 1976, which included a salary increase of $10,000 over his Boston salary—money that would help cover the tuition for his children in private schools and college. So, almost four years to the day after taking the Boston job, di Grazia accepted the position to lead the 784-member Montgomery County police force.

His resignation came with a year remaining on his five-year contract, and with his popularity high in Boston. Some suspected his move to the DC suburbs, so close to the US Capitol, indicated he was aspiring to become head of the FBI, a rumor that di Grazia denied.[77] The new job would, in fact, put him closer to policymakers, as well as the Police Foundation, with whom he was already working. For a person interested in making large scale change, Montgomery County in the 1970s would have been an appealing locale.

"Montgomery County's hardly the center of action," Boston City Councilman Lawrence S. DiCara told the *Washington Post* in 1977. "But it's next door to it."[78]

True to form, di Grazia left Boston with a bang, releasing a 572-page report on corruption in one Boston police district and announcing the separation from his wife of twenty- two years in his last week on the job. Montgomery County Executive James Gleason suggested Montgomery County would be quieter than Boston. "Front page stories about his marital separation," Gleason told the *Washington Post*—"well it's different here, it's not the same atmosphere, it's a smaller place."[79]

Perhaps the opportunity to live life without constant public scrutiny was appealing, but interestingly, di Grazia saw Montgomery County as more progressive than its own County Executive. In news accounts, di Grazia noted that Montgomery County's population of 589,000 in 1976 was only "about 75,000 less than Boston."[80] And looking back years later, di Grazia was quoted as saying, "It struck me as a rather progressive, liberal, affluent county. It had considerably less crime than Boston, and I thought it could become a model police agency for the whole country."[81]

Richard L. Towers

While Chief di Grazia and Superintendent Bernardo were settling into their new positions in Montgomery County, Brian Berthiaume returned to school to pursue a master's degree in special education to finally become certified as a teacher. MCPS, with whom the Health Department was cooperating to run the Other Way school, had a partnership with Trinity College in DC. Trinity provided a special education degree with classes both on-campus and on-site at the Mark Twain School for students with learning disabilities in Rockville. Brian completed his master's degree in 1977, becoming a certified teacher in the process. Brian had come a long way from being the child of two parents who had dropped out of high school and who had finished at the bottom of his own graduating class. His personal experience became something he would draw upon regularly when working with students at the Other Way and for the rest of his career.

"When I was starting back in New Hampshire," said Brian, "I was like, 'Why did I have this desire to succeed?' All I knew is I wanted to do better than my family. My father was an alcoholic. My mother was angry. My dad didn't graduate from high school. You know, something inside me [said] I wanted to be better. I wanted to succeed, and I define success as being educated." The seed his father, Harvey Berthiaume, had planted years before about getting an education was now blossoming, and Brian was getting the attention of people both in the school administrative offices and at the Board of Education.

At the time, Dr. Richard L. "Dick" Towers was the MCPS central office director of programs for exceptional learners, including "special education, disadvantaged, disaffected, gifted, limited English speaking, and drug and alcohol abusing students."[82] He held various titles in the district from 1977 to 1992, including "Director of Interagency, Alternative, and Supplementary Programs," and as an interagency school, the Other Way was one of his programs.[83]

Like Berthiaume, Bernardo, and di Grazia before him, Dick Towers came to Montgomery County from New England in the mid-1970s. Towers was an academic who had consulted on and evaluated alternative schools and adolescent drug abuse programs for several years before coming to Maryland. Towers grew up in Boston, and he received an English literature degree from the University of Massachusetts in 1963 and a Master of Education degree in educational administration and instructional development from Northeastern University in 1966. After teaching high school English in Massachusetts for a few years, Towers moved to South Carolina and completed his PhD in educational administration from the University of South Carolina in 1969. Towers briefly worked as an assistant superintendent in South Carolina before accepting a faculty appointment at St. John's University in New York City in 1970.

New York in the late 1960s and early 1970s was experiencing great change and experimentation in its schools. The city had decentralized its schools in 1968 to give more local control to school systems.[84] Nationally, an alternative school movement had also begun during these years, and decentralized control created opportunities for school innovation. At the same time, Governor Nelson Rockefeller, a Republican who leaned to the left, was trying to handle an exploding drug problem.[85] Though he is better known today for the strict drug enforcement laws he initiated in the mid-1970s, Governor Rockefeller's initial approach was to help people get clean by creating the Narcotic Addiction and Control Commission in 1967, local Narcotics Guidance Councils, and later through opening methadone clinics.[86] The purpose of volunteer Narcotics Guidance Councils was "to develop a program of community participation regarding the control of the use of narcotics at the local level," and its main objective was "educating the community and especially its youth in the field of drug use."[87]

It was into this context of local control, alternative schools, and concerns about drug use that Professor Dick Towers was brought to consult about students with special needs, and he became especially interested in the work happening in alternative schools. From 1971 to 1974, Towers was hired to consult on multiple projects, including English for Speakers of Other Languages, multi-modality instructional skills, long-term effects of Head Start, open classrooms, and adolescent drug use. For most of those projects, he worked with the New York City Central Board of Education.

The adolescent drug abuse project exposed Towers to the drug issues being experienced by teens in the early 1970s, and this became a focus of his for most of the rest of his career in education. Towers resided on Long Island at the time, and the Freeport Community had created its own Narcotics Guidance Council, for which he volunteered from 1971 to 1973.

"Throughout those years working in different places," Towers recalled, "we were involved in looking at all sorts of things to deal with the atypical student, which didn't turn out to be that much atypical really, the alienated. We had the Vietnam war going on. In the '60s and '70s, we were looking at all these alternative approaches to kids. A lot of times, [the approach] would be to pull the kids out and try to put them [in an alternative school]. We had the school without walls in New York, and we had all sorts of things going on. I was looking at a lot of that stuff."[88]

Towers stayed on the St. John's faculty until 1974. The summer of 1974 was the year of the busing decree to desegregate the Boston Public Schools, and that same summer, Towers accepted an offer to return to his home-state of Massachusetts. He became acting principal of Marlborough High School for a year and then Assistant Superintendent for Instruction in the Marlborough Public Schools. It was in this small, industrial city between Boston and Worcester that Towers was working during the same years that Dr. Bernardo was leading the Providence schools and that Commissioner Robert di Grazia and his Whiz Kids were handling the Boston busing crisis with the Boston Police Department. Though Boston is only a forty-five-minute drive from Marlborough, Towers did not work directly with Commissioner di Grazia in Massachusetts.

But, said Towers, "I heard a lot about him."

About one year after di Grazia left Boston to become Chief of the Montgomery County Police and two years after Bernardo left Providence, Towers received his own job offer from Dr. Bernardo and MCPS to direct interagency and alternative programs. Towers was attracted to Montgomery County for many of the same reasons that drew Bernardo and di Grazia.

"I must say I was very, very impressed," said Towers. "[Montgomery County] was innovative and willing to take chances on doing things that others weren't doing. The whole area of alternative education was really in the forefront . . . It just had a lot of great programs. It was a good system."

In Towers view, Montgomery County was a "lighthouse district."

"It was trying things that people would look at. People would come to visit from around the country. School districts would come and say, 'I read about this. I read about that. I'm going to see how this works, how that works.' "

In the wake of winning a national award in 1975, Brian Berthiaume was one of the county's shining lights. The Other Way school started a few years before Towers arrived in Montgomery County, but Towers respected the program and its leader immediately.

"We had a number of places," said Towers. "The Other Way was mostly, but not all drug offenders. They were kids with severe anti-social and behavioral issues, but much of that was infused with drug education. Brian was just an outstanding guy. He was just one in a million, and he was a go-getter. He just spearheaded the whole effort, but it was within that milieu of looking at all these programs that I got to know them, because we supplied the teachers."

Bernardo and di Grazia's Bumpy Roads

Both Bernardo and di Grazia were willing to make difficult decisions to support their progressive agendas. The Phoenix recovery high school emerged in part from those decisions, but the two leaders also drew battle lines with teachers, police officers, unions, and parents.

Bernardo

Bernardo took control of MCPS on October 1, 1975. A few weeks before, he met with the media and described the situation awaiting him as a "formidable challenge."[89] The challenge was complicated even more by a $3.1 million budget shortfall for the fiscal year, due in part to less money coming from the state than expected and the County Council refusing to appropriate additional money to the school district to make up the gap.[90] Bernardo suggested the district might have to take drastic measures such as dropping school building temperatures from 68 degrees to 65, and eliminating four hundred teaching assistant positions, none of which would endear him to parents. He even proposed to the Board of Education that they eliminate all extracurricular activities for the remainder of the school year, including athletics, adult education, and preschool programs.

Administrators and staff did indeed cut building temperatures (aided by warmer than normal weather), and due to what the Board called "heroic conservation efforts," the district saved over $1 million in utility costs and averted the cuts to sports and extracurricular programs.[91] The budget battles, however, continued into the next fiscal year, when Bernardo requested an increase in his first budget proposal. County Executives James P. Gleason countered with a $12 million *cut*. A frustrated Bernardo told his staff, "The effect would be absolutely devastating," and it would amount to the "rape of a fine school system."[92]

Bernardo and the Board ultimately received most of their budget request, but Bernardo still decided to close six under-enrolled schools and change the way coaches would be paid. The coaching-pay redesign led to several coaches heading into the summer break without contracts for the 1976–77 school year, and it led MCPS football coaches to threaten sitting out during the upcoming 1976 season.[93] They ultimately accepted arbitration, but according to one editorial writer at the time, "It will leave a scar that will never heal. The coaches will always be upset with Bernardo."[94]

The Board of Education held an election that November, and Bernardo's performance was a campaign issue. MCPS held board elections on even years, with the number of contended seats alternating between three and four. The November 1976 election was a three-seat year, with the seats held by Marilyn Allen, Thomas Israel, and Harriet Bernstein up for grabs. Bernstein had served just one term, while Allen and Israel had completed two terms, serving since 1968. This had been a liberal Board that had voted 7–0 to hire Bernardo in 1975, but one year into his tenure, integration efforts, declining enrollments leading to school closings, and persistent budget battles had fomented concerns about Bernardo among school board candidates.

A couple weeks into the 1976–77 school year, the six candidates running for those three seats spoke to about one hundred parents representing PTA groups from across the county and responded to the question, "What, in one sentence, is your opinion of Br. Bernardo?" All six candidates expressed disappointment with Bernardo's performance, focusing on his polices, his communication style, and his administrative tactics. Candidate Carol Wallace said, "I often wonder if the dog is wagging the tail, or the tail wagging the dog."[95]

The Board of Education in power from 1974 to 1976 that hired Bernardo was described in Floyd Hayes's study of Montgomery County's educational politics as a "basically liberal" group of "highly educated persons who had been active in civic affairs."[96] Bernardo took many steps to implement the Board's racial balancing vision. The 1976–77 Integration Plan included reorganizing grade levels, creating learning centers to provide specialized academic instruction, increasing community choice in how to achieve racial balance, school clustering options, and alternative schools—which may have indirectly cleared the way for schools like Phoenix, though that was not the stated intention of the plan. Bernardo also submitted a plan to close or consolidate schools with particularly low enrollments (i.e., "small schools").[97] To achieve balanced enrollment across the reorganized schools, MCPS would need to bus students to schools. By 1976, mandatory busing to integrate schools had become a publicized and controversial issue across the nation, highlighted by the eruption of violence under police chief di Grazia's watch in Boston just two years before. By creating such a plan in Montgomery County, the die was cast for Bernardo's eventual ouster, as opposition to the Board's racial balance policy opened the door to more conservative voices on the Board.

Citizens groups, especially in affluent areas like Chevy Chase, appealed the school reorganization, closure, and busing plans.[98] The new busing program to achieve racial balance was of particular concern to candidates Carol Wallace and Marian Greenblatt, according to Hayes:[99]

> The movement to reverse the county's integration policy is best exemplified in the meteoric rise to dominance of Marian Greenblatt and the conservative coalition on the school board.[100]

Greenblatt was a 34-year-old doctoral candidate at the University of Maryland, and she ran a campaign in 1976 as a conservative who pledged to save neighborhood schools.[101] Voters ultimately elected the conservative Greenblatt along with two liberal candidates, Daryl Shaw, EdD, and Blair Ewing, PhD. The 1976–1978 MCPS Board of Education, thus, still leaned left and would be supportive to Bernardo. Still, while Greenblatt was not able to sway policy as a solitary conservative voice on the seven-member board during her first two years, the door was opened for an election in fall 1978 that would alter the balance of power in MCPS.

"Social Workers with Guns"

While Bernardo was busy working with his Board of Education to reorganize the schools, di Grazia had quickly jumped into reforming the Montgomery County police force and was getting crossways with the unions, just as he had in St. Louis County and Boston. By 1978, less than two years into his contract, di Grazia was embroiled in battles with the unions. Using his familiar "whiz kid" staffing approach, di Grazia angered the rank-and-file officers by placing civilians in key posts. He instituted a major reorganization of the department, merging divisions and redefining ranks. He suggested ending the department's traditional four-day week, in part to put more officers on the streets during peak crime hours, thus increasing the risks and pressures of the job. As he assessed the budget, di Grazia declared a moratorium on promotions and fired high ranking officers.

Reform challenges the status quo, and that alone may have upset the established bureaucracy of the Montgomery County police force. Di Grazia, though, added fuel by his tendency to respond through the media and public proclamations. As one newspaper account at the time described it, "Di Grazia seems bent on winning attention by accepting all sorts of speaking requests, whether it be the Rockville Jewish Community Coffeehouse or the Harvard University Institute of Politics."[102]

While di Grazia had also drawn the ire of the union in Boston, his reform efforts tended to garner public acceptance and even attracted suggestions of a mayoral bid. In Montgomery County, on the other hand, his public persona did not lead to mayoral insinuations. Rather, the media scrutiny implied his job was in jeopardy. Di Grazia's view of the police role did not align well with that of the traditional rank-and-file officers, and his quotes never ceased to get media attention.

Serious crimes, said di Grazia, are the products of "poverty, unemployment, broken homes, rotten education, drug addictions . . . and other social and economic ills about which the police can do little, if anything."[103]

His philosophy was embodied by the quote, "Police officers are social workers with guns strapped to the sides."[104]

"Police have been spoon-fed honey," he told *People Magazine*. "And people aren't being honest with them about the problems. People are going to expect more and more from us as a service delivery organization, and we're not going to be able to get by with the macho cops-and-robbers bit anymore."[105]

In an interview for this book, just weeks before he died at the age of 90, di Grazia recalled, "I did feel very strongly about the fact that people always look at the police as storm troopers; and they were out there really working with the people. That's what they spend most of their time with, working with the people. And they *are* social workers. But that didn't sit well with too many police officers."

Di Grazia began to generate attention in the fall of 1978, in the same place he had elevated his stature in Boston—the schools. Unlike the Boston school busing crisis, however, where an explosive situation had been thrust upon his police force to manage, in Montgomery County, di Grazia himself forcefully inserted the police into a place where they had been rather quiet since before his arrival—the local high school drug scene.

By 1978, the Monitoring the Future data revealed that 64% of seniors had used drugs in their lifetime, 59% had smoked pot, and 93% had drunk alcohol.[106] His troops were seeing the effects of this on the ground, and they were begging him to do something about it.

"The troops," said di Grazia, "came back at me saying, 'Nobody's paying attention to these kids in there.' Basically, the department members felt it was rampant and that we should do something about it."

Di Grazia saw a chance to align with the rank and file to show that "somebody in the higher ranks was listening to them." After a student overdosed on a high school front lawn and a student newspaper ran an investigative story about the ease of buying drugs during the school day, di Grazia could ignore the drug problem no longer. He chose to act, and he chose to act with a bravado that garnered national attention and unwittingly helped launch the recovery high school movement.

5
Crackdown

Bethesda-Chevy Chase High School, known as "B-CC" to the locals, opened in 1926, when Montgomery County, Maryland, celebrated its 150th year as a county. B-CC was the fourth high school to operate in Montgomery County. The first, Richard Montgomery High School, had opened in 1892 and was christened after the county's namesake, a major general in the Continental Army who died in battle invading Canada during the Revolutionary War.

Bethesda and its neighboring community of Chevy Chase touch the northwest border of Washington, DC, and Bethesda-Chevy Chase High School moved to its permanent location on Bethesda's East-West Highway in 1935. Montgomery County has since renovated B-CC several times. The remodeling project completed in 1976 expanded the size of the school to over 250,000 square feet.[1] B-CC observed its golden anniversary that year, just as the United States and Montgomery County each commemorated their bicentennials.

The enrollment at Bethesda Chevy-Chase High School by 1978 was fourteen hundred. The school grounds featured a lawn between the busy East-West Highway and the redbrick school building (see Figure 5.1). The trees had matured to create a shady oasis that attracted students during their breaks.[2] Students would congregate on the lawn to chat and play, and in the late 1970s, many might be seen smoking tobacco or pot. B-CC was following the national trends. According to alums, the school was known as much for its easily accessible drugs as it was for its academics.

Montgomery County had developed a reactive policy to handle drug use at its schools, which numbered 186 by 1978. When a student was caught with drugs, school officials would notify parents and the police, and the police would then come to the school. The policy, though, was not particularly effective. During the school years of 1976–77 and 1977–78, there were about 420 student arrests after administrators caught students with drugs and contacted police—an average of over 2 per school day.[3] School spokesperson, Kenneth Muir, told a *Washington Star* reporter that there was "at least one such reported incident a week in the county school system."[4] According to Muir, school personnel were struggling to prevent drug use on school grounds, "because students can spot you a mile away."[5]

Montgomery County Police Chief Robert di Grazia agreed that the reactive policy was ineffective. "I'm not trying to belittle [the schools] part in it," said di Grazia. "However, if we talk about 2 to 3 [arrests] per day across the whole school system, with as much drug use as there is, we're not doing anything."[6]

Salvaging a Teenage Wasteland. Andrew J. Finch, Oxford University Press. © Oxford University Press 2024.
DOI: 10.1093/oso/9780190645502.003.0005

Figure 5.1. Bethesda-Chevy Chase High School featured a lawn between the busy East-West Highway and the redbrick school building that attracted students during class breaks. In the late 1970s, many students might be seen by passersby smoking tobacco or cannabis. According to alums, the school was known as much for its easily accessible drugs as it was for its academics, and it would become ground zero for a police crackdown on drug use in the fall of 1978. This photo taken in 2013 shows a view of Bethesda Chevy Chase High School from the East-West Highway. (Source: Joliv/ Wikimedia.)

Robin de Silva, herself a Montgomery County parent, shared her experience with the growing drug problem in the DC-area at the time in an enlightening essay published by the *Washington Post* in the summer of 1977:

Children can get marijuana, LSD, barbiturates, amphetamines, and PCP on almost any junior high school campus in the area and in countless shopping center parking lots. Armed with a blend of myth, partial truth, and complete trust in their dealers, they think they know what they're buying and are always sure that they can "handle" it. One of the most popular drugs today is PCP, and psychiatrists and toxicologists are not only finding it elusive to measure, but in light of its potential for explosive manifestations, they agree that it is probably more harmful than any other drug. Finding a pattern among young chronic drug users is equally elusive. They are not the oldest, youngest, middle children; not the brightest or slowest;

not primarily from divorced or transient families, though these and other factors have been cited as causes.[7]

A newer drug of concern for youths was PCP, also known as "Angel Dust." When added to cannabis, PCP creates a product with a stronger psychoactive experience than marijuana alone. It had become a drug of choice for Montgomery County teenagers and a priority for drug enforcement. De Silva shared the story of one young PCP user:

> Susan is in the ninth grade at a junior high school in Bethesda. She began smoking PCP the summer after seventh grade. She didn't really seek it out, but she'd smoked pot, had heard bad things about acid, and, well, PCP was a hallucinogen. Just an animal tranquilizer. She smoked it on parsley or on grass that would otherwise have been mediocre. But the PCP got scary after a while. Sometimes she thought she was losing her mind, long after she'd taken it. She couldn't see straight or hold a conversation.[8]

School administrators had been doing their best to contain the not-so-secret story of teenage drug use, and they wanted people to believe they had things under control. One Rockville High School student felt the school officials there were taking the right approach. In a letter to the editor of the *Montgomery Journal* reflecting upon how Rockville administrators had handled drug use at their school "for several years," the student wrote, "By keeping the initiation of arrests internal, the administration kept publicity and controversy to a minimum while effectively dealing with the drug problem."[9]

Then, on an early-spring day in 1978, a high school girl overdosed on PCP and collapsed on the front lawn of Bethesda-Chevy Chase High School in public view. Anybody driving by the school that day on the heavily traveled road may have seen the incident as it unfolded. With an overdose in such a public space, the life-threatening potential of drug use was now on display for all to see.[10]

Local authorities responded to the incident, and according to later reports, the police department had taken note and realized that the reactive stance they had been taking toward teenage drug use on school grounds might not be sufficient. As Chief di Grazia explained, though, the police were in a bind, especially considering the wealthy and influential families attending certain schools in Montgomery County, such as B-CC.

"There was people from foreign countries, councils, and so forth," said di Grazia. "They were all in there. It was a difficult spot to try and really do something. They sort of expected us to be around, but 'don't step on the wrong toes' sort of thing."[11]

The B-CC students themselves were well aware of the drug use on campus. David Simon, who would go on to earn fame as a television producer for shows such as *The Wire*, was editor-in-chief for the student newspaper, *The Tattler*, and a senior in the spring of 1978.

"We used to say," Simon recalled in a 2012 blog post, "that [Walt] Whitman [High School] had all the national merit scholars, that the [Winston] Churchill [High School] kids had the money—as if we were ghetto, that the [Montgomery] Blair [High School] kids had the ability to kick our ass and take our lunch money. But B-CC, we argued, had the best drugs."[12]

To illustrate that last point, *The Tattler,* with Simon at the helm, sent a reporter on a mission to buy drugs during the school day (see Figure 5.2). Simon's *Tattler* "Insight" column explained the assignment:

> For curiosity's sake, we sent a reporter to roam around B-CC two weeks ago with instructions to secure up to $75 in marijuana and cocaine. While we realized that $75 is not a vast sum, it was estimated that the reporter would need at least a

Figure 5.2. David Simon, who would go on to earn fame as a television producer for shows such as *The Wire*, was editor-in-chief for the Bethesda-Chevy Chase High School student newspaper, *The Tattler*, in the spring of 1978. *The Tattler* sent a reporter on a mission to buy drugs during the school day, and Simon's story about it was later mentioned by police as being one of the catalysts for their drug raids the next fall. This is a yearbook photo of the 1977–1978 *Tattler* staff, and Simon is in the front row on the left. (Source: Ancestry.com.)

day to exhaust his cash supply. However, less than four hours later the reporter had made arrangements to purchase four "dime" bags of marijuana, two to four "nickel" bags, and two "lines" of cocaine. Ironically, the reporter could have exhausted his cash supply within the first two hours had he been searching for larger quantities of drugs. It seems that it's easier to buy dope by the ounce and cocaine by the gram. . . . It should be noted that no purchase was ever completed, since the reporter was instructed to refuse the transaction once the deal had been arranged. Most importantly, every one of these "purchases" occurred on school grounds. Three of them took place in hallways and bathrooms and one, involving cocaine, in a classroom.[13]

Simon added that the reporter himself was not "especially familiar with the 'drug culture' at B-CC," and the transactions came from four separate sources. His article goes on to detail how easy it was to purchase liquor as an under-age person in the local community as well.[14]

The article closed by quoting an unnamed senior, who essentially called out the police for overlooking teenage drug usage.

"I've been picked up twice for beer, and twice for dope, but the [police] never busted me. I guess they didn't want to be hassled. Each time they take your name, in case they catch you again."[15]

The benign warnings were about to cease. The overdose on the front lawn of the school earlier that spring and *The Tattler's* undercover reporting served as a call to arms for local police. Captain Ralph Robertson was head of the Bethesda station of the Montgomery County Police Department. He claimed that police began looking into drug use at B-CC in part because of these two incidents.

"All you have to do is ride down East-West highway [B-CC's location] and you can see kids smoking dope" on school grounds, Robertson said at the time.[16]

The police department thus decided to take control of the situation and began devising a scheme to catch students in possession of or distributing drugs on or near school grounds during the school day. An anonymous source told the *Montgomery Journal* that County Executive Gleason met with police over the summer to ask about student drug use, and he was informed at that time of di Grazia's plan.[17]

"The troops were saying, 'That stuff's gone crazy in these high schools. Nobody's paying attention to these kids in there,' said di Grazia. So, we talked a little bit to the different principals and vice principals, and we said what we were going to do. And they said, 'Go ahead.' "[18]

"So, we did."

Their plan was designed over the summer, but they had to wait until fall to act. On September 5, 1978, the day after Labor Day, the fourteen hundred students at Bethesda Chevy-Chase headed back to school. Unbeknownst to them, during the second week of the fall semester, plainclothes police officers started patrolling the grounds outside B-CC, looking for suspicious drug use activity. While the officers did not notice much overt use of other drugs, they did see "open and blatant use" of marijuana.[19]

Maureen Dowd, who would win the Pulitzer Prize as an op-ed writer for the *New York Times* in 1999, was a young staff reporter for the *Washington Star* in 1978 (see Figure 5.3). Chief di Grazia had informed the media that the police would be enforcing alcohol and drug laws for minors, and he told Dowd, "We're placing the schools under strict surveillance to see what's going on and to make arrests when we see what's occurring."[20]

The week of covert investigation was enough to learn where to target their plan, and during the third week of the school year, on Monday, September 18, the Bethesda police officers launched the first drug raid in a massive operation that would last almost four months.

Figure 5.3. Maureen Dowd, who would win the Pulitzer Prize as a writer for the *New York Times* in 1999, began her career in journalism with the *Washington Star*, where she worked as an editorial assistant and later as a metropolitan reporter. Dowd was assigned to cover the Montgomery County high school drug raids and filed several stories about the crackdown in 1978. (Source: Janet Fries /Hulton Archive/Getty Images.)

Outside the school, at 7:50 a.m., before the start of classes that Monday, officers from the Bethesda police station saw a 15-year boy give marijuana to a 15-year-old girl, and the officers arrested both students without much fanfare, one for possession and another for distribution.[21] The arrests garnered such little attention that other students still chose to keep their drugs on school property during the day.

Then, shortly after noon, seven members of the Montgomery County police tactical squad, dressed in civilian clothes, stormed the tree-shaded lawn between B-CC and the East-West Highway and arrested six more students, five on possession charges and one for hindering a police officer trying to make an arrest. One of the arresting officers, Randy Crittenden, told reporters that marijuana possession that day was so widespread and obvious that "we didn't have enough manpower to clear out the whole school yard."[22]

The students arrested for possession and distribution were all 15 or 16 years old. One 18-year-old was arrested for trying to interfere with the arrests, and because he was legally an adult, his name was printed in the local paper the next day.[23] The youths were handcuffed in front of their peers, taken away to the district police station, booked on a misdemeanor citation, and then released into parental custody to await a court hearing. The seven students arrested on drug charges were later given three-day suspensions, while the student charged with interfering with police was not disciplined by the school.[24]

Some students claimed the police had been unnecessarily forceful in apprehending their classmates. Students maintained that one of the arrested students was peacefully drawing a picture on a bench when police grabbed him by the neck and threw him to the ground.[25] Another student asserted police "grabbed a student and rammed him against a car before arresting him."[26] Angry students protested by walking out into the East-West Highway to stop traffic, chanting, "No narcs!!" About fifty students actually walked the short distance to the Bethesda police station and hung out while their classmates were processed. Later, a few students held a sit-in on the school lawn. While students did not deny their friends had been using drugs on school property, they felt violated by how the police had invaded their space.[27]

Police spokesperson Nancy Moses told reporters that the students were exaggerating the use of force, saying, "I think you're experiencing middle-class kids being arrested for the first time."[28]

Police Chief di Grazia had anticipated student unrest, and, in fact, one of his goals was to make students scared and uncomfortable. The chief laid out his plans to reporters after the raid, saying he had given each of the four district police captains discretion in how to carry out the plan.[29] He instructed the media to foster the narrative of an intense police presence in the schools.

"Say we have 500 officers working undercover in the schools," said di Grazia. "If the kids believe that, they'll be afraid to do anything."[30]

He also emphasized this was only the beginning, calling the Monday raid on B-CC just the "opening thrust against the teen-age drug scene."[31]

B-CC was just one of twenty-two high schools in the Montgomery County Public Schools district in 1978. According to Captain Robertson, the initial investigation had included one other high school and a junior high, both unnamed, and the police intended to expand the search across "all other secondary schools in the district."[32]

To this point, standard procedure had been for school administrators to notify parents and police first if a student had been caught with drugs on school grounds. The shift this time was that even though Chief di Grazia said he had gotten approval from school administrators for their plan, B-CC Principal, F. Thornton Lauriat, told reporters, "he and other school officials were not notified of the arrests" before the Monday raid. This had allowed police to maintain an element of surprise.[33]

Chief di Grazia confirmed that the B-CC principal had been kept in the dark regarding timing of the raid. "We were concerned about the principals and vice principals not being with us all the way. So, we thought it was best not to let them know we're coming. We were hidden because of the fact that maybe they would warn and be ready for us so that we didn't look good." He asserted there was no pattern to the raids.[34]

Principal Lauriat also told the *Washington Post*, "I don't think drugs are any more or less a problem here than in any other high school. Our high school just has more visibility than other high schools because of its location and because several years ago this school got the reputation as having a drug culture. That past image may still be hanging around."[35]

The next day, police continued observing the school, patrolling the grounds in civilian clothes and even watching the school through binoculars from a building across the street from the school. No arrests were made at B-CC, as students reportedly refrained from smoking pot on campus. As one student told a reporter, "A lot of people went off the grounds to get high. A lot of them said they aren't going to party at school anymore."[36]

The drug crackdown did continue elsewhere, however, and school staff asserted the interventions would not be conducted exclusively through covert raids. School administrators could still employ the traditional strategy of reporting drug use to police themselves, and that is just what they did on September 19 at Winston Churchill High School, which was about fifteen minutes northwest of B-CC in Potomac, located in the Rockville police district. The administration notified the police that three fifteen-year-old sophomore girls were smoking marijuana outside the school. Police responded by arresting the girls and taking them to the Rockville station, where they stayed until their parents picked them up.[37] Then, on Wednesday, Rockville police arrested a student at the Mark Twain alternative school in Rockville. That brought the total to twelve arrests in three days.

Police from the Wheaton-Glenmont district, in the eastern part of the county, made their first arrests of the crackdown on Thursday at two different locations. Starting early in the morning, officers arrested four Wheaton High School students at 8:45 a.m. for possession on public property adjacent to the high school. Four hours later, Wheaton-Glenmont officers took nine students into custody for marijuana possession during lunch at Albert Einstein High School in Kensington. Like the B-CC raids on Monday, the Einstein principal, Allan Harper, told reporters that police had not notified him ahead of time. He also said they did not enter the school.[38]

Police also served notice on Thursday that their strategy would not be contained to high schools. Undercover police from the Silver Spring district were patrolling White Oak Junior High School, when a hall monitor was tipped off about their presence. They were not able to make the arrest this time, but the next day Silver Spring officers targeted another junior high, this time Eastern Junior High, where they nabbed four girls close to the school—the first arrests of the crackdown in their district.[39]

The Friday sweep covered all four police precincts, and most of the arrests took place off school grounds. Apparently aware that many students were simply moving off-campus to use, officers from the Bethesda district swept through the woods near B-CC on Friday to arrest five students. Silver Spring officers picked up a 16-year-old Springbrook High School girl outside school property. Rockville police struck off-campus twice, targeting a park close to the county's flagship Richard Montgomery High School, and arresting seven students—two at 11:00 a.m. and five at 3:00 p.m. And Wheaton-Glenmont police arrested a male student from Albert Einstein High School. The boy had been one of the nine students caught at school on Thursday, and just one day later, he was arrested for smoking pot just off school grounds.[40]

With nearly twenty arrests on Friday, the first week of the Montgomery County drug crackdown had come to a close. Chief di Grazia's police department had sent a bold message to the community, and one pattern that had emerged was that police were picking up students either at school or at hangouts near the school where students would "party."[41]

Otherwise, the attack showed no bounds. Officers had struck schools in all four police districts. They had made forty-three arrests from high schools, a junior high school, and an alternative high school . . . both off-campus and on-campus . . . and both minors and a legal adult. They arrived both under-cover and in response to calls from administrators.

"We want to instill a little paranoia in these kids," di Grazia had said when the raids began. "So that they don't know when or where it will happen next."[42]

And it appeared as though di Grazia's "opening thrust," as he called it, had accomplished that goal.[43] One sophomore girl from the academically elite Walt Whitman High School in Bethesda told the *Washington Star*, "It was pretty much of a shocker. A lot of us are scared. It's made us more careful."[44]

The prior week's raids were featured prominently in the Sunday papers, including an article by Calvin Zon in the *Washington Star* with the headline, "Paranoia Replaces Partying After Undercover Police Raids: Montgomery's Week of the Big Drug Bust." Chief di Grazia's plan was creating a reaction across the county. One senior at Walt Whitman was quoted as saying, "Everyone's expecting it here very soon."[45]

Walt Whitman's grounds featured an area called "The Hill" where students usually gathered to "party" by smoking pot, and one student noted during the first week of raids, "There aren't many people up here today. And not many are skipping classes."[46]

On Monday, September 25, the police picked the bust up where they had left off on Friday, arresting ten students across three new high schools, Damascus and Seneca Valley in the northern, less populated region of the county, as well as Montgomery Blair in Silver Spring. Tuesday brought a dozen more, as police arrested twelve students in the Gaithersburg High School parking lot.[47] At the time, Gaithersburg was still mostly rural, as the county was just beginning to suburbanize.[48]

While police were making their first arrests at Gaithersburg High School—the second oldest school in the county—Chief di Grazia was meeting with County Executive James Gleason, Superintendent Charles Bernardo, and the Board of Education president, Elizabeth Spencer. They all agreed in principle with the strong-armed nature of the intervention. Bernardo, who had once been a police officer himself, issued a memo to school principals that stated, "I encourage all principals to continue our joint efforts with police officials. Student leaders particularly need to be informed about the law that the school is not a sanctuary."[49]

After the first week of raids, it appeared as though most school leaders and county executives were aligned with the police department's aggressive approach to stopping drug use at school by students. Once arrested, a student's case was sent to the intake office of the Maryland Department of Juvenile Services. Juvenile Services would then hold a conference with the student, the student's parents, and an attorney. This conference would determine whether the student's case would go on to Juvenile Court. Most students arrested for possession would receive family counseling or community service instead of a court hearing unless the youth was charged with distribution. Maryland officials in the 1970s considered drug and alcohol use to be a "social problem better treated by social agencies rather than law enforcement agencies." This suggests why Montgomery County would seriously consider finding a way for schools to create new programs to address the youth drug problem.[50]

The leaders agreed that the strain placed on law enforcement resources along with the disruption of the school climate were not things they wanted to embrace as a permanent solution. During the meeting, the county leaders agreed on a framework to eventually phase out the raids and take the following measures to prevent further problems:

- Training school monitors to identify illegal substances and serve as trusting referral sources for students with drug problems;
- Increasing drug education classes in early grades to shape attitudes before junior high;
- Using the PTA for parent education;
- Making sure the arrested teens were enrolled in drug education programs;
- Holding meetings between school officials and student leaders to create peer pressure discouraging drug use on campus.[51]

After the media reported on the meeting and the planned phase out of the drug raids, "scores of angry parents called the offices of the county executive and the chief of police" demanding the raids continue.[52] In fact, no time line had been set as to when to stop the raids, and they continued unabated.

After seven days of busts, police had not yet targeted the largest high school in the county. Walt Whitman High School, located in the wealthy area of Bethesda, enrolled about two thousand students, and it was known as a strong academic school. Whitman and its prominent "Hill" had avoided the crackdown so far, which helps explain why so many students chose to openly smoke weed outside during lunch on Wednesday, September 27, despite the prior week's events.[53]

Whitman shared its Hill with the former Whittier Woods Elementary School, which had been converted into administrative offices. That morning, painters had arrived at Whittier, which likely escaped the notice of the teenagers. These painters, though, were police in disguise, and they were actually there to spy on the students. Once students started "partying" at lunch, the police converged on their space. According to one news account, some of the police arrived on motorcycles.[54]

As the seen unfolded, student shock transformed into rage. The *Washington Star* reported that one girl threw a punch at a female officer, knocking her off her motorcycle.[55] Police went about their business, arresting eight boys and three girls, all aged 15 or 16. And during this raid, officers found not only marijuana but also LSD on students.

The Whitman bust instigated an uprising. About 300 students walked out of school after lunch, and they launched a protest that would last three hours. School officials urged students to go back to class, but the students refused to do so. The student protesters blocked traffic on Whittier Boulevard, one of the main thoroughfares near the school. They occupied the area through dismissal and pickup at the school, sitting or standing in the street, and not allowing buses or parents in cars to pass. They blocked the road with garbage cans and dumped bags of lawn clippings in the street.[56] According to one news account, "some in the crowd smoked marijuana and drank beer in defiance of police."[57]

At one point, a woman tried to drive through the crowd of students and knocked a couple out of her way.[58] The crowd finally dispersed around 3:30 in the afternoon. Interestingly, police chose to monitor the protest at a distance but not to intervene, as they felt their presence would make matters worse due to student anger about the police raiding their schools.[59] As the Whitman Student Government Association (SGA) president said, "You could say there's a strong feeling of resentment towards the police."[60]

The following week, the *Washington Star* published a letter from a person claiming to be the father of one of the girls arrested at Whitman that day, and he pointed out "several errors in your reporting of the case."[61] He wrote that the three girls arrested at Whitman were "in no way involved with the group of boys who apparently were smoking marijuana. The girls were seated in a separate group, some three or four feet away from the boys, who were seated in a large circle, facing each other." They were part of a larger gathering of some fifty or sixty people on the Hill. He wrote that the protest was triggered in part by "anger over the arrest of the innocent girls," and not because of the presence of police on campus.

The parent also explained a law known as "constructive possession," which allowed people to be convicted if they were "construed to be in possession" due to proximity to smokers—he called it "Guilt by Proximity." The idea was that students could be charged if they were close enough to have immediate access to a substance. In fact, many of the students arrested during the raids, though it is unclear how many, would be charged with constructive possession. While the parent clarified that he supported the raids and thought the Whitman action "was long overdue," he felt the problem was that "innocent people are sometimes swept up with the guilty in the enthusiasm of the moment."[62] The *Montgomery Journal* interviewed students about their knowledge of the constructive possession law. The paper claimed the "constructive possession charge was fairly widely understood by youth a decade ago" (i.e., the late 1960s), but quoted a student named Richard Montgomery as saying, "This generation which has never before been prosecuted for drugs never heard of it."[63]

September 27 was one of the most ambitious days of the busts. In total, schools in all four police districts were targeted, including three high schools and one middle school. In addition to the eleven students nabbed at Whitman High School, four students from Seneca Valley High School in Germantown and four from Sherwood High School in Sandy Spring were arrested for marijuana position.[64] The Seneca Valley students were also charged for cocaine possession, which was the first time a student was charged with possessing something other than marijuana. The day also featured the second Junior High raid. The prior week, police had been thwarted in a bust at White Oak Junior High when students were tipped off about their presence, so they returned on Wednesday, nabbing four boys and a girl for marijuana possession. One of the boys was carrying a concealed knife, and he picked up an additional charge for that. The total of twenty-four arrests in one day would remain the largest single daily tally of the raids. Police returned to Seneca Valley High School on Thursday to arrest two more students on marijuana charges, bringing the overall total to ninety-three arrests across fifteen high schools and junior highs.[65]

There had not been a day without a raid since the crackdown began on September 18, and after they reached a crescendo with the two dozen arrests in one day, it appeared the busts were having the desired effect. The Magruder High School student government president told a reporter, "[Students] are becoming very paranoid . . . very suspicious of persons coming from outside the school." And a B-CC student was quoted as saying, "People are afraid. They wouldn't even bring rolling papers to school anymore."[66]

Then, on Friday, September 29, Superintendent Charles Bernardo did something extraordinary. For the first time since taking office over three years earlier, Bernardo hosted a meeting with almost all the student leaders from the county's junior and senior high schools. The meeting lasted ninety minutes, after which "students mobbed him with questions after the formal meeting broke up."[67]

Jeannette Belliveau, who reported on the meeting for the *Montgomery Journal*, interpreted the meeting as part of the effort to exert peer pressure to stop drug use at schools. She wrote that leaders from two high schools that had not been raided yet (Robert E. Peary and Charles Woodward) supported the drug raids, while leaders from Walt Whitman, B-CC, John F. Kennedy and Thomas Sprigg Wootton High Schools voiced "substantial opposition."[68]

The Peary High School SGA president said, "We feel it's been a long time coming but is just the tip of the iceberg. The students who have been arrested should be prosecuted to the full extent of the law."[69]

Representing the opposing view, the SGA president at Walt Whitman High School—site of eleven arrests just forty-eight hours before—said, "The Whitman SGA takes a strong position against the arrests. While the school is not a sanctuary, it is also not a place for police . . . While the use of drugs on school grounds may be antagonistic to education, so is the presence of police."[70]

If the goal was in fact to get student leaders to pressure their classmates to stop using drugs at school, some of the class presidents felt that would not work. Wootton's SGA president, said, "Standing on a moral soapbox isn't going to do any good. The credibility of the SGA would go down the drain. A large percentage of the students [who do not use drugs themselves] are sympathetic to the drug users."[71]

Upon reflection, one student was particularly prescient. The editor of the Poolesville High School student newspaper presaged later criticisms of school-based anti-drug programs, complaining about drug education films, which along with peer pressure had been another tactic suggested by the county leadership. She described the films as "gory and rather than scare kids away from drug use, it may make it look more exciting."[72]

Instead, the Poolesville student newspaper editor recommended having ex-drug addicts go into schools to speak of their experience. Bernardo seemed to shoot down such an approach by recalling that when he was in Providence, some ex-addicts attempted to deal drugs during their visits. Still, having students in recovery visit schools was something that would later become a prominent feature of the Phoenix recovery high school program.[73]

Following the meeting, Bernardo said the plan for after the raids included stronger anti-drug education and referrals for help, but "I am grasping at what the ultimate solution is."[74]

David Naimon, the first-ever student representative on the MCPS Board of Education, had been working with Superintendent Bernardo since the beginning of the school year, and he summarized the student views as a set of "competing values—the disruption of drugs or the disruption of police."[75]

Bernardo seemed to have grasped the student mentality, saying, "Even if it is not a successful effort, it is not a loss. Even if I learn I'm being unrealistic, it's a very important accomplishment."[76]

"No," he said, "I was very pleased and encouraged by the results of the meeting. I do understand the sensitivities . . . There's an awful lot of pressure on these youngsters to represent opposing points of view."[77]

The Beat Goes On

Whatever people may have hoped for as an outcome of the meeting between the student leaders and the superintendent, the police crackdown did not subside. Day after day, more police would arrive at schools and more students would be cited for drug possession. While most of the arrests continued to involve cannabis, occasionally there would be variety, such as Friday, October 6, when twelve students were arrested near Thomas W. Pyle Junior High in Bethesda—five girls and seven boys, all of them 13 or 14 years old. This time, police seized both marijuana and LSD. By the end of the third week of the crackdown, 129 students had been arrested.[78]

With no end in sight, ideological battle lines were drawn. Reporter Calvin Zon wrote that the issue had shaped into "a battle between the generations reminiscent of student rebellions in the late 1960s and early 1970s."[79] During that time about a decade earlier, a volunteer organization called the Drug Action Coalition had been created to provide drug education. Mary Drury, head of the organization, recalled that concerns about the drugs in the early 1970s had "withered," and she hoped that would not happen again.[80]

"Kids are not going to change unless the whole community owns up to the role of drugs in our lives and the home environment changes," said Drury. "It's not just how they use illegal drugs but how we use illegal drugs."[81]

Indeed, the community was now embroiled in a debate taken up on two fronts: teenage drug use and the use of force by the police to stop it. For some, the critical issue was whether adolescents should use drugs at all, and, if so, whether school was an appropriate place to do so. For those that felt teenagers should not use drugs, or at least not at school, the discussion centered on whether the police tactics were warranted. Everyone, including the police, seemed to agree that the raids had to end eventually, but what should replace the raids was a mystery. The environment was ripe for innovation, but it would take months for a solution to emerge. In the meantime, tempers flared, and the raids continued.

Parents initially responded in support of the raids. One parent told the *Washington Star*, students "should realize that it's not legal and that if they participate in it, they're going to get locked up. Maybe they think it's fun and games, but they should know that they may find themselves on the wrong side of the law. They complain that the police were a little rough, but it's a rough world out there."[82]

Calvin Zon reported that when the raids began, di Grazia had received "nearly a hundred supportive telephone calls from parents and school personnel."[83]

Parents and teachers also were targets of blame. A *Washington Star* editorial pointed a finger at "parents reluctant to function as parents, or who can't find the time; teachers hesitant to enforce the discipline which is the basis of education; teenagers heedlessly—but predictably and naturally—exploiting the great loosening in social structure that results."[84]

The students, however, thought police should have better things to do. One senior said, "They treat us like we're criminals or something. We're no worse than people drinking underage at bars. It's just ridiculous. It makes me sick. For us, [cannabis] is a part of our daily lives—just like our parents who come home and have a cocktail. I don't want to have to hide it. It just makes you resent the system even more. The nickname, 'pig,' now you know where it comes from. There are lots of burglaries in my neighborhood I wish they'd take care of instead. It won't stop anything—Prohibition is a perfect example. It just causes a lot of needless tension."[85]

One Whitman High School student said, "If we can party and keep our scholastics up too, why do they bother us?"[86]

Students, however, were not united in their opposition to the raids or in their acceptance of drug use. One Einstein High School student called B-CC students "spoiled brats," saying, "They are rich kids who didn't like getting arrested." A B-CC junior added about their classmates, "If they were stupid enough to smoke on the front lawn, they deserved to be arrested."[87]

Interestingly, even though one of the Juvenile Services offices indicated preferring prevention programs and increasing the number of counselors, Superintendent Bernardo was quoted in the *Montgomery Journal* as saying, "While I believe in preventive education, I support arrests as the law is being violated. The schools can and do refer [drug users already]. The use of marijuana on school grounds sets a poor example in that it is a flagrant violation of law. The effects as I have observed them preclude the student from maximum growth in relation to potential. Good students get high on learning—not on pot!"[88]

Superintendent Bernardo added his support of di Grazia, "The chief of police, being the father of, I believe, five students in the school system, as a good citizen . . . decided to move. He acted as a competent, conscientious police officer."[89]

County Executive James P. Gleason voiced support for Chief di Grazia's intervention, but he also said, "I don't think it's a healthy situation for police to do permanent surveillance of school environments."[90]

As the debate played out in the media, there were reports of disunity among school administrators. According to reporter Belliveau, "Some school assistant principals felt their educational duties were a higher priority than inspecting school grounds for drug users."[91] This focus on academics over the crackdown prompted parents to telephone the central office, asking Superintendent Bernardo to force principals to enforce drug rules. Parents had also called the county executive and chief of police offices with their demands.

On Thursday, October 5, Superintendent Bernardo "hastily called" a press conference at the central office in Rockville to address the rumored dissent. Bernardo lined up behind the police, saying the drug raids were "needed and welcome."[92] Bernardo then presented his own hardline stance, announcing a new program to include a one-year suspension for selling drugs at school, after a school system hearing separate from a juvenile court hearing.[93] He also was going to allow stiffer penalties than the existing three-day suspension for possession or use. Going further, Bernardo proclaimed the expulsion policy would "apply retroactively to all students arrested this school year for distribution."[94]

In addition to the harsher punishments, Bernardo would implement a new seven-point plan that matched a one-year-old anti-drug program that Northwood High School principal Bobby Mullis had recently presented to Chief di Grazia. Northwood had been enrolling students with drug problems in a drug counseling program run by the nonprofit Guide, Inc., started by Catholic University.[95] Guide provided therapy for drug users and their families. Five MCPS schools (Northwood, Seneca Valley, Magruder, Gaithersburg High. and Gaithersburg Junior High) were using Guide's services. In all, the seven-point program included the following:

1. Drug education in science classes, emphasizing dangers of PCP and MJ;
2. Intensified drug education in elementary schools;
3. Counseling;
4. Training for school monitors;
5. Staff meetings on drug abuse;
6. Warnings on consequences for drug use;
7. Parent drug course/education.[96]

Principal Mullis said, "I've seen so many kids ruin their lives on drugs. It just bothers me. I've seen them become psychologically addicted so that school, their boyfriend, their girlfriend, is not important. Only the pot is important. I'm determined to do something about it."[97] At one time, Mullis had even sent a letter to former presidential advisor Peter Bourne opposing the Carter Administration push for decriminalization of cannabis.

Bernardo told the press he felt the raids had caused administrators to take a closer look at the drug problem. He also asserted that the district administrators were in alignment. Bernardo claimed he had taken a vote of all twenty-two high school principals, and they each had supported strict application of existing rules, which included expulsion for drug offenses.[98]

On the other side of the divide, student leaders had met the previous week and passed a resolution calling for an end to the drug raids. A senior at John F. Kennedy High School, Phil Erh, president of the Montgomery County Region of the Maryland Association of Student Councils, said the resolution was approved by the executive board by a 14-0 vote.[99] The Peary High School SGA president—the same student who had suggested in the September 29 meeting with Superintendent Bernardo that arrested students should be prosecuted to the full extent of the law—abstained. The student resolution advanced to the sixty-delegate General Assembly for a vote on October 12; it requested ending the raids and emphasizing drug education. The students also requested a meeting with Chief di Grazia and Superintendent Bernardo.

"It's a small minority that smoke on school grounds during school hours," President Erh acknowledged, "But the arrests create a disturbance for the vast majority of students."[100]

And the disturbances continued into a fifth week. On October 10, eight students—four boys and four girls—were arrested at Einstein High School in Kensington. One of the students had two previous arrests, and all were charged with marijuana possession. On the same day, near Northwood High School in Silver Spring (where Principal Mullis had implemented the seven-point exemplar program), three students were arrested on marijuana charges. One was 18 and charged as an adult.[101]

Also on October 10, the student member of the MCPS Board of Education, David Naimon, presented questions and concerns on behalf of his classmates in a memorandum to Superintendent Bernardo.[102] Bernardo responded with an indication that students caught distributing drugs would be expelled no matter what the drug.

"I share your concern for the long-term welfare of the student expelled for distribution of drugs," wrote Bernardo. "However, the destructive effect on the total school caused by the introduction of drugs into the school environment is of greater concern to me. By such ruinous behavior, the distributor of drugs forfeits his place in the normal school setting. My anguish over the problem of drug abuse among our students is real, and my strategies for coping with this problem are not intended to be precipitous or to grab headlines."[103]

If Bernardo thought the threat of expulsion would bring an end to drug use on school grounds, and thus wind down the raids, he was mistaken. The next day, at the monthly convention of the Montgomery County Region (MCR) of the Maryland Student Government Association, the county's high school student leaders passed the resolution opposing "police initiated drug arrests on campus," but also "strongly condemned the use of drugs on campus."[104] The vote to halt arrests, however, was a divided one.[105] The Maryland Association of Student Councils also planned to meet on Friday, October 20, in Columbia, Maryland, to develop a proposal "in favor of decriminalizing private use of marijuana."[106]

Police nabbed thirteen students at Paint Branch High School in Burtonsville on Friday the Thirteenth, the largest haul at one school in the four weeks of raids. And while marijuana possession was still the most common citation, other drugs, like PCP, were becoming more frequent, and students were arming themselves. It is not clear if the drug raids themselves had prompted more students to come to school armed, or if students had been bringing weapons all along and were now being discovered due to increased police presence. What is certain was that several students were cited for bringing armaments to school along with violence toward officers. A 16-year-old girl carrying a knife was charged with assault and battery on a police officer at Sherwood High School in Sandy Spring on October 19. That week alone, police charged teens with carrying many concealed weapons, such as a sawed-off shotgun, a .22-caliber rifle, a 16-gauge shotgun, a knife, and brass knuckles.[107]

Students were also continuing to protest. Even though the largest raid on Friday the Thirteenth occurred at Paint Branch High School, a demonstration had been planned for a different site. About ten-to-twenty "chanting, sign-carrying picketers" from several schools protested during the school day at Montgomery Blair High School in Silver Spring.[108] During lunch, many students who did not march watched from a grassy hill in front of the school. The principal had warned students that anyone skipping class to join the protest would be suspended, and one student was quoted as saying the threat had put "a damper" on the demonstration.[109] Apparently, flyers announcing the protest had been circulated across the county, and the intention was "general opposition to campus drug raids by casual clothes police."[110] In response, uniformed police patrolled the school grounds in their cars in case the protest got out of hand. It did not, but the tensions were continuing to escalate.

As the raids continued through a fifth week, the arrest total climbed to 215, and student unrest erupted in violence at the beginning of week six. On Monday, October 23, nine students were caught and charged with marijuana possession. Two boys and four girls were arrested at a playground at Whittier Woods Elementary School near Walt Whitman High School in Bethesda. Four of the students actually attended a private school, the Chautauqua School, in Glen Echo, and the arrests prompted an hour-long demonstration by about one hundred Whitman students, according to police spokesperson Nancy Moses. During the protest, students reportedly hurled rocks at police cars, which was reminiscent of the earlier outburst on the Whitman campus in September.[111]

Soon after the October Whitman protest, an editorial appeared in the *Washington Star* that provided an unflattering view of Montgomery County families and suggested the police raids were not going far enough:[112]

> For ours is the 'Me Decade' according to Tom Wolfe, America's foremost historian. It is the decade in which Montgomery County parents are pursuing the dream of Me . . . The emphasis . . . is Me—My space, My thing, My desires, My head. It is as if Montgomery County . . . had begun to revolve slowly around its own golden navel. Montgomery County children are mostly not the children of missionaries, or social workers helping the indigent, or teachers taking low-paying jobs to work with the disadvantaged. Rather they are the children of professionals whose decisions have often centered on maximizing their personal income, of government workers often doing non-jobs behind a protective Civil Service fence, of government contractors whose frequently shoddy products are hidden behind the grasping for the next contract. . . , Using police to chase the students around the lawn at lunchtime is a very limited response.[113]

By the end of the sixth week of drug raids, the student arrest total had reached 251. That week, police were active in all four districts and cast a broad net, charging students from a private school, two alternative schools in Rockville—Mark Twain and Gateway—and two junior high schools. Then, suddenly, the raids ceased. There were no arrests reported for four consecutive school days; the longest dry spell since they had begun in September.

Into the midst of the calm came a major protest on Halloween Day, instigated not by students but by adults. Jeannette Belliveau had reported in mid-October on the front page of the *Montgomery Journal* that a flyer was "being distributed in Bethesda area high schools and record shops" calling for a student protest on Halloween Day.[114] Belliveau described the bill as "reminiscent of the counterculture confrontations of the late 1960s."[115] The event was called the "Chief di Grazia Memorial Smoke-In," and the flyer asked people to bring "friends, pot, signs" and papier-mache props such as marijuana joints. The smoke-in was scheduled for October 31 at 3:00 p.m. in front of the Bethesda District Police Station and was to be preceded by a protest at 1:00 p.m.

The group distributing the flyer called itself the "Rockville Yippie People's Reefer Party." Yippie stood for the "Youth International Party," a counterculture movement founded in the late 1960s by Abbie Hoffman, among others.[116] Two people were seen passing out the papers, and they were described as a man "with long, dark hair and a full beard who wears the saffron-colored robes associated with the Hare Krishna cult," and "a young woman, perhaps a student, with long, unruly red hair wearing a faded denim halter top and jeans." According to the newspaper account, the man "came to B-CC High at lunchtime and was asked to leave by B-CC principal Thornton Lauriat and a policeman."[117]

The demonstration occurred as advertised in front of the Bethesda district police station, and Montgomery County had never experienced anything quite like it. As Belliveau recounted, the county had "remained a relative oasis" in the years when college students marched, and people flocked to DC to protest the Vietnam War, President Richard Nixon, and other causes. It was thus notable when fifty five people "chanted and carried signs" as a prelude to a drug "smoke-in" named in honor of the reigning police chief.[118] As Belliveau wrote, the demonstration was "something of a watershed . . . Montgomery County's first big youth protest."[119]

According to news accounts, two Yippies in their mid-20s, Rupert Chappelle and Leatrice Urbanowicz, led the crowd. They were presumably the same couple distributing flyers in the school two weeks earlier.[120] Chappelle had "bushy black hair and a beard" and wore a "knee-length white robe and a Yippie button." Urbanowicz, his roommate, described herself as an "on-again, off-again pre-med student"; [she] had "long red hair and freckles." Urbanowicz brought her three-year-old son to the event, with "red-designs painted on his face." Like his mom, the child had long red hair, and during the protest, he "pretended to smoke an eighteen-inch-long papier-mache marijuana joint."[121] Chappelle had developed a following as a musician, playing "ozone music" at Montgomery College in Rockville.[122]

Protesters marched for hours, carrying signs with slogans such as "Free the Weed" and "Narcs Out of Our Lives." Chappelle spoke against laws prohibiting marijuana, "Refined sugar is a drug. It smashes your body. It's not illegal to be wired on caffeine, and people are drunk all the time." A 14-year-old junior high school student was quoted as saying he attended the smoke-in because he "respected the reason for the gathering," and he periodically screamed, "Marijuana!"[123]

After about two hours, police officers in riot gear confronted the protesters and asked the crowd to leave the grounds of the Bethesda police station. The protesters then went across the street and "gathered in front of a statue of a pioneer woman beside the Bethesda post office." About eighteen police officers tracked the demonstrators, who marched up the road and back to the statue, and at 4:00 p.m., three hours into the event, they arrested the "Yippie leaders," Chappelle and Urbanowicz. Urbanowicz "was carried into the station house carrying her screaming three-year-old son." The police were able to disperse the crowd before the marijuana smoke-in began, and the newspaper reported "only two pipes of pot had been lit by the time police began attempting to clear the area." Police eventually arrested nine adults and eighteen juveniles, with charges including loitering, disturbing the peace, carrying a concealed weapon, and marijuana possession.[124]

While the Halloween arrests were not technically part of the school raids, the crackdown began again with three arrests the next day, and one of the most violent episodes erupted on November 2. Once again, the site was the academically elite Walt Whitman High School in Bethesda. Five students were arrested on marijuana charges in a wooded area near the school around lunch time, which "triggered an angry confrontation during which students threw rocks at arresting officers, who were forced to radio for reinforcements."[125] Students on their lunch hour then surrounded the officers, who radioed for help, and "more than a dozen squad cars rushed to the scene."[126]

Police arrived at this protest in riot gear, and as the students began to move toward the street, the police pushed them back. Enraged students hurled rocks, pieces of cinderblock, full milk cartons and fruit (since it was lunch time). Witnesses said about fifty students were in the group, according to news accounts, while "several hundred looked on."[127]

Never one to shy away from the spotlight, Police Chief di Grazia—the namesake target of the Halloween Memorial Smoke-In—decided to pay a visit to Whitman that day. He had been invited by the students "to give his view of the crackdown and answer questions." He spoke to about two hundred angry students in the cafeteria and said, "We're only doing our duty when we arrest you people for smoking pot." This statement received boos, but the chief continued to field questions and comments for two hours.[128] Di Grazia described the protesters as "a small cadre not representative of the Whitman student body. They want to take on the establishment and do their own thing and it doesn't matter what the consequences are."[129]

According to one news account, "The chief earned their respect. After he spoke with them, di Grazia was presented with a banana cream pie that was to have been thrust in his face."[130]

The tide seemed to be turning, though, with regards to support of the raids from county leadership. County Executive Gleason said, "I want to have the jurisdiction back with the school officials as soon as possible. It's not healthy in the long run to have a heavy police presence there."[131]

Indeed, the latest Walt Whitman uprising had created concerns about conducting future raids there. The *Montgomery Journal* reported that "one police officer said privately that police would not go back to Whitman High School, fearing that either police or students might get seriously hurt if another raid is conducted there."[132] Even though Lt. John Baker of the Bethesda police district denied this was the case, there in fact would not be another raid at Whitman High School during the crackdown.

The police presence, however, persisted throughout the rest of the county. "We'll have to continue doing this," di Grazia said after the Whitman riot. "Especially if the students don't appear to be learning a lesson. We brought the problem to everyone's attention, but it hasn't been solved."[133]

By the end of the eighth week, 289 students had been arrested, and after nine weeks, the number had risen to 309—many more than once. The county's Drug Office Director, Donald J. MacCallum, released a report that showed the "more than half of the students arrested for drug use on school grounds have previously been arrested for other offenses," such as running away, larceny, drug offenses, burglary, shoplifting, vandalism, and assault and battery.[134] One senior, for example, had been arrested four times on drug charges: twice for smoking a pipe with friends in the woods near campus, once with pot in his pocket walking down street behind the school, and a fourth time in a "secluded partying spot behind the school."[135]

The number of arrests kept creeping higher, and by mid-November, the *Montgomery Journal* had moved daily reports from the local news to a "Drug Crackdown" report within their police blotter summary, along with events such as thefts, assaults, and public indecency. It was as if daily drug raids at high schools in affluent Montgomery County were no longer all that newsworthy locally.

When the November 20th edition of *PEOPLE* magazine hit the stands, though, the raids and their leader, Chief di Grazia, became national news. Calvin Zon, who had been covering the drug raids for the *Washington Star* since they began in September, had submitted an article to *PEOPLE* that provided readers with both the details of the county's drug crackdown and a bio of its colorful police chief.[136] With Thanksgiving just a few days after the dateline on Zon's article, it is reasonable to assume Montgomery County's drug problems were discussed around more than a few American dinner tables that week. Di Grazia's brash and radical style had brought national attention to the Boston police before fleeing to Montgomery County a year before his contract ended. Now, Chief di Grazia had brought notoriety to Montgomery County about something for which its wealthy, powerful, suburban residents likely did not want to be known—the drug use and rebelliousness of their children.

The Montgomery County Board of Education happened to have its monthly meeting scheduled for the Monday after Thanksgiving, and it was clear their patience with the drug raids had worn thin. Even before the *PEOPLE* magazine article put their schools' drug use into the national consciousness, they had put the drug issue on their November agenda, and they had invited local educator Brian Berthiaume to present a solution. Politics were about to bring the raids to an end.

6

"The Greatest Show in Rockville"

In the midst of the Montgomery County police drug raids, members of the Board of Education had paid a visit to the Other Way School and met with Brian Berthiaume. The program was five years old by that time, and it had been presented an Achievement Award by the National Association of Counties as an innovative county government program in 1975. Though the program had a broader focus than alcohol and drug treatment, Berthiaume had started the school with a priority of stopping drug use soon after his first trip to India, where he met with Eruch Jessawala, an interpreter of Meher Baba's alphabet board. Jessawala had instructed that one of the best things people could do was to help others get off drugs.

Berthiaume was technically a health department employee, but MCPS had been supplying the Other Way with two teachers employed by the public school system. The school thus was one of about a dozen "interagency programs." This meant that as a mental health department program, it had a formal agreement to function cooperatively with the education department. Over the years, several students had enrolled in the Other Way, gotten good results in the program, returned to MCPS, and continued doing well. The Other way had become so popular, the waiting list to enroll had grown long.[1]

The Other Way School students' success and consequent waiting list had gotten the attention of educators in the district. One of those who was impressed by the Other Way was Board of Education member Verna Fletcher. Fletcher was a former elementary school teacher who had been elected to the Board of Education in 1974. She was considered one of the liberal members of the Board of Education, and she was on the Board that hired Superintendent Charlie Bernardo in 1975. Fletcher also was one of the Board members who chose to visit the Other Way during the drug raids, and Fletcher was particularly interested in how Berthiaume's program might provide an option for addressing the district's drug problems.

Berthiaume recalled Fletcher telling him, "We're kicking kids out who are smoking pot in the schools. Why don't you come start a school for us?"

"Of course, I was flattered," said Berthiaume. "And I said, 'Yeah, okay.' I could work with kids that were just drug involved, whereas at the Other Way, they had the whole panorama of problems."

Fletcher was so enamored with Berthiaume's work that she had personally introduced him during a Board of Education meeting that fall. Rita Rumbaugh, who later became the Safe and Drug-Free Schools and Communities program coordinator

Salvaging a Teenage Wasteland. Andrew J. Finch, Oxford University Press. © Oxford University Press 2024.
DOI: 10.1093/oso/9780190645502.003.0006

for MCPS, was a Parent Peer Group Coordinator in fall 1978. She recalled being at a Board of Education meeting one evening, when Fletcher presented Berthiaume's program.

"Verna Fletcher came in huffing and puffing; not unusual for Verna," said Rumbaugh. "Heavy woman, very exuberant and bright and brilliant. She had Brian Berthiaume by the hand. She was leading him into the board room. It was a startling scene for everybody because most of the time it's very formal. She brought Brian, and she said, 'Tell them; tell them all about it.' "[2]

"Brian went into the issue of how marijuana use was affecting kids in schools. Verna put it on the board's agenda right at that moment. She said, 'We need to do something about this. Let's put it on the agenda. Let's do something about it.' "

As the Montgomery County Board of Education was elected by the residents, its members were essentially politicians, and politics had played a major role in the drug raids. Tuesday, November 7, 1978, was an election day in the county, and four of the seven seats were up for grabs on the board, a majority which could potentially alter its ideological direction as well as its president. The county executive would also be on the ballot. Since the Board of Education approved the Superintendent, and the county executive appointed the police chief, this meant the three people most responsible for the drug raids and the subsequent school drug programming (i.e., police chief, school superintendent, and Board of Education chair) would be chosen that fall.

From the beginning of the school drug crackdown in September, some people suggested politics were the sole reason for the raids. Calvin Zon reported in the *Washington Star* that students held an early meeting on the B-CC lawn in September to discuss how to respond to the raids. They discussed options such as a protest petition drive, a demonstration, a smoke-in legal challenge, and even the removal of Chief Robert di Grazia.[3] Reporter Jeannette Belliveau interviewed students for the *Montgomery Journal*, and the Woodward High School SGA president said, "A lot of [students] felt it's just an attempt on the part of di Grazia to make him look good. di Grazia has been having trouble lately and did it to improve his reputation."[4]

Superintendent Bernardo visited with student leaders on September 29, and students wondered aloud if the raids would stop after the November Board of Education election. They also agreed with the opinion that Chief di Grazia was just trying to enhance his reputation. Di Grazia had been criticized by the county's two police associations for his progressive approach.[5]

"I think di Grazia is playing a political game of trying to save his job," said Phil Erh, a senior at John F. Kennedy High School and president of the Montgomery County Region of the Maryland Association of Student Councils.

"It's interesting that he's chosen now to move."[6]

Di Grazia countered, "If that had been the case, I would have done it a long time ago. We feel we don't really belong on the school campuses, and the only reason we moved there was that the situation had escalated. We needed a two-by-four approach to hit them over the head to draw attention to the problem. Something had to be done and we've done it."[7]

Di Grazia noted that "his office has received hundreds of phone call and letters in support of the crackdown and only three calls in opposition."[8]

Bernardo and the Board

Charlie Bernardo had been given a four-year contract by the left-leaning Board of Education in the summer of 1975. That contract was set to expire in 1979, but the board, perhaps sensing a possible ideological shift to the right in the November 1978 election, voted in June 1978 to renew Bernardo's contract early for four more years—through 1983. The early vote, though, caused a stir with the teacher's union, which was upset with some of Bernardo's policies and his "systems analyst" style.[9] The fact that the board had acted a full year before the end of Bernardo's term fueled the controversy. Reporter Calvin Zon wrote how "school morale dropped because of the way he has handled an administrative reorganization this year."[10]

In actuality, Bernardo had created disputes since his first months on the job, but he had had a supportive Board of Education on his side. The Montgomery County Education Association (MCEA), however, was planning to challenge the early renewal of his contract in court, charging it "was an effort to circumvent a new state law" that would require all contract renewals to occur in "February of the year in which a county school superintendent's term is to expire." That would have been February 1979—after the November 11 election.[11]

The board itself had started to shift to the right in the last election. Bernardo had been closing under-enrolled schools, and parents upset with school closures and consolidation helped lift Marian Greenblatt to election in 1976. Greenblatt was a conservative who pledged to save neighborhood schools.[12] Voters had elected Greenblatt along with two liberal candidates, Daryl Shaw and Blair Ewing, which made her the lone conservative voice on the seven-member Board for the next two years.

Even though the board was still friendly toward Bernardo, the door had been opened for an election in November 1978 that would alter the balance of power in MCPS. Three liberal Board members—Herbert Benington, Verna Fletcher, and Roscoe Nix—had decided to retire after only one term, and just one—the president, Elizabeth Spencer—was running for reelection. Those four seats would be up for election, and only three needed to be conservatives to tip the scale. (Liberals Daryl Shaw and Blair Ewing and conservative Greenblatt each had two more years on their terms). Most teachers and administrators were members of the MCEA, and they were supporting Board candidates who were openly critical of Bernardo and his policies.

The primaries were held on September 12—six days before the first drug raid. Drugs were not even considered one of the major issues for the thirteen candidates in the primaries. The school budget, busing and race relations, the curriculum, and the closing of small schools occupied much more of their focus.[13] The eight candidates that emerged from the primaries included the incumbent board president, Elizabeth Spencer, the top vote-getter, who was considered liberal and supported Bernardo. On the other side, the conservative Montgomery Citizens for Education backed the second and third place finishers, Joseph Barse and Carol Wallace. Five others advanced: Fredrica Hodges, Sandra King-Shaw, Eleanor Zappone, Nancy Wiecking, and Barry Klein.[14]

In the eight weeks between the primary and the election, two slates emerged. The conservative, antiestablishment, anti-Bernardo, Citizens for Education backed Zappone, Barse, and Wallace. Mickey Greenblatt, Marian Greenblatt's spouse, was their manager. Their election would tilt the board in favor of Greenblatt, who had lost many votes in her two years on the board. The opposing slate was the Team for Positive Action, which supported Spencer, Wiecking, King-Shaw, and Hodges. Klein was running as an independent candidate.

The eight-week campaign corresponded with the acceleration of the drug raids, and by October 4, just over two weeks into the crackdown, all eight candidates expressed support for the drug busts. Even though Bernardo also backed the raids, Citizens for Education manager Mickey Greenblatt found a way to link his slate's opposition to Bernardo to the crackdown. Recall, principals were reportedly not in agreement with the secretive nature of the undercover raids. Greenblatt also said Bernardo's idea of using peer pressure to stop drug use was "so naïve as to boggle the mind."[15]

"The main thing that bothers us," said Greenblatt, "is the difference in attitude between one set of principals and another, and that Bernardo has not been one, uniform, and two, strict."[16]

The Team for Positive Action was considered a moderate slate, and they included the only incumbent candidate, Spencer. They, too, agreed with the police raids, but their platform called for "a stronger anti-drug curriculum for the schools."[17] This would seem to have more closely aligned with expanding programs like Brian Berthiaume's Other Way School, and, indeed, Verna Fletcher, an Other Way advocate, was part of a more left-leaning Board.

The independent candidate, Barry Klein said, "I have emphasized in my campaign all summer that the breakdown of discipline in our schools—as exemplified by the drug problem—is the result of weak and misguided policies of our present Board of Education and superintendent."[18]

The landscape was not looking favorable for Bernardo. Even though his contract had been extended, a shift in the board would put that contract at risk, so Bernardo felt a need to take his own stance on the drug raids. The day after Greenblatt's quote about Bernardo's not being uniform or strict was published in the papers, Bernardo called a press conference at the central office in Rockville. He expressed the schools' support for the police action and then presented his own firm stance, announcing a new program to include a one-year suspension for selling drugs at school.

Di Grazia's Struggles

While police chief di Grazia denied unleashing the raids to help his image in the county, the accolades he was receiving from parents and county leaders did not translate into acceptance from the rank-and-file officers he was commanding. As one editorial writer put it, "If the school superintendent has not won hearts and minds, the police chief has alienated them by the gross, especially among members of the department."[19] By the autumn of 1978, less than two years into his contract, di Grazia's own battles with the unions had started coming to a head. They did not appreciate his appointing "whiz kid" civilians to administrative posts or his reorganizing of the tradition-proud divisions. Some felt he added risk and pressure to the officers by putting more of them on the streets during certain hours of the day that were more likely to experience criminal activity. He also froze promotions at the same time he fired high-ranking officers.[20]

In the same way Bernardo angered the MCEA and had himself become one of the key issues in the Board of Education race, di Grazia's views and tactics were a focus of the campaign for county executive. County Executive Gleason—di Grazia's boss—had chosen not to seek reelection, and his term of office was set to expire on December 4, 1978. The Democratic candidate for county executive, Charles Gilchrist, realizing that many parents and, hence, voters, approved of the crackdown, called the drug raids "appropriate. Young people, like the rest of us have to abide by the laws."[21] Gilchrist, however, criticized di Grazia's other policies as causing low police morale and indicated he might appoint a new chief if elected.

Di Grazia's bombastic style was in fact causing him as many problems as his policies. In particular, three opinions he had expressed publicly about officers during his tenure had received national attention, and would later be cited as putting his job in jeopardy:

- He claimed 50% of police officers were unsuited for their line of work;
- He called police officers "social workers who carry guns";
- At a public forum in November 1978, di Grazia said he planned to begin human relations training in the police department, because he said police officers "see the community as the enemy."[22]

Reflecting on di Grazia's comments years later, Gilchrist said, "My own feelings were negative towards that kind of statement," and he felt they were "disparaging, or thought to be disparaging, about the qualification of officers."[23]

With regards to harming police morale, candidate Gilchrist could point to the police organizations. Montgomery County had three police officer professional organizations—the Police Association, the Fraternal Order of Police, and the Coalition of Black Police Officers. All had given di Grazia votes of no confidence. The Fraternal Order of Police cited a lack of promotions and a critical report. The Police Association pointed to an interview he gave in October 1978, on the *Panorama* television talk show, where di Grazia said, "The people involved in [the police department] were operating to a great degree, especially the ones in the higher ranks, for their own benefit and not the benefit of the community." And the Coalition of Black Police Officers charged that his firing of two Black officers was racially motivated.[24]

Similar to Bernardo's troubles with the early contract renewal, di Grazia was also involved in a legal process. A citizens group headed by the wife of a county officer demanded an investigation into a long list of complaints it had compiled against di Grazia. The claims worked their way through both the county council and a grand jury.[25]

"There isn't the involvement by the people who I thought would be the leaders in the community," an exasperated di Grazia later said of the police department and the county leadership. "All those people are just too involved in Washington and not involved in where they live. That left the department to the good ol' boys, who were used to doing things their way."

As to whether the drug raids were motivated to help his image and potentially save his job, some claim di Grazia was political to his core. Chester Broderick chaired the Boston Police Patrolmen's Association (BPPA) while di Grazia was in Boston. The BPPA was the union which represented most of Boston's police officers.

"The man had a great personality. He was easy to talk to and he won a lot of hearts," Broderick said. "But you soon found out it was all talk. He was a hypocrite who was using the people and the press for his own political moves."[26]

When di Grazia himself was asked years later why he instigated the drug crackdown, he claimed it was showing responsiveness to his officers.

"I know that it really did help boost the morale of the troops," said di Grazia. "That was, you know, one thing that really happened, because they felt somebody was listening to 'em . . . Somebody in the higher ranks was listening to them."

A Convergence

One regret di Grazia had about the raids was not involving the school leadership early enough.

> I think that we failed to pass it along to [Superintendent Bernardo] in time, which was incorrect on our part . . . We were concerned about the principals and vice principals not being with us all the way. So, we thought it was best not to let 'em know we're coming. And with school, we were hidden because of the fact that maybe they would warn and be ready for us so that we didn't look good. But actually, I think there was a lot of problems that rotated around those raids . . . We thought it was gonna go well, and that I think it didn't go well, and thinking back on it . . . I don't know if it was a smart move.[27]

In hindsight, the crackdown per se ultimately did not play a major role in Montgomery County's decision to retain or fire Bernardo and di Grazia. Their own personalities, policies, and timing (i.e., an election year) were the determining factors. It is also true that their high-profile tenures, coupled with the explosive and undercover nature of the drug crackdown forced the county's leaders to react in a public way, and for parents to demand something be done to address drug use in the schools and to stop the arrests of their children. And the Phoenix recovery high school program emerged from that reaction. When the election season started in the late summer of 1978, drugs were not considered one of key issues, but by November, teenage drug use in general, and the drug raids in particular, had become topics to which the Board of Education and the county executive candidates felt compelled to respond. It was the seeking of solutions that led board members to visit the Other Way and to invite Brian Berthiaume to present his ideas for a "model program" at the November 28 Board of Education meeting.

But first, there was the election, which was scheduled for November 7. No Board of Education candidate opposed the police raids, and all supported Bernardo's new anti-drug plan. The difference was in emphasis, with some supporting an even harder line.[28] Citizens for Education, the anti–status quo group backing candidates Zappone, Barse, and Wallace, felt the drug raids were warranted and that school leaders had not been firm enough in addressing the drug problems in the schools.

"[The raids] pointed up a problem everyone knew was there," said Eleanor Zappone. "It's been a matter of not wanting to face the problem or hoping it would go away."[29]

Barry Klein, the board candidate running as an Independent, laid the blame for the drug problems at lax enforcement on the part of the current administration.

"I have expressed dismay at the failure of the present school administration to enforce the drug ban," said Klein. "[It is] a result of the weak and misguided policies of our Board of Education and the superintendent."[30]

The teacher's union, MCEA, supported that stance. Hank Heller, the MCEA president noted the association's delegate assembly voted "to commend the chief" for the drug raids. "We cannot teach if students are in the classroom under the influence of drugs or out of class because of something drug related."[31]

The left-leaning Team for Positive Action, which supported candidates Spencer, Wiecking, King-Shaw, and Hodges, agreed with the raids as well, but they suggested emphasis should also be placed on the *causes* of drug abuse, including student alienation.[32]

Election

The election for the Board of Education and county executive that would ultimately determine the fate of both Bernardo and di Grazia was held on November 7. At the time, just four years after Watergate and two years into the Carter Administration, there were twice as many registered Democrats as Republicans in Montgomery County.[33] And that was almost the margin of victory for the Democratic candidate for county executive, Charles Gilchrist, the first Democratic executive ever elected in the county.[34] Gilchrist, who had criticized di Grazia's leadership during his campaign, would officially take office on December 4.

Just as di Grazia's future in Montgomery County was dimmer after election night, so was Bernardo's fate. In what the *Montgomery Journal* called "the most dramatic Board of Education election since 1962," the anti–status quo group, Citizens for Education, won all three seats for which it campaigned—the first time Montgomery County voters had elected an entire slate of Board of Education candidates.[35] While one left-leaning candidate, the current board president Elizabeth Spencer, was reelected to her seat, the balance of power had shifted away from Bernardo's supporters.

"Suddenly," reported Jeannette Belliveau and Jude McShea in the morning paper, "Board of Education member Marian Greenblatt, a maverick who was often outvoted 6–1 on the current board, appears likely on December 5 to become the next board president."[36]

"The Problem Is Complex—the Need Is Urgent"

Marian Greenblatt would indeed become the new board president. There was however one more meeting scheduled for the existing Board of Education on Monday, November 27, and Brian Berthiaume had been invited to attend. When the board returned to work after the Thanksgiving weekend, they prepared to work through an agenda with a long list of items to consider. As this was a transitional meeting, the roll was more full than usual. Elizabeth Spencer, who had been reelected, was presiding over her last meeting as board president. Returning members Blair Ewing, Daryl Shaw, and student representative David Naimon attended, as did Superintendent Bernardo. Retiring members Herbert Benington and Roscoe Nix were absent and tardy, respectively. Marian Greenblatt did not attend, but the three newly elected board members, Joseph Barse, Carol Wallace, and Eleanor Zappone did.

Retiring member Verna Fletcher also attended, and she chose her last meeting on the board to bring a motion to the floor on a "Proposed Model School Program for Students with Drug Involvement."[37] In many ways, the timing was ideal. Fletcher had visited Berthiaume's Other Way School during the height of the drug crackdown, and this would be her last opportunity to bring her idea for a drug-recovery high school to the board. That morning, the first day after their Thanksgiving Break, seven more students—three from Winston Churchill and four from Montgomery Blair—had been arrested for possession of marijuana, bringing the total to 328. The *Washington Star* reported: "If the current rate of drug arrests—an average of about 30 a week—continues, county policy will exceed last year's total number of juvenile drug arrests nationwide in six weeks."[38]

Board members who had just been elected on promises to do something about student drug use were in attendance, as were outgoing members who believed schools had a role to play in stemming the drug problem. The drug raids had brought unwanted attention to their schools, and they had the power change it.

Fletcher believed the solution lay with Berthiaume's program, and she helped create the political contingencies for his idea to get implemented. Prior to the meeting, it had been announced on the front page of the newspaper on the Friday after Thanksgiving that Berthiaume had created a proposal for five "centers for helping young people get off drugs and back studying in school."[39] The centers would be opened over the next year. The first would enroll twenty students and begin immediately, with expansion to ultimately put a school in "each of the five administrative areas of the school system."[40] Reporter Jeannette Belliveau had interviewed Berthiaume earlier in the week, and he described the centers as following the model of his award-winning Other Way School with less emphasis on family therapy. As conceived by Berthiaume, students would stay from six to eighteen months and then transfer back to their regular school. He suggested the school could be housed in an existing school building and predicted enrollment of thirty-five students per year per program, with a cap of twenty at any one time. What he was describing was the design of the first full-fledged recovery high school:

- A curriculum of regular education classes in English, math, social studies, and the sciences;
- Weekly family meetings;
- "Strict rules," including "not coming to class high on drugs";
- Student input into decision-making, including discipline (like the democratic alternative schools of the 1970s); and
- "Wilderness camping," to foster relationship-building, reduce isolating behaviors, and lessen the focus on "drug-related sensations."[41]

The last point in particular aligned closely with the philosophy of Meher Baba, who once told spiritual seeker Robert Dreyfuss, "Go back to the U.S.A. Spread my love among others, particularly among the young, and persuade them to desist from taking drugs, for they are harmful physically, mentally, spiritually."[42] Brian Berthiaume, still a "Baba Follower," was proposing a school that would create the conditions for students to "desist from taking drugs."[43] While the original design called for allowing students "who are still using drugs (and in some cases, alcohol) who are experiencing obvious acute problems: bad grades, behavioral problems, or flunking out or expulsion from school," the focus on creating activities without drugs and "not coming to class high" was a step toward what would one day evolve into a requirement for abstinence in order to be admitted at all.[44]

Fletcher and Berthiaume had been erecting political scaffolding for the proposal prior to the board meeting. In addition to promoting the program through the media, they helped form a twenty-five-person advisory committee to explore new "centers for drug abusers." They had invited key stakeholders from Montgomery County for the committee, including a juvenile court judge, a high school principal, a police captain, and various social service workers.[45] Two dozen letters of support arrived at the Board of Education office before the Monday board meeting, and on the night of the meeting, there were about one hundred citizens in the audience, most of whom were there to support Berthiaume's Model School proposal.[46] While it is impossible to know who all the citizens were, Berthiaume claimed many were his allies, and some were parents from his school.

"I had a lot of parents that I had worked with at that point from the Other Way," said Berthiaume. "So those parents wrote letters. They went to Board of Education meetings."

Others, according to Berthiaume, were from his spiritual community.

"Believe it or not," he said, "the Meher Baba community was about 80 people. They all went to the meetings. So, whenever I've had a meeting of the Board of Education, 80 people would walk in with me, and they were all calling the board, writing letters; all of them because they were Baba people, and they liked to be supportive, you know. Baba work, I guess, just as fate would have it."

With those many supporters in attendance, Verna Fletcher presented her motion late in the meeting. Roscoe Nix, the other retiring board member in attendance, seconded it, and thus began a passionate debate.[47] The motion noted the following:

- The need for a "comprehensive program to deal with problems of drug use in schools";
- That the "Model School" program, as Berthiaume's proposed school was called, would meet the immediacy of student needs;
- Plans to provide $30,000 for operation of the first center to begin in January 1979, and to fund the program "either from the required surplus accumulation caused by an MCPS hiring freeze or by a county emergency supplemental appropriation"; and
- That the accountability office would be evaluating the program.[48]

According to one news account of the meeting, discussion of the motion was "heated."[49] Despite all the preparation and supporters in the room, not every board member was ready to support the motion. Superintendent Bernardo recommended a delay "until school staff complete an examination of various programs in the country."[50]

Board member Blair Ewing agreed, "The problem is complex—the need, of course, is urgent."[51] The drug raids had contributed to, if not created, that sense of urgency. But Ewing agreed with Bernardo that the board should wait to approve until they knew "the ultimate costs and responsibilities to the school system." Ewing moved to postpone action on the motion until the next Board of Education meeting, December 18.[52] This would give the board a chance to review drug programs and "budgetary implications."[53] Even though Nix had seconded the original motion, he sided with Ewing on the delay, as did board president Spencer. Fletcher and Daryl Shaw, however, voted against the delay, and student board member Naimon abstained, killing the motion to delay.

Speaking against a delay, Shaw said, "If we don't, we'll never get started. If it costs $35,000 to save 35 kids, it's worth it!" The *Montgomery Journal* reported he made his comments "forcefully," drawing applause from the crowd.[54]

"We'll be sitting here three or four months from now [still] thinking about it," said Shaw. "We're going to spin our wheels and we're not going to come up with anything better than what we have now."[55]

Ultimately, though, Fletcher was persuaded to go along with taking time to discern and revisit in December, and she moved to reconsider the failed motion to delay. Ewing renewed his motion to postpone action, and Nix once again seconded. Fletcher and Spencer joined them in voting affirmative, as student Naiman again abstained, and only Shaw held to his vote against delay. The motion to delay action thus passed, and the decision was sent onto the new board, which would be seated in December. Fletcher was leaving the board, and thus would not be able to vote in favor of the program she had championed. Spencer would no longer be board president, and Nix, who had seconded the original motion would also roll off the board. Interestingly, the person who would become board president in December, Marian Greenblatt, had missed the meeting, and thus was not even involved in the first discussion of Berthiaume's idea.

Jeannette Belliveau interviewed former Other Way students who had attended the board meeting, and one told her he thought the Board of Education's decision to wait was "stupid—it made no sense at all."[56]

For his part, Berthiaume said he was disappointed the program wasn't approved, but glad it wasn't killed entirely and would be reconsidered in a few weeks.[57] The model program would be taken up at the December 18 board meeting. It was scheduled as the final item of the night, just before "items of information" and "adjournment," but the fate of Berthiaume's program would be decided that evening.

Denouement

The three weeks between the November and December board meetings were some of the most eventful in the history of the Montgomery County government. While the drug raids and the decision about the Model Drug Program were not necessarily the main events, virtually all the leaders who brought those issues into the public consciousness would lose their jobs in that brief period—the police chief, the superintendent, the county executive, and the Board of Education president. At the same time, several ideas other than the Model Drug Program surfaced as a solution to ending the drug crackdown and reducing student drug usage, thus casting some doubt over whether the Model Drug Program would be approved in December.

Special Board of Education Meeting

Realizing the complexity of the drug issue, the board held a special meeting on November 30, just three days after tabling the Model Drug Program motion in their regular monthly meeting, but before the new board members were seated. The purpose of the special meeting was to "discuss how heavily the schools should get involved in treating drug users."[58]

One of the critiques to emerge from the monthly board meeting earlier in the week had been not including more county agencies in the process. The Other Way School was a product of the Health and Education departments, and the drug crackdown had been conducted by the police. Many other groups, however, had been battling the adolescent drug problems in Montgomery County for years. The Drug Action Coalition (DAC), for example, was a coalition of community groups founded in 1970. Guide, Inc., affiliated with Catholic University's psychology department, was another program that had been providing individual and family counseling in seven Montgomery County schools.[59] The special board meeting was open to the public, and attendees expressed their displeasure both with the inadequacy of the current MCPS drug education courses, the lack of inclusivity in preparing a plan, and the "inconclusive discussion of what steps the Board of Education will take."[60]

Mary Drury, representing the Drug Action Coalition explained that the DAC had tried repeatedly and unsuccessfully to meet with the Board of Education on drug abuse in August 1978, a month before the drug raids began. Drury felt the county needed a variety of approaches, because "what you do at Whitman, you don't do at Blair."[61]

"We have volunteered and been the generous jerks over the last two years," said Drury. "You [the Board of Education] have been in a castle for years. You've got to drop the drawbridge and join with the rest of the county. You can't do it if you're going to [just] do it the Board of Education's way."[62]

Dirk Thompson, the DAC's legal counsel, added his opinion that MCPS's current drug education approach was "inadequate, superficial, and to a certain extent shows benign neglect."[63]

Superintendent Bernardo also attended the special meeting and agreed: "There's some justification to criticism that we have not built alternatives around the drug population."

"There's also the question," said Bernardo, who had supported the board's decision to delay action on the Model School Program concept, "Should one isolate drug involved youngsters?"[64]

Jeannette Belliveau reported in the *Montgomery Journal* that the audience aimed "bitter remarks" at Bernardo and the board during the meeting. While Bernardo agreed more needed to be done, he hesitated to say the county should provide drug treatment until it "had exhausted all available county agencies."[65]

Bernardo's comments suggested that implementation of Brian Berthiaume's Model Drug Program was far from certain. After the meeting, Superintendent Bernardo said he would "probably recommend one specific program to be started the second semester of the current school year." Costs and nature of the program, though, were not decided yet at the time, and "are still the subject of heavy debate among Bernardo's so-called 'administrative team' of top school officials."[66]

The superintendent instead outlined three possible approaches. The first was Berthiaume's proposal; the second was adding more individual and peer counseling in the student's regular school; and the third was providing family counseling.

For Verna Fletcher, the special meeting would be her last official meeting as a Board of Education member, and she still hoped the board would adopt the Model Drug Program.

"The school system," said Fletcher, "has a responsibility to educate youngsters and to help them stay in school."[67]

Daryl Shaw, who had cast the lone vote against delaying a decision on Berthiaume's school said, "It bothers me to see really bright kids throwing their lives down the drain because they can't stay away from pot . . . I don't think the school system has really attacked the problem in an educational therapeutic sense."[68]

Shaw still had two years remaining on his term, and he would be attending the December 18 board meeting in support of the Model Drug Program. The stage was set for a robust debate in the coming weeks.

Task Force on Drug Problems

The drug problem discussion was not limited to the Board of Education. The same week as the two board meetings, the Montgomery County Region of the Maryland Association of Student Councils (MCR), in partnership with the Montgomery County Police Department and MCPS, formed a thirty-member "Task Force on Drug Problems." The broadly stated purpose of the task force was to "tackle the drug-abuse problem,"[69] and the group planned to release a report in June 1979 that recommended programs. Chuck Lane, a senior at Bethesda-Chevy Chase High School—site of the first drug raid—was appointed as cochair, and the task force would include parents, students, police, teachers, local agencies, staff personnel, and citizen experts, committed to do the following:[70]

1. Study the incidence of drug use in Montgomery County;
2. Study community attitudes toward drug use and abuse;
3. Evaluate past and current and "successful drug awareness programs elsewhere in the United States";
4. Inform the public of its findings; and
5. Recommend programs and policy changes to the appropriate government agencies.[71]

With a B-CC student tapped to cochair the task force, the school newspaper, *The Tattler*, which had figured in the launch of the raids with its undercover drug-buying story in spring of 1978, prominently featured an article announcing the committee's formation. The Student Government Association president was quoted as saying "the force was created as an alternative to the solutions presented by Chief di Grazia."[72]

MCPS students, however, were not united against the drug raids. At the same time the task force was introduced, Chief di Grazia announced that Wootton High School students had sent him a petition the same week with "more than 100 student signatures" *in favor* of the crackdown.[73] And the raids had continued. In its now-regular "Drug Crackdown" report, the *Montgomery Journal* reported the Rockville High School administration called police to the school at 8:00 a.m. Monday, December 4, to arrest three more students for marijuana possession, bringing the total number of student drug arrests to 337.[74]

Di Grazia Fired

The Tattler article about the task force featured a picture of Superintendent Bernardo and Police Chief di Grazia together at the meeting to announce the committee's formation.[75] As it turned out, the photo captured one of the last times Bernardo and di Grazia appeared together in public, as well as their last project for the county. Both would be relieved of their jobs within a week, and the drug crackdown would suddenly end.

The victors of the November election took office in December, and they immediately acted against the status quo. The first to go was Chief di Grazia. Di Grazia had been at odds with the unions for most of his brief tenure in Montgomery County. He had angered the rank-and-file officers by reorganizing the department, placing civilians in leadership positions, ending the four-day workweek, declaring a moratorium on promotions, and firing high-ranking officers. All the while, his bombastic public comments rankled officers in the force. In late November 1978, another di Grazia statement provided some of the final ammunition against him. Di Grazia proclaimed that human relations training for county police officers was "almost completely lacking," which was leading to, among other issues, racial problems involving county police. The Fraternal Order of Police quickly responded, saying di Grazia was "trying to raise the spectre of nonexistent problems, which he can then take credit for solving, in order to distract attention from real problems in the police department."[76]

The timing of di Grazia's latest statement was particularly poor, as the newly elected county executive, Charles Gilchrist, officially took office just days later, on Monday, December 4. Gilchrist had campaigned against di Grazia's leadership style, and now that style was on full display. In fact, the same *PEOPLE Magazine* article that had brought national attention to the drug crackdown days before Thanksgiving had also featured an expose of di Grazia, branding him a "controversial cop."[77] The article shined a light on some of di Grazia's more colorful comments, describing him as "a liberal who has publicly characterized many of his fellow police chiefs as 'pet rocks' and 'archaic Neanderthals.'"[78]

Gilchrist wasted no time on disposing of di Grazia. One of the first public events scheduled for the new county executive was a promotion ceremony scheduled for Friday evening, December 8. Di Grazia had implemented a career development plan as part of the reorganization of the department Gilchrist opposed during his campaign, and the promotion of about 100 privates was to occur during the ceremony. After first researching potential legal ramifications, Gilchrist decided to fire di Grazia to "avoid the embarrassment of sharing a podium with him" at the event.[79]

Gilchrist met with di Grazia on Thursday morning and asked for his resignation. Di Grazia refused, saying that Gilchrist had violated the "Law Enforcement Officers' Bill of Rights" and that he needed to "show cause" to remove di Grazia. Gilchrist countered that the bill of rights applied to active-duty policemen, but not the chief. Gilchrist said, "Chief di Grazia would not resign, consequently he will be relieved of his position effective at 12 noon today [December 7]." Di Grazia was placed on administrative leave, which allowed him to continued getting paid until he could "straighten out his affairs."[80]

According to anonymous news sources at the time, di Grazia "took the news calmly," and he told Gilchrist that "he was making the wrong decision, he would regret it, and he was getting bad advice on the matter."[81] Di Grazia had cleared out his desk by the time Gilchrist addressed the media later that morning, and his term was finished just over two years after it had begun.

In explaining his rationale for the firing, Gilchrist told reporters that di Grazia "was no longer effective."[82] Gilchrist suggested that two of di Grazia's statements in particular were problematic. One of his statements included the sentiment that officers "see the community as the enemy," and the other was that "50 percent of police officers are not qualified."[83] Years later, Gilchrist told the *Washington Post,* those statements were not the only reason he chose to fire di Grazia. He cited a problematic police training project and too many civilians holding important posts.[84]

"He was not the sort of chief of police I had confidence in," said Gilchrist.[85]

Di Grazia chose not to comment publicly until Friday, and when he did, it was through a statement released by his lawyers, because he was considering legal action against a wrongful firing. In the statement, di Grazia delivered some parting shots at the Montgomery County Police Department, saying he had tried to modernize an "outwardly polite but inwardly stagnant department. In doing this, I met resistance from the entrenched interests of the 'good ole boys' presently or formerly in that department. I was fired for implementing these programs and speaking out on these issues—and for demanding the best for Montgomery County citizens."[86]

Adding some credence to di Grazia's claims, Gilchrist appointed longtime Montgomery County officer, Major Donald Brooks, as acting chief. Di Grazia had tried to fire Brooks during his reorganization of the department two years earlier. According to a news account of that reorganization, di Grazia had "ordered two high-ranking officers to clear out their desks, one of them by the end of the day. When union leaders objected to the officers' curt dismissal, one of them—technical services chief Donald Brooks—was allowed to stay."[87]

Now, Brooks was in charge, and in his own statement, Brooks said his "first priority is to try to reunite the various elements in the department."[88]

As was his style, di Grazia did not go quietly. He alleged the firing was improper, and he should be allowed a disciplinary hearing before the Law Enforcement Trial Board.[89] The case wound up in court for years. His arguments were initially rejected by a Montgomery County judge in 1979, but di Grazia successfully appealed in 1980 to the Maryland Court of Appeals, which sent the case back to circuit court.[90] The case was reheard, and a Montgomery County Circuit judge ruled in 1983 that Gilchrist had acted legally in firing di Grazia. The judge ruled Gilchrist's action was not to "punish di Grazia," but rather "the result of irreconcilable differences" over policies.[91]

The B-CC High School student newspaper, *The Tattler*, published an editorial on di Grazia's dismissal a couple weeks after his firing. Unlike other media outlets, *The Tattler* chose to highlight the potential impact of the firing on the "future drug enforcement policy of the County Police." According to the article, Gilchrist had said the drug crackdown "had no effect" on the firing decision, and added he thought the raids had been "appropriate." The paper also reported Gilchrist "did not want the current drug crackdown to become a permanent feature of county drug policy."[92]

The editorial writers commended di Grazia for his "willingness to talk with students about his drug policy," and added, "We believe that Mr. Gilchrist should choose a new chief who not only shares [Gilchrist's] belief that drug busts cannot go on forever, but who also is willing to work with the community to find alternative solutions to the drug problem."[93]

The drug raids did in fact stop with di Grazia's ouster. According to a letter to the editor of the *Montgomery Journal* submitted by a Rockville High Student, "the last police-initiated arrest" occurred on Wednesday, December 6—the day before Gilchrist fired di Grazia. "Since that time, the only drug arrests occurring in MCPS were those initiated by the Rockville High School administration," which was the process prior to the drug raids. While no official, final tally appears to have been published, the letter states the police crackdown had resulted in 343 student arrests.[94]

"The Greatest Show in Rockville"

The new Board of Education was installed on December 1, hence transforming, in the words of *Washington Post* staff writer Neil Henry, "once sedate, almost somnolent sessions into the greatest show in Rockville."[95] Marian Greenblatt had operated in virtual isolation as the lone conservative on the board for two years, but with the installation of Joseph Barse, Carol Wallace, and Eleanor Zappone, the balance of power shifted to the right.

With the ideological shift came challenges to programs implemented by the liberal board, and its superintendent, and emotions at meetings intensified.

"The new tension at board meetings, and the histrionics that sometimes accompany it," wrote Henry, "are the results of the November election, which put a conservative majority on the board for the first time in more than a decade. As a result, the board is now composed of two factions, each of which is inexorably opposed to the political tactics and philosophy of the other."

The new board held their first executive session on Tuesday, December 5—the day after Gilchrist took office as county executive, and two days before Gilchrist fired di Grazia—to discuss the fate of Bernardo's early contract renewal which had been opposed from the beginning by Greenblatt. During that meeting, Greenblatt was elected the new board president and Barse vice president, each on 4–3 votes, with the liberal faction of Blair Ewing, Daryl Shaw, and Elizabeth Spencer voting against them each time.[96]

Untethered by the constraints she had felt for the last two years, Greenblatt presided over meetings in which resolutions were "rammed through with little discussion," causing Blair Ewing to decry a "lack of consideration for due process."[97] One such move was a vote to rescind a requirement that all MCPS employees take a course in Black culture to build cultural sensitivity. Greenblatt's vote upset the county's Black community, bringing accusations of racism that would hound her throughout her tenure as board president (and which she always denied).[98]

"So angry is the Montgomery NAACP," wrote Henry, "That it is threatening to picket all future school board meetings."[99] One of the first meetings they planned to protest was on December 18—the night of the reconsideration or the Model Drug Program. With such philosophical differences emerging and charges of due process violations, supporters of former member Verna Fletcher's motion had to wonder what the outcome would be.

Bernardo's Contract Extension Voided

Years later, in an interview for this book, Robert di Grazia recalled, "Bernardo was a pretty good man to deal with, but he didn't last long down there, either." Indeed, his fate in Montgomery County was sealed the same week as di Grazia's, though it took a bit longer to unfold.

During the same December 5 executive session in which Greenblatt was elected board president, the new conservative majority also voted immediately to invalidate Superintendent Bernardo's new contract.[100] In June, the prior board had voted 5–2 to renew Bernardo's contract for another four years. The vote had been cast more than sixteen months before his contract would have expired on September 30, 1979. The debate had been robust, and Greenblatt led the dissent. She and board president Elizabeth Spencer cast the two *no* votes. Spencer, who did not side frequently with Greenblatt, said she wanted the board to decide on the renewal before September 30, but felt a June 15 vote was too early. One of the points of contention was that a new law had been passed that would have delayed the renewal until February 1979, but that law did not take effect until July 1. Critics suggested the board was rushing to extend Bernardo's contract prior to the law change, and thus to circumvent it.[101] Greenblatt argued the board had acted "prematurely."[102]

"The intent of this early consideration," said Greenblatt in June, "is to avoid placing this question before a new board, the majority of whom will be elected in November. Many of those running will vote to remove him and this board senses it."[103]

Roscoe Nix, who had voted in favor and would not be running for reelection, claimed the board simply wanted to take Bernardo's contract out of the election platforms.

"I've heard from some potential candidates," said Nix, "that regardless of how they stood on other issues, the crucial issue would be how they stand on the contract if they wanted to get the teachers association endorsement."[104]

The MCEA did indeed oppose the early renewal, the contract became a centerpiece of the election, and as Greenblatt had predicted, many of those running would vote to remove him. Bernardo had been upsetting the teachers' union from the start of his tenure with his reorganization plans.

"I was hired to deal with specific problems, and I felt the old organization was inappropriate to meet the needs of things that should have been addressed earlier," Bernardo said.[105]

According to the *Washington Post*, high-ranking bureaucrats had been shifted to less powerful posts and lines of authority were changed, giving Bernardo more direct control over teachers and administrators:

> Many teachers, accustomed to a broad measure of autonomy, objected to Bernardo's detailed directives on such matters as individual course curriculums. They also disliked having to compile enormous amounts of statistics on their students' progress. These statistics were a part of what Bernardo called the 'accountability of educators toward the children.' But teachers complained the forms wasted their time and kept them from their basic mission of teaching.[106]

The teachers also coalesced around opposing the new Black culture course, which was seen as yet another unreasonable time demand. For parents in the community, the most prominent issue was that after years of declining enrollment, Bernardo had led the charge to close twenty-six neighborhood schools and to integrate MCPS. When he had been hired, students of color were mainly concentrated into a handful of schools, and Bernardo was overseeing integration plans similar to those being implemented nationwide in the 1970s.

Conservative organizations such as the Montgomery County Taxpayers League and Montgomery County Citizens for Education, led by Mike Goodman, harnessed the anger of affected parents, who resisted both integration and school closures, and they helped sweep the new slate of board members into power. Greenblatt's husband, Mickey Greenblatt, had been their campaign manager. At the same time, the MCEA, under the leadership of Hank Heller, had decided to battle Bernardo in court. On Monday, September 18—the same day di Grazia ordered the first drug bust at B-CC—the MCEA asked a circuit court judge to void Bernardo's contract renewal. The MCEA filing went further, suggesting even Bernardo's original contract in September

1975 had been illegal. Heller hoped that the court would side with the MCEA, and thus postpone consideration of Bernardo's contract to February 1979, after the new Board of Education had been seated.[107]

Whereas the old board had voted to extend Bernardo's contract and opposed the lawsuit, the new conservative board, led by Greenblatt, reversed course and voted to void Bernardo's new contract. The vote was 4–2 to join MCEA's court action, with Greenblatt, Barse, Wallace, and Zappone voting in favor. Shaw and Spencer (who had just completed her term as president with the election of Greenblatt) voted against.[108] In a sign of the fireworks to come for this new board, Blair Ewing "stormed in anger" out of the five-hour closed session that preceded the public vote and was thus not present for the actual poll.[109] The Circuit Court ultimately took until March to rule against Bernardo and to void the contract, so Bernardo retained his role for a few more months—long enough to participate in the December 18 board meeting that would decide the fate of the Model Drug Program, but still enough to slide him into lame duck status for the remainder of his term.

Berthiaume Forced to Resign from Department of Health

Brian Berthiaume had designed the Model Drug Program based on the Other Way School he had started for the county. Berthiaume, who had completed a Master of Art's Degree in Special Education at Trinity College in DC in 1977, was not, however, an independent actor. He was an employee of the Health Department, and the Other Way School was a Health Department program. Technically, it was considered an "interagency" program, as Health had contracted with MCPS to hire teachers, and Berthiaume's boss was Dr. Bob Jardin, who at the time held the title of Chief of Alternatives and Counseling Programs for Adolescents and Their Families for the Health Department.

Berthiaume recalled first mentioning his idea to convert the Other Way into a drug recovery program to Dr. Jardin.

"I was telling [Jardin] that I was trying to start a recovery high school. He said, 'You're not going to be able to start a recovery high school in the public school system.'

"And I said, 'Why not?'

"He says, 'The public school system will not be receptive to the clinical issues, so it's not a match. You can't do a recovery high school in a public school.'

"And I was just arrogant enough to think, "Oh no, just watch me.' Because I knew I could get the support. I knew I could convince the school board members."

The fact that MCPS was interested in the Other Way as a solution to the drug crackdown was public knowledge by November 1978. The *Montgomery Journal* had featured an interview with Berthiaume in anticipation of the November Board of Education meeting at which the concept would be first considered.[110] Even though Berthiaume had been the director of that program and had received an award for it, the Other Way School was still under the leadership of Dr. Jardin. And according to Berthiaume, Dr. Jardin had plans to replicate the model himself.

"I'm just young and naïve, you know," said Berthiaume who turned 35 in October 1978. "My boss [Jardin] got wind of this, and he fired me.

"[Jardin was] planning on expanding the Other Way model throughout the whole county. [He said] we're going to build a bunch of programs like that all over the (health) department, and you're doing this thing in the school system. You're interfering with my ultimate plan, and I'm firing you."

While the timeline is unclear, Berthiaume claims he received a letter notifying him that he was being fired, and that he appealed to the union for the Health Department. By Berthiaume's account, his evaluations had been positive, and there were no grounds to fire him, so the discharge was overturned. The damage, however, had been done.[111]

"Little did I realize that my whole career was right on the precipice," said Berthiaume. "Because what I found out is my health department environment was pretty much gone, and I mean, you don't want to be some place where they don't want you, because it's only a matter of time before they get you anyway."

Dr. Jardin would remain his boss, so Berthiaume decided it would be best to look for other employment—and the logical next step would be to become program coordinator of the Model Drug Program. That program, though, had not yet been approved.

"I'll leave," Berthiaume told Dr. Jardin, "But . . . give me a few weeks, because I figured the [Model Drug Program] was looking promising.

"Then I went about trying to get all the (school board) votes, but I was not working for the school system. I was still working for the health department."

As Berthiaume was shepherding votes from the Board of Education, requesting testimonial letters from parents, and garnering support from fellow Baba followers, he was not only trying to solve the county's teenage drug problem. He was setting up the next step in his career.

"I'm Not Going to Wait, and Neither Are the Children"

Berthiaume had spent the weeks between the November and December Board of Education meetings courting board members and other stakeholders.

"I did it by taking them out to restaurants and talking to them," said Berthiaume.

Berthiaume did not stop with the board members themselves. He also reached out to power brokers, such as Mike Goodman, chairman of the Citizens for Education.

"I found out whose ears were important to get to and he was one," said Berthiaume. "I went; he listened."[112]

Monday, December 18, would be the first regular session for the new majority of the board. As they headed to the Educational Services Center in Rockville for the meeting that night, most of the attendees must have realized the meeting would be eventful. Still, they could not have been fully prepared for the drama before them. Superintendent Bernardo knew he would be sitting next to Marian Greenblatt, who had led the charge to void his contract extension, setting in motion the process to remove him from his job. Verna Fletcher was no longer on the board, but she would have her name on the final agenda item—the tabled Model Drug Program. She would be attending to offer her support. Berthiaume knew the board would debate Fletcher's proposal for his program, which in essence would be a deliberation about his future career path. Dozens of Baba followers would again fill the seats on his behalf. The now-former police chief di Grazia would not attend, and years later had no memory of the Model Drug Program that had emerged from his drug crackdown. But the drug raids he conceived were a driving force behind the evening's deliberations. Jeannette Belliveau, who had covered the drug crackdown for the *Montgomery Journal*, had been assigned to write about this meeting as well.

The event that stole the show that night was not actually the Model Drug Program. Instead, the Black Experience and Culture Course took center stage. The course, which had been "mandated since 1974 but widely ignored" to build cultural awareness and competence for all MCPS employees, had been receiving almost as much attention as the drug crackdown during the fall semester.[113] The course would meet three hours per week for fifteen weeks, and the teachers' union felt that was a heavy imposition on teachers' time, especially during after-school hours. The former left-leaning board had voted in September to strengthen enforcement and implement the required course. Greenblatt had voted against it at the time, but the board passed it anyway. By December, she was in the majority.

According to news accounts, about 40 of the 120 people in the audience at the board meeting were Black, who wanted their voices heard in support of the course—leaving about 80 others. Interestingly, Brian Berthiaume claimed years later that "the Baba community was about 80 people; they all went to the meetings, so whenever I've had a meeting of the Board of Education, 80 people would walk in with me." While it is impossible to know how many Baba followers were in attendance, it is reasonable to assume, based on Berthiaume's description, that many if not most of the rest of those attending the Board meeting were from the Baba community.

Greenblatt, presiding over her first regular session of the board, called the meeting to order at 5:30 p.m. While vice president Barse was late, all the board members would attend the meeting that night. The agenda was full, covering such basic topics as the annual test report, student trips, appropriations, commencement dates, and the monthly financial report. A few hours into the meeting, the board took up HR-18, which was the official code for the Black studies course. According to Belliveau, this launched "a three-hour shouting match."[114] With Berthiaume, the Baba followers, Verna Fletcher, and supporters of the Model Drug Program looking on and waiting their turn, Vice President Barse said the mandatory nature of the course had "done considerable damage to human relations."[115]

"So did the freeing of the slaves," responded Hanly Norment, a member of the Black fraternity, Alpha Phi Alpha. "Freeing the slaves should have been voluntary too."[116]

At one point, Greenblatt threatened to remove all attendees other than the board and school officials. An audience member yelled out, "Call the police if you want to."[117]

According to Belliveau's account of the meeting, Mickey Greenblatt then "gestured to his wife [President Marian Greenblatt] to throw out persons shouting in the audience," prompting someone to yell at her, "Ask Mickey what to do!"[118]

When President Greenblatt said, "We ask everyone who's not a staff member to leave the room," Gladys Young of the Minority Relations Monitoring Committee said, "We will not leave. This is a public meeting." They refused to vacate, and the audience was allowed to stay.[119]

Around midnight, six-and-a-half hours into the meeting, the board finally held a vote on a motion which stated that "the mandatory nature of H.R. 18 damages human relations in MCPS" and resolved to "rescind the mandatory aspects" of the course.[120] As they were voting, a member of the audience shouted, "All racists raise your hand!"[121] The new conservative members, Greenblatt, Barse, Wallace, and Zappone, then cast the four votes needed to pass the motion. The remaining members, Ewing, Shaw, and Spencer, voted against, and they were supported by the nonvoting student member of the board, David Naimon.[122]

Racial tensions erupted. Belliveau's story quoted a Black woman in the audience as saying, "The Jews of Montgomery County are doing it to the blacks." The chair of the NAACP education committee, Frank Morris, said they planned to distribute leaflets and might picket the homes and meetings of the four board members who voted against the Black studies course.[123]

Rumors had surfaced that the board had stationed undercover police at the meeting for the Black studies course discussion. Greenblatt denied the rumors, telling Belliveau the board "had invited police representatives Monday to discuss possible drug programs."[124] That discussion was finally ready to begin after midnight, but the explosive nature of the meeting had worn out some on the board. After the H.R. 18 vote, Blair Ewing moved to adjourn the meeting. The other two left-leaning members, Shaw and Spencer, voted with him, with Naimon's support, but the conservative block of Greenblatt, Barse, Wallace, and Zappone voted against adjournment. Thus, the meeting would continue.[125]

First, the board tackled more benign items that all members agreed upon—or at least did not have the energy left to debate. They unanimously approved motions to develop a proposal for a "community center for the handicapped," to host a community conference on drug abuse, and to schedule action on a peer counseling course and a health education requirement during a January 1979 all-day meeting.[126]

They then turned their attention to the Model Drug Program proposal. The first action was procedural. As Fletcher had brought forth the original motion, but was no longer on the board, Carol Wallace presented a "substitute motion." Ewing, who had motioned to delay the original vote at the November meeting, abstained, but all others voted in favor of accepting Wallace's new motion. The board then amended Wallace's motion to direct Superintendent Bernardo to "return to the Board for approval of the complete plans before implementation." The board had been concerned that some of the details, such as location and staffing, were not clear, and wanted to approve those items before the program began. Once again, Ewing abstained, but all others voted in favor.[127]

Blair Ewing later explained his hesitancy to support the Model Drug Program. Dr. Ewing had more familiarity with the topic than others on the board, as he evaluated drug programs for the US Department of Justice. He said he found the proposal, "vague." Berthiaume had claimed the Other Way School had "an 80-percent success rate in getting young people off drugs and back into the classroom," and Ewing "questioned whether claims made for the effectiveness of the proposal could be met."[128]

New board member Carol Wallace had attended the November meeting, but she had not been eligible to vote. When her time came to consider the program in December, Wallace chose to sponsor the program, and returning member Daryl Shaw seconded her motion. In so doing, he said, "We recognize this as only a very initial start," and noted that he had "received telephone calls from families backing a pilot program for drug users, with the parents of one boy saying such a program 'might be salvation' for their son."[129] Berthiaume's canvassing to build support for the proposal had apparently been successful.

Despite no longer being a member of the board, Verna Fletcher was given the opportunity to speak about the program she had introduced. And she spoke passionately in its favor.

"I'm really quite upset that no one has pulled things together. I'm not going to wait, and neither are the children."[130]

In its motion, the board affirmed that it was "incumbent upon the Montgomery County Board of Education to act in affirmation of its concern for all Montgomery County public school students," and that "the program proposed by Brian Berthiaume and reviewed and edited by several concerned individuals and groups should be the prototype for this pilot."[131]

The program's goals would be as follows:

1. To reduce student drug/alcohol involvement;
2. To provide the student with a peer support group for reducing drug/alcohol usage;
3. To enable the student to return to the regular public-school environment within six to eighteen months;
4. To increase parental awareness of adolescent drug/alcohol involvement;
5. To provide the parent(s) with a support group for implementing and maintaining a drug/alcohol-free home environment for the student;
6. To provide a drug/alcohol-free educational environment within the MCPS arena for those students in need of such placement;
7. To serve as a prototype for possible future programs.[132]

The program would be installed within the Alternative Centers Department, and it would serve "20 students between the ages of 13 to 18 at any one time." Eligible students would include "(1) students whose drug/alcohol involvement interfers (sic) with their academic performance, school attendance, and/or behavior, and (2) students who request help with their drug/alcohol involvement." Interestingly, the motion also stated explicitly "this program is strictly voluntary on the part of those students enrolled . . . (1) the student must be willing to make a commitment to the program, (2) the student's parent(s) must be willing to attend regular family meetings, and (3) the student must exhibit the potential of functioning on grade level."[133] In contrast to typical alternative school dumping grounds, the voluntary nature of the program was thus built into its mandate, and would be consistent with the creation of most other recovery high schools in the future.

The motion also spelled out costs, which would be $36,000 per semester, or $72,000 per school year, and most importantly that "adequate funding be provided in the FY 1980 operating budget for the continuance and/or expansion of the program."[134] By creating a line item in the MCPS operating budget rather than tying funding to enrollment, the board was creating a sustainable model rather than a financially volatile one. Most schools of choice and recovery high schools to emerge later would instead have their budgets funded almost entirely based on enrollment, actual or projected, which would prove to be unsustainable for many of them. The MCPS board was willing to take the risk that Berthiaume's concept would work, and students would enroll. Further, by starting with a fixed budget amount, the board was willing to let the program start small and grow.

Before approving the motion, the board amended it to require Superintendent Bernardo to "return to the Board for approval of the complete plans before implementation."[135] Bernardo did not have free reign to do whatever he wanted, which was understandable considering the lack of trust and how disconnected the new board was with Bernardo's ideas. There were also several other ideas which had been suggested, and Bernardo had always said he wanted to look at all options rather than settling on the Other Way model.

Student member David Naimon also moved that the program change its name. Naimon proposed the word "pilot" be included in the resolution before the word "program." He also wanted to remove the word "prototype" from the plan and replace it with "pilot."[136] While the full discussion of this motion is not in the record, it is worth noting that a "pilot" serves as "an experimental or trial undertaking prior to full-scale operation or use."[137] By comparison, a "prototype" is "the original or model on which something is based or formed."[138] A prototype would suggest something complete and ready for testing, whereas a pilot would connote the exploratory nature of program, as well as signal its possible revision prior to expansion. The full motion did, however, still say Brian Berthiaume's program "should be the prototype for this pilot," and the goal would be for this program "to serve as a prototype for possible future programs." The revisions, though, did provide a subtle shift, perhaps to gain more board votes, or even to sway Blair Ewing. Ewing abstained from this vote as well as the one to require Bernardo to return to the board for final approval, while all others supported those amendments. Henceforth, the program would be referred to as the Pilot Program.[139]

By the time amendments and discussion concluded, the meeting had moved into the early morning hours of December 19. The board finally called the question and registered their votes. Ewing and Spencer had not been convinced enough by the adjustments or the debate to support the program, and they voted *no*. One liberal member, Dr. Shaw, had cosponsored the proposal, and he voted with the conservative bloc of Greenblatt, Barse, Wallace, and Zappone, along with the affirmation of student-member Naimon, whose vote did not count. With that, the motion carried, 5–2. The Board considered one additional brief item, received a couple documents, and President Greenblatt adjourned the meeting at 1:30 a.m.[140] Berthiaume, Fletcher, and the Baba followers would head home to their beds knowing they had won, and a public high school for students in recovery had been born.

7
Phoenix Rises

After the board meeting, the actualization of a new program began with a realization for Brian Berthiaume.

"So, I had all that going on, and I got the votes. And then I realized I didn't have a job.... I was doing something that doesn't typically happen. Usually, programs in the school system are started by people in the school system. They're not started by outsiders."

Berthiaume had forged a connection with the Board of Education and its power brokers, and that had secured approval for his program. At that point in time, though, early in the new board leadership, there was a divide between the superintendent's office and the newly elected board. The board had required final approval of whatever superintendent Charlie Bernardo decided to do with the Pilot Program, and Berthiaume's concept was named as the prototype for the pilot. Still, everything was essentially only on paper.

"There wasn't a program," said Berthiaume. "And I was just working with the school board. I wasn't working with the people in the school system, the personnel department, you know. I was up here with the school board, and they really don't do the hiring. That's all up to the personnel department."

One of the people with whom Berthiaume had collaborated in crafting the Model Drug Program proposal for the board was Dr. Richard "Dick" Towers, the MCPS director of programs for exceptional learners and of "Interagency, Alternative, and Supplementary Programs." Towers's department paid the teacher positions for the interagency programs such as the Other Way School, and through his work with those programs, he came to see Berthiaume as a "go-getter."

"It was Brian's suggestion," said Towers. "I had met him, and I would go around to these different [interagency programs]. He wanted to see if we could do something with the board. He would frankly lobby them on his own, and he got to know several of them."

Thanks to the drug crackdown, the board and their constituents were interested in the teenage drug problem in their county.

"We had a very interested and socially conscious group of board members," said Towers. "They were receptive, but it mostly was because we had a lot of public interest in it. The public interest, as you know, would get very high when there was some incident going on in the schools."

In the weeks leading up to the board approval, superintendent Bernardo had assigned various people across MCPS to consider ways to tackle the drug problem.

Salvaging a Teenage Wasteland. Andrew J. Finch, Oxford University Press. © Oxford University Press 2024.
DOI: 10.1093/oso/9780190645502.003.0007

Bernardo included Towers because drug and alcohol education and treatment was under his purview.

"We just started looking at it," said Towers, "and we basically were using the similar model to what the Other Way was using."

Berthiaume claimed his boss at the Health Department, Bob Jardin, had given him a month to find a new job.[1] As that month wound down, and the Pilot Program was not yet operational, Berthiaume needed to find work. His Board of Education connections thus stepped in to help him get hired as a consultant in the district.

"[The MCPS administration] had known I had been up to all this with the school board," said Berthiaume.

He found work with the MCPS Secondary Learning Centers, which were eight regional centers for secondary school–age students with learning disabilities in grades 5–12.[2] The director of those centers, David Litsey, provided administrative support and training programs, and Berthiaume was hired to be his consultant in January 1979.[3]

"I would go and visit the various programs and watch what was happening and troubleshoot, and I was a consultant. I did that for about a month or two, but also, I was trying to figure out how do I get hired [to run the Pilot Program]."

Berthiaume's Board of Education connections may have helped him land the consulting position, but in time, they also brought a sense of marginalization.

"It wasn't like [the Pilot Program] emerged among educators, or in the Department of Alternative Programs," recalled one of his future teachers, Steve Baddour. "It emerged from the school board, who approached Brian. I think for a while, he felt very much like an outsider, that he had been brought in from the outside. This was their baby, these people in the school board, and they wanted it to go well. They wanted it to be successful."

Once the Board of Education approved the Other Way School as the prototype, Bernardo assigned it administratively to Towers's department.

"While such an alternative school would have to have strong drug rehabilitative expertise from other agencies," said Bernardo, "they needed our participation to offer the standard course of study, facilities, seek Southern Association accreditation, and ultimately grant credits toward a Maryland State high school diploma. Thus, the close collaboration."[4]

The district settled on April 1, 1979, as the target date to open the Pilot Program.[5] Towers recalled that there were many steps to implement in the roughly one hundred days between the board resolution and the first day of school.

"We got the positions; we started filling them. We had workshops and decided what the approaches would be, what each person's assignment would be, how we would screen, who the clientele would be, how we would publicize it, and what kinds of curriculum would be introduced, what kind of counseling incorporation we were going to do."

Bernardo's contract issue was working its way through the courts, and he had been ordered to submit all Pilot Program details to the board for approval. Berthiaume believed these political realities led to him getting the job, as he claimed Bernardo essentially ordered Towers to hire him.

"Charlie Bernardo knew that I was one of the people applying," said Berthiaume. "And because he was trying to curry the favor of the school board, (Bernardo) got me hired."[6]

"[Towers] often would tease me about it," Berthiaume continued. "He said, 'Yeah, I caught wind that you were politically connected, and I had to hire you.'"

Towers later recalled having positive feelings about Berthiaume, regardless of the politics. Still, according to Berthiaume, Towers would remind him that he had doubts about hiring him.

"He said, 'Brian, you came to the interview in a three-piece suit, but you had sandals on.' I wasn't quite over my hippie phase yet. I don't know if he would have hired me anyway [without Bernardo's influence], but he did."

Staff

Once Berthiaume was in place as the coordinator of the Pilot Program, he worked with Towers to hire additional staff. They advertised for teaching positions, and the first person they hired was Steve Baddour, a teacher at an alternative program operating out of Gaithersburg Junior High School.

"That program was winding down," said Baddour, who was 31 when he was hired. "I had come into the county doing that, so I didn't really know what to do. Then I saw an ad in the superintendent's bulletin, about this school that they called the Pilot Program that was going to be for kids that were involved with drugs and alcohol, and they were looking for a couple teachers in it. I decided to apply, and I interviewed with Brian and Dick Towers."

Baddour was originally from North Carolina, and Berthiaume described him as "a Southern gentleman" and a "pure teacher."

"Professionally, I was always in education," said Baddour.

Baddour had worked in an alternative program, but like Berthiaume, he did not have specific training with regards to substance use disorders. He had majored in English and graduated college in 1969. He had taught Language Arts and Social Studies in North Carolina and Northern Virginia. Baddour went to graduate school at George Washington University, graduating in 1972 with a master's degree in Diagnostic and Prescriptive Education. Baddour explained the program focused on "working with teachers and trying to get them to accommodate kids in their classroom, try and make accommodations for them."

After completing graduate school, Baddour took a year to travel with his wife, and he substitute taught, often in alternative programs in Montgomery County. He took a full-time job at the alternative program in Gaithersburg Middle School for six years before applying for the Pilot Program.

The second teacher they hired was Carol McGinn.[7] According to Berthiaume, McGinn had taught at Walt Whitman High School, where she was "dealing with all kids on their way to Harvard and Yale and ivy leagues," and then she had moved to Albert Einstein High School, which had a heavy immigrant population. As Berthiaume described it, "People from El Salvador, South America, a lot of people who don't speak English... The kids didn't speak English a lot of times and couldn't do the work; opposite problem."

Like Baddour and Berthiaume, McGinn was not certified in addictions counseling, though Baddour had taken counseling courses. MCPS was doing the hiring, and they were seeking educators who had experience teaching students with a range of needs. It would have been unusual in 1979 to find teachers who also had clinical mental health or addictions certifications, and indeed that was not who they found.

"I had taken courses in counseling," said Baddour. "And actually, while I was at [Gaithersburg Middle School], I did a group with the school nurse. It was for kids who were grieving, and I liked that a lot. I felt like I was sitting down in counseling with kids a great deal. Also, with teachers. Not about their personal problems, but about issues in the classrooms. That was the focus of it.

"I really enjoyed the group counseling a lot," said Baddour. But he added, "I don't have a degree in that. I don't have any certifications."

Berthiaume and Towers rounded out the staff with a secretary, Mary Treacy.[8] The Pilot Program now had the staff of four with which they would open the school.

Location

As they were building their staff, the Pilot Program also needed to find a location, and MCPS had an abundance of space in schools that had been closed in recent years. One of the issues that had swept the new board into power was parental unrest around the issue of school closings. By the time Charlie Bernardo arrived in 1975, the enrollment declines had become a source of concern. The media at the time typically noted the declining birth rate of the generation following the baby boom. In retrospect, some of the declining enrollment was likely due to what sociologists call "White flight" caused by changing demographics in the county. Many families were likely relocating or enrolling in private schools to escape the changing faces in the neighborhoods and schools.[9]

Historical accounts of Montgomery County note that legislation removing racial discrimination in housing and business codes, as well as efforts to desegregate schools prompted by the federal *Brown vs. Board of Education* decision, had impacted the county.[10] There had also been an influx of immigrants to the county in the 1960s and 1970s.[11] Historian David Rotenstein wrote, "White flight in the 1960s and 1970s that included the relocation of businesses to nearby shopping malls turned Silver Spring's business district into a distressed area with many vacancies and neglected buildings and streetscapes."[12]

Blogger Dan Reed suggested both positive and negative effects of the change happening in Montgomery County's Silver Spring community:

> The opening of Wheaton Plaza in 1959, the Capital Beltway in 1964, and new suburban developments further out attracted people who could afford to move away, leading to waves of white flight. By the 1970s, Silver Spring inside the Beltway was losing population, and much of downtown was boarded-up and vacant. Several local schools closed due to falling enrollment; by the late 1970s, MCPS was planning to close Montgomery Blair High School. However, there were also positive signs. The area had a growing minority and immigrant population, who were opening businesses and restaurants that attracted people from across the Washington region. The Silver Spring Metro station opened in 1978, and anticipating the people it would bring, developers built offices, apartments, and hotels around it.[13]

MCPS enrollment had peaked at 126,311 in 1972, and the district then lost over 18,000 students by 1978. During Bernardo's three years in office, the Board of Education had closed twenty-one schools, and on December 8, he had asked the board to close three more.[14] The district kept many of the buildings and repurposed them as special education centers, office space, or temporary sites for students while renovating other schools.

One of the schools that had closed and been recycled during those years was Spring Mill Elementary in Silver Spring.[15] In 1979, MCPS was divided into five geographical administrative areas, each managed by its own Area Associate Superintendent.[16] The Area 2 administrative headquarters was being housed in the former Spring Mill Elementary School building.[17] The area superintendent's office was there, along with offices for his staff, personnel workers, school psychologists, curriculum specialists, and so forth. According to Dick Towers, only about three-quarters of the building was being used, leaving unused classroom space available for the Pilot Program (see Figure 7.1).

"It was in the lower portion of the building," said Towers. "There [were] still classrooms, bathrooms. It was beautiful for us because we could just take over that whole bottom part. It was somewhat removed, and yet it was attached to the building. But there were no other pupils in that building. They [would be] the only kids."

While the site may have been ideal for the school district, some residents did not want the program in their neighborhood. Since Towers oversaw alternative programs, he was used to parents being afraid of kids with behavioral issues being placed in their community.

"I have lots of memories for lots of programs we put into various places," said Towers—"initial responses, the NIMBY, Not in My Neighborhood. Different people would get riled up by whoever was upset. We were always pretty successful in calming them. You'd meet with them, you'd listen to them, you'd let them come through, give them some tours, come and observe, and it would be fine."

Figure 7.1. The former Spring Mill Elementary School building in Silver Spring was the original site of the Phoenix School. The area superintendent's office was there, along with offices for district staff, personnel workers, school psychologists, and curriculum specialists. The school was located in the lower portion of the building, where there were classrooms and bathrooms. (Source: Andy Finch.)

The Pilot Program was no exception. On March 14, about two weeks before the school was scheduled to open at the Spring Mill site, MCPS hosted a community meeting in a multipurpose room at the former elementary school. Board of Education members and district administrators attended the meeting and sat at a table in the front of the room.[18] About seventy community members showed up, many ready to express their displeasure with the plans to house the Pilot Program in their back-yard. Reporter Jeannette Belliveau, who had covered the drug raids and the Board of Education meetings, also covered this meeting:

> Parents fearful that the drug program would attract "pushers" to the neighborhood and hurt real estate values berated school board members and school officials involved with the program. At one point in the meeting . . . about half the audience was on its feet shouting and gesturing at officials at the front table. A handful of parents who supported the Spring Mill site, however, said after the meeting that a large silent majority of the community backed having the drug program.[19]

Belliveau quoted one parent as saying, "You don't force things on people! My children come first to me, yours come second."[20]

The district had decided that students would not be bused under supervision to the school, and instead would be required to be driven by their parents. This would later come to be seen as an integral part of the family component of the school, but at the time, it upset the neighborhood.

Busing "would have quieted the concerns of three-fourths of the people here," said a parent. "You're underestimating the concerns of the community as to busing in, busing out . . . Whoever advises you on communal relations is stupid . . . really zero. I'm surprised that a school board, who are supposed to be political animals, don't realize this."[21]

The cosponsors of the board resolution approving the Pilot Program, Carol Wallace and Daryl Shaw, both attended the community meeting.

"It's our understanding that it's a small group in the community closest to the school," said Shaw of the opposition. People in support of locating the program at Spring Mill suggested many of the opposed parents actually enrolled their children in private schools, "primarily the Hebrew Academy and Jewish Day School, who comprise 40 percent of the community around Spring Mill."[22]

One supporter said, "I know a lot of our children need this help. I can't believe someone would walk along by someone who's fallen down and not stop to help."[23]

"I spent 37 years in this county as a principal," said Shaw. "I know these kids and they're kids with problems. We're talking about the kid who has a chance to survive. I wish you'd look upon them as all your children."[24]

Indeed, this first protest would signal similar opposition for future recovery high schools, often confusing the students who were trying to stop using drugs (i.e., the intended population for recovery schools) with those who were actively using (i.e., many of the students in non-recovery high school settings). The local parents were afraid drug dealers would be drawn to the area, when, in fact, the kids who would ultimately enroll in the school would want to avoid "pushers."[25] In most cases, once parents have been given a voice and have a chance to understand the purpose of the program, the opposition subsides. Apparently, that was also the case with the Spring Mill community.

"Generally," said Towers, "if you went through and made sure they were familiar and they weren't dealing with just rumors, but they actually saw it and met them, and met the staff, and met the people, and were listened to, it almost always died down."

Indeed, even though the newspaper account said parents planned another meeting to continue their discussion, the school moved forward and still opened weeks later. It would remain in that same location for the next twenty-four years.

Training

As the staff hired beyond Berthiaume did not have training and experience specific to working with mental health and substance use disorders, Berthiaume and Towers decided to have them attend workshops both before and after the school opened its doors.

"[Our department] had regular summer workshops," said Towers. "We had lots and lots of curriculum development, lots and lots of counseling. We used to do a lot of counseling; [facilitating counseling] groups in high schools, as you know, is not uncommon. All the stuff, we used to try to hone and review and redevelop and so forth.

We had a very extensive summer training and development program in that school district. This just folded in."

Towers also noted, "Brian did have a regular approach that he had used." In 1979, adolescent drug treatment programs were not common, and there was not an evidence-based way of handling teenage drug problems—especially in a school setting. Most schools would address drug and alcohol through a prevention approach. Mutual aid programs such as AA and NA did exist, but Berthiaume was not trained in traditional addictions treatment methodology. Phoenix would eventually adopt a Twelve Step philosophy, but that came later.

"We were all hired, and we all had two or three weeks where we would have training, orientation," said Berthiaume. "I hired an in-service trainer to come and do workshops with us as a group."

The approach Berthiaume had used at the Other Way included a heavy emphasis on family therapy, and that was one of the trainings he had his staff attend. Jay Haley, along with Salvador Minuchin and others had created a family counseling approach in the 1970s that emphasized the client's environment, and specifically their family system, rather than the individual alone as the root of issues such as addiction.[26] Haley had founded the Family Therapy Institute of Washington, DC, in 1976, where he studied and taught what was called "strategic family therapy."[27] Berthiaume decided to take the staff to the institute for an intensive training.

"I took the two teachers and my secretary all over to the Jay Haley Institute for a week-long training before we had any kids," said Berthiaume. "We were in a room with a dysfunctional family, and somebody was watching me through a mirror, when I would be dealing with mom and dad and kid. All of a sudden, the phone would ring. So, you would be sitting there and listening. The phone would ring. You'd have to pick it up, and they'd say, 'Tell the wife . . . to go over and sit on the sofa next to her husband and have her put her right hand on his leg.' Meanwhile, he's screaming, and everybody would want to go [the other] way, you know, because he's being obnoxious.

"So, I say [to the wife], 'I want you to go over there and sit next to [your husband] and take your right hand and put it [on his leg].' And so, she did that. He calmed down so much; you would not believe it. It was like giving the guy a tranquil pill, because all of a sudden, he's connected with someone, some TLC. It was like one of the most powerful learning experiences. So, I learned a lot from that."

While the family therapy training may have helped Berthiaume learn ways to work with families in a clinical way, it also helped him realize that not every staff person would or could serve the same role. Teachers might want and need to just teach.

"My one teacher that I hired [Steve Baddour], he was Lebanese, from North Carolina, a Southern gentleman," said Berthiaume. "He couldn't do it . . . Some of the stuff they told you to do was sort of off the wall. It seemed off the wall anyway, and he said, 'Oh, I can't, I can't do that. I can't say, 'Tell them' or whatever.'

"Steve wasn't able to do the stuff, so he was a pure teacher," said Berthiaume. "I wasn't. I was sort of like always half in teaching, half in the therapy world. When they would tell me to do these weird things, I was just like. 'Oh, sure.'"

Steve would ultimately teach English and math, Carol would teach science and history, and Brian taught drug education, which later evolved into a "recovery" class.

School Name

"We didn't have a name for a while," said Baddour.

When first proposed to the Board of Education in November 1978, it was the "Model Drug Program." The name had been changed to the "Pilot Program" in the final December resolution, and that was its working title while Towers and Berthiaume set up the school.

Though the exact time and process of selecting the school's ultimate name has been lost to history, Baddour recalled that in the first couple months of the school's operation "we did come up with a name.

"It was the staff and Brian saying, 'We have to come up with a name,' and so maybe we had talked about that a little bit. I feel like we were bantering names around, and I don't think it was me. I think that somebody else said the name 'Phoenix,' and I liked it."

Berthiaume recalled liking the name "Phoenix," in part because Meher Baba had used the pen name "Huma," which was a mythical bird in Iranian folklore and poetry.[28] The Huma Bird is similar to a phoenix in that it consumes itself in fire every hundred years (see Figure 7.2).[29] Dutch religious scholar Roelof Van den Broek told the traditional story of the phoenix:

> The bird dies on the nest it has built of aromatic plants . . . The old phoenix burns with the collected aromatics, which are usually ignited by the heat of the sun; from its ashes the new phoenix arises.[30]

"Once [Phoenix] was said, I pushed for it," Baddour remembered. "I really liked that name, because I understood the mythology around the Phoenix bird."

The phoenix had been associated with addiction treatment since 1967, when the Phoenix House program was started in New York City as an alternative to prison for narcotics addicts.[31] The Phoenix House Academies began much later as residential treatment schools, but the Montgomery County school had no connection to the Phoenix House or the Academies. The Phoenix House programs were created as *primary treatment centers* with embedded schools, and they remain so today. In contrast, the Phoenix School program in Maryland was designed and staffed as a *school* providing drug education and recovery support. Berthiaume made it very clear the Phoenix School never intended to be a primary treatment center.

Figure 7.2. "Phoenix" was chosen as the name for the first Montgomery County recovery high school. Brian Berthiaume liked the name, because Meher Baba had used the penname "Huma," which was a mythical bird in Iranian folklore and poetry that has a story similar to the legend of the phoenix. This photo shows Berthiaume's business card, with a phoenix drawn by his wife, Cathleen. (Source: Brian and Cathleen Berthiaume.)

Referrals and Enrollment

The Board of Education resolution had called for the Pilot Program to enroll "20 students between the ages of 13 to 18 at any one time." When Berthiaume first proposed the model to the board, he predicted a total of thirty-five students per year would attend. Of course, as Berthiaume recalled, "It started with zero."

While Towers and Berthiaume were setting up the school, they also had to figure out how to get students to attend. Berthiaume wanted students to enroll voluntarily, as they had at the Other Way School, rather than by mandate or court order. The school had received media attention because of the drug crackdown and the board meetings, so many parents were aware of the program. Berthiaume, however, also needed the schools to identify and refer kids.

"You could let the schools know, and then . . . the schools whose kids weren't making it, maybe they could refer the parents."

Berthiaume and Towers informed school staff, including teachers, principals, counselors, and pupil personnel workers, both in person and through MCPS communications. Berthiaume would meet with parents personally, and once Phoenix had students of its own, he would frequently take a student or two to tell their stories at the local high schools. Visiting local schools would become a central feature of the Phoenix School.

"The way I got the kids half the time was I had to go to the school, meet with the parents because of the stigma about going to a druggy high school," said Berthiaume. "So, I had to go to the school, meet with the parents in the school, and convince them that it was going to be okay. And based on their opinion of me or whatever, then they would come over to Phoenix."

A school brochure later said, "Referrals may be made at any time during the year, including summer school."[32] This meant that the school population was ever-changing. A multi-step enrollment procedure was developed to follow a referral. The procedure included a meeting with the student, the student's family, and Berthiaume. The student would then be interviewed by school staff and students, and if it they felt the student was a good fit for the program, they would attend the school for a two-week trial period before being fully enrolled.

Berthiaume used the referral and enrollment procedures as a screening process to make sure students really wanted to be at the school and were willing to reduce their drug usage and not use during the school day, as the program initially did not expect complete abstinence from the start.

The discernment process was seen by some as limiting access. An evaluation of the school later declared, "The referral process is slow and cumbersome for the most part and seems to ensure that Phoenix is to some degree underutilized in a context in which there are many students out there who could readily qualify for Phoenix's services."[33]

Berthiaume would counter that because the program was not a treatment program, students had to be ready for its requirements, and the staff wanted to make sure students had a chance of succeeding.

The First Students

The Pilot Program that became the Phoenix School opened with a handful of students, some of whom had been arrested in the drug crackdown. Berthiaume could not recall exactly how many students attended on the first day, and no records of daily enrollment counts could be located. An article in the *Washington Post* said there were nine youths in the program in September 1979, about five months after the school opened.[34] In addition, two evaluations of the Phoenix School and a testimonial report were prepared in 1981. The first, completed for the Board of Education by the MCPS Department of Educational Accountability in February 1981, found twelve students had attended the school for at least six months between its inception in April 1979 and September 30, 1980.[35] A second evaluation of the school, conducted by the Pacific Institute for Research and Evaluation under contract with the MCPS Department of

Educational Accountability was completed in December 1981. It noted that nineteen students had been admitted to the school from July 1, 1979, through June 30, 1980.[36]

While it could not be officially established who was the actual first student at Phoenix, one of the parents wrote that their son "was the first student to be accepted by Phoenix School. He had been in the tenth grade at Montgomery Blair High School. He had a drug problem, his attendance was very poor, and his marks were all D's and E's (sic). His counselor, Dr. Stevens, suggested Phoenix School and we thank him for this. Since [our son] entered Phoenix School, his attendance has been almost 100 percent perfect, his marks have improved to A's and B's, and his drug problem has been practically abolished."[37]

With the stated age ranged being 13 to 18, the school was available to younger students, and at least one of the first students was a middle schooler. He was in eighth grade at Newport Middle School when the Phoenix School launched.

"At this time (March 1979) we also learned of his involvement with drugs," wrote his parents in a letter dated November 19, 1979. "Indeed, we later learned that drugs were undoubtedly the root cause of the other problems. Fortunately, we learned about the Phoenix School program which was about to get underway.

"Shortly after entering the Phoenix School there was a remarkable change in his attitude and behavior. No longer was every Monday morning marked by complaints of illness, real or imagined. There were no calls about cutting class or cutting up in class. There were no calls to discuss either deportment or failing grades . . . Regrettably, we can't say for sure that our son is now drug free. But there has been notable progress."[38]

In the beginning, there were no requirements for students to have received treatment or even to have stopped using alcohol and drugs before attending the school.

"If I ever required that," said Berthiaume, "I would have gotten nobody in 1979."

The Board of Education's first two program goals were not complete abstinence or treatment continuing care. They were (1) "to *reduce* student drug/alcohol involvement," and (2) "to provide the student with a peer support group for *reducing* drug/alcohol usage" (italics added).[39] According to the December 1981 evaluation, a stated goal of Phoenix was that students "eliminate their drug use within the one year they are typically permitted to remain in the program," but it appears few of those first students attained complete abstinence in a year.[40]

Teacher Steve Baddour recalled that one of the first students had gone through an alcohol and drug treatment program before coming to the Pilot Program, as it was still called at the time.

"He came to us," said Baddour, "And my memory is he stayed sober the whole time he was with us. . . . He changed his name while he was with us . . . I think he (adopted) his middle name, and I think he just wanted a change from being (his original name)."[41]

"I'm a gay man," continued Baddour. "I was not ever out at school. I was to the staff sometimes, but not ever with the students. Plenty of them knew—and I think just intuitively—and so was (this student). He was out to the staff. I don't remember how many of the staff knew, but I knew he was."

According to Baddour, the student was an alcoholic, and he drank again after leaving the school. He remembered running into him at an AIDS walk years later.

"I remember him saying to me he had been seven months sober. He was an alcoholic . . . He ultimately died, and I think he died of cirrhosis. Eventually his nephew came to the school; his mother was (the student's) sister . . . Boy was he a sweet kid, but we never were able to get him sober, really. (The nephew) was a druggy; he wasn't an alcoholic. After he left us, a while after he left us, he died of an overdose. Brian and I went to his funeral. It's very sad."

Baddour's story suggests certain elements of recovery high schools that existed from the start. One is that the small schools created communities of acceptance for populations marginalized for reasons other than only substance use disorders, such as sexual orientation. Another was the intergenerational nature of addiction, as evidenced by the first student's nephew later coming to the school. And finally, his story exemplifies the chronicity of substance use disorders. Even though the first student had received treatment and stayed sober while enrolled, he later returned to drinking and died of cirrhosis. There are also many stories of students who never used again. Recovery high schools may help a person stay clean and sober for a while and develop essential life skills during their stay, but no program can guarantee a lifetime of abstinence.

Two interesting appendices of the February 1981 program evaluation conducted by MCPS were student case studies compiled from the composite data of their twelve-student sample. One was "The Typical Student Who Completed the Phoenix Program," and the other was "The Typical Student Who Did Not Complete the Phoenix Program." These two case studies provide insight into the student population at the first recovery high school. Of the twelve students, ten were male; hence, the case studies referred to the "student" as "he."[42] Excerpts from each of these case studies are quoted below:

Case Study 1: The Typical Student Who Completed the Phoenix Program

Previously, he had been enrolled in a regular educational program in a regular setting . . . Prior disciplinary actions included suspensions, detentions, and loss of credit. The majority of the infractions were related to attendance or substance abuse, rather than related to violent or disruptive behavior. At the time of the student's referral to Phoenix, he was failing in all courses, and had a history of class failures, withdrawals, and incomplete courses. He was known to local police and Juvenile Services, having been involved in illegal activities such as drug dealing and theft. He and his family had received short-term counseling at a public counseling center.

The student was referred to Phoenix by his high school counselor, the reasons for referral being chronic truancy and inability to function in a regular school setting as a result of substance abuse. He attended Phoenix during one summer school session and one full school year. He indicated upon entry that his substance use was nearly daily both in and out of school. While at Phoenix he maintained a 93% average daily attendance rate and a 3.32 grade point average. Upon completion of the Phoenix program, his substance use was estimated by him to be less than once a month in school, and about four times a month outside of school. . . .

His current self-reported substance use, seven months after completing the Phoenix program, has decreased to not at all during school, and remains once or twice a week outside of school. His parents and current school staff concur with that assessment. His parents' description of him prior to Phoenix is of a potential drop-out who was alienated from their family and society, who was destroying family relationships, and wasting his life. His parents feel the care and concern of Phoenix staff, the drug education, and the support of the peer counseling groups were instrumental in changing his attitude toward substance usage, and giving him the confidence and encouragement he needed to reha-bilitate himself.

The student reported that the program gave him the opportunity to participate with peers in social and recreational activities without being "stoned," and that the staff intro-duced him to responsible ways of coping with his problems, encouraged and praised him, and educated him to the physical and social consequences of substance abuse.[43]

Case Study 2: The Typical Student Who Did Not Complete the Phoenix Program

Typically, the student who did not complete the Phoenix Program was 15 years old at entry and attended the program for nine months. He had previously been enrolled in a special educational placement, and had a history of special services . . . Prior disciplinary actions included expulsions, suspensions, and referrals, with the majority of infractions involving verbal and physical threats to staff and peers, and seriously disruptive and/ or dangerous behavior. At the time of the student's referral to Phoenix, he was failing in all courses, all had a history of class failures, withdrawals, and incomplete courses. He was known to local police and Juvenile Services, having been involved in illegal activities such as drug dealing, assault, and vandalism. The student was referred to Phoenix by his Pupil Personnel Worker, the reasons for referral being seriously disruptive behavior and inability to function in a regular school setting as a result of substance abuse. He indi-cated upon entry that his substance use was nearly daily both in and out of school.

The student attended Phoenix for nine months. While in the program he maintained an average daily attendance rate of 81% and a grade point average of 2.1. During his enrollment at Phoenix he was suspended once for disruptive behavior and twice for use of drugs in school. Typical behaviors included acting out, insubordination, fighting, and the use and distribution of drugs or drug paraphernalia in school.

Phoenix staff counseled him on the program regulations to which he had agreed upon entry—for example, to make an effort to reduce substance abuse and refrain from sub-stance usage in school. He and the staff eventually acknowledged that he was unable or unwilling to abide by program regulations. The student subsequently withdrew from Phoenix. He was referred to the Area Admissions Review and Dismissal Committee (AARD) for a more appropriate placement.[44]

These two case studies make evident that in the early days of the Phoenix School, the school experienced more success with students who came from more traditional schools and had less severe behavioral histories. In its initial design, staffed almost entirely by educators rather than social workers or counselors, this is not surprising. Research would find, in time, that recovery high schools tend to enroll students with more severe symptomology than non-recovery high schools.[45] In 1979 though, Phoenix was enrolling a wide variety of students, and the students with less severe behavior issues appeared to be doing better.

Programming

Even though the Phoenix School started in April, they mandated summer school attendance that first year, so they could continue working with students through the summer.[46] An informational brochure said of Phoenix, "This day program operates year-round."[47]

Steve Baddour compared the experience of teaching at Phoenix with its small number of students, blended across grade levels in each subject, on one floor of a building, with teaching in an old, rural, one-room schoolhouse.

"Phoenix was a good place for me to be," said Baddour. "It was suited to me and my skills and my interests, and I wouldn't have flourished being in front of a lectern, lecturing thirty kids at a time, five times a day. That would have been deadly for me. Who would I have had a relationship with?

"That relationship with the kids, and even the closeness with the staff, and having the feeling of 'Wow, we got this problem, man; we gotta work this out.' Or 'Those kids are really doing, you know, what are we going to do here?'

"I always had the notion that a one-room schoolhouse would be the ideal place to teach in. That you had kids from first to twelfth grade, and they were all together and figuring it out. That was the closest I could get to it."

Berthiaume described the physical space. "When we opened Phoenix, we had one wing of the Spring Mill building," he said.

"You walked in, and then as soon as you get into the middle of the building, you hung a left. You went down the stairs," remembered Berthiaume.

Baddour said the Phoenix School shared the facility with "psychologists, and social workers, and this and that with the school system."

"We were downstairs, and we were on one side," said Baddour. "I was in the kindergarten classroom, which was exceptionally large, and there were two classrooms and an office. That's all that was on that side of that downstairs wing.

"Both of us teachers had a door to the outside. Which was great, because when kids were out for break or lunch, we could see them without having to go outside. It meant the kids were rarely in the building [halls], except to go from one classroom or the other. We were in that hallway, and there were the bathrooms there and all. Boy, I really felt like I could spread out."

Sharing a facility with district administrative staff was also a challenge.

"It was 70% administrators," said Berthiaume. "And then there was us."

"I don't know, it felt like there was always that tension between us and them," said Baddour. "We had students, and our students didn't always behave perfectly."

A number of testimonial letters were given to the Board of Education during budget hearings in December 1981, and at least four of the parent letters were from students who were enrolled during the first weeks of the school's operation.[48] In one of the testimonial letters, handwritten and dated December 4, 1980, a parent suggested that the parents and students also felt the tension between administrators stationed in the Spring Mill building, residences of the surrounding neighborhood, and the Phoenix community:

"The one thing that I feel is very wrong, and it makes me very angry, is the way the Area [2] office people and the neighborhood feel about and treat these kids. They look upon them as monsters and outcasts when in fact they should be highly comended (sic) for their effort in trying to straighten out their life."[49]

Baddour described a typical day at the Phoenix School. "This was fairly consistent for the twenty-five years that I was there," said Baddour.

Baddour tended to teach two English classes ("I taught English to everybody"), and two math classes, ("I taught Math to everybody"). McGinn would do something similar with science and history. Baddour would sit in on a counseling group, and he had a planning period.

"I had the students in two groupings, so they were in four grades, 9 through 12," said Baddour. "I didn't even always know what grade they were in in terms of their English. I don't think they always knew either, because a lot of them had failed so much when they came to us, and they were obviously on a variety of skill levels. My purpose was to get them reading, and get them writing, and to get them talking about and writing about what they were reading.

"I tended to feel very good about the English because I'm an English major," said Baddour. "The math, I think I made the mistake of telling them, 'Well, I can teach math.' We all taught more than one thing, so I ended up with that. I did the best that I could, although quite frankly over the years, the math got more difficult.

"When we had P.E., we were all involved with P.E.," said Baddour. "And we did that as best we could outside with team things."

For the Phoenix school, "physical education" often meant excursions off-campus, some overnight. The promotional brochure highlighted these "camping trips:"

Camping trips and day outings are organized to provide the students with positive drug free experiences. Moreover, they create self-confidence and group cohesiveness.[50]

Many parent testimonial letters spoke favorably of the camping trips.

"Highlights for [our child] were the field trips, especially caving and whitewater canoeing," wrote one parent. "Canoeing trips became a family activity for us."[51]

Another wrote, "The Phys Ed program is something that these kids need. It gets them out in the fresh air, and it is tough. They learn to work out problems."[52]

The field trips were not limited to camping, as the small size of school allowed them take academic excursions as well.

"It was always as struggle to find novels that none of them had read," said Baddour. "A lot of times, I did plays, because so many of them had not done that. If I could coordinate that with going to that play in DC, that was wonderful." Traveling to plays and museums became a main activity.

"One of the things that I liked about it," said Baddour. "Was that it was so small, and so I knew the students well, and there were either four or five of us on the faculty, so it wasn't big. There was a lot more control over how the days went, and how we structured it."

The *Washington Post* Visits Phoenix

In September 1979, *Washington Post* staff writer Katherine Ellison visited the Spring Mill building and wrote a story on the new Phoenix program.[53] She interviewed students, parents, and staff, quoting Berthiaume and a 16-year-old, who Ellison says was one of the students arrested in the drug raids the year before. This article was one of the first to provide a journalistic account of a recovery high school, and it described the Phoenix School as an "experimental program." At the time of the article, nine students were enrolled, and Ellison noted the students and their parents "speak highly of the program."[54]

"He hasn't been late once," said the student's father. "In fact, he gets anxious if a stop light or something on the way to school slows us up." As the article explained, the school buses were not routed to Phoenix, so families provided their own transportation. Parents also were attending "weekly discussion sessions focused on ending drug use at home."[55]

The article highlighted the voluntary nature of the school, and Berthiaume said, "These are kids who want to change."[56]

Berthiaume was described in the article as 36 years old (though he was still three weeks away from his 36th birthday), and he was wearing "immaculate white slacks making him conspicuous among the blue jeans and 'Led Zeppelin' T-Shirts." While the article does not mention Meher Baba, it does note Berthiaume's life had become a "full-time crusade against drug use."[57]

"I do feel the biggest threat to America is drugs."

According to Berthiaume, though, complete abstinence was not a goal of the school at first. While its approach was not called so at the time, Phoenix was essentially using harm reduction rather than abstinence-based recovery in its first years of operation. In an interview for this book, Berthiaume recalled students were enrolled "without any AA or NA, without urine screens also."

"Most of the kids are down to getting stoned once a day," Berthiaume told the *Washington Post*. "And considering their use before, that's progress."[58]

First Graduation Ceremony

Students attending the Phoenix School would typically stay up to a year in the program before returning to their regular schools to graduate. This was the case for all the students in the first school year, 1979–1980, and three of the four students who graduated in the 1980–1981 school year. One student, however, chose to break that pattern in May 1981.[59] According to an article in the *Washington Star*, a student named Carl decided he did not want to return to his old school for commencement exercises.[60] Instead, a graduation ceremony was held on Friday, June 5, 1981, in the Spring Mill building, and Carl was the only graduate in the Phoenix School's first commencement.

The ceremony honored both the significance of the moment and the informality of a recovery school. J. Edward Andrews, who had succeeded Charlie Bernardo as superintendent, attended along with Carol Wallace, who was by then the MCPS board president, as well as former board members, Daryl Shaw and Verna Fletcher, the latter by then on the Maryland State Board of Education. Wallace and Shaw had jointly sponsored the board proposal, originally drafted by Fletcher, to start the school back in 1978. The article featured a photograph of Carl in a tuxedo with black tails and a white tie. In the picture, though, Carl is receiving a bouquet of balloons from a clown. According to the story, "The audience sang 'Happy Graduation' to the tune of 'Happy Birthday.'"[61]

The article noted there were "more than 20 students" in attendance at the ceremony, and his classmates were proud of Carl for choosing to graduate at Phoenix.

"He's our very first graduate," said one classmate. "No one else chose to graduate here."[62]

It would become common for recovery high schools to allow their graduates to speak at their ceremonies, as most typically have small numbers of students graduating each year. On this day, Carl became the one of the first to give such a speech. According to the article, Carl pulled a handwritten speech from his back pocket and spoke to the crowd "with tears in his eyes and a tremble in his throat."

"At this moment I feel higher than I ever have on any drugs," said Carl. "This is the first day of the rest of my life."[63]

The moment effused symbolism. MCPS had received national attention just over two years earlier for its students' drug use and the subsequent police crackdown during a simmering fall of 1978. That semester had ended with the removal of both the police chief and the superintendent, the installation of a new majority on the Board of Education, and the approval of a model school called the Pilot Program.

That program had chosen a name, "Phoenix," from a myth about birth and renewal, and prominent figures from the fiery transition period were in attendance to view a commencement. A student whose life had been consumed by drug use was starting his life anew, with his family and friends there for the occasion. MCPS had emerged from the anger and the shame with a program to celebrate.

Carl's mother spoke at the ceremony, and she captured the meaning of the moment not only for Montgomery County but for the nascent recovery high school movement.

"It ought to be shouted all over the country," she said. "There is help for our kids [at the Phoenix School]. Don't sweep it under the rug."[64]

8
Evaluation

The Phoenix School had been called a "pilot program" from its inception, and the Board of Education continued to use that moniker even after the school adopted the name "Phoenix." Holding onto the word "pilot" suggests the board was considering expansion of the model if it was deemed successful.[1] As such, the board had ordered the Educational Accountability Department to conduct "continual assessment" of the program and to provide "periodic reports."

It is not clear how many periodic reports were produced, but in December 1980, the board took up the question of program effectiveness, not only for Phoenix but for all specialty programs in the district. On Tuesday, December 9, 1980, the day much of the United States was mourning the murder of former Beatle John Lennon, the MCPS Board of Education awarded a contract for $5,991 to the Pacific Institute for Research and Evaluation in Bethesda for "an evaluation of the Phoenix School Pilot Drug Program." The length of the contract was December 10, 1980, to August 31, 1981, which meant they would collect data during the 1981 spring semester.[2]

Two days later, on December 11, the Board convened a special session to discuss an external evaluation regarding "special education programs, movement into programs, and progress of the children in the programs."[3] That meeting would continue until Monday, December 15, when Board member Blair Ewing inquired about the effectiveness of all the alternative programs in the district. Dr. Joy Frechtling, the director of program monitoring for the accountability office, noted that her office was "doing this in pieces regarding studies that were looking at particular programs. They were looking at Mark Twain and Phoenix in small very tailored studies."[4]

Interestingly, according to the report later published about Phoenix from Dr. Frechtling's office, it was on Friday, December 12, the day between the two special session meetings, that the Board asked the Department of Educational Accountability (DEA) to produce "a follow-up report on students who had been participants in the Phoenix School Program, a pilot program for treatment of students with drug and/or alcohol problems."[5] The purpose of this evaluation would be "to determine whether the effects of the program, especially in the areas of reduction of substance abuse and improved academic functioning, persisted once the student reentered the regular school [or work] environment.[6] They would ultimately profile twelve students who had attended the school for at least six months between its beginning in April 1979 and September 30, 1980. After nearly two years of operation, Berthiaume and the Phoenix School thus were suddenly under the microscope of

Salvaging a Teenage Wasteland. Andrew J. Finch, Oxford University Press. © Oxford University Press 2024.
DOI: 10.1093/oso/9780190645502.003.0008

evaluation by two groups—one internal and one external—and the findings would be mixed.

The MCPS Department of Educational Accountability would issue preliminary findings quickly, producing a report in February 1981.[7] The second evaluation conducted by the Pacific Institute for Research and Evaluation was released ten months later in December.[8] Its sample included students who had been admitted to the school from July 1, 1979, through June 30, 1980.[9]

The internal preliminary report was a post hoc follow-up study, and its findings were based on surveying twelve students (nine of whom had successfully "completed" the Phoenix program), eleven parents, and nine MCPS staff (eight counselors and one teacher). There was no comparison group, and the surveys considered data for students pre-, during, and post-Phoenix enrollment. Limited as it may have been, their report was the first known study of recovery high school outcomes, and as such, it represented a landmark. It should also be noted that the study was holistic in nature, as substance use was only one of the outcomes considered. Nine students had completed the Phoenix objectives, and three had not. Overall, the students who completed fared better than those who had not. Findings included the following:[10]

- **Student Behavior:** Students did not have drug-related disciplinary actions in their post-Phoenix placement.
- **School Attendance:** Attendance improved for students while in the Phoenix program, with post-Phoenix attendance slightly better than pre-Phoenix attendance.
- **Grades:** Overall, students' grades in their post-Phoenix places were far superior to the pre-Phoenix grades.
- **Substance Use:** All nine students who completed Phoenix reported they currently did not use alcohol or drugs during school or work. Substance use outside of the school or work setting was still occurring for seven of the nine students, though the frequency of usage for these students was reported to be less than prior to Phoenix participation. Eight of nine students reported that they reduced their use of drugs/alcohol, and that Phoenix helped change their attitudes toward substance use.
- **School/Work Behavior:** All nine students who completed Phoenix reported that they were having no problems at school or work, though some parents and school staff disagreed with that assessment.
- **Perceptions about Phoenix—Students:** The students rated the Phoenix program as excellent, saying they *liked* the concern of Phoenix staff for the students; wilderness trips; supportiveness of the peer group sessions; and the inducements provided by the reward/privilege system. Some students *disliked* the punishments associated with the reward system, the lack of challenge of the academic program, the lack of a post-Phoenix support group, and having been placed in a special school such as Phoenix.

Perceptions about Phoenix—Parents: The parents indicated they *liked* the small class size, field trips, concern of staff, and counseling support; and they *disliked* transportation difficulties, inadequate time or resources for parent/staff communication, lack of relevant training for parents, and inadequate academic preparation for future reentry into a regular school. Two parents questioned the appropriateness of removing a student from a drug abuse program because of continued drug use.

Phoenix School Staff : Seven of the nine post-Phoenix school staff felt the Phoenix program had met the needs of the students around substance abuse, but only five felt their academic needs had been met, and only four felt their emotional/behavioral needs had been met.

The report stated three strengths, three weaknesses, and a few "overall perceptions."[11] **Strengths:**

(1) Though few students (two of the twelve) became completely drug-free, almost all reported changes in the desired direction.
(2) The drug education component was considered to be an outstanding feature of the program.
(3) The continuing concern of Phoenix staff for students who completed the program was perceived as a program strength.

Weaknesses:

(1) The lack of intensive psychological counseling/therapy during Phoenix participation, as well as lack of ongoing support post-Phoenix . . . It was felt that the services provided by Phoenix did not meet the needs of students whose drug usage was related to severe emotional problems.
(2) Reports of the post-Phoenix school staff indicated that the academic program at Phoenix was not sufficiently challenging or varied . . . Therefore, some students were not adequately prepared to resume their educational programs when they returned to a regular school setting.
(3) Parents of students who withdrew or were removed from Phoenix did not feel the program met their children's needs.

While most students, parents, and school staff said they would recommend the program for other students experiencing drug/alcohol abuse problems, some students qualified this recommendation by stating that "they would only recommend Phoenix for those students who are serious about eliminating their substance abuse problems."[12] There was concern that students were continuing to use drugs after leaving Phoenix, but this preliminary, internal study basically affirmed the Phoenix program while noting some areas of improvement. The Board of Education continued supporting the program, attended the school's first graduation ceremony in

May 1981, and allowed funding to continue for the 1981–1982 school year. Two footnotes in the February report, however, were included as cautionary points. First, the researchers clarified, "No attempt was made to gather data descriptive of the program but rather to describe the students who participated in it."[13] And second, "An evaluation including pre- and post-measures and a comparison group is currently being conducted by DEA. The preliminary results of this study should be available in the summer of 1981."[14] It would be that report that would sound the alarm bells for the Phoenix staff.

While the preliminary results may have been made available for board and staff review earlier, the Pacific Institute for Research and Evaluation released its full 59-page report to the public in December.[15] Their student sample was only slightly larger, nineteen instead of twelve, but this number included a comparison group. In reality, only ten Phoenix students were in the sample. The other nine were "matched comparison" students, selected for each Phoenix student. "One friend for each Phoenix School student was selected for study participation" from two names of friends provided by each Phoenix student.[16] While the number of Phoenix students (n = 10) was fewer than the MCPS preliminary study, the fact that a comparison group was used improved the rigor of the evaluation. The authors emphasized the purpose of the evaluation was to examine the "short term goals and objectives" of the Phoenix Pilot Drug Program.[17] They stated, "The fundamental goal of the Phoenix program is to provide a drug/alcohol free educational environment for students involved with drugs/alcohol to reduce their drug/alcohol usage and to enable them subsequently to function effectively in the regular school program."[18] As with the MCPS preliminary report in February, these researchers did not see short-term complete abstinence as a goal of the program, and they were primarily concerned about the environment of the school itself. Their lens would include the adequacy of counseling services, the academic environment, and the parent–school relationships.

The study obviously had many limitations, including a small sample size, a lack of achievement measures, and reliance on self-reports. Still, just as the February preliminary study had broken ground as the first-ever study of recovery high schools, this project represented another first by including a comparison group. Limited as they may have been, though, the findings were mixed, and the data were negative enough to cause concern for Brian Berthiaume and his staff.

The study commended the "outstanding attendance record" of the students, as well as the "strong, well-planned, and carefully executed disciplinary program." One of the key facets of the program was to create "positive peer pressure," described as "a counter-culture movement within a well-defined culture, trying to direct youth away from drug use."[19] The authors praised the staff as "a group of outstanding teachers."[20] With the supportive staff and students in place, the study found that the program was "effectively providing a drug-free school environment," and they felt Phoenix appeared to be "strengthening the students' commitment to school and rebuilding good school habits."[21]

The positive findings about drug use and school habits, however, were lukewarm. The researchers said they could only "hope" the students "would carry with them the habit of being drug-free during the school day." Lacking any evidence of good habits and being drug-free in their regular schools post-Phoenix, the researchers were less than sanguine these changes would "survive the transition back to a regular school."[22]

From there, the findings went downhill:

- For the Phoenix students, the pre- and post-test drug abuse prevalence was essentially the same.
- For the comparison students, the pre- and post-test drug abuse prevalence was essentially the same.
- For both the pretest and post-test scores, the was no difference between the Phoenix group and the comparison group.
- For both groups, the researchers found "some very frequent use of what are generally regarded to be serious substances."

These data led the authors to claim, "In outcome evaluation, it is hard to imagine a more compelling picture of 'no effect.'"[23]

The researchers added, "Self-reports by students indicate that the program is having no effect in reducing overall drug and alcohol usage," even though "all parents report their children use drugs less than before." Ultimately, the "weight of the data," including the "lack of difference between treatment and comparison groups," led the authors to believe "the picture painted by student self-report" over that of the parent surveys.[24]

Regarding the school's counseling services, the most the study could say was "the program does provide counseling." Their observations of the counseling program revealed "the blurring of boundaries in the school," such as "the dual roles of leaders of group counseling sessions and of teachers" and of time boundaries between being supportive persons and disciplinarians.[25] Overall, they found the services to be ambiguous, and said they did not seem to "be achieving the explicit outcomes" of decreased drug and alcohol use and improved self-esteem.[26]

Regarding the school's academic services, the authors were unequivocal: "The program is not providing an individualized academic environment, and its resources and physical setting are not conducive to doing so." They did think the school was "doing very well in repairing learning habits," but not in "achieving significant academic gains." In fact, they questioned if it was even appropriate for Phoenix to be expected to do both.[27]

And regarding the strength of the parent–school partnership, the authors felt they did not have enough evidence to make a claim one way or the other, even though "the school has put a great deal of effort into it." They wrote, "It looks like it needs a great deal more experimentation to bring it off, if such a partnership can be built at all."[28]

Phoenix School Reaction

It was standard procedure for the Pacific Institute to share their findings with program staff "prior to its finalization and public release," and that is exactly what they did in the case of the Phoenix report.[29] It hit the Phoenix staff hard, and Brian Berthiaume was compelled to push back.

After reading the report, Berthiaume met with the senior evaluator, Dr. Robert Emrich. According to the authors, Berthiaume stated, "The evaluation report had missed the point because it dealt with the Phoenix School as though it were a drug and alcohol abuse treatment program when in fact it is not a treatment program."[30]

Berthiaume and his staff were so upset with the report that Dr. Joy Frechtling, the director of Instructional Evaluation and Testing, who would sign off on the report, and the director of the Department of Educational Accountability, Dr. Steven Frankel, hosted two roundtable discussions "to reconcile some of the apparent discrepancies between the researchers' findings and the program director's views of the program." The roundtables included both staff and students—"some of whom were in the study."[31]

To the evaluators' credit, the final report included details on how they elicited feedback, specific concerns of staff and students, and a response from the authors to those critiques. It does not appear, however, that the additional conversations and roundtables changed the conclusions of the evaluation. They did add an affirmative sentence to the introduction, presumably based on the response:

> The program is (underlining included) helping [the students] change their attitudes about drugs and drug use, does result in their reducing their drug usage or even being drug free for at least short periods of time, and may reduce their long-term usage."[32]

They immediately qualified that statement though:

> However, it seems unlikely that many students will achieve the stated goals of the program: that they eliminate their drug use within the one year they are typically permitted to remain in the program. As they describe their progress, it seems to be a series of taking two steps forward and moving one step back.[33]

In affirming their report in the face of the school's reaction, the authors wrote, "We feel comfortable that the report presents a fair picture of the program during the 1980–81 school year."[34]

A negative evaluation is never a good thing for a new program, and in the case of the Phoenix School, the timing was particularly bad. The Board of Education was holding its annual budget hearings in December, and the only existing comparative data now suggested the pilot program had no effect.

"It showed that [students] didn't really stay off drugs," said Berthiaume. "They [the school board] were going to close the school based on this evaluation."

Rather than only focusing on the threat posed by the looming budget hearings, however, Berthiaume saw an opportunity. While the report had included staff interviews along with the self-reports of ten students, their parents, and their friends, the researchers acknowledged one of their shortcomings was evidence about the parent–school partnership. "We know least about how well the school is doing with regard to this objective."[35] Furthermore, unlike the February preliminary report, which interviewed nine staff members of the schools to which Phoenix students returned, the December report only included external interviews about the *referral* process—with two school counselors, a pupil personnel worker, and a principal. The evaluators interviewed no other external stakeholders, such as teachers or treatment providers. Berthiaume thus shepherded the school's stakeholders to exploit these gaps.

"I had to do some fancy footwork to get PPW's (pupil personnel workers) and principals and therapists in the community to write letters; parents to write letters [that explained that] even though they weren't abstinent after they left, they were a lot better than they were before they came."

The Phoenix Parents Advisory Committee, led by Jo Ann Nolen, compiled a report containing "the names and present situations of 72 students who have been served by the Phoenix School during the last 2½ years," meaning it chronicled stories of students dating back to the school's inception in April 1979.[36] It was titled *The Phoenix School: An Impact Report,* and while the two professional evaluations may have been more rigorously conducted, the *Impact Report* collected the stories of many more participants.

The Board of Education held budget hearings from December 8–10, 1981, during which constituents were invited to speak on behalf of the MCPS specialty programs, and Nolen made sure the report was completed in time for those hearings. Nolen represented the Phoenix Parents Advisory Committee at the December 9 meeting, and for maximum effect, she brought along "five young people who have become completely drug and alcohol free since enrolling in the Phoenix School."[37] This statement contradicted the doubts portrayed by the December evaluation about the potential of complete sobriety for Phoenix students. Nolen's *Impact Report* painted a picture of the early years of the school, colored heavily by satisfied parents, students, and stakeholders. The report included thirty-five letters from parents, many of them handwritten, that described their children's histories, how they heard about and selected the Phoenix School, the school's staff and programming, and how their children were doing currently.

The report, a copy of which is now kept at the Montgomery County Historical Society, provided a rich, first-person narrative of the beginning of the recovery high school movement. Just as the professional evaluations had their limitations, so too did this report. It was not really a "study" at all; the *Impact Report* was simply a collection of letters, with an introduction by Nolen. All the letters included were supportive of the school and its programming, and no comment was made as to collection procedures, decisions for inclusion, or if any negative letters had been withheld. No effort was made to conduct a content analysis. Indeed, some of the letters were dated as late as December 9, which suggests Nolen was receiving letters up to the day of the school's hearing. It also included a few letters composed long before the evaluation period, the oldest being dated June 18, 1979—just months after the opening of the school. The vast majority, however, were dated between October 29 and December 4, suggesting the level of anxiety that had been generated by previewing the final evaluation. One parent responded directly to the December report, as parents had been invited to the roundtables during the fall. The parent addressed their letter to Dr. Frechtling, saying, "Your letter of 21 November 1980 caused us to reaffirm our commitment to write because we felt obligated to participate in the evaluation process of the Phoenix School."

The letters were all supportive of the program, and suggestions for improvement tended to be directed at the district to open more schools like Phoenix and to provide the school with more resources. Beyond the thirty-five parent letters, the report included fifteen letters from MCPS staff, such as principals, pupil personnel workers, and counselors. While many provided a positive outcome story about a Phoenix School alum, others were from elementary and middle school principals expressing gratitude for the outreach program in which Phoenix students had spoken to their students about drugs. The report thus described a community drug prevention influence not emphasized by the prior evaluative studies. In a county not far removed from getting national attention for drug raids in its high schools, the concept of high school students spreading an anti-drug message to young children was no small item.

The *Impact Report* closed with nine student letters—eight from alums, and one from a friend of an alum.[38] While only one student pronounced themselves as "drug free," the rest proudly said they had reduced their usage, and most gave a precise amount (such as now only drinking alcohol once per week). All expressed support for the program. A representative comment was, "Any thought of taking away this program would extinguish the possibility of helping young people, like me, who have strayed from the path of achieving their maximum ability."[39] Another said, "Without Phoenix, I would still be messed up and massively into drugs."[40]

Continuation and Expansion

The efforts of Berthiaume and Nolen apparently worked. The MCPS Board of Education minutes recorded that board members all received a copy of the evaluation on January 12, 1982.[41] The board had met in special session to discuss its priorities for the year, which they presented at the two regular session meetings—January 25 and February 9.[42] They ultimately adopted fourteen priorities for the year, and number seven was to "continue steps to discourage student drug, alcohol and tobacco use," in part by supporting students "to participate in programs to discourage drug use."[43] The board then expanded funding for the school's "outdoor education trips" and added

$5000 to their budget for urinalysis—something the school had not been doing before the evaluation period.[44] Then in May, responding to a board inquiry about "the status of the Phoenix program," the meeting minutes simply state, "The superintendent indicated that the Board's budget had been approved for Phoenix."[45]

The board didn't stop there. On June 1, 1982, Berthiaume's boss, Dr. Towers, the director of the Department of Interagency, Alternative, and Supplementary Programs, made a presentation during an all-day board meeting. He was joined by Charles Short, from the Children and Youth Division of the county government, and Terry Baxter, chairman of the Business/Community Team on Drug and Alcohol Abuse. They were invited by the superintendent to give a report on the district's "drug and alcohol abuse activities." Dr. Towers said they had a "continuing effort to enforce the school board's policy on drug abuse." He reported that "their statistics on suspension for drug use or distribution showed a decline; however, the police were arresting about the same number of youngsters."[46]

Dr. Towers had attended the first Phoenix graduation just one year earlier, and he had been moved by it. Berthiaume remembered how Dr. Towers "came up to me, and he said that it was the most meaningful graduation he had ever attended." Now, in his presentation to the board, Towers emphasized the positive effect Phoenix was having. He told the board, "They could not draw any conclusions from these statistics except to say that a great many more youngsters were being helped."[47]

The superintendent, Dr. Edward Andrews, to whom Towers reported, then concluded the board report by saying that the MCPS drug advisory council "wanted to see the Phoenix program expanded, the curriculum beefed up, and the PACT II (interagency drug counseling) program continued . . . He felt that they needed to renew their pledge to be as aggressive as they could in this area, and he intended to follow up this meeting with a memorandum to principals."[48]

Not only had Phoenix emerged from the turbulent evaluation process with a renewed budget, but there was also now a call from the superintendent to *expand* the program. A second Phoenix campus was now almost a certainty.

9
Phoenix II

Berthiaume's original proposal to the board in November 1978 had been an ambitious one. He had planned to create five sites by the end of 1979, and ultimately to put a school in "each of the five administrative areas of the school system."[1] Almost four years later, the Phoenix School was still only operating at its one, original site in the Spring Mill administration building. By the spring of 1982, the Phoenix School was regularly at or near capacity, and its location made it difficult to equally serve all residents of Montgomery County.

"The demand was getting high," said Dr. Towers. "We couldn't deal with everybody that we would like to, because we were limited not only by the philosophy, in terms of the small group, but also our space limitation."

Berthiaume had long felt Phoenix needed another site, and, in June 1982, the superintendent had gone on the record in support of expanding the program.

"I don't remember it coming from the board or any place else," said Towers of the idea to add a second school. "It came from the staff. We were agitating for more ways to develop it, and we decided, 'Well, let's see if we can't get another facility put together.'"

Months before a second school officially opened or even had a location, Berthiaume was thinking about who might run the new site.

"I needed somebody," said Berthiaume, who had envisioned a three-person leadership team. "I couldn't be in two places, right? So, I needed somebody in each place to be the immediate onsite coordinator, and I [would be] the director."[2]

The person who would emerge as the leader of the second recovery high school was a middle school special education teacher at William H. Farquhar Middle School in Olney, a city in the northeastern part of Montgomery County. Sally Eller was two years older than Berthiaume, and she too had moved to Maryland from the North, though not until 1971. As the child of two teachers, Eller had been immersed in education for as long as she could remember. Running a school was almost natural to her.

She was born Sally VanRiper in October 1941, weeks before the United States entered World War II. She was raised in the Finger Lakes Region of New York State, near Seneca Falls, which was the birthplace of the Women's Rights Movement. Sally was the oldest child of Barton and Emily VanRiper, and her professional path closely followed theirs. Barton and Emily were both from Varick, New York, just south of Seneca Falls. They were born twenty-two months apart—Barton in January 1910 and Emily in October 1911.[3] Barton, from a farming family, was the valedictorian of his

Salvaging a Teenage Wasteland. Andrew J. Finch, Oxford University Press. © Oxford University Press 2024.
DOI: 10.1093/oso/9780190645502.003.0009

class at Interlaken High School in 1928, before getting a degree in electrical engineering at Syracuse.

The Depression began while Barton VanRiper was studying at Syracuse; so, although he graduated from the university with honors in 1932, he could not get an engineering job. He thus stayed in school, getting a master's degree in education at the New York State College for Teachers at Albany, which would soon become the State University of New York (SUNY). Sally's mother, Emily Lisk, actually completed two undergraduate degrees: a Bachelor of Arts in English, with a minor in French and history, in Houghton, New York; and a Bachelor of Science in library science at Albany State. Both Emily and Barton started teaching in Seneca County in the same year, 1934—Emily teaching English in Waterloo (known as the "birthplace of Memorial Day"), and Barton teaching physical science and math at Romulus High School.

Barton and Emily married in December 1936. She was 25, and he was just shy of 27 years old. Barton continued teaching math and science at Romulus High School, and he was promoted to supervising principal of the school in 1948. Emily had become a librarian as well as an English teacher in 1935.

In the summer of 1941, the US War Department, preparing for a possible entrance into World War II, approved a multimillion-dollar project to store munitions for planes guarding the Atlantic coast. They selected a site in the townships of Varick (where both Barton and Emily had been born) and Romulus, which was where the VanRipers and their family were living. According to a history of the area, the chosen site of approximately eleven thousand acres would quickly disrupt "the lives of about 150 farm families. Options on the farm lands were signed between June 12 and July 26, with August 1 as a deadline for complete exodus. The displaced families would have to move rather quickly . . . Some farmers only had three days' notice to vacate their property."[4]

A steel fence was built to wall off the new Seneca Army Depot, and, decades later, the Depot was revealed to have been a major nuclear weapons storage site, as well as a place to store uranium for the Manhattan Project to build the atomic bomb.

The VanRipers were one of the families forced to relocate. Sally VanRiper was born just a few months later, and she was raised hearing stories about it.

"There's an article in the newspaper about my grandmother saying she would rather give up her home and her land than to have any mothers' son killed in World War II," Sally recalled. "They felt they needed to sacrifice for the war effort."

Sally's mother felt differently than her grandmother about sacrificing their home. Having lost so much during the Depression, she was not ready to support having their community uprooted and losing their home.

"Um, my mother did not feel [the same way as my grandmother]," said Sally. "I probably heard about that and the Depression almost every day of my life; living at home, that topic came up. I didn't live in the times of the Depression, but it certainly had a huge shadow over us. And being forced out of the farms and the home was another aspect of that."

Barton and Emily VanRiper would have three children, all of whom were raised in central New York. Sally's sister was almost exactly one year younger, making her Sally's constant companion. According to Sally, they were "pretty much raised as twins." Her brother was just over six years younger. Their father, Barton, did not have to spend much time away from the family during World War II, as he served as an East Coast airplane spotter.

Like education, activism was in Sally's blood. She had been raised near Seneca Falls, the home of the women's suffrage movement; something about which her mother and grandmother felt great pride.

"I went to most of the marches and events for celebrating women's suffrage," said Sally. "I remember my mother telling me my grandmother was so proud when she could go to vote, and she didn't have to tell anyone how she voted."

"That whole suffrage thing was very big in our family, particularly with my mother," she continued. "My mother had also been a teacher, and she was much more active in . . . women's issues." Sally's mother, Emily, had been upset at being displaced by the Seneca Army Depot in 1941, and Sally was raised as a peace activist.

"I've always had an interest in different things [such as] during the Vietnam War," said Sally. Years later, just as she was launching the second Phoenix School in 1983, Sally returned to New York to join her mother and thousands of other women in protesting the scheduled deployment of nuclear missiles from the Seneca Army Depot.[5] They were rallying both against nuclear weapons and the "'patriarchal society' that created and used those weapons."[6]

"My mother was one of the few in the [Seneca Falls] community who was supportive of these women," said Sally. "She visited their house/headquarters, but never actually climbed a fence." At the time, Emily VanRiper was 71 years old.

Sally graduated from Ovid Central High School in 1959, and by then, her mother was an English teacher and librarian at the school. For Sally and the other girls in her school, the vocational path was narrow.

"There weren't very many careers for women," said Sally. The limited options for a woman with no money in mid-twentieth century rural New York included teaching, working at the army depot, farming, retail sales, and nursing. In fact, many of Sally's friends and family would become nurses at the infamous Willard Asylum for the Chronic Insane, which had opened in Seneca Falls in 1869 as a state-run "better alternative" for the mentally ill.[7]

"I liked science," said Sally. "I went into science, and I would have loved to have been a researcher in biology. But my family, having gone through the Depression and being very practical said, 'No. You need to be a teacher. You'll have a retirement; you'll have a secure job.'"

So, that is what Sally did. Just as both her parents had done before her, Sally matriculated to Albany State, which had just been renamed the State University of New York at Albany. She studied to become a science teacher, like her father, though her focus was the biological sciences.

"As a woman," said Sally, "The high school counselors just kind of said, 'Okay, you're going to be a teacher. You're going to go to Albany, if you want.'"

While studying at SUNY-Albany, she met Tim Eller, who was an engineering student at Rensselaer Polytechnic Institute, or "RPI." Sally received her Bachelor of Science degree in biology and education in May 1963, and a few months later, at the age of 22, Sally married Tim Eller—becoming Sally Eller. The wedding was held in New Lebanon, New York, in December 1963.

Sally and Tim Eller's wedding was less than a month after the assassination of President John F. Kennedy, but before their second anniversary, another tragedy would strike much closer to home. By the summer of 1965, Sally's father, Barton VanRiper, had become a prominent person in Seneca County. Sally described him as "a quiet man who loved building boats." Mr. VanRiper had spent his entire life in that area, protecting them during the war, and teaching or administrating in the local schools for decades. He had been appointed principal of the entire Romulus Central School District, essentially becoming its superintendent. He also was known as an expert in running rural schools.

"He was well known in the state," said Sally. "The State of New York budget committee [of the] Education Department depended on him for knowing how to run small rural schools, to do the budgeting for a small rural school, and all the tax implications. So, he was at Albany pretty often when it was budget time."

His school was on summer vacation in 1965 when a car Mr. VanRiper was driving collided with a tractor-trailer shortly after noon on Thursday, August 5. The accident was front-page news in the Rochester regional section of the *Democrat and Chronicle*.[8] The news account reported that his car was "demolished," and he was rushed to a hospital in Waterloo, where he died at 1:45 p.m.[9] Barton VanRiper was only 55.

"It was a shock," said Sally. "Deaths by accident are pretty much a shock."

At the time, Sally and Tim still did not have children, and Tim accepted a job with Sylvania in Buffalo, about two hours from Seneca Falls. Barton VanRiper had been so well-respected that his reputation got Sally hired by a Buffalo-area junior/senior high school.

"That principal had a huge amount of respect for my father," said Sally. "He taught for my father, and he's like, 'Okay, you're kinda quiet in the interview, but if you are Barton's daughter, I'm hiring you, because you'll be great.'"

Sally stayed in that job until she became pregnant with her first son.

"You have to leave when you're five months pregnant. There's no 'if, ands, or buts' about it, even though no one knew I was pregnant. You didn't want the students to know that their teacher was pregnant," said Sally, facetiously. "That would be a terrible thing. So, I went home and waited for the baby."

Their first son was born in 1967, and their second son was born in 1969. Though Sally was not teaching at the time, she was active in various movements—continuing her family tradition. As a teacher and an activist, Sally Eller joined in the fledgling free school movement of the 1960s. A. S. Neill had published *Summerhill: A Radical Approach to Child Rearing* in 1960,[10] while Sally was pursuing her teaching degree at SUNY-Albany. *Summerhill* had launched a movement aimed at empowering students; it was followed by John Holt's *How Children Fail*,[11] Jonathon Kozol's *Death at an Early Age*,[12] Herbert Kohl's *36 Children*,[13] and Ivan Illich's *Deschooling Society*.[14] These authors had criticized the existing public schools, promoting social consciousness and civic engagement in schools free of traditional bureaucracy. Free schools supported student agency and relationships between teachers and the children.

Sally and her siblings had attended small, rural schools in central New York, and their parents worked in small schools as well. Like the free schools of the 1970s, those types of schools fostered community between students, faculty, and administration.

"There were twenty, maybe twenty-one, kids in my graduating class from high school. The whole school, K through 12 was about five hundred students," said Sally. The small school experience left a deep, lasting positive impression that would carry into her work at Phoenix decades later. One of her first teaching assignments was in a small, junior high school within a school.

"I always thought that was the very best way to run a middle school," said Sally. "Having a successful school experience is pretty dependent on your relationships between the students, among the students, and the teachers."

With the birth of their second son in 1969, the Ellers had moved back to Seneca Falls. Eisenhower College, a small, liberal arts college had just opened there in 1968, funded partially by a $5 million grant from Congress.[15] The founders promoted the school as a living memorial to Dwight D. Eisenhower, and they created a unique liberal arts philosophy centered on an international curriculum. Sally and Tim became friends with several of the faculty at Eisenhower. She helped develop a cooperative nursery school there, and they based it on the tenets of the free school movement.

"Several of the professors' wives and I did this thing, and the husbands built the playground stuff," said Sally. "It was a family community effort to get, because, mostly, women up there in those days just kept their kids at home, and they stayed at home. We knew we wanted a school for our one-year-olds and three-year-olds. That's what we developed."

Tim Eller accepted a job in Virginia as an electrical engineer developing programs for defense contractors in 1971. The Ellers had friends in Gaithersburg, Maryland, just over the state line from Virginia, so they settled in Montgomery County. They found a house in Brookeville, and, at first, Sally stayed home with their two sons, who were by then ages 3 and 5.

After two years, with both boys now in school, Sally returned to teaching. She took a job as a biology teacher at Gaithersburg High School, where she taught for two years, from 1973 to 1975. Eller returned to school in 1975, enrolling at Trinity College to get her master's degree in special education—the same program in which Brian Berthiaume would enroll one year later, though neither remembered crossing paths.

"We both did the master's program, where all the courses were taught at the Mark Twain School (level 5 Special Ed program for emotional diagnosis)," said Eller. "We never had any classes at Trinity itself. The program was free to teachers, and we got 50% of our step salary."

Eller did her field work at various MCPS schools. She interned as an industrial arts teacher at Mark Twain, and she continued on there as a science teacher for summer school. Eller also was a student resource teacher at Ridgeview Middle School and Rockville High School. She earned her master of arts in teaching degree in 1976, and Rockville hired her to be a student resource teacher.

"I was at Rockville High as the PCP (drug) crisis was exploding," said Eller. "No one knew what was wrong with those kids. I was in the resource room, an alternative program working with students and teachers."

Eller worked as a special education resource teacher at Rockville for two years, where she developed a program for "disruptive and learning-disabled students." According to Eller's resume, at Rockville, she "taught science classes to unmotivated, underachieving students."[16]

"They got rid of that position because they did not want to admit that they had kids with problems," said Eller. "That was the heyday of PCP. Kids were throwing chairs around the school and in the rooms, and nobody knew what was going on. Nobody knew what was going on because those kids ended up in the resource room."

Eller continued, "It's like, 'We'll just get rid of this program, and then we won't have that reputation that we have kids with drug problems.'"[17]

Interestingly, it was just weeks after MCPS eliminated Eller's position at Rockville in 1978 that Chief di Grazia began planning the drug raids. The crackdown began in September 1978. While only four of the arrests occurred at Rockville High School, the last three reported by the media were there on December 4, 1978. Di Grazia was fired three days later.

As the drug raids were beginning, Sally Eller was starting her new job as a special education teacher at Farquhar Middle School, which was in the Sherwood High School cluster. She developed a "mainstreaming program" and was a team specialist in learning disabilities.[18] It was a more traditional special education position, and it was with younger students. While many middle schools were targeted during the fall drug crackdown, no arrests were reported at Farquhar.

Still, the "disruptive" students with drug problems at Rockville had made an impression on Eller. She realized the schools were ill-equipped to handle the large numbers of students using alcohol and drugs.

"I was in middle schools and high schools, and there's just a lot of kids," said Eller.

So, when Rita Rumbaugh invited her to join one of the first School Community Action Teams in 1981 to combat teenage drug problems in Montgomery County, Eller gladly accepted.[19] Rumbaugh had been a special education teacher herself, and she was a Parent Peer Group Coordinator in Montgomery County. She had been asked to build community coalitions, and she was given funding to host a series of development conferences. The coalitions and conferences were funded by the Maryland Department of Education, under the leadership of Health Coordinator Doris Terry. Terry was a pioneer in the creation of school-based prevention programs throughout the 1970s.

"Doris Terry took on the issue of alcohol and other drug use among teens as part of her job responsibility," said Rumbaugh. "She was a person who moved the system by her personal power."

Like Phoenix, the School Community Action Teams had been a response to the rapid rise of alcohol and drug use among US teenagers in the late 1970s, and a lack of awareness about how substance use and student behaviors were linked. According to the design, each high school cluster (i.e., a high school and the elementary and middle schools that fed it) would have a team of school counselors, nurses, administrators, teachers, and others, including aides/assistants and security guards. At that time, nurses were employed by the county health and human services department rather than MCPS. The school personnel and nurses would then be linked to the police district in which the school resided. The teams ranged in size from sixteen to twenty-five members, and Rumbaugh aimed for eighteen.

"At that time, the school didn't know the police, the police didn't know the school, and there were a lot of stereotypes about each other," said Rumbaugh. "You know, 'the police don't do this'; 'the schools don't do that'; 'I don't like those people in the schools'; 'I would never call a police officer.' "

When the Montgomery County police districts had conducted the drug raids on their local schools in 1978, they sometimes did so in response to a school call, but often did so unannounced. The lack of collaboration created a tension between the police, schools, parents, and students, which often played out in the media. The School Community Action Teams, in contrast, were designed to communicate and coordinate across the continuum of care, from prevention to intervention. To prepare the teams, Rumbaugh hosted five-day team development meetings in nice conference centers, and Maryland paid for all the expenses, including substitute teachers while the teachers were out of their classrooms.

"They would have to commit to those days," said Rumbaugh. "And the school would release them, and they would be lodged [for five days]."

With twenty high school clusters in MCPS at the time, the planning was intense. Rumbaugh tried to do at least four conferences per year.

"It about killed me," said Rumbaugh. "I didn't know it; I was young, and I loved what I was doing."

To build the teams, Rumbaugh had to recruit members. She would typically begin by contacting a high school principal to get permission and "get that rolling." One of the first to express interest was Jim Fish, the principal at Sherwood High School.

"He was really motivated to do something about this," recalled Rumbaugh. "He had that personal energy and vibrancy to bring a team together and inspire people. So, he was a great one to start with.

"And from then, I got an okay from the old-boys network at that time, at the administrative level. These principals would talk to each other, and it would become a thing to do."

Sally Eller's school, Farquhar Middle School, was in Jim Fish's Sherwood cluster, and Eller was selected to participate in one of the first School Community Action

Team development conferences. It was held at the conference center in New Windsor, Maryland.

"We brought together speakers, and people talked about this problem," said Rumbaugh. "It wasn't even well-defined at that point, but these behaviors among young people could be attributed to their alcohol or other drug use, and principally, marijuana use, because nobody knew anything about marijuana."

By 1981, the Phoenix School had been operating for two years, and while Berthiaume did not attend the conference in New Windsor, his Phoenix program was discussed at the development conferences. Eller was only a few years removed from working closely with students at Rockville High School who were struggling with alcohol and drugs. So, when she heard someone talk about the Phoenix School, it resonated with her.

"I went [to the conference], and I really was intrigued by the whole thing," she said.

However interesting she found Phoenix, though, the program was not easily accessed by students in Olney (where Farquhar was located) or Sandy Spring (home to Sherwood High School). Those cities were up-county, and the Phoenix School was down-county in Silver Spring, a half hour away. Morning bus service was not available to students enrolled at Phoenix, so parents had to transport them.

"[Phoenix] wasn't reaching that part of the county, and it wasn't easily accessible," said Rumbaugh. "We couldn't access that program. Sally knew that."

"It was hard for the parents who lived at the upper end of the County to get their kids [to the Phoenix School]," said Eller. "That was a big reason, just location."[20]

Expansion had been a part of the Phoenix plan from the beginning, and, as previously mentioned, Berthiaume was considering who would be best to lead the day-to-day operations at a new site. One of the major facets of Phoenix was taking students to speak in Montgomery County schools, including middle schools. MCPS had requested funds from the federal Safe and Drug Free Schools grant to pay for buses to transport students during the speaking engagements and for substitutes to fill in while Berthiaume and/or other staff chaperones were away from Phoenix. Rita Rumbaugh was Maryland's Safe and Drug Free Schools Coordinator, and she felt students speaking about their alcohol and drug issues and the Phoenix School fit nicely into the School Community Action Team philosophy. So, she approved the transportation funding for Phoenix speakers.

"By that time, see, we had trained the administration and nurses, teachers, and others to be aware and to be able to receive that information," said Rumbaugh. "So, it didn't just come out of 'there are these troubled kids telling us about their life.' No. It was part of that fabric of what we could do together."

One of the schools Berthiaume visited in the 1981–1982 school year was William H. Farquhar Middle School. Sally Eller had been trained at the development conference, where she had first learned about the Phoenix School, and she attended the student presentation with great interest. After the talk, Eller and another staff member introduced themselves to Berthiaume.

"I always took two charismatic kids to tell their story," Berthiaume recalled. "And Sally and this other [person] came up, and they both were really interested in Phoenix and what was going on.

"I had mentioned, 'Oh, we're going to open another one,' and I could tell they were both interested."

Even though Eller had never run a school herself, Berthiaume felt she was a good fit.

"She was very, very nurturing but also tough," said Berthiaume. "I just go by my intuition mostly on everything, and I offered the position to Sally."

Eller was offered a job at the Phoenix School before the second site had opened, and while she was still employed at Farquhar (see Figure 9.1). She thus quit her teaching job at the end of the 1982 school year and taught in the Phoenix School's extended school year program that summer. That job extended through the fall semester while the second site was prepared.

The second site came to be known as "Phoenix II," and the original site became "Phoenix I." The organizational structure was set up for Berthiaume to oversee both Phoenix schools. He would spend time at each school, but both would have their own site coordinators. Plans were made for Phoenix II to open in January 1983, to start the

Figure 9.1. Sally Eller was selected to be the Phoenix II coordinator. She taught at the Phoenix School in the summer and fall of 1982, while the second site was prepared, and she moved to Phoenix II in Gaithersburg, Maryland, when it opened in January 1983. Eller remained in that position for eighteen years. (Source: Mike Bucci.)

spring semester. Teacher Steve Baddour would be the site coordinator for Phoenix I, and Sally Eller was chosen to coordinate Phoenix II.

"[Sally] was the other teacher at [Phoenix I] for a semester," said Baddour. "We always knew that she was going to be opening Phoenix II, so that was coming, and that she was just sort of with us to get the lay of the land."

While Berthiaume had been running Phoenix I for nearly four years by the time Phoenix II started, Eller was in some ways the more seasoned educator. She had gotten her teaching degree in 1963, and she had grown up the daughter of a veteran school principal. Eller got her master's degree a year before Berthiaume, and she had worked at both middle and high schools. While she was a special education teacher the last few years before coming to Phoenix, most of her experience was teaching biology in traditional school settings. Berthiaume, on the other hand, had worked almost exclusively in nontraditional or alternative schools, and he had made preventing drug use a mission since his early teaching days. Berthiaume had trained in marriage and family counseling, and he incorporated those types of activities along with yoga and meditation into his approach at Phoenix I. Eller brought a more structured approach to Phoenix II.

"My duties were total supervision of that program," said Eller. "You know, preparing the schedules, overseeing the day's activities, supporting the teachers."

"We wanted somebody experienced, and she did a good job," said Dick Towers. "She really ran with it."

In addition to Eller, there were two teachers and an assistant. There was an English and social studies teacher, and a math and science teacher. Over time, the school added a third full-time teacher, so there was a total of five staff.

Phoenix II went through a few different staff members to start. The first two teachers at Phoenix II were the English and social studies teacher Sally Houlton, and a math teacher who, according to Eller, was not the best fit for the school.

"He didn't mesh with the kids too well," said Eller. "He didn't mesh with the whole thing. I would say a nice guy, but it really wasn't what he wanted to do."

She found his replacement at her place of worship. After Eller moved to Maryland, she had begun attending Quaker meetings in Sandy Spring.

"There's a very strong Quaker community [in Sandy Spring]," said Eller. "I was raised as a Methodist in little ol' Varick [New York], right up there where I grew up and spent all my first 18 years. But my neighbors down here were Quaker, and it just was a nice place to be. It was good spiritually, and nice people."

The current website for the Sandy Spring [Quaker] Friends Meeting notes it is "a warm and welcoming community where we support each other in our shared journeys of the Spirit. When we gather in worship, we seek the indwelling Spirit through receptive silence, listening for the piece of the Divine that resides in everyone . . . We celebrate the diversity of expression that every member brings, understanding that the Light of God lives and shines within each and every one of us."[21]

It was in that Quaker community one summer that Eller met a 30-year-old public elementary school teacher named Mike Bucci. Bucci had received a bachelor's degree in elementary education and begun teaching in Montgomery County in 1973, the same year Eller had returned to teaching biology in Gaithersburg. He completed his master's in mathematics education at the University of Maryland in 1978, the year of the drug crackdown. Bucci, though, had no background in substance use counseling or recovery, and he had spent his career teaching fifth and sixth grade. In 1985, he was preparing to move from a sixth-grade classroom to fourth grade, which he saw as being pretty daring at the time, but Eller had a different idea.

"I knew he would be really a great asset [for Phoenix II]," said Eller. "He was a nice guy, interested in people and what they're doing. Actually, I thought the elementary background would be good. And he loves the outdoors."

"Parallel paths," said Bucci. "There was a need in my life, and so I started attending a Quaker meeting, got on a committee with Sally Eller, who saw my interest in lots of different things and taught at this school for kids with substance abuse problems, and [she] sent me a note one summer and said, 'You know we need a male teacher.'" One of the reasons the school wanted a male on staff was to help with the new urinalyses the school was implementing.

"It was definitely divine intervention," he added. "It was like a calling. You know, you hear about people having a calling—I definitely feel that this was. I was fortunate enough to find a place for me to be able to feel like I made a difference and had some gifts to offer."

Bucci would teach at Phoenix for the next twenty years. He started teaching both math and science, but the school later hired a third teacher, Izzy Kovach. Kovach would teach science and social studies, which freed Bucci and Houlton to focus exclusively on math and English, respectively. Former Phoenix student, Leaf Van Boven, went on to complete a PhD at Cornell in social psychology and become a college professor, but he remembered the academics as not being extremely rigorous.

"When I look at the work that my [own] kids do in high school, I did not get the rigor, depth, and variety that my kids got in terms of education. There's no denying that, but again, it's not as though there was a feasible alternative," said Van Boven, who transferred back to Damascus High School in Damascus, Maryland, after finishing his time at Phoenix.

"In Phoenix, there were kids who hadn't cracked a book or who could barely read. That's just not a setting where you're gonna read a lot of Shakespeare. I was fortunate that I was able to go back into a high school setting [in Damascus] where I could get some of that, and I made an effort to kind of retrofill some of the educational gaps when I was in college. It is true that the school has to, to some extent, serve the lowest common denominator, but it's gotta be so that everyone can be successful if they put forth a reasonable amount of effort. There's no version of, like, AP classes at a Phoenix School, but again, the alternative is those kids not being in school."

At first, Phoenix II ran similarly to Phoenix I. The school provided individual counseling once per week or as needed and a daily counseling group.;[22] Berthiaume would come to the school at least three days a week, meet with students individually and also help with the groups. Nobody on either staff yet had a counseling or social work degree, and Berthiaume had the most experience running therapeutic groups. Both Phoenix programs had similar underlying philosophies.

"The purpose of [Phoenix]," said Eller, "was always to have the students graduate from high school. This was a program for kids in [grades] nine through twelve. These are kids that had basically stopped going to school."

"We did not get kids from court. We got students from their counselors referring them from the high schools, because they stopped coming to school, because they were too involved with drugs and alcohol. Our mission was to get them to come to school, to teach them the classes that they needed, and to have them graduate. In order to do that, they had to be clean and sober, or else they weren't going to accomplish anything. They weren't going to graduate. That was always the purpose."

When Phoenix II started, most of its students, like the Phoenix I students, had not been receiving prior alcohol or drug treatment. Like Berthiaume, Eller would take students to speak in schools, and most referrals would come from MCPS high school staff rather that treatment providers.

Phoenix alum, John Edmonds, was attending Thomas S. Wooten High School in Rockville when Eller and a few Phoenix II students paid a visit. Edmonds said Wooten "very upper-middle class," and he described the meeting:

"It was early morning, and I got a pass. You know they would send these passes to whatever classroom, and the principal would want you down in the office, which was a regular occurrence for me. And I remember it was early in the morning . . .

"I think there was two or three kids [from Phoenix II]. We got called into an empty classroom. There was maybe twelve of us, and each one [of the Phoenix students] told, you know, very briefly, you know, what life was like for them before they got into a recovery school; how their lives had gotten better since being in a recovery school. And then there was some Q & A at the end about, you know, what a recovery school is; you know, what do they do there, how it's different which, you know, of course, is incredibly different. They told a little bit about what it was like then and what it's like now.

"I remember these kids told their story and, you know, I heard their experience, you know, as they say, and I really wasn't much excited about it. I mean it was just, you know, one more chore, one more kinda punishment. Sally Eller says that I asked her in there whether or not alcoholism was hereditary. My father died from alcoholism, and at the time was just having recovered from a liver transplant, so sorta was a concern of mine at the time. You know, she told me that, but I don't remember asking that but, you know, it was very quick. It was thirty–forty minutes, you know, and back to class we were sent."

Edmonds did not transfer immediately to Phoenix II. A few months later, he was in court on drug charges, and he was given the option of enrolling at Phoenix II during their summer period.

"I only went to the Phoenix School to get out of going to jail," said Edmonds.

In the early 1980s, there still were not many adolescent treatment programs in the United States. Eller was clear, however, that the Phoenix Schools were not intended to be treatment centers.

"We were education," said Eller. "We were a school with a specialized component." Of the many alternative schools in Montgomery County, only two were Phoenix Schools. The others had different foci, such as attendance, hands-on instruction, or behavior.

"The kids [at the other schools] would say they didn't have a drug problem," said Eller. "They had a behavior problem, so they would go to another program. Well, it turns out probably 90% of them had a drug problem, but they were able to get away [with it]. They didn't want to admit that part because that freaked their parents out."

The Phoenix schools, though, would require students to admit to their alcohol or other drug use prior to admission.

"We had a series of interviews before they came in, and they had to agree to want to be there," said Eller. "It was a voluntary program." The voluntary nature of the school would remain a hallmark for future recovery high schools.

"Each student said they wanted to come," said Eller. "They had to pretty much admit that they had a problem, such that this would be a good school for them. They had to agree that they were going to work on getting clean and sober, and the parents had to agree that they were going to be supportive."

At the same time, because so few students in the early years of the program had received treatment, Phoenix built in a therapeutic curriculum for that purpose. At both Phoenix I and Phoenix II, the main components included individual and group counseling, drug education, experiential activities, and parent support groups.

There were counseling groups each day, co-led by a teacher, Eller and/or Berthiaume. Berthiaume would come to Phoenix II most days, and he'd sit in on the counseling group.

"I was basically learning a lot from Brian on how to run these groups," said Eller. "That was his skill, and the individual counseling. I really learned from Brian while we were getting Phoenix II off the ground."

The required parent groups were a centerpiece of Phoenix I, and they also were required at Phoenix II. The schools hosted a parent support group every week, and Phoenix contracted with social workers to lead the groups.

"The parents had to agree to participate in the program," said Eller. "That is get the kids to school and come to the weekly required parent counseling session. I always said no one got to the Phoenix School by accident."

While much of the framework of the two Phoenix schools was the same, the personalities of the staff varied, and Phoenix II thus evolved differently from Berthiaume's original program. The three most prominent examples of this divergence were the drug education class, the outdoor programming, and the ultimate requirement that students be abstinent and attend outside Twelve Step meetings. Indeed, these changes transformed the Phoenix Schools from drug and alcohol intervention programs into recovery high schools that would meet best practice standards today.

Drug Education Class

While both schools featured drug education as part of the curriculum, English teacher Sally Houlton developed a full curriculum for a drug education class that in time came to be called the Recovery Class. Like Berthiaume and Eller, Houlton had a special education degree, and her material served as both an education in alcohol and other drug addiction recovery as well as an orientation to Phoenix itself.

"Sally Houlton did the majority of the work on developing this. I would say probably 95%," said Mike Bucci.

Before most of the incoming Phoenix students had received treatment, and before abstinence was an expectation more than an aspiration, the drug education class served as an intervention and motivation for sobriety. Over time, it became a way of supporting the recovery of the students.

Eller taught the class, and said, "There's where we got a lot of work on what addiction was, and a lot of work with encouraging them to use AA or NA and various life skills. They were huge parts of our program.

"They basically had almost two counseling sessions a day. The Drug Education was a little more, 'Let's learn about this.' And the group therapy was a therapy group about what the issues were for the students for that day."

The school hired Marianne Smyth in 1986 as a para-educator, and she highlighted the recovery plans that were part of Houlton's curriculum. She explained it was an elective credit for graduation that students took every day, and the course incorporated a level system.

"They would have an English, and a social studies, and then they'd have recovery class," said Smyth.

"Kids had to do journals. They had to do step work. It just wasn't something out of a book. And the journals, if they didn't want anyone to read it, they could turn the page over. Sally Houlton could spot it in a second if something was going on."

In fact, what Houlton and Phoenix II had created was one of the first formal recovery plans ever devised for adolescents.

Outdoor Experiential Activities

One advantage of the small school size was the opportunity to venture off campus with the entire school, and Brian Berthiaume had been incorporating field trips and other experiential activities about once a month since the first days of Phoenix I. Parents writing letters of support to the School Board in 1981 had suggested these trips were one of the main benefits of Phoenix. One parent had written, "The field trips which involved overnight exercises in a wilderness setting . . . are in effect positive extracurricular disciplines to keep you and idle minds busy and hence, free of mischief."

While the Phoenix I students did some camping excursions, their field trips more frequently involved cultural and artistic experiences.

"We did field trips [at Phoenix I]," said teacher Steve Baddour. "We did camping trips. It could be a lot of fun and really bonding. Other than that, I did most of the field trips, and they would be to go and see a play, or even sometimes a movie, if we were studying something and there was a movie of it, or somehow related to the kids' lives or whatever. We didn't have VCR's then and so forth. A lot of the times, we would get on the subway and go downtown, or even a lot of times, the teachers would drive."

Sally Eller continued such activities at Phoenix II and expanded upon them. Berthiaume admitted the outdoor component was a key difference that emerged between the two programs.

"[Sally] did things that I wouldn't do," said Berthiaume. "She would go on four and five camping trips in the woods with the kids, and I wouldn't do it. I'd go for one or two days at the most. She would go for four or five days, and I just couldn't handle being out. I didn't like camping; she did, and that extra component of all that camping made more cohesiveness in her school than in mine."

Student John Edmonds remembered selecting Phoenix II over Phoenix I because of the camping component, even though it would require a thirty-five-minute drive from his home in Potomac to the school in Gaithersburg.

"I remember having some choice cause Phoenix I was closer to where we lived," said Edmonds. "Phoenix I was described as a more artsy school, and Phoenix II was described as more of an outdoor school. You know they took you on backpacking trips and rock-climbing trips and whitewater rafting trips. So that was a no-brainer for, you know, a sixteen-year-old boy."

Eller acknowledged one of the assets that she felt Mike Bucci would bring to Phoenix II was his interest in the outdoors, and Bucci embraced that opportunity. He even gave it a name that aligned well with the school's title, "Student Outdoor Adventure in Recovery," or "SOAR."

"Because of my interest, we expanded the outdoor adventure program," said Bucci. Using state and county funding set aside for peer leadership and recreation activities, trips often were multiday, overnight excursions.

"The state of Maryland had a peer leadership program where they would fund an outward-bound expedition, and that could be a seven-day program," said Bucci. "So, we took kids out on basically a lifesaving boat that had two masts, so they learned how to sail. They learned how to navigate, and it was the metaphor for, 'What kind of world do you want to have,' 'cause you know everything that we have is on this boat, including each other, so how do you communicate with each other' and all of that."

Student John Edmonds had fond memories of Mike Bucci and his passion for the outdoors (see Figure 9.2).

"Mike Bucci," said Edmonds, "He's a, you know, Teva wearing, flip-flopper, granola, ponytail type of guy. You know, one day someone throws an apple out the school bus

Figure 9.2. Mike Bucci taught at Phoenix II for twenty years. One of the assets he brought to the school was his interest in the outdoors. Bucci created a program of outdoor excursions called "Student Outdoor Adventure in Recovery,", which included activities such as backpacking, rock-climbing, and whitewater rafting. This is a picture of Bucci in his rock-climbing gear. (Source: Mike Bucci.)

window, and he slams on the brakes of the school bus. We're all, you know, sliding to the front, and he made you go out and get the apple core. And he explained why: deer were going to come across and get hit by a car, you know, eating an apple. He had a great love for the outdoors—you had to to have that job, but it was great."

Utilizing a county government program for kids at risk, Phoenix II had access to canoes, climbing gear, backpacking gear, and government employees to serve as guides. To create cohesion, Bucci and the guides would sometimes take half the students one day and half the students another day. In addition to state and county resources, Eller got the local Rotary Club to give the school grant money for kids who couldn't afford it.

"We did a lot of outdoor stuff," said Eller. "Caving, skiing, rock climbing, biking. We'd go on five-day bike trips, and they'd have to live in their tents and pack their food every morning and get on their bikes."

Indeed, the outdoor trips became one of the defining features of Phoenix II, something alums remembered decades later. Cheryl and Del Gendron met as students at Phoenix II from 1985 to 1987 and later married when they were in their 30s. They have picture albums from their years in Phoenix, and these albums have many photos from the camping trips. In an interview for this book, they both reminisced about those outdoor adventures:

CHERYL: We had these trips that we went to. Seneca Rocks. I mean how far away is that, that's like four hours way—Seneca Rocks or Western Pennsylvania or West Virginia—and we went camping, hiking, and rock climbing. And the rec center would bring these real guides, like these people that had this experience.

DEL: Caving, we went caving.

CHERYL: Yeah, spelunking.

DEL: With like miner's caps . . . Some people might have been afraid of heights and just said I can't do it, you know. They might have said, "I can't, I'm too claustrophobic. I can't do it." And, I mean, we wouldn't push people or make them do something they didn't want to do, but . . .

CHERYL: They definitely did though. I remember hiking and being, "I can't believe you're making me do this" and whine, whine, whine, and then you just get to the top and you're like . . .

DEL: Grateful.

Abstinence and Twelve Step Groups

Perhaps the most significant transformation made by Phoenix II was the requirement that students be abstinent from alcohol or other substances upon admission, and that they attend outside Twelve Step groups while enrolled. This involved revising admission policies, modifying therapeutic supports, and adding accountability procedures, such as urinalysis and meeting attendance logs.

The external evaluation contracted by the MCPS Department of Educational Accountability in 1981 noted "the stated goal of the [Phoenix] program: that [students] eliminate their drug use within the one year they are typically permitted to remain in the program." It was not expected that students entering the program already be alcohol and drug free. Indeed, "changing their attitudes about drugs and drug use" and "reducing their drug usage or even being drug free for at least short periods of time" were seen as successes for the school.[23] Unfortunately, the report also concluded the following:

> Despite the program's effectiveness in virtually eliminating drug usage during the school day, self-reports by students indicate that the program is having virtually no effect on reducing overall drug and alcohol usage.[24]

This finding hit hard, because, as Berthiaume said, "They were going to close the school based on this evaluation."

While Berthiaume and his parents were able to present testimonial evidence that persuaded the school board not only to save Phoenix I but later to fund Phoenix II, it appears the report had stated what the staff already knew. The school needed to modify its approach to student alcohol and drug use, and the evaluators included a musing that set the stage for reformation:

> The Phoenix School may well be too brief and superficial a program to impact such profound habits. It is probably correct in thinking that it does not belong in the treatment business, and *its goal should be reformulated to reflect this* (italics added), or the program should be profoundly redesigned so as to have the "weight" required to do effective treatment.[25]

Neither Berthiaume nor Eller recalled the report's suggestion as driving the decision to start requiring abstinence and Twelve Step meetings. While just such a change occurred early in the life of Phoenix II, it was not immediate. Phoenix I had used a level system with incentives to encourage reductions in drug usage, and this system relied on student self-report.

"You can imagine how reliable that is, right?" said Steve Baddour.

Still, when Phoenix II started in January 1983, it incorporated the same approach to reducing drug usage, using group therapy and a behavior modification level system to educate and motivate students to change. A newspaper article about the school published in December 1985 mentioned individual counseling, daily groups, and "programs on drugs and self-awareness."[26] Another article reported, "The Phoenix School relies on students applying peer pressure on newcomers to stop taking drugs and involves parents in counseling sessions."[27] Neither story mentioned Twelve Step meetings or expectations of abstinence. At the time, Dr. Towers called Phoenix a "treatment program for teenage addicts,"[28] and Eller said, "They all come in in denial. It's about a month before they admit it. That's hard work and they do have slip ups . . . You replace drugs with caring about one another." She also said most students would return to their former schools "after a year or a year and a half."[29]

And just like Phoenix I, none of the Phoenix II staff was trained in addictions. Eller started to feel uncomfortable with that design.

"I thought, 'I don't know what I'm doing here,'" said Eller. "You see, Brian just talked the school system into having this program, copying what the health department had been doing [at the Other Way School], where they had teachers, and then they had therapists. The therapist was Brian.[30]

"He talked the school system into having their own program, and he would be the therapist; although Brian never had any formal training in addictions treatment.

"I realized there was a lot of work to be done with parents with the family counseling," said Eller. "You just couldn't do this in a vacuum without including the families, the parents, and I really had no training as a counselor."

So, Eller decided to enroll in the University of Maryland School of Social Work in 1985. Berthiaume followed suit, and in 1988, they both received Master of Social Work degrees.

"That was kind of rough, leaving half day, once a week," said Eller. "Most of the classes were at night, but I convinced my staff to let me out a half day."

Starting with her time at Phoenix I in 1982, Eller had been formulating her own ideas about how to best help the Phoenix students in their recovery. She felt the original level system was "half-hearted," and at Phoenix II she decided to revise it.

"I spent untold hours of time working on that," said Eller, noting she began using it as a way to measure progress during a student's time at the school.[31]

"I am much more practical [than Berthiaume], and [I decided to go] step-by-step and lay it all out."

Several things had converged for Eller to help her reconceive the recovery program at the Phoenix Schools. She had learned about Alcoholics Anonymous and Narcotics Anonymous through Rita Rumbaugh's materials from the Safe and Drug Free Schools program, and she had read the recovery literature from the Hazelden Foundation—one of the most prominent addiction treatment publishers at the time. As she rewrote the level system and recovery policies, she started to include attendance at Twelve Step meetings, asking students to get slips signed to prove they had actually gone to the meeting.

Eller's training as a science teacher also had shown her the value of urinalysis as an accountability measure. Berthiaume noted that soon after Eller had come to Phoenix, a student had enrolled and was doing drug screens on his own.

"He started doing urine screens," said Berthiaume. "I don't think it was for court, but I remember he did it. He was a nice kid; one that we all liked, and everybody looked up to . . . Sally was big on the urine screens, too, because she had all that training. And so, we started doing the urine screens at both the schools after she came on board."

Eller's social work training affirmed the inclusion of both urinalysis and Twelve Step meetings, which at the time were the primary mode of treatment for substance use disorders. The late 1980s were also a time of the expansion of residential treatment for adolescents. While most students enrolling in the Phoenix Schools still had not received treatment, urinalysis, Twelve Step meetings, and more clinically based counseling services provided evidence and impetus to refer students to treatment after they had enrolled.

"I guess if we evolved to anything," said Eller, "it was sending more and more of the students to treatment who came into our program, because if they weren't making progress, passing the levels, getting clean, then, working closely with the parents—the parents were a big factor in all this—we became pretty skilled at getting them into treatment for thirty days, sixty days, something like that. So then, they would come back to the Phoenix School.[32]

"As more residential treatment programs opened up in the eighties and nineties, because there weren't very many at the beginning, then it was easier to get kids in."

This expectation of abstinence and accountability for maintaining it had shifted the school into an abstinence-focused recovery support program, and thus a recovery high school more representative of the dozens of schools that would emerge later.

"Phoenix II," said Eller, "was much more involved in the recovery part of the whole process for the kids. I just got very involved in that and knew that if I couldn't get these kids clean and, at least, committed to being clean while they were in high school, then they weren't going to graduate, and that was our overall goal."

Phoenix II alum, John Edmonds, affirmed the value of a having a strong recovery component. Having struggled to stay sober prior to enrolling—"I couldn't put together three weeks of success anywhere else," he said—Edmonds arrived at Phoenix II after they had instituted required Twelve Step meeting attendance and urinalysis for accountability. He recounted attending a wedding where alcohol was being served about ninety days into his time at Phoenix:

"[Phoenix II] was very peer-pressure oriented toward sobriety, and three months in I was at a family wedding and my mother, of all people, said, 'You know, you can have a glass of champagne, right? It's not really drinking.' That, you know, certainly sounds like an attractive idea but, you know, I had known enough by now, three months into treatment basically, you know, I knew that was drinking.

"So I, for the first time, really had a decision to make, and so I called one of the guys from the [Twelve Step] program, Aaron, who was my running buddy after that point for the next year. You know, I said, 'Hey, this is the deal.' And he said, 'Hey, I'll come pick you up, and I'll take you to [an AA] meeting.'

"And I just walked out of the wedding, and he picked me up outside, and we went to a meeting. So that was really the first time I decided, right? You know, I, I gotta try this thing."

"I can tell you this," said Phoenix I teacher Steve Baddour of both schools. "Once we embraced the recovery program, it was wholehearted. That was the way it was going to be, and we never looked back. It made much more sense, and it was far more effective. I liked it a lot better."

Hadley Farms House

Another key difference between Phoenix I and Phoenix II was the facility. Whereas Phoenix I had found space alongside district administration offices in a recently closed urban elementary school building, Phoenix II opened in a less developed area. Gaithersburg had been home to the Hadley Farms Dairy for decades until it ceased operations in 1977, and over time the dairy farm property had been sold and subdivided.[33] The county allowed MCPS to use a house from the old farm for the new Phoenix program.[34] Eller described it as a little "ranch house" (see Figure 9.3).

Longtime Phoenix staff member, Marianne Smyth recalled, "It was a working dairy farm. Now, when we were there, it was just the barn and silo were left [in addition to the house]."

"It was very challenging to provide school and recovery in a private house," said Eller.

Figure 9.3. The farmhouse pictured here was the original site of Phoenix II and is now home to the Hadley Farms Community Center in Gaithersburg, Maryland. Phoenix II operated at this site from 1983 to 1988. (Source: Andy Finch.)

Bucci recalled the house was about a mile off the main road.

"It was a gravel road," said Bucci. "And there was nothing between."

According to Bucci and Eller, the social studies/English teacher (Sally Houlton) was in the dining room, and math/science (Bucci) was in the living room, with tables arranged in a U-shape. Groups were held in one of the bedrooms. The space gave the classes a seminar-feel, and there were not many doors in the house.

"My classroom would be a step-down living room with a stone fireplace and a sliding glass door backing up to the woods," said Bucci. "I'd see the fox and deer. Part of my science curriculum was a bird feeder and identifying species. You know, 'Is that a deer?' Class would stop.

"And then, the English teacher [Houlton] would have a question, 'Okay, Dickens wrote this, but Mike, did you know whether Dickens wrote . . . what else did Dickens write?' You know, kind of this back-and-forth kind of thing."

The Hadley Farmhouse along with the many camping trips no doubt contributed to a strong sense of cohesiveness at Phoenix II, but the house was a temporary home. According to Bucci, the house, which had a pool, had been promised to the local area as a community center once the land had been developed.

"So, we had to find a new home," said Bucci.

They considered a few places, but the school system had set aside forty acres for a new elementary school on the Hadley Farms property. If the school could be put there, they would not have to buy additional property. As they were considering that option, though, Bucci recalled a meeting by the new homeowner's association in which a community member said, "We don't want those kids in our neighborhood."

"Excuse me," thought Bucci. "Those kids are currently in your neighborhood, and it's not been an issue for you. Tell me how it's impacted you." Still, according to Bucci, the head of the homeowners' association at the time "was a real ally and advocate for having the school there."

In April 1987, though, the school board rejected a proposal to amend the 1987 capital budget to appropriate $285,000 to "plan, construct, and equip" a new facility for Phoenix II on that property.[35] No details were provided in the meeting minutes as to why, but just two months later, on June 22, the board unanimously approved amending the 1988 capital budget with an "emergency appropriation of $150,000 for supplies, materials, and equipment . . . to provide a facility."[36] The rationale provided was that "the Student Construction Trades Foundation, Inc., can build the facility at almost one-half the cost of contracting the project, and students will benefit from the experience of construction [of] a nonresidential facility."

"We were talking with some of the vocational people," said Dick Towers. "They were looking for a project, so we said, 'Let's try that.' We got the superintendent to agree, and yeah, we just went with it."

The new Phoenix II facility would thus be built by MCPS construction trades students. The school was designed by the same external architectural firm that would draw up plans for the Hadley Farms Elementary School on a hill overlooking the new Phoenix building, and the students built it in a year. Bill Wilder, the MCPS director of school facilities, said the final cost was $230,000, and having students do the project saved the district almost $500,000.[37] This would be the first-ever facility constructed specifically for a recovery high school, and still one of the few in the United States built for that purpose. Most recovery high schools today either share facilities or repurpose existing structures.

According to news accounts, the school was built in a "residential style" to blend into the surrounding neighborhood (see Figure 9.4).[38] There were three classrooms, a large multipurpose room that could be divided, a staff lounge, a kitchen, and two offices that could also serve as conference rooms. Years later, alum Edmonds could still picture the layout of the school.

"It looked like a A-frame house," said Edmonds. "I mean, I can draw the map in my head. It was two classrooms and then a third classroom in the corner, a kitchen, and Sally [Eller]'s office, and the administrative office, and that was it. Kind of a restroom area in the middle; you know there was one restroom, tiny little, you know. It was a typical tiny kitchen, nothing to it. You brought your lunch. You brought it back to your desk; you ate it, and there [were] times when you get to a certain level, you could, they'd take you to Burger King or whatever was up the road. But, it kinda looked like a

Figure 9.4. The second Phoenix II site was built by Montgomery County Public Schools construction trades students, and it was dedicated June 1, 1988. The building was rebuilt after a fire and looked similar to the original structure. This photo shows the back of the rebuilt facility. (Source: Andy Finch.)

house. It was a little bit, you know, bigger than a traditional house, I guess. The house was right here, and then everything else was, you know, neighborhood. It was like just removed from the neighborhood, which I don't know how they got that piece of property."

The building was dedicated at a ribbon-cutting ceremony on June 1, 1988, and it hosted a graduation ceremony for thirteen Phoenix students two days later. The occasion drew attention from First Lady Nancy Reagan, who had been promoting her Just Say No campaign to prevent drug abuse since 1982.[39] By 1988, near the end of President Ronald Reagan's second term, Just Say No had become a household phrase, and the First Lady sent a letter to commemorate the opening of the new Phoenix II facility. The letter expressed her "warm greetings" and extended her "heartfelt thanks for all you are doing in this vital campaign" against drug abuse.[40] "We can win this battle because of people like you," wrote the First Lady.[41]

Dr. Towers attended the ceremony and said the new structure was "more than nails and wood and brick and mortar. It's a symbol of the cooperative effort in Montgomery County in fighting drugs and alcohol the likes of which don't exist anywhere in the country."[42] Apparently referring to President Reagan's War on Drugs, he added,

"While others are talking about using armed force in fighting drugs, our officials are working together to do something, and it has borne fruit."[43]

Sally Eller told the attendees the new school was "a symbol of the faith that adults have in [the students'] recovery as they struggle to turn their lives around from the destruction of alcohol and drugs."[44]

Berthiaume concurred, summing up the week, "It's as if we've died and gone to heaven."[45]

Philosophical Differences

Even though Berthiaume and Eller shared a stage and pride in the new facility, by the time the new Phoenix II building opened in 1988, the two programs had grown apart, due both to the geographical distance and the different personalities of their leaders.

Berthiaume acknowledged their differences. "I was always a little more on the affective side than [Eller] was. She was more kind of strict. She was more demanding than I was. I'm not saying that's good or bad, but she did things that I wouldn't do."

Most people who were involved with both programs recall there being some tension between the two leaders. Dr. Towers referred to it as an "interpersonal rivalry."

"I would bring in a consultant once a month," said Berthiaume. "That guy would go to Phoenix II, and he would go to Phoenix I, but always the issues at Phoenix I were different than the issues at Phoenix II. At Phoenix II, the issues were always like Sally and I were 'mom' and 'dad,' and his workshops would often focus on Brian and Sally's relationship with each other, because there were some problems there between mom and dad. Whereas at Phoenix I with Steve [Baddour], I didn't have that kind of conflict with him."

"I'd say it gradually shifted," said Eller. "[Brian] was very busy with all the things at the Phoenix I program, and it was a little hard for the kids to have someone coming in two or three days a week. You'd have the rest of the time, so it evolved that he did the Phoenix I program, and I did the Phoenix II program."

"Sometimes I'd call Phoenix II and say, 'I can't make it today,' because I knew Sally could run the groups," said Berthiaume. "Steven [Baddour] always wanted me [at Phoenix I]; Sally didn't really care. She was just as happy without me being there I think."

"We just drifted apart," said Eller. "I said, 'Brian, why don't you do Phoenix I. You're really busy down there. I'll do Phoenix II.' We did collaborate quite a bit, but eventually, we split, became two different staffs totally. I wouldn't say there was any real animosity, but it just didn't quite work out."

Years later, Eller, Berthiaume, and their staffs and administrators eventually reached a point where their differences had faded to the background, and they developed a mutual respect for what they originated.

"Her school was very effective," said Berthiaume.

"I really learned from Brian while we were getting Phoenix II off the ground," said Eller.

"Brian was very good at selling the program to people that were in charge; he did a great job with them."

Thanksgiving Celebration

When Phoenix II opened their new facility, one of the newspaper stories specifically emphasized that the school included "a large double classroom that can be opened up for . . . the annual Thanksgiving dinner."[46] Both sites had developed a tradition of hosting a meal for Thanksgiving, during which they would invite not only current families but also alumni and community members. It became a way of getting together and expressing gratitude, which is an essential part of Twelve Step recovery programs.

"My favorite day in the whole world was Thanksgiving," said Phoenix II para-educator, Marianne Smyth. "Because we would cook; the alumni would cook and come back; parents brought dishes. I loved it. It was so neat."

"It was a very emotional gathering," remembered student Leaf Van Boven.

The dinners were elaborate occasions. Parents would cook multiple turkeys, and Eller recalled having a large group in attendance.

"Often we had one hundred people there," said Eller. "All their counselors from their schools, all the people who had helped them, their families. The students would cook their favorite Thanksgiving dish."

Thanksgiving, in reality, was not a peaceful time for many of the students, and Bucci recalled for a lot of them, the Phoenix event was the only Thanksgiving dinner they had.

"One year," said Eller, "I remember I had a student who did not have a very good home life, and he said, 'I'm not coming to Thanksgiving. Thanksgiving is always a terrible time. There are family fights.' He didn't have any good feeling for Thanksgiving, so he would not come. And he was totally amazed when the students told him how wonderful it was, and nobody argued. He had had a shooting or something like that [at his house], and it was just really eye opening for him that people could get along at a holiday and not have fights and arguments and hitting and all that violence."

Phoenix, in a sense, had created a holding environment for its students to get an education and work on their sobriety in the midst of their challenging lives. Thanksgiving was a way of opening that safe haven to others, including the students who had come before them, and expressing their appreciation. Berthiaume noted that the guest list included the Montgomery County Board of Education. Over time, most of the names on the board would change, but each year, Thanksgiving would provide a concrete way of acknowledging the significance of what the county had created after the tumultuous drug crackdown in 1978. The Phoenix School was a program borne out of police raids, political squabbles, leadership upheavals, and an attempt to tame a growing drug problem for the county's youth. The two schools had developed their own cultural distinctions, but, for one day, the chasm of ideologies, personalities, and family dynamics was bridged through sharing a meal and giving thanks.

The attendees would gather "while the food was cooling," said Bucci. "All in attendance joined hands in a circle, and each person stated what they were grateful for."

Eller recalled this tradition fondly. "[There] was a big, huge gratitude circle," said Eller. "And that was the kind of thing that really brought people together."

Berthiaume, Eller, and their fellow Phoenix pioneers were years ahead of their time in developing high schools for teenagers in recovery from alcohol and other substance use disorders. Their primary intent was to help *their own students* graduate from high school, however they could, and most of the focus on the Phoenix Schools was local. Still, while the Freedom Road and PDAP GED schools never received traction beyond their local communities, something was different with the Phoenix Schools. Significant expansion of recovery high schools was still years away, but the First Lady's letter indicated a broader impact. With the schools increasingly garnering attention from national media outlets as well as the White House, it is safe to say a recovery high school movement had been kindled.

10
Sparks

Both Phoenix schools seemed to be hitting their stride in the summer of 1988. Montgomery County had just built a new facility for Phoenix II, which was commemorated by a letter from the First Lady, Nancy Reagan, herself. The county would in fact continue supporting both schools for the next two decades. Many of the staff and students saw the late 1980s and early 1990s as the halcyon years for the Phoenix schools.

"The school was very solid," remembered alum John Edmonds. "I think it was probably the most controlled solid environment that most of those people had, you know, including myself. You knew what you were getting every day, which is huge."

Phoenix celebrated the fifteenth anniversary of its first campus with a gala at the Bethesda Marriott on May 25, 1994. The program for the event provided evidence of how renowned and politically connected the school had become in the Washington, DC, community. The honorary chair of the Phoenix Anniversary Committee was J. W. Marriott Jr., who was a resident of Montgomery County. Marriott contributed a letter for the program, as did the current president of the United States, Bill Clinton. President Clinton wrote, "Our nation relies on schools like yours to supply our students with the knowledge and skills necessary to face the daunting challenges of the 21st century. I am confident that the Phoenix School will build on its record of success and continue to endow future generations with the same expertise and guidance demonstrated over the years."[1]

The acknowledgments extended beyond the celebration that night. The day before the event, honorary host Connie Morella, Montgomery County's representative in the US House, rose on floor of the House to "pay tribute to the Phoenix School on the occasion of its 15th anniversary celebration."[2] Rep. Morella's speech gave a description and brief history of the school, and she said, "The Phoenix School, with its innovative approach to helping teenagers overcome alcohol and drug abuse, is a model for the rest of the Nation." With that proclamation, legislators from across the country became aware of recovery high schools, and the Phoenix schools were officially documented in the Congressional Record.

Beyond media pieces and political recognition, Montgomery County leaders also were making efforts to promote Phoenix outside the state. Brian Berthiaume recalled traveling to Wisconsin and Virginia to speak with school administrators about drug use in schools, during which he spoke about Phoenix.[3] Dr. Dick Towers, the MCPS director of programs for exceptional learners and of "Interagency, Alternative, and

Salvaging a Teenage Wasteland. Andrew J. Finch, Oxford University Press. © Oxford University Press 2024.
DOI: 10.1093/oso/9780190645502.003.0010

Supplementary Programs" during the 1980s, recounted speaking about the school at national conferences, such as the National Education Association (NEA). The NEA published a book by Towers a few years after Phoenix II opened titled *How Schools Can Help Combat Student Drug and Alcohol Abuse*. The book, which Towers said was well-circulated, described Phoenix as a "special school" for "drug-abusing students."[4]

"There," wrote Towers, "students with mild-to-moderate drug problems are allowed to attend a small drug-free day school removed from the influence of drug-using friends."[5]

During the same period that the Phoenix schools were getting established, and Dr. Towers was promoting the schools on a national level, the First Lady made stopping youth drug use her signature campaign. The letter commemorating the opening of the Phoenix II facility had been delivered near the end of a crusade Nancy Reagan had begun years earlier, during her husband's 1980 run for the White House. While on the campaign trail, Mrs. Reagan had visited a youth therapeutic community called Daytop Village in New York.[6] She was "stunned to find out just how large the problem of drug abuse really is," and was "impressed by what [she] saw at Daytop Village—children who were climbing out of the mess that they had made of their lives because of their dependency on drugs."[7]

After her husband's election, Mrs. Reagan initially said she would not embrace a cause as all the other First Ladies in the twentieth century had done. By 1982, though, with her husband's reelection campaign on the horizon, White House staff felt Nancy Reagan had become a political liability due in part to her lavish tastes. The liberal media had branded her as "too rich, too snobbish, too conservative."[8] The staff felt Mrs. Reagan needed an image makeover, and their strategy included befriending the press corps and developing a project of her own.[9] Her own children's drug use had alarmed her in the 1970s, and after her Daytop Village experience, Mrs. Reagan had continued to visit adolescent drug treatment centers to offer her support. When confronted by the fact that President Reagan had cut funding for drug prevention programs, Mrs. Reagan faced a dilemma. She wanted to help with the drug problem, but she also needed to support her husband's fiscal conservativism. Mrs. Reagan saw independent organizations like Twelve Step programs as exemplars, but initially could not identify a similar low-cost option for universal drug prevention.

"Throughout 1982," wrote Pierre-Marie Loizeau, "she crusaded against drug abuse, crisscrossing the country, touring drug prevention and treatment facilities. She enjoyed talking with teenagers, giving them moral support and publicized the testimonies of former addicts. She gave numerous speeches and hosted countless lunches.... The war against drugs increasingly became the First Lady's label."[10]

During an event at Longfellow Elementary School in Oakland, Mrs. Reagan was asked by a young student, "Mrs. Reagan, what should I say if someone offers me drugs, if someone wants to give them to me?"

Mrs. Reagan replied, "You just say no! That's all you have to do. Just say no and walk away."[11]

The phrase stuck and took popular culture by storm, appearing in public service announcements, on school posters, and even making its way into popular television series such as *Diff'rent Strokes* and *Dynasty*.[12]

While simply saying a phrase would require no government funding, NIDA sponsored a program called Just Say No—clubs which offered "pins, buttons, and tee shirts emblazoned with the slogan."[13] The idea was to help students refuse to use drugs when peers pressured them. Soleil Moon Frye, then an eight-year-old star of the *Punky Brewster* show, hosted a weekly half-hour community service television program and became the national chairperson of the Just Say No groups.[14] Over time, more than five thousand Just Say No clubs were created.[15]

By the time Mrs. Reagan sent her letter to acknowledge Phoenix II's new building in 1988, Just Say No had become part of the pop-culture lexicon. As First Lady, Mrs. Reagan gave more than twelve hundred media interviews, delivered forty-nine speeches, and motivated more than 5 million people to march in seven hundred cities to promote the Just Say No campaign (see Figure 10.1).[16] While its actual effectiveness at stopping drug use and its cultural competency have been questioned, with some suggesting it did as much harm as good, the Just Say No campaign did give a political boost to programs aimed at reducing youth drug use.[17]

The burgeoning drug war, the Just Say No campaign, media coverage of the Phoenix School, and Dr. Towers's efforts to shine a light on the program did not translate into rapid expansion of recovery high schools like Phoenix. While other high schools that focused on substance use did open around the United States during the 1980s, they were solitary efforts. In the four years following the start of Phoenix II in January 1983, there were a few other recovery high schools that opened in Texas, Missouri, and Washington state. Each, however, was an isolated case, and the growth resembled kindling sparks rather than a massive movement. Unfortunately, all those schools had closed or repurposed by 1991, and while their seeds of influence can be seen in schools that came later, none, including the Phoenix schools, were closely associated with the expansion of recovery high schools that occurred in the late 1990s and early 2000s. The Phoenix School 15th Anniversary Celebration program even noted the slow growth of recovery high schools, stating awareness of only one other school in 1994, and asking, "Why doesn't every community in America have one?"[18]

There are many possible reasons why the Phoenix School innovation and the corresponding national concern about youth drug use did not give rise to recovery high schools at the same rate as the explosion of Just Say No clubs. Obviously, starting a school is much more complex and costly than launching a club or support group. Beyond that, though, campaigns like Just Say No focused on preventing drug use more so than treatment and recovery. The Just Say No clubs were targeted as much at elementary and middle school–age children as they were at high school students—hence an eight-year-old national spokesperson. Even high school programs such as Student Assistance Programs, typically emphasized prevention and early intervention.[19]

Figure 10.1. First Lady Nancy Reagan sent a letter to acknowledge Phoenix II's new building in 1988. Her Just Say No campaign aimed to educate and discourage young people from using illicit drugs, and as First Lady, Mrs. Reagan gave more than twelve hundred media interviews and delivered forty-nine speeches to promote her program. (Source: US National Archives and Records Administration/Wikipedia.)

Ironically, the explanation for lack of rapid growth could also have been timing. While the First Lady was focused on youth drug use, her husband's Secretary of Education, Terrel H. Bell, had convened the National Commission on Excellence in Education to report on the state of the nation's public schools. On April 26, 1983, just under five months after the Montgomery County Public Schools had opened its second Phoenix School, Bell's commission released its report. It was under fifty pages long, but it sent shockwaves through the US public education system, starting with its opening sentences, which drew heavily on Cold War fears of the time:

Our Nation is at risk. Our once unchallenged preeminence in commerce, industry,
science, and technological innovation is being overtaken by competitors
throughout the world . . . We report to the American people that while we can
take justifiable pride in what our schools and colleges have historically accomplished and contributed to the United States and the well-being of its people,
the educational foundations of our society are presently being eroded by a rising
tide of mediocrity that threatens our very future as a Nation and a people. What
was unimaginable a generation ago has begun to occur—others are matching
and surpassing our educational attainments. If an unfriendly foreign power had
attempted to impose on America the mediocre educational performance that
exists today, we might well have viewed it as an act of war. As it stands, we have
allowed this to happen to ourselves.[20]

With that, the report presented its case that the nation's public schools were to
blame for that "rising tide of mediocrity." While the alternative school movement was
not mentioned explicitly, many alternative schools during the 1970s, such as Freedom
Road and Phoenix, had emphasized mental health and emotional needs as much as
academic outcomes, and that mentality was deemed as contributing to America's
decline. While the Commission's methods and findings have since been rebuked, *A
Nation at Risk* impacted school reform and federal policy for decades to come.[21]

"What we now call school reform isn't the product of a gradual consensus emerging among educators about how kids learn," wrote Tamim Ansary in a commentary for EduTopia. "It's a political movement that grew out of one seed planted in
1983. I became aware of this fact some years ago, when I started writing about education issues and found that every reform initiative I read about—standards, testing,
whatever—referred me back to a seminal text entitled 'A Nation at Risk.'"[22]

The free school ideology had faced stiff critique virtually from its beginnings.
Education historian Lawrence Cremin (1973) compared the free school movement of
the 1970s to John Dewey's era of the early twentieth century and essentially predicted
its downfall, writing, "It is utter nonsense to think that by turning children loose in an
unplanned and unstructured environment they can be freed in any significant way.
Rather, they are abandoned to the blind forces of the hucksters."[23] Ten years later, *A
Nation at Risk* held the nation's schools in contempt, and schools were jolted back to
basics. As Ansary wrote, "For one thing, its language echoed the get-tough rhetoric
of the growing conservative movement. For another, its diagnosis lent color to the
charge that, under liberals, American education had dissolved into a mush of self-
esteem classes."[24]

None of that rhetoric or fearmongering gave school boards an incentive to open
more schools like Phoenix that embraced flexibility and emphasized alcohol and
drug recovery groups and camping trips as much as academics. Dr. Leaf Van Boven
attended Phoenix II as a student, and he felt flexible alternative schools made an important contribution to the education landscape. He suggested critics were using the
wrong rationale.

"I think the mistake that people make when they have those reactions to these kinds of unstructured schools is it's almost as though they're evaluating a school for the average student," said Van Boven. "I think it's probably true that a totally unstructured flexible school, where you got a lot of variability in the level at which people are performing and the learning and so on, is not going to work for several thousand students in a standard high school who are just all over the place. These schools, the students you're dealing with, is contingent on the fact that they have essentially failed in that other environment. The lens of evaluation doesn't mean, is this a good school for the average student? Is this a good school for students who can't or haven't been succeeding in the standard kind of school setting? Those are very different questions."

In fact, the lights did not go completely dark for therapeutic supports in schools after the *A Nation at Risk* report. Interestingly, the much-maligned "self-esteem movement" is considered to have risen in schools about the same time as *A Nation at Risk* sounded its bell.[25] Cuban wrote that many of the reformers believed "that in raising children's esteem, academic improvement, social kindness, and personal success in life would occur."[26] Cuban cited as an example John Vasconcellos's bill to establish a California Task Force to Promote Self-Esteem and Personal and Social Responsibility called the "Self-Esteem Commission" in 1986.[27]

Between 1983 and 1987—the years immediately following the release of *A Nation at Risk* and coinciding with the rise of both the self-esteem and Just Say No movements—recovery high schools opened in Texas, Missouri, and Washington state. The Washington program was a public alternative school called the Henderson Bay Alternative High School. The school had begun as an alternative school in 1972 and developed an alcohol and drug recovery focus in 1986–1987. John Riebli, a teacher at the school years later, posted this history of the program:

> The first Henderson Bay (1972) was called Huloima Wehut (Hue-low-ma Way-hut), an Indian name for "a different way." The school was housed at the Key Peninsula Civic Center. The staff and students would have to pack up their books on Friday so that the Civic Center could run their weekend activities. They would unpack again on Monday. In 1977, the school was in a portable outside of Peninsula High School . . . [In](approx. 1987) the school officially became Henderson Bay Alternative High School. Lots changes. (sic) A drug and alcohol program was developed and every teacher took the required drug/alcohol classes for certification. Additional staff was added to include a special education teacher and a secretary. Jim Baker was named the first principal of HBHS at this time. We had 5 teachers and 50 students.[28]

In a 1986 newspaper article promoting alcohol and drug programs in the local school district, Principal Jim Baker said, "We see this as being a life-and-death situation. Unless we can break [the habit], there's no point in doing anything else." Not much else has been published about this program, but a delegation from an Albuquerque group called Parents Against Drugs visited Henderson Bay in the early

1990s as they were planning their own recovery high school.[29] At some point, the school returned to a more general alternative student population, and little institutional memory has survived.

Sober High School/Carrington Academy

While Henderson Bay played only a small role in the larger recovery high school movement, two other schools that opened in Texas and Missouri in the 1980s were directly descended from one of the original recovery schools—the PDAP GED School. These two schools were branches of the same private school organization, which just so happened to be run by John Cates, the founder of the GED school. While these schools may not have been widely replicated and have been largely forgotten, they resumed a school connection with alternative peer groups (APSs), which is becoming increasingly common today. Indeed, since these Cates schools offered more than GED preparation—albeit still with a limited curriculum—they were the first high schools affiliated with APGs and thus are noteworthy.

The Palmer Drug Abuse Program's GED Schools had closed following negative news coverage for PDAP and a subsequent organizational restructuring in 1980. The founder of the GED program, John Cates, left PDAP at that time to follow other interests he had started pursuing while still in leadership at PDAP, including video production.

"At the time, the video age was coming on," said Cates. "It was real easy to get into. That was when I was producing and directing commercials and industrial films, because I'd been in a rock and roll band, and we made an album . . . On the side was my plan."[30]

"When [PDAP] blew up," Cates said, "[it] broke my heart. I didn't know what to do."[31]

That "blow up" occurred in early 1980, in conjunction with the airing of features about PDAP on both *20/20* and *60 Minutes*. The news reports, both of which aired in January 1980, suggested financial improprieties on the part of PDAP's leadership, and they painted an unflattering picture of Meehan's leadership style and motives as cultish. In the wake of the Jonestown massacre in 1978, such accusations were damning. The PDAP board removed Meehan from his director role, retroactive to January 1, 1980. He became a consultant for PDAP and moved to California.[32]

In 1981, Meehan started a new program in San Diego similar to PDAP which he called "Freeway," like his band. The San Diego program would meet a comparable fate as PDAP a few years later, after critics claimed Freeway members "simply exchanged one addiction—to drugs and alcohol—with another addiction—to a lifestyle of self-gratifying antisocial behaviors, dependency on one another at the expense of their home life, and a cult-like adoration of Meehan." Pressure had mounted to shut the program down, and the board ultimately voted to close the organization "because it had run out of money."[33]

Cates would continue partnering with Meehan on various projects through the 1980s while promoting "enthusiastic sobriety" until they had a falling out over a business deal with a hospital 1992.[34] Immediately after the PDAP shakeup, though, Cates pursued other projects. While in Dallas, he had met Susan Perry, who was a counselor there. Like so many other PDAP counselors, Perry had been expelled from high school at age 16, but eventually finished her diploma. She and Cates had started dating, and a few months after the PDAP restructuring, Susan and John were married on June 21, 1980. Newly remarried and soon to be a parent, Cates needed work, and so his side projects became his main occupations for the next few years. In the wake of PDAP falling apart and the GED schools closing, Cates made a living by producing commercials and videos, which was a lucrative line of work in the early 1980s. Cates claims he even turned down a Budweiser account because the alcohol focus clashed with his recovery principles. Susan Cates matriculated to college and got a degree in physics from the University of Houston and a PhD in biochemistry and cell biology from Rice University. She would become an assistant chair of biosciences at Rice University in 2014.

Cates had made enough money by 1985 to purchase a ranch in Texas. He started a nonprofit organization, John Cates and Associates (JCA), and he opened a residential substance use treatment program, which he called "Yellow Rose." He then added an extended care program that would function like the PDAP program. Initially the program was simply called, "JCA," but eventually the program was called "Lifeway." The "enthusiastic sobriety" model he had followed at PDAP, which he began calling "enthusiastic recovery," was the basis of his new treatment and recovery initiative and would come to be known as an "alternative peer group."[35]

Richardson, TX (1986–1991)

Cates also remained passionate about education. He was still a teacher at heart, so he wanted to create an academic option for teenagers similar to the GED program for PDAP members in the seventies. He decided, though, to take the GED idea a step further—this school would be a diploma-granting high school for the teens who were getting recovery support in the JCA program. The school would also be the first private recovery high school, and it was initially called "Sober High."[36] The school opened in Richardson, Texas, a suburb north of Dallas, on September 15, 1986.

Marketing pamphlets proclaimed "Sober High will be like no other school you have ever attended. As far as we know this is the first school of its kind, but needless to say it will not be the last."[37] While it was true that Sober High was the first independent recovery high school, this comment also indicated that Cates was not aware of the Freedom Road School in South Carolina or the Phoenix Schools in Maryland. The pamphlet's prediction of future recovery high schools, however, proved to be accurate.

The school continued to reference itself as "Sober High" in some correspondence, but Cates decided to use his middle name instead, so the school officially changed its name to "Carrington Academy" in 1987. Similar to the PDAP GED school, Carrington Academy focused on academic instruction, while the recovery support and social activities occurred within the alternative peer group, JCA. The counselors worked for the JCA program. One of the early counselors that Cates hired had gotten sober through PDAP in the mid-1970s, just like Cates. Jon Sholeff had been a PDAP counselor, and he had met John Cates when Cates was the director of Houston programs. Years later, he met some teenagers at an AA meeting in Dallas.

"Then I ran into them again at coffee after a meeting," said Sholeff. "And they said that they were in JCA. I said, 'What's JCA?' They said, 'Well, John Cates and Associates.' I called him and went out and talked to one of his kids, and one thing led to another, and he hired me [as a counselor]."

Sholeff had not seen Cates in years, so he felt the job was meant to be.

"There was such a serendipity-ness to it that I figured this is what I was supposed to do, you know?" said Sholeff. "I understood what they were doing, and I understood what John wanted to accomplish. I always enjoyed that. I've always enjoyed working with adolescents and their parents."

Carrington Academy was located in the same building as other JCA services. The first location of the school was as a commercial office complex on South Central Expressway in Richardson, not far from where PDAP had started in Dallas. The school moved to a new building in Dallas before the 1989 school year.

"There were several levels of care [at JCA]," said Sholeff. "There was primary treatment, which was licensed as an intensive outpatient program that required people to be in group three or four hours a day. The next level of care down was aftercare, which also included continued involvement with going to the alternative peer group that JCA had started and continuing in the sober high school."

The students from the school could attend an alternative peer group meeting each day there. Many would attend AA meetings at night as well. JCA had three APG meetings a week in addition to sober social functions. This approach of attending school during the day and participating in APG activities on nights would later become the predominate model for many recovery high schools in Texas in the 2000s.[38]

"It just made that transition a lot more tenable for the kids, I think," said Sholeff. "The kids from the school or the new kids could meet some other kids who were a little bit further down the road to recovery at these meetings and develop relationships. The dynamics of peer pressure took over, and it was a lot easier for them to stay sober because going to Carrington Academy was pretty cool and pretty attractive to them."

The school had three eligibility requirements for students:

1. Be between the ages of 14 and 19;
2. Stay sober;
3. Seriously be working a Twelve Step program.

"It's really amazing to watch what happens after the fog lifts and kids can begin to recover their true self," said Sholeff. "They rediscover the fact that they enjoy learning, and they have a facility for that. All of the sudden they find value in it, and they get a lot of affirmation from their family and a sense of accomplishment that when you're high you don't really care about."

Many of the official documents at the school included a statement that encapsulated the sentiment of recovering one's true self:

At Carrington School, you will have the opportunity to grow in academics and much more. For we believe that you "have only been half educated unless you have acquired survival techniques, a sense of human dignity and worth, an appreciation of life, the ability to give and receive love, the knowledge of how to use your time wisely, and the determination to leave the world a better place for your having been in it." Sobriety is absolutely essential to meeting these goals.[39]

Students embraced this philosophy. Carrington Academy would ask students to write out their expectations for the school each year, and a few handwritten notes have survived. One student wrote, "What I expect from school is too (sic) have teachers that aren't assholes and to have teachers that can fuckin teach, and I expect too (sic) have fun, and learn . . ."

A number of the comments suggest the school atmosphere was relaxed. One of the students wrote, "I think the school is great, and we can turn it into something that every school wants to be like . . . The only area I think needs to change is that they should come down on people who don't want to be there and work 'cause I do, but it's hard when more than half the room is talking.

"We really want to see how far we can push it," she added, "Cause, you know, we're addicts and shit."

According to school literature, Carrington Academy was not a grade-level program, meaning they taught every student "on his or her own level," self-paced. Student files show that some students were enrolled for as long as two or three years, and unlike the PDAP GED program, this school gave high school credits aligned with Texas state requirements. When students applied to the school, they were asked to "list the level you feel you attained in the following courses: Math, Science, Social Studies, and English." This would indicate their academic progress-to-date.

The school day had a morning session (8:00 to 11:00) and an afternoon session (noon to 3:00), Monday through Friday. Students had the option of attending class all day or enrolling in a "work program," meaning they would work mornings and attend school in the afternoons or vice versa. Peer supports were emphasized both during and outside school hours.

"They'd go to an AA meeting until nine o clock, and then go drink coffee at Joe Joe's until eleven or twelve o clock, and then go over to somebody's house, and then get up and try to be at school the next day," recalled Sholeff.

Over time, the school accommodated the late-night student lifestyle and adjusted school hours. By its second year, the schedule was 9:00 a.m. to noon and 1:00 p.m. to 4:00 p.m., with a fifteen-minute tardiness window. One undated document said, "Students must be in the classroom by 9:15AM. If this is impossible, wait until after lunch to come to school . . . Students must return from lunch and be in the classroom by 1:15. If that is impossible, wait until the next morning to return to school."

The school had teachers and curriculum covering each of the major subjects and electives needed for a Texas high school diploma, but the school emphasized it was "not grade leveled."[40] Upon completion, students would graduate and receive actual high school diplomas—albeit they were likely nonaccredited. The school applied for accreditation from the Southern Association of Colleges and Schools (SACS), but there is no indication that the school ever actually received accreditation. It is also not clear if students encountered difficulty transferring credits to other schools, though that is possible. One records request from a school in Austin said, "Since your school is not listed in the 1989–90 Texas Nonpublic School Directory, we would like to know something about your accreditation and the basis for awarding credits." To give itself an "out," JCA informed parents, "As with any other school, there is no way Carrington Schools can control how a school being transferred to will evaluate accumulated credits of a school being transferred from."

A comprehensive list of teachers and staff could not be found in the surviving records, but two people listed on most of the correspondence were John Cates and Loyce Sydow. Most letters to parents were from Sydow, who died in 2014. Her letters were not only informational, they were inspirational. Sydow often would punctuate correspondence with statements like, "We Love You," or "This school year is going to be great."[41] One of those letters announced that Carrington Academy had hired two new teachers, both age 26.[42] Steve Marshall was "from England and is an English major with abilities to teach almost any subject." And Karen Jones was "our new math whiz." It is not clear, though, how many teachers were on the staff at one time.

Ellisville, MO (1987–1988)

After JCA changed the name of the school to Carrington Academy in 1987, it also expanded its services by opening an alternative peer group and a second school campus in Ellisville, Missouri, a suburb west of St. Louis.[43] As an entity, JCA called the two schools the "Carrington Schools," and administration occurred from the JCA home office in Texas. Sholeff called the expansion an opportunity "to respond to needs."

"You know, it was just a lot," said Sholeff. "John was new to the business. We got sober in a place that says you never say no to anybody because God has blessed you with this gift and you got to give it away to be able to keep it. When you're a nonprofit like PDAP, that was one thing, but when you're proprietary like JCA, it means that you just worked a lot and tried to help as many people as you could. It just would become overwhelming at times."

It appears the Ellisville Campus closed in 1988 after just one year of operation. School documents note Carrington Schools applied in 1987 to the National Association of Independent Schools, the Missouri Independent School Association, and the Independent School Association of the Central States for accreditation.[44] Similar to the application to SACS, the school documents do not indicate the school received those accreditations either.

Carrington Academy in Texas would continue operating for a few more years after the closure of the Missouri campus, and through the connection to the JCA alternative peer group, Carrington Academy students had access to extracurricular activities. JCA held social activities and field trips, such as a ski trip and a talent show, and the school had a student council.[45] In the beginning, the school had six ground rules, and each of these rules were analogous to rules for participation in PDAP and its GED school years before:[46]

1. No fighting or violence at any time.
2. No drugs at school or in the building—holding or abusing.
3. No sexual activities.
4. Participation in all activities.
5. Any damage to school or JCA property—you will be responsible for.
6. You will be responsible for your own program and sobriety.

One example of how the school differentiated itself from traditional school policies was its dress code: "We will expect you to dress."[47] The school also eschewed homework, stating, "There will be no assigned homework, however if a student by some strange quirk chooses to progress at a faster pace, he/she can certainly take work home."[48]

Similar to the families that had moved to Houston in the 1970s for the PDAP program, many students relocated to the Dallas area for the JCA program and the Carrington Academy in Texas. Those students would live with host families, and the enrollment for the school was limited to ten students at a time, ages 14 through 19. Families signed a waiver form that stated:

> JCA/Carrington Academy . . . will not be responsible for your son/daughter except during regular school hours. Total responsibility for him/her outside of school will be dealt with between the parents/legal guardians of the student and the head of the household in which they live.[49]

One annual event the school held was a "Roast and Graduation/Reception," and they invited all parents to attend.[50] The school also said parents were "welcome at the school anytime. We encourage parents to take part in our program."[51] Such parental involvement aligned with the approach emphasized by PDAP since its earliest days.

By 1989, Carrington Academy had expanded the ground rules from the six original rules to twelve. While no rationale is provided as to why new regulations were being imposed, the wording suggests the school had experienced issues with relapse, absenteeism, cheating, and sleeping at school. The new rules proclaimed students were "responsible for your own program and sobriety"; "responsible for your own attendance to class"; "responsible for your own [academic] progress"; and no sleeping was allowed in the school building.[52]

Unlike the GED program, which had eliminated fees after Cates turned it over to PDAP, Carrington Academy charged $3000 per year, or $300 per month for ten months. The tuition increased over time. By 1988, the tuition was $4,500 per year, and the marketing brochure included $300/month "room and board for students needing housing with a host family."[53]

After just five years in operation, Carrington Academy closed abruptly in January 1991, in the middle of the school year. Jon Sholeff was tasked with trying to find new schools for the students, and Loyce Sydow with refunding tuition and handling communication with the parents. There was no explanation given in correspondence as to the reason for the immediate shuttering.

"I think it goes back to that thing where it just got so unwieldy that John [Cates] said, 'Everybody has to be autonomous here,'" said Sholeff. "That's what I remember. I don't remember any kind of crisis occurring, any specific crisis other than there was just a lot to do. Understanding that people in recovery are pretty needy, so not only was John [Cates] the chief executive officer of the business, but he was also the one who tended to sponsor a lot of the staff in Houston, in Dallas."

"[Cates] had a hard time," Sholeff added. "One of the downsides of this is that you don't want to say no to anybody who needs you, but [Cates] just got to the point where he couldn't do it anymore. There's no fault in that, in being human."

Another reason for the school closing was the advent of managed care coordinating insurance companies, which led to insurers becoming more restrictive about paying for services. While this may not have directly impacted the school, it did hurt funding for Cates's other programs.

"Insurance companies began tightening restrictions," wrote Daniel Kolitz. "This meant that providers went from covering as much as six weeks of inpatient treatment to just three or four days . . . Everyone was affected."[54]

According to Cates, the FBI had also started investigating service providers about fraudulent referral and billing schemes. He recalled that the investigations and reduced insurance availability caused many programs to shut down or reconfigure over the next few years. Though he was personally never charged, he said, "Everybody was terrified."

John Cates did not give up; he would continue trying new high school initiatives over the next two decades. Even when there was not a formal school, Cates's programs continued providing schooling, paying a staff person to facilitate distance learning and computer-based curricula if needed, harkening back to his PDAP GED school days. When recovery high school growth finally caught fire, though, it was not in Texas, South Carolina, or Maryland. After Carrington Academy closed, growth stalled in Texas for the next six years. South Carolina did not open another recovery high school after Freedom Road closed in 1980. And the Phoenix schools were the only recovery high schools in Maryland until alum John Edmonds opened his own school, Phoenix Recovery Academy, in 2020. One northern state, though, would experience an explosion of recovery high schools—twenty-five between 1987 and 2016—and became the epicenter of growth. Minnesota, whose state motto is *L'Étoile du Nord* ("Star of the North"), had deep roots in both the alternative school and adolescent treatment sectors dating to the early 1970s. And when a Minneapolis social worker could not find a suitable school for her son, she started the school that would finally propel recovery high schools into a national movement.

PART III
A MOVEMENT BEGINS

11
Normalized Alternatives

As morning broke in Minneapolis the day after Valentine's Day, 1971, the area looked like an image from the movie *Frozen*. An early fog had lifted to reveal tree branches "white with frost." With little wind that morning, the fog particles had essentially settled and frozen in place.[1] It was a glorious beginning to what would be a mild President's Day in the Twin Cities, with temperatures warming to thirty-two degrees. It was also the day social worker Carol Robson delivered her first and only child. From the day her child was born to the year he became a legal adult in 1989, the growth of alternative schools of choice in Minnesota dovetailed with his experience as a child growing up in the Minneapolis Public Schools. By the time Carol's son graduated high school, Minnesota had fully embraced school choice so much that recovery high schools took root and blossomed there more than in any other state. In fact, his parents would launch the state's first recovery high school and inspire the second, all in an effort to create an alternative school just for him.[2]

Carol Robson was 33 years old and had not wanted to bring a child into what she saw as a turbulent world. Born in the small Minnesota town of Hills (pop. 450) in Rock County in December 1938,[3] Carol had gotten married at age 20 to Sheridan Robson with the explicit understanding they would not become parents.

"We were engaged in the 1950s," said Robson. "I'd been a political junkie my whole life. I decided I didn't want children because the world was in too bad a shape. We broke our engagement, and then we went on and got married and agreed not to have any children."

After twelve years of marriage, Carol's pregnancy was a surprise.

"It was a wonderful accident, which led to a whole new era in my life," said Robson. "My son is incredible. I'm so thrilled I had him."

In addition to his birth being unplanned, Carol's son had been born with cerebral palsy. Cerebral palsy affects movement, muscle tone, and posture, and it is caused by damage to the cerebral motor cortex. Most commonly developed before birth, symptoms appear in early childhood.[4] According to the Mayo Clinic in Minnesota, cerebral palsy impairs movement, causing "floppiness or rigidity of the limbs, abnormal posture, involuntary movements, unsteady walking, or some combination of these."[5] Cerebral palsy, however, does not, by itself, impair intellectual functioning. A team of Turkish researchers studied 107 children with cerebral palsy and found no relationship between cerebral palsy type and intellectual level.[6] Still, symptoms can impact a child's ability to perform required school activities,

Salvaging a Teenage Wasteland. Andrew J. Finch, Oxford University Press. © Oxford University Press 2024.
DOI: 10.1093/oso/9780190645502.003.0011

such as writing, and as he grew up, his physical limitations became a factor in his education.

"Every time I picked him up [from elementary school], he was standing in the hall being punished because of whatever happened," said Robson. "It was not a fault of his own. He was born with a birth defect from CP, and he has an IQ over the moon. In fact, he came out I think it was second or third (in the) citywide test in all of Minneapolis in third grade. He's very, very bright, but he was being punished. He didn't write fast enough, but on multiple choice he could do anything."

"If he did not write the spelling words fast enough to finish, because he couldn't," recalled Robson, with tears in her voice, "then the teacher would make him stand up in front of the class and spell them out—of course, just humiliating him. Then he would get angry, and he'd end up out in the hall."

When their child was ten, the Robsons had had enough and started looking for a school different than the public school they had been assigned, but they could not find a good fit. The Robsons considered a few religious schools and expensive private schools, such as the Blake School in Hopkins.

Robson recalled, "When I pulled my son out, I said (to him), 'What are we going to do?' All that was available at the time was these small little Christian schools in basements. I'm not anti-Christian, I don't mean that, but they definitely did not meet his needs . . . Then there were a couple of very expensive schools for the high rollers. He would never have fit in there either, nor financially could I afford it."

Eventually, the family chose a small, private alternative school near the University of Minnesota campus called the Second Foundation School, which had opened in 1970, just months before their child was born. Second Foundation billed itself as "a small school with an open school philosophy, nurturing creativity and independence" for students in grades K–12.[7] It was nonsectarian, though it operated in the basement of the University Baptist Church.[8]

"We don't force people to learn," its director, Starri Hedges, told a newspaper reporter in 2012. "We encourage learning, but they learn naturally and through things that they enjoy doing."

The Second Foundation School had opened as part of a counterculture "free school" movement in the United States that began in the 1960s. "In creating its own schools," wrote Greg Pinney in an article describing the half dozen such schools that had started operating around the Twin Cities, "the movement primarily wants to liberate young people from 'repressive' public schools and allow them to develop naturally as human beings."[9]

Minnesota was one of the national leaders in developing alternative schools.[10] The Alternative Education Resource Organization has created an open-source "Alternative Education Hall of Fame" to honor "individuals in the field of educational alternatives who have been inspirational to the one or many people who have named them. The list is not nor will it ever be closed." As of 2022, nine of the Hall of Famers posted were involved with the Minnesota alternative school movement.[11]

Minnesota had begun building a culture of choice years earlier. The state had been allowing income tax deductions for qualifying expenses such as tuition, transportation, instructional materials, and tutoring since 1955.[12] In 1946, when Carol Robson was just 11 years old and still going by her family name Carol Reyne, the Minnesota Department of Education issued a bulletin embracing the progressive policies of the time, saying all classrooms should operate as miniature democratic societies.[13] One such democratic school opened in the private sector in August 1962, when thirty people who had formed the Minnesota Summerhill Society based on A. S. Neill's book, *Summerhill: A Radical Approach to Child Rearing,* decided to start a school on Lake Minnetonka's Spray Island. The Minnesota Summerhill Community School opened with seven students, mostly children of the Summerhill Society board, ages 5 to 14, and moved to a farmhouse in Wayzata in its second month.[14] They hired Cortland Smith, from Albert Lea, Minnesota, and Susan Barenholtz, from New York, as unpaid instructors. Smith was only 22, and Barenholtz was only 21, and they worked for lodging and meals.[15] The two had met at Vermont's Goddard College, which was also known for self-directed study, but they had left before graduating. Cortland and Susan would eventually marry, and they would remain directors of the school, which moved twice more before purchasing the entire seventeen-acre Spray Island about twenty-five miles west of Minneapolis for $35,000 in spring 1966.[16]

Minnesota was part of a national wave that began in earnest in the 1960s, due in large part to the availability of federal funding through the Elementary and Secondary Education Act of 1965. Title III of that act provided for supplementary educational centers, attendance supports, English language learning, special education, rural education, and educational programs when school was not in session.[17] School systems, such as St. Paul in Minnesota, used Title III to fund their early public alternative schools.[18] Minnesota's first public alternative school, the Wilson Open Campus School in Mankato, opened in 1968, becoming one of the earliest public alternative schools in the United States.[19] Don Glines founded the Wilson Open School, and according to historian Dr. Wayne Jennings, Mankato's alternative school was so innovative that "thousands of people visited from around the nation."[20]

Dr. Jennings himself would help start a public open school in 1971 based on the Mankato model, the St. Paul Open School, which also received national acclaim as a demonstration school.[21] The St. Paul School was a nongraded, K–12 school, where about five hundred students progressed at their own rate "with the emphasis on learning rather than teaching; on cooperation, no competition, with imaginative and flexible teachers acting as guides, counselors, and facilitators rather than lecturers, authoritarians, and examiners."[22] St. Paul's school set the stage for braided budgeting now commonly utilized by specialized schools by combining a federal Elementary and Secondary Education Act Title III grant, three private foundation grants, individual contributions, and state and local tax levies to cover the nearly half-million dollars in annual expenses and provide a free, public education.[23]

That same year, just three weeks prior to the birth of Carol's child, the superintendent of the Minneapolis Public Schools, Dr. John Davis Jr., had written to Dr. Robert Binswanger, the director of the Experimental Schools Program for the United States Office of Education. The correspondence was a letter of interest in the federal Experimental School Program, which was providing five-year grants to districts to fund alternative school systems. "Piecemeal" and individual reform efforts inside conventional schools had not been as effective as hoped, so the US Office of Education had decided to fund "large-scale experiments of comprehensive programs" to fuel innovation and to "bridge the gap between basic educational research and actual school practices," as described in this letter:[24]

The Minneapolis experimental school will be comprised of eight buildings with approximately 2500 students in the southeast part of the city. Parents and their students will be able to select educational options ranging from "conventional" programs to "open schools" and "schools without walls." The program will integrate educational programs for children now classified as kindergarten through twelfth grade into a learning curriculum.[25]

In response to the letter, the Minneapolis Public Schools were invited to submit a full proposal that spring. A community coalition of about thirty faculty, students, administrators, and community members received a $10,000 as a two-month planning grant to design the final proposal, called the Southeast Alternatives Project. On June 1, they received word they would be one of just three systems selected out of the 489 applicants nationwide, along with Berkeley, California, and Tacoma, Washington. The initial grant award was for twenty-seven months, and an additional thirty-three-month contract was awarded in 1973, boosting the overall funding to $6.6 million over five years. The plan was designed for the school district to assume the costs at the close of the grant, so the schools could continue operating.[26]

As requested in the initial inquiry letter, students would be given a choice of the following educational models:

- **Contemporary School** at Tuttle—a traditional K–6 school with "promising practices";
- **Continuous Progress** Primary School at Pratt and Intermediate School at Motley—ungraded elementary schools in which children would advance at their own pace;
- **Open School** at Marcy—elementary school with a flexible curriculum, schedule, and age grouping emphasizing affective learning and a community playground (the "Marcy Playground");[27]
- Southeast **Free School**—a K-12 school;
- Marshall-**University High School**—a secondary community school with a "flexible array of courses and activities being located at community learning sites," with participation in small counseling groups.[28]

The location for the project was Southeast Minneapolis, an area near the University of Minnesota, where about thirty thousand of the city's residents lived at the time. It was also home to the private Second Foundation School, which had opened a year earlier.

"Widely differing life styles, income levels, religious beliefs, educational backgrounds and occupations characterize this unique area," said a brochure for the project. "Near the factories, railroad yards and flour mills where independent small business flourish (sic), the imposing presence of the University of Minnesota makes its contribution to that diversity."[29]

"On Southeast Main Street, overlooking the Mississippi River, stands the first school house in Minneapolis," the brochure proclaimed. "It is indeed appropriate that the innovative alternative program occurs in Southeast, where education for Minneapolis had its origins."[30]

Peggy Hunter was a teacher in Southeast Minnesota in the late 1960s, including the Marcy school from 1968–1970, and she recalled wanting to teach in those early alternative programs.

"I went back to school in education after my daughter entered school," said Hunter. "I decided there's got to be a better way to teach kids. So, I went back and got my K-through-six degree."

"I started teaching in '68. I've always been in alternative education," said Hunter. "The principal gave me that first year 'substitute days' to go visit alternative programs around the state, because there were a number of programs that were really doing some exciting things."

That summer of 1971, families living in the area received information on their new public-school options. There were mailings, door-to-door visits, workshops, and community meetings, with only a few weeks to prepare the newly funded programs. The Southeast Alternatives brochure presented a vision for the schools:

Education is a philosophy—a position on the quality of life.
Participants in education seriously ask themselves,
"What do we want the world to be?" and
"What kind of education will contribute to that world?"[31]

Students would not be required to participate in one of the experimental schools and could choose instead to transfer to other Minneapolis public schools. Hunter recalled the facilities for the experimental schools were dated.

"It was in an early section of Minneapolis," said Hunter. "Southeast is kind of a beginning of Minneapolis sort of thing, on the other side of the river. They were old buildings."

Still, the alternative programs proved to be popular.

"The availability of choices of programs for students within the project was an immediate hit with parents," wrote Dr. Jennings in a history of Minnesota alternative schools.[32]

The multimillion-dollar grant cemented a burgeoning culture of school choice in Minnesota and placed Minneapolis at the heart of the national alternative school movement. Over the next two decades, both public and private alternative school options would steadily continue to expand until the state became the first to pass charter school legislation in 1991.

While the original alternative schools of the 1960s were often created as a response to the perceived dehumanizing conventional schools of the time, the 1970s had seen a diversification of purpose and design that led to a proliferation in number across the nation. Mario Fantini noted the alternative schools of the 1960s were actively promoting civil rights (i.e., "freedom schools" and "democratic schools") or the counter-culture movement (i.e., "free schools" and "open schools").[33] A federal report titled *Free and Freedom Schools: A National Survey of Alternative Programs* was released in November 1971, stating the following:

> In the last five years the United States has experienced a remarkable growth in the number of radical alternative schools. The increasing popularity of this new educational form stands as a reminder of the pervasive problems of public education. Thousands of parents, students, and teachers, oppressed by the mindless bureaucracy of public education and motivated by a common counter-ideology, are taking direct and radical action by operating private alternative schools. This report intends to portray the already fertile reality of the alternative school movement. There are presently 350 alternative schools in thirty-nine states. These schools serve a small number of participants—perhaps 12,500 students.[34]

Through the 1970s, such value-laden descriptors were gradually amalgamated into the more common label of "alternative" schools and practices.[35] This fostered rapid growth in schooling alternatives, especially as the public sector tried to emulate the private models to make them more accessible to their local families. Dr. Mary Anne Raywid, a proponent of small schools who wrote extensively on alternative schools, stated there were about one hundred public alternative schools in the United States in 1970, and by 1981, there were over ten thousand:[36]

> Supporters of alternatives in education were quick to point out that the notion is highly consistent with the principles of a democratic society, a pluralistic culture, the need for community involvement in education, the need for institutional self renewal in schools, and the need for financial austerity.... They have a remarkable capacity to respond to a wide spectrum of concerns.[37]

Dr. Raywid added, "Many groups with disparate agendas have seen alternatives as the means to achieve their own purposes."[38]

Minnesota's alternative schools grew in both the private and public sectors through the 1970s, and the lines delineating public and private often blurred. Blending public and private sources of funds became a hallmark of Minnesota school choice that fostered an expansion of programs statewide and created stability for alternative programs like the Southeast Alternatives after federal funding expired. Minneapolis Public Schools assigned one school counselor, Robert Jibben, to work full time with all alternative programs in 1971, and that same year, the district forged its first contracts with nonprofit organizations, allocating $18,000 to four organizations for "educational materials and supplies."[39] The intent was to create school options for students not succeeding in the district's conventional school programs.[40]

Five Minneapolis nonprofit organizations running alternative schools partnered in 1972 to create an umbrella organization, the Minnesota Federation of Alternative Schools (MFAS), in part to coordinate discussions and agreements with Minneapolis Public Schools.[41] While MFAS itself did not operate schools, its member organizations did. The original MFAS included the following:

- **The City, Inc.**—funded in part by the Junior League, which started tutoring services in 1969 and later opened an alternative school.
- **Loring-Nicollet-Bethlehem Center**—In 1969, Loring-Nicollet had started a GED program and the Bethlehem Community Center had begun offering space for a probation worker to offer educational services. They merged to run the Loring-Nicollet School.
- **The Neighborhood Center**, run by Episcopal Community Services, which opened the Center School in 1972.
- **Plymouth Christian Youth Center**, which had allowed North High School students to attend classes there in 1969 and receive credit from MPS.
- **Minneapolis Urban League**, which began the Street Academy in 1971.

Through its arrangement with Minneapolis Public Schools, MFAS allowed students in its member schools to be listed on MPS rolls, receive high school diplomas certified by MPS, and receive support services, often limited in smaller school programs, from the district. In return, MPS would be able to count the MFAS students in its allotments for state dollars.[42] James Storm recounted the history of MFAS in his dissertation for the University of Minnesota.[43] Storm interviewed people familiar with the early alternative programs in the state, and he determined that the private alternative schools that sustained themselves over time were more open to working with Minneapolis Public Schools. Storm quoted an unnamed MPS employee: "Early there were many alternatives, but most weren't willing to work with the district. The ones that survived were the ones that found a way to work with the district."[44]

Much of the impetus for the Minneapolis school district to collaborate with private alternative schools came from its superintendent, Dr. John Davis Jr., who had also led the development of the Southeast Alternatives public alternative schools. He coauthored a manuscript titled "Alternatives: Strategies for Getting Started," in which he wrote, "There is clear evidence that alternatives are education's future direction!"[45]

By the late 1970s, Minnesota's alternative schools had become a last step option for students dropping out of the traditional high schools. Instead of calling them "dropouts," Minneapolis adopted the term "Early School Leavers."[46] In July 1978, an Early School Leavers Committee made a presentation to the Minneapolis City Council to recommend Title III funds be targeted for this particular student group. Their report found that 19% of all Minneapolis Public School students entering 10th grade in 1974 had dropped out prior to their anticipated year of graduation day in 1977. The demographics of the Early School Leavers were predominantly BIPOC: 51% of Native American students and 29% of Black students had dropped out. Further, by August 1977, only 12% of the Indigenous students and 29% of Black students had graduated high school.[47]

Beyond race, the committee addressed the "cause and effect" of dropping out of high school:

> Family strife, chemical dependency, failure in school, crime, pregnancy, health, unemployment and other socioeconomic factors show up as cause and effects of early school leaving. Early school leavers must be served in terms of their total situation—personal, social, familial, and occupational. The public schools neither have the capability nor the resources to meet the total needs of early leavers.[48]

The committee suggested that private organizations partner with public agencies to fund independent alternative schools for the early leavers, but by the late 1970s some of the enthusiasm for funneling public dollars into private alternative schools had waned. Following Dr. Davis's departure in 1975, the new superintendent, Richard Green, was not as fond of private alternative schools, as he saw them as a "mark of failure of the public system" to serve those students. One of Storm's interviewees even claimed, "Richard was very fearful of alternative programs leading to all-black schools."[49] The 1970s were a period of desegregating the public schools, so programs that could intentionally resegregate publicly funded schools would have been anathema to many educators at the time.

MFAS continued to operate, however, receiving accreditation from the North Central Association of Schools in 1981 and legally becoming a 501c3 nonprofit organization in 1982.[50] Still, while its five member organizations added a few more school sites, the membership remained the same size until the late 1980s, when the number of school options—and students accessing them—would jump. In 1987 and 1988, alternative schools were fused with school choice in a way that would open doors to public funding that had never existed before. This change had been driven by the governor's desire for his children to attend suburban schools.

"The Godfather of School Choice" and the Second Chance Laws

Rudy Perpich, the late Minnesota governor, has been called the "godfather of school choice," and he was in his second stint as governor in the 1980s.[51] Not only was Perpich, a member of the Democratic-Farmer-Labor Party, the longest-serving Minnesota governor, but he was also the only one to serve nonconsecutive terms (1976–1979 and 1983–1991). Perpich had worked at the capital for decades, having served as a state senator and the lieutenant governor in the late 1960s and early 1970s. The *Star Tribune* published a history of Minnesota school choice and cited an anecdote from Dan Loritz, who was an education lobbyist.

> Perpich started thinking about open enrollment when, as a legislator in the 1970s, he would move his family to the Twin Cities during the legislative sessions. One year, Loritz said, Perpich tried to move his kids from the St. Paul schools into (suburban) Roseville, but St. Paul officials wouldn't approve the transfer.[52]

After Perpich returned to the governor's mansion in 1983, he would help lead the charge to pry open the doors for school choice.

While Minnesota had been a school choice pioneer, Perpich initially faced opposition to school choice when he first proposed open enrollment in 1985 for two reasons—potential for schools to lose per pupil enrollment revenue and a tarnished image for the school should students withdraw.[53] School choice would eventually be codified in Minnesota through a series of statutes passed beginning with two "second chance laws" in 1987. The first was called the High School Graduation Incentives program (HSGI). Through HSGI, students considered "at risk of dropping out" could, by their own choice, transfer to schools or programs that met their particular educational and/or social needs. The other second chance law created "Area Learning Centers" (ALCs). Area Learning Centers were to be spread over the state and were to offer individualized programs focusing on academics and workforce preparation. These centers would offer year-round, flexible programming, individualized instruction, training and work experience opportunities. ALCs were to serve both high school students at-risk of dropping out as well as residents over 21 years old who had not received a high school diploma.[54] Furthermore, students who had been assessed with chemical dependency (the term being used at that time) were considered "at risk" by Minnesota state law, thus programs within the alternative schools could be developed to target students with substance use disorders.

Then, in 1988, an open enrollment law went into effect for schools enrolling one thousand or more students. This open enrollment policy stated that students could enroll in any public school located outside their resident district. Applications to enroll in a nonresident district could be denied *only* if space was unavailable in the school of choice. The open enrollment law would become mandatory for *all* Minnesota school districts for the 1990–1991 school year.

Any one of these three new laws would qualify as a boon for school choice, but it was how they worked in tandem that made them so potent. While it was the last to pass, the open enrollment law provided the proverbial grease for the other gears to run smoothly. Open enrollment allowed ANY student to choose a school outside their resident district, and per pupil funding would follow them to whichever school they chose, if space was available. While open enrollment was available to all students for any school, it might have been interpreted to apply only to regular-education schools. The HSGI program, thus, focused specifically upon students at-risk of dropping out, which assured that students at-risk of dropping out also would be able to choose among both traditional and alternative schools, which most other states reserved primarily for punitive placements. Finally, the ALC policy mandated the creation of schools (ALCs) designed specifically for individualized academic needs (such as alcohol and drug recovery supports) and workforce development, pushing alternative schools beyond mandated disciplinary alternative schools that were the norm in other states.[55] Without open enrollment, students might have been restricted only to ALCs in their zoned districts, and without the HSGI, students could have been excluded from choosing alternative schools at all. As a result of the 1987 legislation, the first State-Approved Alternative Programs (SAAPs) were approved in 1988, with four sites serving four thousand students.[56]

School Choice and Exceptional Education

Despite all the school options emerging in the Twin Cities as Carol's son grew up, few of the alternative schools, public or private, were designed for students like him who needed exceptional learning supports. Due to staff and resource limitations, many alternative schools at the time simply did not offer special education services. Schools, instead, leaned on their individualized instructional approach as sufficient.

"(Some) schools incorporate special education methods into the curriculum used for all students and therefore do not offer special education as a separate entity," wrote Traci Teas in a 1998 master's thesis.[57] "Still other schools have directors who believe that students in special education do not belong in alternative schools because of lack of special education personnel, the open, unstructured environment of many of these programs, and accessibility issues," wrote Teas. "If a student has a learning disability, or any other mental, physical, or emotional impairment that require special education services, they may not be able to receive these services in the alternative schools."[58]

The Robsons discovered this was indeed the case at the Second Foundation School.

"I brought [my son] over there, and all they did was play Dungeons and Dragons all day," said Carol Robson. She recalled the school, which operated from a church basement, did not have its own library, so she and her son helped set one up. While the school helped her son accelerate his spelling and other interests like role-playing games, she felt he needed something more geared to his needs.

As a professional and as a parent, Carol Robson had learned something about accommodations, and helping others had become central to her identity. Robson had received a social work degree from the University of Minnesota in 1966, and she worked as a social worker for Hennepin County in the "Mentally Retarded and Epileptic" Division (MRE). MRE served youths with mental health and trauma histories as well as physical and cognitive disabilities. Her caseload covered a broad range, from adults with mental health disorders to children in foster homes with autism, Down's Syndrome, and myriad developmental disabilities, as well as higher functioning youths. "Back in those years, things were so incredibly different," recalled Robson. "We had one social worker that followed everyone, whether it was a child abuse case or mental health. Now everything is contracted out, and you'll have five and six contracted."[59]

With funds from Carol's social work position and her husband's job as a bartender, the Robsons bought a sixty-five hundred square-foot house for $155,000 in Minneapolis in 1970, not realizing Carol was about four-months pregnant.[60] The prior owners had employed two elderly nannies who were living on the top floor of the house, and when the Robsons realized they were expecting, they retained the nannies for themselves.[61]

"I was able to keep them on until my son was four years or five years old, I guess," said Robson, "so we had wonderful live-ins on the third floor that were fabulous."[62]

Similar to the educational movement occurring in Minnesota to relocate students from large public schools into smaller, community-based alternative schools in the early 1970s, an effort had begun to relocate people with physical and intellectual disabilities from large, state-operated hospitals into the least restrictive environment possible. Interestingly, the term for the housing process was different from "alternative"; it was called "normalization."[63] In Minnesota, the normalization movement led to transitioning people from the eight state hospitals into smaller community-based facilities and group homes. By the end of the decade, the number of people with intellectual disabilities living in community housing outnumbered those in state hospitals 3,843 to 2,854.[64] In Carol Robson's view, though, even those smaller residences were not ideal.

"When I was working for Hennepin County," recalled Robson, "all we had was foster homes. We'd have places where we'd take people in from the state hospitals, and we called them graveyards because they'd all be sitting in these big mansions and crazy places just rocking and watching TV. [A foster home] was the cream of the crop that came out of the state hospitals."

After her own son was born with cerebral palsy in the winter of 1971, Robson experienced firsthand, both personally and professionally, the gaps in care in the system, as well as the continuum of needs for children.

"I always felt that their needs were not being met," she said.[65]

By 1974, when her son was three years old, Robson had had enough of her Hennepin County job and was ready to convert their large house into a group home. After briefly considering hiring staff as "live-ins," she decided she wanted to run it herself. The nannies moved out, and the Robsons became live-in custodians in what they called "Summit House." Along with their own child, they housed six residents ages 9 to 25.

"There was a big demand for that type of house, and this was perfect," Robson recalled. "They came up to this beautiful big mansion, and they all had their own rooms and bathrooms and stuff. It was just perfectly set up. Most places would move them in, and they'd have a three-bedroom house and put two kids in each room, and they were cramped; but this was really great."[66]

The house was so successful the Robsons opened a second group home in 1978. Then, in 1980, they helped a nonprofit organization purchase a two hundred-acre farm on the central Minnesota prairie near Sauk Centre to house one of the first Camphill Villages in the United States. Camphill Village was similar to a group home, but it was a community unto itself where people with intellectual disabilities lived and worked alongside those without intellectual disabilities. While it faced some criticism at the time from people who felt moving people from a state hospital to a farm went against the principle of normalization because it was a "closed setting" with limited access to alternatives, the criticism was mild, and media accounts were positive.[67]

Camphill was part of a movement rooted in anthroposophy, a concept developed by philosopher Rudolf Steiner.[68] "Anthroposophy" is a Greek term meaning "human wisdom," and Steiner established it as both an educational and therapeutic system based in natural means. It was a spiritual philosophy, as Steiner believed all people had spiritual potential and a capacity for growth. One of Steiner's students, an Austrian doctor named Karl König, started the Camphill Movement in Aberdeen, Scotland, in 1939 with the goal of helping disabled people "unfold to their fullest spiritual potential and help them find a place in society."[69] The first Camphill Village in the United States opened in Copake, New York, in 1961, and after a group from Minnesota traveled to visit in the late 1970s, they decided to bring a village to Minnesota.

According to the Copake, New York, website, "The founding of Camphill Village in 1961 was part of a transformative movement in the United States to reform how society treats people with special needs."[70] The Robsons resonated with the philosophy deeply and helped make it a reality.[71]

"It's based on man's humanity to man," said Carol Robson. "It's literally all volunteer, and I was devoting tons of money."[72]

Camphill Village opened in the fall of 1980, just months before their son turned 10, and not long after that, the Robsons decided to find him a new school. After they determined their first option, the Second Foundation School, was unsatisfactory, Carol Robson originated something yet again. This time it was not a home or a village, but a school that captured the essence of both and aligned well with Steiner's anthroposophy. The Robsons gave it a fitting name: the New Dimensions School.

12
A New Dimension

When Carol Robson saw a need, she created something to meet it.

"I'm a loner, and I start things," said Carol Robson.

By 1981, Carol and her husband, Sheridan Robson had become experienced at launching ventures. They had started two group homes and had played a major role in beginning Camphill Village.[1] These three programs aligned well with Carol's social work training and drive for advocacy, and they had seeded from trying to build stronger services for her child when he was an infant.

A school, of course, is far different from a group home or a farming community. While Carol's first inclination for accommodating her son's basic needs had been to run their own, live-in group home, his school needs were farther afield from her and Sheridan's background. At first, they had pulled him from a traditional school and moved him into an alternative one, the Second Foundation School. When Second Foundation fell short of meeting the needs of a young person with cerebral palsy, the Robsons drew upon their inclination to "start things" and created a private alternative school that could provide the necessary services. They created an independent school ("very private" in Carol's words), which would give it autonomy from the regulations imposed on the alternative schools that were receiving public school allocations. It was a new dimension for their businesses as well as for local schools in Minneapolis, and they gave it that very name, the "New Dimensions School," a name Carol says was inspired by her belief in reincarnation.

"I believe in reincarnation," said Carol. "That's also why Camphill and anthroposophy is very important to me—the belief of man's humanity to man. Being involved in those, I came up with (the idea that) there have to be new dimensions, new exploratory ways to think of children."

Every business Carol and Sheridan Robson had begun to that point represented a new exploration of understanding and serving young people, and not just children with cerebral palsy like their son. New Dimensions would be open to any child with a disability or a need not being accommodated sufficiently in other programs, and this meant the school would veer into territory not even imagined by the Robsons when they conceived it. They filed articles of incorporation in December 1981 for New Dimensions School, Inc., a general for-profit business, with the purpose of operating a school by the same name. Six months later, they earned nonprofit status under a slightly different corporate moniker, "New Dimensions Schools," and dissolved the original corporation.

Salvaging a Teenage Wasteland. Andrew J. Finch, Oxford University Press. © Oxford University Press 2024.
DOI: 10.1093/oso/9780190645502.003.0012

As New Dimensions was a private school, funding would need to come from fees and other fundraising. While the school would not forge contracts with the state and local school districts like the larger private alternative schools had been able to do, there were other public sources of funding for youth, as Carol Robson knew from her many years as a social worker and group home operator. According to Robson, Minnesota had provided a per diem allotment to schools for students at-risk of dropping out. While she could not recall the specific details, she noted that a state legislator, Don Samuelson, had helped her school get some of that funding.[2] Samuelson led key welfare panels as a member of the House in the 1970s, and he later became chairman of the Senate Health, Welfare, and Corrections Subcommittee of the Senate Finance Committee.[3]

"I had worked with St. Louis Park High for a long time, and I knew the teachers for many years," said Carol. "So, when I suggested to them I was starting my own program, they (said they) would like to send three boys who were really impossible in school. I said, 'Well, I'll take 'em.'"

Robson recalled the local schools were receiving a $21 per diem fee to provide services for students who were deemed at-risk, and it retained 17% for each student who transferred to New Dimensions. That left New Dimensions with about $17.50 per diem. Most of the other students, including her son, came from her group homes. For those students, the school charged families a $150 per month fee, which most parents did not have the money to pay; so few paid tuition.

"I was able to take some of my children out of my own treatment home; [my son] knew all of them at the time," said Carol. "I had some high functioning kids that had, you know, borderline IQ, but that were really a problem (at) school."

The Robsons covered the rest of the costs with their own funds, including the money to hire a teacher. Later, they added a volunteer teacher as well. She remembers having about eight students when they started in 1982.

"I formed this school and hired my own teachers, and I never made a penny out of it," said Carol. "I just worked and tried, through hook and by crook, to keep the thing going financially."

They initially found space at the Eliot Center in St. Louis Park.[4] The community center had been home to the Eliot School, an elementary school from 1926 to 1977, presumed to be named after Charles W. Eliot, the legendary president of Harvard.[5] The building was, among other things, prone to lightning strikes, and had been converted into a fine arts center. A newspaper ad from March 1982 promoted enrollment for that fall in the Eliot Center. The promo described New Dimensions, Inc., as a "private non-denominational day school serving all grade levels," featuring a "small highly individualized program that address (sic) the basic-skills and also allow (sic) the student room to explore, be challenged intellectually and pursue special interests. Flexible scheduling available."[6]

"I was very involved in my small one-classroom school," Carol recalled. "Oh my god, I have a picture of the first day of school and my sister said, 'What a motley crew' when she saw it. She didn't like my pulling my son out of the public school.

I didn't really have any criteria, except my own son who was about eleven at the time. Then we took in a couple of Black children from the community who heard about it from a single mother who had a child and blah, blah, blah. I'd get them from several places."

By the fall of 1982, the school had relocated to a different community center in St. Louis Park called Brookside (see Figure 12.1).[7] A newspaper ad cited Brookside as the new site for the school and proclaimed, "We believe in students believing in themselves and in learning from our environment. We maintain very small class sizes. Most of all, we really believe that . . . Learning really can be fun!"[8]

Like the Eliot Center, the Brookside Community Center had housed a St. Louis Park elementary school, in this case from 1922 to 1975. Whereas Eliot had been converted into a fine arts center, Brookside was transformed in fall 1975 into a true multi-purpose facility more in line with the mission of New Dimensions. The center would house "adult education, day care, nursery, health service, ESL, children's library, general recreation, college-level classes from Mankato State, adult leisure classes and more."[9] There were other schools as well, including the Metropolitan Open School and the Discoveries for Children Montessori School. Carol Robson's school would spend almost ten years in that building.

Figure 12.1. The second location of Carol Robson's New Dimensions School was the Brookside Community Center. The school had opened in the spring of 1982 in the Eliot Center in St. Louis Park, Minnesota, but after a few months, the school relocated to Brookside, which had been converted from an elementary school a few years earlier. New Dimensions would remain at this site for ten years, which included its transformation into a recovery high school in 1987. This photo of the former Brookside School was taken in 1962. (Source: St. Louis Park Historical Society.)

Finding a Teacher

The Robsons brought myriad experiences to New Dimensions, but neither Carol nor Sheridan had been a teacher. For all of Carol's involvement in the school, New Dimensions would need someone to run the classroom, and the breadth of ages and content meant this would not be a standard teaching position. Their first choice was a person close to home. The wife of an employee at Summit House had been a teacher at a local public school, and she happily accepted the offer to be the first teacher at New Dimensions. They also had a volunteer teaching assistant, and Carol helped as much as she could.

Carol remembers the first teacher staying with the school for a couple years, but she turned out not to be the best fit.

"She turned out to be just a nut, you know; really, really too strict and very mean to my own son, as a matter of fact," said Carol.

So, they searched for a new teacher. While newspaper ads for a teaching assistant and an assistant teacher were posted in 1983[10] and 1984,[11] respectively, it is not clear when or how Bruce McLean heard about the opening for a teacher at New Dimensions.

"I went and interviewed, and they hired me," said McLean.

While McLean's description makes the decision sound mundane, his presence would change the course of the school and eventually open the door for recovery high schools in Minnesota. Considering the impact this one school would have on the expansion of recovery high schools in the United States, hiring Bruce McLean could be considered one of the most impactful decisions in the history of the movement.

McLean had been a substitute teacher in Minnesota schools for twenty years, and he also had been in theater since childhood, both as an actor and director. This affinity for drama would prove an excellent fit for working with students whose lives in active addiction had been dramatic in their own way, and whose attempts to build new lives in recovery would involve crafting new narratives. Initially, though, New Dimensions was not focused on substance use. Exceptional education was the primary focus, and McLean had been attracted to New Dimensions because of its alternative design.

"I hated regular schools, *hated* regular schools," said McLean. "Whenever I'd sub [at a regular school], I'd think, 'God, I couldn't do this, not in a regular school.'

"[Alternative school students] were easier to work with, I thought. I never had any trouble with any kid, any alternative kid. . . . I love the alternative school because you can play with them, you can joke with them."

This sense of play was always there for him. Robert Bruce McLean was born on May 6, 1941, in Roseau, Minnesota, about 10 miles from the Canadian border, but his family settled in Winona, about 115 miles southeast of Minneapolis. Bruce developed a love for acting at a young age. According to a local news account, the young McLean took part in a presentation in which fifth and sixth grade students at the Madison School "entertained with several folk dances and square dance numbers which they had learned in the school's physical education classes."[12] He made the honor roll at Winona High School, and stayed near home for college, attending Winona State University, where he earned a bachelor's degree in speech and art and worked on becoming a teacher.

At Winona State, McLean participated in several university theater productions. He played Col. Wainwright Purdy III in *Teahouse of the August Moon* as a freshman. A reviewer for the play said he played with a "mixture of bluster and futility."[13] As a sophomore, he was the House Manager for a production of *Candida*, and as a senior, he played the title role in *Othello*, the first recognized open stage production of Othello in the state.[14] He later pursued a master's degree in theater at Mankato State, but teaching provided him a steady job and consistent income. Bruce earned a Minnesota teaching license and took his first teaching job in 1965 in Eveleth, a town in northern Minnesota.[15]

"Oh, what a horrible place," said McLean, referring to the weather. "Eveleth is way up on the Iron Range in Minnesota. Cold, cold, cold."

Like many young people born during World War II and coming of age in the 1950s, Bruce's life would reflect the turbulence of the sixties. His father, Robert, was a veteran of World War I, and both of his siblings served in the military.[16] His brother, Tom, served in the Navy during Vietnam, and his sister, Nancy, relocated to California, near the Naval Station in San Diego. After his time in chilly Eveleth, Bruce moved closer to Minneapolis and was living in suburban Robbinsdale when the McLean family suffered a tremendous loss in 1968. His mother, Florence, died of leukemia in March at the relatively young age of 60.[17] His newly widowed father died a few months later, at the age of 72, just before Thanksgiving.[18] According to family lore, he "died of a broken heart."[19] Bruce's dad had moved in with Nancy in California after Bruce's mom died that spring. With his brother Tom still serving in the Navy during the Vietnam War, Bruce had no immediate family remaining in Minnesota. Glad to escape the brutally cold winters of northern Minnesota, McLean also moved to San Diego where he lived into the early 1970s. Later describing himself as a hippie, he continued acting and teaching in California for a few years, briefly joining the faculty of Southwest College, a community college in Chula Vista.[20]

McLean stayed heavily involved with the theater community in California, both as an actor and a director. From 1970 to 1971, he appeared as an actor in four different plays at the Old Globe Theatre and the Cassius Carter Center State Theater, both in the San Diego area.[21] As a member of the Southwest College faculty, McLean directed *Tobacco Road* for Southwestern College.[22] He then played Polonius in Tom Stoppard's *Rosencrantz and Guildenstern Are Dead* at the Old Globe Theatre in 1972.[23]

After a few years in sunny California, McLean decided to return home to Minnesota. McLean's "old friend and theater compatriot," Tom Leuchtenberg, had started converting a seventy-four-year-old grocery store near the commercial center of Maple Plain, about twenty miles west of Minneapolis.[24] Leuchtenberg was a teacher in the Orono school district and had begun working on constructing the theater in late 1972. McLean returned to Minnesota in 1974 to help him finish renovating the building into an eighty-four-seat playhouse. They dubbed it the "Orono Ensemble Theater," naming it after the school district rather than the town, because they felt "Maple Plain" was not "alluring" enough.[25] A year later, McLean invited David Bell-Lee from the San Diego theater community to assist with the renovation.

The Orono Ensemble put on an eclectic slate of plays. Their first production was *Hay Fever* in summer 1975, and, in the next year, they produced six more shows, both classic and modern: *The Knack; Tobacco Road; The Innocents; And Miss Reardon Drinks a Little; Little Murders;* and *Cat on a Hot Tin Roof*.[26] In 1976, McLean directed Herb Gardner's comedy, *A Thousand Clowns,* and the review called it "a treat not to be missed.... McLean's direction is sure-handed with an eye on the comic pacing that keeps the laughs coming while never sinking to farce."[27] McLean was in the director's chair again for Albert Camus's *Caligula* in 1977. This time, the reviewer deemed it "an artistic disappointment," but said "the theater is to be praised for even attempting" the play.[28]

McLean had taken a break from teaching when the Orono theater was in full swing, but substitute teaching remained a fallback for him.

"Through all of this, I've taught English, History, Social Studies; no math, no Science. That's not me," said McLean, who was certified to teach language arts.[29]

McLean taught as a sub in an array of school settings, and two would influence him profoundly. The first was one of the original schools from the Minnesota alternative school movement in the early 1970s—Plymouth Christian Youth Center. The youth center began running an alternative school called the Northside Street Academy in 1971, and the school is still in operation as the Plymouth Youth Center Arts & Technology High School.[30] The location may have been attractive to McLean from the start. The Plymouth Christian Youth Center had moved into a building in North Minneapolis in 1969, off West Broadway, directly behind the Capri Theater. The theater, built in 1927, was one of thirteen theaters on the North Side, showing movies and hosting recitals.[31] Known for many years as the Paradise Theater, it was renamed the Capri in 1967. In 1979, Prince, who was a Minnesota native, performed in a fundraiser there. It was thought to be his first solo professional concert.[32]

Due to affordable housing and proximity to downtown, the north side of Minneapolis historically has drawn marginalized communities. Initially much of the Twin Cities Jewish population settled there along Plymouth Avenue. By the 1920s, a sizable Black population had moved there as well. According to one historical account, "When blacks arrived in the Twin Cities, they often did not have access to the same community-based agencies as whites, so black churches, social organizations, and barber and beauty shops provided support."[33] One of those organizations was the Plymouth Christian Youth Center (PCYC). The Capri was one of the venues the Center used to promote the arts. The PCYC would eventually purchase the Capri in 1984, and the alternative high school would use the space for classrooms, sharing it with local 4-H program, which ran the American Variety Theater Company there.[34]

McLean remembered teaching at the alternative school, where the students taught him about his own privilege as a White man.

"I was teaching at the Plymouth Youth Center, which was for troubled kids and kids who had got kicked out of school," recalled McLean years later in an interview for this book. "I figured out not to react like I'm a White man, because (of how Black children had been treated) over the years."

"I learned about White privilege and how it still exists, and why this country is still too racist. I'm not that anymore."

While New Dimensions was predominantly White, McLean brought with him lessons of inclusivity learned at PCYC, as well as how to work with marginalized communities who had backgrounds different from his own. His acceptance of diversity also may have been aided by the fact that Bruce identified as a gay man, though it is not clear when or if he was out to his colleagues and students. It was a teaching job at another school in the 1980s that gave McLean experience with a different marginalized group—teenagers with alcohol and drug issues.

Adolescent Treatment Finds New Dimensions

As McLean was returning to Minnesota to start the Orono Ensemble Theater in the mid-1970s, two movements had dovetailed in the state. The first was the alternative/free school movement, which had taken root in many other states as well. The other was treating adolescents for substance use disorders, spurred by the growing number of teenagers using drugs in the 1970s, as well as the Drug War that had been declared by the Nixon administration in 1971.[35]

After Riverside Hospital in New York City began offering treatment especially for teenagers from 1952 to 1961, growth in adolescent treatment had occurred slowly. In addition to hospitals, churches had started providing services in the 1950s and 1960s, including St. Mark's Clinic in Chicago, and the Addicts Rehabilitation Center, Astoria Consultation Service,[36] and Exodus House, all in New York.[37] There were also unaffiliated religious ministries, such as Teen Challenge, which began with David Wilkerson's outreach to street gangs in New York in 1958.[38]

The National Institute on Drug Abuse (NIDA) issued a national directory of all the "drug abuse programs" that existed in the United States and Puerto Rico in 1975.[39] The directory claimed the Drug War had prompted an explosion of federally funded programs from 36 in 1971 time to 376 in 1975. Dr. Robert DuPont, the first NIDA director, wrote, "These programs, combined with the resources from state, local, and private organizations, support over thirty-eight hundred treatment service points."[40] Of those thousands of "treatment service points," only thirteen specifically included adolescents in their names, with such varied titles as crisis unit, clinic, rehabilitation unit, neighborhood program, drug detox, reception rec center, development program, and medicine program. An additional 113 were labeled as "youth" programs, most labeled as youth "centers" providing outpatient "treatment/rehabilitation."[41]

In Minnesota, the appearance of adolescent chemical dependency programs based on a "Minnesota Model" helped accelerate the growth of adolescent treatment even more.[42] The Minnesota Model originated as an abstinence-based approach for adults in the Willmar State mental hospital in the early 1950s and was thus called the "Willmar Model." Dr. Daniel Anderson was one of the cofounders of the model, and in a coauthored first-person account of its evolution through the 1950s and 1960s, he wrote, "The key element of this novel approach to addiction treatment was the blending of professional and trained nonprofessional (recovering) staff around the principles of Alcoholics Anonymous (AA). There was an individualized treatment plan with active family involvement in a twenty-eight-day inpatient setting and participation in Alcoholics Anonymous both during and after treatment."[43] In 1961, Anderson became executive director of the then small, nonprofit Hazelden Foundation, and he took his burgeoning treatment model with him, renaming it the Hazelden Model.[44]

In the early 1960s, most people seeking (or forced into) treatment had experienced what was called "hitting rock bottom."[45] This concept was even given a shape by the classic "Jellinek Curve," an image emerging from the work Dr. E. M. Jellinek at Yale, who conceived a developmental progression of addiction in his 1946 publication, "Phases in the Drinking History of Alcoholics,"[46] and further elaborated upon in his classic 1960 book, *The Disease Model of Alcoholism*.[47] Jellinek's model focused on the downward projection, and, in 1958, Dr. Max M. Glatt, the founder of the Alcoholism Treatment Unit at Warlingham Park Hospital in England, added the right, upward trend of recovery, thus generating the appearance of a trough at the bottom.[48] While the full curve was a combination of the ideas of Jellinek and Glatt, neither of which had much empirical support nor focused on the "rock bottom," the graphic became known simply as the "Jellinek Curve" and propagated the idea of hitting a bottom. One of the earliest statements of this belief was published in the *British Medical* in 1965:

If treatment is to be successful the addict must be advised that he is suffering from a disease which precludes his returning to normal drinking: he must never touch a drop again. A man who has been struggling for years unsuccessfully to control his drinking may find this simple statement enormously helpful, while others unfortunately have to "hit rock bottom" before accepting the truth.[49]

As Dr. Anderson's nascent Hazelden Model started getting noticed, the question remained what to do with people who had not yet hit bottom and had not been "struggling [for] years unsuccessfully to control" their drinking and other drug use. How could a person be "advised" they were suffering from a disease if they had not arrived in the rooms of AA nor checked into a treatment center? This distinction would become especially relevant for young people who had not been using drugs or even living for many years, let alone unsuccessfully trying to stop their use.

An answer came by way of Irene and Wheelock Whitney. Wheelock was an investment banker, philanthropist, and politician who was a fraternity brother of George H. W. Bush at Yale.[50] He and Irene married in 1948, and in 1964, Wheelock campaigned for the US Senate. He earned the Republican nomination, but ultimately lost the election to Eugene McCarthy.[51] As he was making his run for the Senate, it was also becoming apparent that Irene's drinking was getting out of control. Irene was not ready to admit it, but her friends and family were quite aware.[52]

Vernon Johnson was an Episcopal priest who had received treatment at Hazelden in 1962, about a year after Dan Anderson took over and installed his new approach. After getting into recovery himself, Johnson began meeting with a group at St. Martin's-by-the-Lake Episcopal Church in Minnetonka Beach, Minnesota, which included others in recovery and their families.[53] That treatment prompted Johnson to begin meeting at the church with a parish action group that included families in recovery from alcoholism.

In a memorial article published by the Episcopal News Service following his death in 1999, Johnson was quoted as saying, "Why do the people who have the disease wait so long to get treatment? Why do they suffer so long? Since alcoholism is progressive and fatal, we see an urgent need to stop the progress of the disease as early as possible."[54]

Johnson thus developed a process to have the family and friends meet with the person struggling with alcohol and other drugs to help convince them to enter treatment. He called the approach an "intervention," and Wheelock Whitney asked Johnson to organize one for Irene. Johnson's intervention was so impactful that after Irene got into recovery, she and Wheelock provided the financial backing for an institute named in his honor—the "Johnson Institute"—to promote interventions and referrals to treatment, which opened in 1966.[55]

The Hazelden Model paired nicely with interventions promoted by the Johnson Institute to get more and more people into treatment. The model also started to spread beyond Hazelden, and the director of the private St. Mary's Hospital in Minneapolis, Sister Mary Madonna, took notice. At that time, though, private hospitals had not yet started providing inpatient treatment.

"People resented that we would treat addiction as an illness. Private hospitals just didn't have in-treatment programs," Sister Mary Madonna was quoted as saying in a newspaper article commemorating the evolution of the Minnesota Model.[56]

"But we decided to take a risk."

St. Mary's opened its treatment center for adults in 1968, incorporating the Hazelden Model.[57] By the early 1970s, with the Hazelden Model now being embraced by multiple programs not affiliated with Hazelden, Dan Anderson's treatment became known as the Minnesota Model.[58]

The Whitneys also provided financial support to the Pharm House, which, in March 1970, transformed a condemned antebellum home into a walk-in crisis intervention program for people ages "15-51" to deal with "bad trips and other drug emergencies or questions."[59]

"It was kind of crazy at the time because half the people that were volunteering and were staff, they were using," recalled Betty Triliegi, who had worked for Vern Johnson at the Johnson Institute. "It was weird, but anyway, it was the beginning."

About a year later, the program opened a residential treatment center ("Pharm House 2") with a program lasting "six weeks to six months."[60] One of the founders, Terry Troy, also had previously worked at the Johnson Institute, and he brought that programming with him. Pharm House billed itself as a "drug training, counseling, and treatment center," and it was effectively the first program in Minneapolis to treat teenagers with substance use disorders—albeit along with adults.[61]

St. Mary's Hospital expanded beyond adult services in 1974 when it began offering an adolescent detoxification program, and the hospital opened a full treatment center for adolescents a year later—the first inpatient treatment program exclusively for adolescents in the state.[62] With the Johnson Institute creating an avenue to intervene early, and the Minnesota Model joining other youth treatment designs from outside the state, such as Teen Challenge and therapeutic communities, in providing templates for adolescent treatment, more and more programs began operating in the state. Minnesota was well on its way to becoming known as the "Land of Ten Thousand Treatment Centers," and the Whitneys were leading advocates of that growth.

After getting into recovery, Irene had earned her master's degree in counseling psychology at the University of Minnesota in 1970.[63] In addition to the Johnson Institute, St. Mary's, and Pharm House, she and Wheelock were involved in starting the first halfway house for teenagers—the Shanti House (which was later renamed the Irene Whitney Center for Recovery) in 1976.[64] That same year, the Wheelocks organized Freedom Fest to coincide with the Bicentennial celebrations happening across the nation.

"Irene wanted to show the rest of the country what Minnesota had done with addiction," said Betty Triliegi.

Billed as a "celebration of freedom from alcoholism and drug dependency,"[65] it drew about thirty thousand people to Metropolitan Stadium in Bloomington, despite "threatening skies and tornado watches."[66] Many celebrities attended, including Dick van Dyke, who was the master of ceremonies. The event drew national attention, and further cemented Minnesota as the hub of recovery in the United States.

"We're here to celebrate a real freedom," van Dyke was quoted as telling the crowd. "It's an internal freedom—from our addiction. We're here to help overcome the stigma about alcoholism, which is an illness, and show that there is hope. People can recover."[67]

By the early 1980s, for-profit treatment centers had entered the Minnesota scene, sometimes based in other states. One such example was the Addiction Recovery Corporation (ARC) of Waltham, Massachusetts. New Englander Lawrence E. Bienemann started ARC in 1983 and soon expanded beyond the Northeast into Arizona, Illinois, New York, Pennsylvania, and Tennessee.[68] The treatment approach was very similar to the Minnesota Model, using an abstinence-based, Twelve Step approach, as well as incorporating Al-Anon and family support. The thirty-day treatment program cost about $11,000.[69] ARC opened two facilities in Minnesota—one in St. Louis Park, near the New Dimensions school, and another in Eden Prairie, about twenty miles from Minneapolis.[70] The Eden Prairie program was an adolescent residential unit, and like other residential and day-treatment programs, they provided a school for the students while they were in treatment, so students could stay on track with their academics. Those schools, of course, needed teachers, and one of teachers ARC hired for Eden Prairie was Bruce McLean.

McLean had returned to teaching as his primary source of employment after the Orono Ensemble Theater closed around 1980, and the adolescent unit gave him a chance to teach teenagers actively working on their recovery.[71] While he could not recall exactly when he started working at ARC in Eden Prairie, it was most likely in 1983 or 1984. Teaching at ARC was a different experience for McLean than working in a student's regular school.

"They had with them what schoolwork they had been doing," said McLean. "They would identify what they were working on in school, and we would provide that to them."

He noted, however, "I was only a substitute because they needed a teacher. I only taught those kids in that program; there were no other teachers."

In other words, a full-time teaching position at another school would provide a more sustainable job, especially if it was at an alternative school with more support staff. So, when he heard about an opening at the Robsons' New Dimensions school, likely from a newspaper ad, McLean jumped at the opportunity.

Recalling the early days of the school, Carol Robson said, "I had a teacher, always a fully licensed teacher, and then I got rid of her. Then I hired Bruce [McLean], who was with me the rest of the time, and he was fabulous.

"He was a wonderful, wonderful man."

While New Dimensions was open to students of any age, most were around the age of her son, who was eleven when New Dimensions opened its doors. As the school evolved, there were fewer elementary-age children, and more and more junior high and high school students. Though neither Robson nor McLean remembered the exact year he was hired, it was likely 1985 or 1986, which means her son would have been about 14 or 15.

"By that time, he was (high school) age, and we didn't keep grade school kids in it," said Carol. "As he grew, the school grew. It all depended on where [my son] was, I guess, at the time. He fit in beautifully. All of them got along. We had quite a mix.... (They had) different needs like my own son."

The enrollment included youths living in the Robsons' two group homes, students referred from the community, and families who were looking for an alternative school option. Families heard about the school through newspaper ads or open houses held at the school. An ad from September 1985 promoted the following (bullet points included):

- A full academic program
- Class ratios of 1:6
- Diagnostic evaluation
- Weekly field trips

- Licensed, experienced staff
- A positive, nurturing environment, conducive to creative learning, growth, and expression
- Summer school[72]

The second-to-last point may have signaled Bruce McLean's input and theater background, as the focus on "creative learning" and "expression" was an expansion from previous ads. One constant in promos over the years, though, was their motto: "Learning really can be fun!"

"The superintendent of schools was delighted to get two or three of my worst residents in my group home facilities out of his classrooms," said Robson.

She noted the students were diverse.

"One of our first students used to be delivered in a limo from Wayzata. She was 15 years old, and she'd had a couple of abortions and the whole thing. The students coming in there were from various backgrounds, from single family mother, young girl who's seventeen with a child. We had a very mixed group; a wonderful mixed group."

According to Robson, her son did not have a substance use disorder, but an increasing number of the New Dimensions students did. Bruce McLean started noticing many similarities between the students at New Dimensions and those he had taught at ARC in Eden Prairie.

"I noticed that those kids I was working with [at New Dimensions] had chemical dependency problems, because [ARC in Eden Prairie] was a chemical dependency center," said McLean. "I had worked with those kids at [ARC], because their problem was with drugs and alcohol."

By the mid-1980s, there were at least four other recovery high schools that had received media coverage in the United States: Freedom Road in Charleston, the PDAP GED School in Houston, and both Phoenix 1 and 2 in Montgomery County, Maryland. The Phoenix programs were both still in operation and had been featured in the *Washington Post* as well as in articles that had been syndicated nationwide. This was long before the internet and social media, though, and Bruce McLean had never heard of any of those programs. He was a schoolteacher and a theater person, with no awareness of those innovative schools. But he did realize the potential value of a school for youths in recovery, just as those other visionaries had before him.

McLean was featured in a newspaper article a few years after becoming a teacher for New Dimensions, and the article noted that at the ARC residential treatment school, he "saw firsthand that most students who left treatment became lonely at their regular schools and would relapse."[73] This would lead to students bottoming out.

"They feel terrible about themselves," said McLean. While he did not identify as a person in recovery himself, he had felt a connection with those students in some ways. In the article, McLean called himself "a former hippie" and said he could empathize with the students because of his own drug use as a young person.

"I smoked everything and did my share of hallucinogens," he said. "I stopped doing that. It fogged everything up too much."[74]

A school that could help students stop using drugs and maintain the progress gained in treatment made sense to McLean, and he saw an opportunity in the small, private New Dimensions school. So, he decided to suggest that idea to the Robsons.

"Sheridan and Carol and I went to lunch one day, because I said I had something I wanted to talk to them about," recalled McLean. "I introduced this idea of maybe having troubled kids, alcohol or [drug-]dependent kids, in the program. They thought that was a really good idea."

One reason the idea of a recovery high school resonated with Carol Robson was that she *did* identify as a person in long-term recovery. Robson had received residential treatment at Hazelden in February 1974, and she remembered her child celebrating his third birthday while she was in treatment. She said she had a recurrence of use "two or three times in the first six-to-eight months," but by the fall of 1974, Robson had begun an extended period of sobriety that would last fifteen years. It was something that framed most of her son's childhood. She recounted a story when he was only 7 years old.

"When I came in [to recovery], you know, it was pretty shameful to be an alcoholic," said Robson. "I had [my son] at a clinic at the hospital. I'd gone down to get eyeglasses at one part of the clinic, and my son was waiting for me in the waiting room in another part of it, where he was seeing a speech therapist. And as I came walking back there, the waiting room was really full of people. And he said, 'Mom, Mom! I was telling everybody now you're an alcoholic! Now the president's wife is an alcoholic just like you!' It was Betty Ford. And he was so thrilled to announce it to the whole group."

Indeed, former First Lady Betty Ford's openness about her own treatment for a substance use disorder had been a major step towards removing stigma around addiction and encouraging others to seek treatment themselves. On the heels of Hazelden's model becoming the Minnesota Model, and Vernon Johnson's use of interventions to move people into treatment earlier, this was another step towards destigmatizing treatment in the United States.

NIDA director, Robert DuPont, was quoted by the *Washington Post* at the time, saying, "I believe the nation is going to go through a major change because of this. Mrs. Ford has made a big contribution—there are hundreds of thousands of other Americans who need this rehabilitation."[75]

By the time Carol Robson sat down for lunch with Sheridan and Bruce McLean, she had over ten years of sobriety, and during that time, treatment had been experiencing rapid growth in the number of residential treatment beds. By Hazelden's own accounts, the number of inpatient beds in the United States had doubled between 1978 and 1984, due to "liberal insurance coverage."[76]

According to an historical account by White, Dennis, and Tims, treatment models were also being modified in the early 1980s to be more developmentally appropriate for adolescents by the following practices:

- using youth-oriented, multidimensional assessment instruments;
- developing youth-focused family and group treatment modalities;

- using younger and more educated staff at agencies and hospitals;
- dealing more flexibly with rule violations;
- shifting from confrontation to motivation/engagement;
- coordinating care with schools and the juvenile justice systems;
- defining clinical subpopulations requiring special approaches of engagement and treatment (e.g., ethnic minorities, runaways, and adolescents with conduct disorder, ADHD, depression, HIV/AIDS and other co-occurring disorders); and
- refining the use of pharmacological adjuncts in the treatment of comorbid conditions.[77]

Carol Robson would have agreed with all these changes. As a person who valued both innovation and running programs best suited for youth, she thought a "sober school" was particularly salient. Hazelden, where she had gone for treatment herself, had just acquired the Pioneer House in Plymouth, Minnesota, to create its own specialized treatment for adolescents in 1981.[78] The program would become known as the Hazelden Center for Youth and Families (HCYF). The HCYF program and others around the Twin Cities were producing dozens of young people who might want recovery supports beyond the twenty-eight-day treatment which was standard for the Hazelden/Minnesota Model.

"I got funding eventually through the Student-At-Risk program [for the New Dimensions School], but, along the way, we weren't getting any of those students [place at-risk due to special education needs]. We were getting chemically dependent kids coming in. Hey, this was really a going thing," said Robson.

While the exact date of the McLean and Robsons' lunch has been lost to memory, it was likely in 1987, because it was in fall of that year that the New Dimensions School officially changed its focus. A newspaper article featuring the revised school model noted, "The program, new this fall [1987], is designed to meet the needs of students in grades nine through twelve who have recently completed an alcohol/chemical or emotional/behavior treatment program."[79] The description called it a "program for post-treatment adolescents," and initially most, but not all, the students had a substance use disorder. This would allow Carol Robson to continue enrolling students from her group homes, as well as her own sixteen-year-old son, while making the transition to exclusively students in recovery. That first fall with the new focus, New Dimensions enrolled eight students.

McLean was referred to in the article as the "Lead Teacher," and the school offered math, social studies, communications, science, and electives, providing individualized accommodations for each student. As would be a feature of many recovery high schools, students had the option to transfer back to their home school at some point or stay and graduate from New Dimensions.[80]

"We are dedicated to help these students regain educational competence in a setting which reinforces and builds upon the positive qualities established in the student's treatment," McLean said in the article, comparing the atmosphere to a one-room schoolhouse. "It's mostly an esteem-building educational program.[81]

"They deserve an awful lot of attention. The advantage here is that those kids do get that attention positive attention. You can afford to be patient with them, and you can afford to be flexible. It's a much more personalized approach to education."[82]

Like the Phoenix schools in Montgomery County, Maryland, the New Dimensions students took frequent field trips as part of the curriculum. According to the feature article, by November, the schools had already visited the airport, the zoo, the Art Institute, and museums, and they had taken driving tours of the city to study architecture. They even attended the Minnesota Twins' World Championship parade after their 1987 World Series victory over the St. Louis Cardinals. And, of course, with Bruce McLean as their teacher, the school took trips to see local theater productions.[83]

The school had begun its transformation into becoming the first recovery high school in Minnesota, and many more changes were on the horizon. By the end of that school year, the school would adopt a French name, and new characters would enter a story that was about to resemble a soap opera.

13
Becoming Sobriety High

Not long after helping form Camphill Village, a farming community for people with developmental disabilities, Carol Robson had decided to take up farming herself.

"All of a sudden, I decided I wanted a hobby farm," said Robson. "Within three days I had purchased a hobby farm. I moved out there and lived there for twelve years running a full farm operation, starting an organic farm, way before my time."[1]

The farm was forty-five acres in Center City, about sixty miles from Minneapolis.

"A wonderful area," said Robson. "It was just going to be a small thing, and because I have an addictive personality, I ended up with a hundred sixty/seventy sheep and cattle and horses, and everything. I stopped at llamas and buffaloes."

She and her husband, Sheridan, also started using the hobby farm as the main office for all their other businesses. In December 1981, they used its Center City address when they filed the Articles of Incorporation for New Dimensions School, Inc., and then again when they refiled as a nonprofit in June 1982.

Carol attended Alcoholics Anonymous meetings in Center City. This was something she had been doing regularly since moving out to the farm, and they were meetings that were frequently attended by staff and alums of the Hazelden Foundation, which was only a ten-minute drive from the hobby farm. By that time, Hazelden had become a popular destination for the rich and famous to get treatment. Ozzy Osbourne (early 80s), Eric Clapton (1982 and 1987), Natalie Cole (1983), Liza Minnelli, (1985), Calvin Klein (1988), and Melanie Griffith (1988) were among the celebrities to check into Hazelden in the 1980s.[2] Robson recalled meeting many of those celebrities during her days living on the farm.

One day, she stepped into an AA meeting and encountered a relative newcomer who was not a celebrity himself, but who counted them among his friends and former business associates. The impact of this meeting upon her, her marriage, and the New Dimensions School would be profound. The person's name was Ralph Neiditch.[3]

Neiditch had been an advertising executive in New York, and he had come to Hazelden for treatment in 1982.[4] When Carol met Neiditch, he was living in a third-floor attic room at a rooming house in Center City.[5] At some point, not long after they met in that AA meeting, Carol and Ralph became romantically involved, and it was a complicated relationship from the beginning. On the one hand, Carol recalled, "We had a great relationship for eight years." On the other, she learned, "Never get [romantically] involved with AA."

Salvaging a Teenage Wasteland. Andrew J. Finch, Oxford University Press. © Oxford University Press 2024.
DOI: 10.1093/oso/9780190645502.003.0013

One complication was her marriage. Carol and Sheridan were friends and business partners, but their marriage had grown apart. About a year after launching the New Dimensions School to give their son a better education, the Robsons separated in 1983.[6] Carol was living mainly in Center City by then, and she was immersed in running the school, the group homes, and the farm. Their separation would last five years, until they finalized their divorce in July 1988, after twenty-nine years of marriage. According to Carol, she maintained a relationship with Ralph Neiditch during that time, and after her divorce with Sheridan, she got remarried to Neiditch. He also had been married before when they met.[7]

Carol and Sheridan remained friends and business colleagues during their separation and after their divorce. "We have a son together; we're still friends," said Carol in an interview for this book. Her relationship with Neiditch, though, was not entirely a secret.

"It was a lot of drama," said Bruce McLean. "A lot of drama in all of that. That's how I knew [about Neiditch and Carol Robson]. I didn't know anything else."

And that "drama" would have been going on when McLean sat down to lunch with Carol and Sheridan to suggest turning New Dimensions into a recovery high school. It is difficult, if not impossible to fully untangle the time lines and determine who ultimately deserves credit for the school becoming a recovery high school. In later interviews, Neiditch claims credit for creating the school and funding it, even though he is not mentioned in any media coverage of the school prior to 1989. There were at least two full-length feature stories about the school in the *Minneapolis Star-Tribune* in 1987[8] and 1989,[9] and both focused on McLean and the students. Neither mentions Neiditch at all. Of course, they do not mention the Robsons either, and they clearly were involved in the start-up.

The pivotal year was 1988. To that point, all official documents filed on behalf of the school were filed in the names of Carol and Sheridan Robson. In the original Articles of Incorporation, Carol was listed as president, and Sheridan as secretary-treasurer. Then, on April 29, 1988, Carol Robson prepared and signed new Articles of Incorporation for the school.[10] This time, she had a new partner—Ralph Neiditch. Sheridan Robson was not included on the paperwork. Additionally, the organization had been given a different name: "*Ecole Nouvelle*, Inc." The name is French for "New School," not a complete departure from "New Dimensions School."[11] The official address of the corporation was the hobby farm, which was now listed as Carol Robson and Ralph Neiditch's address, and they were named as the "original members of the corporation."[12] The purpose of this corporation was listed as "general educational and community welfare."[13]

Twelve days later, Carol and Sheridan took a trip to the Chisago County Courthouse to pay the $350 fee and make their divorce final.

"To keep it simple, when I went to the courthouse and the judge was asking me about alimony and child [support], I said, 'No problem, no problem: fifty/fifty all the way. No problem,' " she said in an interview for this book.

The transformation was becoming complete. While Carol was still listed as president of the corporation, Neiditch had replaced Sheridan as the secretary (see Figure 13.1). And the school had a new name, though its origin is unclear. Robson said the

Figure 13.1. Ralph Neiditch (left) and Carol Robson (right) officially changed the name of New Dimensions to "Ecole Nouvelle" in April 1988. While New Dimensions had already transformed into a recovery high school, Neiditch's involvement would propel the school from a small program in a St. Louis Park community center into an influential and internationally recognized sober school with multiple locations. (Source: Carol Robson.)

new name, *Ecole Nouvelle*, "absolutely came from Ralph at the time," though she was does not recall why. "Probably some flight of fancy." Interestingly, Ralph's former wife, Mary, was the daughter of a knight of the country of Malta, and she had received her college diploma from the Sorbonne.[14] Though there is no indication that was an influence for the name, the French language would have been familiar to Neiditch.

Changing the name also would have been a way to mark a new school purpose, and adopting a French name may have been a way to imply a certain, international sophistication that "New Dimensions" did not. The latter point would have helped in fundraising, which was something Neiditch embraced much more than the Robsons ever had. He was seeking to make this school his own, and a new name signaled a fresh start.

The original name for the school, New Dimensions, had come from Carol's belief in reincarnation and the philosophy of anthroposophy, which emphasizes the belief of "man's humanity to man."[15] Regarding finances, Carol said, "I formed this school and hired my own teachers, and I never had a penny out of it. I just worked and hired, through hook and by crook, kept the thing going financially."

By changing the school population to move completely away from her son, his friends, and residents of her group homes, keeping the school afloat financially would become increasingly difficult.

"Carol and Sheridan, they were good people," said McLean. "They just didn't get it."

Years later, Ralph Neiditch reflected upon the first couple years of his involvement in Sobriety High and said they were "tough ones for the school."[16] There was no guide for how best to run a recovery high school; to their knowledge, no such school had ever been attempted. The staff and board gave no indication that they were aware of the Freedom Road, PDAP, or Phoenix schools, let alone using the experience from those school leaders as guidance. In addition, the fee to attend the school limited who could enroll, and the financial burden was getting worse for families seeking recovery for their children.

Michael Schiks was program director for the Pioneer House at Hazelden, which operated a seventy-five-bed primary care facility for 14–25-year-olds. That program would be a key referral option for Robson and Neiditch, especially considering their relationship with Hazelden. By the late 1980s, though, Schiks noted middle-class families were being "shut out of residential treatment programs," as the only families able to afford Hazelden's residential program were those wealthy enough to self-pay, those who had elite insurance policies, and young people placed there by the county.[17] With the shift toward servicing students who had received prior treatment, *Ecole Nouvelle* would be constrained by the same forces that would limit treatment access.

One of those forces was the War on Drugs, which was almost eighteen years old by the summer of 1989. As part of that War, Congress passed two Anti-Drug Abuse Acts in the 1980s (1986 and 1988) that facilitated mass incarceration of Black people.[18] Those laws along with the financial disparities built into the cost of treatment further segregated the treatment system between wealthy White children and Black youths. The 1986 legislation established mandatory minimum sentences, including a 100-to-1 ratio between sentences for crack cocaine (used more by black drug users) and powder cocaine (used more by White drug users).[19] The Act of 1988 was signed into law by Ronald Reagan on November 18, just days after his vice president, George H. W. Bush had been elected to succeed him, and it went further, creating the policy goal of a "drug-free America"; establishing the Office of National Drug Control Policy; and restoring the use of the death penalty by the federal government.[20] More salient to treatment disparities, the 1988 law also made crack cocaine the only drug with a mandatory minimum penalty for a first offense of simple possession.[21] These policies would ultimately create a pathway to recovery high schools accessible mainly to White students from higher income families.

Ralph Neiditch and the High Rollers

As Ralph Neiditch increasingly took over leadership of the school, he would need to be creative in raising funds as well as marketing the program to align with societal and economic forces increasingly not in their favor. Neiditch thus had a business plan in mind that was less aligned with Rudolf Steiner's anthroposophy and rooted more in his familiar corporate world. Neiditch had worked for decades in that world, and Carol recalled that his alcoholism had recently cost him his own company.

"He had fabulous jobs in New York, and when I met him, he had just lost his own advertising agency that he had started due to chemical dependency," said Robson. "He always ran with the crowd in New York City from [record-industry executive] Mitch Miller and all these people going back. I mean the history there is incredible. He came to Minneapolis, and he had lost his ad agency. The board in fact came out to Hazelden to kick him off and throw him out of the agency because of his alcoholism, and that's how he ended up out in Center City."

Neiditch had come from New York, which was home to the renowned Ogilvy-Mather Advertising Agency. Its founder was David Ogilvy, and his 1963 book, *Confessions of an Advertising Man* was a classic text considered required reading for people studying advertising in the United States for the next fifty years. Having started his own ad agency, it is likely Neiditch was familiar with the book and its maxim, which included these nuggets of wisdom offered in the chapter titled "How to Manage an Advertising Agency":

- Many of the greatest creations of man have been inspired by the desire to make *money* (italics included).
- In the modern world of business, it is useless to be a creative, original thinker unless you can also sell what you create.
- Finally, I have observed that no creative organization, whether it is a research laboratory, a magazine, a Paris kitchen, or an advertising agency, will produce a great body of work *unless it is led by a formidable individual* (italics included) . . . Few of the great creators have bland personalities. They are cantankerous egotists, the kind of men who are unwelcome in the modern corporation.[22]

Each of those ideas was apparent in Neiditch's actions in promoting *Ecole Nouvelle* and taking the school in a different direction.

"[Ralph] was involved with this whole group of high rollers, I call them, and they were fundraisers," said Robson. "He had all of these core groups around him, and Ralph knew how to pick friends."

Running with "high rollers" was something Neiditch had done most of his professional life, and according to his recovery story, it had contributed heavily to him landing at Hazelden in Center City. An expose on the school summarized one version of Neiditch's story, delivered during a fundraising dinner at a Minneapolis restaurant in the spring of 1995. Personal stories are a core element of Twelve Step recovery, and they tend to include three major sections: "what it was like," "what happened," and "what things are like now."[23] According to the account of his story published in *Education Week*, Neiditch was working for Columbia Records by the early 1980s as an art director, which allowed him to socialize with major musicians, such as Paul Simon and Liza Minnelli. Drug use was part of the culture, "and that included drinking and using cocaine, hashish, and opium."[24]

"It was part of the business," Neiditch told the audience at the fundraising dinner. "I continued to drink and do drugs even though I'd already been through six treatment centers, a handful of psychiatric facilities, and had attempted suicide more than once." This led him to seek treatment in Center City, Minnesota:

An overdose of alcohol and barbiturates that plunged him into a coma finally made Neiditch decide to check himself into the Hazelden Foundation. He credits the renowned treatment center an hour's drive north of Minneapolis with his recovery. The pace, the people, and the contemplative setting persuaded him to uproot himself from his frenetic New York existence and start a new life.[25]

The article also alludes to his relationship with Carol Robson, without mentioning her by name: "The Brooklyn-born Neiditch bought a farm a few miles from Hazelden and settled in to raise sheep and cows for eight years." Over time, Robson had renovated her farmhouse, likely with support from Neiditch, and made it into a tranquil and beautiful retreat. Hazelden even approved the farm as a place for patients to visit, including celebrities such as Ozzy Osbourne and Calvin Klein.[26] But Robson had been erased from the *Education Week* story. In fact, none of the articles published about the new recovery high school included Robson's name. It was as if she had not been involved in the creation of the program, which was clearly untrue.

The story went further with a partially true origin story, saying, "In 1989, Neiditch rented a room in a community center in Minneapolis for $400 a month, placed an advertisement for a teacher in the local paper, and several weeks later, had a student body of six." While Neiditch was one of the school's owners by 1989 and could have been the one to submit a rent check, the location was actually the same Brookside Community Center in St. Louis Park where Robson's school had been located since 1982. Furthermore, while Neiditch may have advertised for a teacher, Bruce McLean was still teaching at the school in 1989, and he was even profiled in an article about the school published that September.[27] McLean was referred to as the "director of education," and the article quoted several students, some who had been at the school for years.

The article, written by staff writer Rob Hotakainen, provided one of the clearest published descriptions of the physical space and climate for Minnesota's first recovery high school:

It's a school with many different twists: Students, who pay $400 a month in tuition, have little homework but say that's good because they have to go to Alcoholics Anonymous or Narcotics Anonymous meetings at least once a week. With rock 'n' roll music playing softly in the background, students eat potato chips and candy and drink Cokes at their desks. They can smoke on the church steps across the street (and nearly all of them do) if they bring along a coffee can for their cigarette butts. It's a cozy schoolroom with a hardwood floor, housed in the Brookside Community Center, which is tucked in a tranquil neighborhood at 41st St. and Vernon Av., just west of Hwy. 100. The serenity prayer is inscribed on a wall plaque. There are no lockers: Students keep their books and papers in plastic milk cases. Students drive or take the city bus to school.[28]

Hotakainen gave hints of the changing philosophy as well, noting the school "operates on tuition and private donations. It receives no state aid, but McLean said he intends to approach the legislature. Last year, private donations helped pay the way for some needy students, but the school *rejected two students this year because they couldn't afford tuition* (italics added)."[29]

"I don't think it's a healthy situation to serve only those who can pay," said McLean in the article. "I want the school to succeed. I can see the difference it makes."[30]

Though Carol Robson had allowed students to stay at New Dimensions even if they could not pay, and an ad placed in the paper during the summer of 1989 promoted the availability of "a limited number of partial scholarships,"[31] the school was now refusing admission to those who could not afford it. This would make the school difficult for low-income families to enroll and would impact the racial and economic demographics of the school, which were already being strained by the expensive and increasingly segregated treatment system.

"They were all white kids except one young Black (student)," recalled McLean. "He was so nice. He wasn't sure he liked me, but pretty soon he did because I treated him with respect. That's all it takes. You treat any person with respect no matter what color they are. That's the key to effective education. That happens so little these days."

Hotakainen's article quoted Minnesota's commissioner of education, Ruth Randall, as seeing the school as supportive, but the tuition was an "expensive proposition for parents."[32] The story mentioned "private donations" aiding with the costs, and that was something Neiditch did help with immensely. Whereas other published accounts may have been stretching the truth, this was a detail confirmed by all sources. Neiditch focused heavily on raising money for the school. While he may have surrendered his corporate advertising and music-industry career, he had maintained his contacts, and even met some of those people at Hazelden as they made their own pathways into recovery.

"When I met (Ralph), he was living in a third-floor attic room at a rooming house out there. Then Hazelden finally hired him as a night [tech/watchman]," said Carol Robson. "When he got involved out there, of course, that's when Ozzy Osborne and Eric Clapton and what's his name, Calvin Klein, were all residents."

One of Neiditch's jobs at Hazelden was working in the relatively new Center for Youth and Families, and according to his story as told by *Education Week,* he was "struck by the seriousness of the problem among adolescents."[33]

Week after week, he would see young people leave treatment, relapse, and return to detoxify. He wanted to put a stop to that revolving door. He reasoned that a school where no one drank or used drugs, one that provided structure and a sense of family, could help these kids avoid the tragic consequences that almost cost him his life. So he lobbied his old crowd of New York investors, including billionaire Donald Trump and entertainment industry executives."[34]

While it is not clear how much, if any, the future US president contributed to the school, many others did. Carol Robson remembered one particularly well-connected patron—Walter Yetnikoff, who had become president of the CBS Records Group in 1975. Yetnikoff died of cancer in 2021, and his *New York Times* obituary described him as living "the sex, drugs and rock 'n' roll life more indulgently than many of his stars did." The story claimed, "Mr. Yetnikoff was one of the most powerful, insatiable and abrasive figures in music in the years just before the digital revolution upended the business."[35] Among the stars on the CBS roster were Michael Jackson, Billy Joel, Bruce Springsteen, and Barbra Streisand.

Similar to Neiditch, the rock'n'roll lifestyle drove Yetnikoff to Hazelden in 1989, just as Neiditch was becoming deeply involved in raising money for the school. So, Ralph asked Yetnikoff for his help.

"He was the promoter that made Michael Jackson and all of these people famous," said Robson. "Through all these connections, we'd go to New York, and limos would pick us up and he's driving us all over.... Walter Yetnikoff was really involved, and one contact led to the next of all of this stuff."[36]

While Neiditch was successful in helping make the school financially viable, the school's culture was changed.

"These were guys that were self-serving; you know, they're big shots," said Robson, "When I was doing it, you know, it was on us. If you couldn't pay and couldn't come, then I subsidized it. I was paying for the teacher and everything. But anyway, it became this whole group of people that were all involved in money."

The transformation of the school was nearly complete, especially after the Robsons' son graduated. Carol said he was 17 when he began his transition to college, which would have been 1988, the year she and Sheridan divorced, and Ralph took over as secretary of the corporation. As her own son moved onto college, Robson began to lose interest in the school.

"I graduated him, and I wasn't interested in carrying on," said Robson. "He's not chemically dependent. I was going to close it."

Neiditch, though, wanted to keep it open, and part of transforming the school involved a rebranding, including the creation of a logo. Neiditch was an artist, and he had designed album covers as well as ads for prominent campaigns such as Revlon. He helped lead a rebranding by designing a new logo for the school. Then, there was the name. They had already switched from "New Dimensions School" to "*Ecole Nouvelle*" (New School), but the students wanted to emphasize a complete focus on recovery. A vote was conducted, and the students selected a new name, one that would more neatly position the school as a "sober school." It would be the name most people remembered when they thought of this program, and perhaps the best known of all the early recovery high schools: "Sobriety High." All the legal paperwork already had been filed to change the corporate name to *Ecole Nouvelle* when Ralph Neiditch had replaced Sheridan Robson on the executive board. The board thus decided to keep that name for the company, and for the school; they filed a "doing business as" (DBA) application with the Secretary of State to make the name Sobriety High official. They filed this on July 18, 1988, exactly one week after the Robsons had filed for divorce in the Chisago County courthouse.[37]

In August 1989, after its first full year as Sobriety High and with Neiditch in a leadership role, the school placed ads in the paper for students, something New Dimensions had done many times as well. These ads clearly stated the school's narrower purpose. Calling Sobriety High "a private school specializing in academics for recovering teens in grades nine through 12," the advertisement limited enrollment to high school students in recovery.[38]

"The focus is on renewing educational goals and working toward graduation from Sobriety High or the student's previous school," the ad stated, situating the school as either a transitional placement or a final destination.

The site remained the "cozy schoolroom with a hardwood floor" in the Brookside Community Center in St. Louis Park.[39] From 1987 to 1989, twenty-five students had enrolled in the school, including eighteen during the 1988–89 school year, and their profile had almost completely transformed as the school evolved from New Dimensions to *Ecole Nouvelle* to Sobriety High. One student had attended since 1987, and two had earned diplomas from the school, but the average length of stay was only one year.[40] Most of the students who enrolled in fall 1989 were juniors and seniors. At the time of a feature article published in September, school had been in session for two weeks, and there were six students enrolled. Such a small number would not be considered unusual now for the start of a year at a recovery high school, as students make their way to the school throughout the year when they finish treatment or just decide they need a more supportive school environment. The school was not yet accredited, as accreditation was not required for schools in Minnesota at that time.[41]

The profiles from the article give a sense of the severe trauma, mental health, and substance use histories that students brought with them to Sobriety High, and they would be recognizable to anyone working in a recovery high school today. The writer calls them "shattered souls."[42]

The student who had been enrolled since 1987 had experienced the evolution of the program. According to the article, the student had "once begged a judge to shoot her. She slit her wrists with a razor and has survived three suicide attempts."

"I asked God to take me while I was sleeping," she is quoted as saying, "because I don't like pain."

According to the story, prior to enrolling at Sobriety High, she would get high every day and "saw no reason for living."[43] Since becoming a student there, though, she had built two and a half years of sobriety.[44]

Another student profiled in the article was 16 at the time, and he was described as "a former cocaine dealer." This student had grown up in Austin, Texas, and he had begun using at 11. His drug use had gotten so bad that his mother kicked him out of their home, which forced him to drop out of school.

"Every time I put a needle in my arm, it hurt," he was quoted as saying. "Sometimes I would cry, but I had to do it."

The student from Austin claimed to have been to treatment nine times, the last time being Hazelden. The story implied that enrolling at a private school after multiple treatment episodes was possible because he had come from a family wealthy enough to provide a trust fund to cover his tuition.[45] At the time of the article, he was living with a roommate and working at a grocery store.

One student interviewed was a local kid, having grown up in St. Louis Park. He began using in seventh grade and "used to sniff glue or gasoline if he ran out of marijuana." According to the article, he had tried to end his life before running away. He was now 16 and a junior in his second year at Sobriety High. By the time of the article, he had achieved fifteen months of sobriety.

Each student account described how difficult their lives had been prior to getting sober, and how much better their lives had become—typical recovery narratives. The students noted many aspects of Sobriety High that had supported them on their recovery journeys, including taking away the stress of large regular schools, not getting approached regularly to get high, and not having to use drugs to be accepted. The story also emphasized the impact Bruce McLean was having. He was the only staff member named in the piece, and it was clear how vital he was to the success of the school in the views of the reporter and the students.

"Students see McLean as a confidant first and teacher second," according to the article. "'Bruce is my best friend,' said the student who had been enrolled for two years. 'I can talk to Bruce about anything. He listens.'"[46]

McLean had reached the apex of his time with Sobriety High—being featured on the front page of the *Star Tribune* for a school he had largely conceived, having spent years directing the curriculum and supporting a small group of teenagers trying to make it one day at a time—a program that may have saved the lives of many young people. In the next couple of years, things would take an unfortunate turn for both Bruce McLean and Carol Robson, but they had already inspired others to start a recovery high school that would ultimately outlast Sobriety High. Ironically, the source of inspiration for the next recovery high school in the Twin Cities was *not* their teaching and administrative prowess. Rather, two of Robson's group home staff came to watch the innovative school in action and determined they could do it better. And they set out to do just that.

14
All Things Are Connected

Carol and Sheridan Robson's group homes required staffing seven days per week, including technicians ("techs") on weekends. Ken Simon was one of their techs in the mid-1980s. Simon was a 29-year-old graduate student in 1987, piecing together jobs to pay the bills while pursuing his Minnesota teaching certificate. During the week, Simon worked in a Minneapolis public school, and then he reported for a weekend shift as a counselor/technician at the Summit House, the Robsons' group home for youths with emotional and behavioral disabilities and cognitive impairments. He went to work at four on Friday afternoons and stayed until nine Sunday nights. At the Summit House, Simon and other staff taught social skills and took the residents to community activities like shows and museum tours.

"We had weekend staff and then, you know, depending on the residents who were very needy, behavior-wise and stuff, that was a tough job, a really tough job," said Carol Robson. "And Ken was a wonderful young man."

While working at Summit House, Simon met a young intern in his mid-thirties named Howard Pearson.[1] Pearson was from a wealthy family that had made major contributions in education, medicine, and the arts. He had developed a charitable soul like others in his family, and when Pearson met Ken Simon, he was also a person in recovery.[2] Like so many others seeking sobriety, Pearson's journey had led him to Minnesota, where he would apply for a position at the Robsons' group home, Summit House. One of Carol Robson's employees hired him.[3]

"He was wonderful, big, heavyset guy," said Robson. "A style fashionista and the whole thing. He was just a fabulous person . . . He was wonderful with the residents."

Working long hours at Summit House, Pearson became close with Ken Simon, and they started talking about the future.

"I was pretty young [about 29]. We just got to be friends," said Simon. "He was a really super man; just a really good heart and extremely wealthy."

Simon and Robson both remembered Pearson saying he had a trust worth $40 million. Simon, on the other hand, was making ends meet and finishing his teacher training. When he became aware that Carol Robson was also running a school (still called New Dimensions at that point), it piqued his interest.

"I was getting my teaching certificate, because I had gotten a BA earlier [in politics and government from Ripon College in Wisconsin]," said Simon. "I was really near the end [of my certificate program] . . . I think I just hit my student teaching. The

Salvaging a Teenage Wasteland. Andrew J. Finch, Oxford University Press. © Oxford University Press 2024.
DOI: 10.1093/oso/9780190645502.003.0014

people who owned the group home (the Robsons) also owned or sponsored a school in St. Louis Park. I remember going out and watching it."

Simon had worked in experiential education such as wilderness programs that involved taking kids on long trips. Simon went to observe the Robsons' school, and he described what he saw:

> It had one teacher [Bruce McLean]. He was a theater teacher. I can picture him now. Kids sat around and did worksheets all day, and then they'd do group. Everything was geared around the group stuff, and nothing was geared around the education. I'm sitting here in education thinking, 'Well, you could do this a lot better,' just educationally. I had no background, and I still really don't have much background, in [substance] abuse.

One day, Simon mentioned to Pearson the Robsons' school he had recently visited. Pearson said that he too had visited the school, and he thought the Robsons wanted him to make a financial contribution—something that was common for a person from his family.[4]

"I didn't think a whole lot of it," said Simon, "but I told him I was graduating and had a real interest in alternative education. I wasn't a great student myself and didn't like regular school."

Simon and Pearson went together to visit the school that would become Sobriety High, and they continued to talk regularly about the school. Simon was struck by how interested Pearson was in the Robsons' program. Pearson was likely attracted to the new substance use recovery focus of Carol Robson's school. The small school was still called New Dimensions, but by fall 1987, it had transitioned into enrolling students in recovery, based in part on teacher Bruce McLean's suggestion.

"[Howard] kept bringing it up," said Simon. "He had really talked about how he would sponsor a school."

Barbara Schmidt—Director of Holos

Simon had gotten a teaching job that year at Osseo Middle School,[5] just northwest of Minneapolis, where he met a long-term substitute teacher in her thirties named Barbara Schmidt in the teachers' lounge.[6] Like Simon, Schmidt had developed an interest in alternative education, but her attention was in a more spiritual direction.

Barbara "Barb" Schmidt was born in 1954 and had grown up in Minnesota.[7] She attended Forest Lake High School, about thirty-five minutes northeast of Minneapolis. She was drawn early to leadership and participated in numerous activities, such as student council, cheerleading, Spanish club, the student newspaper, and choir.[8] Along the way, Schmidt had earned a bachelor's degree in secondary education, after which she completed a master of divinity (MDiv) degree at United Theological Seminary in

Dayton, Ohio—one of the thirteen seminaries affiliated with the United Methodist Church.[9] Her MDiv had an emphasis in pastoral care and counseling, which required one year of clinical pastoral education and two years of advanced training. Schmidt continued studying theology by working on a post–master's degree in pastoral care and social change, finishing the coursework but not the thesis. She did initial PhD coursework in human sciences but did not complete her doctorate. With each subsequent academic experience, Schmidt had deepened her spiritual awareness—from pastoral care within the United Methodist Church to social change and consciousness studies. All her higher education programs emphasized giving to others, and another theme had been human consciousness.

"I followed the yellow brick road," said Schmidt. "Began—oops, didn't get very far!"

While Schmidt did not complete the last two degree programs she started, she did apply what she learned, working in myriad occupations and internships, including youth director in an urban church, chaplain for the Hennepin County juvenile court system, social justice minister for the Lutheran Church in America, and case manager/therapist. In her role as chaplain, she had cofacilitated over two hundred family groups in two years and started a grief group for the sex offenders' unit. She also worked in a mental health clinic focusing on clients with eating disorders and sexual addiction.

"And always," Schmidt pointed out, "when in transition—which was a lot of the time—I did substitute teaching."

She was substitute teaching while working on her PhD when she met Ken Simon (see Figure 14.1).

"She lived in a really nice place in a very nice neighborhood [in Minnetonka]," said Simon. "I think she was sort of looking for her next step in this world. She was a fascinating woman, very passionate." Simon and Schmidt got along well, and eventually he mentioned the recovery high school idea he had been discussing with Pearson.

"I really hadn't done a whole lot of work on it," said Simon. "It had been [Howard] and me, back and forth. She right away said, 'Can I meet with [Howard]?' I said, 'Yeah.' "

"We'd share info on occasion, so [Ken] knew about my background as a court chaplain, addictions therapist, knew I was 'into' consciousness . . . and students called me the 'elevator music lady,' because [when substitute teaching] I always brought my boom box along with relaxation/focusing music and played in classrooms whenever possible," said Schmidt.

"That intrigued [Ken], so much so that one day he asked, 'Would you be interested in helping to start a sober school? Because I know this guy [Howard Pearson] who would fund it, has been through treatment a lot, wants to leave a legacy/do something for young people with drug issues.' Ken was aware, based on our series of conversations, that if I was involved it would be a nontraditional approach, which he was more than OK with."

The three of them set up a time to meet, and Schmidt learned all about Pearson's interest in and ability to fund the school.

Figure 14.1. While he was completing his teaching certification, Ken Simon worked part time as a counselor/technician at Carol Robson's Summit House. After observing Robson's New Dimensions school, he and a fellow counselor/technician worked with Barbara Schmidt to create their own recovery high school, Holos. This photo was featured in the first Holos yearbook in 1989. (Source: Joan Vogt.)

"I was pretty emphatic," recalled Schmidt. "This will succeed. It's a great idea. I'm glad you [Howard] approve of the [nontraditional] approach we'd take, and I want you to know, it will succeed."

That was also the last time Schmidt recalled seeing Pearson. She said he pledged $10,000 seed money and another $10,000 to follow, but she does not remember receiving any of that money.[10]

"I think what I said ended up scaring him, to be honest," said Schmidt. "I never saw him again. He disappeared."

The meeting, though, provided both a spark and a direction to drive Schmidt forward. Carol Robson, Bruce McLean, and the New Dimensions School had motivated Pearson, and his offer to fund a similar school for kids in recovery from alcohol and other drug addictions set a foundation, even though he ultimately would not be active in its early development. Without Pearson's initial interest, though, it is unlikely Simon would have suggested the school idea to Barb Schmidt, and it was even less probable they would have created a *recovery* high school. Still, after that first meeting, they would have to find financial support elsewhere.

"My own personality type happens to be the kind where, when inspired, I can remain quite focused, so [I] decided to just dig in and keep going, regardless," said Schmidt.

"From the very beginning she took over, which was right," said Simon. "She was a really super-sharp, super-committed woman."

Schmidt had held many leadership positions before, such as a director of Christian education, an advocacy coordinator, and a facilitator of groups and programs. Taking the lead in developing the new school concept came naturally to her, and with Schmidt at the helm, they started laying the groundwork for a school.

"With start-ups, most times those who begin the process of putting things in motion wear just about every kind of hat imaginable," said Schmidt.

"We put the school together, and by 'we,' I mean primarily Barb and I, but Barb primarily," said Simon. "We really put a lot of effort into it."

Schmidt recalled she wrote the paperwork for the 501c3 nonprofit organization application, found a lawyer to review the documents, got the federal tax identification number, opened a bank account, found a volunteer to do accounting, set up a payroll system, hired staff, recruited both regular board members and advisory board members, made countless community contacts, did grant-writing, devised an outcome-based curriculum framework, initiated and followed through with the accreditation process, and personally interviewed each prospective student, most times at their homes, with family members involved as well.

Their first step to making the school official was to file Articles of Incorporation, which they did on June 10, 1988.[11] Interestingly, they filed their paperwork less than two months after Carol Robson drew up the paperwork to add Ralph Neiditch to her own Articles of Incorporation and changed the name of New Dimensions to Ecole Nouvelle.[12] Schmidt was listed as program director, and Simon was the treasurer and chairman of the board. They called their new corporation the "Holos Foundation," and it would be a nonprofit 501c3 organization operated for charitable and education purposes.[13]

"Holostic Learning"

The word "Holos"[14] had special meaning for Schmidt, and it reflected concepts she was studying in her PhD program at the time. According to lore, Barb Schmidt had a vision while walking around the Lake of the Isles in Minneapolis that adolescents coming out of treatment needed a safe and sober school, and that was where she got the idea to start a school.[15] In reality, the idea for a recovery high school came from Ken Simon and Howard Pearson, who had gotten the idea from watching Bruce McLean teach at Carol Robson's school. But there was still an inspiration.

"Is it possible I had an out-of-the-middle-of-nowhere idea popping up related to a chemical-free school as I danced around Isles? Yes, I guess it's possible," said Schmidt in an interview for this book. "But I think closer to the truth is those juices started flowing primarily after I'd met Ken. Look, a number of years had passed from my juvenile court days to the late eighties. Big shifts in my life . . . My focus at that time was primarily on learning everything I could about energy, the quantum fabric of space/time, what 'reality' truly is or can be.

"My interest wasn't on a sober school per se," Schmidt said. "Only after Ken approached me—that's when things started coming together—a school where consciousness was in some way acknowledged and integrated into the core of the 'what' and 'how'—though I didn't use the word much because it's such a confusing concept—even now, not much agreement among scientists on what 'consciousness' is, where it's located, etc. What this all eventually translated into was an emphasis on unlimited possibilities: observer-effect unlimited possibilities. So, I attempted to bring in at least some of what I was learning—I had a long way to go, I might add—by referring to the expansion of 'personal capacities and potentials' . . . and putting it smack-dab in the middle of a school that would offer support to teens who I knew, based on that years-ago experience in the juvenile court job—I knew they needed it."

The word "Holos" embodied the concepts of consciousness, unlimited possibilities, personal capacities, and potentials. Jeff Aronson, a clinical pharmacologist at Oxford, explained the etymology of the word "holos":

The Greek ολοσ comes from an Indo-European root SOLO, meaning whole, firm, sound, or correct. A holograph is written entirely in one's own hand, and a holocaust was originally the burning of a whole body, before it came to mean the destruction of a whole nation.[16]

Michael Durchslag, an early teacher in the school who would later become its principal, defined Holos as he understood it, and how he thought the original board of directors meant it:

"Holos is Greek, I think, which, as the story goes, is all things are connected," said Durchslag. "You know, it was a holistic approach to the student."

This was partially correct, but for Barbara Schmidt, the idea ran much deeper. As a PhD student in a human sciences program, her emphasis was "consciousness studies," and she was reading the literature of that field. That was the work that informed her understanding of "Holos":

For a number of years prior to 'Holos,' I had been dipping my toe into the [scientific] topic of consciousness, starting with Robert Ornstein's *The Psychology of Consciousness*, in turn leading me to Willis Harman's book *Higher Creativity*, which then nudged me in the direction of the Institute of Noetic Sciences (IONS) and its founder, astronaut Dr. Edgar Mitchell [the sixth man to walk on the moon] who had a deeply profound experience on his way back to earth . . . an experience that "opened" him to multi-layers of "reality" and a kind of spirit-based sense of the universe and its interconnected consciousness—way overly-simplified. As a result, IONS came into being, with a mandate to research all of the above.[17]

Schmidt explained that she had enrolled in a doctoral program after having read many books on her own. "Countless books related in some way to consciousness and most especially, the observer effect and [Werner] Heisenberg's riveting work [on the uncertainty principle], along with physicist David Bohm and his Holomovement Theory.[18] Which brought in the entanglement thing, non-locality thing, and the beginnings of a hypothesis—perhaps now a more formal theory—of universe/multiverse as a (projected) hologram."

Stephanie Burt wrote a history of the multiverse concept in storytelling, and she described a story from Philip K. Dick's book, *The Man in the High Castle,* which imagines a world in which the Allies lost World War II. In this alternate universe, Dick writes of a banned novel telling of an Allied victory. "The [banned] book . . . 'showed that there's a way out'—another world, and therefore 'nothing to want or hate or avoid' in this one."[19]

This multiverse concept showing a "way out" and no need to "hate or avoid" this world appealed to Schmidt. While the full concepts and theories are far too complex to unpack here, Schmidt's passion for the ideas helps explain the breadth and depth of her intention for the school. The goals of the school would transcend helping teenagers stay sober.

"Holos arose from these concepts, concepts of connected consciousness, concepts of 'reality' as holographic," she said. "I would not have founded [the school] without this holistic consciousness element . . . Holistic. Holism. Holographic."

In some ways, recovery was a path to a goal for Schmidt—a suggestion by Ken Simon that had aligned with and ignited her larger vision years in the making. Her previous experience working with at-risk youth in the juvenile justice system had shown her how many young people had drug use issues after their release. Watching those kids struggle had upset Schmidt, similar to how Bruce McLean had been bothered watching students return to use after being discharged from the Eden Prairie treatment program. Removing the threat of being offered drugs at school would help clear the way for students to grow and attain an authentic consciousness rather than a chemically altered one. As Philip K. Dick had suggested, there was no need for teenagers to hate this world or to use drugs to avoid it. There was another way.

"It wasn't as much of a 'recovery' school concept for me as it was 'You don't have to worry, no drugs around this place' kind of school . . . recovery pieces offered, of course. But the big problem was as much drug availability on school campuses as it was 'doing' recovery steps.

"So, there were two things that inspired: Having had the honor of meeting so many youth [in the justice system] who were smart, savvy, clever, humane, full of heart, capable of real flashes of brilliance—youth who deserved a kind of genuine support I knew they very much needed. And the holism consciousness piece. It was that particular combo which did it for me."

"Without [Howard Pearson]," she added. "The recovery part of the school more than likely wouldn't have factored in."[20]

Location

Barb Schmidt, Ken Simon, and Howard Pearson worked through the fall of 1988 to plan the school, though Simon said Pearson's support came more from the periphery.

"That fall we started planning the school, mostly her and I," he said. "[Howard] was sort of involved. By that time, he was going back to [the Northeast] where he lived. He could come to town every once and a while. We looked for buildings. And I remember there was one building he almost bought, and Barb wouldn't . . . I don't remember the whole story, but it's a bank building on Franklin Avenue. And it was an old, abandoned bank. And [Howard] was like, 'This would make the greatest school.' [Barb and I] toured it, and he never did. I mean, I think he was really excited for a weekend, sort of."

Schmidt had not really liked the site, according to Simon. That could have been because the sense of place would have mattered to her, and a former bank likely did not provide the appropriate environment. The right site emerged through a connection from her former employer, the Lutheran Church of America, and it was about a block from where Ken Simon lived at the time. Some of the early paperwork for Holos used Ken Simon's address on Elliot Street in Minneapolis as the corporate headquarters, which was just a few blocks from what thirty years later would become George Floyd Square. That square commemorates one of the largest mass protests in US history following the death of Floyd, a Black man who was killed by a Minneapolis police officer in May 2020. A memorial is located at the 38th and Chicago Avenue North intersection.

Both Simon's former house and George Floyd Square occupy the Powderhorn Park neighborhood of South Minneapolis, which is part of the larger, eight-neighborhood Powderhorn community. When Simon and Schmidt started searching for a school site, they were offered, free of charge, a large room on the second floor of a community center situated almost exactly between those two locations. Simon could easily walk to it from his house.

"I had previously worked as a social justice minister for the Lutheran Church in America," said Schmidt. "And in that capacity, I was fortunate to work with some fairly fantastic pastors—outside-the-box types. David Anderson was one of them."

Anderson had recently taken a job as director of the community center called "Pillsbury House."[21] The facility had been built in 1979 and was operated by Pillsbury United Neighborhood Services (PUNS).[22] PUNS had a long history in Minneapolis, beginning in 1879 as the Bethel Mission, a program run by the Plymouth Congregational Church. In the subsequent century, the organization had established settlement houses throughout the city with the same purpose: "working with our communities to co-create enduring change towards a just society." Among other programs, the Bethel Mission offered the city's first free kindergarten.[23] As part of the settlement house movement, exemplified by Hull House in Chicago, the Mission became the Bethel Settlement in 1897, providing services, including education and health care, to immigrants and the urban poor.[24] In the early twentieth century, more houses were added, starting with one funded by a grant from the Pillsbury family and given the name, Pillsbury House. It lasted until the 1960s, when urban renewal led to its demolition.[25] The other settlement houses were consolidated at that time, and a new organization emerged—Pillsbury-Waite Neighborhood Services. In 1979, to commemorate the centennial of the Bethel Mission, ground was broken in the Powderhorn Park neighborhood, and a new Pillsbury House opened on Chicago Avenue in 1981. It was just a few years later that Barb Schmidt paid director Anderson a visit there to explain her new venture (see Figure 14.2).

"I tracked him down and asked if there was a room available in his building for a school, filled him in on the details—including, 'Oh, one more thing David—[we] don't have any money to pay rent.' I think it was probably less than an hour later, and a location was born!

"He couldn't have been more gracious. Generous," said Schmidt. "Through the first part of June 1989—[we] paid not a dime. And he never asked for money from me. Not

Figure 14.2. Pillsbury House was the original site for the Holos school in 1989. Located on Chicago Avenue in the Powderhorn Park neighborhood of Minneapolis, the school remained there for just over one year. (Source: Andy Finch.)

once. Would stop in every once in a while to see how things were going—such a ter-
rific guy. Very grateful for him."

Powderhorn Park was one of the most economically and racially diverse neighborhoods in the Twin Cities and a hub of arts culture.[26] The neighborhood hosted
numerous arts festivals, including May Day. This description of Powderhorn's May
Day celebration shows how aligned that area was with Barb Schmidt's vision for the
school:

> The park and lake are used as the setting for the last act in the city's annual May
> Day parade [actually occurring on the first Sunday in May], which is a play in mo-
> tion that has been put on by the In the Heart of the Beast Puppet and Mask Theatre
> since 1975. As the parade runs south along Bloomington Avenue, participants wear
> a variety of costumes, and many manipulate giant puppets, all to produce a story
> that is based on sociopolitical themes including peace, environmentalism, current
> events, and others. After the parade story ends, the tail end of the parade is a "free
> speech" section which includes representatives of community groups and cam-
> paigning politicians. After the parade, there is an intermission as people gather on
> a hillside at the west end of the park for the Tree of Life ceremony. Many details of
> the final act change from year to year, but there are several figures that consist-
> ently appear: River, Woods, Prairie, Sky, Sun, and the Tree of Life. At the end of the
> ceremony, a flotilla comes across the lake with the Sun figure in the central boat.
> The Sun awakens the Tree of Life [a figure which includes a traditional maypole],
> and the crowd sings "You Are My Sunshine" to mark the banishment of another
> season of winter.[27]

The Holos School would fit right in.

Funding

Even though Anderson offered the Pillsbury House site for free to start, by the fall of
1989, Holos would need to pay a modest $250 monthly rent. They also would need to
pay staff and buy supplies. While Howard Pearson had offered funding for the school
and had paid $1,574 in November 1988 for legal fees to create the bylaws, he had not
yet contributed any money toward operating costs.[28] Schmidt knew the school would
need more sustained funding, and they did not want to charge tuition—something
the Robsons had done from the beginning of the New Dimensions School, even if the
Robsons did not always collect the money.

"I—and as others got involved, others, too—were nearly always looking for ways
to fund [the school]," said Schmidt. "Never once considered charging tuition—never.
Completely contrary to my own spiritual values, and my guess is, of staff and board
members as well."

The Holos School asserted this principle in documents filed with the state for tax purposes: "Because we do not charge tuition, there is no need for scholarship or loan monies. Our school is open to any and all students, regardless of financial status."[29]

Beyond Pearson's promised donation and other philanthropic opportunities, Schmidt and Simon wanted to learn more about public sources of funding for private alternative schools—something for which Minnesota had been at the forefront since the early 1970s. The second-chance laws recently passed in 1987 allowed students meeting certain criteria to attend public or private schools, with their per pupil allocations to follow them, but the private schools would be available to students only if a public school district agreed to contract with these schools. Such schools were called "contract alternative schools."[30]

While they had been able to get a publicly funded per diem for a few at-risk students, the Robsons' school had yet to become a full-fledged contract alternative. Schmidt and Simon, though, wanted to consider every option. So, they reached out to one of the trailblazers of Minnesota's alternative school movement, Robert "Bob" Jibben. Jibben had been involved almost from the start of the movement. Minneapolis Public Schools assigned him to be the one school counselor to work full time with all alternative programs in 1971. He would serve as the school coordinator for the Minneapolis Federation of Alternative Schools and later would direct the organization. Michael Durchslag called him a "guru."

"[Bob Jibben] was great. He was a pioneer," said Simon. "At that time Minneapolis had interesting stuff going on. One of the roles that I played was to work with Bob to get resources for the school, and Bob helped us get placed."

Jibben knew as much as anyone about the alternative schools in the area, and he confirmed for Schmidt and Simon that no other public or contracted alternative school was completely focused on recovery.

"Not really," said Jibben. "I mean, programs dealt with [drug use]. And of course, I mean, that was a major problem. The district had a few drug counselors on staff that would go out and intervene with kids and help with problems. I think at one time, we had about four or five of those guys that were designated as chemical dependency counselors . . . But not a school as such, no. They may have run some groups and stuff like that in schools for kids, but I don't know how many or how much."

Jibben explained to Schmidt and Simon the contract alternative school model, a precursor to charter schools—Minnesota was, in fact, the first state to legalize charter schools, but not until 1991.

"They called them contract alternatives," said Jibben, "because eventually we actually got a legal contract with the district to provide education services." And that is what Holos decided to do. With Jibben's help, Holos arranged a contract with the Minneapolis Public Schools, using the Minnesota Graduation High School Incentives Act of 1987 as support.

"It was in place from the start—it was the only money I had available to pay the teachers," said Schmidt.

Funding would be a constant issue, as contracted schools only got a percentage of the state per pupil allocation, not the entire amount.

"Which didn't cover full costs by any means," said Schmidt. "Plus, public schools get to float bond issues and receive funds from property taxes. We got none of that, of course. So, I—and as others got involved, others, too—were nearly always looking for ways to fund it."

Ken Simon explained in detail how the public funding stream was always insufficient.

"It was a tiny school and you're trying to make this up on what the state gives you. You're a contract alternative, so you contract with the district, who is going to take 10% right off the top of the school aid, so you're getting less than everybody else. Then you're not going to get any federal dollars, so you're not getting any Title I [funding] or anything. That goes to the district, and then it goes to district services. You're supposed to go to the district for special ed services. Ha! That's not going to happen. What you get is basically the core or a part of the core that all schools get per pupil, which is nothing."

One creative solution was admitting court-ordered students, as the school could get paid for enrolling them.

"To emphasize," clarified Schmidt, who had once worked as a chaplain for the juvenile court. "It was important those who were court-ordered were involved in making the decision to attend. It wasn't about having any student coerced, forced into attending—it was about helping us fund the school since we got paid for court-ordered students. That's what it was about. Everyone understood that."

Grants would also be important. The Emma P. Howe Foundation, which was part of the Minneapolis Foundation, awarded Holos $30,000 shortly after they established their contract with Minneapolis Public Schools, and after they received their 501(c)3 designation, which qualified them to apply for a grant.

"Pat Cummings, my contact person/advocate there—yet another spectacular individual who went above and beyond—gave great advice all along the way regarding what it took to secure grant funding from the Minneapolis Foundation," said Schmidt. "My background in the court system helped, my background in ministry helped, and when she saw it took only eight months from the time I initially went to see her to the time we had our first students—she was an enthusiastic supporter from that point on. . . . Lovely, lovely woman."

Curriculum

One important element in earning the 501c3 nonprofit status as well as the contract with the district was a business plan and curriculum. Documents filed with the IRS in support of earning tax exempt status provide excellent detail as to the design of the school, including the initial full name of the school: "Holos Foundation, Inc. Transition School for Recovering Chemically Dependent Youth."[31] The word "transition" suggested the original intention of the school was a temporary placement for students between leaving treatment or recovery housing and returning to their homes and a regular school.

"The original idea was that the Holos School would provide a transitional school for students coming out of treatment to be here for anywhere between three and six months and then transition back to their home school after they got a little more sobriety under their belt," explained Michael Durchslag.

As such, the school would have two main goals:

1. To help recovering youth make a positive, healthy [i.e., chemical free] transition back into the public school system;
2. To help recovering youth develop skills which will assist them in succeeding academically within the public school.

The curriculum had a clear connection to Barbara Schmidt's holistic consciousness philosophy, emphasizing "the development of self-esteem, socialization skills, personal responsibility-taking, and academic success." with "additional instruction in stress management, nutrition, exercise, and relaxation" (see Figure 14.3).[32]

Figure 14.3. Barbara Schmidt installed a curriculum at Holos that embraced a holistic consciousness philosophy, emphasizing life skills such as the development of self-esteem, socialization, personal responsibility, exercise, relaxation, and nutrition. This drawing was made by a student for the first Holos yearbook in 1989. (Source: Joan Vogt.)

"Absolutely critical for me to have that kind of link," said Schmidt. "I would not have involved myself if given the directive that it had to be a 'typical' school. Would never have done it."

One document found in the early Holos files was an article written by the Merrill Harmin, who at the time was an education professor at Southern Illinois University. The article, titled, "Teaching Inner Self-Responsibility," was written around the time Schmidt and Simon started planning the school. The one-page article provided a guide of sorts for their recovery high school curriculum.[33]

"There is something deep inside us that feels right about things—even when it serves us not at all. Call it justice. Or caring. Or conscience," wrote Harmin. "In short, humans have inner sources of motivation and respond to more than a current advantage. As teachers, we can help students become more aware of that inner motivation and learn how to tap into it when facing learning tasks."[34]

Harmin's article spoke directly to the development of addictions and mental health issues and suggested that inner motivation was the pathway to health.

"Many of our personal and social problems cannot be well handled when our daily choices reflect only superficial advantages," wrote Harmin. "Choosing that way leads to addictions (TV, food, alcohol, drugs) and to disrespect of others (and lots of divorce and lawsuits). It also contributes to disorganization and despair (job burn out, general depression, social violence, suicide)."

Learning inner motivation would be "healthful," get students to study harder, and was the faculty's "professional responsibility." This language echoed the words of Meher Baba, who taught that drugs "enslave the individual in greater binding" and called his followers to persuade youth "to desist from taking drugs, for they are harmful—physically, mentally and spiritually.[35] Those ideas had inspired Brian Berthiaume to start the Phoenix School in Montgomery County, Maryland, in the late 1970s, and the related concepts of holism, consciousness, and inner responsibility were similarly motivating Barbara Schmidt a decade later. As the Harmin article recommended, Schmidt wanted to teach her students "to be increasingly themselves, spontaneously, naturally and comfortably, as they go through their daily chores."[36]

Harmin closed the article with three suggestions in designing a school to promote inner responsibility and consciousness: "(1) Talk that includes respect for inner selfhood; (2) Classroom procedures that exercise self-responsibility; and (3) Life skill education."[37] The activities that would promote these objectives included "cooperative learning, peer instruction, explicit standards of excellence, learning options, and discovery learning," each of which would be evident in Holos's programming.

"We wanted them to learn to think for themselves, come to their own conclusions as a result of finding data and evidence that was 'solid' and in support of whatever their belief was," said Schmidt. "There was also something related to engaging with the world on an individual, communal, global level as well."

While the school would not be accredited when it started, it could earn accreditation after building a few years of operation, and the academic program thus offered the four traditional primary subjects—English, social studies, science, mathematics—as well as health, communications, and creative arts (music, theatre, art). Credits would be awarded by the Minneapolis Public Schools "for Minneapolis district residents and non-district residents who qualify to register in Minneapolis under the Minnesota Graduation High School Incentives Act of 1987 (all youth diagnosed as chemically dependent qualify)."[38]

Schmidt emphasized, though, that the philosophical design was "circular in nature, not linear." The main areas, thus, were not separated into academic subjects like traditional curricula.

"Reading, writing, speaking, using numbers as in mathematics was a first ring of 'essential' skills required, yes," said Schmidt. "As were 'High Potential Learning' practices, including the use of relaxation, focusing, visioning, NLP (neurolinguistic programming), and other super-learning techniques. But these were taught only as a means of 'getting there,' as in getting into the core areas of study, which were Emotional Well-Being, Physical Well-Being, Relational Well-Being, Aesthetic Well-Being, Spiritual Well-Being, Recreational Well-Being. And at the center of the circle: 'Everyone and everything is sacred'—our starting point."

The school also had an outcome-based design in which credits were awarded based on demonstrating competence in a particular outcome or outcomes, not simply due to seat time. Schmidt's work designing curriculum would also carry over to other alternative schools in the district.

"She also did some really interesting work around pre-standards at that time. The standards weren't out, and Barb was working with [other schools]," said Simon. "One of the things that Barb did which was really interesting—she was really an interesting thinker about this—was she was doing some interesting work with state folks around academic outcomes for kids."

"The curriculum," said Schmidt, "when possible, awarded credits that could be earned by cross-disciplinary courses and projects that lent themselves to this kind of learning. Although our state aid payments were beholden to that seat time, so we were kind of stuck due to how educational financing was being done. It didn't matter so much if you learned, didn't matter what you learned—what did matter was showing up at school, filling a seat. So, this outcome-based approach was definitely restricted in many ways."

As a recovery high school, the curriculum also needed to have recovery supports, and this was something provided by all the staff.

"Although [later] we had a family health coordinator on staff and a part-time therapist—we all did [recovery support]," said Schmidt. "No strict lines of demarcation [such as] you're the therapist, you do that and nothing else. You're the teacher, you can't do anything 'therapeutic.' The therapist helped teach several classes—one which reenacted a trial; not her licensure, not her 'expertise,' and she was fabulous. Teachers and even some of our volunteers who hung around a lot—did they provide counseling? If it fit, if the student could benefit, felt comfortable with it, wanted it, absolutely. Casually done, by the way. We didn't make a big deal out of it. Casual and (I) will use that word one more time: organic."

Faculty

Barbara Schmidt and Ken Simon were the first two staff members for Holos, and they had enough funding to hire two more teachers. Because of funding limitations and small enrollment, though, all four would be part time, as the teachers would have to share a 1.0 position in their first few months. Simon was half time, teaching both writing and social studies for two of the four paid teaching slots. This required him to work at another alternative school called "SOAR" (Students on a Rebound) to make ends meet.

"I started my day teaching at SOAR," said Simon. "They were all drop-out kids. It actually was a pretty decent school."

With Simon teaching two of the classes, Holos only had salary space for two more part-time teachers, so Schmidt worked pro bono to start.

"I myself didn't take any salary at first," said Schmidt. "(I) continued working as an outpatient therapist in order to keep afloat financially."

All four staff in place on opening day would have teaching degrees and licenses, albeit from different states. Two were Minnesota state certified, one was certified in Iowa, and the other was certified in Colorado. Of those four, three (including both Schmidt and Simon) had master's degrees. Schmidt had also completed one and a half years of doctoral study.[39]

"Frankly, certificates, licenses, 'formal training' doesn't mean all that much to me," said Schmidt. "I genuinely could care less if someone has jumped through licensure hoops, for example—because they're just hoops. Rarely indicators of whether or not a meaningful 'connection' will be made with a student or family member. Rarely indicators of ability. Rarely indicators of true knowledge or multiple intelligences. And absolutely no indicator of 'Soul.'

"So, I'll just say, we had licensed people on staff, unlicensed people on staff. Trained people on staff, untrained people on staff. Some paid, some volunteer. Made no difference to me—outside of whatever we had to do to keep our contract with Minneapolis and our accreditation—at that time both parties were supportive of our eclectic bunch. Bob Jibben and the folk at NCA (North Central Accreditation) gave us as much leeway as they could, but that was also due to the outcome-based ed structure in place—they knew it was pretty solid, which raised their confidence quotient."

The original Holos staff other than Schmidt and Simon included Alison Miller and Patricia Field. Miller had a master's degree in foreign language education, and Field was working her master's degree in math education. Alison Miller taught Spanish and was trained in the Lozanov Method, a teaching method developed by the Bulgarian psychotherapist Dr. Georgi Lozanov, which, by the late 1970s, had become a popular way of teaching foreign language.[40] Lozanov, known as the "father of accelerated learning,"[41] had developed a theory of Suggestology, which was the scientific study of suggestion.[42] As described by W. Jane Bancroft, it is clear why such an approach would have been welcome at Holos:

> Suggestology investigates the subsensory signals or subliminal stimuli which come from the physical or social environment and which are absorbed into the unconscious mind before receiving a conscious expression. Suggestion, especially spoken suggestion, activates the reserve capacities of the mind or the memory. Suggestopedia increases memorization capacities. Hypermnesia is facilitated by relaxation techniques (derived from yoga and autogenic therapy) which increase the subject's suggestibility to spoken suggestions or unconscious stimuli.[43]

The method featured the "suggestopedic cycle," which had three distinct parts: (1) review of the previous day's material; (2) new material presented in the foreign language, but largely through emotionally relevant dialogues and situations based on real life; and (3) "the only truly original feature," called the séance (or session). According to Bancroft, the one-hour séance "provides for reinforcement (or rather, memorization) of the new material at an unconscious level. Based on the two forms of yoga concentration: outer/inner, the séance is divided into two parts: active and passive (or 'concert'), with active or outward concentration on the material preceding the rest and relaxation of passive meditation on the text."[44]

Schmidt thought Miller and her Lozanov methods would be an excellent fit for Holos, calling her "absolutely brilliant."

"She got it," said Schmidt. "Got what this holism thing was about."

Patricia Field was hired to teach math, though she and Miller essentially split one half-time position, according to Simon.

"We had a quarter-time math teacher," said Simon.

Field, who was British, had earned a bachelor's degree in education, and was a graduate student at the University of Minnesota.[45] Field would come to the school at Pillsbury House, and the students would all go to math.

"We didn't have the flexibility to create interdisciplinary projects in units," said Simon. "I had a block of time, and that block of time would both be for social studies and writing. I had about two, two-and-a-half hours every day with the kids."

Beyond the paid teachers on-staff, Holos relied on volunteers and contracted-partners from the community, including those already working in the Pillsbury House. One of those was an art teacher.

"We had the art teacher in the art room [of Pillsbury House]," recalled Simon. "The art teacher was amazing and loved our kids. He was great. He was an African American guy, didn't say much, but he was the resident artist for Pillsbury House.... We bought his services. We had an art program, and he ran it."

"What I cared about when it came to serving students and their families," said Schmidt, "regardless of licenses, certificates, trainings, [was] that [the students] felt safe, respected, listened to, and valued. That students felt as if they were learning about things that mattered to them, and that they had at least some input into the process. That they were able to claim both their inner voice and outer voice. And that ultimately, families were able to live together in more harmonious, appreciative ways.

"All more possible, in my estimation, by mixing it up—there were no strict lines of demarcation re: OK, you're the licensed social worker, so only you get to meet with families, or OK, you've got the teacher license so only you can do the teaching thing. If someone offered to make a contribution, and I could see enthusiasm, passion, a desire to help make a difference—let's sit down and talk about it; oh, how cool, yes, let's give it a go."

With a site, funding, curriculum, and staff in place, Holos was set to open on January 30, 1989, the first day of the spring semester for Minneapolis Public School students.[46] All that was still needed were students. While nobody interviewed remembers exactly how many students were present on day one, someone recalled about three students attending the first day, and by March there would be ten students enrolled. Holos would enroll sixteen total in that first spring; fourteen of whom finished the semester. Two young people would earn their high school diploma. The Holos School was off and running, but the students would almost immediately suggest changes to the name of the school and to its mission. And Barb Schmidt, being who she was, listened.

15

Peers Enjoying a Sober Education

Joanie Hannigan[1] grew up in Hastings-on-Hudson, New York, in Westchester County, and by the time she was 16, her drug use had become problematic. In her words, she was "doing a lot of bad stuff" and had started to bottom out. She dropped out of high school, periodically left home, and toured with the Grateful Dead. The Dead had formed as a band in Northern California in 1965, and thousands of teenagers had followed them around the country to attend their concerts in the twenty-plus years since. Some of their first gigs were as the house band for Ken Kesey's Acid Tests, including a three-day psychedelic rock event called the Trips Festival, in January 1966, which has been credited with launching the hippie counterculture.[2] Frank Mastropolo wrote about that festival and described the Acid Tests as "wild parties in the Bay Area that featured music, dancing, theater, strobe lights, Day-Glo paint and free access to LSD, which was legal at the time."[3] Drug use by both the band and the audience remained synonymous with Dead Shows, as their music would provide the soundtrack for a fan's acid trip. LSD became one of Joanie Hannigan's favorite drugs.

"I don't remember exactly what happened," said Hannigan. "I know the bottom line was that whoever I was living with, hanging out with, they split, and I didn't have any place to go, and I called my mother and said, 'I'm coming home.' She was like, 'No, you're not coming home.'"

Hannigan had broken into her own house and stolen items, in part to support her drug use. The theft, as well as the emotions brought on by Hannigan's absence, had forced her mother to intervene. Her mom had researched options and realized that Minnesota had become a hub for adolescent treatment. By then, three of the oldest hospitals in the Twin Cities—St. Mary's (opened in 1887), Lutheran Deaconess (1891), and Fairview (1916)—had joined together to form Riverside Medical Center. This partnership allowed the original adolescent program in the Twin Cities, St. Mary's Hospital, to evolve into a multitiered system with psychiatric care, outpatient detox, and in-patient treatment.

"If you want to come home, you have to go to this place for thirty days," her mother told her. "If you go to this place, you'll never bottom out again or do drugs."

Hannigan was particularly motivated to fly in an airplane.

"I really thought it over," she said. "I'm like, 'Well, that's a pretty good deal.' Plus, I didn't have any place to go, right? I literally had no place to go. I was sick at that point. I didn't look good. I was really emaciated. I was in really bad shape. I agreed to

Salvaging a Teenage Wasteland. Andrew J. Finch, Oxford University Press. © Oxford University Press 2024.
DOI: 10.1093/oso/9780190645502.003.0015

go. I thought I was going to Mississippi. I kept thinking I was in Mississippi, because the Mississippi River was there.

Months went by until I figured out I was not in Mississippi."

The joint-venture hospital called Riverside Medical Center was indeed on the banks of the Mississippi River, but near the river's origin in Minnesota, and all those services had a steep cost. A thirty-five-day stay at St. Mary's-Fairview-Deaconess had a price tag of $13,775, with $5000 due at admission. Insurance would not cover the program, so in late 1988, Hannigan's parents mortgaged their home, and she and her mom boarded a flight to Minneapolis and its burgeoning adolescent treatment system.[4] With so many programs offering a range of services, it is beyond the scope of this book to describe them all—though many were aligned with the Johnson Institute and the Minnesota Model. Additionally, the client experience might stretch from gratitude to disgust. Some people would credit these treatment programs with saving their lives, while others would blame them for destroying their lives. Capturing a representative client assessment of adolescent treatment in Minnesota during the 1970s and 1980s is not possible here, but Hannigan's experience had many negative memories.

"The experience was kinda terrible," recalled Hannigan. "Fairview Deaconness was a machine . . . very regimented." She and some of her fellow youth residents dubbed the center "Fairview Decatraz" based on its dehumanizing, rigid, and "systematized" culture.[5] One technique involved them writing her an embarrassing and shaming song about herself that Hannigan had to sing in front of everybody every day.[6]

"Ultimately when I thought I was going home, on the day I was going home, my parents and I, we had a conference call, and it was like, 'Well, you're not going home.' I had a real epiphany moment of like, 'Well, okay. I'm going to go where I'm going to go.'"

St. Mary's was one of the programs that had received generous support from Irene and Wheelock Whitney in the mid-1970s. When Hannigan finished her stay at Fairview-Deaconess, her family had decided she would move into the Irene Whitney Center for Recovery,[7] which had changed its name from "Shanti House" after Irene's death in 1986. The program, which opened in 1976, had been the first halfway house for teenagers, serving residents ages 14 to 25. The house where Hannigan lived for the next seven to eight months was a converted church into which the program had moved in 1979 (see Figure 15.1).[8]

Betty Triliegi was the director of Shanti House from its beginning, and she explained how the various programs were linked.

"Irene Whitney is the one that started everything, really," said Triliegi. "We were pretty connected. We had former clients from Pharm House [treatment center] that worked [at Shanti House]. We hired them, and they came over, and we did group. When we opened our doors, I think we had seventeen clients; they all moved in. By that time, we had a lot of treatment centers around town here. They all needed a place for these young people to go. Their parents didn't want them home."

"It was a halfway house," she explained. "Which meant it was halfway from the treatment center to independent living. It was still a program. We had counselors,

Figure 15.1. Shanti House, which opened in 1976, was the first halfway house for teenagers, serving residents ages 14 to 25. The program changed its name to the Irene Whitney Center for Recovery after Whitney's death in 1986. This is an image of a brochure with a drawing of Shanti House. (Source: Betty Triliegi.)

and we did family group, and we did therapy, and we did interventions. We did everything. Whatever was needed, we did."

The house had about forty beds, and it was co-ed, with women on one floor and men on the other. Every room had four residents in it.

"We never trusted two; we always wanted four," said Triliegi. "Hazelden had done that, also. There was always accountability with four."

Shanti House took referrals from multiple treatment programs, not just the Twin Cities but also from around the country, including California, Florida, and Texas.

"There were a lot of adolescent units that were feeding Shanti House," said Triliegi. "Plus, we were the only one in the country.... There was nowhere in the country you could put a fifteen or a sixteen-year-old, and there was a big need. Parents didn't want them home; schools didn't want them."

Triliegi had worked for years under Vernon Johnson at the Johnson Institute, and the halfway house was founded by Irene Whitney. The Minnesota Model's emphasis on abstinence and the blending of professional and trained nonprofessional recovering staff around the principles of Alcoholics Anonymous (AA) was thus apparent at Shanti House. But Triliegi had also visited Phoenix House in New York, one of the original therapeutic communities, which emphasized accountability to the group with "only two rules, no drugs and no physical violence."[9] That, along with the Johnson Institute's intervention mindset, made Shanti House a confrontational environment.

"Our program ran every day from eight in the morning until ten at night, so we had programming all day long," said Triliegi. "We had family groups weekly, and I had twenty staff people. It was a lot of programming, a lot of therapy. They did not have a lot of time alone."

The culture worked well for many people. In an interview for this book, Triliegi said she had received a letter years later from one of Shanti House's graduates.

"She said, 'Betty, I'm writing to you because now I'm 39 years sober and just so grateful. My brother's been sober, I don't know, twenty years.' She said it never would have happened if we hadn't gone to Shanti House."

The experience, however, was not as pleasant for Joanie Hannigan, who called the Shanti House/Irene Whitney Center a "Darwinian therapeutic community . . . very big brother . . . encouraging kids to rat out each other." She referred to the counseling as "attack therapy" and said it would last as long as three hours per day.

"It was really intense. Like I said, it was like a therapeutic community [with a level-system], and so there was lots of, you know, 'you are on male/female. You are on phase one. You can't listen to the radio. You're on pots and pans every night for three months.'"

Doug Guion was another resident of the Irene Whitney Center at the time Hannigan lived there. He was a couple years younger and had grown up in Connecticut. Doug had gotten treatment in Arizona and Tennessee, before arriving in Minnesota for a six-month stay at the halfway house. His memory of the culture was more mixed.

"I was in a halfway house; I went to school; I made friends; we did group therapy. It was a completely crazy, wild ride," said Guion. "We did encounter therapy and bataka bats[10] and screaming, and you'd sit in a room, and they'd scream at you, and it was a pretty insane time. I sort of weathered that. I found it abstractly interesting and just sort of the way my mind works, I was sort of objectively aware of how interesting the situation was. I was both a part of it, and I was also somewhat detached from it."

As Guion said, when school was in session, the teenage residents of the Irene Whitney Center attended Southwest High School in the Linden Hills neighborhood of Minneapolis—a fifteen-minute walk from the house.

"The Crips and the Bloods [gangs] were there," said Guion. "People were getting chased down and beaten up. It was a violent, dangerous school."

Hannigan said the school was "gigantic," with about twenty-five hundred students, and "I was doing really poorly in many ways. I was ending up in the nurse's office all the time because I was having flashbacks. I was having symptomatic post-LSD kind of stuff going on. Some long-term withdrawal from that, those kinds of issues."

The months that students like Joanie and Doug were in treatment and transitional housing—late 1988 to early 1989—coincided with the months Ken Simon and Barb

Schmidt were planning the Holos school. They had decided to open the school on the first day of the spring semester—Monday, January 30—and during the first weeks of 1989, Schmidt was reaching out to multiple agencies promoting the new school and recruiting students. Unlike Carol Robson at New Dimensions/Sobriety High, Schmidt did not place ads in the paper. In fact, there was no media coverage of the school at all before it opened or during its first semester. Schmidt instead relied on personal connections, and her network was large based on her prior professional experience. She met in person and made many phone calls trying to find teens to come to the school.

"Halfway houses made referrals. As did aftercare programs in the Twin Cities. As did probation officers," said Schmidt. "I made personal contacts with all of the preceding to tell them about the school and give info regarding how to refer and answered their questions. Basically [I] began establishing relationships with them from the beginning."

By that time, Sobriety High was in its second school year as a recovery high school, and these same sources had been referring students there. According to Bob Mowatt, the director of Hennepin County's juvenile probation office, they only placed three students at Sobriety High in its first two years.[11] But Holos had differences that made it a more amenable option. First was its commitment to being tuition-free, meaning money would not be a barrier to entry. In addition, because it was working through alternative school director Robert Jibben to establish a contract with Minneapolis Public Schools, the process would be more seamless than referring a student to an external independent school.

"Robert Jibben, amazing man," said Schmidt, "incredibly supportive, can't say enough about him."

Their location on Chicago Avenue in Minneapolis may have also helped for students living in the city, though Sobriety High's site in St. Louis Park was not that much longer a drive, especially for students living in the suburbs west of town. Simon and Schmidt also built an advisory board that would not only help with funding, but also with identifying students from a diverse number of sources. Juvenile Probation Director Mowatt was one of them, as were the following:

- Vincent DeLusia, Vice President, Black Educators of Twin Cities and Minneapolis Community College
- Sandra Hilary, Minneapolis City Council
- Michael LaBrosse, President, Human Development Industries in Minneapolis
- Judge Allan Oleisky, Juvenile Court
- Barb Ross, Education Specialist
- Janet Witthuhn, Assistant to the Superintendent of Minneapolis Public Schools

This group was well positioned to advocate for the school and help with networking; and families responded. Schmidt remembers there being three students present on day one—two referred by probation officers and one from Jibben.

"If you've got kids coming out of treatment," director Mowatt told a newspaper reporter, "it's just so overwhelming for them. If you put kids back in a typical high school, you have all kinds of social pressures."[12]

This was certainly the case for Joanie Hannigan.

"I had a really hard time functioning in school," said Hannigan. "From what I remember, the school had started to really wean me out of certain classes. I think that I was probably a little unwanted in the school."

Thus, when Barb Schmidt paid a visit to Betty Triliegi at the Irene Whitney Center, Hannigan was one of the first residents that came to Triliegi's mind as a potential student. Schmidt recalls Triliegi as being "thrilled."

"Those youth were attending a nearby public school where drug access was easy, and they didn't feel as if they fit in," said Schmidt. "Some were not from the local area, which made things even more difficult for them."

Triliegi recommended a few students she thought would be a good fit, and Schmidt recalled meeting with each student individually first, so they "could have some say in the decision regarding whether or not to try it out."

Doug Guion was another resident recommended by Triliegi. While neither he nor Hannigan remember the exact circumstances around being selected or meeting with Schmidt, Guion does recall having some input.

"It didn't feel compulsory. I'm sure it was a choice," said Guion. "I'm sure it was something that was offered. I mean, it may have been that I was selected for it, or a few of us were selected for it, because we either showed promise or had a specific aptitude that they thought would make a good match for the curriculum. We also might have been in a certain phase in the rehab. It was a three-stage system [at the Irene Whitney Center], so I'm certain it was choice-based.

"And quite honestly," he added, "the alternative of staying with gangs [at Southwest High School] or sitting in a room in a nonstructured environment [at Holos], where we could smoke cigarettes downstairs and watch movies, it was hardly a choice."

Guion's family lived in Connecticut, so they were deferring many decisions to the halfway house staff. His mother had no recollection of being contacted about Holos, but she shared Doug's assumption that the house thought it would be a good fit for me and simply called to inform her—"to which she would have and obviously did agree."

Hannigan recalls four total residents, including herself, choosing to transfer from Southwest High School. In addition to her being from New York and Guion from New Canaan, Connecticut, the others were from Dallas, Texas, and Burnsville, Minnesota, about a thirty-minute drive south.

"The first year we had lots of people in very different places, but they were close in age," said Ken Simon.

The referral sources listed in legal documents were high school chemical dependency counselors and "at risk youth" coordinators, local adolescent treatment centers, probation officers and court judges, and area halfway houses.[13] Despite the diverse referral network and tuition-free attendance, though, Simon noted, "most of the kids in the first year came from affluent families."

This may have been in part because the Irene Whitney Center did have a fee of sixty-eight dollars per day.[14] While modest for adolescent residential care, the cost to families was still over $2000 each month. Also, like Sobriety High, Holos required a student to have had prior treatment, so that limited eligibility to only those families who had access to treatment.

"They had to have successfully gone through treatment," said Simon. "And they had to stay sober."

Holos was proactive about trying to have a diverse enrollment. Beyond writing a standard inclusivity clause stating the school would be available to all "chemically dependent" students, "regardless of race, religion, ethnic background, or sexual preference,"[15] the board outlined concrete steps to doing that, starting with being tuition-free and having juvenile court and urban school representation on their advisory board. "To encourage a multi-cultural/ethnic student population and curriculum," the board would reach out to "the Minneapolis Urban League Street Academy; the Institute on Black Chemical Abuse; the Inter-Cultural Center in the St. Paul Public Schools; Heart of the Earth [American Indian] Survival School."[16]

Enrollment grew to ten in March and fourteen in April. In all, Schmidt accepted sixteen students into the Holos School during its first semester, and there was some diversity: 25% of the students were BIPOC—three of the sixteen (19%) were Black, and one was "American Indian." Two of the sixteen students dropped out before the end of the year because of a return to use, including one of the three Black students. This meant fourteen students finished the year at the school.[17]

Once the students were there, Schmidt and Simon made sure to get their input in the running of the school, which aligned well with the holistic philosophy.

Doug Guion said, "Ken and [Barb] would talk about this as, 'We sort of want you guys [the students] to help create the school with us [the staff]; you're part of the process. This is less about taking a specific design and executing it here. It's let's design it together. Let's co-create.' We were actively involved in that, and we felt like we were a part of the school, and we did know that we were the first class."

One of the things the students were asked to do was name the school. The school began as "Holos" due to the 501(c)3 corporation name, "Holos Foundation." In time, the foundation would be involved in multiple programs, with the recovery high school being the first.

"It was very important for the students themselves to name," said Schmidt. "It was their school, and they were the ones who'd be 'passing it on' to other young people in recovery."

Schmidt and Guion both remembered the naming of the school being a class project.

"I do remember it was sort of like a project we took on," said Guion. "We had discussions about it, and we ideated on it.... We talked about it. I don't remember the process specifically or how long it lasted."

At the end of the process, the students chose "Imagination—P.E.A.S.E. Academy." The acronym stood for "Peers Enjoying A Sober Education (see Figures 15.2a and 15.2b).

Figure 15.2a. Joanie Hannigan and Doug Guion were two of the first graduates of P.E.A.S.E. Academy. They each wrote text for the school's first yearbook, and these are their yearbook photos. (Source: Joan Vogt.)

Figure 15.2b. Joanie Hannigan and Doug Guion were two of the first graduates of P.E.A.S.E. Academy. They each wrote text for the school's first yearbook, and these are their yearbook photos. (Source: Joan Vogt.)

"Who knows how we came up with it," said Guion. "I'm sure we came up with a lot of horseshit first, then we settled on P.E.A.S.E., and it's a play on words, and it's also an acronym which is literal so . . . We all liked it."

"That initial group of students was fantastic," said Schmidt, "very simpatico with ideas of PEACE. I think when I told them, 'OK, time to name the school,' they sort of collectively said out loud, 'Wouldn't it be cool to be able to align it with PEACE?' And I don't think it took them long to come up with the brilliant 'Peers Enjoying A Sober Education.' Gave pretty much everyone goosebumps."

The cover of the spring 1989 yearbook has the full name, in all caps: "IMAGINATION—P.E.A.S.E. ACADEMY OF HOLOS, INC." By fall, "Imagination" had been dropped, and the name Holos, Inc., referred only to the non-profit. The origin of "Imagination" has been lost, though it was consistent with the school's mindfulness and human consciousness approach. Schmidt simply felt the long name was too complicated for the general public.

"My practical side took over in the end," said Schmidt. "I thought that extra word could make it difficult for others to understand/navigate around, so decided to stick just with P.E.A.S.E. Academy. One of my not-so-smart decisions—in hindsight, [it] probably should have remained." Perhaps, but the shortened name has endured and is now one of the most recognizable of all recovery high school monikers.

The name "Holos" may have gone into the background, but its spirit remained evident in the school.

"There is literally no comparison between any school I had ever been to and Holos," said Guion. "Not just comparing it against the Minnesota Public School that I described, but I remember it being very unstructured. There wasn't a rigorous process or a rigorous sort of path for the curriculum; we didn't have specific days where it was math and then science and English. It was very exploratory. I mean, I remember doing a science project where . . . I've always been interested in physics, and so you got to sort of choose what you wanted to do, so I did a project to explain to everyone how gravity functioned in the universe."

Schmidt and Simon had created a school which harkened back to the original democratic schools that launched the alternative school movement in the 1960s. It was as if Summerhill had arrived at the Pillsbury House on Chicago Avenue.

"I remember watching *Cry Freedom*, I think it was called," said Guion. "I remember it was [about South African activist Steven] Biko. I remember watching that, and then we would deconstruct it and talk about it. It was an interesting place where we're sort of this new, like unschooling, homeschooling movement where the child chooses what they want to learn for the day. It wasn't directly like that, but it was similar in that let's change the learning process to instead of trying to have you learn core curriculum, let's do things that are on a specific topic that's interesting to you and then you'll explore them more fully. I remember going for walks. Again, I remember smoking downstairs a lot. We were all teenagers, and we all smoked, and we're all in rehab. It never felt like school, that's for sure. I liked all of my classmates and we had fun and we all enjoyed each other's company, so I really enjoyed my time at Holos."

The contrast with the Irene Whitney halfway house was clear.

"You couldn't walk out the door [at Irene Whitney]," said Joanie Hannigan of the halfway house's therapeutic community approach. "It was this group therapy session. It would be like twenty girls with three counselors in a circle in a ballroom or in the dining room on one end of the house and the boys on the other end in the dining room. Inevitably these horrible, horrible modalities or whatever . . . I can't even explain it. . . . It was really popular to do these sessions where [several] girls would hold one girl down and scream obscenities at them until they 'broke.' It's sad when you think about it."

"It was completely different [at school]," said Guion. "There was absolutely none of that. It was ostensibly . . . from what I remember . . . the mission was let's take kids who are in trouble and give them a positive educational experience that is entirely different from the set curriculum that you might experience in a normal school because . . . [maybe] the thinking was they're unlikely to do as well in a structured environment because of the nature of their issues and so this might give a more positive experience for them. Not only strengthening their sobriety but also, strengthening their education.

"It was supportive and open. Again, very unstructured. You felt safe, and you felt cared for, and it felt like it was an important thing to do. It was very, very different than just being in a regular school. It wasn't about grades or performance in a traditional way, it was let's be together, let's create this community and let's do interesting things and use our mind in an interesting way."

It was no wonder the school reminded the students of "peace."

"Going to school was like a respite," said Hannigan.[18]

The pedagogy may have felt unstructured to the students, but they were not just sitting around all day. The school incorporated biofeedback, daily guided meditation, yoga, and even past life regressions.

"We used to joke about it all the time," said Hannigan, "because we'd be like, 'We're the only school meditating.'"

With Powderhorn Park being so close, Ken Simon would take the students to the park for lunch and tell stories for English class.

"I remember Ken bringing us outside a lot to walk," said Hannigan. She also remembered going to the art room in Pillsbury House. "The art teacher, I distinctly remember because that was just fun, you know?"

Despite all the holistic wellness activities woven into the curriculum, one thing that was missing in the beginning was traditional recovery work, such as Twelve Step meetings, Big Book readings, or even psychotherapy. That would be added later, but at first those activities were absent.

"These were not 'sick' kids," said Schmidt. "They weren't 'crazy' kids. 'Irrational' kids. Dysfunctional? Yeah, they could be. Just like you sometimes. Like me. Because the culture at large is dysfunctional. Once they knew we understood that—or at least got glimpses of us acknowledging that it wasn't just about them—it wasn't all about 'treatment' or 'recovery.' Yes, of course we addressed issues of sobriety—one of the staff had to deal with it herself.... I think it was almost a collective sense among staff—we didn't act as if that was the only thing going on."

Most of the students were attending mutual aid groups outside school, and the kids in the halfway house were going to meetings every day in addition to their therapy sessions at the house. In the beginning, P.E.A.S.E. Academy did not require Twelve Step meetings, but Schmidt did encourage students "to assess what worked best for them, and then go for it."

"The addiction stuff was coming from within us and then being filtered through them I would say," recalled Hannigan. "We were all over. It was all over us, you know? We were coming from a place where we were having therapy sessions every single day when we left school."

P.E.A.S.E. Academy did not screen the students for drug use either.

"They'd tell us if they had a slip—or it would eventually come out some other way, including behaviors that changed," said Schmidt. "Didn't happen very often. Did we miss times/not catch on regarding students who may have been back to using? Using on a permanent basis, I honestly don't think so. Relapses—yeah, might have not been aware at times. But again, don't think it occurred very often—one of the main benefits of keeping the school enrollment under thirty. Hard to get lost in the shuffle. Actually, nearly impossible. Operating under the radar is pretty difficult with such a tight-knit group."

In filing its original documents requested nonprofit status, Schmidt called the school, "Holos Foundation, Inc. Transition School for Recovering Chemically Dependent Youth," and that first semester, the intention was for students to stay for three-to-six months and then return to traditional schools to graduate after they had some sobriety under their belt. For the most part, that is what the first group of students did.[19] One student did finish her credits at P.E.A.S.E. that spring, and she described herself as the "valedictorian" in the yearbook. Joanie Hannigan returned to New York to finish school; Doug Guion went back to Connecticut; another student returned to Texas, and the rest eventually returned to schools in Minnesota. But they had one more legacy they wanted to leave . . . they wanted future students to be able to stay.

Michael Durchslag recalled, "Those original students said, 'Barb, we can't go back. We don't want to go back. This is where we feel comfortable. This is where we feel safe. This is where we're learning. We can't go back to the home school, because if we go back, we'll use, or we're worried that we'll use.' "

So, according to Durchslag, Schmidt went back and renegotiated the contract with Minneapolis Public Schools, and P.E.A.S.E. Academy became a four-year graduating program when they opened the doors for the fall of 1989.

As a farewell, Joanie Hannigan wrote an essay for page one of the yearbook titled "Holos (Holostic Learning)," and it closed with these insightful lines:

We were nervous, scared, and excited. This was a chance for us. Our classroom was small, few teachers, and text books. How could this be educational? We had a fixed definition of learning. But at Holos we learned, it started out slowly; a way we were comfortable with. Showing talents we didn't know we had. We were amazed by our creativity. We taught each other. We were talented and smart.

Coming from all over Minnesota, Texas, Connecticut, and New York, we're all different and unique people, with one thing in common, we're recovering chemically dependent learning how to learn. This school was put together for us. It is not for everyone, that is what is special about it. Soon we will be going back to high schools and college, but we will be preparred [sic]. We can look past the page to the value of the literature, past solution of the problem. We have smart insightful, courageous, and important young minds. We are pioneers of learning.[20]

16
Sock and Buskin

Doug Guion composed a "Dear Friend" letter for the first P.E.A.S.E. Academy year-book, but he never knew the intended person's identity. None of the students did, but the letter thanked the "friend" for "giving us the tools to help create this community." While the letter was titled "Dear Friend by Doug" in the Table of Contents, the salu-tation was "DEAR, SIR" (*sic*).[1] According to Guion, they knew the person was a "he," and they were told the funds came from an endowment, but that was all.

"We generally assumed it was a person connected in some way to the Irene Whitney Center or a local AA member who heard of the school and decided to help out, but I can't be certain of either," said Guion.

"There was this mysterious private donor that gave [Barb Schmidt and Ken Simon] money to do this," said Joanie Hannigan. "We didn't know who they were, but we were very thankful."

Hannigan still did not know the person's identity thirty years later, but without their involvement, P.E.A.S.E. Academy may never have come into existence as a re-covery high school. That is because the friend was the third member of the creation team—the one who was in recovery and had promised to fund the project: Howard Pearson.

"[Barb Schmidt] was into this holistic stuff and had met . . . an extremely wealthy guy who said, 'If you start a sober school, you won't have to worry about the funding. I'll fund it,' " said Steve Massey, who was hired to teach at P.E.A.S.E. Academy in the fall of 1989.

Without the possibility of funding, Barb Schmidt might never have gone beyond the teacher's lounge conversation with Ken Simon. And Howard Pearson wanted to fund a *sober* school like New Dimensions/Sobriety High, thus charting the course for a recovery high school—in essence, putting the "S" in P.E.A.S.E. (Peers Enjoying A Sober Education).

The P.E.A.S.E. Academy yearbook that featured Joanie Hannigan's essay and Doug Guion's "Dear Friend" letter displayed many pieces of student artwork (see Figure 16.1). Art was a focus at the school, and the cover drawing was credited to two stu-dents, both from Minnesota. The black and white image is a circle divided in half by a diagonal line. The left hemisphere is dark with a full moon, two puffy clouds, and three stars. The right half has a clear background with three clouds and a sun rising through one of the clouds. In the middle of the circle, on top of the diagonal line, is a dove—a universal symbol of peace—flying from left (dark) to right (light). Many

Salvaging a Teenage Wasteland. Andrew J. Finch, Oxford University Press. © Oxford University Press 2024.
DOI: 10.1093/oso/9780190645502.003.0016

Figure 16.1. The cover art for the first Holos/P.E.A.S.E. Academy yearbook was credited to two students, both from Minnesota. Originally printed on a purple background, many symbols can be construed from the work, including a circle representing connectedness and holism, and the peaceful dove linking to the acronym for the school name chosen by the students—Peers Enjoying A Sober Education. (Source: Joan Vogt.)

symbols can be construed from the work, including a circle representing connect-edness and holism, and the peaceful dove linking to the name students chose for the school. The night-darkness and the day-light could certainly represent the lives of the students, before and after P.E.A.S.E., but also just the struggles of living in recovery one day at a time. As an added touch, the drawing was printed on top of a purple cover. Purple is thick with symbolism that would align with the school, including being the color of the amethyst, the gemstone that represents sobriety.[2]

What the artists could not have known was how representative and prescient their work would be for the recovery high schools in Minnesota. In creating Holos, Barb Schmidt had been influenced by consciousness studies, and she tried to infuse con-sciousness and mindfulness in the school. Philosopher Rollo May defined conscious-ness as "the awareness that emerges out of the dialectical tension between possibilities and limitations,"[3] and this tension was apparent not only in the students' lives but also in the recovery high school movement itself. With P.E.A.S.E. Academy and Sobriety High being the first of twenty-five recovery high schools that would eventually op-erate in the state (up to sixteen at one time), the sunrise on the P.E.A.S.E. Academy yearbook cover could have represented the dawn of a movement. And, going deeper, the picture displayed the dialectical nature of what was actually happening. Positive steps would frequently be cloaked in difficulty. Joy was often followed soon by sad-ness. The possibilities almost always revealed limitations; the sunshine would regu-larly be obscured by clouds. And many of the Minnesota schools would become rivals, divided by finite levels of funding and ideological differences. Over time, none would draw more ire than Sobriety High, in part because of how successful they would be-come. It would be years before there was peace among the schools in Minnesota.

Dear Friend

In June 1989, many of the divisive issues were a long way away. As reflected in their yearbook comments—"Nothing we can't do!!"; "I can be anything I wanna be"; "You were (are) all adventurers"—those first P.E.A.S.E. Academy students no doubt were filled with more hope than fear about their lives as they finished the spring.[4] But what happened after Doug Guion's "Dear Friend" letter appeared in the yearbook was illus-trative of the shadow and the light; for all the joy and imagination Howard Pearson brought to the world, there was sadness and a tragic, early end.

Of all the people featured in this book, Howard Pearson brought forth the heaviest emotions from those interviewed. Carol Robson and Barb Schmidt did not really know each other, but both knew Pearson, and both teared up when telling stories about him. At some point, Pearson left Minneapolis to travel overseas. Robson remembered him going to Morocco, and Schmidt thought he went to Spain, but both recalled he was scheduled to return to Minneapolis that summer of 1989—and both would make plans to meet up with him. While Barb Schmidt had lost touch with Pearson, Ken Simon had stayed in contact. Simon tracked him down and sent him a copy of the P.E.A.S.E. Academy yearbook, which featured Doug Guion's letter from the students on page 3.

"He was sort of overwhelmed learning that the school was now up and running, a 'reality' even without his financial backing," said Schmidt, "and a little overwhelmed regarding the dedication to him as well."

"We figured he might benefit from knowing he played a role, regardless of how things had transpired," she added. "Here was a success for him, at least on some level, and we wanted him to know it—a way to help him personally, and in his recovery/ sobriety."

According to Schmidt, Pearson was so "moved" by the yearbook gesture, and by the reality of P.E.A.S.E., that he reached out to her for the first time in months and said he wanted to meet and discuss "how he might be of assistance to keep P.E.A.S.E. Academy going—financially, yes, but possibly in other ways, too."

While he was overseas, Pearson told Schmidt as soon as he traveled back to Minneapolis, he wanted to meet face-to-face.

"He told me he had taken the yearbook with him," said Schmidt, "and was looking at it as we spoke—obviously it meant a lot to him."

As Schmidt recalled, they arranged to meet on a Sunday evening in July at the Whitney, a former grain mill in downtown Minneapolis which had recently been renovated into a luxury hotel.[5] He knew when his flight was due to land, and he wanted to come directly to the hotel from the airport.[6]

"I was there," said Schmidt. "Only he didn't show up. I sat in the Whitney lobby waiting. And waiting. And waiting. He never showed up. After an hour?, I left. And [I] thought, 'Maybe a flight delay, or maybe he was going through another 'rough patch' and felt a need to distance himself again, or maybe [he] got scared again, so (I) just decided to let it be."

Two days later, a family member called Schmidt with tragic news. Howard had died the day they were scheduled to meet.

"The family was left in shock," said Schmidt, "Yet somehow they knew he was supposed to be meeting with me and wanted to let me know why he'd been a no-show."

Howard Pearson died in a hotel room about a month after the end of the school year. The official cause of death was "acute bronchial asthma due to (or as a consequence of) acute cocaine and morphine intoxication"—he had overdosed.[7]

"That was a real tragedy," said Carol Robson.

The recovery high school movement had just begun in Minnesota, and the schools would ultimately help save hundreds of lives and create hope where there had been none. But there was another side—addiction is a chronic condition, and recovery often involves returns to use, sometimes resulting in the end of a life.[8] Most people in the recovery field have experienced the fulfilling rewards and devastating losses inherent in the work. For Carol Robson at Sobriety High and the staff at P.E.A.S.E. Academy, Howard Pearson's story represented both sides of recovery. To the students, he had been an unknown benefactor who had helped create their school. Little did they know he also symbolized death's proximity to recovery high schools.

"When we stepped into the door of Holos for the first time," wrote Guion in his "Dear Friend" letter, "it was more like a gloomy ghost town rather than a school. The one thing that we can all reminisce about is the dream and the feeling that we could actually make it happen" (see Figure 16.2).

June 2, 1989

DEAR, SIR

When we stepped into the door of Holos for the first time, it was more like a gloomy ghost town rather than a school. The one thing that we can all reminisce about is the dream and the feeling that we could actually make it happen.

Although at times trying was a low priority and screwing around seemed to be on everyone's mind, the dream was still there. Holos is not your everyday run of the mill school!

Because we all share dependency of one thing or another, there is a special bond in all of us. That bond enables us to share and laugh together and also to understand, empathize, and help each other.

We have all found special things in ourselves that we either had hidden, or took for granted.

Some things that occur at Holos are out of the ordinary school routine, like: trying to bring down stress while holding hands, learning Spanish with music, and the love that we all feel for the opportunity of not attending, but creating Holos. It is a satisfaction that cannot easily be expressed through words.

The word "Holos" is not just an acronym; it is a feeling that makes us a family. That gloomy ghost town is now a blossoming community, incorporating not only education, but more importantly, trust, empathy, and love.

Thank you for giving us the tools to help create this community.

Love,

The kids from "Holos"

Figure 16.2. This is the complete letter written by Doug Guion on behalf of the entire student body to an anonymous "Dear, Sir." The letter was printed in the first Holos/P.E.A.S.E. Academy yearbook in 1989. (Source: Joan Vogt.)

According to people who knew him, Howard Pearson had shared that dream, and just before his death, he had seen it become a reality.

"That gloomy ghost town is now a blossoming community," Guion concluded the letter, "incorporating not only education, but more importantly, trust, empathy, and love. Thank you for giving us the tools to help create this community."

The students had just begun their summer break, and they had no idea that the person to whom they had dedicated their inaugural yearbook was gone. Barb Schmidt and Ken Simon were told the funeral would be on the East Coast, and they could attend.[9]

"I actually got to be very close friends with [Howard]," said Simon. "I couldn't go (to the funeral). I was in grad school; I was broke; I was living in a one-bedroom apartment with my girlfriend who was also in grad school. There was no way we could go to the funeral, or I could go."

Carol Robson also recalled being told by of Howard's death by a relative, and she too did not attend the funeral. But Barb Schmidt did.

"I flew out (to Howard's funeral)," said Schmidt. "Unfortunately missed the service except the very end of it—was told where family and friends were gathering after. Drove myself there, didn't stay long—enough to meet a few family members and friends. And his dad. I especially wanted to meet his dad."

Before leaving, Schmidt had mailed a letter to Howard's father, the patriarch of a family that would become known for their philanthropy.

"I let him know [Howard] had made a tremendous contribution in helping formulate the school, that his son had 'seeded' the idea, and from that idea, a sobriety school was born. In other words, his son's life had left a legacy of sorts, a legacy he could be proud of.

"[The letter] emphasized he as a father could be proud of his son because the school was [Howard's] initial idea, and from that initial idea—look, it became real. He was the catalyst for its creation.

"We embraced through tears, then he patted the top part of his suit—dug into the inner pocket and took out the letter I'd sent him. He'd had it with him, over his heart, during the funeral. Hand holding ensued. Tight grasp. It was very real."

Barb Schmidt had tears in her own eyes recalling that story. "That elderly gentleman was a gentle man. In so much emotional pain. Absolutely devastated.

"He knew he had to move on to others who were there, but I'll never forget that moment."

How much money Howard Pearson gave to Simon and Schmidt to start Holos while he was alive is uncertain. His interest in P.E.A.S.E. Academy did, however, lead to funds for the school after his death. Obituaries described Howard as a husband, son, brother, uncle, nephew, cousin, and friend. Adjectives included "adored and adoring," "loved and loving," "beloved," and "cherished." In lieu of flowers, Howard's family asked that contributions in his memory be made to the Holos Foundation, in care of Barbara Schmidt and Ken Simon, and included the corporate address.[10] Memorial monies were directed toward P.E.A.S.E. Academy, and Schmidt remembered receiving over $7,000 for the school. Howard Pearson had left behind a lasting legacy, after all.

"As they say in the rooms," reflected school director Michael Durchslag over thirty years later, "everyday clean is a miracle, and to think how many hundreds (thousands?) of people that his kindness and generosity has helped over the past three decades is astounding, not to mention the generations to come—for example, Joanie [Hannigan's] own children. P.E.A.S.E. is a lasting legacy of both [Howard] and Barb. They deserve all the credit in the world for setting the table for a truly special place."

Early Years at P.E.A.S.E. Academy

The table may have been prepared for exciting possibilities, but the stage was also set for several limitations and disappointments for both P.E.A.S.E. Academy and Sobriety High, the school that had inspired it. An early sign of the barriers to come was around the intentions of P.E.A.S.E. Academy to diversify enrollment. Recovery high schools were set up to help teenagers recover from substance use disorders and were designed mostly by progressive and inclusive staff to be welcoming to all. Over time, however, they were attended predominantly by White adolescents from middle to upper-income families and often unused by or inaccessible to children of color and lower-income families. One strategy to attract students of color to a school of choice is to hire staff of color, and that first summer P.E.A.S.E. Academy committed to hiring "a member of the minority community" (i.e., "Black/Hispanic/Indian").[11] While there were some people of color involved with P.E.A.S.E. (an art teacher and the driver/counselor for the Irene Whitney House were both Black), the first four paid administrative/teaching positions had been given to White employees. Schmidt was intentional about changing that pattern, but unfortunately no person of color applied.

"No one of color ever submitted an application," said Schmidt, "nor did anyone who was affiliated with Holos Foundation or who knew me previously as a Hennepin County Juvenile Court chaplain make a recommendation or pass along a name. Ditto Minneapolis Public Schools Alternative Education Office."

Schmidt had to replace two of the school's three teachers after that first spring. Ken Simon remained on the Holos board but became less involved with the day-to-day teaching, and the "absolutely brilliant" Spanish teacher trained in the Lozanov Method, Allison Miller, moved to Washington. Opportunity emerged from these losses, though not in the form of a more diverse staff. Instead, Schmidt was able to bolster the therapeutic element of the school and stabilize the faculty. Schmidt used the available funds to hire a new social studies teacher, Steve Miller, and the first science teacher, Steve Massey. Miller would teach social studies at P.E.A.S.E. Academy for the next six years, and Steve Massey would stay for ten years. In addition, Massey brought a counseling credential, as his teaching license was in school counseling. In Massey, Schmidt also found another person with a more traditional spiritual background who would relieve some of the leadership burden.

"Steve Massey, when he joined up," said Schmidt, "offered to assist with some of these tasks, and I took him up on it—very much wanting to be of help, and he was."

Massey grew up in Dubuque, Iowa, about five hours south of Minneapolis. He graduated from Wahlert Catholic High School, and then stayed in Dubuque to complete a bachelor's degree in psychology with a minor in science from Loras College, a small, private Catholic college.[12] After graduating in 1985, Massey felt called to make an impact beyond his local community, so he moved east.

"I left small town Dubuque and landed at Forty-Second Street and Eighth Avenue in New York City, Times Square, volunteering with street kids through Covenant House," said Massey.

Covenant House was begun by two Catholic priests in the late 1960s in New York's East Village community to provide "a refuge for homeless and runaway youth."[13] They became an official nonprofit organization in 1972, opening an intake center in lower Manhattan.[14] The program was designed to transition youth into independent adulthood, and it provided a range of services that would prepare Massey for working at P.E.A.S.E. Academy, which was created to transition students into recovery. Covenant's many programs included educational support, GED preparation, work readiness, substance use treatment and prevention, and mental health services.

"For a year and a half, I'm in a prayer community and volunteering forty to fifty hours a week in the agency," said Massey.

By the mid-1980s, Covenant House had expanded across the United States and into Canada and Central America. Massey made plans to pursue a graduate degree in educational psychology and then move to Covenant's Los Angeles branch. In 1987, he returned to the Midwest and enrolled at the University of Minnesota at Duluth, where he met his future wife, Kate. She had grown up in Minnesota and wanted to stay. Steve Massey's plans changed.

"She said, 'I'm not leaving here,'" recalled Massey. "She's from this area. I landed in Forest Lake area (coincidentally, where Barb Schmidt grew up), and I had to find a job."

Massey graduated from Minnesota-Duluth in May 1989, just as Holos/P.E.A.S.E. Academy was wrapping up its first spring, and he received his teaching license in guidance and counseling. Neither Massey nor Schmidt recall how he first learned of Holos, but during his job search, he paid the school a visit at the Pillsbury House on Chicago Avenue.

Massey remembered asking Schmidt, "'You looking for a counselor?' She said, 'Heck yeah. Exactly.' I'm like, 'All right. I'm on board.' She said, 'I need somebody to teach some science and some health.'"

"During that spring," said Schmidt, "he came around, more than once, introduced himself and told me he wanted to be involved in some way. [I] have no idea how he heard of us . . . [I] didn't know if we'd have enough money to stay open through the next school year. Just a persistent guy though—loved that about him. He didn't give up and wasn't rattled at all when I told him, 'Hey, this is still in 'iffy' zone, no real job security." He didn't seem concerned—[he] was very dedicated, willing to go the extra mile."

When the school had two positions available that fall, there was the opening for him, and he took it. Though his teaching license was in counseling, the licensure rules at the time were much more relaxed.

"I taught some health, and I taught a little bit of science," said Massey. "I've got a minor in science. I wasn't licensed to teach it. I taught it, gave credit in it. It's crazy."

Massey was not in recovery himself, but he had studied psychology and worked with homeless teenagers in New York who were struggling with substance use. While the official target population was still "any student who has successfully completed chemical dependency treatment,"[15] Massey, like Barb Schmidt, could see the potential of a sober environment like P.E.A.S.E. Academy to support adolescents whether they had been through a treatment program or not. Over time, the school would open its doors to a variety of youths, with the expectation of not using drugs while enrolled.

"I thought our school had value," said Massey. "Any kid who was at risk, who wanted a sober environment, whether they had gone through treatment or not—we evolved to a school where you have to make a commitment to sobriety. You don't have to have a past of sobriety. When I was there for ten years, that didn't resonate with me. I had kids knocking on my door saying, 'I want this place because I'm at risk. I've got some drinking in my past or drugs in my past, but I'm not an addict in the sense of its controlling me.'

"We had those kids [who had received treatment]," he added. "We had many of those kids, but we also had some kids who came because they wanted a sober environment. The expectation for any kid was you make a commitment to sobriety and how are you doing that. [For] some kids it's, 'Twelve Steps, it's the only thing I know.' Other kids it's, 'I just have to stay away from certain people and certain triggers in my life, but I'm not an addict like a kid who's gone through treatment, maybe.'"

For Schmidt, Massey and his counseling training provided a reprieve.

"The first major relief from this 'Need to do everything' syndrome,'" said Schmidt. "That took some of the pressure off."

After a few years, they received a grant from the Minnesota Office of Drug Policy to fund a family health coordinator, and Steve moved into that position while continuing to teach a few classes. In time, the school also had enough money to hire a part-time therapist to help Massey coordinate counseling. One aspect of the school that Massey championed was parent support through periodic check-ins and a monthly "parent potluck."

"Phone calls would be made/meetings set up if something needed addressing— again, not often," said Schmidt. "It was mostly the parent potluck support group— Steve and another staff member ran (the group). Attendance was good—probably at 80% or more. I think they laughed a lot—we wanted it to be joyful, not a funeral dirge full of drama! Yes, issues parents/guardians faced were brought up if that's what they wanted to do—but that wasn't the sole purpose. And although I didn't attend except for maybe the first fifteen minutes or so, Steve [Massey] communicated with me regarding a general gist of things for a while until I got so busy—I just assumed all was well with him at the helm, no discussions really needed."

Even though the staff remained all White after that first summer, Schmidt still had a goal of serving more students of color. Of the sixteen students accepted into the school in the spring of 1989, official documents stated "three were of Black origin and one was American Indian. Out of two students who dropped out due to drug use, one was Black. (Hence, our student body of fourteen.)"[16]

The Pillsbury House location on Chicago Avenue had at least two major enrollment limitations. The physical space was limited and projected to have a cap of fifteen students, which they reached in their first spring. Pillsbury House also was not accessible enough to BIPOC and lower-income families. The Powderhorn community may have been more racially and economically diverse than other areas of the Twin Cities, but poverty and people of color were more concentrated in other parts of town, especially North Minneapolis. While the Whitney House residents could ride a van to the Chicago Avenue site, not everybody had reliable transportation there each day or was willing and able to make the trip. Schmidt thus thought they should have a location in North Minneapolis in addition to the Pillsbury House in South Minneapolis to expand and diversify potential enrollment.

The community called "Near North" had long attracted marginalized communities, in part due to its affordable and allowable housing.[17] In the early 1900s, the region was populated mostly by immigrants of Eastern European and Jewish descent.[18] Real estate covenants had limited where Black folks could reside, and Near North became one of the places they settled in the second half of the century. Community organizations and Black-owned businesses blossomed to service Black residents, and by the 1960s, one-third of Minneapolis's Black citizens lived in Near North.[19] The Jewish population had started to relocate to suburbs like St. Louis Park[20]—which would later become home to Sobriety High.

Pillsbury House's parent organization, Pillsbury United Neighborhood Services (PUNS), had been a presence in North Minneapolis since starting Unity House there in 1897—even pre-dating their affiliation with the Pillsbury family. PUNS was formed in 1984 (five years before the opening of the Holos School), when Pillsbury-Waite Neighborhood Services merged with Northside Neighborhood Services, which had recently purchased a Near North neighborhood center on Oak Park Avenue.[21] That center had been a gathering place for the Northside community for forty-five years.[22] The renamed "Oak Park Community Center" describes itself today as a "highly visible, centrally located facility . . . uniquely positioned to support the needs and ambitions of historically underestimated and underserved adults, youth and families."[23] In the summer of 1989, they had space available, and, as it was under the same umbrella as Pillsbury House, Schmidt encouraged her board to lease it for a second P.E.A.S.E. Academy site.

"It was a more impoverished area, quite a few drug issues," said Schmidt—"an attempt at trying to be 'present' within a fairly tough part of the city."

A second site in Near North would raise the ceiling for student enrollment and position the school to reach more students of color. P.E.A.S.E. Academy would now be able to serve twenty-eight students (up to fourteen at each building) and predicted in legal documents "six to eight should be Black, three to four should be American Indian, and sixteen to seventeen should be Caucasian. This is proportional to the minority population in the Twin Cities area."[24] Schmidt felt the North Minneapolis location would attract teachers of color as well, thus helping diversify the staff.

The second site launched during the 1989–1990 school year, but despite the possibilities, most of the goals were unrealized. The enrollment did grow, but it was not as diverse as hoped, and the staff remained essentially the same. There was not enough funding to provide a full staff for each program, so the teachers commuted between the two locations—a fifteen-to-thirty-minute drive, depending on traffic.

"We had two sites," said Massey. "I taught one day at one site and another day at another site and worked back and forth."

The split became a burden and did not increase the number of BIPOC students.

"Alas— [adding a site] didn't work," said Schmidt. "The split was too hard on the staff, and we didn't get any more referrals from North Minneapolis than the previous year."

Schmidt speculated that cultural affinity may have been one reason for the lack of interest from the BIPOC community.

"Native Americans had their own support systems, and there was an alternative school for Native Americans nearby—not a sober school per se, but I'm sure they addressed chemical issues," she said. "Ditto African Americans—they had their own set of alternative schools and connected agencies—had been around a long time. Yes, segregated. On purpose and by choice. I think the feeling was (just a guess): Black people were better able to serve Black people; Native Americans were better able to serve Native Americans. And they may have been right."

Once more, though, Barb Schmidt was able to turn a constraint into an opportunity. With the stress caused by having two sites, and the North Minneapolis location not reaching its enrollment and staffing goals, Schmidt decided to consolidate the two programs back into one school. As Pillsbury House would always have an enrollment cap, she searched for a larger site that would be more accessible to both north and south. Using her Lutheran Church background and network again, Schmidt located space at the University Lutheran Church of Hope in Dinkytown, near the University of Minnesota campus.[25]

The congregation had formed in 1904, laid its cornerstone in 1908, and was in the midst of recovering from a fire when Barb Schmidt contacted Hope's pastor, Mark Hanson. An arsonist had set fire to the lower-level education wing on August 17, 1989, just months before Schmidt approached the church about using its spaces for P.E.A.S.E. Academy.[26] The smoke had caused extensive damage to the sanctuary and forced the members to worship in the fellowship hall during the reconstruction. The fire prompted "renewal and restoration" ideas, and Pastor Hanson was charged with leading the fundraising efforts.[27] Hosting a tenant would help offset some of those costs, but P.E.A.S.E. Academy would have been a fit for other reasons, including the pastor's own priorities.

Pastor Hanson, who would later become president of the Lutheran World Federation, had just taken over the congregation in 1988.[28] A history of the church published in recognition of its centennial noted, "Hanson was drawn to ministry at Hope because it provided an integration of his first two calls: to urban ministry and to a congregation of intellectual people interested in faith exploration and social justice issues."[29]

One of the ways the church had served the community was opening its doors to Minneapolis' Twelve Step programs, hosting meetings for myriad mutual aid groups and even holding the Narcotics Anonymous New Year's Dance each year.[30]

"This church has a long history with the recovery community," said Michael Durchslag. "They just do.... Their connection to the recovery community is part of their mission. I think it has been for a long time."

The congregation had recently passed an "Affirmation of Welcome to all who may have felt excluded."[31] The statement speaks to why the Board would have allowed a school like P.E.A.S.E. Academy to use its space. Here is an excerpt:

> As a community of faith, we know that the world is often an unloving place and that the experience of alienation is all too common.... To those who have felt excluded, we extend a particular invitation to share in God's reconciling activity among us. To the stranger, we offer hospitality. To all, we extend a most heartfelt welcome and wish them continued joy and peace in the Lord.[32]

"I hadn't known that pastor [Hanson] prior," said Schmidt. "But [I] made a phone call, offered a little info about my background, stopped in to see him, and we clicked— a done deal."

Pastor Hanson brought a recommendation to his Board of Commissioners on July 11, 1990. During their regular meeting, the board approved a contract with Holos to provide P.E.A.S.E. Academy space for $500/month ("dirt cheap" according to Durchslag), beginning in August.

"We were part of their mission, you know, as a community outreach," said Durchslag.

The original three-page contract limited enrollment to twenty, which would be only a modest increase over the Pillsbury House. Space would include two large Sunday School classrooms on its second floor with "adults sized tables and chairs in each room," the small kitchen next to the Youth Room, and use of the Youth Room for morning snack time (juice, fruit, toast), break time (two-to-three times a day), and lunch time (Tuesday, Wednesday, Thursday). Mondays and Fridays, the school could only use the building from 8:00 a.m. to noon. Tuesdays, Wednesdays, and Thursdays, the school could stay until 2:00 p.m. Maintenance of the space was emphasized, and the lease stated in multiple places an expectation "that the leased premises are kept in or returned to a condition appropriate for lessee's next school day." As an acknowledgment that smoking was still considered part of a person's re-covery, P.E.A.S.E. Academy agreed to provide "sand pots for the collection of cigarette butts at the west entrance to the building."[33]

With the signing of the lease agreement, P.E.A.S.E. Academy prepared to move out of the Pillsbury United Neighborhood Services buildings and into a new home, where it remains to this day. The partnership between Holos/P.E.A.S.E. Academy and the United Lutheran Church of Hope would allow the school to survive for decades. The church promoted inclusivity, which aligned with Barb Schmidt's philosophy and vision. The disparities of the treatment system still hindered diversification of the school, but the space was accessible, affordable, and expandable. Interestingly, the new school site was in the community where the Southeast Alternatives Project had launched almost twenty years earlier—the recovery school movement had settled into the epicenter of the Minneapolis alternative school movement.

Sobriety High Transitions

P.E.A.S.E. Academy's new location was in fact only three blocks from the Second Foundation School—the small, private alternative school which had been un-satisfactory enough for her son's needs that Carol Robson had decided to start New Dimensions. By 1990, he had matriculated to college, and Carol was contem-plating closing Sobriety High. Her new partner, Ralph Neiditch, wanted to keep it open, though, and he started making major changes, such as bolstering the Board of Directors. These changes would lead Sobriety High to a new city as well as the re-moval of both Bruce McLean and Carol Robson. Similar to the possibilities and limits being experienced at P.E.A.S.E. Academy, both McLean and Robson's experience at Sobriety High would soon move from joy to despair. As a theater veteran, McLean would have been familiar with the image of the laughing and frowning masks repre-senting drama's coexisting comedy and tragedy. The masks together are often called "Sock" (comedy) and "Buskin" (tragedy). The symbols are associated with ancient Greek theater, where actors in tragic roles wore boots called a "buskin," and the co-medic actors wore a thin shoe called a "sock." In the days before microphones, actors wore the appropriate masks to indicate their emotions, and the names of sock and buskin became associated with the masks.[34] After experiencing so much joy at New Dimensions and Sobriety High, Robson and McLean were about to figuratively don the buskin mask.

Treatment historian William White wrote that from 1985 to 1990, addiction treatment was becoming "increasingly concerned about 'special populations'" and more "specialized treatment tracks for women, adolescents, the elderly, gays and lesbians, and the 'dually diagnosed'" were being launched. "Relapse tracks also be-came a common treatment innovation," wrote White,[35] and programs like P.E.A.S.E. Academy and Sobriety High were filling a needed role. An article in *Star-Tribune* had fostered awareness of both Sobriety High and P.E.A.S.E. Academy, and demand was increasing.[36]

McLean had been the centerpiece of the lengthy *Star-Tribune* article. One of the early students was quoted as saying Bruce was her "best friend."[37] There was a noticeable omission in the piece, however. Carol Robson and Ralph Neiditch were not mentioned at all. Considering Robson had created the school, and Neiditch had just taken over as one of the directors, their absence from the article is puzzling.

"They were very pissed at me," said McLean, "because I didn't talk about the other people that were involved."

The article had appeared around the same time Ken Simon and Howard Pearson had observed Sobriety High and came away unimpressed by McLean's pedagogy.

"I can picture him now," said Simon years later. "Kids sat around and did worksheets all day, and then they'd do group. Everything was geared around the group stuff, and nothing was geared around the education. I'm sitting here in education thinking, 'Well, you could do this a lot better,' just educationally."

Simon was not the only person critical of McLean's approach. One student said she left the school in part due to McLean's emotional volatility. Speaking to staff at her former treatment center, the student described Sobriety High as very small, having "ten or twelve kids" and feeling "weird." She claimed McLean would "get so mad and frustrated with us, he'd tell us to go home at noon because he was crying."[38] Ralph Neiditch also reported that McLean did not feel comfortable with him coming to the school, even though Neiditch was in recovery and McLean was not.[39]

Neiditch decided it was time for some changes. He knew their model was not financially sustainable, as they were relying on tuition and had a cap on the number of students they could admit to their one classroom at the Brookside Community Center in St. Louis Park. One of the first steps Neiditch had taken was bolstering the board and cultivating support by inviting both the pragmatic and the wealthy. While working at Hazelden, Neiditch had met Wally Arntzen, the founder of an organization called Help Enable Addicts to Receive Treatment (H.E.A.R.T.). H.E.A.R.T. would pay for treatment if a family could not afford it, and it also helped with other types of expenses and services that might be causing a person difficulty. Arntzen was not wealthy himself, but he knew people who were, including many on the H.E.A.R.T. board.[40]

"They were fundraisers," said Robson. "Wally Arntzen never had any money . . . He had all of these core groups around him, and Ralph knew how to pick friends."

Jim Czarniecki was the director of the Minnesota Museum of American Art in St. Paul in the early 1990s, and he would later take over as director of Sobriety High in 1998. He named a few volunteers who were "responsible for Sobriety High's existence" by playing "hugely significant roles" in its early years:

- Konrad "Kit" Friedemann provided "thousands of hours of pro bono legal services, much of it in completely uncharted waters as policies, practices, rules, and legislation was crafted," starting in 1988;

- Diane Naas, the founder of Professional Recovery Associates in the Twin Cities, whose several hundred pro bono hours each year, starting in 1989, "ensured that our early years worked well and that our recovery support program (was) the most effective possible"; and
- Kirk M., who "insisted on remaining anonymous," donated "well over a million dollars" from 1987–2005.[41]

While Neiditch was building a team that could give Sobriety High a solid financial foundation and a shared vision of quality and growth, that effort was a signal it was time for Robson to step away.

"In order to expand," said Robson, "You have to eventually get a board with a lot of money, and that's when the high rollers came in. They were very happy to take over. I thought it was going to work, but also I'm not a board member type to sit there. I'm a loner, and I start things, and when I started going to the first meetings . . . I knew I didn't fit in with any of those people."

The Sobriety High leadership determined that the school's survival would be aided by moving out of St. Louis Park, and they looked to the newer suburbs for a space. Edina was a growing suburb just to the south, and they realized there were likely more families in Edina who could afford to pay monthly fees. The Edina Independent School District 273 had also suggested they might be interested in contracting with Sobriety High, just as Minneapolis Public Schools had done with P.E.A.S.E. Academy, which would remove the financial burden for families almost entirely. Whereas P.E.A.S.E. Academy's move to Southeast Minneapolis gave it more space and accessibility for diverse families, Edina could give Sobriety High additional space, better access to affluent families, and possibly public-school funds.

The Community Education Services center in Edina had three rooms available, which would accommodate a couple dozen students and three or four staff.[42] Carol Robson had started to put her energy into her other projects, such as Camphill Village, her hobby farm, and a restaurant she owned with her ex-husband, Sheridan. She assumed, though, Bruce McLean would remain the lead teacher for the new space.

"I loved Bruce dearly," she said, "and if you're gonna go big, I wanted Bruce to go."

Neiditch, however, was making other plans. He was ready to replace McLean. Through his work at Hazelden, Neiditch had gotten to know Harry Swift, a Hazelden stalwart who had helped start the family program and was currently serving as its president.[43] Swift had heard of the work Judi Hanson, Denise Martineau, and Pam Leimer at the Team House in downtown St. Paul, where they were providing academic services for adolescents in the residential program. Swift suggested Neiditch contact Hanson about the program.

Judi Hanson had grown up in Minnesota and was in the Henry Sibley Senior High School Class of 1960 in Mendota Heights, about twenty minutes southeast of Minneapolis. After high school, she had gotten married, had two children, and stayed home to raise them for sixteen years before getting divorced. Looking for employment after her divorce, Hanson turned to her alma mater, Sibley High School, where her own children were then students.

"I needed to have a job, and I graduated from that school," said Hanson. "My kids both went to that school, so I knew the assistant principal and the special ed director, and they were like, 'We need people. We need somebody who can do this, this, this, this, and this,' you know."

Hanson was hired around 1983 to cover any job that needed to be done. She watched the gym locker room for one period; she monitored the nurse's office; she helped in the attendance office; and she even walked the halls and checked the bathrooms.

"I was at Sibley working as an aide or an assistant and I had about six different jobs," said Hanson. "Oh, my God, it was such a training ground. And then I was a special ed aide, and I did books on tape before they had that, you know. I'd stay after school and read books with the kids. I worked with special ed. It was a training ground."

Sibley High School was located in School District 197, and by law, the school needed to provide educational services to any student residing within the district boundaries—just as Southwest High School had done for the residents of the Irene Whitney Center. The Warren Eustis House,[44] an extended care program for adolescents who had completed primary care elsewhere, was in School District 197, meaning their school of zone was Sibley. Named after a prominent attorney, the Warren Eustis House had opened in 1980, and it was one of three residential programs operated in Minnesota by the nonprofit Granville House.[45] Granville's mission was to treat "poor people who are victims of chemical dependency," and it was receiving public funds to do so. The oldest program, Jane Dickman House in Woodbury, had opened in 1963 and served women 16-and-older, and Team House, in St. Paul, had opened in 1972 and served men 17-and-over. While Warren Eustis was the only one of Granville's programs exclusively for adolescents, all three had teenage residents.

For the first few years, the Warren Eustis House in Eagan would use a van to drive their residents about ten minutes to Sibley High School during the school day.

"You know how kids come and go in treatment centers," said Hanson, "and you're trying to get transcripts together, and the teachers were just so frustrated, because it was seemingly unorganized . . . The teachers were like, 'Oh, these kids, they just they come, and they go. It's just a pain, you know?' They were in and out too much."

Dr. Paul Larson, Sibley's special education director, oversaw much of this process, and he happened to attend church with Judi Hanson. One day, Dr. Larson had the idea to send teachers to the house instead of having the students come to the school, and he asked Hanson who she thought might be a good teacher for the job. One of Hanson's responsibilities was arriving at Sibley each day to field calls from teachers who were going to be out, as well as communicating with the substitute teachers who would take their places each day.

"So, I kind of knew who was out there," said Hanson. "[Dr. Larson] said, 'Who do you know, on our list of subs that you think I could send out there [to Warren Eustis House]?'"

Judi Hanson suggested the most reliable of all the subs, Denise Martineau, who was a special education teacher.

"I said, 'Whenever I call her, she will take auto [shop]; she will take band; she will do anything.' And I said, 'She can handle it.' And I hadn't even met her much yet."

The Warren Eustis House agreed, and Martineau began teaching at the extended care facility in Eagan. She soon realized she needed help, so Hanson was assigned there too, sometime around 1988. They were joined by math teacher, Pam Leimer, and the three of them essentially operated a school for the residents during their stay.

"It was an old mansion that had, you know, like, beautiful grounds," said Hanson. "It had a swimming pool—it wasn't filled, because it was too expensive, but [the house] was just charming and quaint. And, you know, one cook to cook the food; there was maybe twenty-some kids, you know, it wasn't big. And you just learned to grow, I mean, just learned to understand and appreciate those kids and learned so much."

"We were upstairs in the top floor where they had two lights on the walls, and that's it; we had some tables. It was crazy, but we really got to know [the students] so much and what their fears [were]. [It was] like a good training room because it wasn't too fast. [It] wasn't like, 'Here's fifty kids, fix them,' you know; it wasn't like that."

The multitude of jobs that had defined Hanson's role at Sibley High School were now paying off, as she became a de facto school administrator for the program. Over the next few years, Hanson, Martineau, and Leimer also provided similar services at Granville House's other two programs—Team House (all males) in St. Paul and Jane Dickman House (all females) in Woodbury—while the Eustis House in Eagan remained their home base. Martineau was a licensed special education teacher, Leimer taught math, and Hanson served as the students' educational liaison between the treatment center and their schools, like the work Bruce McLean had done at the ARC program before coming to New Dimensions. Granville eventually sold the Eustis House property and transferred the residents to Team House in St. Paul. Hanson, Martineau, and Leimer followed them there.

"We went, 'Okay, I guess we're moving now," said Hanson.

Word about their efforts made it around the Twin Cities treatment community, and it was after the move to St. Paul that Ralph Neiditch became aware of Hanson, Martineau, and Leimer and their treatment school program.

"Ralph heard from [Hazelden president] Harry Swift that we were doing a really good job with these kids [at Team House]," said Hanson. "We had them four hours a day [for academics], which was quite a bit. The treatment center really invested in a good program."

Sometime during the late summer/early fall of 1990, Ralph Neiditch gave Judi Hanson a call and asked if he could pay a visit to the Team House to see their schooling in action.

"He came," said Hanson. "He talked to us. He just was very interested in how we did what we did, and he said, 'Do you mind if I call you [for suggestions]?' And he did that. For a year, he called me."

Neiditch was studying the treatment school run by Hanson, Martineau, and Leimer, essentially using them as consultants.

"He used to say," Hanson said of his calls, " 'Now, if you had a sobriety high school, what would you do? How many kids would you put in the class? How would you structure the day?' Basically, he keeps asking things, and then he'd say, 'Okay, bye!' You know, he was so funny."

During the course of that year, Hanson and Martineau moved once again to the Jane Dickman House in Woodbury. By then, though, Martineau had decided to go back to regular school. Her husband was having medical issues, and she could get a job at the junior high with better benefits.

"She was worried, you know; she just needed to do more," said Hanson. "So, she left there. And then I wasn't sure what I was going to do."

Then one day in the summer of 1991, after nearly a year of collecting ideas, Neiditch made Hanson an offer. His board of directors had made the decision to move to Edina in the fall, and Neiditch wanted her to take a leadership role at Sobriety High during the transition.

"He called me," said Hanson, "and he said, 'Here's the deal. We're going to have to shut the school down if we don't figure something else out, so I really want to hire you.'"

The decision was a monumental one for Hanson. Hanson had grown tired, as McLean had, of watching kids struggle in their schools after finishing treatment. She had been raised in the Twin Cities suburbs, and she had worked in treatment settings around Minneapolis during the ascent of adolescent treatment, but Hanson did not have a college degree, and she had never run an entire school before.

"At that point, I had been very frustrated," said Hanson. "Transitioning kids mostly to mainstream schools, in which they do not do well, you know. So, I thought, 'Hmm, should I do this? Should I do this big move?'"

One of the things that helped Hanson discern was a class about drugs and health that she had taken around that time at Inver Hills Community College in Inver Grove Heights, Minnesota—about a ten-minute drive from Sibley High School. The instructor was Dave Hadden, who was becoming a trailblazer in the collegiate recovery movement. Hadden would become one of the most influential people in the youth recovery field, helping start the StepUP Program at Augsburg College and cofounding the national Association of Recovery Schools in 2002. At that time, though, Hadden was an adjunct instructor for Hanson's college course, and he had updated the curriculum to cover current drug and alcohol issues across the continuum of care.[46]

"He had us write a paper," recalled Hanson. "I forget the assignment, but I wrote a paper about how I think that it would be cool to have a school for kids in recovery . . . He was a hoot, and he was a character of a teacher."

Hanson had also been influenced by another innovator along the way: Barb Schmidt, whom Hanson met when she was starting Holos.

"Denise [Martineau] and I met with her, and that's what also helped us thinking about the concept."

Hanson had realized what she wanted to do—she wanted to leave the treatment center and go to Sobriety High (see Figure 16.3).

"I thought, 'This is the most hopeful thing I've ever heard about that kids can do in recovery.'"

During the summer of 1991, Neiditch arranged for a meeting for Carol Robson to meet Hanson, Martineau, and Leimer. Neiditch and Robson had already made arrangements to rent space in the Edina Community Education Center. There was only one issue—even though Robson was ready to step away from Sobriety High, Robson thought Bruce McLean would remain. She also did not know that Neiditch had been meeting with Hanson and the others for months.

"I wasn't aware, because I wasn't aware of Judi until he brought me to the meeting," said Robson. "My first meeting was when he brought me up there, and Judi and they were saying, 'I really want to leave the residential facility that we're in,' and they were the ones pressing for my version of the thing that they wanted to start and go on. . . . They were asking to come to the school, and they were unhappy with their residential thing."

After the meeting, Neiditch campaigned hard to bring Hanson on-board and let McLean go.

Figure 16.3. Judi Hanson took over the leadership of Sobriety High in 1991 and oversaw the move of the school to Edina, Minnesota. She would remain at Sobriety High for twenty-two years. (Source: Judi Hanson.)

"He was pushing to get Judi in there," said Robson. "I'm really stressed out, because I loved Bruce dearly."

The decision was made to terminate McLean—the person who had brought the idea of a recovery high school to Carol and Sheridan Robson, and who had been the only staff person featured in the two major newspaper stories written about the school in 1987 and 1989.

"Sobriety High dumped me," said Bruce McLean. In an interview for this book, almost exactly twenty-five years after the fact, McLean still had hard feelings, calling Neiditch "greedy."

"As soon as Ralph Neiditch got control," said McLean, "then it started to get worse, because they're the ones that forced me out."

Bruce McLean's tenure at Sobriety High was over, and the experience caused a rift from which Robson and Neiditch's relationship never really recovered.

"I know that I cried over it," said Robson. "We really had a falling out at that point, and I felt terrible. It was a terrible emotional thing for me. Ralph was more hardened, [saying], 'Well you gotta go on, and you gotta go forward.'"

Despite the rocky introduction, Robson had a positive impression of Judi Hanson.

"She was wonderful," said Robson. "You know how you know instinctively that somebody's a good person, and their heart is in the job of teaching? That was her, as I perceived her at the time."

"I knew that as long as she was involved, the classrooms would be fabulous."

The feeling was mutual.

"She was instrumental," said Hanson. "We really liked Carol and wished we could have talked to her more. But she was never at the forefront [of the meetings]. It was all [Ralph]. But she was the one that gave the money, I'm sure, to pay the three of us for the whole summer to get that thing all moved and put together and, you know, ready to go."

Sobriety High agreed to match Hanson's salary and give her insurance benefits. Denise Martineau had just taken a regular school position, but she was hired as an hourly consultant in special education, and Pam Leimer, the treatment center's math teacher, would also join the faculty. The staff had been completely replaced.

Robson had already started packing a van to move out of their little classroom in the Brookside Community Center, where New Dimensions had operated since 1982 when her son was just eleven years old. There were lots of memories in that space, including mementos of its original purpose as a school for young children with exceptional needs. Hanson, Martineau, and Leimer did the bulk of the packing.

"Our first assignment was to take everything out of that classroom and its storage room and inventory it, and then move it all over to our Edina location," said Hanson. "And along the way, we discovered there were a lot of manipulatives and special ed types of things too."

"The new facility over in Edina . . . was a wonderful one," recalled Robson. "Judi helped to move it. Then I lost touch, because I was out of there."

The emotions caught up with Carol Robson. Over the course of two years, her son had moved onto college, her marriage to Sheridan had ended, she had turned over control of her school, and she had let go of a teacher to whom she was close. Her relationship with Ralph Neiditch was also ending, and the stress led to a recurrence of substance use and a return to treatment for the first time in fifteen years.

"It was a nasty thing that happened during all this stuff with Bruce and everything," said Robson. "I had a relapse, and it led to a bunch of political stuff."

Robson had considered closing the school when her son was no longer a student. Neiditch helped convince her to keep it open, but as he took over, she eventually left for good.

"I got out," said Robson. "I walked away, and that was it."[47]

The transition was complete. Sparked by Ralph Neiditch, a visionary board of directors, and Judi Hanson's steady leadership, Sobriety High had begun its assent to becoming one of the most prominent recovery high schools, growing to multiple campuses and receiving media coverage in national TV and newspaper outlets—and virtually none of the reporting mentioned Bruce McLean or Carol Robson by name. They were effectively written out of the story.

For Robson, however, the enduring memory of New Dimensions/Sobriety High has been a positive one.

"I was always glad that it went on," said Robson. "All I can say is that the evolution with Ken [Simon] and Judi and Bruce, they were all fabulous people, and I don't have a thing to say bad about them. They were wonderful."

A while after she left Sobriety High, Carol Robson started reminiscing with her son about the journey that had begun with his birth on a frosty President's Day in 1971.

"I said, 'You know, having a birth injury with [cerebral palsy],'—and again, I go from a karma background, my own spiritual beliefs—and I said, 'There's always a purpose and a reason.' And I said, 'If it hadn't been for you being stuck in a terrible school and having to pull you out . . . you know, out of necessity, we started this, and look at what it evolved into, a fabulous project.'"

"He looked at me, and he said, 'Yeah, that's good.'"

Epilogue
The Fate of the Schools

Reporter Jane Pauley traveled to Edina, Minnesota, in the spring of 1995, to do a segment for *Dateline NBC* about Sobriety High.[1] By that time, the school had moved again to the site where it would remain for the next twenty years, going from Edina's Community Education Center to a suburban business park building in 1993. This move would give the students some anonymity at the same time the school was positioning itself nationally as the original and premier "sober school."

"Sobriety High is hard to find," wrote Neal Karlen in a *Life* magazine feature. "If you were a stoner trying to pay a surprise visit to a pal just out of drug treatment and now enrolled in the school, you'd never get past the invisible street sign, unnamed cul-de-sac, and nondescript door. They like it that way.... Hidden amid the cookie-cutter office parks of the wealthy Minneapolis suburb of Edina."[2]

The media spotlight, however, had started shining brightly on Sobriety High, thanks to Ralph Neiditch, who had cut his teeth on the New York advertising scene, and a well-connected board of directors. The *Dateline NBC* episode featured interviews with current students and Judi Hanson, who had become the school director, and it culminated with a moving scene from a commencement ceremony. In the era just before social media, Jane Pauley's story resonated in a way that earlier news coverage had not.

Earlier that same year, the popular and well-respected Bill Moyers[3] hosted a four-hour documentary titled, "What Can We Do About Violence?" The special profiled Sobriety High and about a dozen other non-recovery high school programs.[4] While the Phoenix schools had been on a brief national nightly news segment, had a few articles in the *Washington Post*, and received letters from both President Bill Clinton and First Lady Nancy Reagan commemorating it, nothing had the effect beyond the local community like the Jane Pauley and Bill Moyers pieces. Based on the number of recovery high schools, those two media pieces corresponded with a rapid increase of schools. According to data from the Association of Recovery Schools, thirteen recovery high schools began operation in the twenty-two years from 1973 to 1995, including PDAP's GED school. In the next ten years alone, from 1996 to 2006, forty-three recovery high schools opened their doors, and the national association was launched (in 2002). Media exposure is not the only explanation, but the active marketing of Sobriety High beyond the Minnesota area was certainly a factor.

Salvaging a Teenage Wasteland. Andrew J. Finch, Oxford University Press. © Oxford University Press 2024.
DOI: 10.1093/oso/9780190645502.003.0017

Sobriety High believed it was the first (and best) sober school, and it promoted itself as such to prominent media outlets. *Education Week* proclaimed, "It was the first school of its kind in the country."[5] *Life* described Sobriety High as "the country's first high school devoted to teenagers who have come out of chemical-dependency programs."[6] And in announcing the Moyers special, the *Minneapolis Star-Tribune* noted, "Moyers features Sobriety High as the only school in the United States devoted exclusively to teenagers in recovery."[7] The latter story shows the influence of Sobriety High's marketing. The article was written by a staff writer for the hometown newspaper that made the claim about Sobriety High even though, by then, P.E.A.S.E. Academy was six years old. Additionally, a third recovery high school had started in the Twin Cities in 1992—the Gateway Program for Youth in St. Paul.

While this book has shown that the actual lineage of recovery high schools can be traced further back to the Freedom Road School in South Carolina, the PDAP GED School in Texas, and both Phoenix schools in Maryland, the recovery high school movement arguably owes as much to Sobriety High and P.E.A.S.E. Academy as it does to those older programs in other states. While the two Phoenix schools in Maryland had received modest national publicity and lasted over three decades, there is no evidence that they directly spurred the launch of other schools. The two major historical accounts of recovery high schools[8] to date both cite Sobriety High as the first and oldest recovery high school, and only one mentions the Phoenix schools.[9] Neither acknowledged the schools in South Carolina or Texas. This could be because neither Freedom Road nor the PDAP GED School received national news coverage, and both lasted only a few years in the 1970s.

This section will explore what happened to the programs profiled in this book. While Freedom Road and the PDAD GED School did not have long histories, the Phoenix schools, Sobriety High, and P.E.A.S.E. Academy lasted for decades, and P.E.A.S.E. Academy is still operating today.[10] It will take another book to explore the full impact of each of those programs as well as the schools that came after them to build a movement. The schools profiled in this work, though, are the ones that sparked and launched that movement, and the following is an account of their fate.

Freedom Road School—Charleston, South Carolina: 1973–1980

The Freedom Road School, which had changed its name to the Lowcountry School in 1977, closed its doors in 1980 after losing its favorable lease with the Catholic diocese and not finding another suitable space in Charleston County. There were several reasons for the school's demise—detailed in chapter 2—including a less supportive superintendent, federal budget cuts to mental health services, the removal of substance use disorders from South Carolina's special education funding eligibility, and a "not in my neighborhood" response from the community to the school as it sought a new location. The school district would direct future substance use referrals to a more general alternative school.

Just over one year after D. Ceth Mason died from cancer, Sun Medical Corporation, a Charleston-based organization that sought to "provide alternate forms of treatment" while "containing costs," opened the D. Ceth Mason Treatment Center in June 1984. The center provided "innovative" treatment to both adults and adolescents for "drug addiction or behavior problems," but their philosophy of youth addiction focused less on substance use recovery and more on addressing the underlying behavioral issues.[11]

"I have trouble labeling someone that young a drug addict or alcoholic," said Sun Medical executive, Barry Lines. "I can see they have behavior problems that contribute to addictions, but alcoholism takes years to develop."[12]

The D. Ceth Mason adolescent program did not initially provide a school option, but in 1985, the Southern Pines Psychiatric Hospital opened a private high school near Charleston for patients in their Partial Hospitalization Program (PHP). About a year later, in April 1986, the D. Ceth Mason program followed suit by opening a school for its Adolescent Treatment Center (ATC). The D. Ceth Mason ATC school used the Freedom Road school example by contracting with school districts for teachers. Charleston County supplied ATC with a teacher, while Berkeley and Dorchester Counties each supplied an aide for every six children in the program. ATC also used the public-school curriculum, while PHP hired its own teachers and operated under its own policies.[13]

Unlike Freedom Road, in which the treatment services were embedded in the school, both ATC and PHP were schools embedded in day treatment programs, providing "emotionally handicapped children a program that combines academic education with necessary therapy."[14] On a typical eight-hour day at ATC, patients would have therapy and goal-setting sessions plus meetings with their counselors or doctors. Academic studies were individually planned and provided through classroom instruction.[15] The goal for the patients was to maintain their grade level while in treatment. According to Dr. Robert Sinnott, an ATC psychiatrist and medical director, patients would "get more attention than they can get in a special classroom in a regular school, but they don't have to sleep, eat, and spend weekends in a hospital."[16]

The ATC staff would meet weekly and included representatives of various agencies, including the Department of Social Services, the Department of Youth Services, and the Continuum of Care, an agency aimed at "helping children who fall through the cracks of the system."[17] After patients exited the program, staff would follow up through regular meetings with the various agencies and monitored the youth for at least a year, with monthly aftercare sessions and therapy as needed.

Over time, the D. Ceth Mason ATC program expanded to provide long-term psychiatric care, including wrap-around social work, special education, occupational therapy, and counseling services.[18] The program came to be known as the "New Hope D. Ceth Mason Treatment Center," described as an "intensive holistic approach to chemical dependency and psychiatric treatment for adults and adolescents."[19] New

Hope offered six programs, including both adolescent outpatient and day treatment, as well as a residential treatment center. Services lasted from six to nineteen months, and Monday through Friday residents would attend the accredited school at the New Hope Day Treatment Center, located behind the Trident Regional Medical Center.[20] It is unclear how long the PHP school continued operating, but the New Hope program was enrolling students at least through the 1980s as a treatment-embedded school, the last vestiges of the Freedom Road/Lowcountry School. Despite the innovative and groundbreaking nature of Freedom Road, however, to date, no recovery high school has operated in South Carolina since the Lowcountry School closed in 1980.

PDAP GED School—Houston, Texas: 1976–1980

The PDAP GED School in Houston closed soon after John Cates and Bob Meehan left PDAP following Dan Rather's *60 Minutes* expose on the program. PDAP referred to its GED schools as the "PDAP Continuing Education Program," suggesting plans to expand to other cities.[21] According to Cates, PDAP opened GED schools in Dallas and Denver between 1979 and 1980, using a similar design and curriculum as the Houston program. All the programs ceased operation about the same time.

As detailed in chapter 10, John Cates opened new recovery high schools in Texas in the 1980s. In 1986, the nonprofit John Cates & Associates (JCA) opened a private high school called "Sober High" in Richardson, Texas, a suburb north of Dallas.[22] The school changed its name to "Carrington Academy" in 1987, using Cates's middle name, though it continued to be referenced as "Sober High" in some correspondence. That same year, JCA opened a second campus in Ellisville, Missouri, a suburb west of St. Louis. As an entity, JCA called the two schools the "Carrington Schools," and administration occurred from the JCA home office in Texas. The Ellisville Campus closed in 1988 after just one year of operation, and in 1991, Carrington Academy abruptly shuttered its program as well.

Cates did not give up. Texas legalized charter schools in 1995, and the first charter schools opened in the fall of 1996.[23] At the time, two of the four types of charters in Texas were as follows:

- **Campus Program Charters**, authorized and overseen by independent school districts; and
- **Open-Enrollment Charters**, authorized by the State Board of Education (SBOE) as the authorizer.

Cates had started his own program based on the enthusiastic sobriety/recovery model called Lifeway, Inc., based in Houston. In 1997, Lifeway proposed a "campus program charter school" to be authorized and overseen by the Houston Independent School District (HISD).[24] The charter for the "Carrington Academy Charter School" was approved, and the school operated for one year as an HISD charter, meaning its enrollment was limited to students residing in the school district. In its first year, the Carrington Academy Charter School served 130 HISD students, grades 7–12, and two received diplomas.[25]

In 1998, the Foundation for Recovering Youth, another Cates company, applied for Carrington Academy to become an "open enrollment charter school," which would expand enrollment by allowing students residing outside HISD boundaries to enroll in the school. The charter was approved in 1998, with a targeted opening date of January 11, 1999, but on the application, the school's name was changed to "Heights Academy" or "Heights Charter School."[26] That school opened in 1999, but to a more general population, not limited to students in recovery. The recovery high charter school that had existed in 1997–98 had been dissolved.

Cates's schools had gotten increasingly more structured, moving from the original GED program run out of his Rice Village apartment through the Carrington Academy Charter School that had been authorized by the Houston Independent School District. Even though none of the schools existed for long, Cates's programs left a legacy and had a major influence on the recovery high schools of today. The PDAP GED schools from the late 1970s and Sober High/Carrington Academy in 1986 were the first private recovery high school programs.[27]

More importantly, Cates connected all his programs to Alternative Peer Groups—a model that would become more common in the 2000s, especially in Texas. PDAP was the original APG, and Bob Meehan had expanded the model into other states through the 1980s. Cates continued the growth with his Lifeway organization. Cates's schools largely had avoided the cult accusations that had dogged Meehan's groups, even though Cates remained closely associated with Meehan for many years (see chapter 10 for more details). One reason for the difference was that Cates had attained professional counseling credentials to supplement his teaching license, and as APGs expanded, counseling licenses and their requisite ethical standards became typical for APG staff.

One thing that did hound Cates's schools was financial instability. None of the schools lasted formally more than five years, but Cates said he continued providing educational services all along.

"We never had a period that we didn't have a school," said Cates. "What we had was schools shrinking, growing, shrinking, growing, changing names, those kinda things here in Houston."

After the large Carrington Academy Charter School closed, Cates kept things going by hiring a facilitator to work with a smaller number of students in his Lifeway APG program using Texas Tech's charter school distance curriculum. And the program slowly grew.

"We already had the leftovers of what had been the big Carrington Academy," said Cates. "We started off with just a facilitator. We started working with Texas Tech's curriculum; they had their own charter school curriculum. We brought their curriculum in, we put a facilitator in a room—not a teacher just a facilitator—and he would work with those kids. There were about seven of 'em, six or seven of 'em, and we'd fallen to that point. There were about six or seven kids, and he would meet with them from nine [a.m.] to three [p.m.] and help them work on their computerized curriculum, that's what it came down to. As the numbers grew, we got up to about fourteen, fifteen, and a lady [in recovery] who was in the process of training as a teacher . . . took it over and started to add more structure back into it."

By 2004, they had switched from the Texas Tech curriculum and contracted with a charter school network called Southwest Schools, which provided curriculum and staff.

"We started working with the curriculum provided by Southwest Schools in their charter, and we at first tried it with one of their employees being the director of the school," said Cates. "By this time, we'd gone up to two full-time teachers [in addition to the director]."

A new recovery high school, called Three Oaks Academy, had been born, and it would be the longest operating of all Cates's recovery schools. Three Oaks would last for thirteen years and become one of the earliest schools accredited by the Association of Recovery Schools.

Archway Academy

John Cates was also indirectly involved in launching one of the largest and best-known recovery high schools: Archway Academy in Houston. When Lifeway ran into financial complications in the late 1990s—due in part to managed care restrictions on lengths of stay and the investigations of alleged improprieties—a group of parents, led by Lifeway counselor Kirk Campbell, spun off from Lifeway and formed their own APG called Cornerstone. One of those parents was Steve Roberts.

"[My son and I] originally started out in one of John Cates's programs, LifeWay," said Roberts. "It was having some financial and internal struggles. I, along with several other parents, broke off from LifeWay and formed an APG called Cornerstone.

"What convinced me was that Kirk Campbell and some of the other staff weren't getting paid," Roberts continued. "Trust me, I knew nothing about APGs and how they ran or functioned. I just knew I was paying dues or whatever they were and taking my child to meetings and staying there. I'm there [at Lifeway] literally at most three months. All of a sudden, I'm in a meeting with some parent and they said, 'If we don't do something, our kids are not going to have a place to go. So, you want to join us?' I'm thinking, 'What am I getting myself into now?' Next thing I knew we're forming Cornerstone. We leave on the strength of a guy named Kirk Campbell, who basically says, 'Come with me and I'll show you the way.' At that point I was gullible enough to follow anybody that said, 'I would show you the way.' Fortunately, he was the Pied Piper. He knows what he's doing."

Campbell and Dr. Anette Edens led the creation of the Cornerstone APG in 1999, and it was offered space in, of all places, Palmer Episcopal Church—the place where

PDAP had begun almost thirty years earlier, in 1971. One person familiar with the early years of Cornerstone explained how they got involved in education.

"We were just struggling with this idea that the kids would come to Cornerstone, go back to their school, be around their friends all day, and they were the kids that they used with and bought drugs and sold drugs too," they said. "So, we talked to the leadership of [Palmer Episcopal Church] about starting a school."

The parents initially ran the school themselves, using the Texas Tech University High School correspondence curriculum, just as Cates's program at Lifeway had done.

"We had sort of a home-schooled concept," said Roberts, "where kids got up in the morning and went to a location, not their home. They worked a curriculum that was provided by Texas Tech University before proctors. These parents were incredibly involved and dedicated in the program. It really worked well."

Roberts own son completed his diploma in the program, but as the original group of parents moved on, it became harder to sustain. So, they decided to form a board and hire a principal, Jim Williams, whom they tasked with creating a full-fledged recovery high school. They knew they wanted to do something different from their prior experience with Lifeway.

"I had seen some of John [Cates's] programs, and they were not necessarily the types of programs [we wanted to run]," said Roberts. "I had broken away from one of his programs, and clearly I was not interested in following up with that program."

Once the board was formed, things moved quickly.

"I think the board had been developed either the end of 2002 and/or the beginning of 2003," said Williams. "I think they offered me the position in August [of 2003] and we opened in January [of 2004]."

One of Williams's first assignments was to travel with Cornerstone board members to the second annual conference of the Association of Recovery Schools (ARS), being hosted in Minneapolis by Augsburg College's StepUP program, one of the oldest collegiate recovery programs. Unknown to Williams when he agreed to attend the conference was that he was about to be immersed in the origins of the recovery high school movement. One of the conference organizers was Augsburg's assistant director, Dave Hadden, who had cofounded ARS in 2002. Hadden also was the teacher at Inver Hills Community College who had given Judi Hanson the assignment where she envisioned running a recovery high school (see chapter 16). Among the scheduled activities during the conference were field trips to visit Sobriety High, P.E.A.S.E. Academy, and Hazelden. Just a few months later, Archway Academy would open its doors in the basement of Palmer Episcopal Church, where PDAP had started years before.

At that point, there were multiple APGs operating in Houston, many of which had split from Lifeway. Archway made a decision to enroll students from all of them, which eventually allowed its enrollment to reach about one hundred students.

"We had Archway recognize at that time the APGs were not a functioning group," said Roberts. "They were a group of individuals who not always got along with each other. Their leaders like Kirk [Campbell] had broken off from John Cates. When we established Archway, we didn't want to be Cornerstone High School. We didn't want to service just one APG. We wanted to service the community."

In time, Cates's Three Oaks Academy would follow Archway's example by enrolling students from APGs other than Lifeway, and, by 2004, Houston had become a recovery community with multiple APGs and two recovery high schools. Filmmaker Greg Williams featured both the schools in his 2016 documentary *Generation Found*, which introduced recovery high schools to thousands of new people—similar to the impact Jane Pauley's *Dateline NBC* piece had on the movement over twenty years before.[28] That same year, the Association of Recovery Schools recognized John Cates's contributions to the field by honoring him with its Jim Czarniecki Visionary Award at its 2016 annual conference in Austin, Texas—almost exactly forty years after Cates had started providing GED prep services in his Houston apartment.[29]

The Phoenix Schools—Montgomery County, Maryland: 1979–2012

The two Phoenix Schools existed as separate entities, with Phoenix I opening in Silver Spring in 1979, and Phoenix II launching in 1983 in Gaithersburg. Both schools enjoyed long runs, enrolling hundreds of students over thirty-plus years. But in the end, the schools were merged into one program that ultimately closed, in part due to lack of interest. When Phoenix II moved into its new facility in 1988, it occupied a prominent place in Montgomery County. The White House, district leadership, and the media all hailed the program. By all accounts, the schools both hit their stride in the 1990s, developing their own, unique cultures.

Marianne Smyth worked as support staff, with the title of "peer educator," at both schools. She started assisting during summer school at Phoenix I in 1986 before moving over to Phoenix II. Smyth brought a variety of experiences with her to Phoenix, having started her career driving a school bus, working at the Mark Twain alternative school after finishing her bachelor's degree, and then getting a master's degree in counseling, though she did not complete the practicum required to become a licensed school counselor. Her background had prepared her to do a little of everything at Phoenix, and she jumped right in.

"One summer, there was an opening in Phoenix I," said Smyth. "[I said,] 'Oh, okay, I'll do it.' And I fell in love with the kids, with the program.

"We all had to fill in, you know, and do [different things]."

According to Phoenix alum John Edmonds, "[Marianne] was like the den mother of the school."

Smyth was working at Phoenix II when they moved into their new building, though she preferred their original space in the house.

"I kind of liked the old building," said Smyth. "It was real homey."

Smyth worked at Phoenix II for twelve years, and she described a program that worked well. She felt both schools evolved in different directions, but both were successful.

"Sally took over Phoenix II, and Brian kept Phoenix I," said Marianne. "Different philosophies, I guess, would be the best thing I could say.... [Phoenix I] did more in-town cultural things. We [i.e., Phoenix II] were out in the woods. But we were who we were, and we did what we did, and it worked for most of [the students]. I think statistically, we were pretty successful.

"It goes back to creating enough of an environment for the kids to take risks and grow; be held accountable, but yet, feel cared for. And you do it by [the staff] being real. You know how many times I had to say, 'Look, I'm sorry, I really shouldn't have said that,' or blah, blah, blah. Didn't happen too often, but you know, you have to be real with the kids."

In 1994, Constance Morella, who represented Montgomery County in the US House of Representatives, gave a speech on the House floor to recognize the fifteenth anniversary of the Phoenix School. Her words provided evidence to the impact of both schools.

Since its establishment, the Phoenix School has enabled hundreds of Montgomery County students to stay sober and drug-free. Students attend the Phoenix program from 12 to 18 months, after which they return to their home high schools. More than 86 percent who complete the Phoenix program go on to complete their high school studies, and many go on to college....

The Phoenix School has two locations. The Silver Spring campus is under the able auspices of the founder of the Phoenix School, Brian Berthiaume. Sally Eller is the coordinator of the Gaithersburg campus and an advocate of early diagnosis and treatment as the best prevention for the disease of alcoholism and drug addiction. The Phoenix School, with its innovative approach to helping teenagers overcome alcohol and drug abuse, is a model for the rest of the Nation. I am proud that this outstanding school is in the district that I represent in Congress. I extend my heartiest congratulations and best wishes to the school in celebration of its 15th anniversary, and I wish the winning combination of counselors, health professionals, faculty, parents and students continued success in promoting new programs and ideas to fight drug and alcohol abuse among teens.[30]

That success would continue into the twenty-first century, until disaster struck Phoenix II on Sunday night, May 6, 2001. The school year was nearing its end, and they were already making plans for commencement in a few weeks. Teacher Mike Bucci remembered being at home that night watching *The X-Files*, when a promotion for the ten o'clock news came onto the screen.

"A fire at a local school," Bucci recalled from the report. That was how he first heard the Phoenix II facility had been set on fire by arsonists.

Sally Eller had been out sick that entire week.

"I'd actually been in the hospital, so I wasn't happy," said Eller. "I'm laid down on Sunday night, and I get this call that says the school was on fire. I don't remember who called me, but it was Mike Bucci or the school system or the fire department. I guess the fire department would've called, I don't know . . . I went there, and the school was in flames."

An investigation determined the fire was lit in the back of the school, near a wooded area. According to a media account, a trained sniffing dog detected a petroleum-based product had been used to accelerate the fire.[31]

Capt. Jim Resnick, a spokesperson for the Montgomery County Fire and Rescue said the fire caused $1 million in damage, and he noted, "[The petroleum] and the volume of the fire leads us to believe that it was not an accidental fire."[32]

Since school was not in session, there were no injuries, but it required seventy firefighters, eighteen tanker trucks, and about forty minutes to extinguish the blaze.

Bucci left his house immediately that night to go to the school, and he remembers watching it burn.

"I'm standing at the [site]," said Bucci. "I'm watching the fire and the firemen with the superintendent of schools, you know, and making plans with him that day for taking care of the kids."

The staff decided they would meet with the students at the school on Monday morning.

"They probably could have canceled school," said Bucci, "but we decided that that wasn't probably the best thing. You know, the staff pretty much [had] to hold up the kids.

"We were all devastated."

The Washington Times reported, "Students spent part of Monday together walking the fenced-off perimeter of their school, which fire reduced to roofless walls and blistered, blackened beams."[33]

"I am very good at shutting my emotions off," said Bucci. "I don't know if that's a plus or a minus . . . So, we met at the [Judith A. Resnick] Elementary School [on a hill overlooking the Phoenix II site] and gathered everybody together . . . We stood on the hill, all the staff and students, and held hands in a line and . . . one of the things that I would do frequently was tell the story of the name behind the school, and the Iranian/Persian story of the phoenix who lives it's life, and when it's time, you know, just builds a nest and lights itself on fire to be born anew, more beautiful. And I told that story, and we didn't have class that day."

Nobody was ever charged in the fire, though the staff and students suspected it was started by a student who once attended the school.

"I think someone probably did it because they were mad," said a former student. "They don't realize the teachers are here to help them."[34]

A current student echoed the phoenix story, saying, "We have to rise from the fire, and whoever set this fire, we've learned we have to pray for them. I owe my life to this school."[35]

"Supposedly, they never found out who did it," said Eller, in an interview for this book. "I imagine the kids know … I'm pretty sure it was set by a student. It started in the part of the school where my office was and that kind of thing. I imagine they probably didn't really realize what they were doing. I don't know if their intent was to burn the whole school down."

"We don't know who did it still to this day. [Probably] a local kid," said Bucci. "We had built some benches, partly as an outdoor gathering space; partly as a way to commemorate, because kids die. Kids die from this disease. Kids died during our program, after our program. So, there were markers of remembrance there in this place. And with these benches, and over the weekend it was a nice place for kids to party. You know, we'd show up Monday morning, and there would be beer cans. Were they our kids or not? Can't pick up alcohol very well on urinalysis; [we] rely on honesty, you know; these are kids that are in recovery, their honesty is always in question—trust but verify."

Marianne Smyth could not imagine one of the Phoenix School students setting the fire. "They think that one of the neighborhood kids caused the fire," said Smyth. "It was arson. I think Sally or somebody [had] chased the kids from the [basketball court]. They could play basketball all they wanted, just not when we were, when the kids were there. And I think she made some kids angry, and they came back and torched it. I can't imagine any of our kids doing that."

While the investigation progressed, school began again on Tuesday morning in extra classroom space provided by the Longview School in Gaithersburg. The move represented a radical shift for the Phoenix II school community—from a relatively new facility that had been built expressly for them to an elementary school building constructed in 1950 as a segregated school. The original name for that school had been the Emory Grove Consolidated Colored Elementary School, and in 1961, the school became a school for children with disabilities.[36] Ironically, the Department of Alternative Programs had transferred Marianne Smyth from Phoenix II to Longview a few years earlier to work in the Journey Program for students with severe disabilities. She was working there when the fire occurred.

"I don't know if burnout is a strong enough word," said Smyth. In her final weeks at Phoenix II, she had been experiencing fibromyalgia, which is a chronic disorder that causes pain, fatigue, and sleeping trouble, which she attributed in part to the stress of working in a recovery high school for over a decade. "It was time to move on."

"But it's funny," said Smyth. "We were in housed at [Longview]. . . , That's where Phoenix II came. It was African American. It was a segregated school. It's one of the oldest buildings. The main populace there were kids with severe handicaps. Our little Journey Program, I think we had two classrooms at the end of the building. So, it was particularly difficult for me, because they would bring things in [from the burned Phoenix II site], so the whole hall would smell like fire and smoke. And I'd hear the familiar voices of Mike [Bucci] and you know, but I wasn't part of them anymore."

As fate would have it, plans had already been in the works before the fire to relocate Phoenix II to the Longview building. Dr. Jerry Weast had become MCPS superintendent in 1999, with a mandate to close the achievement gap between diverse populations.[37] He submitted a memo to the Board of Education that provided a historical context for consolidating alternative schools:

> In February 1999, the Board of Education received a report from the Work Group on Alternative Programs that was charged with the responsibility of conducting a comprehensive analysis of existing alternative program services. This work group produced a report that made several recommendations to refine the entry/exit process, develop a continuum of alternative program services, and establish regional facilities to meet the needs of some of the students served by the various alternative programs.[38]

As Mike Bucci recalled, "[The district said] we want to consolidate these alternative programs because the kids don't have a media center or a science lab, you know, and they need that for their high school assessments, and administrators are being evaluated on how many, what percentage of kids pass these tests."

The use of standardized tests to evaluate teachers and determine if a school was "passing" or "failing" had been growing since the *A Nation at Risk* report in 1983, and in January 2001, President George W. Bush had proposed the No Child Left Behind (NCLB) Act as one of his first actions in office. Representative John Boehner of Ohio introduced the act as H.R. 1 on March 22, just six weeks before the Phoenix II fire. It would become law in January 2002. School reform thus provided the backdrop for all decisions regarding Phoenix, and some school administrators were wary of small alternative schools with limited access to resources.

Sally Eller felt the environment was not favorable for a school like Phoenix. "I saw the handwriting on the wall," said Eller, "with the new superintendent [Weast] who was coming in and made many statements about how he wasn't going to support alternative programs, et cetera."

Izzy Kovach taught science and social studies at Phoenix II from 1996 to 2005. She described the strengths and limitations of a specialized school like Phoenix.

"It certainly met all of the objectives," said Kovach. "We used the county curriculum, but we couldn't offer, you know, the range of subjects that a regular high school could. I mean, we didn't have facilities to do lab work. So, rather than teach biology or chemistry, we would, you know, do more ecology to meet science credits. Our math teacher, you know, he could cover all of the fields. He would work with students individually, whatever classes they needed. We couldn't offer art or music, but the classes that we were able to offer were first rate."

The destruction of the Phoenix II building facilitated the consolidation process. The board decided to rebuild the facility, but during the re-build, Phoenix needed a home. So, the district moved forward with opening the first consolidated, regional alternative high school center in its "upcounty" area in September 2001. Students from the Longview School for special education eventually would be moved to a building in Germantown, and Longview's former Gaithersburg site adopted a new name, the

"Emory Grove Center."[39] Phoenix II would remain at the Emory Grove Center, along with the Journey and Gateway alternative programs. Phoenix II thus had become a "school-within-a-school."

Bucci compiled a history of the Phoenix Schools a few years after the consolidation, trying to shine a positive light on the change. "Many community members made contributions to make the transition as painless as possible, especially the staffs at our new school site," wrote Bucci. "Parents, students, and staff were concerned that the mission of the school would carry on, as the plans were to create an alternative school center at Longview School. The Board of Education has recommitted itself to keeping Phoenix as it was, a 'school within a school.'

"Two other alternative programs—Gateway and Journey—were combined into Emory Grove and occupy one end of the building, while Phoenix is in a different wing. We share a cafeteria, media center, computer lab, gym, science lab and administrative staff. Ms. Maniya DesRoches has been our building's administrator since the programs have moved together, guiding us through our growing pains."[40]

The pains never really subsided. Housing three alternative schools in one building, only one of which was focused on recovery, posed challenges that the school had not faced in its own, stand-alone facility. Bucci recalled, "We fought really hard to have a wing for the kids that were involved in recovery instead of the kids, you know, that they were using [drugs] with two years ago or six months ago or whatever. Which they rode on the bus together and then went down their separate line. 'Oh you, I have to take your urinalysis, and you don't.' You know, kids' seriousness about recovery goes up and down."

Sally Eller had been leading Phoenix II over eighteen years, since it opened in 1983, and the transition proved too much for her.

"It's a hard program to run," said Eller. "You have to learn a lot of things. It's not easy. I think they turned it into an alternative school where you could just push the kids who weren't doing anything in high school. Their parents insisted they have the school system provide some kind of school into them, so they push them into these alternative programs which don't have any real clear focus. . . . They all had drug issues. It's just that the parents didn't want to admit that. They would go to one of the other schools.

"Then, I think, they started integrating us some with that. It didn't work because students had to have a place where they felt safe, where they felt people understood their problem or [were] helping them. They didn't want to be mixed in with kids that didn't want to admit they had any kind of drug or alcohol problem, or maybe didn't have, although I always was skeptical of that."

In November 2001, about six months after the fire, Eller decided she could no longer continue.

"I had put in my thirty years in teaching," said Eller. "I was at retirement age, so I chose to retire. My husband felt I was getting totally stressed out. It was not a very good situation, as I said, in that school after the fire. I could retire, so I did."

Interestingly, Brian Berthiaume, the Phoenix School founder and the person who had originally hired Eller, also left Phoenix I in 2001, about a month after the fire that destroyed the Phoenix II building. Over the years, the two schools had become increasingly siloed, and Berthiaume and Eller had grown further apart. As time went by, Berthiaume said he had also gotten crossways with their boss, Director of Alternative Programs Charles D'Aiutolo. Steve Baddour, the first teacher Berthiaume had hired in 1979, was still at Phoenix I, and he reflected on Berthiaume's last years there.

"When Brian left, and he's probably told you about this, administration was never his strength," said Baddour. "He would always rather have been with the students, and doing counseling and so forth, which he really loved, and I think he was really good at. There at the end, it just seemed like a lot of . . . I don't know, it's very interesting."

Baddour suggested one of the changes that occurred in the late 1990s was that the district made it more difficult to remove students who were actively using, and Berthiaume had pushed back about that.

"I feel like I can remember being in a group, and feeling like, 'This isn't a real group,'" recalled Baddour. "Too many of these kids are using, and the ones who are sober, aren't going to open up in front of them, and the ones who are using, they aren't going to open up at all."

"I didn't like to deal with the administrative things either," Baddour added, "but I think I was better [than Berthiaume] at, 'give them what they want, so they stay off my back.' When I look back on it, I do think a lot about, why do these people think about fighting for their turf, and this and that. Some battles were worth it, and the battle to keep a sober school, was a good one. Brian was right. When we couldn't get rid of kids who refused to remain sober, it really had an impact."

In July 2001, things came to a head, and Berthiaume was transferred to a different alternative program.

"They got rid of me," said Berthiaume. "They moved me out to a program where they made me the principal of (a) school with violent kids [the Muncaster Challenge Program],[41] and I got out of there as quick as I could because my verbal, develop-a-relationship approach didn't work with middle school violent kids. You have to be more, kind of intimidating, and have authority, and all that kind of stuff. I was more on the personal-level thing."

The district replaced Berthiaume with the person who had been the instructional specialist at the Muncaster Challenge Program, Stephen Durand.[42] Berthiaume searched for a new position and found one doing transition support services at Albert Einstein High School in Kensington. For the next two years, Berthiaume conducted social skills counseling groups for developmentally disabled students, including those with autism and Asperger's syndrome, and he provided students with job training experiences in the community. He worked at Einstein High School until he retired from MCPS in 2003.

"After they transferred me," Berthiaume recalled, "[Phoenix] was my baby, and I was so invested in it; it was really traumatic. It was like losing your family. And I didn't want anything to do with it at all. So, I divorced myself. I didn't go and visit or anything."

Thus, by 2002, both Brian Berthiaume and Sally Eller were no longer involved in recovery high schools, and the Phoenix School facility that had gotten the attention of First Lady Nancy Reagan had burned. Phoenix II parents were so concerned about the school's future at Emory Grove that they crowded the Board of Education meeting on May 14, 2002. Seventeen people testified that night during the public comments section, and twelve of them spoke on behalf of Phoenix II. One parent said, "The door opens, a breeze comes in, and my son smells marijuana."[43] During the meeting, the superintendent and school administrators from Emory Grove responded to questions from the board about Phoenix II, and the testimony was largely positive. A table was presented showing data since the move, highlighting "the significant improvements made by the Phoenix II students in the areas of withdrawal from school, attendance, suspension, serious incidents, and recommendations for expulsion."[44] Oddly, the table did not include any data about drug use. In the end, the administrators promised the board and the parents to make changes to assure the safety of students in the future, and parents felt heard.

"We got everything that we wanted today," a parent told a newspaper reporter.[45]

Based on the tone of the board meeting, the MCPS administration felt consolidation was the way to proceed. The minutes suggested Phoenix II had even improved its situation with access to more staff and "state-of-the-art" facilities, and Phoenix I was about to be placed on the same path. Later that year, the board approved a similar program as part of the FY 2003–2008 Capital Improvements Program request for the McKenney Hills Center in Silver Spring, "to provide students in the downcounty area with access to the same services."[46]

The programs to be consolidated in the McKenney Hills Center included Phoenix I, which would be moved from the only home it had ever known, in the Spring Mill Center; the NEW School, housed in the Takoma Park Elementary School annex; and Tahoma, housed in the Lynnbrook Center annex in Bethesda. Six programs would have to be moved out of McKenney Hills to accommodate the change.

Superintendent Weast wrote, "By consolidating these programs, a more rigorous instructional program can be implemented, and a more comprehensive curriculum will be available."

The die was cast. When the school year began in September 2003, Phoenix I was operating in the same building with other alternative schools (the NEW School and Tahoma) for the first time in its twenty-four-year history.[47] And in another cruel blow to Phoenix II, after the county rebuilt its former facility on Hadley Farms Drive, Phoenix II was not allowed to move back in. Instead, it remained a "school-within-a-school" at the Emory Grove Center.

Enrollment at the two Phoenix schools steadily declined over the next few years. MCPS released a report stating that, by October 31, 2008, enrollment for Phoenix at McKenney Hills Center (Phoenix I) was only five students, and Phoenix at Emory Grove Center (Phoenix II) had only seven students.[48] The recovery high schools that had maintained rolls of twenty five to thirty students, with waiting lists of thirty or more for decades, now had a total of twelve students *combined*. The next year, MCPS consolidated alternative programs once again, pulling several alternative school programs into the existing Mark Twain school in Rockville. The two Phoenix programs were combined, moved to Mark Twain, and absorbed into the Needwood Academy High School Alternative Program. In fall 2009, Mark Twain was renamed the "Blair G. Ewing Center," honoring the longtime board of education member who had died of cancer that summer.

The Phoenix School thus had returned to being a single program, as it had been from 1979 to 1982, and it was now called "Phoenix at Needwood Alternative School." Advocate Patty Winters studied the decline of the Phoenix School in the early 2000s, and she prepared a public comment document for the MCPS board of education.[49] Winters outlined several challenges faced by Phoenix resulting largely from the decision to consolidate alternative school programs:

1. Policies, hiring staff, and registration requirements that were originally handled by the program coordinator were eventually defined by a central office administrator, resulting in students abusing or selling drugs being allowed into the Phoenix School;
2. Some principals referred students using or selling drugs to Phoenix;
3. Funding initially provided for staff training was ended;
4. Funding initially provided for outdoor excursions with staff and wilderness experts was ended; these field trips contributed heavily to students' self-esteem and motivation to stay sober, and helped staff stay charged; and
5. County and state test scores became a higher priority within MCPS, and the Department of Alternative Programs and resources went toward the consolidation of alternative programs, losing the integrity of the Phoenix program and its successes.[50]

"Consequently," wrote Winters, "the tight community was no longer intact, and students striving to live drug free shared school buses, cafeteria time, and gym, laboratory, and other classes with peers who were not. The net effect over time was that both school personnel who had been referring families and students to Phoenix and families needing a recovery school saw that the critical pieces of the original successful model were lost in the co-location model, and so they were not willing to try it. Referrals and enrollment predictably dropped until only four students were enrolled in the 2012–2013 school year."[51]

MCPS did list Phoenix at Needwood Academy as a "Level 2 High School Recovery Program" in its 2013 long-range planning document, but with almost no families choosing to enroll at Phoenix, the school effectively ceased operations after the 2012–2013 school year.

"[It had] evaporated away," said Sally Eller. The county that Dr. Richard Towers had once considered a "lighthouse district" had extinguished the flame on one of its shining programs, thirty-four years after it began. It was somehow fitting that Phoenix closed not long after moving to a building named for a board member, Blair

Ewing, who had voted against approving the Phoenix/Model Drug Program after the drug raids of 1978.

By the time the school closed, none of its original staff were still involved, and both Berthiaume and Eller had been gone for over a decade. But their programs had left a legacy. The Association of Recovery Schools honored both of them with the 2017 Jim Czarniecki Visionary Award at their annual conference in Washington, DC.[52]

Mike Bucci left Phoenix II in 2004, but he continued to advocate for a recovery high school in Montgomery County. In his history of the school, written not long after the fire, Bucci wrote the following:

> Phoenix alumni include professors, doctors, lawyers, a bouncer at the 9:30 club, musicians, MCPS employees, soldiers, and "ordinary" folks. They also include those in prison and those who have been buried. At the Hadley Farms property, a group of benches are near memorial stones families have placed to remember their children, lost to this disease.[53]

One Phoenix II alumnus, John Edmonds, even opened his own recovery high school in Frederick, Maryland, in 2020, during the COVID-19 pandemic. That school was a private school located outside Montgomery County, but he preserved the memory of his alma mater by naming the new school "Phoenix Recovery Academy."

Sobriety High—Edina, Minnesota: 1987–2011

While the Phoenix Schools in Maryland were named after a mythical bird that set itself on fire, only to emerge as a new, more beautiful bird, Sobriety High's ending resembled another mythological character with wings—Icarus. According to Greek mythology, Icarus's father, Daedalus, had made him feathers that allowed him to fly. Daedalus warned Icarus "to take the middle way, in case the moisture weighs down your wings, if you fly too low, or go too high the sun scorches them. Travel between the extremes." Icarus did not heed his father's warning, and when he flew too close to the sun, his wings melted, causing Icarus to plummet from the sky and into the sea, where he drowned.[54] The story has long served as a cautionary tale of hubris, and it can be argued hubris both spurred the climb and hastened the fall of Sobriety High.

In the early days of the recovery high school movement, Sobriety High garnered more attention than any other. Media attention, most notably from the Bill Moyers PBS special in January 1995 and the Jane Pauley *Dateline NBC* profile in June 1995, sparked schools in multiple states, including California, Texas, and Tennessee.[55] This was by design. As Carol Robson had said, when Ralph Neiditch took over, he assembled a group of "high rollers" with the intent of raising significant funding. Part of the strategy was to promote the school, and eventually to expand the number of campuses, and thus increase enrollment. As a contracted school, Sobriety High received funds from the Edina school district for each student enrolled, so with more students would come more funding. According to an internal report from the fall of 1994, the school had enrolled five students their first September in Edina. That grew to thirty-one in September 1994, and they projected an enrollment cap of forty-five that year. That report stated this rationale:

> We have consciously limited the size of our student body to maintain the quality of our program . . . Although the number of students we may potentially serve is limited, we have demonstrated success at aiding maintenance of sobriety and providing an opportunity to achieve high school graduation. Future goals of our organization are to expand to multiple sites where a duplicate program may be offered in order to increase the number of potential students served.[56]

This statement was an early indication that Sobriety High had realized there was demand for its services, and it would need to expand to meet the demand. In time, the conscious limitation of enrollment faded as costs grew for facilities and staff. The school had moved from a low-cost community center to a wealthy suburban business park site in 1993 that almost tripled its rent.[57] Neiditch also felt it was important that Sobriety High project an elite image.

"We had these big galas, and it was a big deal," said Judi Hanson. "[Neiditch] had to have the pomp and circumstance. And the diplomas that he had for the school right before I came were beautiful wood with bronze plaques engraved. They were just incredible. Oh, my God!"

One of the consequences of the move to Edina, though, was that it became more challenging for Ralph Neiditch, who lived almost an hour away in Chisago County, to get to the school. Judi Hanson said he also struggled with depression, and by 1995, he came into the school less and less.

"He was a crazy, crazy man. He was a big addict who had moved out of New York, so he would drive in from Chisago in a little Mazda, and he did not know how to drive very well," said Hanson. "There were days he'd say, 'I just can't come in today.'"

Neiditch and the Sobriety High board of directors, which he had helped build, parted ways in 1995. He told Hanson, "I'm leaving one of the best places I've seen, and you're doing a great job."[58]

The course Neiditch helped chart for Sobriety High, however, was already in motion. In September 1995, the board amended its bylaws to expand its size and parent involvement, and it moved Sobriety High's registered address from Neiditch's home office in Shafer, Minnesota, to the Edina site.[59] Hanson served as director until the board hired Jim Czarniecki to become chief executive officer in 1998. Czarniecki had been the director of the Minnesota Museum of American Art in St. Paul, and he described himself as a "son and brother of alcoholics and an addict."[60] Jim Czarniecki had a vision to take an already established concept and develop it, and his influence on recovery high schools would be profound.

"My work is to raise the profile of recovery schools among policymakers and bring an already successful idea to a wider realm of influential people," said Czarniecki.

"It is much more about developing, expanding, and funding recovery schools than inventing them."[61]

One of Czarniecki's first steps was adding a second campus, which opened in Oakdale, Minnesota, just east of St. Paul, in 1999. The Oakdale campus was thus called "Sobriety High East," and the Edina campus became known as "Sobriety High West." Each campus would have a capacity of about forty students. While they existed as separate schools, Sobriety High officially operated as one school with two sites, which allowed it to pool its public funding. The organization was savvy in how it funded the schools, using private donations, district contracts, and state and federal grants to cover its costs. The foundation under Czarniecki's leadership launched a capital campaign called *The Campaign for the Second Decade,* which raised $850,000. Private donations for the school doubled from 1998–99 (just under $300,000) to 1999–2000 (just under $600,000). Having a second campus ballooned state funding as well, as Sobriety High went from $172,000 annually with one campus to over $600,000 in 2000–01 with two.[62] By 2001, there were eleven recovery high schools in Minnesota alone, and Sobriety High was the figurehead. The *Star-Tribune* called Sobriety High a "sober school icon."[63]

"Its annual report cites supportive parents, alumni, corporations and foundations, and coverage by *Life* magazine, PBS and the Sunday Times of London," wrote staff writer Pat Doyle. "It awards its own diploma and pays its own teachers, several of whom have stayed for years despite salaries lower than those paid by nearby schools."[64]

Czarniecki's expansionist vision also was embraced by the board.

"Our vision: Within a few years, we would like to have a school within all the congressional districts in the state," board member Doug Wallace told the *Star-Tribune.*[65]

The board targeted prominent politicians to build political capital in hopes of generating funding and establishing favorable policies. Governor Arne Carlson attended the 1995 commencement, First Lady Terry Ventura attended a campus ribbon-cutting ceremony, and Senator Mark Dayton and Representative Jim Ramstad supported funding legislation for the school.[66]

As the school expanded, it did not stop with Minnesota, sharing its design with planners in other states. Bill Cirone, the superintendent of schools in Santa Barbara County, California, worked closely with Czarniecki and the Sobriety High staff to create a public recovery high school in his district, called Summit High School, that opened in 2005.[67] The Sobriety High foundation also worked with Fairbanks Hospital in Indianapolis to help start Hope Academy in 2006.

One of Czarniecki's most ambitious projects was with Massachusetts legislators. William Ostiguy, then head of the employee assistance program at the Boston firefighters' union, was researching programs to help the families of firefighters whose children had substance use problems.[68] Having heard about Sobriety High, Ostiguy contacted Hanson for information, and she connected him with one of her students who had relocated from Massachusetts for treatment.[69] When the student returned home to Massachusetts for summer break in 2004, Ostiguy set up a meeting with the student, Boston Mayor Thomas Menino, State Senator Steven Tolman, the chairperson of the Interagency Council on Substance Abuse, and the executive director of the Gavin Foundation. These efforts led to the state government creating a five-year grant in 2006 for three recovery high schools, which opened in October 2006.[70]

Sobriety High even promoted its model internationally. Larry Schmidt had taught English at the Edina campus since 1993, and he had contributed much to curriculum development and classroom methods across several subjects, which he had shared widely with the other Minnesota schools and treatment centers.[71] In the summer of 2002, seven students from Arzamas, Russia (about three hundred miles east of Moscow), traveled to Minnesota to visit Sobriety High, and Schmidt worked with them to translate the school's curriculum into Russian. The following spring, Schmidt and Denise Martineau, who was then working at the East Campus, traveled to Arzamas to help develop a recovery high school there. While no school ultimately opened there, the planning represents the first known effort to start a recovery high school outside the United States.[72]

Most of Sobriety High's attempts to grow, however, were focused on Minnesota, and those efforts started to upset both legislators and other school leaders. In an annual report, Sobriety High called its approach the "UnCommon School Initiative": "an aggressive expansion plan designed to increase public sector support."[73] Contract alternative schools like Sobriety High did not receive the full per pupil allocation, because private organizations were excluded from federal education funding, property taxes, and certain other forms of state aid. In 1999, State Representatives Tim Mahoney and Mark Buesgens coauthored a bill (House File 1330) for $2 million to fund sober schools.[74] The bill did not pass, but in May 2000, the state legislature did provide a one-time appropriation for one new rural school, the United South Central (USC) Sober School in Freeborn, and $385,000 to Sobriety High to "expand and demonstrate that its . . . outcomes could be replicated and maintained."[75]

According to their annual report, Sobriety High had been extended an "invitation" to return to the legislature in 2001 for more funding. Even though there were at least eight other sober schools in Minnesota at the time, the bill was designed so that only Sobriety High met all the requirements: a contract school, no more than forty-five students per site, a 12–1 student-teacher ratio, no closer than a mile to other secondary schools, at least $250,000 raised in non-state funds for capital projects, and accreditation by the North Central Association of Colleges and Schools.[76]

Sobriety High advocate Morgan Fleming told the *Star-Tribune,* "we meet it all, of course. No surprise."

The bill was not funded, and the attempt generated animosity. One legislator, Mike Wilhelmi, exclaimed, "We were told it was a one-year project [in 2000] . . . that they would not be back." According to Wilhelmi, the new 2001 request had generated "hard feelings."[77]

Other sober school administrators were not happy with the legislation either.

Paul Grehl, who ran the Gateway Program for Youth in St. Paul said, "There are many schools currently doing this very thing, and they don't require one extra penny."[78]

With the failure of the bill, Sobriety High was not able to open a planned campus in Duluth, and animosity would linger between Sobriety High and a few other recovery high schools for years to come. At the same time, the Oakdale city council denied a request to expand its East Campus site, forcing the school to look for a new building, which it found a few miles away in Maplewood.

Sobriety High underwent a transformation in 2003 when they hired Lyle Taipale. Taipale had worked at a treatment center as a teacher and liaison between the home schools and students, similar to what Judi Hanson, Denise Martineau, and Bruce McLean had done earlier in their careers. Frustrated by students' heavy return to use after treatment, Taipale convinced the St. Paul school district to add "chemical health" counselors in the high schools.[79] Later, after Sobriety High and P.E.A.S.E. Academy set examples as recovery high schools, Taipale helped start the Gateway Program for Youth in St. Paul, and Paul Grehl was hired to run it in 1992. Gateway was the third recovery high school in Minnesota, and Taipale and Grehl envisioned the program as an extension of treatment while students transitioned to school. Like P.E.A.S.E. Academy in its early days, Gateway was intended to be a short-term placement for students—a much more clinical and therapeutic-based environment than Sobriety High's recovery support approach. Taipale had accepted an offer to become the director of alternative programs for the Mounds View Area Learning Center—about fifteen miles north of St. Paul—and in 1995 he started another recovery high school there, called the Arona Campus.

Arona's model was more like Sobriety High, and in 2003, Jim Czarniecki offered Taipale the position of chief academic officer. He accepted and became part of implementing major changes. First, the organization split the foundation off from the school and created two separate governing boards: the Sobriety High Foundation would have a Board of Trustees, and Sobriety High would have a Board of Governors. Jim Czarniecki would remain the CEO of Sobriety High, overseeing policies, budgets, and data collection. Czarniecki also was appointed president of the foundation, whose goal was to support and sustain sober schools. At first, that was only Sobriety High campuses, but over time, the design allowed for the Foundation to support other recovery high schools as well. The mission of the Foundation was to provide a sober school in any community that wanted one, and with the help of US Representative Jim Ramstad, who identified as a person in recovery, the Sobriety High Foundation secured a $400,000 federal earmark in 2003.[80]

Next, Sobriety High was granted the status of a charter school by the Intermediate School District 917 in Dakota County, about twelve miles south of Edina, with plans to open a third campus in Burnsville. Minnesota had become the first state to pass a charter school law in 1991, allowing groups of parents, educators, and community members to create new public schools.[81] Recovery high schools initially had avoided applying for charters, as one requirement of the charter legislation was that schools had to accept all applicants up to their enrollment capacity. This meant schools could not screen out students based on their recovery status. Other aspects of charter schools, however, were appealing, such as being independent of most state regulations. Most importantly charter schools were considered "public schools," while contract alternatives were considered "private schools." As such, contract alternatives received a percentage of the per pupil allotment for local schools, and that was it. Charter schools, by comparison, received a higher percentage of the per pupil funding, as well as 90% of the cost of a lease ("lease aid"), and special education funding for qualified students. One estimate suggested the school would increase its funding from $5,200 to $7,500 per student as a charter school compared to being a contract alternative.

The Burnsville campus thus opened in Dakota County as Sobriety High South in the fall of 2004, and all three campuses operated under the same charter.[82] That school adopted the name "Alliance Academy," though people continued to refer to it as "South Campus." Sobriety High now had three schools, and the Foundation also invested in an expansion of the West Campus in Edina, increasing its capacity to fifty-five. But Jim Czarniecki still felt they had only scratched the surface.

"There are 21,000 chemically dependent teenagers in Minnesota, and about 2,000 of them get treatment," said Czarniecki. "The need is huge."[83]

So, the growth continued. One year after Lyle Taipale left Mounds View for Sobriety High, the Mounds View School District elected to close Arona. Taipale and the Sobriety High Foundation rescued it and moved the school to a new campus in Coon Rapids, north of Minneapolis, in June 2005. To expedite the move, Arona Academy was established initially as a private contract alternative, with plans to move it under the Sobriety High public charter in 2006. Czarniecki said the acquisition was a "risk," requiring "considerable financial expense, not to mention political capital."[84] A staff member familiar with the acquisition claimed the foundation had to spend $300,000 to $400,000 on Arona.

"It was not planned ahead for, and it almost sunk whole ship," said the staff member.[85]

There was now a fourth campus called Arona Academy of Sobriety High. Representative Ramstad himself dedicated the Arona facility in Coon Rapids—"our best yet," according to Czarniecki.[86] And the beat went on. In August 2005, the foundation opened a fifth campus called "Libre Academy—A Sobriety High School" in Litchfield, a rural community about seventy miles west of Minneapolis. Like Arona, Libre Academy first was established as a private contract alternative school, but Libre planned to establish its own public charter separate from Sobriety High.

By the end of 2005, Sobriety High thus had five campuses operating in all four poles of the Twin Cities, had reached into rural Minnesota, and had even more grandiose growth plans. In the coming years, Sobriety High, under Czarniecki's leadership, hoped to inaugurate a training institute at Hamline University, place schools across "the entire state," develop a "national model for sober schools," and "promote the vision of a sober school wherever one is needed."[87] Czarniecki even met with representatives of the Gates Foundation about possibly replicating their model nationally. But then, tragically, Jim Czarniecki's body betrayed him. Following an emergency operation for an "intestinal blockage," Czarniecki was diagnosed with stage IV colon cancer and had surgery to remove a tumor, a section of his colon, and adjacent lymph nodes, followed by over a year of chemotherapy.[88]

Lyle Taipale was asked to take the helm during the traumatic time for Sobriety High. On December 16, 2005, while deep into chemotherapy treatment, Czarniecki formally transferred control to Taipale as the new superintendent and CEO of Sobriety High. Czarniecki continued as a consultant to the school and as president of the Sobriety High Foundation, a half-time position he had held since its inception in 2003, as long as he was physically able to do so. Unfortunately, his condition began to worsen about a year after his diagnosis, and Jim Czarniecki died in his sleep, with his wife, Kitty, and four children by his side, on July 9, 2006. He was only fifty-eight years old, and he had continued working on behalf of Sobriety High until the very end of his life.

While Sobriety High mourned the loss of its visionary and inspirational leader, Taipale tried to provide steady guidance. He quickly realized, though, that all the growth had turned Sobriety High into a financial house of cards. Sources familiar with Sobriety High's financial situation explained that private donations had been steadily declining. At one point, contributions had approached nearly half the operating budget, but that had fallen to under 40% in 2004, and it was under 20% by 2006. Taipale thus engineered a paradigm shift, installing a budget that would rely more on public dollars than private contributions, which ultimately required belt-tightening.

Kellie Lund had been a counselor at P.E.A.S.E. Academy before taking over as program director at Sobriety High East in Maplewood.[89]

"[Sobriety High] expanded too quickly," said Lund. "What [Lyle] reported was when he took over from Jim [Czarniecki], it was in such shambles, financially. There was shock. And I do remember that. I started there right at the tail end of the dream phase, kind of when the reality hit. I remember it very well. It was kind of this, 'Oh, my God, we are almost not surviving.'"

"It was all built on sand," said Angela Wilcox, a teacher who had also worked at P.E.A.S.E. Academy before moving to Sobriety High.

Wilcox affirmed that a gilded image had continued to be part of Sobriety High's brand since the Ralph Neiditch years. "They had the promotional material. I mean, it was beautiful. It was a slick marketing department," she said.

"They presented a very different image publicly," said Lund. "They were financially a mess."

Things would not improve. By 2008, Sobriety High and the rest of the recovery high schools were headed into the Great Recession, which reduced the amount of public-school funding available for specialty programs and tightened philanthropy. The federal government also changed the formula for funding the Safe and Drug Free Schools state grants, which led to the elimination of Chemical Health specialists— a key referral source—from most high schools in Minnesota. At least eight sober schools closed their doors in Minnesota from 2008 to 2011.

The toll at Sobriety High was not only financial. Whereas the Edina campus had built a strong culture over years,[90] the rapid expansion had not allowed for such a culture to build in the other schools. The financial challenges forced Sobriety High to reduce staff and to require many existing staff members to split time across campuses.

"It was financial and emotional," said Wilcox. "I remember walking into a meeting and saying [to Taipale], 'You can't just cut our jobs. We're in the middle of the school year. We've got a contract.' And he ripped the contract up and said, 'Yeah, I can fire you on the spot. This contract isn't worth the paper it's printed on.'"

The end proceeded like dominoes falling. In 2009, Libre Academy shut down its separate charter in Litchfield. The two original Sobriety High campuses, West in Edina and East in Maplewood, then allowed their leases to expire in 2010. Considering the impact those schools, especially the Edina campus, had had on the recovery high school movement, their closures were made with relatively little fanfare.

"It was kind of Maslow's hierarchy of needs in the sense that the schools were in such frantic survival mode that there was absolutely no resources, emotional energy, or time to attend to some of those really important things at that time," said Lund.

Staff and students were either let go or transferred to one of the newer campuses in Coon Rapids and Burnsville. Judi Hanson, who had been the face of Sobriety High for two decades was retained in a new outreach role and moved to the South Campus, Alliance Academy, in Burnsville. The Sobriety High Foundation changed its name to the National Youth Recovery Foundation in 2010, essentially shifting its focus away from supporting Sobriety High. The Foundation instead would emphasize continuing care more broadly by establishing boards in other cities without recovery high schools, dealing a major financial blow to Sobriety High. Cathie Hartnett took over as executive director of the foundation and said they had reduced their contributions to Sobriety High from hundreds of thousands to about $20,000 per year.[91]

"A free-standing charter school with multiple campuses called Sobriety High has not worked as a financial model," Hartnett told the *Star Tribune*. "Sobriety High has got to find a model that works."[92]

While Sobriety High had been increasingly reliant on its public-school allocations, thanks to the financial restructuring years before, losing so much foundation support left the school almost completely reliant on public dollars determined by enrollment. Public funding also started dropping as enrollment faltered to "inexplicably low" levels.[93] Taipale left and became the coordinator of the Administrative Licensure Program at the University of Minnesota in 2010. Paul McGlynn, who had been a teacher at Arona Academy, took over as executive director, and he recognized the funding issues immediately.

"It's a difficult business model to sustain," McGlynn told a reporter.[94]

Enrollment was down about twenty students in November 2011, which McGlynn said would amount to a shortfall of $238,000 in the $1.2 million budget.[95]

"We were trying to hold on," said Lund. "I'll never forget, what was it two days before school started, we were told, 'Oh, we guess we can't get you any toilet paper. No copy paper. You're gonna have to fend for yourselves.' We had to call all the families and say, 'Oh, we're adding more to the school supply lists. Bring paper and copy paper. It was just brutal trying to hold those schools together with the resources. Well meaning, but very poor organization. Things were sprung on you."

The last two campuses held on for the 2012–2013 school year, but the fiscal situation continued deteriorating. Even though a combined total of 142 students came through their doors that year, the "daily membership" on which the per pupil allocation was calculated was only 57 per day—just over 28 per campus and far below capacity. They thus ended that year about $400,000 in the red.[96]

"We've had lower enrollment and less cash flow due to that lower enrollment," McGlynn told a reporter at the time. "We've struggled with maintaining our staffing." Cutting staff was not feasible, he added, because "we really don't have any staff left to cut."[97]

The board, therefore, decided to close both schools. Arona Academy's last day was June 7, and Alliance Academy in Burnsville was shuttered a week later. Judi Hanson, who had helped Carol Robson pack up the original St. Louis Park site for Sobriety High's move to Edina in the summer of 1991, was now ending the program almost exactly twenty-two years later.

"[Paul McGlynn and I] were the ones that shut the door and locked it on June 13," Hanson recalled. "I went home with at least twenty boxes of Sobriety High. I mean, it was my life for so long. I couldn't get rid of anything. You know what I mean?"

Hanson sighed deeply and said, "Oh God, it was painful. It was really painful. Blood, sweat, and tears."

The impact of Sobriety High, however, has sustained. Serenity High School in McKinney, Texas, a school inspired by the media blitz of the mid-1990s, is still going. Schools fostered by the Sobriety High Foundation in the mid-2000s, such as Hope Academy in Indianapolis and the Massachusetts recovery high schools, are still in operation. And the Association of Recovery Schools (ARS), for which Judi Hanson served on the nine-member formative steering committee in 2002, continues to set the standards for the field. ARS held its fifth annual conference at Texas Tech University, about three weeks after Jim Czarniecki died in 2006. To honor his immense impact not only on the growth of Sobriety High, but also the establishment of the recovery high school movement, ARS created a Visionary Award that year named in his honor: the Jim Czarniecki Award. When Minneapolis hosted the conference in 2007, ARS gave the award to Czarniecki, posthumously, and his widow, Kitty, delivered an emotional acceptance speech. Nobody would have assumed then that Sobriety High—at the time five campuses strong—would be completely gone only six years later.

P.E.A.S.E. Academy—Minneapolis, Minnesota: 1989–present

Of the six recovery high schools profiled in this book, one remains: P.E.A.S.E. Academy. Interestingly, it too was inspired by Sobriety High, though before the school had that name. P.E.A.S.E. Academy has faced its share of turbulence along the way, but it has remained at the same Lutheran Church building into which Barbara Schmidt moved in 1990.

One of the first issues P.E.A.S.E. Academy faced was losing many of its referrals. During the first years, recovery houses such as the Irene Whitney Center for Recovery made referrals, as did treatment aftercare programs and probation officers. Schmidt had built relationships with multiple referral sources through personal contacts, telling them about the school, giving information regarding how to refer, and answering their questions. About three years into the school's existence, though, Schmidt noticed a change in communication between staff and students. It turned out to be a trust problem.

"As staff, we began noticing students weren't being as open with us," said Schmidt. "They didn't seem as if they were 'connecting' with us anymore—it was palpable. So, we had a school-wide meeting. And I asked them what was up. They didn't hold back. Said they didn't feel as if they could trust us anymore because we'd begun communicating with aftercare programs and those halfway houses when issues were brought up in our discussion groups that affected their sobriety. Which, we didn't hide that fact from them. But they got to the point of realizing: Why are we 'telling it' to P.E.A.S.E. staff if all they're going to do is turn around and pass the details on to aftercare staff?"

The staff considered the issue raised by the students and unanimously agreed the students were correct.

"The students were right," said Schmidt. "We goofed, big time. In our attempt to keep the referral pipeline going, we had inadvertently become a mere extension of aftercare and halfway house staff. Clearly, not our role. Especially considering most times we didn't agree with or support program responses in those instances when students made mistakes, relapsed, etc. For the most part, we found them to be pretty punitive-based and controlling, which wasn't our approach at all. In fact, sometimes I know we cringed when we heard how aftercare programs 'dealt with' these young people if they happened to get themselves in a temporary mess."

Schmidt apologized to the students and said she would be visiting each halfway house/aftercare program personally, letting them know how they were going to approach recurrences of use from that day forward.

"We'd encourage students to tell their aftercare/halfway house staff what had happened [in cases of return to use]," said Schmidt, "but we weren't going to force them, nor were we going to pass along that info ourselves."

Suddenly, P.E.A.S.E. Academy stopped getting referrals from most of their providers.

"No formal announcements or notifications. Nothing said to me directly," Schmidt recalled, "but referrals just started disappearing, pretty much across the board. It seemed as if halfway houses, aftercare programs were not very happy with us. Yet we couldn't do it any other way and maintain our integrity with students. So, from that moment forward—it was mostly word-of-mouth, and occasionally probation officers doing the referring."

Schmidt noted the referral sources were also not happy with how "recovery" had evolved at P.E.A.S.E. In addition to introducing nutrition as part of the holistic curriculum, the school acknowledged there was "not just one way to do this," and they began supporting approaches other than the Twelve Step program.

"Meaning for those who were successful with the traditional Twelve Step program: cool. But we saw it didn't work for everyone."

Psychologist Dr. Charlotte Kasl had just published a book titled *Many Roads, One Journey: Moving Beyond the Twelve Steps*, which introduced a sixteen-step model that was becoming well known in recovery circles in Minnesota.[98] Schmidt felt this program was more amenable to women and BIPOC populations.

"[Dr. Kasl] came and spoke with our students (about) an empowerment model rather than a powerless model as an option, which makes sense if you've been raised in an environment where you had no power to speak of in the first place—women and children/teens, or even people of color, LBGT, etc.," said Schmidt.

As the Twelve Step program was seen as the only road to recovery by most treatment programs at the time, especially those following the Minnesota Model, suggesting it was not necessarily "the" answer for everyone had gotten them further into trouble. After some time had passed, Schmidt tried to rebuild the connections with referral sources, again making personal contact with recovery houses and aftercare providers.

"While they felt they couldn't go on the record when it came to acknowledging the Twelve Step program wasn't the be all/end all, there was more than one person I spoke with who, off the record, said, 'I get it.' And I think after that, some referrals started trickling in again, occasionally," said Schmidt.

The soured relationship with recovery houses, though, got Schmidt to thinking about providing their own housing. The nonprofit Holos Foundation had been created with the realization that they may ultimately develop programs beyond the school, and one of those initiatives was the P.E.A.S.E. House. The board partnered with the Department of Housing and Urban Development to qualify for low-cost housing (i.e., empty properties) under the category of "homelessness." Residents had to be students from P.E.A.S.E. Academy, and there would be room for about six students at a time.

"When we recognized some were in need of temporary shelter," said Schmidt, "we'd sit down with parents/guardians and ask them about it as a possibility. It was never forced, nor were families 'guilted' or shamed into letting their sons/daughter live there, but (the house) was offered as a support mechanism for the family."

"Barb's vision was to create some offshoots of Holos, which was mind, body, spirit, to do some other wellness things and create an umbrella of wellness, with the sober school being part of that," said teacher Steve Massey. "None of those pieces really came to fruition." The house, for example, only lasted a few years before closing.

Steve Massey started assisting Schmidt with many of the administrative tasks, and when the school received a grant from the Minnesota Office of Drug Policy for a family health coordinator, Massey moved into that slot along with teaching a few classes. The school hired a part-time therapist to work with Massey and also leaned heavily on volunteers, such as Paul Willis.

"[Paul Willis] was a super creative guy who was incredibly talented in so many areas—he became my right-hand person," said Schmidt. "Helped me out immeasurably. Later on there was enough [money] to offer him a small stipend—he deserved a lot more. Never complained, just moved right into everything and anything. He would have scrubbed floors if that's what needed to be done."

One of the projects Schmidt championed was a charter school submission under the Holos umbrella for a community learning center in St. Paul serving grades 1–12. This would be a program that could build upon Schmidt's broader holistic education ideals while not exclusively enrolling students in recovery. Schmidt was deeply involved in the movement to pass the nation's first charter school law in 1991.[99]

"I gave testimony at the state legislature several times, all related to P.E.A.S.E. Academy and the difficulties I encountered trying to do a school start-up with few dollars," said Schmidt.

The Minnesota Board of Education approved the charter application on April 5, 1993, though the St. Paul school board rejected it. Schmidt then received approval from the Red Lake Falls school board, as the charter law allowed for a school to be housed outside the sponsoring district. In approving the charter, only the eighth charter school ever approved in Minnesota, Red Falls Lake officials said they believed they would learn from Schmidt's "experimental methods."[100]

For two years, Schmidt had spent so much time on the charter proposal and other activities, she had become less and less active in P.E.A.S.E. Academy.

"I really wasn't as involved with the school on a day-to-day basis anymore," said Schmidt. "I was kind of flying all over the place, with Paul Willis at my side.

"Whenever I showed up at the school it was as if we could start from where we left off. I think I was still interviewing potential new students, for example—and was around enough to make my interest in them known. And they understood what was going on with proposing a charter school community learning center. Very understanding," said Schmidt.

Schmidt's involvement in the charter school was ultimately not to be. Life had taken a toll on Schmidt, complicated by starting one of the first recovery high schools, pushing back against the Minnesota Model's "Twelve Step"–only approach to recovery, opening a sober house, advocating for the nation's first charter law, and eventually shepherding a proposal through hearings by the State Board and two different school district boards.

"She had her ups and downs emotionally, and I don't know any details behind that," said Massey. "She gave me a call one day and said, 'I'm done. Not coming back.

"She really disconnected almost overnight."

"My body was telling me it was time to leave," said Schmidt. "Telling me I needed to let go. Telling me there was something else. . . . So, I listened. The board and staff listened as well."

The exact date has been lost to memory, but by 1994, leadership of P.E.A.S.E. Academy passed to Steve Massey and Paul Willis. After leaving P.E.A.S.E. Academy, Schmidt actually proposed another non-recovery, holistic, one-teacher charter school called "NOETICUS" in 1996, but it was not approved, and Schmidt never again worked in a recovery high school.[101]

"Being the senior staff person, I took over the director role," said Massey. "I did the fundraising, all the enrollment administration, all the board operations and financial reporting, and all that stuff fell to me with no administrative capacity."

Massey and Willis oversaw a tremendous enrollment increase, growing from about fifteen to eighteen students at a time to nearly one hundred in the next five years. One reason for the growth was P.E.A.S.E. Academy's accessible location on public transportation lines near the University of Minnesota. Another major reason was the school's inclusive philosophy. Unlike Sobriety High and other early Minnesota recovery high schools, such as the Gateway Program in St. Paul, P.E.A.S.E. did not limit enrollment to students already in recovery, typically from prior treatment. This was something valued by Schmidt and continued under Massey's leadership.

"We evolved to a school where you have to make a commitment to sobriety. You don't have to have a past of sobriety," said Massey. "I had kids knocking on my door when I was the director saying, 'I want this place because I'm at risk. I've got some drinking in my past or drugs in my past, but I'm not an addict in the sense of it's controlling me. I went through treatment and Twelve Step, and now this is my plan.' Yes, we had those kids. We had many of those kids, but we also had some kids who came because they wanted a sober environment. The expectation for any kid was you make a commitment to sobriety, and how are you doing that? Some kids it's, 'Twelve Steps, it's the only thing I know.' Other kids it's, 'I just have to stay away from certain people and certain triggers in my life, but I'm not an addict like a kid who's gone through treatment maybe.'"

The broader enrollment concept was not embraced by some other professionals in the community.

Massey recalled, "We battled some of the traditional sober schools at the time who felt, 'You're really not a sober school because you take anybody.' I said, 'Call it what you want.' There was some value I think, frankly, between the kid who was in recovery and the kid who wasn't in recovery; both had a common purpose in wanting a sober environment to learn in."

Kellie Lund became a chemical dependency counselor at P.E.A.S.E. Academy in 2001, before later transferring to Sobriety High to run their Maplewood campus, and she suggested P.E.A.S.E. Academy felt more like a harm reduction model, which increased its referral base.[102]

"Interestingly because it was a harm reduction model, [P.E.A.S.E. Academy received] tons of referrals from the justice system," said Lund, who said the approach led to more diversity. Data provided to ARS in 2002 showed that almost 30% of the seventy students in enrolled at P.E.A.S.E. Academy were non-White (11% Native American, 7.5% Black, 7.5% Hispanic, 3% Asian American), and 37% qualified for public assistance for poverty.[103]

Angela Wilcox taught language arts at the school from 1996 to 2005, and she said the inclusivity of the environment created tension.

"There was not a deep level of understanding about recovery," said Wilcox. "It was a sober school. So, kids who had never used but didn't want to be around using could come. There were kids who were dry [but not necessarily sober]. There was no expectation that you were working a [Twelve Step] program, had a sponsor, or anything like that."

At one point, the board began discussing hiring a chemical dependency counselor, as there was not one on staff.

"There was a strong contingent of people saying, 'No, we do not want a C.D. counselor, because we don't want kids to confuse this with treatment,'" said Wilcox. " 'We're a school; we're not a treatment program. Having a C.D. counselor on staff blurs that line. Bad idea.' And other people saying, 'We definitely need that. We need the support for kids. We need to build a culture of recovery in the school.' So, it was pretty contentious."

The broad interpretation of recovery led to challenges at the school, including heavier student drug use. In 2001, the school did hire a chemical dependency counselor, Kellie Lund, who had worked at Hazelden. She described the environment she walked into.

"What I could tell is that there were very few of them who actually were in recovery and wanted to be in recovery," said Lund. "And there were a vast majority of them who really loved the fellowship; really loved the looseness of the school, the community. They got a lot of positives out of the community, but they weren't all that hip to the recovery thing. And a lotta them were using. And there was a really strong subculture of the using kids, and then kind of a weaker culture of the recovery kids, and they were the ones that were struggling."

The complexities also created a revolving door for leadership. Paul Willis left in 1996, and then Steve Massey earned his administrator's license and took a position in the Forest Lake school district in 1999.[104] Michael Durchslag had been hired to replace the original social studies teacher, Steve Miller, in 1997, and he became the lead teacher and interim director in July 1999. He talked about the impact of Massey's exit.

"We were a big school," recalled Durchslag. "We've grown to this size, and we didn't know what to do with the size. Steve [Massey], who was there from the beginning, (was) the only connection to the beginning. Charismatic, great leader; you know, a servant leader. He left, and there was a power vacuum."

The original staff was gone by then, and over the next eight years, there were seven director changes, with the longest stint being John Howitz at just over three years from 2003 to 2006. Durchslag was interim director again in 2003, before being appointed the permanent director in January 2007. Durchslag finally brought stability to the position, which he occupies to this day.

A few major changes created the steadiness to sustain the school, including increasing academic expectations, creating a culture of recovery and restorative practices, and joining a charter school network. Angela Wilcox remembered the academic environment when she was hired to teach language arts in 1996. Like many others such as Bruce McLean and Judi Hanson at Sobriety High, Wilcox had taught at a treatment center for a few years before coming to work at P.E.A.S.E., and she recognized some immediate changes that were needed.

"I prepped my first lesson, and the first day of class, nobody came in," said Wilcox. "And I went out in the hall, and I was like, 'Hey, are there students?' And they said, 'Oh, they're probably in the youth room,' like kids can, kind of depending on where they are that day, if they don't feel like they're in the right headspace to be in a classroom, they can find peer support in the youth room. I go in there, and there's like twenty-three kids playing pool, listening to music, hanging out.

"That was the culture. Kids smoked in the classrooms. Some of the teachers smoked the classrooms. The youth room was kind of the hangout spot. So, it was a school in quotation marks. . . . So, the first year I was there, and there were a couple of other teachers, Michael [Durchslag] was one of them, who were on board with 'can we make this a real school, like can we have real classes where kids have to come in?'" We still had eighth through twelfth graders in one room, right? So, I was the only English teacher in the school, (and) you've got this range of kids, some of whom haven't been in school for three years, some of whom had massive learning disabilities, which is part of, you know, they were self-medicating, couldn't function in school, (with an) undiagnosed, learning disability; so it was challenging.

"I said, 'Not anymore. 'We're gonna actually have class. So, it took a couple of years. Then there was a lot of resentment. [Students said,] 'You're trying to make this into a public school.' I'm like, 'Oh, have you ever been in a public school? This is still not a public school.' But building a culture of academics and learning. There were some real growing pains around that and bringing in licensed teachers instead of, you know, well-meaning people who wanted to hang out with kids in recovery."

The recovery culture change began during Paul Eastwold's years in leadership, from 2000 to 2002. Eastwold had worked in the justice system and studied educational leadership at the University of Minnesota, and Wilcox credited him with installing helpful changes.

"[Paul was] a really solid director who understood recovery, understood academics, understood school leadership," said Wilcox. "He was the first person since Steve Massey who had a vision for what the mission of the school was, and he brought Kelly [Lund] in. And that's when the real transformation started to happen. So, we had a much more solid academic program; we started to build a real recovery culture.

"He also understood the obstacles clearly. He said, 'This is a model that's not sustainable. You cannot have the director playing this role and this role and this role. It doesn't work. So, we've got to . . . rethink the funding formula.' He had a vision to say, 'We have to have a C.D. counselor if we're going to call ourselves [a recovery school]. We need a recovery community.'"

Eastwold thus hired Kellie Lund as the chemical dependency counselor in 2001, and she had a similar reaction to the recovery culture as Wilcox and others had had about the academics.

"I think the most worrisome aspect to me," said Lund, "was the school culture of the staff was . . . a strong belief that you had to be careful with these kids, and that you had to, you know, kind of try to meet their emotional needs. And there was a lot of, 'well, they're having problems at home—of course, they're using.' You know, there was just no understanding of the reality of it as a primary illness or any real reasonable expectations about recovery, because they hadn't seen a whole lot of it. And a lot of enabling and secret-keeping. The kids could go to staff and say, 'If I tell you someone's using, will you keep my secret?' So, I found this staff who was stressed out, because they knew he was using, he was dealing, she really wanted recovery. But they didn't know what to do about it. They felt locked in by the promises they had made to the kids, and just overwhelmed by the enormity of it."

To assist with building a community of recovery, P.E.A.S.E. Academy became one of the first recovery high schools to install practices based on restorative justice.[105] A central tenet of restorative practices is that students take responsibility for recurrences of use and conflicts, acknowledging their use and role in a conflict to the community of students, staff, and parents.

Through methods such as restorative groups/circles, restorative justice lets people say what happened, how they were impacted, what they need, and what they are willing to do to help make things better.[106] Thus, a recurrence of use was no longer hidden as a secret, but rather was treated as a critical event in the recovery process which warranted "significant attention from the school community, additional support services and monitoring, and an opportunity for students to take ownership of their recovery."[107]

Wilcox compared the changes in academics, recovery, and restorative practices that occurred around 2002 to the legs of a stool. She said, "We had a much more solid academic program. We started to build a real recovery culture. And then I think bringing in restorative practices was the third leg."

The final piece in building a stable foundation was moving from being a contract alternative to being a charter school. Rick Bishop took over for Eastwold in August 2002, and he was director only through March 2003, but Durchslag remembered the charter was his idea.

"He planted the seed about maybe becoming a charter school," said Durchslag. "He was a very hands-off director, and a friend of the board. [Bishop] disappeared in March, and that's when Kelly [Lund], myself, and Randy Comfort had to just basically run the school for the last three months of the school [in 2003]."

Minneapolis Public Schools and P.E.A.S.E. Academy then decided to end their contract.

"The [P.E.A.S.E. Academy] board was moving toward becoming a charter school. They were dissatisfied with some of the services that were being provided [by Minneapolis Public Schools]," recalled Durchslag. "Minneapolis was dissatisfied, I think, on their end with some of the things we were doing."

Durchslag cited one point of contention being the fact that more and more of the P.E.A.S.E. students, including students with special education needs requiring additional resources, were coming from outside the district's boundaries.

"One of the big (issues) that I do know is that as we've grown, you know; we started off as twelve students. When I came on-board in '95, we had thirty students, and at that time in 2003, we were serving seventy to seventy-five students and that's what we serve still today," said Durchslag.

Realizing they could not sustain the school over the long-term as an independent charter school, the board pursued other options. One of the offers was through Minnesota Transitions Charter School (MTCS), which had started with one school in 1995 and had grown to become the largest group of charters in the state.[108] Another offer was from Sobriety High, which had just been granted charter school status by the Intermediate School District 917 in Dakota County. Ironically, Sobriety High/New Dimensions had been the school that inspired Ken Simon and Howard Pearson to create a better sober school years before.

"Sobriety High was a very interesting proposal," said Durchslag. "Two things about the Sobriety High proposal that kind of leaned us towards [Minnesota Transitions Charter School]: One was that the board really wanted to make sure that P.E.A.S.E. Academy kept its identity . . . We cooperate with them; they're wonderful. But we didn't want to become a Sobriety High School.

"But I think the real issue was that if Sobriety High was to take us on, they were not going to let us go. [At the time], we were pursuing our own charter. [Sobriety High] said, 'If you want to become a Sobriety High campus, you're a Sobriety High campus. We're not going to take you on for a year or two years and then say goodbye. This is going to become a permanent relationship.' Minnesota Transitions Charter School said, 'Yeah, we'll take you on for a year. We'll take you on for a couple years, you know, whatever, sure.'"

The board chose MTCS, and they never left, and the first full school year under their umbrella was 2004–05. Becoming part of a larger network has allowed P.E.A.S.E. Academy to survive, but as administrative takeovers often are, the transition was rocky.

"When that transition happened," said Angela Wilcox, "It was unhealthy the way [the leadership and the board] navigated it."

Consequently, several of the staff ended up leaving, with Durchslag being one of the few staff members to stay. Interestingly, many of the staff, including Lund, Wilcox, and Lisa Comfort, chose to move over to Sobriety High. The director through the transition was John Howitz, and he left in December 2006. The board asked Durchslag to take his place in January. It was his third stint as director, but this time it would be permanent. The relationship with MTCS stabilized, and P.E.A.S.E. Academy ended up outlasting Sobriety High, which closed all its programs by 2013. It is likely had the board chosen another path, P.E.A.S.E. Academy too would no longer exist. Instead, because of the decision to join MTCS and the transformation that strengthened the academics and the recovery community, P.E.A.S.E. Academy became the longest operating recovery high school in January 2024.

Over time, a Minnesota state administrative rule brought P.E.A.S.E. Academy back into a formal relationship with Pillsbury—the organization that operated the original school site for Holos/P.E.A.S.E. Academy in 1989. Minnesota charter schools have an "authorizer," which is a "public oversight entity approved by the state to authorize one or more charter schools. An authorizer's fundamental role is to hold a school accountable for the terms of its performance contract—the 'charter.'"[109] Pillsbury United Communities (PUC) became a charter school authorizer in 2007, and they are now the authorizer for MTCS, P.E.A.S.E. Academy's charter umbrella. PUC has a stated purpose and long track record of "attacking the institutional racism that plagues education," which essentially means P.E.A.S.E. has come full circle and stayed true to Barb Schmidt's original equity and diversity goals.[110]

Even though Schmidt had fought hard for Minnesota to pass its charter law, she was, of course, no longer involved with P.E.A.S.E. Academy by the time MTCS and PUC took over. After Schmidt resigned from Holos, she completely let go of the school and moved on with her life. In an interview for this book over two decades later, though, she allowed herself to reflect on the origins of Holos and P.E.A.S.E., and her words are salient for all the programs profiled in this book.

"I simply trust we all did the best we could under the circumstances, under the conditions each of us was living under at the time. I truly believe everyone did his or her best. Even on days when we might have tripped.

"And I now send a thought/feeling of love to every single person who was involved. And of appreciation."

Afterword: Findings

As a young counselor helping start a recovery high school in Nashville in 1997, there were many times I wished for people I could call for advice. If there were others who had experienced the same issues before, perhaps their wisdom could be a guide. I had no idea of the depth and breadth of knowledge that existed then, almost twenty-five years after the Freedom Road School had opened in Charleston in 1973. The two Phoenix Schools were completely unknown to me, even though they were experiencing some of their strongest years in the mid-to-late 1990s, as was Sobriety High. While Judi Hanson had helped us some, there were so many other visionaries of whom we were unaware. Reviewing their stories now, many lessons emerge from those trailblazers. This chapter will explore some of the themes from the origin stories, in no particular order.

The Silent Generation

Most of the recovery high school innovators were born during the Silent Generation, which is the name given to people born from 1928 to 1945—encompassing all the children born in the United States during the Great Depression and World War II.[1] While the name of their Generation has been traced to a *Time* magazine article in 1951 that said they were a group "ready to conform," when they became adults, people from the Silent Generation actually led most of the social movements of the 1960s and 1970s.[2] While the Baby Boomers and Generation X children were growing up, it was often people from the Silent Generation that ran their schools and taught their classes. Louis Menand wrote, "It is almost impossible to name a single person born after 1945 who played any kind of role in the civil-rights movement, Students for a Democratic Society, the New Left, the antiwar movement, or the Black Panthers during the nineteen-sixties."[3] Leading innovators associated with the Freedom Road School (Dr. Sid Jordan and Jesse Purvis), the Palmer Drug Abuse Program (Bob Meehan), the Phoenix Schools (Brian Berthiaume and Sally Eller), and Sobriety High (Carol Robson, Ralph Neiditch, Bruce McLean, and Judi Hanson) were all members of the Silent Generation. Shirley Jackson (Freedom Road School) was born in 1946, so she just missed being part of that Generation as well.[4]

There are a few reasons why it is not surprising that people from the Silent Generation would create recovery high schools. First, even though many people from that generation are now associated with the heavy drug usage that emerged in the 1960s and 1970s—such as Timothy Leary, Ken Kesey, and any number of music and film stars from the era—drug usage was still far less common and socially acceptable for youths in their time. Prohibition did not end until 1933, and the propaganda film *Reefer Madness* was released in 1936, meaning negative messages about alcohol and drug usage far outweighed the positive ones in their childhood and adolescence.[5] While youths certainly drank alcohol and used drugs, availability was less, and use was much more a sign of rebellion than the instrument of social conformity it would become in the 1970s. By the time the Summer of Love (1967), Woodstock (1969), and the drug usage associated with creating what Pete Townshend called a teenage wasteland had occurred, the people of the Silent Generation had become the "adults in the room." Some, like Leary and Kesey, saw drug usage as a path toward enlightenment, while others, like the founders of the adolescent treatment programs and recovery high schools saw a need to salvage that wasteland.

Forbes conducted an economic analysis of the various generations and dubbed the Silent Generation "the Lucky Few," as their numbers were smaller than other generations, and noted they had a "booming" economy awaiting them when they finished school.[6] Demographer Richard Easterlin suggested they had excellent timing in life around financial markets and referred to them as the "fortunate" generation.[7] *Forbes* contributing writer Neil Howe wrote, "In their personal lives, this age location has been a source of tension. By the time the Silent Generation were entering midlife, they spearheaded the divorce revolution and popularized . . . the term 'midlife crisis.' But in their economic lives, this age location has been very good to them—and given them a lifetime ride on the up-escalator coming off the American High."[8] It makes sense, then, that people from the Silent/Fortunate Generation would start schools with a therapeutic context that would involve some financial uncertainty. They had always been taken care of financially, so there may not have been as much concern around the economic volatility of the schools.

When the children of the 1970s and early 1980s went to school or needed help, their teachers, principals, counselors, and social workers were often from the Silent Generation, so it was fitting that recovery high schools developed in those years would originate from people of that generation. Two notable exceptions were John Cates (PDAP GED School, born in 1951) and Barb Schmidt (Holos/P.E.A.S.E. Academy, born in 1954). Cates was an early Baby Boomer, who turned eighteen the year of Woodstock. Schmidt was born in the heart of the Baby Boom, as were her partners Ken Simon and Howard Pearson, and it is interesting that their school—the youngest of the ones profiled—pushed back on some of the conventions of adolescent treatment and recovery, such as a Twelve Step-exclusive mentality.

Common Elements

Certain elements of recovery high schools have existed from the start. Even though students of color were underrepresented in the early schools, the small size created communities of acceptance for populations marginalized for substance use disorders, gender, and sexual orientation. Beyond size, the schools have emphasized a client-centered/nondirectional approach with the intention of being welcoming. Dr. Sid Jordan said this about the Freedom Road school philosophy:

> I was trained as a mental health consultant, which is an indirect service, not a direct service. It taught me how to not be an expert, but to listen to people, and help them use their talent. Not come in as an expert but come in as someone to help foster the talent that is sitting in front of you with these agencies that you work with, with the schools, with the people from the community. It's about fostering their competence, and not being an expert with explaining everything and directing everything.

For schools that had no blueprint or evidence-base, this approach allowed the schools to mold to their dynamic populations and to individualize services.

All the early recovery high schools implemented family programs, which addressed the family-nature of substance use disorders as well the generational nature of addiction. Schools would regularly enroll siblings and relatives, and Phoenix lasted long enough to enroll younger relatives. Recovery high schools were also one of the first program modalities to recognize the chronicity of substance use disorders by not forcing students to withdraw after a recurrence of use. Though the first programs were typically transitional and shorter term, most eventually allowed students to stay enrolled until finishing high school rather than only finishing a treatment program. As such, they were able to help students learn how to live in recovery from a substance use disorder rather than simply how to overcome it.

The chronicity also meant recovery high schools always existed under the specter of trauma and loss. Research would find, in time, that recovery high schools tend to enroll students with more severe symptomology than non-recovery high schools.[9] The first site-level evaluation of the Phoenix School suggested the students with less severe behavior issues appeared to be doing better. Some students in recovery high schools find the mental health challenges so daunting that they have died by suicide. Other have returned to use either during or after enrollment, which sometimes has led to overdose and death. Group meetings and sharing of stories allow students the opportunity to process the difficult emotions, but they also expose young people to explicit recounts of trauma and death, over and over again. Furthermore, in communities with fewer twelve step meetings, adolescents can be required to attend meetings outside school in which they might encounter adults who could pose a risk to them physically, psychologically, and sexually. It is a dilemma that remains to this day—the programs designed to provide support and connection also expose teenagers to risk.

Unhealthy Associations

Because teenagers are minors and developmentally vulnerable to influential peers and mentors, some early schools were associated with programs that could be considered unhealthy. An early cautionary tale was represented by the PDAP GED school. PDAP and other "enthusiastic sobriety" programs featured charismatic leadership and an exclusive membership that framed their participants as "winners" and nonparticipants as "losers." This created a cultish atmosphere, and PDAP was eventually accused of being a cult in multiple exposés. Recovery high schools have not faced many other similar accusations, but associating with insular programs can provide a threat to their enrollment. For example, when PDAP reorganized after the *60 Minutes* and *20-20* news pieces, the GED program closed. And when P.E.A.S.E. Academy decided to push back against the Twelve Step-exclusive and behavior modification approach of the therapeutic communities, its referral base dried up for a while.

Most of the early schools used myriad referral sources and created their own policies based on approaches more client and family-centered than behavioral or punitive. Having multiple referral sources protected the schools from being overly affected by one that was unethical or unhealthy. Recovery high schools also were early adopters of the "many pathways to recovery" philosophy currently understood as a best practice in recovery programming. Once again, P.E.A.S.E. Academy was a trailblazer by not requiring every student to work a Twelve Step program, and not having predetermined lengths of sobriety or prior treatment for admission.

Racial and Ethnic Diversity

Recovery high schools developed in the school desegregation era but were predominantly White for decades. Issues of race and poverty were driving forces in education, treatment, and juvenile justice in the 1970s and 1980s. In the 1970s, the school sector was characterized by desegregation efforts such as busing and magnet schools, as well as alternative schools like free and democratic schools. Desegregation efforts were met with White flight to the suburbs and the eventual resegregation of schools in the 1980s and 1990s through school choice laws and charter schools. The justice sector during those years featured the Drug War, the crack epidemic, and a War on Crime, all of which led to mass incarceration of youth from BIPOC communities. Adolescent treatment also grew dramatically during those years, and, with some exceptions such as Canarsie and the Oxford House in New York, were filled with White youths from middle-to-upper income families.

Recovery high school demographics were influenced by each of these sociological factors and were almost exclusively White, as the treatment and justice pathways diverged along racial lines. White children were often referred to counseling and treatment, whereas children of color found themselves forced into a school-to-prison pipeline that detoured around programs like recovery high schools. The founders and staff of the first recovery high schools were mostly people who aligned with the Civil Rights movement and social justice causes, and in the case of Freedom Road in Charleston, included people of color. Yet the students were mostly White, referred from treatment programs that were mostly White, or pursued by families with enough social capital to discover and access recovery high schools. In the case of PDAP, this may have been intentional, as PDAP founder Bob Meehan was accused of not being welcoming to marginalized groups.[10] There was no indication, though, that the people running PDAP's GED School were similarly unwelcoming, and for other schools, the lack of diversity was certainly not intentional. Both Freedom Road and Holos actively recruited staff and students of color. The systems, however, were stacked against them, and in the case of Sobriety High in their early years, charging a tuition did not help. Seeing mainly White staff and students, begat by systemic factors, deterred students of color from enrolling. One recovery high school staff member provided this explanation for the lack of diversity:

> [Juvenile justice referrals] never hit the door. We get calls from [probation officers], and applications are faxed. They try, but it is rare [students of color] make it here, because they are still using. (The) Drug Court mandates primary treatment, but they have no authority over where to go to school. If they did, they would make them go here. There is a racial barrier. [Students of color] say, "I don't want to go to school with all those White kids."[11]

Another deterrent for that school was its neighborhood, as the staff member described their suburban community as "a blue collar, Republican, good ol' boy, White neighborhood."

The lack of diversity in recovery high schools also may have been cultural. A Black woman who had been a loyal volunteer at a recovery high school had invited friends from a local historically Black medical college to the school. She said, "They were all very impressed with our school, but they were not surprised with the lack of diversity. They said, 'This is not how we handle things. We keep it in the family.' "[12]

Ultimately, of the schools profiled, only P.E.A.S.E. Academy drew a racially diverse student body, due to its accessible location, openness to referrals from the justice system as well as treatment programs, and willingness to allow recovery programs like harm reduction and the Sixteen Steps that were more amenable to marginalized groups. The inclusivity also created a dilemma in that the breadth of substance use philosophies caused problems that almost broke the school.

Regardless of how social justice–minded their leaders where, by allowing their enrollments to become so White, at a certain point recovery high schools were contributing to treatment disparities rather than confronting them. When the Association of Recovery Schools was created in 2002, the organization soon recognized the discrepancy between espousing justice and admitting homogenous populations. Organizers for the inaugural conference invited Bonny Beach, the executive director of NDNS4 Wellness, a recovery high school run by the American Indian Prevention Coalition in Phoenix; Mark Kuleta, a school counselor at the Aateshing Program, an indigenous recovery high school in the Cass Lake Area Learning Center on the Leech Lake Indian Reservation in Minnesota; and representatives from the Child Welfare League of America. In 2003, the Association of Recovery Schools was in communication with Johnny Allem, the executive director of the Johnson Institute, about plans to open two urban recovery high schools.[13] The schools were slated to launch in 2004 in Washington, DC, and in Minnesota—the two locations for Johnson Institute offices—but they never did open.[14] The 2007 Association of Recovery Schools conference at Augsburg College in Minneapolis featured a plenary session titled "Under-represented Populations in Recovery Schools: A Discussion." The five panelists represented programs serving marginalized populations:

- Mark Harris: Coordinator of the Recovery Center, a project of the Multicultural Substance Abuse Prevention Program at Lane Community College in Eugene, Oregon
- Will O'Berry: Coordinator of LGBTQIA Support Services at Augsburg College.
- Jonathan Lofgren: Chief Operations Officer of African American Family Services
- Janelle Fischler: Speech and Language Pathologist, ESL teacher, and Seeking Educational Equity and Diversity (SEED) facilitator for Minnesota Independent School District 622
- Mark Kuleta: School counselor of the indigenous Aateshing Program

A lesson from the original programs and those early Association of Recovery Schools meetings was that recovery high schools wanting a diverse student body must not only locate themselves in diverse communities, they must recruit from families of color, hire diverse administrators and staff, and adapt recovery programs to be more inclusive while still respecting the recovery of the community. They must also actively work at dismantling the unjust systems that are creating the disparities. If they do not, recovery high schools risk perpetuating the very systems of segregation they seek to avoid.

Change has been slow, but in 2021, the Association of Recovery Schools joined other recovery organizations in drafting and implementing a policy document titled *North Star Guide for Recovery Leaders,* which "intentionally and unambiguously addresses the needs of Black and Indigenous communities."[15] In recent years, the Association of Recovery Schools has created a Justice, Equity, Diversity, and Inclusion (JEDI) committee, diversified its board, and required implementation of the *North Star Guide* in its accreditation standards. Recovery high school populations have shown more racial diversity, but as the *North Star Guide's* preamble states, there is much more to be done, and "the work continues."[16]

Evolving Definition

The definition of a recovery high school has evolved over time. One characteristic used to define recovery high schools for this book was if recovery was embedded in a school rather than the school being embedded in a treatment program. In the

1970s, however, adolescent treatment programs were scarce. This meant any school providing services to students with substance use disorder was likely also providing hours of treatment-level services as well. This blurred the distinction between a treatment school and a recovery school. The blurriness was especially true for Freedom Road and the first Phoenix School. Sometimes, the best indicator was how the school referred to itself in media . . . did representatives describe it as a treatment program or a school?

Though all the programs discussed in this book are schools, the origins of the South Carolina and Texas recovery schools were more rooted in the substance use treatment and recovery components. Charleston's Freedom Road School evolved from an adolescent treatment program. Houston's Palmer Drug Abuse Program GED School tutored students who were trying to get sober through the support of their alternative peer group. The two Phoenix schools were Montgomery County public schools, staffed by teachers, though their genesis was a semester-long drug raid, and academics were arguably a secondary goal to creating a recovery milieu, at least initially. The schools that emerged in the Minneapolis area were seeded in the alternative school wave of the 1970s and cultivated by the school choice movement of the 1990s. The ecology of Minnesota was arguably more conducive to recovery high schools than any other state both because of its alternative school history and its long-standing commitment to alcohol and drug treatment. But even in Minnesota, the educational expectations took time to evolve, fostered by the standards movement of the 1990s and teachers such as Angela Wilcox and Larry Schmidt who realized the academic potential of their students.

As adolescent treatment expanded nationwide, treatment centers became a primary referral source, and schools like Sobriety High required lengths of sobriety and/or prior treatment for admission. While this allowed for a clearer demarcation between a treatment program and a recovery high school, it also excluded many students who may have benefitted from an abstinence-focused environment. Furthermore, adolescent treatment has always had disparities and gaps between the youth who need treatment and those who receive it, meaning most recovery high schools have enrolled students who may not have been solidly in recovery when they started. While some newer schools have created ancillary programs to help students focus on their substance use before fully integrating into the recovery high schools, most have not had the resources to do so. This has created uncertainty around who to admit, who to exclude, and when to withdraw a student who has had a recurrence of use, which is especially pronounced when funding depends on census. That issue has existed from the beginning, but the pressures have ebbed and flowed based on treatment access in a school's community and how fixed/certain the budget revenue is.

Currently, recovery high schools are dealing with a reduction in adolescent treatment programs driven by the pandemic, a declining perception of harm around cannabis, and a focus on medically assisted treatment for opiates that may not require a treatment stay. Recovery high schools may need to look once again to how the original schools handled a dearth of treatment and broad social acceptability of cannabis use in the 1970s and early 1980s—for example, more inclusive enrollment policies, more treatment-level and wraparound services, and expectations of abstinence to preserve a community of recovery. One difference today is that referrals were not as much of an issue in the 1970s and 1980s when more of society saw adolescent drug usage as problematic, and treatment programs were being promoted to handle the problem. While recovery high schools have decades of experience and evidence today with how to be more inclusive, provide more services, and develop abstinence-focused policies, there are now fewer referral sources and even some disagreement among recovery school leaders as to whether abstinence from substances is possible, necessary, or culturally sensitive for adolescents. Research and open discussion of these disputes will frame the evolution of the next generation of recovery high schools.

Spiritual Foundations

Spirituality has been evident in multiple ways. Many of the original recovery high schools followed Twelve Step principles and required students to participate in Alcoholics or Narcotics Anonymous programs. Spirituality is foundational to the Twelve Steps, with the second, third, fifth, sixth, seventh, eleventh, and twelfth steps each mentioning a higher power, God, or spirituality. No step captures the spiritual and peer support facets of recovery high schools more than the twelfth: "Having had a spiritual awakening as the result of these Steps, we tried to carry this message to alcoholics, and to practice these principles in all our affairs."[17]

The founders of recovery high schools embodied spirituality in various ways. D. Ceth Mason was involved with Alcoholics Anonymous almost from its inception, and he was a powerful advocate for its implementation in South Carolina, which provided a Twelve Step foundation for the Freedom Road School. All the programs, including P.E.A.S.E. Academy that embraced multiple pathways, had linkages to the Twelve Step program and thus its spiritual component.

Beyond the Twelve Steps, spirituality has played a role in other ways. Many of the original recovery high schools were located in Christian churches, including Freedom Road (Catholic), PDAP GED School (Episcopal and Presbyterian), and P.E.A.S.E. Academy (Lutheran). Even though the schools were not run by the churches directly, the mission of the churches aligned well with providing a sober space for youth in recovery to get an education.

The founders of the original schools had connections to a spectrum of faith traditions, some more traditional than others. D. Ceth Mason was on the leadership board of the welcoming Circular Congregational Church in Charleston. Bob Meehan was raised as a Catholic, and the Palmer Drug Abuse Program he started was named after the Palmer Memorial Episcopal Church that housed it. In recent years, John Cates has espoused his Christian testimony publicly on the Sugar Land Baptist Church's YouTube channel.[18] Sally Eller met teacher Mike Bucci at the Sandy Spring Quaker

Friends Meeting. And Barb Schmidt had been a social justice minister for the Lutheran Church in America.

Not all the spiritual connections, though, were Christian. Another common theme was a linkage to Eastern faith traditions and mysticism, which could have been influenced by the founders coming of age in the Sixties. Brian Berthiaume was a follower of Meher Baba, and he received support from an eighty-member strong "Baba Community" at school board meetings. Berthiaume even incorporated yoga into his classroom as a teacher before starting the Phoenix School. Dr. Sid Jordan began teaching meditation in 1971, before the Freedom Road school began. After leaving South Carolina, Jordan moved to Asheville, North Carolina, in 1994 to support the service community of Ananda Girisuta, the "Daughter of the Mountain." He then trained to be a meditation and yoga instructor as an Ananda Marga Family Acarya (which is a spiritual guide or teacher) and adopted the spiritual name, Acarya Vishvamitra.[19] Ananda Marga originated in India in 1955 and is translated as "The Path of Bliss."[20] According to Dada Gunamuktananda, its philosophy is "one of universalism. It is an all-embracing outlook, recognizing God as the one limitless supreme consciousness, with all beings of the universe part of the one cosmic family," and its motto is "Self-Realisation and Service to the Universe."[21] Ananda Marga was also founded by a Baba, Prabhat Ranjan Sarkar, who was a spiritual guru, philosopher, and "social revolutionary."[22] And Barbara Schmidt, who had worked for the Lutheran church, embraced many mystical concepts around holism, consciousness, connectedness, and the multiverse. She too later adopted a name with a non-Western connotation.[23]

While the beliefs of these faith traditions vary, a throughline was a belief in a connection with others and a power that transcends oneself, while also embracing self-actualization and improvement, which aligned well with the Twelve Step philosophy. Most, though not all, of the traditions focused more on inclusivity than orthodoxy. The majority of the founders embraced the power of relationship and acceptance of others, which fostered a community of recovery.

More Research Needed

This theme is less a finding than a question in need of further research: Do the schools work? This project had limits in being able to answer that question. First, it was not designed as an outcome study to determine efficacy or effectiveness. The preponderance of evidence from extant studies does suggest recovery high schools are effective in reducing substance use, improving graduation rates, and reducing societal costs. More studies certainly are needed, but the research so far has been compelling.[24]

Beyond the fact that this project was rooted more in historical artifacts and lived experience than in statistical empiricism, another limit to interpreting outcomes was the undeniable personal history underlying the study. Having run a recovery high school, started a national organization, and conducted multiple research studies, the author did not approach this work as a blank slate. This is something I have tried to address in every project I have ever conducted, including this one, by involving researchers with no formal connection or background with recovery high schools. This has included research faculty, graduate students, and investigators from research centers. If assertions made in the book could not be independently verified, they were noted as such or not included at all.

Since this work was not focused on *if* recovery high schools work, but rather on *how* they began, my over-twenty-five years of personal experience and connections has been an asset. That experience has allowed me to draw upon hundreds of stories from students, some new to recovery and others with anywhere from months to years of sobriety. Those stories have also included interviews and interactions with students who returned to use while enrolled at a recovery high school or after graduating or transitioning out of school. One of the most rewarding aspects of the research conducted for this book was meeting students who attended recovery high schools as long as forty years ago. Some of those students had returned to use at some point, though many others had remained sober for decades.

Those stories also suggest there are other indicators of success than abstinence from drug use. This book is an origin story, but by interviewing students decades later, we get some indication of the impact of schools. Recovery high schools may help a person stay clean and sober for a while and develop essential life skills during their stay, but no program can guarantee a lifetime of abstinence.

Dr. Leaf van Boven attended Phoenix II before matriculating to Cornell for his doctorate. One of the main things he valued was the school's accessibility.

"A number of the kids there were not from well-off backgrounds. They were able to go to this thing because it was a public school. It's frustrating to think about the lack of opportunity for those kids without a school like Phoenix, because a lot of [alternative] schools are expensive."

He said, "In my view, part of what made those [Phoenix] schools so successful is that there was a very strong community of people who were all trying to stay clean and sober. Things might have been messed up in a whole bunch of other areas of life and so on, but at least at that time, everyone was kind of on-board with the program."

He also acknowledged some students continued to use after being enrolled. "There were definitely some students who were continuing to use, and they would definitely get called out.

"Often, I think about these moments of redirection, and if those hadn't been there, who knows what would have happened? In a sense, it feels very far away because it is increasingly far away, but at the same time, like, it's very much a part of how I think of myself and what's important. I think I always understood that the people and the program were designed to help us. There was a lot that I didn't like about that, but I didn't feel like it was wrong ever or misguided."

Having a recovery high school available to them at a vulnerable time of life was invaluable, and it was a consistent theme across every student story, whether they had returned to use or not. Many credited the schools with saving their lives, while others simply acknowledged the importance of having a period in their lives to build life skills, allow their brain to develop, and to finish a high school diploma without the interference of mood-altering substances.

This book is the first publication to examine the trajectories of recovery high school students across decades of their lifespan. More rigorous longitudinal research could help us to understand the long-term effect of recovery high schools on their students beyond basic substance use histories.

School Closures

A final theme to explore here is the closure of the original schools. Five of the six no longer exist, though most had lengthy runs—while two lasted less than ten years, one lasted twenty-six years, and two lasted thirty or more years. P.E.A.S.E. Academy is still open, and it has surpassed Phoenix I to become the longest-operating recovery high school. This book has focused on how schools *opened*, but future compelling research could investigate why schools have *closed* as well as why they have sustained. At least three themes of closure can be gleaned from the stories told in this book.

Funding. Finances were at the root of the closure for most of the five schools no longer in operation. Freedom Road and Phoenix were publicly funded schools that the local districts decided to stop supporting in their budgets. Both Phoenix schools evaporated when Montgomery County Schools decided to no longer keep their students separate from a general school population, in part because it was more economically efficient to operate multiple programs in one building than to have dedicated facilities for every school. And Sobriety High closed its doors because of financial difficulties caused mainly by growing beyond its means.

Philosophical Differences. Finances, though, were not the only reason the early schools closed. Philosophies also played a role. Charleston, South Carolina, and Montgomery County, Maryland, continued to fund alternative schools; they just did not operate small schools for students in recovery. One example of a philosophical shift was having schools perceived to be *inclusive* and not *exclusive*. Recovery high schools are intended exclusively for students with substance use or co-occurring disorders, while education in the 1990s was moving toward more inclusivity and fewer barriers. Advocates for recovery high schools would argue they could be both *inclusive* of students with exceptional needs and *exclusive* of students actively using alcohol and other drugs.[25] Embracing such complexities requires leaders to understand recovery high schools and have a desire to make them work, despite their higher costs. Without that comprehension and commitment from administrators, though, recovery high schools may struggle to survive.

Leadership Changes. Different philosophies and funding priorities occur with new leadership. New superintendents and school boards in the Charleston, South Carolina, and Montgomery County, Maryland, meant lost institutional knowledge, new political allegiances, changed funding priorities, and different philosophies. The

PDAP GED School had one simple reason for closing—its leader left. Innovative programs often get started by creative, passionate, and, sometimes, charismatic individuals. When founders or influential program directors leave or are replaced, programs may dissolve, and that is was happened to the GED school when John Cates left PDAP.

Schools close for multiple reasons, and it would be informative to recovery high school sustainability to understand the various causes and trends behind why recovery high schools have ended, so programs can try to steer away from those roadblocks in the future. Conversely, it can help to comprehend what factors contribute to a school's survival. According to the Association of Recovery Schools, there have been just over one hundred recovery high schools since 1973, with an average lifespan of about ten years, which means there is plenty of data to mine.

Conclusion

Over the years, people have asked my thoughts about the key ingredient of a successful recovery high school. Is it the curriculum? The policies? The budget? Staff credentials and experience? All those pieces are important, but ultimately this book has shown how critical the community is—students working together with themselves and trusted adults, caring for each other, both inside the school and in the surrounding district. The old adage of requiring a village fits well. Phoenix II teacher Izzy Kovach shared a story about her first day on the job, which happened to be a day the school was on an outdoor excursion.

"The best part [of Phoenix] was just how kids were taking responsibility for each other," said Kovach. "It's hard to put a finger on what it came from. . . . It's from the constant small group meetings that we held and large group meetings that we held, and then we had, you know, an active outdoor education program. At least once a month, we'd go off on a one-day or multiple-day trip that would really challenge you—rock climbing or sailing or hiking, yeah, really challenging activities where kids would have to really trust each other. My very first day at Phoenix was a rock-climbing trip, and I had never climbed before. And there I was, at the end of a rope with, you know, some sixteen-year-old boy holding me up, and it was, 'Okay, I guess I have to have some faith here.' You know, it was just that sort of thing. Yeah . . . We needed to care about each other."

For all the differences, strengths, and challenges across schools, the relationships of human beings in recovery with their allies, holding each other up one day at a time, are what have made recovery high schools work from the beginning, and those relationships are what will continue to be the schools' special ingredient.

Notes

Introduction: Opening the Door

1. Casey, J. (1997, June 3). "School to open its door to teen addicts." *The Tennessean*, 1B.
2. The term "recovery school" was not adopted until years later.
3. See note 1, 1B.
4. Tigno, J. (1999, August 19). "Teens get a sobering experience." *The Tennessean*.
5. White, W. L., and Finch, A. J. (2006). "The recovery school movement: Its history and future." *Counselor*, 7(2), 54–57.

Prologue: Setting the Stage for Recovery and Education

1. Quoted from Education Evolving website, explaining the history of charter schools. https://www.educationevolving.org/content/history-and-origins-of-chartering.
2. Fornatale, P. (2009, September). "High times." *Guitar World, 30*(9), 76.
3. The Sound Team. (2019, January 3). "The Who's Roger Daltrey says 'Baba O'Riley' is a warning to kids today." The Sound. https://www.thesound.co.nz/home/music/2019/01/the-whos-roger-daltrey-says-baba-oriley-is-a-warning-to-kids-today.html.
4. Lassiter, M. D. (2015, June). "Impossible criminals: The suburban imperatives of America's War on Drugs." *Journal of American History, 102*(1), 126–140. https://doi.org/10.1093/jahist/jav243.
5. White, W. L. (1999). "A history of adolescent alcohol, tobacco and other drug use in America." *Student Assistance Journal, 11*(5), 16–22, 19.
6. As explained in the 2023 Monitoring the Future Annual Report (81): "All surveys in 2020 were completed before March 15, when national social distancing policies were enacted and data collection was halted due to pandemic concerns. Consequently, results from 2020 and previous years are pre-pandemic, while results from 2021 and 2022 took place after the onset of the pandemic and the associated national response. The COVID-19 pandemic is a historical event of particular interest for the 2022 results. Last year (2022) MTF documented some of the largest one-year declines ever recorded by the survey across a wide variety of drugs from 2020 to 2021": Miech, R. A., Johnston, L. D., Patrick, M. E., O'Malley, P. M., Bachman, J. G., and Schulenberg, J. E., (2023). Monitoring the Future national survey results on drug use, 1975–2022: Secondary school students. Monitoring the Future Monograph Series. Ann Arbor, MI: Institute for Social Research, University of Michigan. https://monitoringthefuture.org/results/publications/ monographs/; Monitoring the Future, 2003.
7. Monitoring the Future, 2017.
8. Monitoring the Future, 2020.
9. Hall, G. S. (1904). *Adolescence: Its psychology and its relations to physiology, anthropology, sociology, sex, crime, religion and education,* Vol. 1. D Appleton & Company. https://doi.org/10.1037/10616-000.

10. Arnett, J. J. (2006). G. Stanley Hall's "*Adolescence*: Brilliance and nonsense." *History of Psychology, 9*(3), 186–197; quote at 186. https://doi.org/10.1037/1093-4510.9.3.186.
11. Ibid.
12. Anslinger, H. (1937). "Marijuana, Assassin of Youth." *American Magazine, 124*(1). https://www.redhousebooks.com/galleries/assassin.htm.
13. Drug Enforcement Administration. (2020, June 5). "*Narcotics—Drug fact sheet.*" Drug Prevention. https://www.dea.gov/sites/default/files/2020-06/Narcotics-2020.pdf.
14. Sloman, L. (1979). *Reefer madness: The history of marijuana in America.* Indianapolis: Bobbs-Merrill.
15. Lassiter, M. D. (2015, June). Impossible criminals: The suburban imperatives of America's War on Drugs. *Journal of American History 102*(1), 127, 126–140. https://doi.org/10.1093/jahist/jav243.
16. Ibid., 129.
17. Lee, M. A. (2012). *Smoke signals: A social history of marijuana: medical, recreational, and scientific.* New York: Scribner, 6.
18. Bard, N. D., Antunes, B., Roos, C. M., Olschowsky, A., and de Pinho, L. B. (2016). "Stigma and prejudice: the experience of crack users." *Revista latino-americana de enfermagem, 24,* e2680. https://doi.org/10.1590/1518-8345.0852.2680.
19. See note 15 earlier, 126–140.
20. Toomey, T. L., Nelson, T. F., and Lenk, K. M. (2009). "The age-21 minimum legal drinking age: A case study linking past and current debates." *Addiction 104*(12), 1958–1965. https://doi.org/10.1111/j.1360-0443.2009.02742.x.
21. Ibid.
22. Johnston, L. D., O'Malley, P. M., Bachman, J. G., and Schulenberg, J. E. (2011). *Monitoring the Future national survey results on drug use, 1975–2010*: Vol. I, *Secondary school students.* Ann Arbor: Institute for Social Research, University of Michigan, 152.
23. Charalampous K. D. (1971). "Drug culture in the seventies." *American Journal of Public Health, 61*(6), 1221, 1225–1228. https://doi.org/10.2105/ajph.61.6.1225.
24. Ibid., 1228.
25. Hudak, J. (2016). *Marijuana: A short history.* Washington, DC: Brookings Institution Press, 42.
26. Readers interested in the years and details about the laws are directed to Hudak in note 25 earlier, and Massing, M. (1998). *The fix: Solving the nation's drug problem* New York: Simon & Schuster.
27. Technically William McKinley was president at the start of the twentieth century, but Roosevelt took over in 1901 following McKinley's assassination, and his administration passed the first major drug law of the twentieth century in 1906.
28. See Massing in note 26 earlier, 86.
29. Ibid.
30. Murphy, M. F., and Steele, R. H. (1971). *The world heroin problem: Report of special study mission.* Composed of Morgan F. Murphy [and] Robert H. Steele Pursuant to H. Res. 109 Authorizing the Committee on Foreign Affairs to Conduct Thorough Studies and Investigations of All Matters Coming Within the Jurisdiction of the Committee. United States: US Government Printing Office, 1.
31. Ibid.
32. PBS. (2014). *Thirty years of America's drug war.* Drug Wars. http://www.pbs.org/wgbh//pages/frontline/shows/drugs/cron/.

33. Nixon, R. (1971). *Remarks about an intensified program for drug abuse prevention and control*. Online by Gerhard Peters, and John T. Woolley, American Presidency Project. https://www.presidency.ucsb.edu/node/240238.
34. Ibid.
35. See Massing in note 26 earlier, 133.
36. Ibid., 119.
37. National Academy of Sciences. (1991). *A brief history of ADAMHA and previous studies of its organization*. Washington, DC: National Academies Press. https://www.ncbi.nlm.nih.gov/books/NBK234556/.
38. Gardner, E. A. (1973). *Final report of the Mental Health Task Force*. Washington, DC: Department of Health and Human Services, 32.
39. National Institutes of Health. (2023, November 8). *National Institute of Mental Health (NIMH)*. https://www.nih.gov/about-nih/what-we-do/nih-almanac/national-institute-mental-health-nimh.
40. Substance Abuse and Mental Health Services Administration. (2023, April 24). *Block grants laws and regulations*. https://www.samhsa.gov/grants/block-grants/laws-regulations.
41. Kleiman, M. A., and Hawdon, J. E. (2011). "Office of drug abuse law enforcement." In *Encyclopedia of Drug Policy* (Vol. 2, 605–605). Thousand Oaks, CA: SAGE Publications, Inc. https://doi.org/10.4135/9781412976961.
42. US Department of Justice. (2017). *Organization, mission, and functions Manual: Drug Enforcement Administration*. Drug Enforcement Administration. https://www.justice.gov/jmd/organization-mission-and-functions-manual-drug-enforcement-administration.
43. See Massing in note 26 earlier.
44. Alexander, M. (2010). *The new Jim Crow: Mass incarceration in the Age of Colorblindness*. New York: New Press.
45. Baum, D. (2016, April). "Legalize it all: How to win the war on drugs." *Harper's*. https://harpers.org/archive/2016/04/legalize-it-all/.
46. Davis, J. C. (2015). "The business of getting high: Head shops, countercultural capitalism, and the marijuana legalization movement." *The Sixties*, *8*(1), 27–49. DOI:10.1080/17541328.2015.1058480.
47. Dufton, E. (2013). "Parents, peers and pot: The rise of the drug culture and the birth of the parent movement, 1976–1980." *Trans-Scripts*, *3*, 211–236, 211.
48. Domestic Council Drug Abuse Task Force. (1975). *White Paper on Drug Abuse*. Washington, DC: US Department of Justice, https://www.ncjrs.gov/pdffiles1/Photocopy/164686NCJRS.pdf.
49. Ibid., 9.
50. Ibid., 2.
51. Ibid., 10.
52. Ibid., 24.
53. Ibid., 20.
54. Ibid., 24.
55. Marro, A. (1978, September 21). "U.S. drug chief hits efforts to legalize pot." *Washington Star*.
56. Carter, J. (1977, August 2). *Drug abuse message to the Congress*. Online by Gerhard Peters, and John T. Woolley, American Presidency Project. http://www.presidency.ucsb.edu/ws/?pid=7908.
57. See note 47 earlier, 212.

58. PBS. (2014). "Interview with Peter Bourne." *Frontline*. https://www.pbs.org/wgbh/pages/frontline/shows/drugs/interviews/bourne.html.

59. See Massing in note 26 earlier.

60. See note 58 earlier.

61. Ibid.

62. See note 47 earlier; see Massing in note 26; and note 46 earlier.

63. See note 47 earlier.

64. Gleaton, T. J. (2006). *Evaluating student safety and drug use with Pride Surveys*. Bowling Green, KY: Pride Surveys, 3.

65. See note 47 earlier, 236.

66. See note 46 earlier.

67. National Institutes of Health. (2010, October). *Alcohol-Related traffic deaths*. National Institute on Alcohol Abuse and Alcoholism (NIAAA). https://www.niaaa.nih.gov/sites/default/files/publications/AlcoholRelatedTrafficDeaths.pdf.

68. SAMHSA. (2018). *Supplemental materials: Definitions of variables in legal policies*. Washington, DC: SAMHSA.

69. A comprehensive history of adolescent addiction and treatment is beyond the scope of this work. Readers interested in exploring the history of adolescent recovery are advised to read William H. White's (2014) *Slaying the Dragon: The History of Addiction Treatment and Recovery in America*. White is the foremost authority on addiction treatment worldwide, and all researchers in this area owe him a debt of gratitude.

70. White, W., Dennis, M., and Tims, F. (2002). "Adolescent treatment: Its history and current renaissance." *Counselor*, *3*(2), 20–23. https://www.chestnut.org/william-white-papers/1/papers/items/.

71. See note 5 earlier; and see note 70.

72. See note 70 earlier.

73. Hubbard, S. (1920). "The New York City Narcotic Clinic and different points of view on narcotic addiction." *Monthly Bulletin of the Department of Health of New York*, *10*(2), 33–47, as cited in M. D. Godley and W. L. White (2005). "A brief history and some current dimensions of adolescent treatment in the United States." In M. Galanter (Ed.), *Progress in the treatment of alcoholism,* Vol. 17. New York: Springer, 369–382. https://www.chestnut.org/william-white-papers/1/papers/items/.

74. See note 70 earlier.

75. Ibid.

76. See Massing in note 26 earlier.

77. See Godley and White in note 73 earlier, 368.

78. See note 70 earlier.

79. See Godley and White in note 73 earlier.

80. Gamso, R., and Mason, P. (1958). "A hospital for adolescent drug addicts." *Psychiatric Quarterly, Supplement*, *32*, 99–109; and see note 70 earlier.

81. Jainchill, N. (1997). "Therapeutic communities for adolescents: The same and not the same." In G. DeLeon (Ed.), *Community as method: Therapeutic communities for special population and special settings*, (161–177). Westport, CT: Praeger Publishers/Greenwood Publishing Group; Winters, K. C., Stinchfield, R. D., Opland, E. O., Weller, C., and Latimer, W. W. (2000). "The effectiveness of the Minnesota Model approach in the treatment of adolescent drug abusers." *Addiction*, *94*(4), 601–612; and see note 70 earlier.

82. See note 5, 16–22.

83. Miller, J. (1973). "The Seed: Reforming drug abusers with love." *Science, 182*(4107), 40. http://www.jstor.org/stable/1736222.

84. Jones, S. (2018). "The Seed: Indeed." The Seed Indeed. https://theseedindeed.wordpress.com/seed-adolescent-fraud/.

85. NIDA. (1975). *National Directory of Drug Abuse Treatment Programs.* Washington, DC: US Department of Health, Education, and Welfare, 145.

86. See note 70 earlier, 20–23.

87. Katz, M. S. (1976). "A history of compulsory education laws." *Phi Delta Kappan Fastback Series, No. 75. Bicentennial Series.* Bloomington, IN: Phi Delta Kappa Educational Foundation.

88. Sarason, S. B., and Lorentz, E. M. (1998). *Crossing boundaries: Collaboration, coordination, and the redefinition of resources.* Hoboken, NJ: Wiley.

89. Taylor, F. W. (1911). *The principles of scientific management.* New York: Harper & Brothers; Tyack, D. B. (1974). *The one best system: A history of American urban education.* Cambridge, MA: Harvard University Press.

90. Fuller, W. E. (1982). *The old country school: The story of rural education in the Middle West.* Chicago, IL: University of Chicago Press.

91. Cremin, L. A. (1961). *The transformation of the school.* New York: Vintage Books.

92. See note 9 earlier, 510.

93. Ravitch, D. (2000). *Left back: A century of failed school reforms.* New York: Simon & Schuster.

94. Cremin, L. A. (1978). "The free school movement: A perspective." In T. E. Deal, and R. R. Nolan (Eds.), *Alternative schools: Ideologies, realities, guidelines* (203–210). Chicago: Nelson-Hall.

95. Elkind, D. (1998). *All grown up and no place to go: Teenagers in crisis* (Revised ed.). Reading, MA: Addison-Wesley.

96. US Supreme Court (1954). Brown v. Board of Education of Topeka, 347 U.S. 483 (1954). https://supreme.justia.com/cases/federal/us/347/483/.

97. US Supreme Court (1955). Brown v. Board of Education of Topeka, 349 U.S. 294 (1955). https://supreme.justia.com/cases/federal/us/349/294/.

98. Neill, A. S. (1960). *Summerhill: A radical approach to schooling.* New York: Hart.

99. See note 93 earlier.

100. Rousseau, J. J. (1762/1979). *Emile or On Education.* New York: Basic Books, 120.

101. See note 98 earlier.

102. See note 93 earlier.

103. Hawkins, J., and J. Wall. (1980). *Alternative education: Exploring the delinquency prevention potential.* Washington, DC: US Department of Justice, Office of Justice Programs, Office of Juvenile Justice and Delinquency Prevention.

104. Holt, J. (1964). *How children fail.* Lanham, MD: Pitman Publishing Company; Kozol, J. (1967). *Death at an early age: The destruction of the hearts and minds of Negro children in the Boston Public Schools.* Boston: Houghton Mifflin; Kohl, H. (1967). *36 children.* New York: New American Library; Illich, I. (1970). *Deschooling society.* New York: Harper & Row.

105. Duke, D. L. (1978). *The retransformation of the school.* Chicago: Nelson-Hall.

106. Ibid., 26.

107. Ibid., 3.

108. Graubard, A. (1972). "The free school movement." *Harvard Educational Review, 42*(3), 364–368.

109. See note 105 earlier, 4.

110. Educational Facilities Laboratories. (1962). *Profiles of significant schools: Schools without walls.* New York: Educational Facilities Laboratories.

111. Ibid., 3.

112. Crabtree, M. (1975). "Chicago's Metro High: Freedom, Choice, Responsibility." *Phi Delta Kappan, 56*(9), 613–615. http://www.jstor.org/stable/20298049.

113. Silberman, C. E. (1970). *Crisis in the classroom: The remaking of American education.* New York: Random House; Etzioni, A. (1971). Review of *Crisis in the Classroom. Harvard Educational Review* (February), 87–98.

114. See note 91 earlier; and note 94 earlier.

115. See note 94 earlier, 207.

116. National Commission on Excellence in Education. (1983). *A nation at risk: The imperative for educational reform.* Washington, DC: National Commission on Excellence in Education.

117. Coleman, J., Hoffer, T., and Kilgore, S. (1982). "Cognitive outcomes in public and private schools." *Sociology of Education, 55*(2–3), 65–76. https://doi.org/10.2307/2112288.

118. Levin, H. M. (1990). "The theory of choice applied to education." In W. H. Clune, and J. F. Witte (Eds.), *Choice and control in American education.* London: Falmer.

119. Finn, C. E. Jr. (1990). "Why we need choice." In W. L. Boyd, and H. Walberg (Eds.), *Choice in education.* Berkeley, CA: McCutchan Publishing, 4.

120. Chubb, J. E., and Moe, T. E. (1990). *Politics, markets, and America's schools.* Washington, DC: Brookings Institution, 206.

121. Peterson, P. E., and Campbell, D. E. (2001). *Charters, vouchers, and public education.* Washington, DC: Brookings Institution Press.

122. Bard, B. (1975, December). "The failure of our school drug abuse programs." *Phi Delta Kappan, 57*(4), 251–255. https://www.jstor.org/stable/20298229.

123. Ibid., 251.

124. Densen-Gerber, J., and Drassner, D. (1974). "Odyssey House: A structural model for the successful employment and re-entry of the ex-drug abuser." *Journal of Drug Issues, 4*(4), 414–427. https://doi.org/10.1177/002204267400400413, 415.

125. Ibid., 416

126. Odyssey House. (2024). "History." https://odysseyhousenyc.org/odyssey-house/history/.

127. See note 124 earlier, 416.

128. Ibid., 420.

129. Lawson, D. (1979, Fall). "The Canarsie Youth Center." *McGill Journal of Education, XIV*(3), 379–385.

130. Ibid., 379.

131. Ibid., 380.

132. Lawson, D. (1979, Fall). "The Canarsie Youth Center." *McGill Journal of Education, XIV*(3), 379–385.

133. The Alpha School was located at 60 Hinsdale Street, Brooklyn, NY.

134. Campbell, B. (1971, March 16). "New city school to help ex-addicts." *New York Times,* 33. https://www.nytimes.com/1971/03/16/archives/new-city-school-to-help-exaddicts.html.

135. Tomasson, R. E. (1971, September 12). "Brooklyn's Alpha School is devoted to rehabilitation of addicts." *New York Times*, A37. https://www.nytimes.com/1971/09/12/archives/brooklyns-alpha-school-is-devoted-to-rehabilitation-of-addicts.html.

136. Ibid., A37.

137. Jones, J. W. (1971). *Drug crisis: Schools fight back with innovative programs*. Washington, DC: National School Public Relations Association, 26. https://hdl.handle.net/2027/mdp.39015002525759.

138. Ibid., 27,

139. See note 103 earlier, 15.

140. See note 122 earlier, 251–255.

141. Edwards, G. (1974). "Perspectives on drug education." *Contemporary Drug Problems*, 3, 485–545; and see note 122 earlier.

142. Finch, A. J., and Hart, C. (2013). "Definitions of school-based recovery support services." In *The 2013 Market Study for Recovery Schools* (17–23). Reno, NV: Stacie Mathewson Foundation.

143. Diehl, D. (2001). "Recovery high school." In S. L. Isaacs, and J. R. Knickman (Eds.), *To improve health and health care: The Robert Wood Johnson Foundation anthology*, Vol. V. San Francisco: Jossey-Bass.

144. Association of Recovery Schools. (2022). "What is a Recovery High School?" https://recoveryschools.org/what-is-a-recovery-high-school/.

145. Nash, A., and Collier, C. (2016). "The Alternative Peer Group: A Developmentally Appropriate Recovery Support Model for Adolescents." *Journal of addictions nursing*, 27(2), 109–119. https://doi.org/10.1097/JAN.0000000000000122.

146. White, W. L., and Finch, A. J. (2006). "The recovery school movement: Its history and future." *Counselor*, 7(2), 54–57.

Chapter 1

1. Ginsberg, A. (1956). *Howl and other poems*. San Francisco: City Lights Books. Kerouac, J. (1957). *On the road*. New York: Viking Press. Burroughs, W. S. (1959). *Naked lunch*. New York: Grove Press.

2. Charters, Ann (2001). *Beat down to your soul: What was the Beat Generation?* London: Penguin Books.

3. The Fugs were a rock band formed in 1964 by poets Ed Sanders and Tuli Kupferberg, and they were a prominent part of the counterculture movement, often performing at Vietnam War protests: NPR Music. (2010, April 6). *The Fugs: At the forefront of the counterculture*. Music Interviews. https://www.npr.org/2010/04/06/125628216/the-fugs-at-the-forefront-of-the-counterculture.

4. Pravda was the official newspaper of the Soviet Union.

5. Hinckley, D. (2019, January 12). *The Summer of Love: Everything was peace and love until the cops showed up*. https://www.nydailynews.com/2017/08/14/the-summer-of-love-everything-was-peace-and-love-until-the-cops-showed-up/?clearUserState=true.

6. Leary, T. (1983). *Flashbacks: A personal and cultural history of an era*. New York: G. P. Putnam's Sons, 253.

7. Ashbolt, A. (2007). "Go Ask Alice: Remembering the Summer of Love forty years on." *Australasian Journal of American Studies*, 26(2), 35–47. http://www.jstor.org/stable/41054075

8. Ibid.

9. "An Open Poem to the Prophets and Their Apostles," Persian Fuckers Anonymous and Unlimited, Berkeley Commune file, Bancroft Social Protest Project, UC Berkeley; see note 7 earlier, 43.

10. In June 1967, UCSF had opened a free health clinic in the Haight. One of the services provided by the health clinic was drug treatment: Bai, N. (2017, June 17). "Born in the Summer of Love: The Haight Ashbury Free Clinic transformed drug addiction treatment." https://www.ucsf.edu/news/2017/06/407286/born-summer-love-haight-ashbury-free-cli nic-transformed-drug-addiction.

11. University of California San Francisco. (2023). *UCSF Langley Porter Psychiatric Hospital.* https://psych.ucsf.edu/lpphc.

12. US Department of Health and Human Services, Administration for Children and Families. (2010). *Head Start Impact Study: Final report.* Washington, DC: Author.

13. US Environmental Protection Agency. (2024). *Superfund Site: Hunters Point Naval Shipyard.* San Francisco, CA. https://cumulis.epa.gov/supercpad/SiteProfiles/index.cfm?- fuseaction=second.Cleanup&id=0902722#bkground.

14. Bayview Hunters Point Foundation for Community Improvement. (2019). *Our history.* https://bayviewci.org/who-we-are/mission-history/.

15. Anti-Eviction Mapping Project. (2016). "Timeline of the Bayview-Hunters Point— Divestment and Development." https://antievictionmap.com/bayview-hunters-point/.

16. Hicks, B. (2015). *The mayor: Joe Riley and the rise of Charleston.* Charleston, SC: Evening Post Books, 29.

17. Ibid., 30.

18. Ibid., 30.

19. Hopkins, G. W. (2016, April 15). *South Carolina Encyclopedia: Charleston hospital workers' strike.* https://www.scencyclopedia.org/sce/entries/charleston-hospital-workers-strike/.

20. Ibid.

21. Ibid.

22. Ibid.

23. See note 16 earlier.

24. See note 19 earlier.

25. "Hospital strike in Carolina ends." (1969, June 28). *New York Times.* https://www.nytimes. com/1969/06/28/archives/hospital-strike-in-carolina-ends-abernathy-refuses-to-leave- jail.html.

26. See note 16 earlier.

27. Richardson, D. F. (2016, June 8). *South Carolina Encyclopedia: Laing School.* https://www. scencyclopedia.org/sce/entries/laing-school/.

28. Blakeney, B. (2020, April 6). "William 'Bill' Saunders: Forgotten warrior." *Charleston Chronicle.* https://www.charlestonchronicle.net/2020/04/06/william-billsaunders-forgot ten-warrior/.

29. Ibid.

30. Avery Research Center at the College of Charleston. (2004). *Inventory of the William (Bill) Saunders Papers, circa 1950–2004.* Charleston, SC: College of Charleston.

31. See note 28 earlier.

32. "The Two-Way Street." (1968, July 11). *News and Courier,* 12-A.

33. Leland, I. (1978, May 7). "The Rev. Henry Grant." *News and Courier,* 3-E.

34. Shoemaker, A. J. (2019). *Building community across walls: A history of an integrated church amid a gentrifying neighborhood in Charleston, South Carolina.* Divinity School of Duke University [Unpublished thesis].

35. South of Broad is an exclusive and historic area of Charleston, located in the southern-most tip of the Peninsula. It features antebellum homes owned by wealthy plantation owners in the eighteenth and nineteenth centuries.

36. "Santee Cooper chased these people into better homes." (1941, December 15). *Greenville News*, 7.

37. Ibid.

38. National World War II Museum. (n.d.) "Research Starters: The draft and World War II." https://www.nationalww2museum.org/students-teachers/student-resources/resea rch-starters/draft-and-wwii#:~:text=On%20September%2016%2C%201940%2C%20 the,to%20register%20for%20the%20draft.&text=Once%20the%20U.S.%20entered%20W WII,the%20duration%20of%20the%20fighting.

39. World War II Draft Registration Card, David Ceth Mason Jr.

40. National Museum of American History. (2009, May 19). *National Museum of American History's New Exhibition Goes "On the Water."* https://americanhistory.si.edu/press/relea ses/national-museum-american-historys-new-exhibition-goes-water.

41. American Merchant Marine at War. (2007, January 31). *US Merchant Marine in World War II.* http://www.usmm.org/ww2.html.

42. USAHS *Samuel F. B. Morse* Passenger Manifest, June 7, 1943 (New York Arrival Papers).

43. USAHS *Thistle* Passenger Manifest, December 4, 1945 (Honolulu Arrival Papers).

44. Simpson, D. (1978, August 13). "Painful past makes Mason realize he's satisfied now." *News and Courier*, 65.

45. Ibid.

46. See note 44, 65.

47. Simpson, D. (1978, July 30). "Revolving door drunks." *News and Courier*, 2-E.

48. See note 44, 65.

49. See note 47, 2-E.

50. Ibid.

51. Ancestry.com. (2012). *1940 United States Federal Census* [database on-line]. Provo, UT, USA: Ancestry.com Operations Inc.

52. Mason-Byrd. (1938, October 21). *Sumter Item*, 2. Miss Byrd Weds Lieutenant Kellogg. (1943, April 17). *Sumter Item*, 3.

53. "Marriage licenses." (1944, October 11). *News and Courier*, 4.

54. See note 44, 65.

55. See note 47, 2-E.

56. "$60,000 alcoholics care program is under consideration." (1948, January 29). *News and Courier*, 7-B.

57. Conroy, P. (2010). *South of Broad: A novel.* New York: Doubleday, 59.

58. "Thurmond to address S.C. school officials." (1948, December 10). *News and Courier*, 10.

59. South Carolina State Hospital. (1949). *One Hundred and Twenty-Sixth Annual Report of the South Carolina State Hospital for the year ending June 30, 1949.* The Joint Committee on Printing, General Assembly of South Carolina, 18.

60. Brown, S. (2005). *A biography of Mrs. Marty Mann: The First Lady of Alcoholics Anonymous.* Center City, MN: Hazelden Publishing.

61. Mann, M. (1944). "Formation of a National Committee for Education on Alcoholism." *Quarterly Journal of Studies on Alcohol*, 5(3), 355.
62. "Gift for speaker." (1961, November 3). *Charleston Evening Post*, 1-B.
63. "A.A.'s first State Assembly to open here tomorrow." (1948, July 15). *Charleston Evening Post*, 2-A.
64. See note 44, 65.
65. Greenberg, G. (2013, April 30). "The creation of disease." *New Yorker*. https://www.newyorker.com/tech/annals-of-technology/the-creation-of-disease.
66. "Institute on Alcoholism opens tomorrow at Medical College." (1949, January 24). *News and Courier*, 6.
67. "300 expected at A.A. meeting here." (1960, May 27). *Greenville News*, 12.
68. "Pioneer in S.C. alcoholism treatment dies." (1983, January 2). *Charlotte Observer*, 20.
69. Le Cook, B., and Alegria, M. (2011). "Racial-ethnic disparities in substance abuse treatment: The role of criminal history and socioeconomic status." *Psychiatric Services, 62*(11), 1273–1281. http://psychiatryonline.org/doi/abs/10.1176/ps.62.11.pss6211_1273.
70. Stockton, R. P. (1971, July 19). "Hospitals aren't punished under new law, Mason says." *News and Courier*, 1-B.
71. "The legacy of Summerton." (2010, March 13). *Newsweek*. https://www.newsweek.com/legacy-summerton-188534.
72. "South Carolina African American History Calendar." (2024). *Pearson v Clarendon County and Briggs v Elliott*. https://scafricanamerican.com/honorees/pearson-v-clarendon-county-and-briggs-v-elliott/.
73. See note 71 earlier.
74. Ibid.
75. National Museum of American History. (2009, May 19). *National Museum of American History's New Exhibition Goes "On the Water."* https://americanhistory.si.edu/press/releases/national-museum-american-historys-new-exhibition-goes-water.
76. "Circular Church congregation elects Mason." (1954, January 12). *Charleston Evening Post*, 5-B.
77. Ibid.
78. Ibid.
79. "Circular Congregational Church." (2024). About Circular. https://www.circularchurch.org/about.
80. Ibid.
81. Calhoun, J. (2008). *The Circular Church: Three centuries of Charleston history.* Charleston, SC: The History Press, 119–120.
82. Jones, J. (2020, October 11). "*First hospital and training school for nurses in Charleston, South Carolina.*" Black then: Discovering our history. https://blackthen.com/first-hospital-training-school-nurses-charleston-south-carolina/.
83. MUSC Library. (2024). *McClennan-Banks Memorial Hospital (Courtenay Street).* http://waring.library.musc.edu/exhibits/mcclennanbanks/Hospital.php.
84. Mikell Interview with author, 2014.
85. Moulton, B. (1970, March 6). "Alcoholism Council plans formulated." *The Item*, 7.
86. See note 83 earlier.
87. Mikell interview with author, February 8, 2021.

88. "Alcoholism Council plans to revamp." (1969, December 4). *Charleston Evening Post*, 19-A.
89. "Special unit." (1971, August 31). *Charleston Evening-Post*, 1-B.
90. Mikell email with author, February 23, 2021.
91. Shirley Jackson was married to Herman Beckett 1968–1999. In 2004, she married Thomas Mikell and became Shirley Mikell. Most of her work in the substance use field was under the name of Beckett, including all the work referenced here. For that reason, she will be referred to as Beckett in the book.
92. Bailey, M. J., and Duquette, N. J. (2014, June). "How Johnson fought the War on Poverty: The economics and politics of funding at the Office of Economic Opportunity." *Journal of Economic History, 74*(2), 351–388 [author manuscript, p. 2].
93. Ibid.
94. "Medical facility to be completed in 6 to 9 months." (1968, March 22). *Charleston Evening Post*.
95. Jordan interview with author, March 5, 2021.
96. "Mental health center plans to seek aid of community." (1969, July 18). *News and Courier*, 12-A.
97. "Hollings to speak a center ceremony." (1970, March 5). *Charleston Evening Post*, 2-A.
98. Mikell interview with author, November 2014.
99. Alcoholics Anonymous World Services, Inc. (1989). *Twelve steps and twelve traditions.* Alcoholics Anonymous World Services, 132.
100. Ibid., 124–125.
101. May, J. (1969, September 17). "Alcohol information center is goal." *News and Courier*, 14-A.
102. "Alcoholism Council plans to revamp." (1969, December 4). *Charleston Evening Post*, 19-A.
103. Ibid., 7.
104. "Drug 'hot line' goes into service." (1970, August 1). *News and Courier*, 1-B.
105. Ibid., 1-B.
106. Ibid.
107. Garrett, M. W. (1971, March 9). "Local facilities are insufficient." *Charleston Evening Post*, 1-A, 3-A.
108. Ibid., 3-A.
109. Ibid., 3-A.
110. Tucker, W. S. (1970, October 8). "Drug treatment facilities proposes." *News and Courier*, 1-A, 17-A.
111. Ibid., 17-A
112. Ibid. 17-A.
113. Ibid.
114. Purvis interview with author, February 5, 2021.
115. "Funding hampers drug program." (1972, April 12). *News and Courier*, 11-A.
116. Purvis interview with author, February 5, 2021.
117. New World Encyclopedia. (n.d.). *Strom Thurmond.* https://www.newworldencyclopedia.org/entry/Strom_Thurmond.
118. "OEO approves one-year grant for county." (1972, May 3). *News and Courier*, 11-A.
119. "Drug counselor grant." (1972, January 8). *Charleston Evening Post*, 2-A.

Chapter 2

1. Alston, J. A. (1974, May 1). "Fetter provides drug education, therapy." *News and Courier*, 1-B.
2. Glass, M. A. (1973, June 7). "Drug program awaits license." *News and Courier*, 8-B.
3. Ibid.
4. Jordan interview with author, March 5, 2021.
5. Ibid.
6. Ibid.
7. Mikell interview with author, February 8, 2021.
8. Grimes, W. (2015, October 24). "Dr. Beny Primm, pioneer in addiction and AIDS prevention, dies at 87." *New York Times*, https://www.nytimes.com/2015/10/25/nyregion/dr-beny-primm-pioneer-in-aids-prevention-dies-at-87.html.
9. Mikell interview with author, February 8, 2021.
10. Drago, E. L., and Hunt, E. C. (1991). *A History of Avery Normal Institute from 1865 to 1954* (Revised and Enlarged). Charleston, SC: Avery Research Center, http://www.averyinstitute.us/history.html.
11. Ibid.
12. Dr. Charles H. Banov was a Jewish physician born and raised in Charleston. He told stories from over fifty years of practice in his 2007 memoir, *Office Upstairs: A Doctor's Journey* (The History Press).
13. Mikell interview with author, February 8, 2021.
14. "Drug counselor grant." (1972, January 8). *Charleston Evening Post*, 2–A.
15. Glass, M. A. (1973, April 6). "Fetter drug center program passed over." *News and Courier*, 7-A.
16. Ibid.
17. Ibid.
18. Ibid.
19. Ibid.
20. Dubois, N. (2023, June 2). "*Immaculate Conception School, 200 Coming Street.*" Discovering our past: College of Charleston histories, https://discovering.cofc.edu/items/show/26. The location of the Immaculate Conception School was 200 Coming Street, Charleston, South Carolina, 29403. The location of the Immaculate Conception School was 200 Coming Street, Charleston, South Carolina, 29403.
21. Dubois. "*Immaculate Conception School, 200 Coming Street.*".
22. Ibid.
23. Jordan interview with author, March 5, 2021.
24. See note 1 earlier.
25. Graham, M. (1975, June 24). "At Freedom Road School | Education reinforces therapy." *News and Courier*, 4-A.
26. Haines, M. J. (1974, November 24). "Center aids substance abusers." *News and Courier*, 10-A.
27. Scott, D. (1976, September 27). "Teen-age drug users in one of a kind school." *News and Courier*, 1-B, 9-B.
28. Ibid.
29. See note 1 earlier.
30. See note 25 earlier.
31. Ibid.

32. Ibid.
33. Scott, D. (1976, September 27). "Teen-age drug users in one of a kind school." *News and Courier*, 1-B, 9-B.
34. Ibid.
35. See note 25 earlier.
36. See note 33 earlier.
37. Mikel interview with author, November 2014.
38. Robinson, S. C. (1978, May 1). "Mason House program aids youthful drug abusers." *News and Courier*, 1–B. The location of the Mason House was 22 Burns Lane, Charleston, South Carolina, 29401.
39. Purvis interview with author, February 5, 2021.
40. Roach, H. (1974, October 25). "Alcohol, drugs masquerade as 'substances.'" *Charleston Evening Post*, 2-A.
41. See note 33 earlier.
42. Beckett interview with author, November 2014.
43. See note 33 earlier.
44. Ibid.
45. See note 25 earlier.
46. Ibid.
47. See note 33 earlier.
48. See note 1 earlier.
49. See note 25 earlier.
50. Beckett interview with author, November 2014;Scott, D. (1976, September 27). "Teen-age drug users in one of a kind school." *News and Courier*, 1-B, 9-B.
51. Beckett interview with author, November 2014.
52. Ibid.
53. Purvis interview with author, February 5, 2021.
54. Beckett interview with author, November 2014.
55. Fantini, M. (1973, March). "Alternatives within public schools." *Phi Delta Kappan*, *54*(7), 444–448, https://www.jstor.org/stable/20373540.
56. "Freedom Road School has first graduates." (1975, June 2). *Charleston Evening Post*, 2-B.
57. Encyclopedia.com. (n.d.). *Office Of Economic Opportunity*, https://www.encyclopedia.com/history/dictionaries-thesauruses-pictures-and-press-releases/office-economic-opportunity.
58. "Franklin Fetter, county programs to merge." (1977, March 25). *Charleston Evening Post*, 2-A.
59. Ibid.
60. Lowcountry is a term used to describe the low-lying geographic and cultural region along South Carolina's coast, including the Charleston, Greenville, Columbia, Myrtle Beach, the Sea Islands, and parts of Georgia. Bluffton, SC. "What does Lowcountry mean?" (n.d.). https://www.blufftonsc.com/what-does-lowcountry-mean/#:~:text=The%20Lowcountry%20is%20a%20geographic,rolling%20hills%20of%20the%20Piedmont.
61. Foster, C. (1979, April 6). "'Too expensive' | Drug program is canceled by county school district." *News and Courier*, 1-B, 2-B.
62. Ibid.
63. Ibid.
64. Lareau, J. (1980, June 12). "Substance abuse budget outlook good." *News and Courier*.

65. White, M. (1982, September 25). "Mason gets Order of the Palmetto." *News and Courier/ Evening Post*, 1-A, 10-A.

66. Ibid.

Chapter 3

1. Bradley, B. S. (2013). *Houston's Hermann Park: A century of community*. Sara and John Lindsey Series in the Arts and Humanities, Vol. 16. College Station: Texas A&M University Press.

2. "The Who—Live at Woodstock '69." (June 9, 2013). *YouTube*. https://www.youtube.com/watch?v=fFCZ49drEh8.

3. "Hoffman calls for takeover." (1970, April 13). *Lubbock Avalanche-Journal*, 4.

4. Ibid.

5. Kolitz, D. (2021). Love bomb. *Atavist Magazine*, 117. https://magazine.atavist.com/the-love-bomb-enthusiastic-sobriety-bob-meehan-abuse-cult-drugs-rehab/.

6. Ibid. See also Palmer Drug Abuse Program. (n.d.). *Our story*. https://pdaphouston.org/about/#history.

7. Many of the details about Meehan's life, including his time in jail, are difficult to verify. While multiple sources have been consulted, ultimately, many of the details were provided by Meehan himself in Meehan, B. (2000). *Beyond the yellow brick road: Our children and drugs, Revised*. Roswell, GA: Meek Publishing, 3.

8. The Lexington Narcotic Farm had changed its name in 1967 to the "National Institute of Mental Health, Clinical Research Center": Kentucky Historical Society. (n.d.). *Lexington Narcotic Farm collection fills gap*. https://history.ky.gov/news/lexington-narcotic-farm-collection-fills-gap.

9. Helmore, K. (1985, April 29). "Ex-drug addict finds self-esteem the key to going straight." *Christian Science Monitor*. https://www.csmonitor.com/1985/0429/hdrug-f2.html.

10. See note 5 earlier.

11. See note 6 earlier.

12. Palmer Drug Abuse Program. (1982). *PDAP*, 2nd ed. Midland, TX: Palmer Drug Abuse Program, 7.

13. See note 9 earlier.

14. See note 12 earlier, 7.

15. "Joseph Meehan, traffic officer, clerical garb salesman, at 64." (1978, June 13). *Evening Sun*, 8.

16. St. Bernadine Church. (n.d.). "*Our history*." https://stbernardinechurch.org/new-page-3.

17. Ibid.

18. Meehan interview with author, June 3, 2020.

19. See note 9 earlier.

20. Brashears, A. D. (1964, May 2). "Three freed in pill cases." *Baltimore Sun*, 22.

21. See note 7, earlier.

22. See note 7, earlier.

23. Ibid.

24. See note 7 earlier.

25. Meehan interview with author, June 3, 2020.

26. Ibid.

27. Massing, M. (1998). *The fix: Solving the nation's drug problem*. New York: Simon & Schuster, 88–102.

28. Johns Hopkins Urban Health Institute. (n.d.). "*History of Johns Hopkins Institutions in East Baltimore*." https://urbanhealth.jhu.edu/about/history-of-johns-hopkins-institutions-in-east-baltimore/.

29. "State drug bill assailed." (1970, June 23). *Baltimore Sun*, 30.

30. Meehan interview with author, June 3, 2020.

31. Ibid.

32. See note 7 earlier.

33. Ibid.

34. Ibid., 2.

35. Ibid.

36. "Father Charlie on Bob Meehan." (2013, October 1). Excerpt from *The group: A documentary*. https://www.youtube.com/watch?v=GfwJm38LKA4.

37. Ibid.

38. See note 7 earlier.

39. Meehan interview with author, June 3, 2020.

40. Pronounced "puh-DAP": Palmer Drug Abuse Program. (1982). *PDAP*, 2nd ed. Midland, TX: Palmer Drug Abuse Program, 7.

41. Palmer Drug Abuse Program. (n.d.). "Historically speaking . . ." http://www.pdap.com/aboutus.htm.

42. See note 7 earlier, 137.

43. Ibid..

44. Ibid.

45. See note 12 earlier.

46. Ibid., 7.

47. Anne Wingfield was later married and changed her last name, but her maiden name is used here, as that was the name she was known by when the events of this book occurred.

48. Wingfield interview with author, May 12, 2020.

49. Ibid.

50. Ibid.

51. It has been suggested the lack of diversity may have been intentional on the part of Meehan. Though nobody interviewed for this book stated that avoiding people of color was a policy at PDAP, Kolitz implied the lack of inclusion may have been on purpose. When leading a training for his "enthusiastic sobriety" program years later, Meehan was accused of listing unacceptable groups for participation, including "Black people, gay people, poor people, Mexicans":see note 5 earlier. This quote was not independently verified, and there is no indication a similar attitude existed for the GED school, which Meehan was not directly involved in running.

52. See note 7 earlier.

53. See note 12 earlier.

54. See note 7 earlier.

55. PDAP GED School (Yearbook). (1978). *Dreams realized*, vol. 1. Houston, TX: PDAP Continuing Education System.

56. General Educational Development (G.E.D.): What Is It? (n.d.). On *Best Accredited Colleges*. https://study.com/articles/General_Educational_Development_GED_What_is_it.html;

National Advisory Council on Adult Education. (1976). *The Annual Report to the President of the United States of the National Advisory Council on Adult Education*. Washington, DC: National Advisory Council on Adult Education, 150.

57. Hanford, E., Smith, S., and Stern, L. (2013, September). "Second-chance diploma: Examining the GED." *American RadioWorks*. http://americanradioworks.publicradio.org/features/ged/.

58. Paxton, J. (Ed.) (1976). *The Statesman's Year-Book 1976–77*. London: Palgrave Macmillan, 702. https://doi.org/10.1057/9780230271050. Lond, J. Paxton, Springer, 702; and see National Advisory Council on Adult Education (note 56 earlier), 150.

59. Odyssey House. (2024). *History*. https://odysseyhousenyc.org/odyssey-house/history/. Lawson, D. (1979, Fall). The Canarsie Youth Center. *McGill Journal of Education*, *XIV*(3), 379–385.

60. Will interview with author, January 28, 2016.

61. See note 57 (Hanford); note 56 (National Advisory Council), 150; and note 58 (Paxton), 702.

62. John Cates testimony video. (2016, March 31). *YouTube*. https://www.youtube.com/watch?v=mq3Fvsiedro.

63. Cates interview with author, February 27, 2014.

64. See note 62 earlier.

65. Cates interview with author, February 27, 2014.

66. "Teacher is charged with selling heroin." (1975, October 16). *Houston Chronicle*, sec. 2, p. 2.

67. Scott, G. (1977, February 14). "Cates works with drug abusers | End of double-life has purpose." *Rosenberg Herald-Coaster*.

68. See note 62 earlier.

69. Cates interview with author, February 27, 2014.

70. See note 66 earlier, sec.2, p. 2.

71. See note 62 earlier.

72. Donovan, S. (1977, November 19). "Witnesses support WISD creation." *Houston Chronicle*, sec. 1, p. 2.

73. See note 67 earlier.

74. Ibid.

75. See note 62 earlier.

76. Ancestry.com. (n.d.). *Texas, U.S., Divorce Index, 1968–2015* [database on-line.]. Lehi, UT: Ancestry.com Operations Inc.

77. Cates interview with author, February 27, 2014.

78. Cates, J. C. (2019, June 29). *APG history, model, & definition of Enthusiastic Recovery*. [Breakout Session.] National Alternative Peer Groups Conference, Boston, MA. Harris County Court Docket. (1976, July 13). The State of Texas vs. Cates, John Carrington.

79. Cates interview with author, January 30, 2023. As an example of how roads can diverge, Cates's roommate, Michael Drane, who was his codefendant in the felony, had kept dealing drugs after the October arrest. "He thought he would just keep dealing and buy his way out of the court case," said Cates. Just before midnight on January 20, 1976, eight narcotics officers went to his residence with a search warrant, looking for heroin. As they entered the premises, Drane barricaded himself in a bedroom and started firing on the officers with a rifle, wounding three of them. The officers fired back, hitting Drane with at least six bullets and killing him in the shootout. (See: "Police kill 2 suspects; 3 officers wounded." (1976, January 21). *Houston Chronicle*, sec. 1, p. 3.)

80. See note 62 earlier.

81. Cates interview with author, January 28, 2016.

82. The Kiva was a meeting room in Farish Hall on the University of Houston Central Campus. It was built in the 1970s, and featured moveable, trapezoid tables that allowed for classroom design training and experimentation.

83. Bill P.'s last name has been removed to protect his privacy.

84. Cates, J. C. (2019, June 29). *APG history, model, & definition of Enthusiastic Recovery.* [Breakout Session.] National Alternative Peer Groups Conference, Boston, MA, slide 26.

85. Ibid.

86. Cates interview with author, January 28, 2016.

87. Wayne Cloud interview with author, May 15, 2020.

88. Will interview with author, January 28, 2016.

89. Cates interview with author, January 28, 2016.

90. See note 7, 149.

91. Bernholz interview with author, April 3, 2020.

92. Wingfield, interview with author, May 12, 2020.

93. Cates interview with author, January 28, 2016.

94. Ibid.

95. Ibid.

96. Bernholz interview with author, April 3, 2020.

97. Meehan interview with author, June 3, 2020.

98. Cates interview with author, January 28, 2016.

99. AW. (n.d.). Historic Houston location, distinguished Texas litigators. https://www.abrahamwatkins.com/firm-overview/firm-history/.

100. Bernholz interview with author, April 3, 2020.

101. St. Luke's Presbyterian Church was located at 8915 Timberside Drive, Houston, TX 77025.

102. See note 55 earlier.

103. Wayne Cloud interview with author, May 15, 2020.

104. As the PDAP website explains, "The 'Monkey Fist' is a mariner's knot used by ships to help them dock. A baseball sized knot with lines attached is thrown from the ship to the dock, the first contact the ship has with land. The crew on shore catches the knot, secures the line to the dock and pulls the ship to shore. At PDAP we have adopted this as a symbol representing our sobriety as we are being pulled in from the sea of drugs and alcohol. The fist symbolizes first contact to solid ground, with the group symbolizing the crew that pulls the newcomer safely to shore. Traditionally, the small leather monkey fist is suspended on a leather cord around the PDAPer's neck. This symbol also serves as the PDAP logo." Palmer Drug Abuse Program. (n.d.). *A symbol of success . . .* https://www.pdap.com/aboutus.htm.

105. Wayne Cloud interview with author, May 15, 2020; Cates interview with author, January 28, 2016.

106. Carol Cloud with author, May 15, 2020.

107. Ibid.

108. Ancestry.com. (n.d.). Calvert Hall High School Yearbook, 1961, 122. *U.S. School Yearbooks, 1900–1999* [database on-line]. Lehi, UT: Ancestry.com Operations Inc.

109. Hard Left. (2008, July 18). *YouTube.* https://www.youtube.com/watch?v=6wsJaMpJwMk&feature=emb_logo.

110. Frank Beard biography. (n.d.). *IMDb*. https://www.imdb.com/name/nm0063896/bio.

111. Ibid.

112. Kielty, M. (2020, February 26). "ZZ Top's Frank Beard details '70s heroin addiction: 'A regret.'" *Ultimate Class Rock*. https://ultimateclassicrock.com/zz-top-frank-beard-heroin/?utm_source=tsmclip&utm_medium=referral

113. See note 109 earlier.

114. Daniel Kolitz published an article critical of Meehan soon after his death in 2021. According to Kolitz, "Meehan booked Freeway at the Houston Astrodome and rented a private plane to fly PDAP participants in from Los Angeles to attend. Carrie Hamilton, an aspiring singer, was the opener. One staff member recalls Meehan and his entourage arriving in limousines. According to several former colleagues, Meehan funded the event by clearing out the bank account of PDAP L.A.—an estimated $50,000 to $100,000 in charitable donations. After the Houston show, Meehan took Freeway on tour through the Rocky Mountains, playing at various PDAP branches. That trip was also allegedly bankrolled with the program's money"; see note 5 earlier, 117.

115. Mike Douglas. (1979, November 18). *Baltimore Sun*, Television Listings, 22.

116. Marks, A. (2018, November 5). "Jim Jones and the lessons of Jonestown." *Rolling Stone*. https://www.rollingstone.com/culture/culture-features/jonestown-jim-jones-lessons-terror-jungle-751924/.

117. See note 5 earlier, 117.

118. Super Bowl ratings history (1967–present). (n.d.). On *Sportsmediawatch.com*. https://www.sportsmediawatch.com/super-bowl-ratings-historical-viewership-chart-cbs-nbc-fox-abc/.

119. A full examination of the PDAP controversy, its business model, and whether it was truly a cult or simply caught up in the Jonestown hysteria, is beyond the scope of this book. The people directly involved with the circumstances have a range of views and emotions over forty years later about what was really happening, how many of the accusations were true, and how much of the upheaval was driven by internal politics. Readers interested in an in-depth critique are directed to Kolitz (note 5 earlier); and Dan Rather's *American Journalist* website: https://danratherjournalist.org/investigative-journalist/60-minutes/pdap.

120. Ibid.

Chapter 4

1. Memorial page for Harvey Bryan Berthiaume (1984, April 2, 1908–October 17). (n.d.). *Find a Grave*, database and images. Memorial ID 100857727, citing Mountain View Cemetery, Swanzey, Cheshire County, NH. Maintained by Franz Martin (contributor 47090189). https://www.findagrave.com/memorial/100857727/harvey_bryan-berthiaume.

2. Ancestry.com. (2010). *1920 United States Federal Census* [database on-line]. Provo, UT: Ancestry.com Operations, Inc.

3. Ibid.

4. Ancestry.com. (2002). *1930 United States Federal Census* [database on-line]. Provo, UT: Ancestry.com Operations Inc.

5. Ancestry.com. (2005). *U.S., World War II Army Enlistment Records, 1938–1946* [database on-line]. Lehi, UT: Ancestry.com Operations, Inc..

6. See note 2 earlier.

7. See note 4 earlier.

8. Ancestry.com. (2012). *1940 United States Federal Census* [database on-line]. Provo, UT: Ancestry.com Operations, Inc..

9. "Berthiaume-Barlow." (1941, June 24). *Greenfield Recorder-Gazette*, 3. Ancestry.com. (2013). *New Hampshire, U.S., Marriage and Divorce Records, 1659–1947* [database on-line]. Provo, UT: Ancestry.com Operations, Inc.

10. See note 8 earlier; see note 4 earlier.

11. See note 5 earlier.

12. Ibid.

13. Ancestry.com. (2013). *Massachusetts, U.S., Birth Index, 1860–1970* [database on-line]. Lehi, UT: Ancestry.com Operations, Inc.

14. Berthiaume interview with author, October 5, 2015.

15. See note 5 earlier.

16. Memorial page for Irene M. Lamoureux Berthiaume (2010, September 8, 1923–August 4). (n.d.). *Find a Grave*, database and images. Find a Grave Memorial ID 100857787. Citing Mountain View Cemetery, Swanzey, Cheshire County, NH. Maintained by Franz Martin (contributor 47090189). https://www.findagrave.com/memorial/100857787/irene_m-berthiaume.

17. Ibid.

18. Durand, Bethel E. (Barlow). (2003, June 12). *Boston Globe*, C20.

19. Ancestry.com. (2015). *U.S. Social Security Applications and Claims Index, 1936–2007* [database on-line]. Provo, UT: Ancestry.com Operations, Inc.

20. "Irene Berthiaume: Obituaries and death notices." (2010, August 6). *Keene Sentinel*. https://www.sentinelsource.com/news/obituaries/irene-berthiaume/article_4abbdffb-0285-5103-8041-91fb752dcedf.html.

21. H. A. Manning Company. (1958). *Manning's Keene, Marlboro, North Swanzey and Hinsdale directory, 1958*. Springfield, MA: H. A. Manning Company.

22. Grant, G. (1964, August 19). "Kennedy High opens this fall with new frontier of teaching." *Washington Post*. https://www.proquest.com/historical-newspapers/kennedy-high-opens-this-fall-with-new-frontier/docview/142189254/se-2.

23. Lee, B. (2000, July 19). "They aren't singing 'Camelot' at Kennedy High." http://www.prstech.com/jfk/letter_blairlee1.html.

24. Schulte, B. (1999, December 11). "Kennedy's melting pot reaches boiling point." *Washington Post*. https://www.washingtonpost.com/archive/politics/1999/12/11/kennedys-melting-pot-reaches-boiling-point/1bfcfbf4-0668-4875-947f-518e3620b809/?utm_term=.8cdca57483fa..

25. "Avatar Meher Baba 1894–1969." (n.d.). *Meher Spiritual Center*. https://www.mehercenter.org/meher-baba/life-and-work/.

26. "Avatar." (n.d.). *Merriam-Webster*. https://www.merriam-webster.com/dictionary/avatar.

27. "History and Legacy." (n.d.). Meher Spiritual Center. https://www.mehercenter.org/the-center/history-and-legacy/.

28. Baba, Meher. (1966). Excerpts from GOD IN A PILL? Walnut Creek, CA: Sufism Reoriented, Inc. http://www.avatarmeherbaba.org/erics/godpill.html.

29. Goldstein, M. (2007, June 1). "Cover story—'Tommy' by Mike McInnerney." *Rockpop Gallery*. https://rockpopgallery.typepad.com/rockpop_gallery_news/2007/06/cover_story_tom.html.

30. Ibid.
31. Bob Jardin Professional Profile. (n.d.). *Bizstanding*. https://bizstanding.com/ng/org-prof-profile/70642546-12202839606655687-2-3-9ecc8.
32. Henry, N., and Volente, J. (1978, November 29). "Students join unit seeking drug solution." *Washington Post*.
33. Sanders, L. (1982, September 13). "Di Grazia still stirs debate in private life." *Law Enforcement News, VIII*(15), 1–10, 10.
34. Johnson, R. W. (1975, March 25). "Montgomery schools superintendent Elseroad accepts Colorado position." *The News* (Frederick, MD), 14.
35. US Bureau of the Census. (1982). *1980 Census of Population, General Population Characteristics (1980 PC80-1-B22); 1980 Census of Housing, General Housing Characteristics (1980 HC80-1-A22)*. Suitland, MD: U.S. Bureau of the Census.
36. Ibid.
37. Joseph, R. (2014). "Montgomery County, MD Public Schools: Student performance and achievement of low-income and minority students." *Graduate Student Capstones, 52*. http://digitalcommons.du.edu/geog_ms_capstone/52.
38. See note 35 earlier (General Population Characteristics).
39. "Montgomery County engages new superintendent." (1975, August 28). *Cumberland News* (Cumberland, MD), 4. Montgomery County Public Schools. (2019). *MCPS Boundary Analysis, 52*. https://www.montgomeryschoolsmd.org/uploadedFiles/departments/publicinfo/Boundary_Analysis/interim-report/01_Introduction.pdf.
40. Hayes, F. W., III. (1985, November). "Politics and expertise in an emerging postindustrial community: Montgomery County, Maryland's search for quality integrated education." [Conference Paper]. Presented at the Annual Meeting of the Southern Political Science Association, Nashville, TN, November 6–9, 1985. https://files.eric.ed.gov/fulltext/ED263266.pdf.
41. Ibid.
42. Committees were influential in Montgomery County politics. Hayes wrote, "It cannot be overemphasized that it is firm and consistent practice in Montgomery County education politics to draw extensively on community participation. Community groups are quick to insist on their right to be involved. It was natural, then, that increasing recognition of a problem would be accompanied by the appointment of community groups": see note 40 earlier, 19–20.
43. See note 34 earlier, 14.
44. "Former policeman fills superintendent's post." (1969, January 14). *Pottstown Mercury*, 15.
45. Ibid.
46. Ibid., 15
47. "Bernardo resigns Roberts position." (1971, January 8). *Pottstown Mercury*, 1, 24.
48. Ibid., 1, 24.
49. Ibid.
50. "Schools remain closed: Ruling banning walkout overturned." (1972, September 7). *Portsmouth Herald*, 2.
51. Parry, R. (1975, August 27). "New Montgomery County school head talk of future plans." *Daily Mail* (Hagerstown, MD), 38.
52. See note 39 ("Montgomery County engages"), 4.

53. "Providence aims at balanced mix." (1974, December 18). *Bridgeport Post* (Bridgeport, CT), 22.

54. Johnson, R. W. (1975, September 3). "Montgomery's school woes are formidable: Bernardo." *Frederick News*, 32.

55. See note 51, earlier, 38.

56. See note 39 ("Montgomery County engages"), 4.

57. Johnston, L. D., O'Malley, P. M., Bachman, J. G., and Schulenberg, J. E. (2003). *Monitoring the Future national survey results on drug use, 1975–2003: Vol. I, Secondary school students* (NIH Publication No. 04-5507). Bethesda, MD: National Institute on Drug Abuse..

58. Domestic Council Drug Abuse Task Force. (1975). *White Paper on Drug Abuse.* Washington, DC: US Department of Justice. https://www.ncjrs.gov/pdffiles1/Photocopy/ 164686NCJRS.pdf.

59. Massing, M. (1998). *The fix: Solving the nation's drug problem.* New York: Simon & Schuster.

60. "High school ring broken." (1975, May 30). *Morning Herald*, 17.

61. Daniels, L. A. (1977, January 4). "Bostonians not neutral on new Montgomery police chief." *Washington Post.* https://www.washingtonpost.com/archive/politics/1977/01/04/bostoni ans-not-neutral-on-new-montgomery-police-chief/2fa9e559-8512-4aab-9c8a-5cbd9 3f51aee/.

62. Ibid.

63. Finfer, L. (2012, June 14). "'What ifs?' about White and Menino." *Dorchester Reporter.* https://www.dotnews.com/columns/2012/what-ifs-about-white-and-menino.

64. See note 33 earlier, 1–10.

65. Belmar, J. M., and Kleinknecht, G. (2014, May 14). *Policewomen on patrol: The results of an experiment.* Project of the St. Louis County Police Welfare Association. According to the report (p. 1), "No other large police department at this time was allowing females to work alone while patrolling in a marked cruiser, a period when the police profession was dominated by both male patrol officers and male supervisors. This new police practice was part of an 'experiment' managed by Professor Lewis J. Sherman, with the results and conclusions used to decide if assigning females to uniform patrol duties would continue."

66. See note 33 earlier, 7.

67. See note 61, earlier.

68. The Boston Police Patrolmen's Association. (2015). *50th Anniversary Book.* Boston, MA: Boston Police Patrolmen's Association.

69. Gellerman, B. (2014, December 19). "How the Boston busing decision still affects city schools 40 years later." *WBUR News.* https://www.wbur.org/news/2014/06/20/boston-bus ing-ruling-anniversary.

70. Ibid.

71. Ibid.

72. National Policing Institute. (n.d.). "About us." https://www.policinginstitute.org/ about-us/.

73. "Police chiefs called pet rocks." (1976, April 14). *Corpus Christi Times*, 8.

74. Ibid.

75. Ibid.

76. See note 61 earlier.

77. Ibid.

78. Ibid.

79. Ibid.

80. Ibid.

81. See note 33 earlier, 7.

82. Towers resume [unpublished].

83. Ibid.

84. Ravitch, D. (2000). *The great school wars: A history of the New York City Public Schools.* Baltimore, MD: Johns Hopkins University Press.

85. Gray, M. (2009, April 2). A brief history of New York's Rockefeller Drug Laws. *Time.* http://content.time.com/time/nation/article/0,8599,1888864,00.html.

86. In 1973, with efforts to help people get clean falling short, Rockefeller implemented mandatory minimum sentences for possessing small amounts of narcotics. This legislation famously became known as the Rockefeller Laws and caused prison populations to expand rapidly: see note 88.

87. Village of Massena, NY. (1970). *Chapter 49: Narcotic Guidance Council (L.L. No. 1-1970).* https://ecode360.com/7084197.

88. Towers interview with author, July 3, 2017.

89. See note 34 earlier, 14.

90. "Tight budget threatens after-school activities." (1975, November 13). *Morning Herald* (Hagerstown, MD), 14.

91. "Montgomery school budget cuts in sports averted." (1976, January 14). *The News* (Frederick, MD), 28.

92. "Cutting budget 'devastating rape of fine school system': Bernardo." (1976, March 11). *The News* (Frederick, MD), 19.

93. Cline, D. (1976, June 26). "Montgomery grid coaches may lose jobs." *The News* (Frederick, MD), 11.

94. Goldberg, S. (1976, July 23). "Grid coaches made right move." *The News* (Frederick, MD), 17.

95. Johnson, R. W. (1976, September 23). "School board candidates evaluate Bernardo deeds." *The News* (Frederick, Maryland), 36.

96. See note 40 earlier, 18.

97. Ibid., 28.

98. Ibid.

99. Eaton, S. E., and Crutcher, E. (1994). *Slipping towards segregation: Local control and eroding desegregation in Montgomery County, Maryland.* Cambridge, MA: Harvard University, 16. https://eric.ed.gov/?id=ED374202.

100. See note 40 earlier, 32.

101. Ibid.

102. Valente, J. (1978, March 28). "Chief Di Grazia and his shadow." *Washington Post.* https://www.washingtonpost.com/archive/local/1978/03/28/chief-digrazia-and-his-shadow/53608ea3-e543-4da5-a1db-b2f067a4f47c/.

103. Shearer, L. (1976, August 22). "Parade's Special: Intelligence Report." *Boston Globe,* J4.

104. See note 102 earlier.

105. Zon, C. (1978, November 20). "A Controversial Cop Shakes Up Maryland Suburbs with Pot Raids on Its High Schools." *PEOPLE, 10*(21). https://web.archive.org/web/20120426125315/http://www.people.com/people/archive/article/0,,20072225,00.html.

106. See note 57 earlier.

Chapter 5

1. "Bethesda-Chevy Chase High School." (n.d.). *Wikipedia*. https://en.wikipedia.org/wiki/Bethesda-Chevy_Chase_High_School.

2. Zon, C. G. (1978, September 19). ". . . And crackdown angers B-CC students." *Washington Star*, B–1.

3. Belliveau, J. (1978, September 27). "Most students won't face judge." *Montgomery Journal*, A-5.

4. See note 2 earlier, B-2.

5. Ibid.

6. See note 3 earlier, A-5.

7. De Silva, R. (1977, July 3). "The young American and the flight toward drugs." *Washington Post*. https://www.washingtonpost.com/archive/lifestyle/1977/07/03/the-young-american-and-the-flight-toward-drugs/e02faf3b-f4ec–49f0-af08-16154bf5cc6e/.

8. Ibid.

9. Letter. "Drug arrests at Rockville." (1979, February). *Montgomery Journal.*.

10. Valente, J., and Tafari, L. (1978, September 19). "7 pupils arrested in drug busts at B-CC High School." *Washington Post*. https://www.washingtonpost.com/archive/local/1978/09/19/7-pupils-arrested-in-drug-busts-at-b-cc-high-school/95bda6da-4931-4d4f-ac08-b3716293046f/.

11. Di Grazia interview with author, February 15, 2018.

12. Simon, D. (2012, June 4). "Graduation remarks, Bethesda-Chevy Chase High School." https://davidsimon.com/graduation-remarks-bethesda-chevy-chase-high-school/.

13. Simon, D. J. (1978, April 21). "Drugs, alcohol easily available to students." *The Tattler*, 1, 3.

14. Ibid. Years later, the *Washington Post* referenced the *Tattler* story in an article: "Simon put the story in the paper without first showing it to the newspaper adviser, and it caused an uproar in the school. Faculty members told him that the story was offensive. His parents were called in for a conference with a teacher that was ostensibly about his grades, but he always felt had something to do with his story. In the end, though, the principal took no action against Simon. It was the era of the Watergate reporting in *The Post*, and there was a pride in journalism. Eventually, the incident faded in the school's history": Judkis, M. (2012, March 28). "David Simon of *The Wire* former high school muckraker." *Washington Post*. https://www.washingtonpost.com/blogs/arts-post/post/david-simon-of-the-wire-former-high-school-muckraker/2012/03/28/gIQAjLHpgS_blog.html.

15. See note 13 earlier, 1, 3.

16. See note 10 earlier.

17. See note 3 earlier, A-5.

18. Di Grazia interview with author, February 15, 2018.

19. See note 2 earlier, B-2.

20. Dowd, M. (1978, September 19). "County gets tough with kids on alcohol and drugs." *Washington Star*, B-1.

21. Belliveau, J. (1978, September 20). "More H.S. drug busts likely." *Montgomery Journal*, A-4. See also note 10 earlier.

22. Ibid.

23. With the passage of time, it is possible some people may not want stories of youthful drug use and/or arrests resurfaced. Names of students connected with drug usage and legal involvement thus will not be used here.

24. Zon, C. G. (1978, September 20). "Pot takes a holiday after B-CC drug bust." *Washington Star*, C-1.

25. See note 2 earlier, B-2.

26. See note 10 earlier.

27. See note 2 earlier, B-2.

28. Ibid.

29. In 1978, the four police districts were Rockville (North and West), Bethesda (South), Silver Spring (SE), Wheaton-Glenmont (East). Germantown (North) and Montgomery Village (Central) were created later.

30. See note 20 earlier.

31. Ibid.

32. See note 2 earlier, B-2.

33. Ibid.

34. Di Grazia interview with author, February 15, 2018.

35. See note 10 earlier.

36. See note 24 earlier, C-2.

37. Ibid., C-1.

38. Ahlers, M. M. (1978, September 22). "13 more students arrested for drugs." *Montgomery Journal*, A-1.

39. Dowd, M. (1978, September 23). "County drug busts net 23 more students." *Washington Star*.

40. Ibid.

41. Zon, C. G. (1978, September 24). "Paranoia replaces partying." *Washington Star*, C-1.

42. See note 39 earlier.

43. See note 20 earlier, B-1.

44. See note 41 earlier, C-4.

45. Ibid., C-1, C-4.

46. See note 41 earlier, C-4.

47. See note 3 earlier, A-1, A-5.

48. Bucci email to author, September 14, 2020.

49. See note 3 earlier, A-1, A-5.

50. Ibid., A-5.

51. Dowd, M. (1978, September 27). "County plans to phase out drug arrests." *Washington Star*, C-2.

52. Belliveau, J. (1978, September 29). "Arrest of 11 at Whitman brings student protest." *Montgomery Journal*, A-4.

53. Ibid.

54. Ibid., A-4.

55. Zon, C. G. (1978, September 28). "Angry students block traffic." *Washington Star*, B-1.

56. See note 52 earlier, A-4.

57. Zon, C. G. (1978, November 3). "Violence breaks out in drug raid." *Washington Star*, B-2.

58. See note 52 earlier, A-4.

59. See note 55 earlier, B-1.

60. Belliveau, J. (1978, September 27). "Student views: Estimates of pot smoking vary." *Montgomery Journal*, A-8.
61. A father. (1978, October 6). "Letters to the editor: Of youth, drugs and tomorrows." *Washington Star*.
62. Ibid.
63. Belliveau, J. (1978, October 18). "School briefs: Innocents arrested?" *Montgomery Journal*, A-11.
64. See note 52 earlier, A-4.
65. Ibid.
66. Belliveau, J. (1978, September 29). "Parents back the drug busts." *Montgomery Journal*, A-1, A-5.
67. Belliveau, J. (1978, October 4). "Most student leaders oppose the drug busts." *Montgomery Journal*, A-2.
68. Ibid.
69. See note 67 earlier, A-2.
70. Ibid.
71. Ibid.
72. Ibid.
73. See note 67 earlier, A-2.
74. Ibid.
75. Ibid.
76. Ibid.
77. Ibid.
78. Zon, C. (1978, October 6). "Montgomery school chief supports police drug raids." *Washington Star*.
79. Zon, C. G. (1978, October 8). "Raids force a look at drug issue." *Washington Star*, C-1.
80. Ibid.
81. Ibid.
82. See note 24 earlier, C-1.
83. See note 41 earlier, C-4.
84. "High school drug busts." (1978, October 1). *Washington Star*, editorials.
85. See note 24 earlier, C-1.
86. See note 41 earlier, C-4.
87. Ibid.
88. See note 3 earlier, A-5.
89. See note 67 earlier, A-2.
90. See note 84 earlier.
91. Belliveau, J. (1978, October 6). "Bernardo says students dealing drugs will be expelled 1 year." *Montgomery Journal*, A-1.
92. Ibid. See also note 78 earlier.
93. The old rule had allowed a student to transfer to another school after being expelled.
94. See note 91, A-4.
95. Belliveau, J. (1978, October 11). "Student leaders act to stop drug busts." *Montgomery Journal*, A-3.
96. Ibid.
97. Ibid.

98. See note 78 earlier.

99. See note 95, A-3; see also note 79, C-1.

100. See note 95 earlier, A-3.

101. "Drug arrests continue." (1978, October 11). *Washington Star*, B-2.

102. Belliveau, J., and Benton, M. J. (1978, November 15). "Student violence has police wary." *Montgomery Journal*, A-1, A-6.

103. Ibid., A-6.

104. Zon, C. G., and McAleer, C. A. (1978, October 14). "Drug raid protest draws few Blair students." *Washington Star*, D-1.

105. Belliveau, J. (1978, October 18). "Protest Smoke-In set for Halloween." *Montgomery Journal*, A-1.

106. Ibid.

107. "Eight more arrests in drug crackdown." (1978, October 13). *Washington Star*, B-2. See also note 104 earlier, D-1.

108. See note 104 earlier, D-1.

109. Ibid.

110. Ibid.; see also note 105, A-1.

111. "Drug-sweeps net 22 more school kids: Total now 228." (1978, October 25). *Montgomery Journal*, A-9.

112. Torrey, E. F. (1978, October 27). "Drug busts and the Me Decade." *Washington Star*, A-9.

113. Ibid.

114. See note 105 earlier (Belliveau), A-1.

115. Ibid.

116. Holloway, D. (2002). "Yippies." *St. James Encyclopedia of Pop Culture*. Archived from the original on January 17, 2021. https://web.archive.org/web/20210117155545/https://www.encyclopedia.com/media/encyclopedias-almanacs-transcripts-and-maps/yippies.

117. Ibid.

118. Belliveau, J. (1978, November 3). "A dying gasp from the 1960's?" *Montgomery Journal*, A-15.

119. Ibid.

120. "Smoke-Ins" and "Free the Weed" protests were common events led by the Yippies in the 1970s, and Leatrice Urbanowicz was one of the more prominent Yippies. She had garnered news coverage in Ohio when she ran for lieutenant governor as a Kent State student. She was the running mate of activist Steve Conliff in his gubernatorial campaign. Urbanowicz was part of a group of students who got close enough to then-Governor Jim Rhodes to throw a banana cream pie at him. Conliff was charged with assault for the incident. Urbanowicz was later removed from the ballot for not gathering the one thousand signatures required to be on the primary ballot. She moved to Maryland in 1978, where she participated in Yippie events. See (1) "Gov. Rhodes is hit in face with a pie by protester." (1977, August 17). *New York Times*. https://www.nytimes.com/1977/08/17/archives/gov-rhodes-is-hit-in-face-with-a-pie-by-protester.html. (2) Rapport, M. (1978, March 29). "Student on ballot with pie thrower: She's candidate for lieutenant governor." *Daily Kent Stater*. https://dks.library.kent.edu/cgi-bin/kentstate?a=d&d=dks19780329-01.2.11&e=-------en-20--1--txt-txIN-------. (3) "Urbanowicz removed from state office race." (1978, April 5). *Daily Kent Stater*. https://dks.library.kent.edu/cgi-bin/kentstate?a=d&d=dks19780405-01.2.25&e=-------en-20--1--txt-txIN---. (4) McGuire,

C. (2016, April 8). "Observations: Leatrice Urbanowicz loves learning, throwing pies." *Frederick News-Post*. https://www.fredericknewspost.com/public/ap/observations-leatrice-urbanowicz-loves-learning-throwing-pies/article_52c90e10-c32d-5651-953f-36fb24ec9104.html.

121. See note 118 earlier, A-15.

122. Chappelle participated in similar events years after the 1978 Halloween protest. Decades later, Rupert Chappelle was on the staff at Montgomery College, and videos of him playing synthesizers could be found on YouTube, including the video "Extreme Theremining —Twin Peaks," posted in 2010. https://www.youtube.com/watch?v=q72tCpzA-b8. See Sargent, E. D. (1983, July 5). "Celebration of family life at park leaves Yippies out in the rain." *Washington Post*. https://www.washingtonpost.com/archive/local/1983/07/05/celebration-of-family-life-at-park-leaves-yippies-out-in-the-rain/4e2d364c-b338-4152-9b39-798882e8ac5f/.

123. See note 118 earlier, A-15.

124. "Drug arrest protest" (photo). (1978, November 1). *Washington Star*. Belliveau, J. (1978, November 1). "8 at police station Smoke-In arrested." *Montgomery Journal*, A-10.

125. Zon, C. G. (1978, November 3). "Violence breaks out in drug raid." *Washington Star*, B-1.

126. Ibid.

127. Ibid.

128. Ibid., B-2.

129. Ibid.

130. Zon, C. (1978, November 20). "A controversial cop shakes up Maryland suburbs with pot raids on its high schools." *PEOPLE*, *10*(21), https://web.archive.org/web/20120426125315/http://www.people.com/people/archive/article/0,,20072225,00.html.

131. See note 126 earlier, B-2.

132. Belliveau, J., and Benton, M. J. (1978, November 15). "Student violence has police wary." *Montgomery Journal*, A-1.

133. See note 132 earlier, B-2.

134. Belliveau, J. (1978, December 1). "Drug users had previous arrests." *Montgomery Journal*, A-7.

135. Zon, C. G. (1978, November 29). "Some students consider arrests badge of honor." *Washington Star*, MC–1.

136. See note 131 earlier.

Chapter 6

1. Belliveau, J. (1978, November 24). "New plan aimed at drug use." *Montgomery Journal*, A-1, A-9.

2. Rumbaugh interview with author, February 16, 2016.

3. Zon, C. G. (1978, September 24). "Paranoia replaces partying." *Washington Star*, C-1.

4. Belliveau, J. (1978, September 27). "Student views: Estimates of pot smoking vary." *Montgomery Journal*, A-8.

5. Belliveau, J. (1978, October 11). "Student leaders act to stop drug busts." *Montgomery Journal*, A-3.

6. Zon, C. G. (1978, October 8). "Raids force a look at drug issue." *Washington Star*, C-4.

7. Ibid.

8. Ibid.
9. Zon, C. G. (1978, September 4). "'Budget, Bernardo, Basics'—Montgomery County school race issues." *Washington Star.*
10. Ibid.
11. "The Superintendent & the Chief." (1978, November 12). *Washington Star* editorial page.
12. Hayes, F. W., III. (1985, November). *Politics and expertise in an emerging postindustrial community: Montgomery County, Maryland's search for quality integrated education.* [Conference Paper.] Presented at the Annual Meeting of the Southern Political Science Association, Nashville, TN, November 6–9, 1985. https://files.eric.ed.gov/fulltext/ED263 266.pdf.
13. See note 9 earlier.
14. Hirzel, D. (1978, September 13). "Basics, discipline win in counties' school contests." *Washington Star..*
15. Belliveau, J. (1978, October 4). "All school board candidates support drug busts." *Montgomery Journal*, A-6.
16. Ibid.
17. Ibid.
18. Ibid.
19. See note 11 earlier.
20. Zon, C. (1978, November 20). "A controversial cop shakes up Maryland suburbs with pot raids on its high schools." *PEOPLE, 10*(21), https://web.archive.org/web/20120426125315/http://www.people.com/people/archive/article/0,,20072225,00.html.
21. See note 6 earlier, C-4.
22. Dowd, M. (1978, November 24). "Montgomery police step up complaints against di Grazia." *Washington Star*, B-1. Vesey, T. (1983, June 28). "Gilchrist calls di Grazia 'destructive.'" *Washington Post..*
23. Ibid.
24. Sanders, L. (1982, September 13). "Di Grazia still stirs debate in private life." *Law Enforcement News, VIII*(15), 9.
25. Ibid., 10.
26. Ibid., 1.
27. Di Grazia interview with the author, February 15, 2018.
28. See note 6 earlier, C-1, C-4.
29. Ibid.
30. Ibid.
31. Ibid.
32. See note 6 earlier, C-1, C-4.
33. Belliveau, J., and McShea, J. (1978, November 8). "Out's win schools race." *Montgomery Journal*, A-1.
34. "Police Chief fired." (1978, December 8). *Baltimore Sun*, 64.
35. See note 33 earlier, A-1.
36. Ibid.
37. MCPS Board of Education Minutes, November 27, 1978.
38. Zon, C. G. (1978, November 28). "County juvenile drug arrests may exceed 1977 national total." *Washington Star*, MC-1.
39. See note 1 earlier, A-1.

40. Ibid.

41. Ibid.

42. Meher Baba. (2005). "November 1965, to Robert Dreyfuss, Meherazad, LA 638." Posted by Patra Chosnyid Skybamedpa, Eastern School of Broad Buddhism. http://www.mehe rbabadnyana.net/life_eternal/Book_One/Drugs.htm. In 1965, Robert Dreyfuss had flown from America and hitchhiked across Europe, Turkey, and Iran to India to meet with Meher Baba in Meherazad. Baba instructed him, "Tell those that are [taking drugs], that if drugs could make one realize God, then God is not worthy of being God." Later Robert gave a talk to some Baba lovers in New York. "I got up in front of all those people and said, 'The journey to Baba is from here to here.' I gestured from my head to my heart. Then I sat down. That was my first Baba talk": Dreyfuss, R. (2012). "The journey to Baba is from here to here." Avatarmeherbaba.org. https://www.avatarmeherbaba.org/erics/firstbabat alk.html.

43. Ibid.

44. See note 1 earlier, A-1.

45. Ibid.

46. Belliveau, J. (1978, November 29). "School board backs off on model drug center." *Montgomery Journal*, November 29, 1978, A-2. Cahill, R. (1978, November 29). "Schools delay action on special drug classes." *Washington Star*, p. MC-2.

47. See note 46 (Cahill), A-1.

48. MCPS Board of Education Minutes, November 27, 1978.

49. See note 46 earlier (Belliveau), A-1 .

50. Ibid.

51. Ibid.

52. See note 46 (Belliveau), A-2.

53. MCPS Board of Education Minutes, November 27, 1978.

54. See note 46 (Belliveau), A-2.

55. Ibid.

56. Ibid.

57. Ibid.

58. Belliveau, J. (1978, December 6). "Board hit for inaction on youth drug problems." *Montgomery Journal*, A-6.

59. Ibid.

60. Ibid.

61. Ibid.

62. Ibid.

63. Ibid.

64. Ibid.

65. Ibid.

66. Ibid.

67. Ibid.

68. Ibid.

69. Belliveau, J. (1978, December 1). "Drug users had previous arrests." *Montgomery Journal*, A-7.

70. Schisgall, L. (1978, December 15). "B-CC student picked to lead new county drug task force." *The Tattler*, 3.

71. Ibid.

72. Ibid.

73. See note 69, A-7.

74. "Drug crackdown." (1978, December 5). *Montgomery Journal*.

75. See note 70, 3.

76. Barton, C. (1978, November 29). "FOP says di Grazia statement untrue." *Montgomery Journal*, A-2.

77. See note 20.

78. Ibid.

79. "Montgomery cop seeks cohesion." (1978, December 8). *Evening Sun* (Hanover, PA), 28. Patterson, R. (1978, December 12). "Di Grazia suing to keep Maryland job." *Boston Globe*, 6.

80. Ibid.; "Di Grazia firing called legal." (1983, August 2). *Star-Democrat (Easton, MD)*, 3.

81. See note 79 ("Montgomery cop seeks"), 28.

82. See note 79 (Patterson), 6.

83. Ibid.

84. See note 22 (Vesey) earlier.

85. Ibid.

86. See note 79 (Patterson), 6.

87. See note 24 earlier, 7.

88. See note 79 ("Montgomery cop seeks"), 28.

89. See note 22 (Vesey) earlier.

90. Ibid.

91. "Di Grazia firing called legal." (1983, August 2). *Star-Democrat* (Easton, MD), 3.

92. "Exit di Grazia." (1978, December 15). *The Tattler*, 8.

93. Ibid.

94. "Drug arrests at Rockville." (1979, February). *Montgomery Journal*, letter to the editor.

95. Henry, N. (1978, December 27). "Disputes enliven sessions of county school board." *Washington Post*, C-1.

96. Valente, J. (1978, December 6). "Board votes to sue on Bernardo pact." *Washington Post*, B-1. Blair Ewing was absent from the meeting, but his colleagues noted his opposition for the record. Student member David Naiman abstained.

97. See note 95 earlier, C-1.

98. Muscatine, A. (1981, December 27). "Greenblatt leads shift to school conservatism." *Washington Post*, B-1.

99. See note 95 earlier, C-1.

100. See note 96 ("Board votes"), B-1.

101. Hall, C. (1978, June 15). "Montgomery Board renews Bernardo contract in 5–2 vote." *Washington Post*, Md 1.

102. See note 96 ("Board votes"), B-1.

103. Ibid.

104. Ibid.

105. Meyers, R. (1978, June 21). "Stepping on toes in Montgomery." *Washington Post*, C–1.

106. Ibid.

107. Henry, N. (1979, September 4). "Montgomery schools to reflect new board's philosophy." *Washington Post*, C-1.

108. See note 96 ("Board votes"), , B-1.
109. Belliveau, J. (1978, December 8). "School superintendent fights ouster." *Montgomery Journal*, A-1.
110. See note 1 earlier, A-1, A-9.
111. Berthiaume provided this story in an interview with the author, and it could not be independently verified, as he technically remained in his position with the health department.
112. Henry, N. (1979, September 4). Montgomery schools to reflect new board's philosophy. *Washington Post*, C-1.
113. Belliveau, J. (1978, December 20). "Blacks may picket 'racist' Board of Ed." *Montgomery School*, A-1.
114. Ibid., A-1, A-4.
115. Ibid., A4.
116. Ibid., A4.
117. Ibid., A4.
118. Ibid., A4.
119. Ibid., A-4.
120. MCPS Board of Education minutes, December 18, 1978, 14.
121. Belliveau, J. (1978, December 20). Blacks may picket 'racist' Board of Ed. *Montgomery School*, A-1, A-4.
122. Ibid., A-1.
123. Ibid., A-4.
124. Ibid.
125. See note 120 earlier, 14.
126. Ibid.
127. Ibid., 15.
128. Belliveau, J. (1978, December 20). "Student drug help approved." *Montgomery Journal*, A-9.
129. Ibid.
130. Ibid.
131. See note 120 earlier, 15.
132. Ibid.
133. Ibid., 15–16
134. Ibid., 16
135. Ibid.
136. Ibid., 15.
137. Pilot definition. (n.d.). *Dictionary.com*. https://www.dictionary.com/browse/pilot.
138. Prototype definition. (n.d.). *Dictionary.com*. https://www.dictionary.com/browse/prototype.
139. See note 120 earlier, 15.
140. See note 120 earlier, 16.

Chapter 7

1. This claim was stated in interviews that the author had with Brian Berthiaume but could not be independently verified.
2. David Litsey profile. (n.d.). *LinkedIn*. https://www.linkedin.com/in/david-litsey-68a68878/.

3. Cathleen Berthiaume email with author, August 6, 2019.

4. Bernardo email with author, August 6, 2019.

5. Belliveau, J. (1979, March 16). "70 come out to fight model drug program." *Montgomery Journal*, A-6.

6. Decades later, in an interview for this book, Charlie Bernardo said via email that he could not recall the specific details surrounding the origin of the Pilot Program or the hiring of its personnel. "While I remember their zeal and integrity regarding the Phoenix concept," Bernardo said, "I don't have a direct recollection of the men themselves."

7. People interviewed for the book had different memories or could not remember at all the last names for some staff. The last names of Carol McGinn (teacher) and Mary Treacy (secretary) were not cited specifically by Berthiaume or Baddour but were confirmed by two separate parent letters in the document *The Phoenix School: An Impact Report*. Details about their staff responsibilities and backgrounds were derived from that document, interviews, and email correspondence with Berthiaume and Baddour. Neither McGinn nor Treacy were interviewed. Source: Nolen, J. A. T. (1981, December 9). *The Phoenix School: An impact report*. [Evaluation Report]. Submitted to Montgomery County Board of Education.

8. See earlier note regarding staff names. Berthiaume also recalled an administrative assistant named "Janice Tracey" (Cathleen Berthiaume email to author, August 5, 2019). Correspondence with Steve Baddour and parent letters in the report *The Phoenix School: An Impact Report* (see note 7) instead used the name cited here, Mary Treacy, though Baddour could not recall the exact last name or its spelling.

9. Eaton, S. E., and Crutcher, E. (1994). *Slipping towards segregation: Local control and eroding desegregation in Montgomery County, Maryland*. Cambridge, MA: Harvard University. https://eric.ed.gov/?id=ED374202.

10. Eaton and Crutcher (1994, 8) explain that MCPS "never faced a desegregation lawsuit and, as a result, have been able to avoid the type of desegregation orders that forced change on many school districts. School officials in this suburban 495-square-mile district of 114,000 students near Washington, DC, found safe haven in 1977 with a voluntary magnet school program. The county passed and refined locally devised, locally controlled desegregation-related policies as it experienced enormous demographic changes [starting in the mid-1970s]. Montgomery County offers a case study of a school district where desegregation methods widely assumed to be preferable to mandatory measures were employed."

11. Cohn, D., and Morin, R. (1991, July 21). "The dispersion decade." *Washington Post*. https://www.washingtonpost.com/archive/politics/1991/07/21/the-dispersion-decade/3a64a0b8-032f-44b2-ab74-42d1889a2cee/.

12. Rotenstein, D. S. (2016, October 15). "Silver Spring, Maryland has whitewashed its past." *History News Network*. https://historynewsnetwork.org/article/163914.

13. Reed, D. (2019, June 5). "These 1970s plans show the Silver Spring that could have been." *Just Up the Pike blog*. http://www.justupthepike.com/2019/06/these-1970s-plans-show-silver-spring.html.

14. "3 Montgomery school closings recommended." (1978, December 9). *Washington Post*, B-4.

15. In source material, the spelling of this building can be found both as one word, "Springmill," and two, "Spring Mill." Today, the building is known as the "Spring Mill Field Office." Since it was most commonly referred to as Spring Mill in documents once Phoenix moved there and is still two words today, that is how it will be noted here.

16. Office of Legislative Oversight. (1979). *An evaluation of the plant maintenance program of the Montgomery County Public Schools.* [Evaluation Report, April 29, 1979]. Rockville, MD: Montgomery County Council.
17. The building was located at 11721 Kemp Mill Road, Silver Spring, MD, 20902.
18. Belliveau, J. (1979, March 16). 70 come out to fight model drug program. *The Montgomery Journal,* A-6.
19. See note 5 earlier, A-6.
20. Ibid.
21. Ibid.
22. Ibid.
23. Ibid.
24. Ibid.
25. Ibid.
26. Shepard, C. F. (2018, February 25). "Remembering Minuchin and the democratization of therapy." *Counseling Today,* https://ctarchive.counseling.org/2018/02/remembering-minuchin-democratization-therapy/#.
27. Wylie, M. S. (2007, November 1). "Jay Haley didn't set out to transform psychotherapy." *Psychotherapy Networker: The Accidental Therapist.* https://www.psychotherapynetworker.org/article/accidental-therapist/.
28. Berthiaume interview with author, May 9, 2023.
29. "Huma Bird: The bird of fortune." (n.d.). MythLok. https://mythlok.com/huma-bird/.
30. van den Broek, R. B. (2015). *The myth of the Phoenix according to classical and early Christian traditions.* Netherlands: Brill, 146.
31. Phoenix House Foundation. (n.d.). *Incite,* hosted by Columbia University in the city of New York. https://incite.columbia.edu/phoenix-house-foundation.
32. Department of Alternative and Continuing Education. (n.d.). *The Phoenix School: A Montgomery County Public Schools program.* [Unpublished Brochure]. Rockville, MD: Montgomery County Public Schools.
33. Emrich, R. L., and Green, P. (1981, December) *Summary of the evaluation of the Phoenix Pilot Drug Program.* [Evaluation Report]. Napa, CA: Pacific Institute for Research and Evaluation, 40.
34. Ellison, K. (1979, September 13). "Md. School tries to raise teen addicts from ashes." *Washington Post,* B-5.
35. Shapiro, A., and Gross, S. (1981, February). *Preliminary follow-up evaluation of participants in the Phoenix School: A Pilot Drug Program.* [Evaluation Report]. Rockville, MD: Montgomery County Public Schools Department of Educational Accountability.
36. See note 33, 3 (footnote).
37. See note 7, 38–39.
38. Ibid., 27–28.
39. MCPS Board of Education minutes, December 18, 1978, 15.
40. See note 33 earlier.
41. The name of this student has been removed to protect their privacy.
42. See note 35, A1–A2.
43. Ibid., A1.
44. Ibid., A2.
45. Tanner-Smith, E., Finch, A. J., Hennessy, E. A., and Moberg, D. P. (2018). "Who attends recovery high schools after substance use treatment? A descriptive analysis of school

aged youth." *Journal of Substance Abuse Treatment*, 89, 20–27. https://doi.org/10.1016/j.jsat.2018.03.003.

46. Berthiaume interview with author, October 2015.
47. Department of Alternative and Continuing Education. (n.d.). *The Phoenix School: A Montgomery County Public Schools program.* [Unpublished Brochure]. Rockville, MD: Montgomery County Public Schools.
48. Student names were redacted to protect their privacy.
49. See note 7 earlier, 36.
50. See note 47.
51. See note 7 earlier, 56.
52. Ibid., 36.
53. See note 34 earlier, B-5.
54. Ibid.
55. Ibid.
56. Ibid.
57. Ibid.
58. Ibid.
59. The student's name has been changed to respect his privacy.
60. Gaines-Carter, P. (1981, June 6). Graduation-for-one fetes singular success. *Washington Star*, B1–B2.
61. Ibid., B2.
62. Ibid.
63. Ibid., B1.
64. Ibid., B2.

Chapter 8

1. The word "pilot" denotes a test case before introducing something more widely.
2. MCPS Board of Education minutes, December 9, 1980, Resolution No. 693-80.
3. MCPS Board of Education minutes, December 15, 1980, 1.
4. Ibid., 4.
5. Shapiro, A., and Gross, S. (1981, February). *Preliminary follow-up evaluation of participants in the Phoenix School: A Pilot Drug Program.* Rockville, MD: Montgomery County Public Schools Department of Educational Accountability, 4.
6. Ibid., 1.
7. See note 5 earlier.
8. Emrich, R. L., and Green, P. (1981, December) *Summary of the evaluation of the Phoenix Pilot Drug Program.* [Evaluation Report]. Napa, CA: Pacific Institute for Research and Evaluation.
9. Ibid., 3 (footnote).
10. See note 5 earlier, 9–15.
11. Ibid., 2–3.
12. Ibid., 3.
13. Ibid., 1, footnote 1.
14. Ibid., 1, footnote 2.
15. See note 8 earlier.

16. Ibid., 3.
17. Ibid., 1.
18. Ibid., 38.
19. Ibid., 35.
20. Ibid., 40.
21. Ibid., 39.
22. Ibid., 39.
23. Ibid., 14.
24. Ibid., 39.
25. Ibid., 29.
26. Ibid., 39.
27. Ibid., 39.
28. Ibid., 39.
29. Ibid., 1.
30. Ibid., 1.
31. Ibid. While the report refers to Brian Berthiaume both as the "principal" and the "program director," his title was technically "program coordinator."
32. See note 8 earlier, 1.
33. Ibid.
34. Ibid.
35. Ibid., E-3.
36. Nolen, J. A. T. (1981, December 9). *The Phoenix School: An impact report*. [Unpublished Report]. Submitted to Montgomery County Board of Education, 2.
37. Ibid., 2.
38. Ibid., 75–89.
39. Ibid., 76.
40. Ibid., 78.
41. MCPS Board of Education minutes, January 12, 1982, 34.
42. MCPS Board of Education minutes, January 25, 1982, 17–18; MCPS Board of Education minutes, February 9, 1982, 21–24.
43. Ibid., 23.
44. MCPS Board of Education minutes, February 18, 1982, 6.
45. MCPS Board of Education minutes, May 11, 1982, 4.
46. MCPS Board of Education minutes, June 1, 1982, 9-11. While the minutes did not specify, it is presumed the arrests referred to by Dr. Towers did not all happen on school grounds.
47. Ibid., 10.
48. Ibid., 11.

Chapter 9

1. Belliveau, J. (1978, November 24). "New plan aimed at drug use." *Montgomery Journal*, A-1.
2. Berthiaume interview with author, October 2015.
3. Barton LeRoy VanRiper (1910–1965). (n.d.). *WikiTree*. https://www.wikitree.com/wiki/VanRiper-26.
4. "Seneca Army Depot—then and now." (2014, November). Seneca County, NY. https://www.co.seneca.ny.us/wp-content/uploads/2020/01/Seneca-Army-Depot-story-ADA.pdf.

5. Espenscheid, A. T. (n.d.). *Women's encampment for a future of peace and justice collection (MS 839)*. Special Collections and University Archives. Amherst, MA: University of Massachusetts Amherst Libraries. http://findingaids.library.umass.edu/ead/mums839.

6. Krasniewicz, L. (1992). *Nuclear summer: The clash of communities at the Seneca Women's Peace Encampment*. Ithaca, NY: Cornell University Press.

7. Willard Asylum operated from 1869 to 1995 and is famous for its collection of patients' suitcases. "A cleaning person stumbled upon hundreds of dusty suitcases in the attic, brought by patients upon their admittance to the hospital . . . The patients died at Willard, and their personal effects went unclaimed by anyone outside the institution. The staff, apparently unable to throw them away, meticulously stored and catalogued the suitcases in the attic . . . Photos of the luggage, carefully packed by the inmates and their families, indicate they believed they were just passing through": Jacobson, M. M. (2016, September 20). *Willard Asylum for the Chronic Insane, Ovid, New York: An abandoned asylum where patients have been forgotten but their possessions remain*. Atlas Obscura. https://www.atlasobscura.com/places/willard-asylum-for-the-chronic-insane.

8. "Romulus crash kills principal." (1965, August 6). *Democrat and Chronicle* (Rochester, NY), C-1.

9. "School principal at Romulus killed in crash." (1965, August 6). *Democrat and Chronicle* (Rochester, NY), C-3.

10. Neill, A. S. (1960). *Summerhill: A radical approach to child rearing*. Oxford, UK: Hart Publishing, Ltd.

11. Holt, J. C. (1964). *How children fail*. New York: Dell Publishing Company.

12. Kozol, J. (1967). *Death at an early age: the destruction of the hearts and minds of Negro children in the Boston public schools*. New York: Bantam Books.

13. Holt, J. (1967). *36 children*. New York: New American Library.

14. Illich, I. (1971). *Deschooling society*. New York: Harper & Row.

15. Sanders, G. F. (1975). "Eisenhower College: From riches to rags—and back?" The Life and Media of Gordon F. Sander. https://www.gordonsander.com/eisenhower-college-from-riches-to-rags-and-back-change-10175.

16. Sally Eller resume.

17. Eller interview with author, January 19, 2016.

18. Sally Eller resume.

19. The proceedings document of the first National Conference on Alcohol and Drug Abuse in 1986 said Rumbaugh had "spent the past six years developing and coordinating School Community Action Teams." Her bio was compiled by Dr. Richard Towers. See National Institute on Alcohol Abuse and Alcoholism (NIAAA) and National Institute on Drug Abuse (NIDA). (1987). *Proceedings of the 1st National Conference on Alcohol and Drug Abuse Prevention: Sharing knowledge for action* (August 3–6, 1986). Washington, DC: US Department of Health and Human Services, 15.

20. Sally Eller interview with author, January 19, 2016.

21. Sandy Spring Friends Meeting. (n.d.). https://www.sandyspring.org/.

22. Boin, S. (1985, December 24). "Phoenix School helps Montgomery students kick the drug habit." *Frederick News*, 6.

23. Emrich, R. L., and Green, P. (1981, December) *Summary of the evaluation of the Phoenix Pilot Drug Program*. [Evaluation Report]. Napa, CA: Pacific Institute for Research and Evaluation, Foreword.

24. Ibid., 20.

25. Ibid., 38.

26. See note 22, 6.

27. Arocha, Z. (1986, June 5). "Day of triumph at Phoenix High." *Washington Post*. https://www.washingtonpost.com/archive/politics/1986/06/05/day-of-triumph-at-phoenix-high/dc6dd64c-d7af-471d-aeaa-2bac7d287d66.

28. Ibid.

29. See note 22 earlier, 6.

30. Eller interview with author, February 13, 2016.

31. Eller interview with author, November 11, 2019.

32. Eller interview with author, January 19, 2016.

33. Hadley Farms Community Association. (n.d.). *Welcome to Hadley Farms!* https://hadleyfarms.org/; "Hadley Farms Dairy discontinues milk processing and distributing." (1977, October 16). *Baltimore Sun*, 199.

34. The farmhouse that was the original site of Phoenix II is now home to the Hadley Farms Community Center and the local pool, and the address is 7420 Hadley Farms Drive, Gaithersburg, MD, 20879.

35. MCPS Board of Education minutes, April 21, 1987, 17.

36. MCPS Board of Education minutes, June 22, 1987, 16–17.

37. "The house that trades built." (1988, June 13). *The Bulletin: A weekly newsletter for MCPS employees*, 1–2.

38. Ibid. The address for the new Phoenix II site was 7305 Hadley Farms Drive, Gaithersburg, MD, 20879.

39. Lilienfeld, S. O., and Arkowitz, H. (2014, January 1). "Why 'Just Say No' doesn't work." *Scientific American*. https://www.scientificamerican.com/article/why-just-say-no-doesnt-work/.

40. See note 37 earlier, 1–2.

41. Boin, S. (1988, June 2). "Montgomery's Phoenix program celebrates completion of home." *Frederick Post*, B-6..

42. Ibid., B-6.

43. Ibid.

44. Ibid.

45. See note 37 earlier, 1–2.

46. See note 41 earlier, B-6.

Chapter 10

1. Phoenix Anniversary Committee. (1994, May 15). *The Phoenix School: Celebrating 15 years of hope and recovery*. [Unpublished Program].

2. Morella, C. A. (1994, May 24). "A tribute to the Phoenix School." *Congressional Record (140)* 66. Washington, DC: Government Printing Office.

3. Berthiaume interview with author, October 2015.

4. Towers, R. L. (1987). *How schools can help combat student drug and alcohol abuse*. West Haven, CT: National Education Association, 174.

5. Ibid.

6. Daytop Village was incorporated in 1964 as a therapeutic community utilizing methods aligned with Synanon, such as "group encounters and addicts confronting each other, demanding self-revelation and responsibility"; see Our history. (2012). *Daytop Village.* https://web.archive.org/web/20151222234947/http://www.daytop.org/history.html.

7. "Mrs. Reagan's crusade." (n.d.). *Reagan Foundation.* https://web.archive.org/web/2006051 5050147/http://www.reaganfoundation.org/reagan/nancy/just_say_no.asp.

8. Loizeau, P-M. (2003). *Nancy Reagan: The woman behind the man.* Hauppauge, NY: Nova Science Publications, 95.

9. Ibid.

10. Ibid., 104.

11. Ibid., 104–105.

12. Mozingo, J., Kohli, S., and Torres, Z. (2016, March 7). "'Just Say No' anti-drug campaign helped define Nancy Reagan's legacy." *Los Angeles Times.* https://www.latimes.com/local/california/la-me-nancy-reagan-drugs-20160307-story.html.

13. See note 4 earlier, 107.

14. Ibid., 108.

15. See note 8 earlier, 105.

16. Ibid.; Stuart, T. (2016, March 7). "Pop-culture legacy of Nancy Reagan's 'Just Say No' campaign." *Rolling Stone.* https://www.rollingstone.com/culture/culture-news/pop-culture-legacy-of-nancy-reagans-just-say-no-campaign-224749/.

17. McGrath, M. (2016, March 8). "Nancy Reagan and the negative impact of the 'Just Say No' antidrug campaign." *The Guardian.* https://www.theguardian.com/society/2016/mar/08/nancy-reagan-drugs-just-say-no-dare-program-opioid-epidemic. "Dr. Herbert Kleber interview." (2000). *Frontline.* https://www.pbs.org/wgbh/pages/frontline/shows/drugs/interviews/kleber.html.

18. The awareness of only one other school shows how little was known about recovery high schools in the years before the improvement of internet technology made information more accessible. The only school cited in the Phoenix celebration program was Recovery High School in Albuquerque, New Mexico, which had opened in 1992. By 1994, however, there were in fact at least ten recovery high schools scattered across the United States, including the two Phoenix schools. See also note 1 earlier.

19. See note 4 earlier, 115.

20. National Commission on Excellence in Education. (1983). *A nation at risk: The imperative for educational reform—A report to the nation and the Secretary of Education,* United States Department of Education. Washington, DC: National Commission on Excellence in Education, 7.

21. Strauss, V. (2018, April 26). "'A Nation at Risk' demanded education reform 35 years ago. Here's how it's been bungled ever since." *Washington Post.* https://www.washingtonpost.com/news/answer-sheet/wp/2018/04/26/the-landmark-a-nation-at-risk-called-for-education-reform-35-years-ago-heres-how-it-was-bungled/; Berliner, D. C., and Biddle, B. J. (1995). *The manufactured crisis: Myths, fraud, and the attack on America's public schools.* Reading, MA: Addison-Wesley Publishing Co.

22. Ansary, T. (2007, March 9). "Education at risk: Fallout from a flawed report." *EduTopia.* https://www.edutopia.org/landmark-education-report-nation-risk.

23. Cremin, L. A. (1978). The Free School Movement: A perspective. In T. E. Deal and R. R. Nolan, (Eds.). *Alternative schools: Ideologies, realities, guidelines.* Chicago: Nelson-Hall, 208 (originally published in *Notes on Education,* October 1973) .

24. See note 22 earlier.
25. Cuban, L. (2019, April 19). "Whatever happened to the self-esteem movement?" *Larry Cuban on School Reform and Classroom Practice*. https://larrycuban.wordpress.com/2019/04/19/whatever-happened-to-the-self-esteem-movement/.
26. Ibid.
27. Online Archive of California. (n.d.). "Inventory of the Task Force to Promote Self-Esteem and Personal and Social Responsibility Records, 2008." http://oac.cdlib.org/findaid/ark:/13030/kt8b69r98n.
28. Riebli, J. (n.d.). Untitled document. Accessed January 15, 2021, but the webpage has since been removed.
29. Diehl, D. (2001). "Recovery high school." In S. L. Isaacs and J. R. Knickman (Eds.), *To improve health and health care: The Robert Wood Johnson Foundation anthology,* Vol. V. San Francisco: Jossey-Bass.
30. "John Cates testimony video." (2016, March 31). *YouTube*. https://www.youtube.com/watch?v=mq3Fvsiedro.
31. Ibid.
32. PDAP. (n.d.). *Dan Rather American Journalist*. Dolph Briscoe Center for American History, University of Texas at Austin. https://danratherjournalist.org/investigative-journalist/60-minutes/pdap.
33. Gorman, T. (1986, April 12). "Cure not worth it, disillusioned drug program backers decide." *Los Angeles Times*. https://www.latimes.com/archives/la-xpm-1986-04-12-me-3553-story.html.
34. Kolitz, D. (2021). "Love bomb." *The Atavist Magazine*, 117. https://magazine.atavist.com/the-love-bomb-enthusiastic-sobriety-bob-meehan-abuse-cult-drugs-rehab/, 16.
35. Lifeway International. (n.d.). *Enthusiastic Recovery APG Manual*. [Unpublished manual]. Houston, TX: Lifeway International Houston, LLC.
36. JCA Information. (1986, September 9). *Unpublished flyer*. John Cates & Associates.
37. Ibid.
38. By the 2000s, the Texas programs had all distanced themselves from Bob Meehan, though three of them had roots in the original PDAP program from the 1970s. Archway Academy opened in 2004 and is located in Palmer Episcopal Church itself—the original PDAP site. Three Oaks Academy was started by John Cates in 2004 and was operated by Lifeway. And University High School opened in 2014, modeled after Archway Academy, and employed a former Archway staff member.
39. JCA Information. (1989). *Unpublished flyer*. John Cates & Associates.
40. JCA Information. (1987). *Unpublished flyer*. John Cates & Associates.
41. Letter from Lydow to Roberts, 1988.
42. Lydow letter, August 21, 1989.
43. The address of the Ellisville campus was 15627 Manchester Road, Ellisville, MO, 63011.
44. JCA Information. (1987, July 24). *Unpublished flyer*. John Cates & Associates.
45. JCA Information. (1986). *Unpublished flyer*. John Cates & Associates.
46. Ibid.
47. See note 40 earlier, 2.
48. Ibid.
49. JCA Information. (1988). *1988–1989 School Year*. [Unpublished flyer]. John Cates & Associates.
50. Lydow letter to Roberts, 1988.

51. Ibid.

52. Carrington Academy. (1989). *1989–1990 School Year*. [Unpublished flyer]. John Cates & Associates.

53. See note 49 earlier.

54. See note 34 earlier, 16.

Chapter 11

1. "Jack Frost pays a midwinter visit (photo)." (1971, February 16). *Star Tribune*, 1.

2. To respect his privacy, the name of Carol Robson's child has not been included.

3. Minnesota Department of Health; Saint Paul, MN; *Minnesota, Birth Index, 1935–2000*. Ancestry.com. 1940 Census record.

4. "Cerebral palsy." (n.d.). *Mayo Clinic*. https://www.mayoclinic.org/diseases-conditions/cerebral-palsy/symptoms-causes/syc-20353999.

5. Ibid.

6. Türkoğlu, G., Türkoğlu, S., Çelik, C., and Uçan, H. (2017). "Intelligence, functioning, and related factors in children with Cerebral Palsy." *Noro psikiyatri arsivi* ("Archives of Neuropsychiatry"), *54*(1), 33–37. https://pubmed.ncbi.nlm.nih.gov/28566956.

7. "Second Foundation School." (1988, January 17). *Star Tribune Private School Directory*, 212.

8. The address of the University Baptist Church, which housed the Second Foundation School, was 1219 University Avenue SE, Minneapolis, MN, 55414.

9. Pinney, G. (1971, March 7). "The free schools: Counter-culture education." *Star Tribune*, 13–14.

10. Raywid, M. A. (1981, April). "The first decade of public school alternatives." *Phi Delta Kappan*, *62*(8), 551–554. https://www.jstor.org/stable/20386018.

11. "AERO Alternative Education Hall of Fame." (n.d.). *Alternative Education Resource Organization* (AERO). https://www.educationrevolution.org/store/resources/halloffame/.

12. Manzi, N., and Michael, J. (2017, June). *Income tax deductions and credits for public and nonpublic education in Minnesota*. [Information Brief.] St. Paul, MN: Minnesota House of Representatives Research Department.

13. Jennings, W. (n.d.). "History of educational reform in Minnesota." *Academia.edu*. https://www.academia.edu/33758789/History_of_Educational_Reform_in_Minnesota.

14. Chastain, S. (1970, September 21). "Minnetonka's loose little island." *Minnesota Star*, 24.

15. Kleeman, R. P. (1962, September 9). "They learn and like it." *Star Tribune*, 21.

16. "Susan Barenholtz 'Susie' Smith." (2017, June 18). *Star Tribune* obituaries. https://www.startribune.com/obituaries/detail/203793/; "Land bought for school of new kind." (1966, March 17). *Minnesota Star*, 66.

17. Jeffrey, J. (1978). *Education for children of the poor: A study of the origins and implementation of the Elementary and Secondary Education Act of 1965*. Columbus: Ohio State University Press.

18. Joiner, L. M. (1972, August). *St. Paul Open School: The St. Paul Public Schools Independent School District Number 625*. [Evaluation Report.] New York: Teaching and Learning Research Corporation; see also note 10 earlier.

19. Ibid.

20. See note 13 earlier.

21. Ibid., and see note 10 earlier.
22. See note 18 earlier.
23. Ibid.
24. See note 10 earlier; see also "Minneapolis Public Schools." (1974). *Southeast Alternatives 1974.* [Unpublished Promotional Pamphlet.] St. Paul, MN: Gale Family Library, Minnesota History Center.
25. Davis, J. B., Jr. (1971, January 27). "Letter of interest in experimental schools program." [Unpublished correspondence.] St. Paul, MN: Gale Family Library, Minnesota History Center.
26. See note 24 earlier ("Minneapolis Public Schools").
27. In the 1990s, an alternative rock-band named Marcy Playground had a hit named "Sex and Candy." Lead vocalist John Wozniak had attended the Marcy Open School, and according to iTunes, many of his songs were inspired by his childhood in that community. See Apple Music—Marcy Playground. https://music.apple.com/us/artist/marcy-playground/633000.
28. See note 24 earlier ("Minneapolis Public Schools").
29. Ibid., 2.
30. Ibid., 2.
31. See note 24 earlier ("Minneapolis Public Schools").
32. Ibid.
33. Fantini, M. (1973, March). "Alternatives within public schools." *Phi Delta Kappan, 54*(7), 444–448. https://www.jstor.org/stable/20373540.
34. Cooper, B. S. (1971, November). *Free and freedom schools: A national survey of alternative programs.* [Commission Report.] Submitted to the President's Commission on School Finance. Accessed on Google Books.
35. Deal, T. E., and Nolan, R. R. (1978). *Alternative schools: Ideologies, realities, guidelines.* Chicago, IL: Burnham Inc.
36. See note 10 earlier.
37. Ibid., 552.
38. Ibid.
39. Storm, J. H. (1993). *The Minneapolis Federation of Alternative Schools: Its programs and organizational development* (Order No. 9328390). [PhD thesis, University of Minnesota]. ProQuest Dissertations & Theses Global, 88 (304039640). https://www.proquest.com/dissertations-theses/minneapolis-federation-alternative-schools/docview/304039640/se-2.
40. At first, the agreements stipulated that funding would flow directly from MPS to MFAS teachers. Storm notes this created confusion for teachers, as they were employed by MFAS schools, but paid by MPS. In 1986, MPS created a formal agreement to contract with MFAS. (Storm p. 147–148). These arrangements were codified by the state legislature and became known as "contract alternative schools"—the mechanism to fund the earliest recovery high schools in the state in the late 1980s and early 1990s.
41. See note 39 earlier, 89.
42. Ibid.
43. Ibid.
44. Ibid., 93.

45. Davis, J. B., Jr., and Hols, M. (1977, April 7) *Alternatives: Strategies for getting started, Revised*, as cited by Storm in note 43, 112.

46. See note 39 earlier, 109.

47. Ibid.

48. Ibid., 109–110.

49. Ibid., 113.

50. Ibid., 118; when MFAS went up for re-accreditation in 1984, one of the team members was the prominent alternative schools advocate, Dr. Mary Anne Raywid.

51. McAuliffe, B. (2004, April 11). "Given the choice: As their options broaden, thousands of students are abandoning traditional public schools, thus creating crisis and opportunity for many school systems." *Star Tribune*, 1–A.

52. Ibid.

53. Ibid.

54. Boyd, W.L., Hare, D., and Nathan, J. (2002). *What really happened? Minnesota's experience with statewide public school choice programs.* [Evaluation Report.] Minneapolis, MN: Center for School Change, Hubert H. Humphrey Institute of Public Affairs, University of Minnesota.

55. Ibid.

56. Ibid.

57. Teas, T. G. (1998). *Chemically dependent teens with special needs: Educational considerations for after treatment.* Master's thesis, Bethel College, St. Paul, MN, 46.

58. Ibid., 48.

59. Robson interview with author, April 22, 2016.

60. The Robson's address was 1004 Summit Avenue, Minneapolis. The purchase price was cited by Carol Robson and confirmed by a records search.

61. According to Carol Robson, the prior owners had been the Sweatt family, who had started the Honeywell Corporation. See "Charles Sweatt." (1977, August 2). *New York Times.* https://www.nytimes.com/1977/08/02/archives/charles-sweatt-long-an-officer-of-honeywell-inc-of-minneapolis.html. Sweatt was long an officer of Honeywell, Inc. of Minneapolis.

62. Robson interview with author, August 10, 2021.

63. Brandt, S. (1979, May 13). "Proposal to create village for retarded raises controversy." *Star Tribune*, 21.

64. Ibid.

65. Robson interview with author, April 22, 2016.

66. Robson interview with author, August 10, 2021.

67. See note 63 earlier, 21.

68. Levy, P. (1985, November 2). "Farm gives meaning to mentally handicapped." *Star Tribune*, 29, 35.

69. Ibid., 29, 35.

70. "Village History." (n.d.). *Camphill Village Copake.* https://camphillvillage.org/about/village-history/.

71. Camphill Village still exists in Sauk Centre, Minnesota, and the movement has grown to one hundred villages worldwide. Rudolf Steiner is also known for founding the Waldorf Schools.

72. Robson interview with author, April 22, 2016.

Chapter 12

1. They also started programs that lasted. While Carol Robson was no longer involved, the Summit House was still operating at the writing of this book, as was Camphill Village. Sheridan Robson remained on the Camphill board into the 2020s, more than forty years after its founding.

2. Don Samuelson from Brainerd was a longtime state representative who became a state senator. He was in the House from 1968–1982, when he was elected to the senate. This means he would have been a representative when New Dimensions opened, but a senator during its first years in operation. See "Samuelson may join race for Oberstar's seat." (1983, December 23). *St. Cloud Times*, 15.

3. "When Forsyth faces Willet, it's rock vs. hard-place." (1986, March 2). *Star Tribune*, 9B.

4. The original address of the New Dimensions School was 6800 South Cedar Lake Road, St. Louis Park, MN, 55426.

5. "North Side/Eliot Elementary School." (n.d.). *St. Louis Park Historical Society*. https://slp history.org/eliotschool/.

6. "New Dimensions School" (promotional advertisement). (1982, March 28). *Star Tribune*, 75.

7. The address of the second location of the New Dimensions School was 4100 Vernon Avenue South, room 101, St. Louis Park, MN, 55416.

8. See note 6 earlier, 88.

9. "Brookside Elementary School." (n.d.). *St. Louis Park Historical Society*. https://slphistory. org/brooksideschool/.

10. "Teacher's Assistant" (classified advertisement). (1983, July 18). *Star Tribune*, 116.

11. "Assistant Teacher" (classified advertisement). (1984, August 19). *Star Tribune*, 124.

12. "Society & Clubs." (1952, March 5). *Winona Republican-Herald*, 12.

13. Murray, M. (1960, February 15). "'Teahouse' wisdom offers myriad chuckles." *Winona Daily News*, 15.

14. Murray, M. (1961, March 22.) "WSC Players delight in Shaw's 'Candida.'" *Winona Daily News*, 10; "Shakespeare's 'Othello' opens tonight." (1964, November 8). *Winona Daily News*, 13.

15. The US Hockey Hall of Fame would open in Eveleth, Minnesota, in 1973.

16. "Winona deaths: Robert Andrew McLean." (1968, November 29). *Winona Daily News*, 13.

17. "Winona deaths: Mrs. Robert McLean." (1968, March 31). *Winona Daily News*, 19.

18. See note 16 earlier, 13.

19. Laura Earp interview with author, June 30, 2022.

20. Hotakainen, R. (1989, September 17). "The war on drug abuse is a one-on-one battle for Sobriety High students." *Star Tribune*, 1A.

21. "'Tobacco Road' to revive era of Depression on Mayan Hall stage." (1971, March 7). *Chula Vista Star-News*, 10.

22. "Tryouts for 2 plays set at Southwestern." (1971, January 10). *Imperial Beach Star-News*, 5.

23. "Bard would relish production at Globe." (1972, April 3). *Times-Advocate* (Escondido, California), 18.

24. Vaughn, P. (1976, February 24). "Love's labor changed grocery into theater." *Minneapolis Star*, 34.

25. Ibid.

26. Ibid., 34.

27. Vaughan, P. (1976, August 12). "Clown's one in a thousand in Orono theater staging." *Minneapolis Star*, 41.

28. Vaughan, P. (1977, January 12). "Play lacks emphasis on Camus' words." *Minneapolis Star*, 24.

29. Hotakainen, R. (1989, September 17). "The war on drug abuse is a one-on-one battle for Sobriety High students." *Star Tribune*, 12A.

30. The address of the Plymouth Youth Center Arts & Technology High School is 2301 Oliver Avenue North, Minneapolis, MN, 55411.

31. Preston, R. (2021, October 1). "Historic Capri Theater in Minneapolis reopens after $12.5 million state-of-the-art renovation." *Star Tribune*. https://www.startribune.com/ renovated-capri-in-north-minneapolis-is-a-beacon-of-hope/600102640/.

32. Ibid.

33. Hankin-Redmon, E. (2020, January 20). "How Near North came to be one of Minneapolis' largest black communities." *MinnPost*. https://www.minnpost.com/mnopedia/2020/01/ how-near-north-came-to-be-one-of-minneapolis-largest-black-communities/.

34. "About PCYC." (n.d.). *PCYC*. https://pcyc-mpls.org/about-pcyc/.

35. Readers interested in a more comprehensive historical overview of adolescent treatment are referred to Godley, M. D., and White, W .L. (2005). "A brief history and some current dimensions of adolescent treatment in the United States." In M. Galanter (ed.), *Progress in the treatment of alcoholism,* Vol. 17. New York: Springer, 369–382. https://www.chest nut.org/resources/0e089536-2c2d-497c-a43d-0701f4a3e5c2/2005-Current-Dimensions- of-Adolescent-Treatment.pdf. A more detailed history is also included in the prologue of this book.

36. Astoria Consultation Service was begun by an Episcopalian priest, Fr. Damian Pitcaithly, in Queens in 1960. It changed its name to the Samaritan Halfway Society in 1965 and Samaritan Village in 1974. In 2015, "Samaritan merged with Daytop to become Samaritan Daytop Village"; see "History." (n.d.). *Samaritan Daytop Village.* http://www.samaritanvill age.org/about-good/history.

37. White, W. L. (2014). *Slaying the dragon: The history of addiction treatment and recovery in America,* 2nd ed. Bloomington, IL: Chestnut Health Systems; White, W., Dennis, M., and Tims, F. (2002). "Adolescent treatment: Its history and current renaissance." *Counselor, 3*(2), 20–23. https://www.chestnut.org/william-white-papers/1/papers/items/.

38. "Our history." (n.d.). *Adult and Teen Challenge.* https://teenchallengeusa.org/about/ history/.

39. National Institute on Drug Abuse (NIDA). (1976). *National Directory of Drug Abuse Treatment Programs.* Rockville, MD: United States Department of Health, Education, and Welfare.

40. Ibid., iii.

41. Ibid..

42. Winters, K. C., Stinchfield, R. D., Opland, E., Weller, C., and Latimer, W. W. (2000). "The effectiveness of the Minnesota Model approach in the treatment of adolescent drug abus- ers." *Addiction, 95*(4), 601–612.

43. Anderson, D. J., McGovern, J. P., and Dupont, R. L. (1999). "The origins of the Minnesota Model of addiction treatment: A first person account." *Journal of Addictive Diseases, 18*(1), 107. DOI: 10.1300/J069v18n01_10..

44. Ibid., 112.
45. DePue, K., Finch, A. J., and Nation, M. (2014). "The bottoming out experience and the turning point: A phenomenology of the cognitive shift from drinker to non-drinker." *Journal of Addictions and Offender Counseling*, 35(1), 38–56.
46. Jellinek, E. M. (1946). "Phases in the drinking history of alcoholics: Analysis of a survey conducted by the official organ of Alcoholics Anonymous (Memoirs of the Section of Studies on Alcohol)." *Quarterly Journal of Studies on Alcohol, 7,* 1–88.
47. Jellinek, E. M. (1960). *The disease concept of alcoholism.* New Haven, CT: Hillhouse Press.
48. Ward, J. H., Bejarano, W., Babor, T. F., and Allred, N. (2016). "Re-Introducing Bunky at 125: E. M. Jellinek's life and contributions to alcohol studies." *Journal of Studies on Alcohol and Drugs, 77*(3), 375–383, 379.
49. "Treatment of alcohol addiction." (1965). *British Medical Jour*nal, *2*(5455), 184–185.
50. "Minnesota businessman, civic leader Wheelock Whitney dies at 89." (2016, May 21). *Star Tribune.* https://www.startribune.com/minnesota-businessman-civic-leader-wheelock-whitney-dies-at-89/380291131/.
51. Ibid.
52. Levy, P. (2000, June 29). "As costs rise, Minnesota Model faces scrutiny: The approach the most emulated in the treatment of chemical dependency may be at a turning point." *Star Tribune,* 1-A.
53. Thorkelson, W. (1999). "Vernon Johnson was pioneer in compassionate chemical dependency treatment." *Episcopal News Service,* 99–104. https://episcopalarchives.org/cgi-bin/ENS/ENSpress_release.pl?pr_number=99-104.
54. Ibid.
55. See note 52, 1-A.
56. Ibid.
57. Ibid.
58. See note 45 earlier, 107.
59. Flanagan, B. (1970, October 6). "Old house has a new aim." *Minneapolis Star,* 33; Hengen, B. (1971, January 13). "Boxing show has purpose." *Minneapolis Star,* 59.
60. "Drugs in the park." (n.d.). *St. Louis Park Historical Society.* https://slphistory.org/drugs-in-the-park/; "The Pharm House." (1974, June 15). *Star Tribune,* 16.
61. Pharm House would later become the Omegon treatment center.
62. See note 39 earlier.
63. "Irene Whitney dies in California." (1986, February 15). *Star Tribune,* 44.
64. "Pharm House Alumni and Friends." (2015, July 31). *It's time for the 3rd Annual Recovery Reunion!* Facebook. https://www.facebook.com/PharmHouseAlumni/posts/pfbid-028Ci6kEuXDUxnfWYo4viZx7g2fzWJgUPRNYkMqqsEgLFHCz8q6defDbAwHLxmNZvPl.
65. "Institute plans freedom from drugs festival." (1976, March 18). *Minneapolis Star,* 34.
66. "Throngs celebrate freedom from narcotics and alcohol." (1976, June 27). *Wichita Beacon,* 1F.
67. Ibid.
68. Longcope, K. (1987, January 2). "Getting the pride back; A facility for alcohol and drug-addicted lesbians and gay men." *Boston Globe,* 11, 12.
69. Ibid.

70. In 1986, ARC converted the adolescent program into the first treatment center in the nation designed expressly for the LGBTQ community, and the name was changed to PRIDE. The adolescent unit had been closed to make space for PRIDE.

71. "I, Simulacrum" (theater listing). (1980, February 29). *Star Tribune*, 35.

72. "New Dimensions School (promotional advertisement). (1985, September 8). *Star Tribune*, 91.

73. Hotakainen, R. (1989, September 17). "The war on drug abuse is a one-on-one battle for Sobriety High students." *Star Tribune*, 1A.

74. Ibid.

75. MacPherson, M., and Radcliffe, D. (1978, April 22). "Betty Ford says that she is addicted to alcohol." *Washington Post*. https://www.washingtonpost.com/archive/politics/1978/04/22/betty-ford-says-that-she-is-addicted-to-alcohol/bd6734d3-0ea1-4eb2-ab97-7279ca6dcc3d/.

76. "Hazelden Foundation History." (n.d.). *Funding Universe*. http://www.fundinguniverse.com/company-histories/hazelden-foundation-history/.

77. See note 37 (White et al.), 20–23.

78. "Hazelden Betty Ford Foundation History." (n.d.). *Hazelden Betty Ford Foundation*. https://www.hazeldenbettyford.org/about-us/history.

79. Williams, J. M. (1987, November 12). "New Dimensions gives students attention they deserve, teacher says." *Star Tribune*, 38.

80. Ibid.

81. Ibid.

82. Ibid.

83. Ibid.

Chapter 13

1. According to one definition, a hobby farm is typically less than fifty-acres, "primarily for pleasure instead of being a business venture. The owner or owners of a hobby farm typically have a main source of income," and "the farm does not have to make money—it can be engaged in on a hobby level." See Arcuri, L. (2022, February 14). "What is a hobby farm?" *Treehugger*. https://www.treehugger.com/what-is-a-hobby-farm-3016957.

2. Janzer, C. (2019, March 20). "8 famous figures who have checked into Hazelden." *Artful Living*. https://artfulliving.com/8-famous-figures-rehab-hazelden/#:~:text=Eric%20Clapton,the%20documentary%20Beware%20of%20Mr.

3. According to multiple sources, Ralph Neiditch was experiencing neurological issues by the time research began on this book. He lived out his life in a nursing home specializing in memory care, and the author was unable to interview him. Neiditch died on November 26, 2021, at the age of 83.

4. Portner, J. (1995, April 26). "Clean and sober." *Education Week*. https://www.edweek.org/education/clean-and-sober/1995/04.

5. Robson interview with author, April 22, 2016.

6. Ibid.

7. According to genealogical records, Neiditch had been married at least twice before—once in 1960 and again in 1971. He married his second wife in New York in 1971, and they filed for divorce in 1984.

8. Williams, J. M. (1987, November 12). "New Dimensions gives students attention they deserve, teacher says." *Star Tribune*, 38.

9. Hotakainen, R. (1989, September 17). "The war on drug abuse is a one-on-one battle for Sobriety High students." *Star Tribune*, 1A.

10. Articles of Incorporation of Ecole Nouvelle, Inc. (1988, April 29). *Corporate Charter Number 1C-374*. Minnesota Secretary of State.

11. The official Certificate of Incorporation was issued by the Secretary of State's office eight weeks later, on June 29, 1988.

12. See note 10 earlier.

13. Ibid.

14. "Miss Foley wed in St. Patrick's." (1971, March 4). *The Item of Millburn and Short Hills* (Millburn, NJ). 12.

15. Robson interview with author, April 22, 2016.

16. See note 4 earlier.

17. Wieffering, E. (1992, March). "Halfway Houses need a fix." *American Demographics*, *14*(3)3; ProQuest 16–17.

18. Taifa, N. (2021, May 10). "Race, mass incarceration, and the disastrous War on Drugs." *Brennan Center for Justice,* 4. https://www.brennancenter.org/our-work/analysis-opinion/race-mass-incarceration-and-disastrous-war-drugs.

19. Ibid.

20. Office of National Drug Control Policy (ONDCP). *FY 2001–FY 2007 Strategic Plan* [OJP Document 189713NCJRS]. Washington, DC: Office of Justice Programs. https://www.ojp.gov/pdffiles1/Photocopy/189713NCJRS.pdf.

21. Anti-Drug Abuse Act of 1988 (H.R. 5210, 100th Congress): Highlights of Enacted Bill. Washington, DC: Department of Justice. https://www.ojp.gov/pdffiles1/Digitization/143053NCJRS.pdf.

22. Ogilvy, D. (1985/1963). *Confessions of an advertising man.* New York: Atheneum. 21–23.

23. Kunst, J. (2023, August 28). "Do's and don'ts of telling your story." *Amethyst Recovery Center*. https://www.amethystrecovery.org/dos-and-donts-of-telling-your-story/.

24. See note 4 earlier.

25. Ibid.

26. Robson interview with author, April 22, 2016

27. See note 9 earlier, 1A.

28. Ibid.

29. Ibid., 1A.

30. Ibid., 13A.

31. "Sobriety High." (1989, August 10). *Star Tribune*, 68.

32. See note 9 earlier, 12A.

33. See note 4 earlier.

34. Ibid.

35. Genzlinger, N. (2021, August 10). "Walter Yetnikoff, powerful but abrasive record executive, dies at 87." *New York Times*. https://www.nytimes.com/2021/08/10/arts/music/walter-yetnikoff-powerful-but-abrasive-record-executive-dies-at-87.html.

36. Robson interview with author, April 22, 2016.

37. Certificate of Assumed Name. (1988, July 22). AN073994. Minnesota Secretary of State.

38. See note 31 earlier.

39. See note 9 earlier, 1A.
40. Ibid., 12A.
41. Ibid., 12A.
42. Ibid., 1A.
43. Ibid., 12A.
44. Ibid., 12A.
45. Ibid., 12A.
46. Ibid., 12A.

Chapter 14

1. Howard Pearson is a pseudonym for a person who died long before this book was written. The author contacted his siblings, and they neither recalled his role with this recovery high school nor agreed to be interviewed for the book. While several subjects who knew Howard confirmed his involvement, and the first yearbook for the Holos school honored him with a letter titled "Dear Sir," that document also did not give his name. Out of respect for his family's privacy, his real name will not be used here, and details specific enough to allow him to be easily identified have not been included. The pseudonym chosen represents "Ho" for Holos (Howard) and "Pea" for "P.E.A.S.E." (Pearson). Additionally, "H.O.W." is an acronym for a well-known saying in Twelve Step communities, "Honesty, Open-Mindedness, and Willingness."

2. Simon and Robson interviews with author, 2016.

3. Robson interviews with author, 2016.

4. While it could not be verified, Simon said he believed the Robsons were hoping to get Pearson to fund a stronger recovery high school. "I think that's what [the Robsons] were trying to do is get him to fund a deeper school," said Simon. "[Howard] told me this later. He was there because they were trying to get to his money, in a sense, and get to him." Carol Robson did not say she had tried to get money from Howard Pearson. She said, "I lost touch with Ken (Simon). I was getting him involved, and then he and [Howard] went off on their own, which was fine with me because my ultimate goal was not that. I'm so thrilled today to hear that Ken (was) at P.E.A.S.E. Academy (the eventual name of the school Simon helped start), because he was another fabulous person along the way."

5. New Dimensions transitioned into a recovery high school in the fall of 1987. Holos records show the nonprofit formed by Barb Schmidt and Ken Simon had a start date of June 10, 1988, and Howard paid the legal fees for a period in May 1988.

6. Long after the main time period covered in this book, Barbara Schmidt changed her name. Since she went by Barbara Schmidt for all the events described here, that is the name that will be used.

7. Ancestry.com. (2010). *U.S., Public Records Index, 1950–1993*, Vol. 2 [database on-line]. Lehi, UT: Ancestry.com Operations, Inc.

8. Forest Lake High School Yearbook. (1970). *U.S., School Yearbooks, 1880–2012. Ancestry. com.* U.S., School Yearbooks, 1900–2016 [database on-line]. Lehi, UT: Ancestry.com Operations, Inc.

9. Ministerial Education Fund FAQ. (2024, February 20). *United Methodist Church.* https:// www.umc.org/en/content/ministerial-education-fund-faq#:~:text=The%2013%20Uni

ted%20Methodist%20seminaries%20help%20students%20to%20discover%20their%20
calling%20through%20challenging%20curriculum.

10. Ken Simon recalled Howard Pearson giving about $35,000 to seed the school, but that could not be verified.

11. The initial draft of the Articles of Incorporation was drawn up on May 20, 1988, and the official documents were dated June 10, 1988, the same day the official Certificate of Incorporation was issued by the Secretary of State's office. See Articles of Incorporation of Holos Foundation. (1988, June 10). *Corporate Charter Number 1C-321*. Minnesota Secretary of State. The official Certificate of Incorporation also was issued by the Secretary of State's office on June 10, 1988.

12. Articles of Incorporation of Ecole Nouvelle, Inc. (1988, April 29). *Corporate Charter Number 1C-374*. Minnesota Secretary of State. The official Certificate of Incorporation was issued by the Secretary of State's office eight weeks later, on June 29, 1988. The dates on these documents later contributed to confusion as to which school came first. *Ecole Nouvelle* had operated as a sober/recovery school under their original New Dimensions School since at least fall 1987. Robson and Neidich also had prepared their new documents for *Ecole Nouvelle* in April 1988, just weeks before Schmidt and Simon drafted their articles of incorporation in May. Robson and Neiditch did not, however, get their official Certificate of Incorporation until *after* Schmidt and Simon. For that reason, the Corporate Charter Number for the Holos Foundation (1C-321) is actually an earlier number than that issued for *Ecole Nouvelle* (1C-374). New Dimensions School, Inc., of course, predated both by many years, becoming legally registered with the State of Minnesota on December 15, 1981.

13. Articles of Incorporation of Holos Foundation. (1988, June 10). *Corporate Charter Number 1C-321*. Minnesota Secretary of State.

14. The first Holos School students created a yearbook in the spring of 1989, in which they described the philosophy of the school. They titled it "Holostic Learning."

15. Michael Durchslag interview with author, 2016.

16. Aronson J. (2003, February 15). "Wholly, holy, holey." *BMJ: British Medical Journal, 326*(7385), 392.

17. Schmidt interview with author, 2016.

18. The uncertainty principle states that it is impossible to measure pairs of complementary properties of a particle (such as position and momentum) precisely and simultaneously, because the more precisely you know one of these properties, the less precisely you can know the other. The observer effect proposes that the act of watching something affects what is being watched. Both were proposed by German physicist Werner Heisenberg as part of quantum theory. See Lindley, D. (2008). *Uncertainty: Einstein, Heisenberg, Bohr, and the struggle for the soul of science*. New York: Random Books.

19. Burt, S. (2022, November 7). "Is the Multiverse where originality goes to die?" *New Yorker*. https://www.newyorker.com/magazine/2022/11/07/is-the-multiverse-where-originality-goes-to-die; Dick, P. K. (1962). *The man in the high castle*. New York: Putnam.

20. Schmidt email with author, 2022.

21. The address of Pillsbury House, and the original location for the Holos School, is 3501 Chicago Avenue South, Minneapolis, MN, 55407.

22. In 2001, PUNS changed its name to "Pillsbury United Communities." See "Our History." (n.d.). *Pillsbury United Communities*. https://pillsburyunited.org/about/history/.

23. Ibid.

24. Ibid.

25. Ibid. In the 1960s, fires damaged the vacated building, and the original Pillsbury House was torn down in April 1968. The original site is now home to a parking ramp.

26. Fagan, C., Martell, N., and Larrimore, S. (2012). "Community partnerships to examine local housing markets: A neighborhood profile." *Undergraduate Journal of Service Learning & Community-Based Research, 1*, 1–23. https://doi.org/10.56421/ujslcbr.v1i0.105.

27. Powderhorn Park, Minneapolis (n.d.). "History." *Wikipedia.* https://en.wikipedia.org/wiki/Powderhorn_Park,_Minneapolis.

28. Holos Foundation records. [Unpublished Financial Documents, 1988.] Courtesy of P.E.A.S.E. Academy administration.

29. Holos, Inc. Curriculum. (1989, July 25). "Documents submitted for Minneapolis Public Schools Contract." Courtesy of P.E.A.S.E. Academy administration.

30. Boyd, W. L., Hare, D., and Nathan, J. (2002). *What really happened? Minnesota's experience with statewide public school choice programs.* [Evaluation Report.] Minneapolis, MN: Center for School Change, Hubert H. Humphrey Institute of Public Affairs, University of Minnesota.

31. Holos Foundation, Inc. (1989). *Application for Recognition of Exemption.* [Internal Revenue Service Form 1023]. Courtesy of P.E.A.S.E. Academy administration.

32. Ibid., 2.

33. The article was adapted from an original article published in the Winter 1987 Celebrations, AHE Newsletter. Harmin, M. (1987). "Holistic education: Teaching inner self-responsibility."

34. Ibid.

35. Meher Baba. (1966). Excerpts from GOD IN A PILL? Walnut Creek, CA: Sufism Reoriented, Inc. http://www.avatarmeherbaba.org/erics/godpill.html.

36. See note 33.

37. Ibid.

38. See note 31.

39. Schmidt, B. (1989, July 31). Additional information for 501(C)3 status. [IRS Correspondence.] Courtesy P.E.A.S.E. Academy administration.

40. Bancroft, W. J. (1978, April). "The Lozanov Method and its American adaptations." *Modern Language Journal, (62)*4, 167–175.

41. "Dr. Georgi Lozanov and Buckminister Fuller." (n.d.). *Quantum Learning Education.* https://quantumlearning.com/ql-conference-history/.

42. Bancroft, W. J. (1976). "Suggestology and Suggestopedia: The theory of the Lozanov Method." *Education Resources Information Center (ERIC),* ED 132 857, 1. https://files.eric.ed.gov/fulltext/ED132857.pdf.

43. Ibid., 1.

44. See note 40 earlier.

45. Schmidt interview with author, 2016.

46. Two different start dates are recorded in official documents filed with the IRS: January 30 and February 1. Considering January 30 was a Monday, it is most likely that was the first official day of the Holos School. February 1 may have been simply an estimated starting point, but none of the people present on that first day remembered in their interviews years later.

Chapter 15

1. Joanie's married name is Joanie Vogt, but since she was still Hannigan during the events of this book, that is the name used here.
2. Mastropolo, F. (2016, January 31). "50 years ago: Grateful Dead and Big Brother & the Holding Company begin the Haight-Ashbury Era at the Trips Festival." *Ultimate Classic Rock (UCR)*. https://ultimateclassicrock.com/trips-festival/.
3. Ibid.
4. By 1990, the National Directory of Drug Abuse Treatment and Prevention Programs listed thirteen youth programs in the Twin Cities alone. See National Directory of Drug Abuse and Alcoholism Treatment and Prevention Programs. (1990). US Department of Health and Human Services, Public Health Service, Alcohol, Drug Abuse, and Mental Health Administration, National Institute on Drug Abuse.
5. Vogt interview with author, June 13, 2022.
6. Ibid.
7. The address of the Irene Whitney Center for Recovery, formerly named "Shanti House," was 4954 Upton Avenue South, Minneapolis, MN, 55410. They had converted the former Lake Harriet Baptist Church into a halfway house. The original location of the Shanti House, which opened in 1976, was 15 Groveland Terrace, Minneapolis, MN, 55403. They moved in 1979 because a larger facility was needed. See "Halfway house is a wholesome success." (1980, July 3). *Minneapolis Star*, 24.
8. According to Sunita Shah, "Shanti is a Sanskrit term meaning 'peace.' In Hindu practices, also in Buddhist and Jain practices, Shanti is often chanted three times to represent three-fold peace in body, mind and spirit." See Shah, S. (2021, April 29). "What does "Shanti" mean?" *Jai Jais*. https://thejaijais.com/blogs/sunitas-blog/what-does-shanti-mean.
9. Mold, A., and Berridge, V. (2010). "The 'Old': Self-help, Phoenix House and the rehabilitation of drug users." In *Voluntary action and illegal drugs. Science, technology and medicine in modern history*. London: Palgrave Macmillan. https://doi.org/10.1057/9780230274693_2.
10. Bataka bats are used in treatment for anger management.
11. Hotakainen, R. (1989, September 17). "The war on drug abuse is a one-on-one battle for Sobriety High students." *Star Tribune*, 12A.
12. Ibid.
13. Holos Foundation, Inc. (1989). *Application for Recognition of Exemption*. [Internal Revenue Service Form 1023.] Courtesy of P.E.A.S.E. Academy administration.
14. Wieffering, E. (1992, March). "Halfway Houses need a Fix." *American Demographics*, (*14*)3, 17.
15. Schmidt, B. (1989, July 31). Additional information for 501(C)3 status. [IRS Correspondence.] Courtesy P.E.A.S.E. Academy administration.
16. Ibid.
17. See note 13 earlier, 2.
18. One interesting similarity between the halfway house and the recovery high school was their names. The former name for the Irene Whitney Center was Shanti, which means "peace." Holos changed its name to P.E.A.S.E., in part because the word resembled "peace."
19. See note 13 earlier, 2.
20. P.E.A.S.E. Academy (yearbook). (1989). "*Imagination P.E.A.S.E. Academy of Holos, Inc.*" Courtesy of Joan Vogt.

Chapter 16

1. P.E.A.S.E. Academy (yearbook). (1989). "*Imagination P.E.A.S.E. Academy of Holos, Inc.*" Courtesy of Joan Vogt.

2. Purple was in the popular consciousness in the late 1980s, on the heels of two Oscar-nominated films: *The Color Purple* (1985) and *Purple Rain* (1984). *Purple Rain* won the Oscar for Best Original Song Score by Prince, who grew up in Minnesota.

3. May, R. (1994). *The courage to create*. [Reprint.] New York: W. W. Norton & Company, 121.

4. See note 1.

5. "Whitney Hotel in downtown Minneapolis takes another step toward becoming condos." (2005, July 11). *Minnesota Lawyer*. https://minnlawyer.com/2005/07/11/whitney-hotel-in-downtown-minneapolis-takes-another-step-toward-becoming-condos/.

6. Schmidt email with author, 2022.

7. Howard Pearson death certificate. The source details of the citation are not included here to protect his family's privacy.

8. Dennis, M., and Scott, C. K. (2007). "Managing addiction as a chronic condition." *Addiction Science & Clinical Practice*, 4(1), 45–55. https://www.ncbi.nlm.nih.gov/pmc/articles/PMC2797101/

9. The precise location of the funeral is not included to respect the family's privacy.

10. Source of the obituary is not included to respect his family's privacy.

11. Schmidt, B. (1989, July 31). Additional information for 501(C)3 status. [IRS Correspondence.] Courtesy P.E.A.S.E. Academy administration.

12. Steve Massey. (n.d.). *LinkedIn*. https://www.linkedin.com/in/steve-massey-68477779/.

13. "Our History." (n.d.). *Covenant House*. https://ny.covenanthouse.org/about/about-us/journey-of-covenant-house/.

14. In February 1990, a few years after Massey left Covenant House, one of the cofounders, Father Bruce Ritter, was forced to resign due to allegations of sexual and financial misconduct. See Barron, J. (1990, February 28). "Ritter and Macchiarola quitting Covenant House." *New York Times*. https://www.nytimes.com/1990/02/28/nyregion/ritter-and-macchiarola-quitting-covenant-house.html?smid=url-share.

15. Holos Foundation, Inc. (1989). *Application for Recognition of Exemption*. [Internal Revenue Service Form 1023.] Courtesy of P.E.A.S.E. Academy administration, 4.

16. See note 11 earlier.

17. Hankin-Redmon, E. (2020, January 20). "How Near North came to be one of Minneapolis' largest black communities." *MinnPost*. https://www.minnpost.com/mnopedia/2020/01/how-near-north-came-to-be-one-of-minneapolis-largest-black-communities/.

18. "Our History." (n.d.). *Pillsbury United Communities*. https://pillsburyunited.org/about/history/.

19. See note 17 earlier.

20. Ibid.

21. The address for P.E.A.S.E. Academy's second site at the Oak Park Community Center was 1701 Oak Park Avenue North, Minneapolis, MN, 55411. In 2001, PUNS changed its name to Pillsbury United Communities.

22. See note 18 earlier.

23. Ibid.

24. See note 11 earlier.

25. The address of the new location of P.E.A.S.E. Academy at the University Lutheran Church of Hope would be 601 13th Avenue SE, Minneapolis, MN, 55414. It remains there to this day.

26. University Lutheran Church of Hope (UCLH). (2003). *The history of University Lutheran Church of Hope 1904-2004*. Minneapolis, MN: University Lutheran Church of Hope.

27. Ibid., 22.

28. Ibid., 33.

29. Ibid.

30. Durchslag interview with author, 2012.

31. See note 26 earlier, 50.

32. Ibid.

33. Lease agreement between University Lutheran Church of Hope and P.E.A.S.E. Academy of Holos, Inc. (1990, July 11). *Holos/ULCH*. [Unpublished contract.] Courtesy of P.E.A.S.E. Academy administration.

34. "Mask (Sock and Buskin/Comedy and Tragedy)." (n.d.) On *Symbols*. https://symbols project.eu/explore/human/profession/civil/mask-sock-and-buskin-/-comedy-and-trag edy.aspx.

35. White, W. (1998). "Significant events in the history of addiction treatment and recovery in America." Compiled from *Slaying the dragon: The history of addiction treatment and recovery in America*. Bloomington, IL: Chestnut Health Systems. https://www.chestnut.org/resources/016b7167-780f-452f-b0e0-7d3b80ea6588/AddictionTreatment-ampersand-RecoveryInAmerica.pdf.

36. Hotakainen, R. (1989, September 17). "The war on drug abuse is a one-on-one battle for Sobriety High students." *Star Tribune*, 1A.

37. Ibid., 12A.

38. Story as told to Judi Hanson. Hanson interview with author, March 11, 2016.

39. Ibid.

40. Smith, R. T. (1973, May 20). "Robert T. Smith Column." *Star Tribune*, 1B.

41. Czarniecki email with author, December 4, 2005.

42. Jim Czarniecki email with author, October 20, 2005.

43. "What's a family to do?" (2012, Summer). *Hazelden Voice*, *17*(1), 4–5.

44. The address of the Warren Eustis House was 720 Blue Gentian Road, Eagan, MN. See "Secretary" [Classified Advertisement]. (1982, August 8). *Star Tribune*, 122.

45. *Granville House v. Dept, Health Human Serv*, 715 F.2d 1292 No. 83-1062 (8th Cir. 1983). https://casetext.com/case/granville-house-v-dept-health-human-serv.

46. Dave Hadden, personal communication with author.

47. In interviews, Robson shared several stories from this time period that implied she felt Neiditch was doing things behind her back to move her out, including moving things out of her office while she was on a trip. As the author was unable to interview Neiditch, and nobody else familiar with the events mentioned those stories, they have not been included in the book.

Epilogue

1. Pauley, J. (Reporter and Host). (1995, June). "Straight times at Sobriety High." *Dateline NBC*, Season 3. Elizabeth Kovetas, Producer; Andrew Finkelstein, Editor.

2. Karlen, N. (1999, February). "Sobriety High: Where troubled teens get a clean start." *Life*, *22*, 72–79; quote from 74.

3. Bill Moyers's son, William Cope Moyers, was a major recovery advocate and would later become president of Hazelden Betty Ford.

4. Moyers, B. (Host). (1995, January 9 and 11). "*What can we do about violence? A Bill Moyers special.*" [Documentary.] Sue Castle, Segment Producer; Andrew Finkelstein, Editor.

5. Portner, J. (1995, April 26). "Clean and sober." *Education Week*. https://www.edweek.org/education/clean-and-sober/1995/04

6. See note 2 earlier.

7. Blake, L. (1995, January 7). "Moyers TV special on curbing violence features Edina school." *Star Tribune*, 21.

8. Diehl, D. (2001). "Recovery high school." In S. L. Isaacs and J. R. Knickman (Eds.), To improve health and health care: The Robert Wood Johnson Foundation anthology, Vol. V. San Francisco: Jossey-Bass. White, W. L., and Finch, A. J. (2006). "The recovery school movement: Its history and future." *Counselor*, *7*(2), 54–57.

9. See note 8 (Diehl).

10. On January 30, 2024, P.E.A.S.E. Academy became the first recovery high school to celebrate thirty-five years in operation.

11. McDowell, E. F. (1984, October 1). "Program puts emphasis on family in treating chemical dependency." *News and Courier*, 4-A.

12. Ibid.

13. McDowell, E. F. (1986, October 16). "Programs offer alternative treatment for children." *News and Courier*, 5-A.

14. Interestingly, the private Partial Hospitalization Program (PHP) program had sixteen patients during the 1985–1986 school year, but after ATC opened a public option, the PHP had no patients in the school by October 1986. It is not clear what happened to the PHP treatment school, but the ATC school was still in operation in 1988.

15. See note 13 earlier.

16. Ibid.

17. Ibid.

18. "D. Ceth Mason Treatment Center advertisement." (1987, October 4). *Greenville News*, 226.

19. Ingram, B. (1988, June 2). "Treatment center lives up to its name." *News and Courier / Evening Post*, 1–2.

20. Ibid.

21. PDAP GED School (Yearbook). (1978). *Dreams realized*, vol. 1. Houston, TX: PDAP Continuing Education System.

22. JCA Information. (1986, September 9). Unpublished flyer. John Cates & Associates.

23. "Charter schools – History of charter schools." (n.d.). *Texas Education Agency*. https://tea.texas.gov/texas-schools/texas-schools-charter-schools/charter-schools-history-of-charter-schools.

24. The address for the Carrington Academy Charter School was 6255 Corporate Drive, Houston, TX, 77036.

25. Carrington Academy charter school application. (1998, July 24). Courtesy John Cates.

26. Ibid.

27. New Dimensions/Sobriety High in Minneapolis was also a private school, but it did not become a *recovery* school until 1987.

28. One of the issues *Generation Found* explored was the racial divide of substance use programs in Houston. At the time, APGs and the two recovery high schools in Houston were still predominantly White. Spurred in part by the film but also by other community members, an APG and a new high school were opened in areas more accessible to people of color. See Williams, G. (Director). (2017). *Generation found* [Documentary Film]. Gathr Films.

29. ARS initiated the Jim Czarniecki Visionary Award in 2006 to honor visionaries and to recognize his immense impact on the establishment of the recovery high school movement. (ARS personal communication with author.)

30. Morella, C. A. (1994, May 24). "A tribute to the Phoenix School." *Congressional Record (140)* 66. Washington, DC: Government Printing Office.

31. Pope, C. (2001, May 9). "Phoenix II school destroyed by fire." *The Gazette.*

32. Ibid.

33. Hyslop, M. (2001, May 8). "Arson suspected in school fire: Phoenix pupils suspect arsonist is one of them." *Washington Times*, C1.

34. Ibid.

35. Ibid.

36. The Longview School moved to Germantown in the fall of 2001, and it is still in operation as a special education day school. According to the Longview School website, the original school was built in 1950 in Gaithersburg, MD, as "one of the first all-black schools in Montgomery County." A renaming committee selected "Longview to represent the 'long' distance traveled by the students and the beautiful view seen from the school (Sugarloaf Mountain off in the distance). The school housed a general education population until 1961 when Longview became a special education school for children with disabilities. The original building is still in use and is now known as the Emory Grove Center." See "About our school: Longview history." (n.d.). *Longview School.* https://www2.montgomeryschool smd.org/schools/longview/about/#:~:text=Longview%20was%20originally%20built%20 in,Grove%20Consolidated%20Colored%20Elementary%20School.

37. Dessauer, C. (2011, February 25). "The last lessons of Jerry Weast." *Bethesda Magazine MOCO 360.* https://bethesdamagazine.com/2011/02/25/the-last-lessons-of-jerry-weast-2/.

38. Weast, J. (Memo). (2002, November 12). "Supplemental appropriation—Alternative High School Program." MCPS Board of Education.

39. The address of the Emory Grove Center, the site of Phoenix II beginning in fall 2001, was 18100 Washington Grove Lane, Gaithersburg, MD, 20877.

40. Undated and unpublished historical essay written by Mike Bucci. Document provided to author as archival material.

41. The Muncaster Challenge Program was a yearlong alternative program, which combined academics with outdoor adventure activities. It was open only to students who faced expulsion from their regular schools for offenses such as carrying a knife or hitting a teacher. See Rasicot, J. (1998, April 30). "Wheeling to succeed." *Washington Post.* https://www.was hingtonpost.com/archive/local/1998/04/30/wheeling-to-succeed/ca76b477-ec01-4337-80e5-058d3cbf7be9/.

42. According to Durand's LinkedIn profile, he had been the instructional specialist at Muncaster for four years, and he served the same role for Phoenix I from 2001–2005. He also says he ran Parent Support groups at Phoenix from 1991 to 2001. See Stephen Durand Profile. (n.d.). *LinkedIn.* https://www.linkedin.com/in/stephen-durand-6ba34132/.

43. Hsu, C. (2002, May 17). "A troubled school for troubled teens." *The Montgomery Journal,* 3.

44. MCPS Board of Education minutes, May 14, 2002, 6.

45. See note 43 earlier.

46. See note 38 earlier. The address of the McKenney Hills Center, site of Phoenix I beginning in fall 2003, was 2600 Hayden Drive, Silver Spring, MD, 20902.

47. See note 38 earlier.

48. MCPS Committee on Special Populations Minutes, November 7, 2008.

49. Winters, P. (2017, August 25). "Why America's first recovery school closed in 2013." [Public Comment Document.] https://marylandpublicschools.org/programs/Docume nts/BSASW/08252017/BSAWpubliccomment20170825.pdf.

50. Ibid., 3. The final point was the continued legacy of the No Child Left Behind law.

51. Ibid.

52. See note 29 earlier.

53. See note 40 earlier.

54. "The Myth of Daedalus and Icarus by Ovid." (n.d.). *CommonLit*. https://www.commonlit. org/en/texts/the-myth-of-daedalus-and-icarus.

55. Harris, S. (1999, March 7). "Making the grade, clean & sober." *Los Angeles Times*, A1, A22–A23. See also Louey, S. (1998, November 14). "Board to hear Serenity High plan." *Dallas Morning News*. And see Casey, J. (1997, June 3). "School to open its door to teen addicts." *The Tennessean*, 1B.

56. Frequently Asked Questions (FAQ) document. (1994). Courtesy of Judi Hanson.

57. Robson interview with author, August 10, 2021; Czarniecki interview with author, October 20, 2005.

58. Attempts to reach Neiditch were unsuccessful. According to sources familiar with Neiditch, after leaving Sobriety High, he was treated for a brain tumor. He lost contact with others at the school and died in 2021.

59. Amendment of Bylaws. (1995, September 14). *Resolution of the Board of Directors of Sobriety High*. State of Minnesota: Secretary of State Office. See also Sobriety High. (2001). *Annual Report*. Edina, MN. Courtesy Judi Hanson.

60. Czarniecki personal communication with author, December 4, 2005.

61. Ibid.

62. Doyle, P. (2001, April 29). "School-Aid bill blasted as biased." *Star Tribune*, B1, B6.

63. Ibid., B6.

64. Ibid., B6.

65. See note 62, B6.

66. Ibid., B6. See also Hopfensperger, J. (2002, April 5). "First Lady helps carry a message to kids." *Star Tribune*, B2. And see "Sobriety High says goodbye to its fifth class." (1995, June 8). *St. Cloud Times*, 6. Note, this article covers the graduation that was portrayed in the *Dateline NBC* episode and notes the program was to air in June 1995.

67. Hatfield, M. (2005, September 4). "High school helps maintain teen sobriety." *Santa Maria Times*.

68. Hanson interview with author, January 12, 2014.

69. Hanson interview with author, April 16, 2006.

70. Finch, A. J., Karakos, H., and Hennessy, E. (2016). "Exploring the policy context of recovery high schools." In T. Reid (Ed.), *Substance abuse: Influences, treatment options and health effects*, 109–139.

71. Czaniecki email with author, December 5, 2005.

72. "Helping out Russia." (2003, July 18). *Star Tribune*, B4.
73. See note 59 earlier (annual report).
74. Hoffman, J., and Hadden, D. T. (2001, March). *Recovery based sober school programs in Minnesota*. [Unpublished Report.] Courtesy Association of Recovery Schools archives.
75. Ibid. See also note 59 earlier (annual report).
76. See note 62 earlier, B1, B6.
77. Ibid.
78. Ibid.
79. By the early 2000s, most Minnesota high schools employed at least one chemical health specialist. One job description for a "Chemical Health Prevention Specialist" position said it was to, "develop, promote, and sustain chemical health prevention and education services to students, families, and the school community, in collaboration with schools, county, and community agencies." Many of these positions were funded at least in part by money from federal Safe and Drug Free Schools grants. As that mechanism was re-vised to become a competitive grant during the Obama administration, the budgeting for these positions became more difficult to maintain, and, as a result, schools had to self-fund Chemical Health specialists, resulting in a staffing reduction across the state. See Chemical Health Prevention Specialist. (n.d.). *Position standard*. Anoka Hennepin Independent School District #11. https://www.ahschools.us/cms/lib/MN01909485/Centricity/Dom ain/12024/Chem%20Hlth%20Prev%20Spec%20-%202-21.pdf.
80. "What the federal government gave to Minnesota in 2003." (2003, December 11). *Star Tribune*, A24. Questions were raised about the legitimacy of Sobriety High's receipt and expenditure of a federal earmark. One school administrator contended Sobriety High did not have enough adequately licensed staff (i.e., licensed alcohol and drug counselors) and did not spend the money as expected. No wrongdoing was ever proven or formally charged.
81. Minnesota Session Laws. (1991). *Laws of Minnesota 1991*. [Chapter 265-H.F. No. 700, ar-ticle 9, section 3]. Minnesota Legislature: Office of the Revisor of Statutes. https://www.revisor.mn.gov/laws/?id=265&year=1991&type=0.
82. The address for the Sobriety High South Campus ("Alliance Academy") was 12156 Nicollet Avenue South, Burnsville, MN, 55420.
83. Ford, T. (2003, October 8). "High school for students with addictions to open next year." *Star Tribune*, S3.
84. Czarniecki email with author, December 5, 2005.
85. The staff member did not agree to be identified.
86. Czarniecki email with author, October 20, 2005.
87. See note 59 earlier (annual report).
88. "Jim Czarniecki celebration." (n.d.). Journal history. *Caringbridge*. http://caringbridgeclas sic.org/mn/jimcz/history.htm.
89. During the events recounted in this book, Kellie Lund went by the last names of "Lund" and "Winter." While she was at P.E.A.S.E. Academy, she was known as Kellie Winter, but during her time at Sobriety High and during interviews, she was known as Lund, the name used here.
90. See note 1 earlier.
91. Levy, P. (2011, November 13). "Sober outlook for famed school." *Star Tribune*, B1, B4.
92. Ibid.

93. Ibid.

94. Kennedy, C. (2013, May 3). "Sobriety High to close after school year concludes." *Patch* (Burnsville, MN). https://patch.com/minnesota/burnsville/sobriety-high-to-close-after-school-year-concludes.

95. See note 91 earlier.

96. Gessner, J. (2013, May 14). "Sobriety High's Alliance Academy in Burnsville closing." *Sun This Week.* https://www.hometownsource.com/sun_thisweek/sobriety-highs-alliance-academy-in-burnsville-closing/article_04f78cf2-603c-538b-a66d-d8b99a1958a8.html.

97. Ibid.

98. Kasl, C. D. (1992). *Many roads, one journey: Moving beyond the Twelve Steps.* New York: Harper Perennial.

99. Even though Holos was granted a charter for a grade 1–12 community learning center, the P.E.A.S.E. Academy recovery high school maintained its contract alternative school status until 2004, when it came under the umbrella of the Minnesota Transitions Charter School.

100. "2 more charter schools OK'd by school board; Total is now 8." (1993, April 6). *Star Tribune*, 4B.

101. "'Woman of peace, serenity' pushes holistic learning." (1996, June 17). *St. Cloud Times*, 4. See also Hotakainen, R. (1996, June 17). "Woman wants to start one-teacher holistic school." *Star Tribune*, 11.

102. Kellie Lund went by the name Kellie Winter during her years at P.E.A.S.E. Academy.

103. ARS Inaugural Conference Participant Information. (2002). Courtesy of Association of Recovery Schools archives.

104. Massey would become the superintendent of schools in that district.

105. Riestenberg, N. (2005). "P.E.A.S.E. Academy: The restorative recovery school." *Restorative Practices E-Forum.* https://www.iirp.edu/news/pease-academy-the-restorative-recovery-school.

106. Wilcox, A. (2007). "Restorative justice." *Journal of Groups in Addiction & Recovery, 2* (2-4), 162–179. https://doi.org/10.1080/15560350802080670.

107. Moberg, D. P., Finch, A. J., and Lindsley, S. M. (2014) "Recovery high schools: Students and responsive academic and therapeutic services." *Peabody Journal of Education, 89*(2), 165–182. https://doi.org/10.1080/0161956X.2014.895645.

108. As of 2024, MTCS had eight programs, including P.E.A.S.E. Academy. The MTCS mission states, "We are a student-centered learning community that inspires and supports all learners to achieve excellence through equitable, relevant learning experiences." See MTCS Mission. (n.d.). *Minnesota Transitions Charter School.* https://mtcs.org/about/mtcs-mission/.

109. "Authorizer Performance." (n.d.). *Minnesota Department of Education.* https://education.mn.gov/MDE/dse/chart/auth/.

110. "Codifying community wisdom for educational equity." (2022, September 9). *Pillsbury United Communities.* https://pillsburyunited.org/category/prosperity/education/.

Afterword: Findings

1. Menand, L. (2021, October 18). "It's time to stop talking about generations." *New Yorker.* https://www.newyorker.com/magazine/2021/10/18/its-time-to-stop-talking-about-generations.

2. Ibid.

3. Menand, L. (2019, August 18). "The misconception about Baby Boomers and the Sixties." *New Yorker.* https://www.newyorker.com/culture/cultural-comment/the-misconception-about-baby-boomers-and-the-sixties.

4. Louis Menand listed notable cultural figures from the Silent Generation: "Gloria Steinem, Muhammad Ali, Tom Hayden, Abbie Hoffman, Jerry Rubin, Nina Simone, Bob Dylan, Noam Chomsky, Philip Roth, Susan Sontag, Martin Luther King Jr., Billie Jean King, Jesse Jackson, Joan Baez, Berry Gordy, Amiri Baraka, Ken Kesey, Huey Newton, Jerry Garcia, Janis Joplin, Jimi Hendrix, and Andy Warhol." Interestingly, the first US president from the Silent Generation was Joe Biden: see note 1 earlier.

5. Sloman, L. (1979). *Reefer Madness: The history of marijuana in America.* Indianapolis, IN: Bobbs-Merrill.

6. Howe, N. (2014, August 13). "The silent generation, "The lucky few" (Part 3 of 7). *Forbes.* https://www.forbes.com/sites/neilhowe/2014/08/13/the-silent-generation-the-lucky-few-part-3-of-7/?sh=1539cb7d2c63.

7. Easterlin, R. (1987). *Birth and fortune: The impact of numbers on personal welfare,* 2nd ed. Chicago, IL: University of Chicago Press.

8. See note 6 earlier.

9. Tanner-Smith, E., Finch, A. J., Hennessy, E. A., and Moberg, D. P. (2018). "Who attends recovery high schools after substance use treatment? A descriptive analysis of school aged youth." *Journal of Substance Abuse Treatment, 89,* 20–27. https://doi.org/10.1016/j.jsat.2018.03.003.

10. Kolitz, D. (2021). "Love bomb." *Atavist Magazine,* 117. https://magazine.atavist.com/the-love-bomb-enthusiastic-sobriety-bob-meehan-abuse-cult-drugs-rehab/.

11. This quote is from an interview conducted by the author, but the source asked not to be identified.

12. Finch, A. J. (2003). *A sense of place at Recovery High School: Boundary permeability and student recovery support.* Nashville, TN: Vanderbilt University, PhD dissertation, 83.

13. The Johnson Institute was founded in 1966 and advocated for programs on recovery. Hazelden took over the Institute in 2009. See Salmassi, M. (2009, March). "Hazelden Foundation absorbs Johnson Institute programs." *Partnership to End Addiction.* https://drugfree.org/drug-and-alcohol-news/hazelden-foundation-absorbs-johnson-institute-programs/.

14. Johnny Allem interview with author, October 3, 2002.

15. "North Star Guide for recovery leaders." (2021, June 19). *Faces and Voices of Recovery.* https://facesandvoicesofrecovery.org/wp-content/uploads/2021/06/Race-Equity-in-Recovery-North-Star-final-2.pdf.

16. Ibid.

17. Alcoholics Anonymous World Services, Inc. (1989). *Twelve steps and twelve traditions.* Alcoholics Anonymous World Services.

18. "John Cates testimony video." (2016, March 31). *YouTube.* https://www.youtube.com/watch?v=mq3Fvsiedro.

19. Sid Jordan. (n.d.). *Neohumanist College.* https://nhcollege.gurukul.edu/conference/presenters/sid-jordan-2/.

20. Gunamuktananda, D. *Ananda Marga: Path of bliss.* http://www.anandamarga.org/pdf/AMPathofBliss.pdf. See also History. (n.d.). *Ananda Marga*—*New York Sector.* https://ampsnys.org/history/.

21. Ibid.

22. Pandey, R. (2016). *Sarkar, you can not be forgotten. The life and work of Prabhat Ranjan Sarkar*. Munich, Germany: GRIN Verlag.

23. Since all her recovery high school work was done under the name of Barbara Schmidt, she asked that be the name used in this book.

24. Finch, A. J., Tanner-Smith, E., Hennessy, E., and Moberg, D. P. (2018). "Recovery high schools: Effect of schools supporting recovery from substance use disorders." *American Journal of Drug and Alcohol Abuse*, 44(2), 175–184. https://doi.org/10.1080/00952 990.2017.1354378.

25. Teas, T. G. (1998). *Chemically dependent teens with special needs: Educational considerations for after treatment*. St. Paul, MN: Bethel College, master's thesis.

Index

For the benefit of digital users, indexed terms that span two pages (e.g., 52–53) may, on occasion, appear on only one of those pages.

Figures are indicated by an italic f following the page number.